LOCKE'S
PHILOSOPHICAL WORKS.

IN TWO VOLUMES.

VOL. II.

WITH A GENERAL INDEX.

THE
WORKS
OF
JOHN LOCKE.

VOL. II.
PHILOSOPHICAL WORKS.

WITH A PRELIMINARY ESSAY AND NOTES,

BY J. A. ST. JOHN.

Select Bibliographies Reprint Series

 BOOKS FOR LIBRARIES PRESS
FREEPORT, NEW YORK

First Published 1877
Reprinted 1969

STANDARD BOOK NUMBER:
8369-5049-6

LIBRARY OF CONGRESS CATALOG CARD NUMBER:
74-94275

PRINTED IN THE UNITED STATES OF AMERICA

CONTENTS.

AN ESSAY CONCERNING HUMAN UNDERSTANDING.

BOOK III.

	Page.
CHAP. 1.—Of Words or Language in general	1
2.—Of the Signification of Words	4
3.—Of General Terms	9
4.—Of the Names of Simple Ideas	21
5.—Of the Names of Mixed Modes and Relations	30
6.—Of the Names of Substances	40
7.—Of Particles	74
8.—Of abstract and concrete Terms	77
9.—Of the Imperfection of Words	79
10.—Of the Abuse of Words	94
11.—Of the Remedies of the foregoing Imperfections and Abuses	113

BOOK IV.

CHAP. 1.—Of Knowledge in general	129
2.—Of the Degrees of our Knowledge	134
3.—Of the Extent of Human Knowledge	142
4.—Of the Reality of Knowledge	169
5.—Of Truth in general	181

vi CONTENTS.

	Page.
CHAP. 6.—Of Universal Propositions, their Truth and Certainty	188
7.—Of Maxims	201
8.—Of trifling Propositions	219
9.—Of our Knowledge of Existence	228
10.—Of our Knowledge of the Existence of a God	229
11.—Of our Knowledge of the Existence of other Things	243
12.—Of the Improvement of our Knowledge	252
13.—Some further Considerations concerning our Knowledge	263
14.—Of Judgment	265
15.—Of Probability	267
16.—Of the Degrees of Assent	271
17.—Of Reason	282
18.—Of Faith and Reason, and their distinct Provinces	303
19.—Of Enthusiasm	311
20.—Of wrong Assent, or Error	321
21.—Of the Division of the Sciences	336

APPENDIX.

CONTROVERSY WITH THE BISHOP OF WORCESTER.

Introduction by the Editor 339

AN EXAMINATION OF P. MALEBRANCHE'S OPINION OF SEEING ALL THINGS IN GOD; WITH REMARKS UPON SOME OF MR. NORRIS'S BOOKS.

Introduction by the Editor 413

ELEMENTS OF NATURAL PHILOSOPHY.

CHAP. 1.—Of Matter and Motion	472
2.—Of the Universe	475
3.—Of our Solar System	475

CONTENTS.

	Page.
Chap. 4.—Of the Earth, considered as a Planet	478
5.—Of the Air and Atmosphere	479
6.—Of Meteors in general	481
7.—Of Springs, Rivers, and the Sea	483
8.—Of several Sorts of Earth, Stones, Metals, Minerals, and other Fossils	485
9.—Of Vegetables, or Plants	486
10.—Of Animals	488
11.—Of the five Senses	490
12.—Of the Understanding of Man	495

SOME THOUGHTS CONCERNING READING AND STUDY FOR A GENTLEMAN.

Introduction by the Editor	497
INDEX	505

OF

HUMAN UNDERSTANDING.

BOOK III.

CHAPTER I.

OF WORDS, OR LANGUAGE IN GENERAL.

1. *Man fitted to form articulate Sounds.*—GOD, having designed man for a sociable creature, made him not only with an inclination, and under a necessity to have fellowship with those of his own kind, but furnished him also with language, which was to be the great instrument and common tie of society. Man, therefore, had by nature his organs so fashioned, as to be fit to frame articulate sounds, which we call words. But this was not enough to produce language; for parrots, and several other birds, will be taught to make articulate sounds distinct enough, which yet by no means are capable of language.

2. *To make them Signs of Ideas.*—Besides articulate sounds, therefore, it was further necessary that he should be able to use these sounds as signs of internal conceptions, and to make them stand as marks for the ideas within his own mind, whereby they might be made known to others, and the thoughts of men's minds be conveyed from one to another.

3. *To make general Signs.*—But neither was this sufficient to make words so useful as they ought to be. It is not enough for the perfection of language, that sounds can be made signs of ideas, unless those signs can be so made use of as to comprehend several particular things; for the multiplication of words would have perplexed their use, had every particular thing need of a distinct name to be signified by. To remedy this inconvenience, language had yet a further improvement in the use of general terms, whereby one word was made to mark a multitude of particular existences; which advantageous use of sounds was obtained

only by the difference of the ideas they were made signs of: those names becoming general, which are made to stand for general ideas, and those remaining particular, where the ideas they are used for are particular.

4. Besides these names which stand for ideas, there be other words which men make use of, not to signify any idea, but the want or absence of some ideas, simple or complex, or all ideas together; such as are nihil in Latin, and in English, ignorance and barrenness: all which negative or privative words cannot be said properly to belong to, or signify no ideas; for then they would be perfectly insignificant sounds; but they relate to positive ideas, and signify their absence.

5. *Words ultimately derived from such as signify sensible Ideas.*—It may also lead us a little towards the original of all our notions and knowledge, if we remark how great a dependence our words have on common sensible ideas; and how those which are made use of to stand for actions and notions quite removed from sense, have their rise from thence, and from obvious sensible ideas are transferred to more abstruse significations, and made to stand for ideas that come not under the cognizance of our senses; v. g., to imagine, apprehend, comprehend, adhere, conceive, instil, disgust, disturbance, tranquillity, &c., are all words taken from the operations of sensible things, and applied to certain modes of thinking. Spirit, in its primary signification, is breath; angel, a messenger; and I doubt not, but if we could trace them to their sources, we should find in all languages the names which stand for things that fall not under our senses, to have had their first rise from sensible ideas. By which we may give some kind of guess what kind of notions they were, and whence derived, which filled their minds who were the first beginners of languages; and how nature, even in the naming of things, unawares suggested to men the originals and principles of all their knowledge; whilst, to give names that might make known to others any operations they felt in themselves, or any other ideas that came not under their senses, they were fain to borrow words from ordinary known ideas of sensation; by that means to make others the more easily to conceive those operations they experimented in themselves, which made no outward sensible appearances; and then, when they had got known and agreed

names, to signify those internal operations of their own minds, they were sufficiently furnished to make known by words all their other ideas; since they could consist of nothing but either of outward sensible perceptions, or of the inward operations of their minds about them, we having, as has been proved, no ideas at all, but what originally come either from sensible objects without, or what we feel within ourselves, from the inward workings of our own spirits, of which we are conscious to ourselves within.

6. *Distribution.*—But to understand better the use and force of language, as subservient to instruction and knowledge, it will be convenient to consider:

First, To what it is that names, in the use of language, are immediately applied.

Secondly, Since all (except proper) names are general, and so stand not particularly for this or that single thing, but for sorts and ranks of things, it will be necessary to consider, in the next place, what the sorts and kinds, or, if you rather like the Latin names, what the species and genera of things are, wherein they consist, and how they come to be made. These being (as they ought) well looked into, we shall the better come to find the right use of words, the natural advantages and defects of language, and the remedies that ought to be used, to avoid the inconveniences of obscurity or uncertainty in the signification of words, without which it is impossible to discourse with any clearness or order concerning knowledge; which, being conversant about propositions, and those most commonly universal ones, has greater connexion with words than perhaps is suspected.

These considerations, therefore, shall be the matter of the following chapters.*

* See, in Condillac, (Origine des Connoissances Humaines, Part II. § 1.) an attempt at reconciling the common method of philosophising on the origin of language, with the account delivered in Scripture. He believes that language was originally revealed to man in Paradise; but in order to gratify the appetite for speculation, indulges in the very improbable supposition, that two children may have wandered away into the desert before they could speak, and there founded an empire with a new language; after which he sets himself about discovering the method which in such a case they would be likely to pursue. And this is what a hundred years ago was called philosophy in France! Most persons are acquainted with the story told by Herodotus, concerning the children who were nursed by the she-goats, beyond the reach of human language.

CHAPTER II.

OF THE SIGNIFICATION OF WORDS.

1. *Words are sensible Signs necessary for Communication.*—MAN, though he has great variety of thoughts, and such from which others as well as himself might receive profit and delight, yet they are all within his own breast, invisible and hidden from others, nor can of themselves be made to appear. The comfort and advantage of society not being to be had without communication of thoughts, it was necessary that man should find out some external sensible signs, whereof those invisible ideas, which his thoughts are made up of, might be made known to others. For this purpose nothing was so fit, either for plenty or quickness, as those articulate sounds, which with so much ease and variety he found himself able to make. Thus we may conceive how words, which were by nature so well adapted to that purpose, come to be made use of by men as the signs of their ideas;* not by any natural connexion that there is between particular articulate sounds and certain ideas, for then there would be but one language amongst all men; but by a voluntary imposition, whereby such a word is made arbitrarily the mark of such an idea. The use, then, of words, is to be sensible marks of ideas; and the ideas they stand for are their proper and immediate signification.

2. *Words are the sensible Signs of his Ideas who uses them.*—The use men have of these marks being either to record their own thoughts for the assistance of their own memory, or, as it were, to bring out their ideas, and lay them before

for the purpose of discovering what was the original dialect of mankind, and how their first word was Bèkos, simply the *bèc* of the goats, with the Greek termination. Quintillian, alluding to the same story, supposes the children to have been brought up by dumb nurses, and to have been, therefore, themselves dumb. (L. x. c. 1.)—ED.

* Though much has been written on the origin and progress of language, we have hitherto arrived at nothing like the philosophy of the subject, chiefly perhaps from our neglecting to observe the mode by which savages enlarge their vocabulary. There are, indeed, no tribes of men without language, but many among whom it is exceedingly scanty. A philosopher who should study the efforts of such tribes to multiply their words, by expressing influxes of new ideas, might throw some light on a subject still very little understood.—ED.

the view of others; words, in their primary or immediate signification, stand for nothing but the ideas in the mind of him that uses them, how imperfectly soever or carelessly those ideas are collected from the things which they are supposed to represent. When a man speaks to another, it is that he may be understood; and the end of speech is, that those sounds, as marks, may make known his ideas to the hearer. That, then, which words are the marks of, are the ideas of the speaker; nor can any one apply them, as marks, immediately, to anything else but the ideas that he himself hath; for this would be to make them signs of his own conceptions, and yet apply them to other ideas; which would be to make them signs and not signs of his ideas at the same time, and so in effect to have no signification at all. Words being voluntary signs, they cannot be voluntary signs imposed by him on things he knows not. That would be to make them signs of nothing, sounds without signification. A man cannot make his words the signs either of qualities in things, or of conceptions in the mind of another, whereof he has none in his own. Till he has some ideas of his own, he cannot suppose them to correspond with the conceptions of another man; nor can he use any signs for them, for thus they would be the signs of he knows not what, which is in truth to be the signs of nothing. But when he represents to himself other men's ideas by some of his own, if he consent to give them the same names that other men do, it is still to his own ideas; to ideas that he has, and not to ideas that he has not.

3. This is so necessary in the use of language, that in this respect the knowing and the ignorant, the learned and the unlearned, use the words they speak (with any meaning) all alike. They, in every man's mouth, stand for the ideas he has, and which he would express by them. A child having taken notice of nothing in the metal he hears called gold, but the bright shining yellow colour, he applies the word gold only to his own idea of that colour, and nothing else; and therefore calls the same colour in a peacock's tail gold.*

* "All," says the proverb, "is not gold that glitters;" but, like children, travellers sometimes forget the wisdom contained in this saying. A propos of this, Navarette remarks:—"They report the apartments and rooms are very stately and noble, especially the

Another that hath better observed, adds to shining yellow great weight: and then the sound gold, when he uses it, stands for a complex idea of a shining yellow and a very weighty substance; another adds to those qualities fusibility, and then the word gold signifies to him a body, bright, yellow, fusible, and very heavy; another adds malleability. Each of these uses equally the word gold, when they have occasion to express the idea which they have applied it to; but it is evident that each can apply it only to his own idea, nor can he make it stand as a sign of such a complex idea as he has not.

4. *Words are often secretly referred, first to the Ideas in other Men's Minds* —But though words, as they are used by men, can properly and immediately signify nothing but the ideas that are in the mind of the speaker; yet they in their thoughts give them a secret reference to two other things.

First, They suppose their words to be marks of the ideas in the minds also of other men, with whom they communicate; for else they should talk in vain, and could not be understood, if the sounds they applied to one idea were such as by the hearer were applied to another, which is to speak two languages. But in this, men stand not usually to examine whether the idea they and those they discourse with

emperor's bedchamber; but I never heard there were seventy-nine, as Bishop Marolus writes, where he follows Mendoza, in his second chapter, quoted above; nor are there any rooms of gold, silver, or precious stones, as the same author says, and J. Lazenna affirms. How could these things be hid from us, who lived so many years in that country, and some time at the court, inquiring diligently, and examining into the most remarkable things there? The Chinese history tells us, the arched roof of an ancient emperor's state-rooms was of gold, which I do not find any difficulty to give credit to; and I am satisfied he that now reigns might have the same if he pleased. Nor are there tiles of gold, as others have reported, but they are glazed yellow, which is the emperor's colour; when the sun shines on them, they look like gold, or polished brass. The petty kings of the blood-royal use exactly the same; and they are on the temples of deceased emperors. There are other tiles, blue glazed, which I have seen on some temples, and look very graceful. I have sometimes seen the tiles with which the floors of the palace are laid; they are square, and as large as the stones of the floor of St. Peter's church at Rome; some were glazed yellow, and others green, as smooth and glossy as a looking-glass, and must doubtless be a great ornament to a room." (Account of China, I. vi. § 9.)—ED.

have in their minds be the same, but think it enough that they use the word, as they imagine, in the common acceptation of that language; in which they suppose that the idea they make it a sign of is precisely the same, to which the understanding men of that country apply that name.

5. *Secondly, to the Reality of Things.*—Secondly, Because men would not be thought to talk barely of their own imaginations, but of things as really they are; therefore they often suppose the words to stand also for the reality of things. But this relating more particularly to substances, and their names, as perhaps the former does to simple ideas and modes, we shall speak of these two different ways of applying words more at large, when we come to treat of the names of fixed modes and substances in particular; though, give me leave here to say, that it is a perverting the use of words, and brings unavoidable obscurity and confusion into their signification, whenever we make them stand for anything but those ideas we have in our own minds.

6. *Words by Use readily excite Ideas.*—Concerning words, also, it is further to be considered: First, that they being immediately the signs of men's ideas, and by that means the instruments whereby men communicate their conceptions, and express to one another those thoughts and imaginations, they have within their own breasts; there comes, by constant use, to be such a connexion between certain sounds and the ideas they stand for, that the names heard, almost as readily excite certain ideas as if the objects themselves, which are apt to produce them, did actually affect the senses. Which is manifestly so in all obvious sensible qualities, and in all substances that frequently and familiarly occur to us.

7. *Words often used without Signification.*—Secondly, That, though the proper and immediate signification of words are ideas in the mind of the speaker, yet, because by familiar use from our cradles we come to learn certain articulate sounds very perfectly, and have them readily on our tongues, and always at hand in our memories, but yet are not always careful to examine or settle their significations perfectly; it often happens that men, even when they would apply themselves to an attentive consideration, do set their thoughts more on words than things. Nay, because words are many

of them learned before the ideas are known for which they stand : therefore some, not only children but men, speak several words no otherwise than parrots do, only because they have learned them, and have been accustomed to those sounds. But, so far as words are of use and signification, so far is there a constant connexion between the sound and the idea, and a designation that the one stands for the other ; without which application of them, they are nothing but so much insignificant noise.

8. *Their Signification perfectly arbitrary.*—Words, by long and familiar use, as has been said, come to excite in men certain ideas so constantly and readily, that they are apt to suppose a natural connexion between them. But that they signify only men's peculiar ideas, and that by a perfect arbitrary imposition, is evident, in that they often fail to excite in others (even that use the same language) the same ideas we take them to be signs of: and every man has so inviolable a liberty to make words stand for what ideas he pleases, that no one hath the power to make others have the same ideas in their minds that he has, when they use the same words that he does. And therefore the great Augustus himself, in the possession of that power which ruled the world, acknowledged he could not make a new Latin word ; which was as much as to say, that he could not arbitrarily appoint what idea any sound should be a sign of in the mouths and common language of his subjects. It is true common use, by a tacit consent, appropriates certain sounds to certain ideas in all languages, which so far limits the signification of that sound, that, unless a man applies it to the same idea, he does not speak properly : and let me add, that, unless a man's words excite the same ideas in the hearer which he makes them stand for in speaking, he does not speak intelligibly. But whatever be the consequence of any man's using of words differently, either from their general meaning, or the particular sense of the person to whom he addresses them ; this is certain, their signification, in his use of them, is limited to his ideas, and they can be signs of nothing else.

CHAPTER III.
OF GENERAL TERMS.

1. *The greatest Part of Words general.*—All things that exist being particulars, it may perhaps be thought reasonable that words, which ought to be conformed to things, should be so too,—I mean in their signification: but yet we find quite the contrary. The far greatest part of words that make all languages are general terms; which has not been the effect of neglect or chance, but of reason and necessity.

2. *For every particular Thing to have a Name is impossible.*—First, It is impossible that every particular thing should have a distinct peculiar name. For the signification and use of words depending on that connexion which the mind makes between its ideas and the sounds it uses as signs of them, it is necessary, in the application of names to things, that the mind should have distinct ideas of the things, and retain also the particular name that belongs to every one, with its peculiar appropriation to that idea. But it is beyond the power of human capacity to frame and retain distinct ideas of all the particular things we meet with; every bird and beast men saw, every tree and plant that affected the senses, could not find a place in the most capacious understanding. If it be looked on as an instance of a prodigious memory, that some generals have been able to call every soldier in their army by his proper name, we may easily find a reason why men have never attempted to give names to each sheep in their flock, or crow that flies over their heads; much less to call every leaf of plants, or grain of sand that came in their way, by a peculiar name.

3. *And useless.*—Secondly, If it were possible, it would yet be useless; because it would not serve to the chief end of language. Men would in vain heap up names of particular things that would not serve them to communicate their thoughts. Men learn names, and use them in talk with others, only that they may be understood: which is then only done when by use or consent the sound I make by the organs of speech, excites in another man's mind who hears it the idea I apply it to in mine, when I speak it. This cannot be done by names applied to particular things, whereof I

alone having the ideas in my mind, the names of them could not be significant or intelligible to another, who was not acquainted with all those very particular things which had fallen under my notice.

4. Thirdly, But yet, granting this also feasible, (which I think is not,) yet a distinct name for every particular thing would not be of any great use for the improvement of knowledge: which, though founded in particular things, enlarges itself by general views; to which things reduced into sorts under general names, are properly subservient. These with the names belonging to them, come within some compass, and do not multiply every moment, beyond what either the mind can contain, or use requires: and therefore, in these, men have for the most part stopped; but yet not so as to hinder themselves from distinguishing particular things by appropriated names, where convenience demands it. And therefore in their own species, which they have most to do with, and wherein they have often occasion to mention particular persons, they make use of proper names; and there distinct individuals have distinct denominations.

5. *What things have proper Names.*—Besides persons, countries also, cities, rivers, mountains, and other the like distinctions of place, have usually found peculiar names, and that for the same reason; they being such as men have often an occasion to mark particularly, and, as it were, set before others in their discourses with them. And I doubt not, but if we had reason to mention particular horses as often as we have to mention particular men, we should have proper names for the one, as familiar as for the other; and Bucephalus would be a word as much in use as Alexander. And therefore we see that, amongst jockeys, horses have their proper names to be known and distinguished by, as commonly as their servants; because, amongst them, there is often occasion to mention this or that particular horse when he is out of sight.

6. *How general Words are made.*—The next thing to be considered is, how general words come to be made. For, since all things that exist are only particulars, how come we by general terms, or where find we those general natures they are supposed to stand for? Words become general by being made the signs of general ideas; and ideas become

general by separating from them the circumstances of time and place, and any other ideas that may determine them to this or that particular existence. By this way of abstraction they are made capable of representing more individuals than one; each of which having in it a conformity to that abstract idea, is (as we call it) of that sort.

7. But, to deduce this a little more distinctly, it will not perhaps be amiss to trace our notions and names from their beginning, and observe by what degrees we proceed, and by what steps we enlarge our ideas from our first infancy. There is nothing more evident, than that the ideas of the persons children converse with (to instance in them alone) are, like the persons themselves, only particular. The ideas of the nurse and the mother are well framed in their minds; and, like pictures of them there, represent only those individuals. The names they first gave to them are confined to these individuals; and the names of nurse and mamma the child uses, determine themselves to those persons. Afterwards, when time and a larger acquaintance have made them observe that there are a great many other things in the world that, in some common agreements of shape, and several other qualities, resemble their father and mother, and those persons they have been used to, they frame an idea, which they find those many particulars do partake in; and to that they give, with others, the name man, for example. And thus they come to have a general name, and a general idea; wherein they make nothing new, but only leave out of the complex idea they had of Peter and James, Mary and Jane, that which is peculiar to each, and retain only what is common to them all.

8. By the same way that they come by the general name and idea of man, they easily advance to more general names and notions. For, observing that several things that differ from their idea of man, and cannot therefore be comprehended under that name, have yet certain qualities wherein they agree with man, by retaining only those qualities, and uniting them into one idea, they have again another and more general idea; to which having given a name, they make a term of a more comprehensive extension: which new idea is made, not by any new addition, but only as before, by leaving out the shape, and some other properties signified

by the name man, and retaining only a body, with life, sense, and spontaneous motion, comprehended under the name animal.*

9. *General Natures are nothing but abstract Ideas.*—That this is the way whereby men first formed general ideas, and general names to them, I think is so evident, that there needs no other proof of it but the considering of a man's self, or others, and the ordinary proceedings of their minds in knowledge: and he that thinks general natures or notions are anything else but such abstract and partial ideas of more complex ones, taken at first from particular existences, will, I fear, be at a loss where to find them. For let any one reflect, and then tell me, wherein does his idea of man differ from that of Peter and Paul, or his idea of horse from that of Bucephalus, but in the leaving out something that is peculiar to each individual, and retaining so much of those particular complex ideas of several particular existences as they are found to agree in? Of the complex ideas signified by the names man and horse, leaving out but those particulars wherein they differ, and retaining only those wherein they agree, and of those making a new distinct complex idea, and giving the name animal to it; one has a more general term, that comprehends with man several other creatures. Leave out of the idea of animal, sense and spontaneous motion, and the remaining complex idea, made up of the remaining simple ones of body, life, and nourishment, becomes a more general one, under the more comprehensive

---

* It formed part of Berkeley's system to deny the existence of general ideas, which accordingly he ridicules with great pertinacity in his Introduction to the Principles of Human Knowledge. (§ 7, et seq.) His reasoning, however, is that of a sophist, and the sneering tone of his language wholly unsuited to philosophical discussion. Making use—as far as he judged favourable to his purpose—of the language in the text, he says:—"The constituent parts of the abstract idea of animal are body, life, sense, and spontaneous motion. By *body* is meant body without any particular shape or figure—there being no one shape or figure common to all animals, without covering, either of hair or feathers, or scales, &c., nor yet naked: hair, feathers, scales, and nakedness being the distinguishing properties of particular animals, and, for that reason, left out of the *abstract idea*. Upon the same account, the spontaneous motion must be neither walking, nor flying, nor creeping: it is, nevertheless, a motion; but what that motion is, it is not easy to conceive. (§ 9.)—ED.

term, vivens. And, not to dwell longer upon this particular, so evident in itself, by the same way the mind proceeds to body, substance, and at last to being, thing, and such universal terms, which stand for any of our ideas whatsoever. To conclude: this whole mystery of genera and species, which make such a noise in the schools, and are with justice so little regarded out of them, is nothing else but abstract ideas, more or less comprehensive, with names annexed to them. In all which this is constant and unvariable, that every more general term stands for such an idea, and is but a part of any of those contained under it.

10. *Why the Genus is ordinarily made Use of in Definitions.*—This may show us the reason why, in the defining of words—which is nothing but declaring their significations—we make use of the genus, or next general word that comprehends it. Which is not out of necessity, but only to save the labour of enumerating the several simple ideas which the next general word or genus stands for; or, perhaps, sometimes the shame of not being able to do it. But though defining by genus and differentia—I crave leave to use these terms of art, though originally Latin, since they most properly suit those notions they are applied to—I say, though defining by the genus be the shortest way, yet I think it may be doubted whether it be the best. This I am sure, it is not the only; and so not absolutely necessary. For, definition being nothing but making another understand by words what idea the term defined stands for, a definition is best made by enumerating those simple ideas that are combined in the signification of the term defined: and if, instead of such an enumeration, men have accustomed themselves to use the next general term, it has not been out of necessity, or for greater clearness, but for quickness and dispatch sake. For I think, that, to one who desired to know what idea the word man stood for; if it should be said, that man was a solid extended substance, having life, sense, spontaneous motion, and the faculty of reasoning; I doubt not but the meaning of the term man would be as well understood, and the idea it stands for be at least as clearly made known as when it is defined to be a rational animal: which, by the several definitions of animal, vivens and corpus, resolves itself into those enumerated ideas. I have, in explaining

the term man, followed here the ordinary definition of the schools; which, though perhaps not the most exact, yet serves well enough to my present purpose. And one may, in this instance, see what gave occasion to the rule, that a definition must consist of genus and differentia; and it suffices to show us the little necessity there is of such a rule, or advantage in the strict observing of it. For, definitions, as has been said, being only the explaining of one word by several others, so that the meaning or idea it stands for may be certainly known; languages are not always so made according to the rules of logic, that every term can have its signification exactly and clearly expressed by two others. Experience sufficiently satisfies us to the contrary; or else those who have made this rule have done ill, that they have given us so few definitions conformable to it. But of definitions more in the next chapter.

11. *General and Universal are Creatures of the Understanding.*—To return to general words, it is plain, by what has been said, that general and universal belong not to the real existence of things; but are the inventions and creatures of the understanding, made by it for its own use, and concern only signs, whether words or ideas. Words are general, as has been said, when used for signs of general ideas, and so are applicable indifferently to many particular things: and ideas are general when they are set up as the representatives of many particular things; but universality belongs not to things themselves, which are all of them particular in their existence, even those words and ideas which in their signification are general. When therefore we quit particulars, the generals that rest are only creatures of our own making; their general nature being nothing but the capacity they are put into by the understanding, of signifying or representing many particulars; for the signification they have is nothing but a relation, that, by the mind of man, is added to them.*

* To this, the Bishop of Worcester objects :—" The abstracted ideas are the work of the mind, yet they are not mere creatures of the mind; as appears by an instance produced of the essence of the sun being in one single individual : in which case it is granted that the idea may be so abstracted that more suns might agree in it, and it is as much a sort, as if there were as many suns as there are stars. So that here we have a real essence subsisting in one individual, but capable of being multiplied into more, and the same essence remaining. But in this one

12. *Abstract Ideas are the Essences of the Genera and Species.*—The next thing therefore to be considered is, what kind of signification it is, that general words have. For, as it is evident that they do not signify barely one particular thing—for then they would not be general terms, but proper names—so, on the other side, it is as evident they do not signify a plurality; for man and men would then signify the same, and the distinction of numbers (as the grammarians call them) would be superfluous and useless. That, then, which general words signify is a sort of things; and each of them does that, by being a sign of an abstract idea in the mind, to which idea as things existing are found to agree, so they come to be ranked under that name; or, which is all one, be of that sort. Whereby it is evident that the essences of the sorts, or, if the Latin word pleases better, species of things, are nothing else but these abstract ideas. For the having the essence of any species, being that which makes anything to be of that species, and the conformity to the idea to which the name is annexed being that which gives a right to that name; the having the essence, and the having that conformity, must needs be the same thing; since to be of any species, and to have a right to the name of that species, is all one. As, for example, to be a man, or of the species man, and to have right to the name man, is the same thing. Again, to be a man, or of the species man, and have the essence of a man, is the same thing. Now, since nothing can be a man, or have a right to the name man, but what has a conformity to the abstract idea the name man stands for; nor anything be a man, or have a right to the species man, but what has the essence of that species; it follows, that the abstract idea for which the name stands, and the essence of the species, is one and the same. From whence it is easy to observe, that the essences of the sorts of things, and, consequently, the sorting of this, is the workmanship of the understanding, that abstracts and makes those general ideas.

<small>sun there is a real essence, and not a mere nominal or abstracted essence. But suppose there were more suns, would not each of them have the real essence of the sun? For what is it makes the second sun, but having the same real essence with the first? If it were but a nominal essence, then the second would have nothing but the name."—(For Locke's reply, see Letters to the Bishop of Worcester. Appendix No. VII)—ED.</small>

13. *They are the Workmanship of the Understanding, but have their Foundation in the Similitude of Things.*—I would not here be thought to forget, much less to deny, that Nature, in the production of things, makes several of them alike: there is nothing more obvious, especially in the races of animals, and all things propagated by seed. But yet, I think, we may say the sorting of them under names is the workmanship of the understanding, taking occasion, from the similitude it observes amongst them, to make abstract general ideas, and set them up in the mind, with names annexed to them, as patterns or forms, (for, in that sense, the word form has a very proper signification,) to which as particular things existing are found to agree, so they come to be of that species, have that denomination, or are put into that classis. For when we say this is a man, that a horse; this justice, that cruelty; this a watch, that a jack; what do we else but rank things under different specific names, as agreeing to those abstract ideas, of which we have made those names the signs? And what are the essences of those species set out and marked by names, but those abstract ideas in the mind; which are, as it were, the bonds between particular things that exist, and the names they are to be ranked under? And when general names have any connexion with particular beings, these abstract ideas are the medium that unites them; so that the essences of species, as distinguished and denominated by us, neither are nor can be anything but those precise abstract ideas we have in our minds. And therefore the supposed real essences of substances, if different from our abstract ideas, cannot be the essences of the species we rank things into. For two species may be one, as rationally as two different essences be the essence of one species: and I demand what are the alterations may or may not be in a horse or lead, without making either of them to be of another species? In determining the species of things by our abstract ideas, this is easy to resolve: but if any one will regulate himself herein by supposed real essences, he will, I suppose, be at a loss; and he will never be able to know when anything precisely ceases to be of the species of a horse or lead.

14. *Each distinct abstract Idea is a distinct Essence.*—Nor will any one wonder that I say these essences, or abstract

ideas (which are the measures of name, and the boundaries of species) are the workmanship of the understanding, who considers that, at least, the complex ones are often, in several men, different collections of simple ideas; and therefore that is covetousness to one man, which is not so to another. Nay, even in substances where their abstract ideas seem to be taken from the things themselves, they are not constantly the same; no, not in that species which is most familiar to us, and with which we have the most intimate acquaintance: it having been more than once doubted, whether the fœtus born of a woman were a man;* even so far as that it hath been debated, whether it were or were not to be nourished and baptized; which could not be, if the abstract idea or essence to which the name man belonged were of nature's making, and were not the uncertain and various collection of simple ideas, which the understanding put together, and then, abstracting it, affixed a name to it. So that, in truth, every distinct abstract idea is a distinct essence; and the names that stand for such distinct ideas are the names of things essentially different. Thus a circle is as essentially different from an oval as a sheep from a goat; and rain is as essentially different from snow as water from earth: that abstract idea which is the essence of one being impossible to be communicated to the other. And thus any two abstract ideas, that in any part vary one from another, with two distinct names annexed to them, constitute two distinct sorts, or, if you please, species, as essentially different as any two of the most remote or opposite in the world.

15. *Real and nominal Essence.*—But since the essences of things are thought by some (and not without reason) to be wholly unknown, it may not be amiss to consider the several significations of the word essence.

* That is, in the case of monstrous births. This subject once gave rise to a long controversy between Mr. Limony and Mr. Winslow; not, indeed, with a view to determine what is the real essence of man, and consequently whether anything born of woman be of the human species or not; but simply as to their origin. The remarks of Maupertuis, however, though exceedingly brief, throw more light upon the controversy than the reasonings of the disputants themselves: (Venus Physique, c. 14:) and M. Sauvage, in our own day, has made monsters the subject of long investigations, and considers himself to have explained the whole mystery.—ED.

First, Essence may be taken for the being of anything, whereby it is what it is. And thus the real internal, but generally (in substances) unknown constitution of things, whereon their discoverable qualities depend, may be called their essence. This is the proper original signification of the word, as is evident from the formation of it; essentia, in its primary notation, signifying properly, being. And in this sense it is still used, when we speak of the essence of particular things, without giving them any name.

Secondly, The learning and disputes of the schools having been much busied about genus and species, the word essence has almost lost its primary signification: and, instead of the real constitution of things, has been almost wholly applied to the artificial constitution of genus and species. It is true, there is ordinarily supposed a real constitution of the sorts of things; and it is past doubt there must be some real constitution, on which any collection of simple ideas co-existing must depend. But it being evident that things are ranked under names into sorts or species, only as they agree to certain abstract ideas to which we have annexed those names; the essence of each genus or sort comes to be nothing but that abstract idea which the general, or sortal* (if I may have leave so to call it from sort, as I do general from genus) name stands for. And this we shall find to be that which the word essence imports in its most familiar use. These two sorts of essences, I suppose, may not unfitly be termed, the one the real, the other nominal essence.

16. *Constant Connexion between the Name and nominal Essence.*—Between the nominal essence and the name there is so near a connexion, that the name of any sort of things cannot be attributed to any particular being but what has this essence, whereby it answers that abstract idea whereof that name is the sign.

17. *Supposition, that Species are distinguished by their real Essences useless.*—Concerning the real essences of corporeal substances—to mention these only—there are, if I mistake not, two opinions. The one is of those, who, using the word essence for they know not what, suppose a certain number of

* I do not find that this word, though not worse than many in constant use, took root in the language. It might, however, be useful where *special* could not so well be employed.—ED.

those essences, according to which all natural things are made, and wherein they do exactly every one of them partake, and so become of this or that species. The other, and more rational opinion is of those who look on all natural things to have a real, but unknown constitution of their insensible parts; from which flow those sensible qualities which serve us to distinguish them one from another, according as we have occasion to rank them into sorts under common denominations. The former of these opinions, which supposes these essences as a certain number of forms or moulds, wherein all natural things that exist are cast, and do equally partake, has, I imagine, very much perplexed the knowledge of natural things. The frequent productions of monsters, in all the species of animals, and of changelings, and other strange issues of human birth, carry with them difficulties, not possible to consist with this hypothesis; since it is as impossible that two things partaking exactly of the same real essence should have different properties, as that two figures partaking of the same real essence of a circle should have different properties. But were there no other reason against it, yet the supposition of essences that cannot be known, and the making of them, nevertheless, to be that which distinguishes the species of things, is so wholly useless and unserviceable to any part of our knowledge, that that alone were sufficient to make us lay it by, and content ourselves with such essences of the sorts or species of things as come within the reach of our knowledge; which, when seriously considered, will be found, as I have said, to be nothing else but those abstract complex ideas, to which we have annexed distinct general names.

18. *Real and nominal Essence the same in simple Ideas and Modes, different in Substances.*—Essences being thus distinguished into nominal and real, we may further observe, that, in the species of simple ideas and modes, they are always the same; but in substances always quite different. Thus, a figure including a space between three lines, is the real as well as nominal essence of a triangle; it being not only the abstract idea to which the general name is annexed, but the very essentia or being of the thing itself—that foundation from which all its properties flow, and to which they are all inseparably annexed. But it is far otherwise concerning

that parcel of matter which makes the ring on my finger, wherein these two essences are apparently different. For it is the real constitution of its insensible parts, on which depend all those properties of colour, weight, fusibility, fixedness, &c., which are to be found in it; which constitution we know not, and so having no particular idea of, have no name that is the sign of it. But yet, it is its colour, weight, fusibility, fixedness, &c., which makes it to be gold, or gives it a right to that name, which is therefore its nominal essence: since nothing can be called gold but what has a conformity of qualities to that abstract complex idea to which that name is annexed. But this distinction of essences belonging particularly to substances, we shall, when we come to consider their names, have an occasion to treat of more fully.

19. *Essences ingenerable and incorruptible.*—That such abstract ideas with names to them, as we have been speaking of, are essences, may further appear by what we are told concerning essences, viz., that they are all ingenerable and incorruptible: which cannot be true of the real constitutions of things which begin and perish with them. All things that exist, besides their author, are all liable to change; especially those things we are acquainted with, and have ranked into bands under distinct names or ensigns. Thus, that which was grass to-day is to-morrow the flesh of a sheep; and, within a few days after, becomes part of a man: in all which and the like changes it is evident their real essence—i. e., that constitution whereon the properties of these several things depended—is destroyed, and perishes with them. But essences being taken for ideas established in the mind, with names annexed to them, they are supposed to remain steadily the same, whatever mutations the particular substances are liable to. For, whatever becomes of Alexander and Bucephalus, the ideas to which man and horse are annexed, are supposed nevertheless to remain the same: and so the essences of those species are preserved whole and undestroyed, whatever changes happen to any or all of the individuals of those species. By this means the essence of a species rests safe and entire, without the existence of so much as one individual of that kind. For, were there now no circle existing anywhere in the world, (as perhaps that figure exists not anywhere exactly marked out,) yet the idea annexed to that name

would not cease to be what it is; nor cease to be as a pattern to determine which of the particular figures we meet with have or have not a right to the name circle, and so to show which of them, by having that essence, was of that species. And though there neither were nor had been in nature such a beast as an unicorn, or such a fish as a mermaid; yet, supposing those names to stand for complex abstract ideas that contained no inconsistency in them, the essence of a mermaid is as intelligible as that of a man; and the idea of an unicorn as certain, steady, and permanent as that of a horse. From what has been said, it is evident that the doctrine of the immutability of essences proves them to be only abstract ideas; and is founded on the relation established between them and certain sounds as signs of them, and will always be true as long as the same name can have the same signification.

20. *Recapitulation.*—To conclude: this is that which in short I would say, viz., that all the great business of genera and species, and their essences, amounts to no more but this:— That men making abstract ideas, and settling them in their minds with names annexed to them, do thereby enable themselves to consider things, and discourse of them as it were in bundles, for the easier and readier improvement and communication of their knowledge; which would advance but slowly were their words and thoughts confined only to particulars.

CHAPTER IV.

OF THE NAMES OF SIMPLE IDEAS.

1. *Names of simple Ideas, Modes, and Substances, have each something peculiar.*—THOUGH all words, as I have shown, signify nothing immediately but the ideas in the mind of the speaker; yet, upon a nearer survey, we shall find the names of simple ideas, mixed modes, (under which I comprise relations too,) and natural substances, have each of them something peculiar and different from the other. For example:—

2. *First, Names of simple Ideas and Substances intimate real Existence.*—First, the names of simple ideas and sub-

stances, with the abstract ideas in the mind, which they immediately signify, intimate also some real existence, from which was derived their original pattern. But the names of mixed modes terminate in the idea that is in the mind, and lead not the thoughts any further, as we shall see more at large in the following chapter.

3. *Secondly, Names of simple Ideas and Modes signify always both real and nominal Essence.*—Secondly, The names of simple ideas and modes signify always the real as well as nominal essence of their species. But the names of natural substances signify rarely, if ever, anything but barely the nominal essences of those species, as we shall show in the chapter that treats of the names of substances in particular.

4. *Thirdly, Names of simple Ideas undefinable.*—Thirdly, The names of simple ideas are not capable of any definition; the names of all complex ideas are. It has not, that I know, been yet observed by anybody what words are, and what are not, capable of being defined: the want whereof is, as I am apt to think, not seldom the occasion of great wrangling and obscurity in men's discourses, whilst some demand definitions of terms that cannot be defined; and others think they ought not to rest satisfied in an explication made by a more general word, and its restriction, (or to speak in terms of art, by a genus and difference,) when, even after such definition made according to rule, those who hear it have often no more a clear conception of the meaning of the word than they had before. This at least I think, that the showing what words are, and what are not capable of definitions, and wherein consists a good definition, is not wholly besides our present purpose; and perhaps will afford so much light to the nature of these signs and our ideas, as to deserve a more particular consideration.

5. *If all were definable, it would be a Process in infinitum.*—I will not here trouble myself to prove that all terms are not definable from that progress in infinitum, which it will visibly lead us into, if we should allow that all names could be defined. For, if the terms of one definition were still to be defined by another, where at last should we stop? But I shall, from the nature of our ideas, and the signification

our words, show why some names can and others cannot be defined, and which they are.

6. *What a Definition is.*—I think it is agreed, that a definition is nothing else but the showing the meaning of one word by several other not synonymous terms. The meaning of words being only the ideas they are made to stand for by him that uses them, the meaning of any term is then showed, or the word is defined, when by other words the idea it is made the sign of, and annexed to, in the mind of the speaker, is as it were represented or set before the view of another; and thus its signification ascertained. This is the only use and end of definitions; and therefore the only measure of what is or is not a good definition.

7. *Simple Ideas, why undefinable.*—This being premised, I say that the names of simple ideas, and those only, are incapable of being defined. The reason whereof is this, that the several terms of a definition, signifying several ideas, they can all together by no means represent an idea, which has no composition at all: and therefore, a definition, which is properly nothing but the showing the meaning of one word by several others not signifying each the same thing, can in the names of simple ideas have no place.

8. *Instances: Motion.*—The not observing this difference in our ideas, and their names, has produced that eminent trifling in the schools, which is so easy to be observed in the definitions they give us of some few of these simple ideas. For, as to the greatest part of them, even those masters of definitions were fain to leave them untouched, merely by the impossibility they found in it. What more exquisite jargon could the wit of man invent, than this definition:— " The act of a being in power, as far forth as in power?" which would puzzle any rational man, to whom it was not already known by its famous absurdity, to guess what word it could ever be supposed to be the explication of. If Tully, asking a Dutchman what "beweeginge" was, should have received this explication in his own language, that it was "actus entis in potentia quatenus in potentia;" I ask whether any one can imagine he could thereby have understood what the word "beweeginge" signified, or have guessed what idea a Dutchman ordinarily had in his mind, and would signify to another, when he used that sound?

9. Nor have the modern philosophers, who have endeavoured to throw off the jargon of the schools, and speak intelligibly, much better succeeded in defining simple ideas, whether by explaining their causes, or any otherwise. The atomists, who define motion to be a passage from one place to another, what do they more than put one synonymous word for another? for what is passage other than motion? And if they were asked what passage was, how would they better define it than by motion? For is it not at least as proper and significant to say, passage is a motion from one place to another, as to say, motion is a passage? &c. This is to translate, and not to define, when we change two words of the same signification one for another; which, when one is better understood than the other, may serve to discover what idea the unknown stands for; but is very far from a definition, unless we will say every English word in the dictionary is the definition of the Latin word it answers, and that motion is a definition of motus. Nor will the successive application of the parts of the superfices of one body to those of another, which the Cartesians give us, prove a much better definition of motion, when well examined.

10. *Light.*—" The act of perspicuous, as far forth as perspicuous," is another peripatetic definition of a simple idea; which, though not more absurd than the former of motion, yet betrays its uselessness and insignificancy more plainly, because experience will easily convince any one that it cannot make the meaning of the word light (which it pretends to define) at all understood by a blind man; but the definition of motion appears not at first sight so useless, because it escapes this way of trial. For this simple idea entering by the touch as well as sight, it is impossible to show an example of any one, who has no other way to get the idea of motion, but barely by the definition of that name. Those who tell us that light is a great number of little globules, striking briskly on the bottom of the eye, speak more intelligibly than the schools; but yet these words ever so well understood would make the idea the word light stands for no more known to a man that understands it not before, than if one should tell him that light was nothing but a company of little tennis-balls, which fairies all day long

struck with rackets against some men's foreheads, whilst they passed by others. For granting this explication of the thing to be true, yet the idea of the cause of light, if we had it ever so exact, would no more give us the idea of light itself, as it is such a particular perception in us, than the idea of the figure and motion of a sharp piece of steel would give us the idea of that pain which it is able to cause in us. For the cause of any sensation, and the sensation itself, in all the simple ideas of one sense, are two ideas; and two ideas so different and distant one from another, that no two can be more so. And therefore, should Des Cartes's globules strike ever so long on the retina of a man, who was blind by a gutta serena, he would thereby never have any idea of light, or anything approaching it, though he understood ever so well what little globules were, and what striking on another body was. And therefore the Cartesians very well distinguish between that light which is the cause of that sensation in us, and the idea which is produced in us by it, and is that which is properly light.*

11. *Simple Ideas, why undefinable, further explained.*—Simple ideas, as has been shown, are only to be got by those impressions objects themselves make on our minds, by the proper inlets appointed to each sort. If they are not received this way, all the words in the world made use of to explain or define any of their names, will never be able to produce in us the idea it stands for. For words, being sounds, can produce in us no other simple ideas than of those very sounds; nor excite any in us, but by that voluntary connexion which is known to be between them and those

* To abridge the labour of the reader, I subjoin Hobbes' theory of light.—"His suppositis accedamus, ad causarum dictiones, et inquiramus primis loco causam lucis solara. Quoniam ergo corpus solare motu simplice circulari circumstantem æthereem substantiam modo ad unam, modo ad aliam partem, a se rejicit ita ut quæ partes proximæ soli sunt motæ ab ipso sole proxime remotiores rursus urgeant necesse est ut in quacunque distantia positi oculi prematur tandem pars anterior et ea parte pressa propagetur motus ad intimam organi visorii partem cor A motu autem cordis oreagentis oritur per eandem retro viam conatus desinens in conatu versus exteriora tunicæ quæ vocatur retina. Sed conatus iste ea exteriora illud ipsum est quod vocatur lumen, sive phantasma lucidi; nam propter hoc phantasma est quod objectum, vocatur lucidum." (Phisica, ch. 27, § 2.)—ED.

simple ideas which common use has made them the signs of. He that thinks otherwise, let him try if any words can give him the taste of a pineapple, and make him have the true idea of the relish of that celebrated delicious fruit. So far as he is told it has a resemblance with any tastes, whereof he has the ideas already in his memory, imprinted there by sensible objects not strangers to his palate, so far may he approach that resemblance in his mind. But this is not giving us that idea by a definition, but exciting in us other simple ideas by their known names; which will be still very different from the true taste of that fruit itself. In light and colours, and all other simple ideas, it is the same thing: for the signification of sounds is not natural, but only imposed and arbitrary. And no definition of light or redness is more fitted or able to produce either of those ideas in us, than the sound light or red by itself. For, to hope to produce an idea of light or colour by a sound, however formed, is to expect that sounds should be visible or colours audible, and to make the ears do the office of all the other senses. Which is all one as to say, that we might taste, smell, and see by the ears—a sort of philosophy worthy only of Sancho Pança; who had the faculty to see Dulcinea by hearsay. And therefore he that has not before received into his mind by the proper inlet the simple idea which any word stands for, can never come to know the signification of that word by any other words or sounds whatsoever, put together according to any rules of definition. The only way is by applying to his senses the proper object, and so producing that idea in him, for which he has learned the name already. A studious blind man, who had mightily beat his head about visible objects, and made use of the explication of his books and friends, to understand those names of light and colours which often came in his way, bragged one day that he now understood what scarlet signified. Upon which, his friend demanding what scarlet was, the blind man answered, It was like the sound of a trumpet. Just such an understanding of the name of any other simple idea will he have, who hopes to get it only from a definition, or other words made use of to explain it.

12. *The contrary shown in complex Ideas, by Instances of a*

CHAP. IV.] NAMES OF SIMPLE IDEAS. 27

Statue and Rainbow.—The case is quite otherwise in complex ideas; which, consisting of several simple ones, it is in the power of words standing for the several ideas that make that composition, to imprint complex ideas in the mind, which were never there before, and so make their names be understood. In such collections of ideas passing under one name, definition, or the teaching the signification of one word by several others, has place, and may make us understand the names of things which never came within the reach of our senses; and frame ideas suitable to those in other men's minds when they use those names: provided that none of the terms of the definition stand for any such simple ideas, which he to whom the explication is made has never yet had in his thought. Thus the word statue may be explained to a blind man by other words, when picture cannot; his senses having given him the idea of figure,* but not of colours, which therefore words cannot excite in him. This gained the prize to the painter against the statuary: each of which contending for the excellency of his art, and the statuary bragging that his was to be preferred, because it reached further, and even those who had lost their eyes, could yet perceive the excellency of it, the painter agreed to refer himself to the judgment of a blind man; who being brought where there was a statue made by the one, and a picture drawn by the other, he was first led to the statue, in which he traced with his hands all the lineaments of the face and body, and with great admiration applauded the skill of the workman. But being led to the picture, and having his hands laid upon it, was told, that now he touched the head, and then the forehead, eyes, nose, &c., as his hands moved over the parts of the picture on the cloth, without finding any the least distinction: whereupon he cried out, that certainly that must needs be a very admirable and divine piece of **workmanship**, which could represent to them all those parts, where he could neither feel nor perceive anything.

* In this view of the power of feeling to create true ideas of figure I perfectly concur; but it is wholly at variance with the crotchet advocated in a former part of the work, (book 2. ch. ix. § 8. where see note 45,) that a man who obtains from the touch only an idea of a cube and the idea of a globe, would not be able by sight to distinguish the one from the other.—ED.

13. He that should use the word rainbow to one who knew all those colours, but yet had never seen that phenomenon, would, by enumerating the figure, largeness, position, and order of the colours, so well define that word, that it might be perfectly understood. But yet that definition, how exact and perfect soever, would never make a blind man understand it; because several of the simple ideas that make that complex one being such as he never received by sensation and experience, no words are able to excite them in his mind.

14. *The same of complex Ideas when to be made intelligible by Words.*—Simple ideas, as has been shown, can only be got by experience from those objects which are proper to produce in us those perceptions. When by this means we have our minds stored with them, and know the names for them, then we are in a condition to define, and by definition to understand the names of complex ideas that are made up of them. But when any term stands for a simple idea that a man has never yet had in his mind, it is impossible by any words to make known its meaning to him. When any term stands for an idea a man is acquainted with, but is ignorant that that term is the sign of it, then another name of the same idea which he has been accustomed to, may make him understand its meaning. But in no case whatsoever is any name of any simple idea capable of a definition.

15. *Fourthly, Names of simple Ideas least doubtful.*— Fourthly, But though the names of simple ideas have not the help of definition to determine their signification, yet that hinders not but that they are generally less doubtful and uncertain than those of mixed modes and substances; because they standing only for one simple perception, men for the most part easily and perfectly agree in their signification; and there is little room for mistake and wrangling about their meaning. He that knows once that whiteness is the name of that colour he has observed in snow or milk, will not be apt to misapply that word as long as he retains that idea; which when he has quite lost, he is not apt to mistake the meaning of it, but perceives he understands it not. There is neither a multiplicity of simple ideas to be put together, which makes the doubtfulness in the names of mixed modes ; nor a supposed, but an unknown real essence, with properties depending thereon, the precise number whereof is also un-

known, which makes the difficulty in the names of substances. But, on the contrary, in simple ideas the whole signification of the name is known at once, and consists not of parts whereof more or less being put in, the idea may be varied, and so the signification of name be obscure or uncertain.

16. *Simple Ideas have few Ascents in lineâ prædicamentali.*— Fifthly, This further may be observed concerning simple ideas and their names, that they have but few ascents in prædicamentali, (as they call it,) from the lowest species to the summum genus. The reason whereof is, that the lowest species being but one simple idea, nothing can be left out of it; that so the difference being taken away, it may agree with some other thing in one idea common to them both; which, having one name, is the genus of the other two: v. g., there is nothing that can be left out of the idea of white and red to make them agree in one common appearance, and so have one general name; as rationality being left out of the complex idea of man, makes it agree with brute in the more general idea and name of animal: and therefore when, to avoid unpleasant enumerations men would comprehend both white and red, and several other such simple ideas, under one general name, they have been fain to do it by a word which denotes only the way they get into the mind. For when white, red, and yellow are all comprehended under the genus or name colour, it signifies no more but such ideas as are produced in the mind only by the sight, and have entrance only through the eyes. And when they would frame yet a more general term to comprehend both colours and sounds, and the like simple ideas, they do it by a word that signifies all such as come into the mind only by one sense: and so the general term quality, in its ordinary acceptation, comprehends colours, sounds, tastes, smells, and tangible qualities, with distinction from extension, number, motion, pleasure, and pain, which make impressions on the mind, and introduce their ideas by more senses than one.

17. *Sixthly, Names of simple Ideas not at all arbitrary.*— Sixthly, The names of simple ideas, substances, and mixed modes have also this difference;—that those of mixed modes stand for ideas perfectly arbitrary; those of substances are not perfectly so, but refer to a pattern, though with some latitude; and those of simple ideas are perfectly taken from

the existence of things, and are not arbitrary at all. Which, what difference it makes in the significations of their names, we shall see in the following chapters.

The names of simple modes differ little from those of simple ideas.

CHAPTER V.
OF THE NAMES OF MIXED MODES AND RELATIONS.

1. *They stand for abstract Ideas, as other general Names*— THE names of mixed modes being general, they stand, as has been shown, for sorts or species of things, each of which has its peculiar essence. The essences of these species also, as has been shown, are nothing but the abstract ideas in the mind, to which the name is annexed. Thus far the names and essences of mixed modes have nothing but what is common to them with other ideas: but if we take a little nearer survey of them, we shall find that they have something peculiar, which perhaps may deserve our attention.

2. *First, The Ideas they stand for are made by the Understanding.*—The first particularity I shall observe in them, is, that the abstract ideas, or, if you please, the essences of the several species of mixed modes, are made by the understanding, wherein they differ from those of simple ideas: in which sort the mind has no power to make any one, but only receives such as are presented to it, by the real existence of things operating upon it.

3. *Secondly, Made arbitrarily and without Patterns.*—In the next place, these essences of the species of mixed modes are not only made by the mind, but made very arbitrarily, made without patterns, or reference to any real existence. Wherein they differ from those of substances, which carry with them the supposition of some real being, from which they are taken, and to which they are conformable. But, in its complex ideas of mixed modes, the mind takes a liberty not to follow the existence of things exactly. It unites and retains certain collections, as so many distinct specific ideas, whilst others, that as often occur in nature, and are as plainly suggested by outward things, pass neglected, without particular names or specifications. Nor does the mind, in

these of mixed modes, as in the complex idea of substances, examine them by the real existence of things; or verify them by patterns containing such peculiar compositions in nature. To know whether his idea of adultery or incest be right, will a man seek it anywhere amongst things existing? Or is it true because any one has been witness to such an action? No: but it suffices here, that men have put together such a collection into one complex idea, that makes the archetype and specific idea, whether ever any such action were committed in rerum natura or no.

4. *How this is done.*—To understand this right, we must consider wherein this making of these complex ideas consists; and that is not in the making any new idea, but putting together those which the mind had before. Wherein the mind does these three things: first, it chooses a certain number; secondly, it gives them connexion, and makes them into one idea; thirdly, it ties them together by a name. If we examine how the mind proceeds in these, and what liberty it takes in them, we shall easily observe how these essences of the species of mixed modes are the workmanship of the mind; and, consequently, that the species themselves are of men's making.

5. *Evidently arbitrary, in that the Idea is often before the Existence.*—Nobody can doubt but that these ideas of mixed modes are made by a voluntary collection of ideas, put together in the mind, independent from any original patterns in nature, who will but reflect that this sort of complex ideas may be made, abstracted, and have names given them, and so a species be constituted, before any one individual of that species ever existed. Who can doubt but the ideas of sacrilege or adultery might be framed in the minds of men, and have names given them, and so these species of mixed modes be constituted before either of them was ever committed; and might be as well discoursed of and reasoned about, and as certain truths discovered of them whilst yet they had no being but in the understanding, as well as now, that they have but too frequently a real existence? Whereby it is plain how much the sorts of mixed modes are the creatures of the understanding, where they have a being as subservient to all the ends of real truth and knowledge, as when they really exist. And we cannot doubt but law-

makers have often made laws about species of actions which were only the creatures of their own understandings—beings that had no other existence but in their own minds. And I think nobody can deny but that the resurrection was a species of mixed modes in the mind, before it really existed.

6. *Instances:—Murder, Incest, Stabbing.*—To see how arbitrarily these essences of mixed modes are made by the mind, we need but take a view of almost any of them. A little looking into them will satisfy us that it is the mind that combines several scattered independent ideas into one complex one, and, by the common name it gives them, makes them the essence of a certain species, without regulating itself by any connexion they have in nature. For what greater connexion in nature has the idea of a man, than the idea of a sheep, with killing, that this is made a particular species of action, signified by the word murder, and the other not? Or what union is there in nature between the idea of the relation of a father with killing, than that of a son or neighbour, that those are combined into one complex idea, and thereby made the essence of the distinct species parricide, whilst the other makes no distinct species at all? But, though they have made killing a man's father or mother a distinct species from killing his son or daughter, yet, in some other cases, son and daughter are taken in too, as well as father and mother: and they are all equally comprehended in the same species, as in that of incest. Thus the mind in mixed modes arbitrarily unites into complex ideas such as it finds convenient; whilst others that have altogether as much union in nature, are left loose, and never combined into one idea, because they have no need of one name. It is evident then that the mind by its free choice gives a connexion to a certain number of ideas, which in nature have no more union with one another than others that it leaves out: why else is the part of the weapon the beginning of the wound is made with taken notice of to make the distinct species called stabbing, and the figure and matter of the weapon left out? I do not say this is done without reason, as we shall see more by and by; but this I say, that it is done by the free choice of the mind, pursuing its own ends; and that, therefore, these species of mixed

modes are the workmanship of the understanding: and there is nothing more evident than that, for the most part, in the framing these ideas, the mind searches not its patterns in nature, nor refers the ideas it makes to the real existence of things, but puts such together as may best serve its own purposes, without tying itself to a precise imitation of anything that really exists.

7. *But still subservient to the End of Language.*—But, though these complex ideas or essences of mixed modes depend on the mind, and are made by it with great liberty, yet they are not made at random, and jumbled together without any reason at all. Though these complex ideas be not always copied from nature, yet they are always suited to the end for which abstract ideas are made: and though they be combinations made of ideas that are loose enough, and have as little union in themselves as several other to which the mind never gives a connexion that combines them into one idea, yet they are always made for the convenience of communication, which is the chief end of language. The use of language is, by short sounds to signify with ease and dispatch general conceptions; wherein not only abundance of particulars may be contained, but also a great variety of independent ideas collected into one complex one. In the making therefore of the species of mixed modes, men have had regard only to such combinations as they had occasion to mention one to another: those they have combined into distinct complex ideas, and given names to; whilst others, that in nature have as near a union, are left loose and unregarded. For, to go no further than human actions themselves, if they would make distinct abstract ideas of all the varieties which might be observed in them, the number must be infinite, and the memory confounded with the plenty, as well as overcharged to little purpose. It suffices, that men make and name so many complex ideas of these mixed modes as they find they have occasion to have names for, in the ordinary occurrence of their affairs. If they join to the idea of killing the idea of father or mother, and so make a distinct species from killing a man's son or neighbour, it is because of the different heinousness of the crime, and the distinct punishment is due to the murdering a man's father and mother, different from what ought to be inflicted on

the murder of a son or neighbour; and therefore they find it necessary to mention it by a distinct name, which is the end of making that distinct combination. But though the ideas of mother and daughter are so differently treated, in reference to the idea of killing, that the one is joined with it to make a distinct abstract idea with a name, and so a distinct species, and the other not; yet, in respect of carnal knowledge, they are both taken in under incest: and that still for the same convenience of expressing under one name, and reckoning of one species such unclean mixtures as have a peculiar turpitude beyond others; and this to avoid circumlocutions and tedious descriptions.

8. *Whereof the intranslatable Words of divers Languages are a Proof.*—A moderate skill in different languages will easily satisfy one of the truth of this; it being so obvious to observe great store of words in one language which have not any that answer them in another. Which plainly shows that those of one country, by their customs and manner of life, have found occasion to make several complex ideas, and given names to them, which others never collected into specific ideas. This could not have happened if these species were the steady workmanship of nature, and not collections made and abstracted by the mind, in order to naming, and for the convenience of communication. The terms of our law, which are not empty sounds, will hardly find words that answer them in the Spanish or Italian, no scanty languages; much less, I think, could any one translate them into the Caribbee or Westoe tongues: and the Versura* of the Romans, or Corban† of the Jews, have no words in other

* This Roman law-term is thus explained by Festus:—"Versuram facere, mutuam pecuniam sumere ex eo dictum est, quod initio, qui mutuabantur ab aliis, non ut domum ferrent, sed ut aliis solverent, velut verterent creditorem." (p. 1004, ed. Lond.) A man was said "versuram facere," when he borrowed from one person to pay another. (Dacier, in locum.)—ED.

† Mr. Trollope, in his note on Matthew xv. 5, furnishes a very brief and satisfactory explanation of this term. From Mark xv. 11, it appears that δῶρον here interprets the Hebrew word κορβᾶν. The notion of Corban was this: that if a man wished to avoid supporting his parents, or any other duty, he devoted the means of doing so to God; not indeed with the intention of applying the thing so devoted to sacred purposes, but that the mere saying *Let it be Corban*, might make it impossible to assign it to the use against which the vow was made."—ED.

languages to answer them; the reason whereof is plain, from what has been said. Nay, if we look a little more nearly into this matter, and exactly compare different languages, we shall find, that, though they have words which in translations and dictionaries are supposed to answer one another, yet there is scarce one of ten amongst the names of complex ideas, especially of mixed modes, that stands for the same precise idea, which the word does that in dictionaries it is rendered by. There are no ideas more common and less compounded than the measures of time, extension, and weight; and the Latin names, hora, pes, libra, are without difficulty rendered by the English names, hour, foot, and pound: but yet there is nothing more evident than that the ideas a Roman annexed to these Latin names, were very far different from those which an Englishman expresses by those English ones. And if either of these should make use of the measures that those of the other language designed by their names, he would be quite out in his account. These are too sensible proofs to be doubted; and we shall find this much more so in the names of more abstract and compounded ideas, such as are the greatest part of those which make up moral discourses; whose names, when men come curiously to compare with those they are translated into, in other languages, they will find very few of them exactly to correspond in the whole extent of their significations.

9. *This shows Species to be made for Communication.*—The reason why I take so particular notice of this, is, that we may not be mistaken about genera and species, and their essences, as if they were things regularly and constantly made by nature, and had a real existence in things; when they appear, upon a more wary survey, to be nothing else but an artifice of the understanding, for the easier signifying such collections of ideas as it should often have occasion to communicate by one general term; under which divers particulars, as far forth as they agreed to that abstract idea, might be comprehended. And if the doubtful signification of the word species may make it sound harsh to some, that I say the species of mixed modes are made by the understanding; yet, I think, it can by nobody be denied that it is the mind makes those abstract complex ideas, to which specific names are given. And if it be true, as it is, that the mind makes

the patterns for sorting and naming of things, I leave it to be considered who makes the boundaries of the sort or species; since with me species and sort have no other difference than that of a Latin and English idiom.

10. *In mixed Modes it is the Name that ties the Combination together, and makes it a Species.*—The near relation that there is between species, essences, and their general name—at least in mixed modes—will further appear when we consider that it is the name that seems to preserve those essences, and give them their lasting duration. For the connexion between the loose parts of those complex ideas being made by the mind, this union, which has no particular foundation in nature, would cease again, were there not something that did, as it were, hold it together, and keep the parts from scattering. Though therefore it be the mind that makes the collection, it is the name which is as it were the knot that ties them fast together. What a vast variety of different ideas does the word triumphus hold together, and deliver to us as one species! Had this name been never made, or quite lost, we might, no doubt, have had descriptions of what passed in that solemnity: but yet, I think, that which holds those different parts together, in the unity of one complex idea, is that very word annexed to it; without which the several parts of that would no more be thought to make one thing, than any other show, which having never been made but once, had never been united into one complex idea, under one denomination. How much, therefore, in mixed modes, the unity necessary to any essence depends on the mind, and how much the continuation and fixing of that unity depends on the name in common use annexed to it, I leave to be considered by those who look upon essences and species as real established things in nature.

11. Suitable to this, we find that men speaking of mixed modes, seldom imagine or take any other for species of them, but such as are set out by name; because they being of man's making only, in order to naming, no such species are taken notice of, or supposed to be, unless a name be joined to it, as the sign of man's having combined into one idea several loose ones; and by that name giving a lasting union to the parts, which would otherwise cease to have any, as soon as the mind laid by that abstract idea, and ceased actually to think

on it. But when a name is once annexed to it, wherein the parts of that complex idea have a settled and permanent union, then is the essence, as it were, established, and the species looked on as complete. For to what purpose should the memory charge itself with such compositions, unless it were by abstraction to make them general? And to what purpose make them general, unless it were that they might have general names for the convenience of discourse and communication? Thus we see, that killing a man with a sword or a hatchet are looked on as no distinct species of action; but if the point of the sword first enter the body, it passes for a distinct species, where it has a distinct name; as in England, in whose language it is called stabbing; but in another country, where it has not happened to be specified under a peculiar name, it passes not for a distinct species. But in the species of corporeal substances, though it be the mind that makes the nominal essence; yet since those ideas which are combined in it are supposed to have an union in nature, whether the mind joins them or not, therefore those are looked on as distinct names, without any operation of the mind, either abstracting or giving a name to that complex idea.

12. *For the Originals of mixed Modes, we look no further than the Mind, which also shows them to be the Workmanship of the Understanding.*—Conformable also to what has been said concerning the essences of the species of mixed modes, that they are the creatures of the understanding rather than the works of nature; conformable, I say, to this, we find that their names lead our thoughts to the mind, and no further. When we speak of justice, or gratitude, we frame to ourselves no imagination of anything existing, which we would conceive; but our thoughts terminate in the abstract ideas of those virtues, and look not further, as they do when we speak of a horse, or iron, whose specific ideas we consider not as barely in the mind, but as in things themselves, which afford the original patterns of those ideas. But in mixed modes, at least the most considerable parts of them, which are moral beings, we consider the original patterns as being in the mind, and to those we refer for the distinguishing of particular beings under names. And hence I think it is that these essences of the species of mixed modes are by a

more particular name called notions, as, by a peculiar right, appertaining to the understanding.

13. *Their being made by the Understanding without Patterns, shows the Reason why they are so compounded.*—Hence, likewise, we may learn why the complex ideas of mixed modes are commonly more compounded and decompounded, than those of natural substances; because they being the workmanship of the understanding, pursuing only its own ends, and the conveniency of expressing in short those ideas it would make known to another, it does with great liberty unite often into one abstract idea things, that, in their nature, have no coherence; and so under one term bundle together a great variety of compounded and decompounded ideas. Thus the name of procession, what a great mixture of independent ideas of persons, habits, tapers, orders, motions, sounds, does it contain in that complex one, which the mind of man has arbitrarily put together, to express by that one name! whereas the complex ideas of the sorts of substances are usually made up of only a small number of simple ones; and in the species of animals, these two, viz., shape and voice, commonly make the whole nominal essence.

14. *Names of mixed Modes stand always for their real Essences.*—Another thing we may observe from what has been said, is, that the names of mixed modes always signify (when they have any determined signification) the real essences of their species. For these abstract ideas being the workmanship of the mind, and not referred to the real existence of things, there is no supposition of anything more signified by that name, but barely that complex idea the mind itself has formed, which is all it would have expressed by it, and is that on which all the properties of the species depend, and from which alone they all flow: and so in these the real and nominal essence is the same, which, of what concernment it is to the certain knowledge of general truth, we shall see hereafter.

15. *Why their Names are usually got before their Ideas.*—This also may show us the reason why for the most part the names of mixed modes are got before the ideas they stand for are perfectly known; because, there being no species of these ordinarily taken notice of but what have names, and those species, or rather their essences, being abstract complex ideas

made arbitrarily by the mind, it is convenient, if not necessary, to know the names, before one endeavour to frame these complex ideas; unless a man will fill his head with a company of abstract complex ideas, which, others having no names for, he has nothing to do with, but to lay by and forget again. I confess, that in the beginning of languages it was necessary to have the idea before one gave it the name, and so it is still, where, making a new complex idea, one also, by giving it a new name, makes a new word. But this concerns not languages made, which have generally pretty well provided for ideas which men have frequent occasion to have and communicate; and in such, I ask whether it be not the ordinary method, that children learn the names of mixed modes before they have their ideas? What one of a thousand ever frames the abstract ideas of glory and ambition, before he has heard the names of them? In simple ideas and substances I grant it is otherwise; which, being such ideas as have a real existence and union in nature, the ideas and names are got one before the other, as it happens.

16. *Reason of my being so large on this Subject.*—What has been said here of mixed modes is, with very little difference, applicable also to relations; which, since every man himself may observe, I may spare myself the pains to enlarge on: especially, since what I have here said concerning words in this third book, will possibly be thought by some to be much more than what so slight a subject required. I allow it might be brought into a narrower compass; but I was willing to stay my reader on an argument that appears to me new and a little out of the way, (I am sure it is one I thought not of when I began to write,) that, by searching it to the bottom, and turning it on every side, some part or other might meet with every one's thoughts, and give occasion to the most averse or negligent to reflect on a general miscarriage, which, though of great consequence, is little taken notice of. When it is considered what a pudder is made about essences, and how much all sorts of knowledge, discourse, and conversation are pestered and disordered by the careless and confused use and application of words, it will perhaps be thought worth while thoroughly to lay it open; and I shall be pardoned if I have dwelt long on an

argument which I think, therefore, needs to be inculcated, because the faults men are usually guilty of in this kind, are not only the greatest hindrances of true knowledge, but are so well thought of as to pass for it. Men would often see what a small pittance of reason and truth, or possibly none at all, is mixed with those huffing opinions they are swelled with, if they would but look beyond fashionable sounds, and observe what ideas are or are not comprehended under those words with which they are so armed at all points, and with which they so confidently lay about them. I shall imagine I have done some service to truth, peace, and learning, if, by any enlargement on this subject, I can make men reflect on their own use of language, and give them reason to suspect, that, since it is frequent for others, it may also be possible for them to have sometimes very good and approved words in their mouths and writings, with very uncertain, little, or no signification. And therefore it is not unreasonable for them to be wary herein themselves, and not to be unwilling to have them examined by others. With this design, therefore, I shall go on with what I have further to say concerning this matter.

CHAPTER VI.

OF THE NAMES OF SUBSTANCES.

1. *The common Names of Substances stand for Sorts.*—THE common names of substances, as well as other general terms, stand for sorts; which is nothing else but the being made signs of such complex ideas, wherein several particular substances do or might agree, by virtue of which they are capable of being comprehended in one common conception, and signified by one name. I say do or might agree, for though there be but one sun existing in the world, yet the idea of it being abstracted, so that more substances (if there were several) might each agree in it, it is as much a sort as if there were as many suns as there are stars.* They want not their reasons who think there are, and that each fixed star would answer the idea the name sun stands for,

* Modern astronomy has ascertained, that the stars are in reality suns; that is, the centres of systems like our own.—ED.

to one who was placed in a due distance; which, by the way, may show us how much the sorts, or, if you please, genera and species of things (for those Latin terms signify to me no more than the English word sort) depend on such collections of ideas as men have made, and not on the real nature of things; since it is not impossible but that, in propriety of speech, that might be a sun to one which is a star to another.

2. *The Essence of each Sort is the abstract Idea.*—The measure and boundary of each sort or species whereby it is constituted that particular sort, and distinguished from others, is that we call its essence, which is nothing but that abstract idea to which the name is annexed; so that everything contained in that idea is essential to that sort. This, though it be all the essence of natural substances that we know, or by which we distinguish them into sorts, yet I call it by a peculiar name, the nominal essence, to distinguish it from the real constitution of substances, upon which depends this nominal essence, and all the properties of that sort; which, therefore, as has been said, may be called the real essence; v. g., the nominal essence of gold is that complex idea the word gold stands for, let it be, for instance, a body yellow, of a certain weight, malleable, fusible, and fixed. But the real essence is the constitution of the insensible parts of that body, on which those qualities and all the other properties of gold depend. How far these two are different, though they are both called essence, is obvious at first sight to discover.

3. *The nominal and Essence different.*—For though perhaps voluntary motion, with sense and reason, joined to a body of a certain shape, be the complex idea to which I and others annex the name man, and so be the nominal essence of the species so called, yet nobody will say that complex idea is the real essence and source of all those operations which are to be found in any individual of that sort. The foundation of all those qualities which are the ingredients of our complex idea, is something quite different: and had we such a knowledge of that constitution of man, from which his faculties of moving, sensation, and reasoning, and other powers flow, and on which his so regular shape depends, as it is possible angels have, and it is certain his

Maker has, we should have a quite other idea of his essence than what now is contained in our definition of that species, be it what it will; and our idea of any individual man would be as far different from what it is now, as is his who knows all the springs and wheels and other contrivances within of the famous clock at Strasburg, from that which a gazing countryman has for it, who barely sees the motion of the hand, and hears the clock strike, and observes only some of the outward appearances.*

4. *Nothing essential to Individuals.*—That essence, in the ordinary use of the word, relates to sorts, and that it is considered in particular beings no further than as they are ranked into sorts, appears from hence: that, take but away the abstract ideas by which we sort individuals, and rank them under common names, and then the thought of anything essential to any of them instantly vanishes; we have no notion of the one without the other, which plainly shows their relation. It is necessary for me to be as I am; God and nature has made me so; but there is nothing I have is essential to me. An accident or disease may very much alter my colour or shape; a fever or fall may take away my reason or memory, or both, and an apoplexy leave neither sense nor understanding, no, nor life. Other creatures of my shape may be made with more and better, or fewer and worse faculties than I have; and others may have reason and sense in a shape and body very different from mine. None of these are essential to the one or the other, or to any individual whatever, till the mind refers it to some sort or species of things; and then presently, according to the

* Several of our older travellers have spoken of the great-clock at Strasburg, but Skippon's brief description will suffice to give the reader who happens not to have the others at hand, a sufficient idea of this curious piece of mechanism: "We saw here the famous clock described by Tom Coryat. Towards the bottom is a great circle, with the calendar, (a figure pointing to the day of the month,) and within that are fifteen other circles, each being divided into one hundred parts, the calendar lasting from 1573 to 1672. In the middle is a map of Germany, and on it is written, '*Conradus Dasypodius et David Wolkenstein Vratist designabant Thobias Stunner, pingebat,* A.D. MDLXXIII.' The clock-work was made by one Isaac Habrechtus, of Strasburg. When the clock strikes, a little figure keeps time at every stroke, with a sceptre, and another figure turns an hour-glass, and twelve apostles follow one another, and a cock crows." (Ap. Churchill, Vol. VI 457.)—ED.

abstract idea of that sort, something is found essential. Let any one examine his own thoughts, and he wil find that as soon as he supposes or speaks of essential, the consideration of some species, or the complex idea signified by some general name comes into his mind; and it is in reference to that, that this or that quality is said to be essential. So that if it be asked, whether it be essential to me or any other particular corporeal being to have reason? I say, no; no more than it is essential to this white thing I write on to have words in it. But if that particular being be to be counted of the sort man, and to have the name man given it, then reason is essential to it, supposing reason to be a part of the complex idea the name man stands for; as it is essential to this thing I write on to contain words if I will give it the name treatise, and rank it under that species. So that essential and not essential relate only to our abstract ideas, and the names annexed to them; which amounts to no more than this, that whatever particular thing has not in it those qualities which are contained in the abstract idea which any general term stands for, cannot be ranked under that species nor be called by that name, since that abstract idea is the very essence of that species.

5. Thus, if the idea of body with some people be bare extension or space, then solidity is not essential to body; if others make the idea to which they give the name body to be solidity and extension, then solidity is essential to body. That, therefore, and that alone is considered as essential, which makes a part of the complex idea the name of a sort stands for, without which no particular thing can be reckoned of that sort, nor be entitled to that name. Should there be found a parcel of matter that had all the other qualities that are in iron, but wanted obedience to the loadstone, and would neither be drawn by it nor receive direction from it, would any one question whether it wanted anything essential? It would be absurd to ask, whether a thing really existing wanted anything essential to it; or could it be demanded, whether this made an essential or specific difference or not, since we have no other measure of essential or specific but our abstract ideas? And to talk of specific differences in nature, without reference to general ideas in names, is to talk unintelligibly. For I would ask any one, what is

sufficient to make an essential difference in nature between any two particular beings, without any regard had to some abstract idea, which is looked upon as the essence and standard of a species? All such patterns and standards being quite laid aside, particular beings, considered barely in themselves, will be found to have all their qualities equally essential; and everything in each individual will be essential to it, or, which is more, nothing at all. For though it may be reasonable to ask, whether obeying the magnet be essential to iron? yet I think it is very improper and insignificant to ask, whether it be essential to the particular parcel of matter I cut my pen with, without considering it under the name iron, or as being of a certain species? And if, as has been said, our abstract ideas which have names annexed to them are the boundaries of species, nothing can be essential but what is contained in those ideas.

6. It is true, I have often mentioned a real essence, distinct in substances from those abstract ideas of them, which I call their nominal essence. By this real essence I mean the real constitution of anything, which is the foundation of all those properties that are combined in, and are constantly found to co-exist with the nominal essence; that particular constitution which everything has within itself, without any relation to anything without it. But essence, even in this sense, relates to a sort, and supposes a species; for being that real constitution on which the properties depend, it necessarily supposes a sort of things, properties belonging only to species, and not to individuals; v. g., supposing the nominal essence of gold to be a body of such a peculiar colour and weight, with malleability and fusibility, the real essence is that constitution of the parts of matter on which these qualities and their union depend; and is also the foundation of its solubility in aqua regia and other properties, accompanying that complex idea. Here are essences and properties, but all upon supposition of a sort or general abstract idea, which is considered as immutable; but there is no individual parcel of matter to which any of these qualities are so annexed as to be essential to it or inseparable from it. That which is essential belongs to it as a condition, whereby it is of this or that sort; but take away the consideration of its being ranked under the name of some abstract idea, and then there is

nothing necessary to it, nothing inseparable from it. Indeed, as to the real essences of substances, we only suppose their being, without precisely knowing what they are; but that which annexes them still to the species is the nominal essence, of which they are the supposed foundation and cause.

7. *The nominal Essence bounds the Species.*—The next thing to be considered is, by which of those essences it is that substances are determined into sorts or species; and that, it is evident, is by the nominal essence; for it is that alone that the name, which is the mark of the sort, signifies. It is impossible, therefore, that anything should determine the sorts of things, which we rank under general names, but that idea which that name is designed as a mark for; which is that, as has been shown, which we call nominal essence. Why do we say this is a horse, and that a mule; this is an an animal, that an herb? How comes any particular thing to be of this or that sort, but because it has that nominal essence, or, which is all one, agrees to that abstract idea that name is annexed to? And I desire any one but to reflect on his own thoughts, when he hears or speaks any of those or other names of substances, to know what sort of essences they stand for.

8. And that the species of things to us are nothing but the ranking them under distinct names, according to the complex ideas in us, and not according to precise, distinct, real essences in them, is plain from hence: that we find many of the individuals that are ranked into one sort, called by one common name, and so received as being of one species, have yet qualities depending on their real constitutions, as far different one from another as from others from which they are accounted to differ specifically. This, as it is easy to be observed by all who have to do with natural bodies, so chemists especially are often, by sad experience, convinced of it, when they, sometimes in vain, seek for the same qualities in one parcel of sulphur, antimony, or vitriol, which they have found in others. For, though they are bodies of the same species, having the same nominal essence, under the same name, yet do they often, upon severe ways of examination, betray qualities so different one from another, as to frustrate the expectation and labour of very wary chemists.

But if things were distinguished into species, according to their real essences, it would be as impossible to find different properties in any two individual substances of the same species, as it is to find different properties in two circles, or two equilateral triangles. That is properly the essence to us, which determines every particular to this or that classis; or, which is the same thing, to this or that general name: and what can that be else, but that abstract idea to which that name is annexed; and so has, in truth, a reference, not so much to the being of particular things, as to their general denominations?

9. *Not the real Essence, which we know not.*—Nor indeed can we rank and sort things, and consequently (which is the end of sorting) denominate them by their real essences; because we know them not. Our faculties carry us no further towards the knowledge and distinction of substances, than a collection of those sensible ideas which we observe in them; which, however made with the greatest diligence and exactness we are capable of, yet is more remote from the true internal constitution from which those qualities flow, than, as I said, a countryman's idea is from the inward contrivance of that famous clock at Strasburg, whereof he only sees the outward figure and motions. There is not so contemptible a plant or animal, that does not confound the most enlarged understanding. Though the familiar use of things about us take off our wonder, yet it cures not our ignorance. When we come to examine the stones we tread on, or the iron we daily handle, we presently find we know not their make, and can give no reason of the different qualities we find in them. It is evident the internal constitution, whereon their properties depend, is unknown to us; for to go no further than the grossest and most obvious we can imagine amongst them, what is that texture of parts, that real essence, that makes lead and antimony fusible, wood and stones not? What makes lead and iron malleable, antimony and stones not? And yet how infinitely these come short of the fine contrivances and inconceivable real essences of plants or animals, every one knows. The workmanship of the all-wise and powerful God in the great fabric of the universe, and every part thereof, further exceeds the capacity and comprehension of the most inquisitive and intelligent man, than the best

contrivance of the most ingenious man doth the conceptions of the most ignorant of rational creatures. Therefore we in vain pretend to range things into sorts, and dispose them into certain classes under names, by their real essences, that are so far from our discovery or comprehension. A blind man may as soon sort things by their colours, and he that has lost his smell as well distinguish a lily and a rose by their odours, as by those internal constitutions which he knows not. He that thinks he can distinguish sheep and goats by their real essences, that are unknown to him, may be pleased to try his skill in those species called cassiowary and querechinchio, and by their internal real essences determine the boundaries of those species, without knowing the complex idea of sensible qualities that each of those names stand for, in the countries where those animals are to be found.

10. *Not substantial Forms, which we know less.*—Those, therefore, who have been taught that the several species of substances had their distinct internal substantial forms; and that it was those forms which made the distinction of substances into their true species and genera, were led yet further out of the way by having their minds set upon fruitless inquiries after substantial forms, wholly unintelligible, and whereof we have scarce so much as any obscure or confused conception in general.

11. *That the nominal Essence is that whereby we distinguish Species, further evident from Spirits.*—That our ranking and distinguishing natural substances into species consists in the nominal essences the mind makes, and not in the real essences to be found in the things themselves, is further evident from our ideas of spirits; for the mind getting only by reflecting on its own operations those simple ideas which it attributes to spirits, it hath or can have no other notion of spirit but by attributing all those operations it finds in itself to a sort of beings, without consideration of matter. And even the most advanced notion we have of God is but attributing the same simple ideas which we have got from reflection on what we find in ourselves, and which we conceive to have more perfection in them than would be in their absence; attributing, I say, those simple ideas to him in an unlimited degree. Thus, having got from reflecting on our-

selves the idea of existence, knowledge, power, and pleasure —each of which we find it better to have than to want; and the more we have of each the better—joining all these together, with infinity to each of them, we have the complex idea of an eternal, omniscient, omnipotent, infinitely wise and happy being. And though we are told that there are different species of angels; yet we know not how to frame distinct specific ideas of them: not out of any conceit that the existence of more species than one of spirits is impossible, but because having no more simple ideas (nor being able to frame more) applicable to such beings, but only those few taken from ourselves, and from the actions of our own minds in thinking, and being delighted, and moving several parts of our bodies, we can no otherwise distinguish in our conceptions the several species of spirits one from another, but by attributing those operations and powers we find in ourselves to them in a higher or lower degree; and so have no very distinct specific ideas of spirits, except only of God, to whom we attribute both duration and all those other ideas with infinity; to the other spirits, with limitation. Nor, as I humbly conceive, do we, between God and them in our ideas, put any difference by any number of simple ideas which we have of one and not of the other, but only that of infinity.* All the particular ideas of existence, knowledge, will, power, and motion, &c., being ideas derived from the operations of our minds, we attribute all of them to all sorts of spirits, with the difference only of degrees, to the utmost we can imagine, even infinity, when we would frame as well as we can an idea of the first being; who yet, it is certain, is infinitely more remote, in the real excellency of his nature, from the highest and perfectest of all created

* Hence the employment of angels as agents in poetry always proves a cold and lifeless contrivance, compared, at least, with the introduction of human actors. We can scarcely be made to sympathize with natures entirely unknown to us; and it is only by regarding God as the author of our existence, as our great parent, that we can be said actually to love him. He is to us what a father is to the child who has never seen him. Our own existence proves his—our intelligence his wisdom—our happiness his goodness—our afflictions the existence of sin, and the necessity of chastisement. We can therefore love God with an affectionate love, with a love which constitutes the purest bliss of all who feel it. But of angels we know nothing.—ED.

beings, than the greatest man, nay, purest seraph, is from the most contemptible part of matter; and consequently must infinitely exceed what our narrow understandings can conceive of him.

12. *Whereof there are probably numberless Species.*—It is not impossible to conceive nor repugnant to reason, that there may be many species of spirits, as much separated and diversified one from another by distinct properties whereof we have no ideas, as the species of sensible things are distinguished one from another by qualities which we know and observe in them. That there should be more species of intelligent creatures above us than there are of sensible and material below us, is probable to me from hence, that in all the visible corporeal world, we see no chasms or gaps.* All quite down from us the descent is by easy steps, and a continued series of things, that in each remove differ very little one from the other. There are fishes that have wings, and are not strangers to the airy region; and there are some birds that are inhabitants of the water whose blood is cold as fishes, and their flesh so like in taste, that the scrupulous are allowed them on fish-days. There are animals so near of kin both to birds and beasts that they are in the middle between both: amphibious animals link the terrestrial and aquatic together; seals live at land and sea, and porpoises have the warm blood and entrails of a hog, not to mention what is confidently reported of mermaids, or sea-men. There are some brutes that seem to have as much knowledge and

---

* Pope has clothed this opinion with exquisite versification; and, in itself, it is not, though a mere conjecture, inconsistent with philosophy. It will, however, occur to every man, that between the highest of created beings and his Creator, there must always be an infinite gap. The very terms Creator and created suggest thus much. However, Pope escapes all difficulties by the brevity of his exposition, which will admit of more than one interpretation:—

" See, through this air, this ocean, and this earth,
All matter quick, and bursting into birth.
Above, how high progressive life may go!
Around, how wide! how deep extend below!
Vast chain of being! *which from God began,*
Nature's ethereal, human, angel, man,
Beast, bird, fish, insect, what no eye can see,
No glass can reach *from infinite to thee,*
From thee to nothing."—ESSAY ON MAN, 1. § 8.—ED.

reason as some that are called men; and the animal and vegetable kingdoms are so nearly joined, that, if you will take the lowest of one and the highest of the other, there will scarce be perceived any great difference between them; and so on, till we come to the lowest and the most inorganical parts of matter, we shall find everywhere that the several species are linked together, and differ but in almost insensible degrees. And when we consider the infinite power and wisdom of the Maker, we have reason to think that it is suitable to the magnificent harmony of the universe, and the great design and infinite goodness of the Architect, that the species of creatures should also, by gentle degrees, ascend upward from us toward his infinite perfection, as we see they gradually descend from us downwards: which if it be probable, we have reason then to be persuaded that there are far more species of creatures above us than there are beneath: we being, in degrees of perfection, much more remote from the infinite being of God than we are from the lowest state of being, and that which approaches nearest to nothing. And yet, of all those distinct species, for the reasons above-said, we have no clear distinct ideas.

13. *The nominal Essence that of the Species, proved from Water and Ice.*—But to return to the species of corporeal substances. If I should ask any one whether ice and water were two distinct species of things, I doubt not but I should be answered in the affirmative: and it cannot be denied but he that says they are two distinct species is in the right. But if an Englishman bred in Jamaica, who perhaps had never seen nor heard of ice, coming into England in the winter, find the water he put in his basin at night in a great part frozen in the morning, and, not knowing any peculiar name it had, should call it hardened water; I ask whether this would be a new species to him different from water? And I think it would be answered here, it would not be to him a new species, no more than congealed jelly, when it is cold, is a distinct species from the same jelly fluid and warm; or than liquid gold in the furnace is a distinct species from hard gold in the hands of a workman. And if this be so, it is plain that our distinct species are nothing but distinct complex ideas, with distinct names annexed to them. It is true every substance that exists has its peculiar constitution,

whereon depend those sensible qualities and powers we observe in it; but the ranking of things into species (which is nothing but sorting them under several titles) is done by us according to the ideas that we have of them: which, though sufficient to distinguish them by names, so that we may be able to discourse of them when we have them not present before us; yet if we suppose it to be done by their real internal constitutions, and that things existing are distinguished by nature into species by real essences, according as we distinguish them into species by names, we shall be liable to great mistakes.

14. *Difficulties against a certain Number of real Essences.*—To distinguish substantial beings into species, according to the usual supposition, that there are certain precise essences or forms of things, whereby all the individuals existing are by nature distinguished into species, these things are necessary:—

15. First, to be assured that nature in the production of things always designs them to partake of certain regulated established essences, which are to be the models of all things to be produced. This, in that crude sense it is usually proposed, would need some better explication before it can fully be assented to.

16. Secondly, It would be necessary to know whether nature always attains that essence it designs in the production of things. The irregular and monstrous births, that in divers sorts of animals have been observed, will always give us reason to doubt of one or both of these.

17. Thirdly, It ought to be determined whether those we call monsters be really a distinct species, according to the scholastic notion of the word species; since it is certain that everything that exists has its particular constitution: and yet we find that some of these monstrous productions have few or none of those qualities which are supposed to result from, and accompany the essence of that species from whence they derive their originals, and to which, by their descent, they seem to belong.

18. *Our nominal Essences of Substances not perfect Collections of Properties.*—Fourthly, The real essences of those things which we distinguish into species, and as so distinguished we name, ought to be known; i. e., we ought to have ideas of them. But since we are ignorant in these four

points, the supposed real essences of things stand us not in stead for the distinguishing substances into species.

19. *Fifthly,* The only imaginable help in this case would be, that, having framed perfect complex ideas of the properties of things flowing from their different real essences, we should thereby distinguish them into species. But neither can this be done: for being ignorant of the real essence itself, it is impossible to know all those properties that flow from it, and are so annexed to it, that any one of them being away, we may certainly conclude that that essence is not there, and so the thing is not of that species. We can never know what is the precise number of properties depending on the real essence of gold, any one of which failing, the real essence of gold—and consequently gold—would not be there, unless we knew the real essence of gold itself, and by that determined that species. By the word gold here, I must be understood to design a particular piece of matter; v. g., the last guinea that was coined. For if it should stand here in its ordinary signification for that complex idea, which I or any one else calls gold; i. e., for the nominal essence of gold, it would be jargon: so hard is it to show the various meaning and imperfection of words, when we have nothing else but words to do it by.

20. By all which it is clear, that our distinguishing substances into species by names, is not at all founded on their real essences; nor can we pretend to range and determine them exactly into species, according to internal essential differences.

21. *But such a Collection as our Name stands for.*—But since, as has been remarked, we have need of general words, though we know not the real essences of things; all we can do is to collect such a number of simple ideas as by examination we find to be united together in things existing, and thereof to make one complex idea. Which, though it be not the real essence of any substance that exists, is yet the specific essence to which our name belongs, and is convertible with it; by which we may at least try the truth of these nominal essences. For example: there be that say that the essence of body is extension: if it be so, we can never mistake in putting the essence of anything for the thing itself. Let us then in discourse put extension for body, and when

we would say that body moves, let us say that extension moves, and see how ill it will look. He that should say that one extension by impulse moves another extension, would, by the bare expression, sufficiently show the absurdity of such a notion. The essence of anything in respect of us, is the whole complex idea comprehended and marked by that name; and in substances, besides the several distinct simple ideas that make them up, the confused one of substance, or of an unknown support and cause of their union, is always a part: and therefore the essence of body is not bare extension, but an extended solid thing: and so to say an extended solid thing moves or impels another, is all one and as intelligible as to say, body moves or impels. Likewise to say that a rational animal is capable of conversation, is all one as to say a man; but no one will say that rationality is capable of conversation, because it makes not the whole essence to which we give the name man.

22. *Our abstract Ideas are to us the Measures of Species: Instance in that of Man.*—There are creatures in the world that have shapes like ours, but are hairy, and want language and reason. There are naturals amongst us that have perfectly our shape, but want reason, and some of them language too.* There are creatures, as it is said, ("sit fides

* Several French naturalists—as M. Bory de St. Vincent and M. Lesson—finding it difficult to mark the points by which man is distinguished from the inferior animals, appear somewhat desirous altogether to lose sight of them. They seem to be animated by a passion to resemble the brutes, and consequently to catch with extraordinary delight at whatsoever seems, in their view, to establish the relationship of man to the orang-outang. "Homme, enorgueilli de ton enveloppe extérieure!" exclaims Lesson, with ludicrous emphasis, "des traits que dans ta vanité tu as osé comparer à ceux de la Divinité! être fragile, egoïste, dont la vie s'écarte dans des acts vicieux, déguises avec plus ou moins d'art, meconnois si tu le peux, *ta parenté avec les orangs!*" (Histoire des Mammifères, t. iii. p. 260, et seq.) Such a writer may feel in himself some relationship to the orang, and rejoice in it, but it is hardly fair in him to speak thus confidently in behalf of us all. In the same spirit which, among certain classes, obtains the name of philosophy, M. de St. Vincent seeks to humble human pride. "Par une singularité digne de remarque," he says, "pour rejeter les orangs parmi les singes et ceux-ci parmi les bêtes brutes, en conservant à l'homme toute la dignité qu'il s'arroge, on arguë d'un avantage incontestable que possederaient les singes et les orangs. En effet, *quatre mains ne vaudraient elles pas mieux que deux, commes élémens de perfectabilité?*" (L'Homme, i. 44.) But, if so, M. de St. Vincent should explain to us how it has happened that the *two hands* have proved *too many* for the *four*.—ED.

penes authorem," but there appears no contradiction that there should be such,) that, with language and reason and a shape in other things agreeing with ours, have hairy tails; others where the males have no beards, and others where the females have. If it be asked whether these be all men or no,—all of human species? it is plain, the question refers only to the nominal essence: for those of them to whom the definition of the word man, or the complex idea signified by that name, agrees, are men, and the other not. But if the inquiry be made concerning the supposed real essence, and whether the internal constitution and frame of these several creatures be specifically different, it is wholly impossible for us to answer, no part of that going into our specific idea; only we have reason to think, that where the faculties or outward frame so much differs, the internal constitution is not exactly the same. But what difference in the real internal consitution makes a difference it is in vain to inquire; whilst our measures of species be, as they are, only our abstract ideas, which we know; and not that internal constitution which makes no part of them. Shall the difference of hair only on the skin be a mark of a different internal specific constitution between a changeling and a drill, when they agree in shape, and want of reason and speech? And shall not the want of reason and speech be a sign to us of different real constitutions and species between a changeling and a reasonable man? And so of the rest, if we pretend that distinction of species or sorts is fixedly established by the real frame and secret constitutions of things.

23. *Species not distinguished by Generation.*—Nor let any one say, that the power of propagation in animals by the mixture of male and female, and in plants by seeds, keeps the supposed real species distinct and entire. For, granting this to be true, it would help us in the distinction of the species of things no further than the tribes of animals and vegetables. What must we do for the rest? But in those too it is not sufficient: for if history lie not, women have conceived by drills; and what real species by that measure such a production will be in nature, will be a new question: and we have reason to think this is not impossible, since mules and jumarts—the one from the mixture of an ass and a mare, the other from the mixture of a bull and a mare— are so frequent in the world. I once saw a creature that

was the issue of a cat and a rat, and had the plain marks of both about it; wherein nature appeared to have followed the pattern of neither sort alone, but to have jumbled them together. To which he that shall add the monstrous productions that are so frequently to be met with in nature, will find it hard, even in the race of animals, to determine by the pedigree of what species every animal's issue is; and be at a loss about the real essence, which he thinks certainly conveyed by generation, and has alone a right to the specific name. But further, if the species of animals and plants are to be distinguished only by propagation, must I go to the Indies to see the sire and dam of the one, and the plant from which the seed was gathered that produced the other, to know whether this be a tiger or that tea?

24. *Not by substantial Forms.*—Upon the whole matter, it is evident that it is their own collections of sensible qualities that men make the essences of their several sorts of substances; and that their real internal structures are not considered by the greatest part of men in the sorting them. Much less were any substantial forms ever thought on by any but those who have in this one part of the world learned the language of the schools: and yet those ignorant men who pretend not any insight into the real essences, nor trouble themselves about substantial forms, but are content with knowing things one from another by their sensible qualities, are often better acquainted with their differences, can more nicely distinguish them from their uses, and better know what they expect from each, than those learned quicksighted men who look so deep into them, and talk so confidently of something more hidden and essential.

25. *The specific Essences made by the Mind.*—But supposing that the real essences of substances were discoverable by those that would severely apply themselves to that inquiry, yet we could not reasonably think that the ranking of things under general names was regulated by those internal real constitutions, or anything else but their obvious appearances; since languages, in all countries, have been established long before sciences. So that they have not been philosophers or logicians, or such who have troubled themselves about forms and essences that have made the general names that are in use amongst the several nations of men: but

those more or less comprehensive terms have, for the most part, in all languages, received their birth and signification from ignorant and illiterate people, who sorted and denominated things by those sensible qualities they found in them; thereby to signify them, when absent, to others, whether they had an occasion to mention a sort or a particular thing.

26. *Therefore very various and uncertain.*—Since then it is evident that we sort and name substances by their nominal and not by their real essences, the next thing to be considered is, how and by whom these essences come to be made. As to the latter, it is evident they are made by the mind, and not by nature: for were they Nature's workmanship, they could not be so various and different in several men as experience tells us they are. For if we will examine it, we shall not find the nominal essence of any one species of substance in all men the same: no, not of that which of all others we are the most intimately acquainted with. It could not possibly be, that the abstract idea to which the name man is given should be different in several men, if it were of Nature's making; and that to one it should be "animal rationale," and to another, "animal implume bipes latis unguibus." He that annexes the name man to a complex idea made up of sense and spontaneous motion, joined to a body of such a shape, has thereby one essence of the species man; and he that, upon further examination, adds rationality, has another essence of the species he calls man: by which means the same individual will be a true man to the one, which is not so to the other. I think there is scarce any one will allow this upright figure, so well known, to be the essential difference of the species man; and yet how far men determine of the sorts of animals rather by their shape than descent, is very visible: since it has been more than once debated, whether several human fœtuses should be preserved or received to baptism or no, only because of the difference of their outward configuration from the ordinary make of children, without knowing whether they were not as capable of reason as infants cast in another mould: some whereof, though of an approved shape, are never capable of as much appearance of reason all their lives as is to be found in an ape, or an elephant, and never

give any signs of being acted by a rational soul. Whereby it is evident, that the outward figure, which only was found wanting, and not the faculty of reason, which nobody could know would be wanting in its due season, was made essential to the human species. The learned divine and lawyer must, on such occasions, renounce his sacred definition of " animal rationale," and substitute some other essence of the human species. Monsieur Menage furnishes us with an example worth the taking notice of on this occasion : " When the abbot of St. Martin," says he, " was born, he had so little of the figure of a man, that it bespake him rather a monster. It was for some time under deliberation, whether he should be baptized or no. However, he was baptized, and declared a man provisionally;—till time should show what he would prove. Nature had moulded him so untowardly, that he was called all his life the Abbot Malotru; i. e., ill-shaped. He was of Caen." (Menagiana, 278, 430.) This child, we see, was very near being excluded out of the species of man, barely by his shape. He escaped very narrowly as he was; and it is certain, a figure a little more oddly turned had cast him, and he had been executed,* as a thing not to be allowed to pass for a man. And yet there can be no reason given why, if the lineaments of his face had been a little altered, a rational soul could not have been lodged in him; why a visage somewhat longer, or a nose flatter, or a wider mouth, could not have consisted, as well as the rest of his ill figure, with such a soul, such parts, as made him—disfigured as he was—capable to be a dignitary in the church.

27. Wherein, then, would I gladly know, consist the precise and unmovable boundaries of that species? It is plain, if we examine, there is no such thing made by Nature, and established by her amongst men. The real essence of that or any other sort of substances, it is evident, we know not; and therefore are so undetermined in our nominal essences, which we make ourselves, that, if several men were to be asked concerning some oddly-shaped fœtus, as soon as

* What is the rule now observed by those who decide on the execution of monsters? Does the law determine? This should be inquired into: for acts are constantly perpetrated in society, of which public opinion can take no hold, on account of the obscurity that surrounds them.--ED.

born, whether it were a man or no, it is past doubt one should meet with different answers. Which could not happen, if the nominal essences whereby we limit and distinguish the species of substances were not made by man with some liberty; but were exactly copied from precise boundaries set by nature, whereby it distinguished all substances into certain species. Who would undertake to resolve what species that monster was of, which is mentioned by Licetus, (lib. i. c. 3,) with a man's head and hog's body? Or those other, which to the bodies of men had the heads of beasts, as dogs, horses, &c. If any of these creatures had lived, and could have spoke, it would have increased the difficulty. Had the upper part to the middle been of human shape, and all below swine, had it been murder to destroy it? Or must the bishop have been consulted, whether it were man enough to be admitted to the font or no? as I have been told it happened in France some years since, in somewhat a like case.* So uncertain are the boundaries of species of animals to us, who have no other measures than the complex ideas of our own collecting: and so far are we from certainly knowing what a man is; though perhaps it will be judged great ignorance to make any doubt about it. And yet, I think I may say that the certain boundaries of that species are so far from being determined, and the precise number of simple ideas which make the nominal essence, so far from being settled and perfectly known, that very material doubts may still arise about it. And I imagine none of the definitions of the word man which we yet have, nor descriptions of that sort of animal, are so perfect and exact as to satisfy a considerate inquisitive person; much less to obtain a general consent, and to be that which men would everywhere stick by in the decision of cases, and determining of life and death, baptism or no baptism, in productions that might happen.

28. *But not so arbitrary as mixed Modes.*—But though these nominal essences of substances are made by the mind, they are not yet made so arbitrarily as those of mixed modes.

* However this question may be decided, the opinions of learned writers on the formation of monsters are exceedingly curious; but Bartholin, I think, stands alone in attributing the whole to the agency of comets, in his "Consilium Medicum, cum Monstrorem in Danir Natorum Historia."—ED.

To the making of any nominal essence, it is necessary, First, that the ideas whereof it consists have such a union as to make but one idea, how compounded soever. Secondly, that the particular idea so united be exactly the same, neither more nor less. For if two abstract complex ideas differ either in number or sorts of their component parts, they make two different, and not one and the same essence. In the first of these, the mind, in making its complex ideas of substances, only follows nature; and puts none together which are not supposed to have a union in nature. Nobody joins the voice of a sheep with the shape of a horse, nor the colour of lead with the weight and fixedness of gold, to be the complex ideas of any real substances; unless he has a mind to fill his head with chimeras, and his discourse with unintelligible words. Men observing certain qualities always joined and existing together, therein copied nature; and of ideas so united made their complex ones of substances. For, though men may make what complex ideas they please, and give what names to them they will; yet, if they will be understood when they speak of things really existing, they must in some degree conform their ideas to the things they would speak of; or else men's language will be like that of Babel; and every man's words, being intelligible only to himself, would no longer serve to conversation and the ordinary affairs of life, if the ideas they stand for be not some way answering the common appearances and agreement of substances as they really exist.

29. *Though very imperfect.*—Secondly, Though the mind of man, in making its complex ideas of substances, never puts any together that do not really or are not supposed to co-exist; and so it truly borrows that union from nature: yet the number it combines depends upon the various care, industry, or fancy of him that makes it. Men generally content themselves with some few sensible obvious qualities; and often, if not always, leave out others as material and as firmly united as those that they take. Of sensible substances there are two sorts: one of organized bodies, which are propagated by seed; and in these the shape is that which to us is the leading quality and most characteristical part that determines the species. And therefore, in vegetables and animals, an extended solid substance of such a certain figure

usually serves the turn. For however some men seem to prize their definition of "animal rationale," yet should there a creature be found that had language and reason, but partook not of the usual shape of a man, I believe it would hardly pass for a man, how much soever it were "animal rationale." And if Balaam's ass had all his life discoursed as rationally as he did once with his master, I doubt yet whether any one would have thought him worthy the name man, or allowed him to be of the same species with himself. As in vegetables and animals it is the shape, so in most other bodies not propagated by seed, it is the colour we most fix on, and are most led by. Thus, where we find the colour of gold, we are apt to imagine all the other qualities comprehended in our complex idea to be there also: and we commonly take these two obvious qualities, viz., shape and colour, for so presumptive ideas of several species, that, in a good picture, we readily say this is a lion, and that a rose; this is a gold, and that a silver goblet, only by the different figures and colours represented to the eye by the pencil.

30. *Which yet serve for common Converse.*—But though this serves well enough for gross and confused conceptions, and inaccurate ways of talking and thinking; yet men are far enough from having agreed on the precise number of simple ideas or qualities belonging to any sort of things, signified by its name. Nor is it a wonder; since it requires much time, pains, and skill, strict inquiry, and long examination to find out what and how many those simple ideas are, which are constantly and inseparably united in nature, and are always to be found together in the same subject. Most men wanting either time, inclination, or industry enough for this, even to some tolerable degree, content themselves with some few obvious and outward appearances of things, thereby readily to distinguish and sort them for the common affairs of life: and so, without further examination give them names, or take up the names already in use. Which, though in common conversation they pass well enough for the signs of some few obvious qualities co-existing, are yet far enough from comprehending, in a settled signification, a precise number of simple ideas, much less all those which are united in nature. He that shall consider, after so much stir about genus and species, and such a deal of talk of spe-

cific differences, how few words we have yet settled definitions of, may with reason imagine that those forms which there hath been so much noise made about are only chimeras, which give us no light into the specific natures of things. And he that shall consider how far the names of substances are from having significations wherein all who use them do agree, will have reason to conclude that, though the nominal essences of substances are all supposed to be copied from nature, yet they are all or most of them very imperfect. Since the composition of those complex ideas are, in several men, very different: and therefore that these boundaries of species are as men, and not as Nature, makes them, if at least there are in nature any such prefixed bounds. It is true that many particular substances are so made by Nature, that they have agreement and likeness one with another, and so afford a foundation of being ranked into sorts. But the sorting of things by us, or the making of determinate species, being in order to naming and comprehending them under general terms, I cannot see how it can be properly said, that Nature sets the boundaries of the species of things: or, if it be so, our boundaries of species are not exactly conformable to those in nature. For we having need of general names for present use, stay not for a perfect discovery of all those qualities which would best show us their most material differences and agreements; but we ourselves divide them by certain obvious appearances into species, that we may the easier under general names communicate our thoughts about them. For having no other knowledge of any substance but of the simple ideas that are united in it; and observing several particular things to agree with others in several of those simple ideas, we make that collection our specific idea, and give it a general name; that in recording our thoughts, and in our discourse with others, we may in one short word designate all the individuals that agree in that complex idea, without enumerating the simple ideas that make it up; and so not waste our time and breath in tedious descriptions; which we see they are fain to do who would discourse of any new sort of things they have not yet a name for.

31. *Essences of Species under the same Name very different.*—But however these species of substances pass well enough in ordinary conversation, it is plain that this com-

plex idea, wherein they observe several individuals to agree, is by different men made very differently; by some more, and others less accurately. In some, this complex idea contains a greater, and in others a smaller number of qualities, and so is apparently such as the mind makes it. The yellow shining colour makes gold to children; others add weight, malleableness, and fusibility; and others yet other qualities, which they find joined with that yellow colour, as constantly as its weight and fusibility: for in all these and the like qualities one has as good a right to be put into the complex idea of that substance wherein they are all joined, as another. And therefore different men leaving out or putting in several simple ideas which others do not, according to their various examination, skill, or observation of that subject, have different essences of gold, which must, therefore, be of their own and not of nature's making.

32. *The more general our Ideas are, the more incomplete and partial they are.*—If the number of simple ideas that make the nominal essence of the lowest species, or first sorting of individuals, depends on the mind of man variously collecting them, it is much more evident that they do so in the more comprehensive classes, which, by the masters of logic, are called genera. These are complex ideas designedly imperfect; and it is visible at first sight, that several of those qualities that are to be found in the things themselves, are purposely left out of generical ideas. For as the mind, to make general ideas comprehending several particulars, leaves out those of time and place, and such other that make them incommunicable to more than one individual; so to make other yet more general ideas that may comprehend different sorts, it leaves out those qualities that distinguish them, and puts into its new collection only such ideas as are common to several sorts. The same convenience that made men express several parcels of yellow matter coming from Guinea and Peru under one name, sets them also upon making of one name that may comprehend both gold and silver, and some other bodies of different sorts. This is done by leaving out those qualities, which are peculiar to each sort, and retaining a complex idea made up of those that are common to them all; to which the name metal being annexed, there is a

genus constituted, the essence whereof being that abstract idea, containing only malleableness and fusibility, with certain degrees of weight and fixedness, wherein some bodies of several kinds agree, leaves out the colour and other qualities peculiar to gold and silver, and the other sorts comprehended under the name metal. Whereby it is plain, that men follow not exactly the patterns set them by nature when they make their general ideas of substances, since there is no body to be found which has barely malleableness and fusibility in it, without other qualities as inseparable as those. But men, in making their general ideas, seeking more the convenience of language and quick dispatch by short and comprehensive signs, than the true and precise nature of things as they exist, have, in the framing their abstract ideas, chiefly pursued that end, which was to be furnished with store of general and variously comprehensive names. So that in this whole business of genera and species, the genus, or more comprehensive, is but a partial conception of what is in the species, and the species but a partial idea of what is to be found in each individual. If, therefore, any one will think that a man, and a horse, and an animal, and a plant, &c., are distinguished by real essences made by nature, he must think nature to be very liberal of these real essences, making one for body, another for an animal, and another for a horse, and all these essences liberally bestowed upon Bucephalus. But if we would rightly consider what is done in all these genera and species, or sorts, we should find that there is no new thing made, but only more or less comprehensive signs, whereby we may be enabled to express in a few syllables great numbers of particular things, as they agree in more or less general conceptions, which we have framed to that purpose. In all which we may observe, that the more general term is always the name of a less complex idea, and that each genus is but a partial conception of the species comprehended under it. So that if these abstract general ideas be thought to be complete, it can only be in respect of a certain established relation between them and certain names which are made use of to signify them, and not in respect of anything existing, as made by nature.

33. *This all accommodated to the end of Speech.*—This is adjusted to the true end of speech, which is to be the easiest

and shortest way of communicating our notions. For, thus, he that would discourse of things as they agreed in the complex ideas of extension and solidity, needed but use the word body to denote all such. He that to these would join others, signified by the words life, sense, and spontaneous motion, needed but use the word animal to signify all which partook of those ideas; and he that had made a complex idea of a body, with life, sense, and motion, with the faculty of reasoning, and a certain shape joined to it, needed but use the short monosyllable, man, to express all particulars that correspond to that complex idea. This is the proper business of genus and species; and this men do without any consideration of real essences, or substantial forms, which come not within the reach of our knowledge when we think of those things, nor within the signification of our words when we discourse with others.

34. *Instance in Cassowaries.*—Were I to talk with any one of a sort of birds I lately saw in St. James's Park, about three or four feet high, with a covering of something between feathers and hair, of a dark brown colour, without wings, but in the place thereof two or three little branches coming down like sprigs of Spanish broom, long great legs, with feet only of three claws, and without a tail, I must make this description of it, and so may make others understand me; but when I am told that the name of it is cassuaris, I may then use that word to stand in discourse for all my complex idea mentioned in that description; though by that word, which is now become a specific name, I know no more of the real essence or constitution of that sort of animals than I did before; and knew probably as much of the nature of that species of birds before I learned the name, as many Englishmen do of swans or herons, which are specific names, very well known, of sorts of birds common in England.

35. *Men determine the Sorts.*—From what has been said, it is evident that men make sorts of things; for it being different essences alone that make different species, it is plain that they who make those abstract ideas which are the nominal essences, do thereby make the species, or sort. Should there be a body found, having all the other qualities of gold, except malleableness, it would no doubt be made a

question whether it were gold or not, i. e., whether it were of that species. This could be determined only by that abstract idea to which every one annexed the name gold; so that it would be true gold to him, and belong to that species, who included not malleableness in his nominal essence, signified by the sound gold; and on the other side it would not be true gold, or of that species to him who included malleableness in his specific idea. And who, I pray, is it that make these diverse species even under one and the same name, but men that make two different abstract ideas consisting not exactly of the same collection of qualities? Nor is it a mere supposition to imagine that a body may exist, wherein the other obvious qualities of gold may be without malleableness; since it is certain that gold itself will be sometimes so eager, (as artists call it,) that it will as little endure the hammer as glass itself. What we have said of the putting in or leaving malleableness out of the complex idea the name gold is by any one annexed to, may be said of its peculiar weight, fixedness, and several other the like qualities; for whatsoever is left out or put in, it is still the complex idea to which that name is annexed that makes the species; and as any particular parcel of matter answers that idea, so the name of the sort belongs truly to it, and it is of that species. And thus anything is true gold, perfect metal. All which determination of the species, it is plain, depends on the understanding of man, making this or that complex idea.

36. *Nature makes the Similitude.*—This, then, in short, is the case. Nature makes many particular things which do agree one with another in many sensible qualities, and probably too in their internal frame and constitution: but it is not this real essence that distinguishes them into species; it is men, who, taking occasion from the qualities they find united in them, and wherein they observe often several individuals to agree, range them into sorts, in order to their naming, for the convenience of comprehensive signs; under which individuals, according to their conformity to this or that abstract idea, come to be ranked as under ensigns; so that this is of the blue, that the red regiment; this is a man, that a drill; and in this, I think, consists the whole business of genus and species.

37. I do not deny but nature, in the constant production of particular beings, makes them not always new and various, but very much alike and of kin one to another; but I think it nevertheless true, that the boundaries of the species, whereby men sort them, are made by men; since the essences of the species, distinguished by different names, are, as has been proved, of man's making, and seldom adequate to the internal nature of the things they are taken from. So that we may truly say, such a manner of sorting of things is the workmanship of men.

38. *Each abstract Idea is an Essence.*—One thing I doubt not but will seem very strange in this doctrine, which is, that from what has been said it will follow, that each abstract idea with a name to it, makes a distinct species. But who can help it, if truth will have it so? For so it must remain till somebody can show us the species of things limited and distinguished by something else; and let us see that general terms signify not our abstract ideas, but something different from them. I would fain know why a shock and a hound are not as distinct species as a spaniel and an elephant. We have no other idea of the different essence of an elephant and a spaniel, than we have of the different essence of a shock and a hound; all the essential difference whereby we know and distinguish them one from another, consisting only in the different collection of simple ideas, to which we have given those different names

39. *Genera and Species are in order to naming.*—How much the making of species and genera* is in order to general names, and how much general names are necessary, if not to the being, yet at least to the completing of a species, and making it pass for such, will appear, besides what has been said above concerning ice and water, in a very familiar example. A silent and a striking watch are but one species to those who have but one name for them; but he that has the name watch for one, and clock for the other, and distinct complex ideas to which those names belong, to him they are different species. It will be said perhaps, that the inward

---

* On the signification of these terms which occur so frequently in Locke, and in all writers on natural history, see the explanation of Dr. Prichard, in his "Researches into the Physical History of Mankind." Vol. I. p. 105 et seq.—ED.

contrivance and constitution is different between these two, which the watchmaker has a clear idea of. And yet it is plain they are but one species to him, when he has but one name for them; for what is sufficient in the inward contrivance to make a new species? There are some watches that are made with four wheels, others with five; is this a specific difference to the workman? Some have strings and physies, and others none; some have the balance loose, and others regulated by a spiral spring, and others by hogs' bristles: are any or all of these enough to make a specific difference to the workman, that knows each of these and several other different contrivances in the internal constitutions of watches? It is certain each of these hath a real difference from the rest; but whether it be an essential, a specific difference or not, relates only to the complex idea to which the name watch is given: as long as they all agree in the idea which that name stands for, and that name does not as a generical name comprehend different species under it, they are not essentially nor specifically different. But if any one will make minuter divisions from differences that he knows in the internal frame of watches, and to such precise complex ideas give names that shall prevail; they will then be new species to them who have those ideas with names to them, and can by those differences distinguish watches into these several sorts, and then watch will be a generical name. But yet they would be no distinct species to men ignorant of clock-work and the inward contrivances of watches, who had no other idea but the outward shape and bulk, with the marking of the hours by the hand. For to them all those other names would be but synonymous terms for the same idea, and signify no more, nor no other thing but a watch. Just thus I think it is in natural things. Nobody will doubt that the wheels or springs (if I may so say) within, are different in a rational man and a changeling; no more than that there is a difference in the frame between a drill and a changeling. But whether one, or both the differences be essential or specifical, is only to be known to us by their agreement or disagreement with the complex idea that the name man stands for: for by that alone can it be determined whether one or both, or neither of those be a man.

40. *Species of Artificial Things less confused than Natural*

—From what has been before said, we may see the reason why, in the species of artificial things, there is generally less confusion and uncertainty than in natural. Because an artificial thing being a production of man which the artificer designed, and therefore well knows the idea of, the name of it is supposed to stand for no other idea, nor to import any other essence than what is certainly to be known, and easy enough to be apprehended. For the idea or essence of the several sorts of artificial things consisting, for the most part, in nothing but the determinate figure of sensible parts; and sometimes motion depending thereon, which the artificer fashions in matter, such as he finds for his turn; it is not beyond the reach of our faculties to attain a certain idea thereof, and to settle the signification of the names whereby the species of artificial things are distinguished with less doubt, obscurity, and equivocation, than we can in things natural, whose differences and operations depend upon contrivances beyond the reach of our discoveries.

41. *Artificial Things of distinct Species.*—I must be excused here if I think artificial things are of distinct species as well as natural: since I find they are as plainly and orderly ranked into sorts, by different abstract ideas, with general names annexed to them, as distinct one from another as those of natural substances. For why should we not think a watch and pistol as distinct species one from another, as a horse and a dog; they being expressed in our minds by distinct ideas, and to others by distinct appellations?

42. *Substances alone have proper Names.*—This is further to be observed concerning substances, that they alone of all our several sorts of ideas have particular or proper names, whereby one only particular thing is signified. Because in simple ideas, modes, and relations, it seldom happens that men have occasion to mention often this or that particular when it is absent. Besides, the greatest part of mixed modes, being actions which perish in their birth, are not capable of a lasting duration as substances, which are the actors; and wherein the simple ideas that make up the complex ideas designed by the name have a lasting union.

43. *Difficulty to treat of Words.*—I must beg pardon of my reader for having dwelt so long upon this subject, and perhaps with some obscurity. But I desire it may be considered how

difficult it is to lead another by words into the thoughts of things, stripped of those specifical differences we give them: which things, if I name not, I say nothing; and if I do name them, I thereby rank them into some sort or other, and suggest to the mind the usual abstract idea of that species, and so cross my purpose. For to talk of a man, and to lay by, at the same time, the ordinary signification of the name man, which is our complex idea usually annexed to it, and bid the reader consider man as he is in himself, and as he is really distinguished from others in his internal constitution, or real essence, that is, by something he knows not what, looks like trifling; and, yet, thus one must do who would speak of the supposed real essences and species of things, as thought to be made by nature, if it be but only to make it understood that there is no such thing signified by the general names which substances are called by. But because it is difficult by known familiar names to do this, give me leave to endeavour by an example to make the different consideration the mind has of specific names and ideas a little more clear; and to show how the complex ideas of modes are referred sometimes to archetypes in the minds of other intelligent beings; or, which is the same, to the signification annexed by others to their received names; and sometimes to no archetypes at all. Give me leave also to show how the mind always refers its ideas of substances, either to the substances themselves or to the signification of their names as to the archetypes; and also to make plain the nature of species or sorting of things, as apprehended and made use of by us; and of the essences belonging to those species, which is perhaps of more moment to discover the extent and certainty of our knowledge than we at first imagine.

44. *Instances of mixed Modes in kinneah and niouph.*—Let us suppose Adam in the state of a grown man, with a good understanding, but in a strange country, with all things new and unknown about him, and no other faculties to attain the knowledge of them but what one of this age has now. He observes Lamech more melancholy than usual, and imagines it to be from a suspicion he has of his wife Adah, (whom he most ardently loved,) that she had too much kindness for another man. Adam discourses these his thoughts to Eve, and desires her to take care that Adah commit not folly;

and in these discourses with Eve he makes use of these two new words kinneah and niouph. In time, Adam's mistake appears, for he finds Lamech's trouble proceeded from having killed a man : but yet the two names kinneah and niouph, (the one standing for suspicion in a husband of his wife's disloyalty to him, and the other for the act of committing disloyalty,) lost not their distinct significations. It is plain, then, that here were two distinct complex ideas of mixed modes with names to them, two distinct species of actions essentially different ; I ask wherein consisted the essences of these two distinct species of actions ? And it is plain it consisted in a precise combination of simple ideas, different in one from the other. I ask, whether the complex idea in Adam's mind, which he called kinneah, were adequate or not ? And it is plain it was ; for it being a combination of simple ideas, which he, without any regard to any archetype, without respect to anything as a pattern, voluntarily put together, abstracted, and gave the name kinneah to, to express in short to others, by that one sound, all the simple ideas contained and united in that complex one ; it must necessarily follow that it was an adequate idea. His own choice having made that combination, it had all in it he intended it should, and so could not but be perfect, could not but be adequate, it being referred to no other archetype which it was supposed to represent.

45. These words, kinneah and niouph, by degrees grew into common use, and then the case was somewhat altered. Adam's children had the same faculties, and thereby the same power that he had, to make what complex ideas of mixed modes they pleased in their own minds ; to abstract them, and make what sounds they pleased the signs of them ; but the use of names being to make our ideas within us known to others, that cannot be done, but when the same sign stands for the same idea in two who would communicate their thoughts and discourse together. Those, therefore, of Adam's children, that found these two words, kinneah and niouph, in familiar use, could not take them for insignificant sounds, but must needs conclude they stood for something ; for certain ideas, abstract ideas ; they being general names, which abstract ideas were the essences of the species distinguished by those names. If, therefore, they would use these words as names of species

already established and agreed on, they were obliged to conform the ideas in their minds, signified by these names, to the ideas that they stood for in other men's minds, as to their patterns and archetypes; and then indeed their ideas of these complex modes were liable to be inadequate, as being very apt (especially those that consisted of combinations of many simple ideas) not to be exactly conformable to the ideas in other men's minds, using the same names; though for this there be usually a remedy at hand, which is to ask the meaning of any word we understand not of him that uses it.; it being as impossible to know certainly what the words jealousy and adultery (which I think answer קנאה and נאוף) stand for in another man's mind, with whom I would discourse about them; as it was impossible, in the beginning of language, to know what kinneah and niouph stood for in another man's mind, without explication, they being voluntary signs in every one.

46. *Instance of Substances in Zahab.*—Let us now also consider, after the same manner, the names of substances in their first application. One of Adam's children, roving in the mountains, lights on a glittering substance which pleases his eye; home he carries it to Adam, who, upon consideration of it, finds it to be hard, to have a bright yellow colour, and an exceeding great weight. These perhaps, at first, are all the qualities he takes notice of in it; and abstracting this complex idea, consisting of a substance having that peculiar bright yellowness, and a weight very great in proportion to its bulk, he gives it the name zahab, to denominate and mark all substances that have these sensible qualities in them. It is evident now, that, in this case, Adam acts quite differently from what he did before in forming those ideas of mixed modes, to which he gave the names kinneah and niouph: for there he puts ideas together only by his own imagination, not taken from the existence of anything: and to them he gave names to denominate all things that should happen to agree to those his abstract ideas, without considering whether any such thing did exist or not; the standard there was of his own making. But in the forming his idea of this new substance, he takes the quite contrary course; here he has a standard made by nature; and therefore, being to represent that to himself by the idea he has of it, even when

it is absent, he puts in no simple idea into his complex one, but what he has the perception of from the thing itself. He takes care that his idea be conformable to this archetype, and intends the name should stand for an idea so conformable.

47. This piece of matter, thus denominated zahab by Adam, being quite different from any he had seen before, nobody, I think, will deny to be a distinct species, and to have its peculiar essence, and that the name zahab is the mark of the species, and a name belonging to all things partaking in that essence. But here it is plain the essence Adam made the name zahab stand for was nothing but a body hard, shining, yellow, and very heavy. But the inquisitive mind of man, not content with the knowledge of these, as I may say, superficial qualities, puts Adam on further examination of this matter. He therefore knocks and beats it with flints, to see what was discoverable in the inside : he finds it yield to blows, but not easily separate into pieces ; he finds it will bend without breaking. Is not now ductility to be added to his former idea, and made part of the essence of the species that name zahab stands for? Further trials discover fusibility and fixedness. Are not they also, by the same reason that any of the others were, to be put into the complex idea signified by the name zahab? If not, what reason will there be shown more for the one than the other? If these must, then all the other properties, which any further trials shall discover in this matter, ought by the same reason to make a part of the ingredients of the complex idea which the name zahab stands for, and so be the essence of the species marked by that name : which properties, because they are endless, it is plain that the idea made after this fashion by this archetype will be always inadequate.

48. *Their Ideas imperfect, and therefore various.*—But this is not all ; it would also follow that the names of substances would not only have (as in truth they have) but would also be supposed to have different significations, as used by different men, which would very much cumber the use of language. For if every distinct quality that were discovered in any matter by any one were supposed to make a necessary part of the complex idea signified by the common name given to it, it must follow, that men must suppose the same word to signify different things in different men ; since they cannot

doubt but different men may have discovered several qualities in substances of the same denomination, which others know nothing of.

49. *Therefore, to fix their Species, a real Essence is supposed.*—To avoid this, therefore, they have supposed a real essence belonging to every species, from which these properties all flow, and would have their name of the species stand for that. But they not having any idea of that real essence in substances, and their words signifying nothing but the ideas they have, that which is done by this attempt, is only to put the name or sound in the place and stead of the thing having that real essence, without knowing what the real essence is; and this is that which men do when they speak of species of things, as supposing them made by nature, and distinguished by real essences.

50. *Which Supposition is of no Use.*—For let us consider, when we affirm that all gold is fixed, either it means that fixedness is a part of the definition—part of the nominal essence the word gold stands for; and so this affirmation, all gold is fixed, contains nothing but the signification of the term gold. Or else it means, that fixedness, not being a part of the definition of the gold, is a property of that substance itself: in which case it is plain that the word gold stands in the place of a substance, having the real essence of a species of things made by nature. In which way of substitution it has so confused and uncertain a signification, that, though this proposition—gold is fixed, be in that sense an affirmation of something real, yet it is a truth will always fail us in its particular application, and so is of no real use or certainty. For let it be ever so true, that all gold—i. e., all that has the real essence of gold—is fixed, what serves this for, whilst we know not in this sense what is or is not gold? For if we know not the real essence of gold, it is impossible we should know what parcel of matter has that essence, and so whether it be true gold or no.

51. *Conclusion.*—To conclude: what liberty Adam had at first to make any complex ideas of mixed modes, by no other patterns but his own thoughts, the same have all men ever since had. And the same necessity of conforming his ideas of substances to things without him, as to archetypes made by nature, that Adam was under, if he would not wil-

fully impose upon himself; the same are all men ever since under too. The same liberty also that Adam had of affixing any new name to any idea, the same has any one still; (especially the beginners of languages, if we can imagine any such;) but only with this difference, that, in places where men in society have already established a language amongst them, the significations of words are very warily and sparingly to be altered: because men being furnished already with names for their ideas, and common use having appropriated known names to certain ideas, an affected misapplication of them cannot but be very ridiculous. He that hath new notions will perhaps venture sometimes on the coining of new terms to express them; but men think it a boldness, and it is uncertain whether common use will ever make them pass for current. But in communication with others, it is necessary that we conform the ideas we make the vulgar words of any language stand for to their known proper significations, (which I have explained at large already,) or else to make known that new signification we apply them to.

CHAPTER VII.
OF PARTICLES.

1. *Particles connect Parts or whole Sentences together.*—BESIDES words, which are names of ideas in the mind, there are a great many others that are made use of to signify the connexion that the mind gives to ideas or propositions one with another. The mind, in communicating its thoughts to others, does not only need signs of the ideas it has then before it, but others also, to show or intimate some particular action of its own, at that time, relating to those ideas. This it does several ways; as is, and is not, are the general marks, of the mind, affirming or denying. But besides affirmation or negation, without which there is in words no truth or falsehood, the mind does, in declaring its sentiments to others, connect not only the parts of propositions, but whole sentences one to another, with their several relations and dependencies, to make a coherent discourse.

2. *In them consists the Art of Well-speaking.*—The words whereby it signifies what connexion it gives to the several

affirmations and negations that it unites in one continued reasoning or narration, are generally called particles; and it is in the right use of these that more particularly consist the clearness and beauty of a good style. To think well, it is not enough that a man has ideas clear and distinct in his thoughts, nor that he observes the agreement or disagreement of some of them; but he must think in train, and observe the dependence of his thoughts and reasonings upon one another. And to express well such methodical and rational thoughts, he must have words to show what connexion, restriction, distinction, opposition, emphasis, &c., he gives to each respective part of his discourse. To mistake in any of these, is to puzzle instead of informing his hearer; and therefore it is that those words which are not truly by themselves the names of any ideas, are of such constant and indispensable use in language, and do much contribute to men's well expressing themselves.

3. *They show what Relation the Mind gives to its own Thoughts.*—This part of grammar has been perhaps as much neglected as some others over-diligently cultivated. It is easy for men to write, one after another, of cases and genders, moods and tenses, gerunds and supines: in these and the like there has been great diligence used: and particles themselves, in some languages, have been, with great show of exactness, ranked into their several orders. But though prepositions and conjunctions, &c., are names well known in grammar, and the particles contained under them carefully ranked into their distinct subdivisions; yet he who would show the right use of particles, and what significancy and force they have, must take a little more pains, enter into his own thoughts, and observe nicely the several postures of his mind in discoursing.

4. Neither is it enough for the explaining of these words, to render them, as is usual in dictionaries, by words of another tongue which come nearest to their signification: for what is meant by them is commonly as hard to be understood in one as another language. They are all marks of some action or intimation of the mind; and therefore to understand them rightly, the several views, postures, stands, turns, limitations, and exceptions, and several other thoughts of the mind, for which we have either none or very deficient names, are dili-

gently to be studied. Of these there is a great variety, much exceeding the number of particles that most languages have to express them by; and therefore it is not to be wondered that most of these particles have divers and sometimes almost opposite significations. In the Hebrew tongue there is a particle consisting of but one single letter, of which there are reckoned up, as I remember, seventy, I am sure above fifty, several significations.

5. *Instance in But.*—But is a particle, none more familiar in our language; and he that says it is a discretive conjunction, and that it answers to *sed* Latin, or *mais* in French, thinks he has sufficiently explained it. But it seems to me to intimate several relations the mind gives to the several propositions or parts of them, which it joins by this monosyllable.

First, " But to say no more:" here it intimates a stop of the mind in the course it was going, before it came quite to the end of it.

Secondly, " I saw but two plants:" here it shows that the mind limits the sense to what is expressed, with a negation of all other.

Thirdly, " You pray; but it is not that God would bring you to the true religion."

Fourthly, " But that he would confirm you in your own." The first of these buts intimates a supposition in the mind of something otherwise than it should be; the latter shows that the mind makes a direct opposition between that and what goes before it.

Fifthly, " All animals have sense, but a dog is an animal:" here it signifies little more but that the latter proposition is joined to the former, as the minor of a syllogism.

6. *This Matter but lightly touched here*—To these, I doubt not, might be added a great many other significations of this particle, if it were my business to examine it in its full latitude, and consider it in all the places it is to be found; which if one should do, I doubt whether in all those manners it is made use of, it would deserve the title of discretive, which grammarians give to it. But I intend not here a full explication of this sort of signs. The instances I have given in this one may give occasion to reflect on their use and force in language, and lead us into the contemplation of several

actions of our minds in discoursing, which it has found a way to intimate to others by these particles; some whereof constantly, and others in certain constructions, have the sense of a whole sentence contained in them.

CHAPTER VIII.

OF ABSTRACT AND CONCRETE TERMS.

1. *Abstract Terms not predicable one of another, and why.*— THE ordinary words of language and our common use of them, would have given us light into the nature of our ideas, if they had been but considered with attention. The mind, as has been shown, has a power to abstract its ideas, and so they become essences, general essences, whereby the sorts of things are distinguished. Now each abstract idea being distinct, so that of any two the one can never be the other, the mind will by its intuitive knowledge perceive their difference, and therefore in propositions no two whole ideas can ever be affirmed one of another. This we see in the common use of language, which permits not any two abstract words or names of abstract ideas to be affirmed one of another. For how near of kin soever they may seem to be, and how certain soever it is that man is an animal, or rational, or white, yet every one at first hearing perceives the falsehood of these propositions: humanity is animality, or rationality, or whiteness: and this is as evident as any of the most allowed maxims. All our affirmations then are only in concrete, which is the affirming, not one abstract idea to be another, but one abstract idea to be joined to another, which abstract ideas, in substances, may be of any sort; in all the rest are little else but of relations; and in substances the most frequent are of powers: v. g., "a man is white," signifies that the thing that has the essence of a man has also in it the essence of whiteness, which is nothing but a power to produce the idea of whiteness in one whose eyes can discover ordinary objects: or, "a man is rational," signifies that the same thing that hath the essence of a man hath also in it the essence of rationality i. e., a power of reasoning.

2. *They show the Difference of our Ideas.*—This distinction of names shows us also the difference of our ideas: for if we observe them, we shall find that our simple ideas have all abstract as well as concrete names; the one whereof is (to speak the language of grammarians) a substantive, the other an adjective; as whiteness, white, sweetness, sweet. The like also holds in our ideas of modes and relations; as, justice, just, equality, equal; only with this difference, that some of the concrete names of relations amongst men chiefly are substantives; as, paternitas, pater; whereof it were easy to render a reason; but as to our ideas of substances, we have very few or no abstract names at all. For though the schools have introduced animalitas, humanitas, corporietas, and some others; yet they hold no proportion with that infinite number of names of substances, to which they never were ridiculous enough to attempt the coining of abstract ones: and those few that the schools forged and put into the mouths of their scholars could never yet get admittance into common use, or obtain the license of public approbation. Which seems to me at least to intimate the confession of all mankind, that they have no ideas of the real essences of substances, since they have not names for such ideas: which no doubt they would have had, had not their consciousness to themselves of their ignorance of them kept them from so idle an attempt. And therefore though they had ideas enough to distinguish gold from a stone, and metal from wood; yet they but timorously ventured on such terms, as aurietas and saxietas, metallietas and lignietas, or the like names, which should pretend to signify the real essences of those substances whereof they knew they had no ideas. And indeed it was only the doctrine of substantial forms, and the confidence of mistaken pretenders to a knowledge that they had not, which first coined and then introduced animalitas and humanitas, and the like; which yet went very little further than their own schools, and could never get to be current amongst understanding men. Indeed, humanitas was a word in familiar use amongst the Romans, but in a far different sense, and stood not for the abstract essence of any substance; but was the abstracted name of a mode, and its concrete humanus, not homo.

CHAPTER IX.

OF THE IMPERFECTION OF WORDS.

1. *Words are used for recording and communicating our Thoughts.*—From what has been said in the foregoing chapters, it is easy to perceive what imperfection there is in language, and how the very nature of words makes it almost unavoidable for many of them to be doubtful and uncertain in their significations. To examine the perfection or imperfection of words, it is necessary first to consider their use and end; for as they are more or less fitted to attain that, so they are more or less perfect. We have, in the former part of this discourse often, upon occasion, mentioned a double use of words.

First, One for the recording of our own thoughts.

Secondly, The other for the communicating of our thoughts to others.

2. *Any Words will serve for recording.*—As to the first of these, for the recording our own thoughts for the help of our own memories, whereby, as it were, we talk to ourselves, any words will serve the turn. For since sounds are voluntary and indifferent signs of any ideas, a man may use what words he pleases to signify his own ideas to himself: and there will be no imperfection in them, if he constantly use the same sign for the same idea; for then he cannot fail of having his meaning understood, wherein consists the right use and perfection of language.

3. *Communication by Words civil or philosophical.*—Secondly, As to communication of words, that too has a double use.

I. Civil.

II. Philosophical.

First, By their civil use, I mean such a communication of thoughts and ideas by words, as may serve for the upholding common conversation and commerce about the ordinary affairs and conveniences of civil life, in the societies of men one amongst another.

Secondly, By the philosophical use of words, I mean such a use of them as may serve to convey the precise notions of things, and to express in general propositions certain and undoubted truths, which the mind may rest upon and be satisfied with in its search after true knowledge. These two uses are very distinct: and a great deal less exactness will serve in the one than in the other, as we shall see in what follows.

4. *The Imperfection of Words is the Doubtfulness of their Signification.*—The chief end of language in communication being to be understood, words serve not well for that end, neither in civil nor philosophical discourse, when any word does not excite in the hearer the same idea which it stands for in the mind of the speaker. Now, since sounds have no natural connexion with our ideas, but have all their signification from the arbitrary imposition of men, the doubtfulness and uncertainty of their signification, which is the imperfection we here are speaking of, has its cause more in the ideas they stand for than in any incapacity there is in one sound more than in another to signify any idea: for in that regard they are all equally perfect.

That then which makes doubtfulness and uncertainty in the signification of some more than other words, is the difference of ideas they stand for.

5. *Causes of their Imperfection.*—Words having naturally no signification, the idea which each stands for must be learned and retained by those who would exchange thoughts and hold intelligible discourse with others in any language. But this is the hardest to be done where,

First, The ideas they stand for are very complex, and made up of a great number of ideas put together.

Secondly, Where the ideas they stand for have no certain connexion in nature, and so no settled standard anywhere in nature existing, to rectify and adjust them by.

Thirdly, When the signification of the word is referred to a standard, which standard is not easy to be known.

Fourthly, Where the signification of the word and the real essence of the thing are not exactly the same.

These are difficulties that attend the signification of several words that are intelligible. Those which are not intelligible at all, such as names standing for any simple ideas which another has not organs or faculties to attain; as the names of colours to a blind man, or sounds to a deaf man; need not here be mentioned.

In all these cases we shall find an imperfection in words, which I shall more at large explain in their particular application to our several sorts of ideas: for if we examine them, we shall find that the names of mixed modes are most liable to doubtfulness and imperfection, for the two first of these reasons; and the names of substances chiefly for the two latter.

6. *The Names of mixed Modes doubtful. First, Because the Ideas they stand for are so complex.*—First, The names of mixed modes are many of them liable to great uncertainty and obscurity in their signification.

I. Because of that great composition these complex ideas are often made up of. To make words serviceable to the end of communication it is necessary, as has been said, that they excite in the hearer exactly the same idea they stand for in the mind of the speaker. Without this, men fill one another's heads with noise and sounds, but convey not thereby their thoughts, and lay not before one another their ideas, which is the end of discourse and language. But when a word stands for a very complex idea that is compounded and decompounded, it is not easy for men to form and retain that idea so exactly, as to make the name in common use stand for the same precise idea, without any the least variation. Hence it comes to pass that men's names of very compound ideas, such as for the most part are moral words, have seldom in two different men the same precise signification; since one man's complex idea seldom agrees with another's, and often differs from his own—from that which he had yesterday, or will have to-morrow.

7. *Secondly, because they have no Standards.*—Because the names of mixed modes for the most part want standards in nature whereby men may rectify and adjust their significations; therefore they are very various and doubtful. They are assemblages of ideas put together at the pleasure of the mind, pursuing its own ends of discourse, and suited to its own notions, whereby it designs not to copy anything really existing, but to denominate and rank things as they come to agree with those archetypes or forms it has made.* He that

---

* "The words genius and taste are, like the words beauty and virtue, mere terms of general approbation, which men apply to whatever they approve, without annexing any specific ideas to them. They are, there

first brought the word sham, or wheedle, or banter, in use, put together as he thought fit those ideas he made it stand for; and as it is with any new names of modes that are now brought into any language, so it was with the old ones when they were first made use of. Names, therefore, that stand for collections of ideas which the mind makes at pleasure must needs be of doubtful signification, when such collections are nowhere to be found constantly united in nature, nor any patterns to be shown whereby men may adjust them. What the word murder, or sacrilege, &c., signifies can never be known from things themselves: there be many of the parts of those complex ideas which are not visible in the action itself; the intention of the mind, or the relation of holy things, which make a part of murder or sacrilege, have no necessary connexion with the outward and visible action of him that commits either: and the pulling the trigger of the gun with which the murder is committed, and is all the action that perhaps is visible, has no natural connexion with those other ideas that make up the complex one named murder. They have their union and combination only from the understanding, which unites them under one name: but uniting them without any rule or pattern, it cannot be but that the signification of the name that stands for such voluntary collections should be often various in the minds of different men, who have scarce any standing rule to regulate themselves and their notions by, in such arbitrary ideas.

8. *Propriety not a sufficient Remedy.*—It is true, common use (that is, the rule of propriety) may be supposed here to afford some aid, to settle the signification of language; and it cannot be denied but that in some measure it does. Common use regulates the meaning of words pretty well for common conversation; but nobody having an authority to establish the precise signification of words, nor determined to what ideas any one shall annex them, common use is not sufficient

fore, as often employed to signify extravagant novelty as genuine merit; and it is only time that arrests the abuse. Purity, simplicity, grace, and elegance, are, as well as beauty, qualities that are always equally admired, because the words by which they are expressed are terms of approbation. But, nevertheless, these terms are entirely under the influence of fashion; and are applied to every novelty of style or manner, to which accident or caprice gives a momentary currency." (Payne Knight, Analytical Inq. into the Prin. of Taste, p. 111, c. iii. § 5.)—ED.

to adjust them to philosophical discourses; there being scarce any name of any very complex idea (to say nothing of others) which in common use has not a great latitude, and which, keeping within the bounds of propriety, may not be made the sign of far different ideas. Besides, the rule and measure of propriety itself being nowhere established, it is often matter of dispute, whether this or that way of using a word be propriety of speech or no. From all which it is evident, that the names of such kind of very complex ideas are naturally liable to this imperfection, to be of doubtful and uncertain signification; and even in men that have a mind to understand one another, do not always stand for the same idea in speaker and hearer. Though the names glory and gratitude be the same in every man's mouth through a whole country, yet the complex collective idea which every one thinks on or intends by that name, is apparently very different in men using the same language.

9. *The way of learning these Names contributes also to their Doubtfulness.*—The way also wherein the names of mixed modes are ordinarily learned, does not a little contribute to the doubtfulness of their signification. For if we will observe how children learn languages, we shall find that, to make them understand what the names of simple ideas or substances stand for, people ordinarily show them the thing whereof they would have them have the idea; and then repeat to them the name that stands for it; as, white, sweet, milk, sugar, cat, dog. But as for mixed modes—especially the most material of them, moral words—the sounds are usually learned first; and then, to know what complex ideas they stand for, they are either beholden to the explication of others, or (which happens for the most part) are left to their own observation and industry; which being little laid out in the search of the true and precise meaning of names, these moral words are in most men's mouths little more than bare sounds; or when they have any, it is for the most part but a very loose and undetermined, and, consequently, obscure and confused signification. And even those themselves who have with more attention settled their notions, do yet hardly avoid the inconvenience to have them stand for complex ideas different from those which other, even intelligent and studious men, make them the signs of. Where shall one find

any, either controversial debate, or familiar discourse, concerning honour, faith, grace, religion, church, &c., wherein it is not easy to observe the different notions men have of them? which is nothing but this, that they are not agreed in the signification of those words, nor have in their minds the same complex ideas which they make them stand for, and and so all the contests that follow thereupon are only about the meaning of a sound : and hence we see, that, in the interpretation of laws, whether divine or human, there is no end ; comments beget comments, and explications make new matter for explications ; and of limiting, distinguishing, varying the signification of these moral words there is no end. These ideas of men's making are, by men still having the same power, multiplied in infinitum. Many a man who was pretty well satisfied of the meaning of a text of Scripture, or clause in the code, at first reading, has, by consulting commentators, quite lost the sense of it, and by these elucidations given rise or increase to his doubts, and drawn obscurity upon the place. I say not this that I think commentaries needless ; but to show how uncertain the names of mixed modes naturally are, even in the mouths of those who had both the intention and the faculty of speaking as clearly as language was capable to express their thoughts.

10. *Hence unavoidable Obscurity in ancient Authors.*— What obscurity this has unavoidably brought upon the writings of men who have lived in remote ages and different countries it will be needless to take notice; since the numerous volumes of learned men employing their thoughts that way are proofs more than enough to show what attention, study, sagacity, and reasoning are required to find out the true meaning of ancient authors. But there being no writings we have any great concernment to be very solicitous about the meaning of, but those that contain either truths we are required to believe, or laws we are to obey, and draw inconveniences on us when we mistake or transgress, we may be less anxious about the sense of other authors; who, writing but their own opinions, we are under no greater necessity to know them, than they to know ours. Our good or evil depending not on their decrees, we may safely be ignorant of their notions; and therefore in the reading of them, if they do not use their

words with a due clearness and perspicuity, we may lay them aside, and without any injury done them, resolve thus with ourselves,

"Si non vis intelligi, debes negligi."

11. *Names of Substances of doubtful Signification.*—If the signification of the names of mixed modes be uncertain, because there be no real standards existing in nature to which those ideas are referred, and by which they may be adjusted, the names of substances are of a doubtful signification for a contrary reason, viz., because the ideas they stand for are supposed conformable to the reality of things, and are referred to as standards made by Nature. In our ideas of substances we have not the liberty, as in mixed modes, to frame what combinations we think fit, to be the characteristical notes to rank and denominate things by. In these we must follow Nature, suit our complex ideas to real existences, and regulate the signification of their names by the things themselves, if we will have our names to be signs of them, and stand for them. Here, it is true, we have patterns to follow; but patterns that will make the signification of their names very uncertain: for names must be of a very unsteady and various meaning, if the ideas they stand for be referred to standards without us, that either cannot be known at all, or can be known but imperfectly and uncertainly.

12. *Names of Substances referred*, 1. *To real Essences that cannot be known.*—The names of substances have, as has been shown, a double reference in their ordinary use.

First, Sometimes they are made to stand for, and so their signification is supposed to agree to, the real constitution of things, from which all their properties flow, and in which they all centre. But this real constitution, or (as it is apt to be called) essence, being utterly unknown to us, any sound that is put to stand for it must be very uncertain in its application; and it will be impossible to know what things are or ought to be called a horse, or antimony, when those words are put for real essences that we have no ideas of at all. And therefore in this supposition, the names of substances being referred to standards that cannot be known, their significations can never be adjusted and established by those standards.

13. *Secondly, To co-existing Qualities, which are known but imperfectly.*—Secondly, The simple ideas that are found to co-exist in substances being that which their names immediately signify, these, as united in the several sorts of things, are the proper standards to which their names are referred, and by which their significations may be best rectified: but neither will these archetypes so well serve to this purpose as to leave these names without very various and uncertain significations; because these simple ideas that co-exist and are united in the same subject being very numerous, and having all an equal right to go into the complex specific idea which the specific name is to stand for, men, though they propose to themselves the very same subject to consider, yet frame very different ideas about it; and so the name they use for it unavoidably comes to have, in several men, very different significations. The simple qualities which make up the complex ideas being most of them powers in relation to changes which they are apt to make in or receive from other bodies, are almost infinite. He that shall but observe what a great variety of alterations any one of the baser metals is apt to receive from the different application only of fire, and how much a greater number of changes any of them will receive in the hands of a chymist, by the application of other bodies, will not think it strange that I count the properties of any sort of bodies not easy to be collected and completely known by the ways of inquiry which our faculties are capable of. They being therefore at least so many, that no man can know the precise and definite number, they are differently discovered by different men, according to their various skill, attention, and ways of handling; who therefore cannot choose but have different ideas of the same substance, and therefore make the signification of its common name very various and uncertain. For the complex ideas of substances being made up of such simple ones as are supposed to co-exist in nature, every one has a right to put into his complex idea those qualities he has found to be united together. For though in the substance of gold one satisfies himself with colour and weight, yet another thinks solubility in aq. regia as necessary to be joined with that colour in his idea of gold, as any one does its fusibility; solubility in aq. regia being a quality as constantly joined with its colour

and weight as fusibility or any other; others put into it ductility or fixedness, &c., as they have been taught by tradition or experience. Who of all these has established the right signification of the word, gold? or who shall be the judge to determine? Each has his standard in nature, which he appeals to, and with reason thinks he has the same right to put into his complex idea signified by the word gold, those qualities, which, upon trial, he has found united; as another who has not so well examined has to leave them out; or a third, who has made other trials, has to put in others. For the union in nature of these qualities being the true ground of their union in one complex idea, who can say one of them has more reason to be put in or left out than another? From hence it will unavoidably follow, that the complex ideas of substances in men using the same names for them, will be very various, and so the significations of those names very uncertain.

14. *Thirdly, To co-existing Qualities which are known but imperfectly.*—Besides, there is scarce any particular thing existing, which, in some of its simple ideas, does not communicate with a greater, and in others a less number of particular beings: who shall determine in this case which are those that are to make up the precise collection that is to be signified by the specific name? or can with any just authority prescribe which obvious or common qualities are to be left out; or which more secret or more particular are to be put into the signification of the name of any substance? All which together seldom or never fail to produce that various and doubtful signification in the names of substances which causes such uncertainty, disputes, or mistakes, when we come to a philosophical use of them.

15. *With this Imperfection—they may serve for civil, but not well for philosophical Use.*—It is true, as to civil and common conversation, the general names of substances, regulated in their ordinary signification by some obvious qualities, (as by the shape and figure in things of known seminal propagation, and in other substances, for the most part by colour, joined with some other sensible qualities,) do well enough to design the things men would be understood to speak of: and so they usually conceive well enough the substances meant by the word gold or apple, to distinguish the one from the

other. But in philosophical inquiries and debates, where general truths are to be established, and consequences drawn from positions laid down, there the precise signification of the names of substances will be found not only not to be well established, but also very hard to be so. For example: he that shall make malleableness or a certain degree of fixedness a part of his complex idea of gold, may make propositions concerning gold, and draw consequences from them that will truly and clearly follow from gold, taken in such a signification: but yet such as another man can never be forced to admit, nor be convinced of their truth, who makes not malleableness or the same degree of fixedness part of that complex idea that the name gold, in his use of it, stands for.

16. *Instance, Liquor.*—This is a natural and almost unavoidable imperfection in almost all the names of substances in all languages whatsoever, which men will easily find when, once passing from confused or loose notions, they come to more strict and close inquiries. For then they will be convinced how doubtful and obscure those words are in their signification which in ordinary use appeared very clear and determined. I was once in a meeting of very learned and ingenious physicians, where by chance there arose a question, whether any liquor passed through the filaments of the nerves. The debate having been managed a good while by variety of arguments on both sides, I (who had been used to suspect that the greatest part of disputes were more about the signification of words than a real difference in the conception of things) desired, that, before they went any further on in this dispute, they would first examine and establish amongst them, what the word liquor signified. They at first were a little surprised at the proposal, and had they been persons less ingenious, they might perhaps have taken it for a very frivolous or extravagant one: since there was no one there that thought not himself to understand very perfectly what the word liquor stood for, which I think, too, none of the most perplexed names of substances. However, they were pleased to comply with my motion; and upon examination found that the signification of that word was not so settled or certain as they had all imagined; but that each of them made it a sign of a different complex idea. This

made them perceive that the main of their dispute was about the signification of that term; and that they differed very little in their opinions concerning some fluid and subtle matter, passing through the conduits of the nerves; though it was not so easy to agree whether it was to be called liquor or no—a thing, which, when considered, they thought it not worth the contending about.*

17. *Instance, Gold.*—How much this is the case in the greatest part of disputes that men are engaged so hotly in, I shall perhaps have an occasion in another place to take notice. Let us only here consider a little more exactly the fore-mentioned instance of the word gold, and we shall see how hard it is precisely to determine its signification. I think all agree to make it stand for a body of a certain yellow shining colour; which being the idea to which children have annexed that name, the shining yellow part of a peacock's tail is properly to them gold. Others finding fusibility joined with that yellow colour in certain parcels of matter, make of that combination a complex idea, to which they give the name gold, to denote a sort of substances; and so exclude from being gold all such yellow shining bodies as by fire will be reduced to ashes; and admit to be of that

* The controversy here alluded to still remains unsettled; the hypotheses of physiologists on the subject being in fact as numerous as ever. Blumenbach represents the present state of opinion among scientific men; and from his account the reader will probably infer that the dispute is likely to be co-lasting with physiology itself. Speaking of the nature of the nerves, he observes:—"Most opinions on this subject may be divided into two classes: the one regards the actions of the nervous system as consisting in an oscillatory motion; the other ascribes it to the motion of a certain fluid, whose nature is a matter of dispute, by some called animal spirits, and supposed to run in vessels; by others conceived to be a matter analogous to fire, to light, to a peculiar æther, to oxygen, to electricity, or to magnetism, &c. Although I would by no means assent to either of these opinions, I may be allowed to observe, that most arguments brought by one party against the hypothesis of the other, must necessarily be made in proportion to the subtlety either of the oscillations (if any such exist) of the nerves, or to that of the nervous fluid. These two hypotheses may perhaps be united, by supposing a nervous fluid, thrown into oscillatory vibrations by the action of stimulants. The analogy between the structure of the brain and some secreting organs favours the belief of the existence of a nervous *fluid*. But tubes and canals are evidently no more requisite for its conveyance, than they are requisite in bibulous paper, or any other material employed for filtering." (Physiology, § 222, et seq.)—ED.

species, or to be comprehended under that name gold, only such substances as, having that shining yellow colour, will by fire be reduced to fusion and not to ashes. Another, by the same reason, adds the weight, which, being a quality as straightly joined with that colour as its fusibility, he thinks has the same reason to be joined in its idea, and to be signified by its name; and therefore the other made up of body, of such a colour and fusibility, to be imperfect; and so on of all the rest: wherein no one can show a reason why some of the inseparable qualities that are always united in nature should be put into the nominal essence, and others left out: or why the word gold signifying that sort of body the ring on his finger is made of, should determine that sort rather by its colour, weight, and fusibility, than by its colour, weight, and solubility in aq. regia: since the dissolving it by that liquor is as inseparable from it as the fusion by fire; and they are both of them nothing but the relation which that substance has to two other bodies, which have a power to operate differently upon it. For by what right is it that fusibility comes to be a part of the essence signified by the word gold, and solubility but a property of it? or why is its colour part of the essence, and its malleableness but a property? That which I mean is this, that these being all but properties, depending on its real constitution, and nothing but powers, either active or passive, in reference to other bodies, no one has authority to determine the signification of the word gold (as referred to such a body existing in nature) more to one collection of ideas to be found in that body than to another; whereby the signification of that name must unavoidably be very uncertain; since, as has been said, several people observe several properties in the same substance, and I think I may say nobody at all. And therefore we have but very imperfect descriptions of things, and words have very uncertain significations.

18. *The Names of simple Ideas the least doubtful.*—From what has been said, it is easy to observe what has been before remarked, viz., that the names of simple ideas are, of all others, the least liable to mistakes, and that for these reasons: First, Because the ideas they stand for being each but one single perception are much easier got, and more clearly retained than the more complex ones, and therefore

are not liable to the uncertainty which usually attends those compounded ones of substances and mixed modes, in which the precise number of simple ideas that make them up are not easily agreed, and so readily kept in the mind; and Secondly, Because they are never referred to any other essence, but barely that perception they immediately signify: which reference is that which renders the signification of the names of substances naturally so perplexed, and gives occasion to so many disputes. Men that do not perversely use their words, or on purpose set themselves to cavil, seldom mistake in any language which they are acquainted with, the use and signification of the names of simple ideas. White and sweet, yellow and bitter, carry a very obvious meaning with them, which every one precisely comprehends, or easily perceives he is ignorant of, and seeks to be informed; but what precise collection of simple ideas modesty or frugality stand for in another's use is not so certainly known, and however we are apt to think we well enough know what is meant by gold or iron; yet the precise complex idea others make them the signs of, is not so certain, and I believe it is very seldom that, in speaker and hearer, they stand for exactly the same collection; which must needs produce mistakes and disputes when they are made use of in discourses, wherein men have to do with universal propositions, and would settle in their minds universal truths, and consider the consequences that follow from them.

19. *And next to them, simple Modes.*—By the same rule, the names of simple modes are, next to those of simple ideas, least liable to doubt and uncertainty, especially those of figure and number, of which men have so clear and distinct ideas. Who ever that had a mind to understand them mistook the ordinary meaning of seven, or a triangle? and in general the least compounded ideas in every kind have the least dubious names.

20. *The most doubtful are the Names of very compounded mixed Modes and Substances.*—Mixed modes, therefore, that are made up but of a few and obvious simple ideas, have usually names of no very uncertain signification. But the names of mixed modes, which comprehend a great number of simple ideas, are commonly of a very doubtful and undetermined meaning, as has been shown. The names of substances being

annexed to ideas that are neither the real essences nor exact representations of the patterns they are referred to, are liable to yet greater imperfection and uncertainty, especially when we come to a philosophical use of them.

21. *Why this Imperfection charged upon Words.*—The great disorder that happens in our names of substances proceeding, for the most part, from our want of knowledge and inability to penetrate into their real constitutions, it may probably be wondered why I charge this as an imperfection rather upon our words than understandings. This exception has so much appearance of justice, that I think myself obliged to give a reason why I have followed this method. I must confess, then, that, when I first began this discourse of the understanding, and a good while after, I had not the least thought that any consideration of words was at all necessary to it; but when, having passed over the original and composition of our ideas, I began to examine the extent and certainty of our knowledge, I found it had so near a connexion with words, that, unless their force and manner of signification were first well observed, there could be very little said clearly and pertinently concerning knowledge, which being conversant about truth, had constantly to do with propositions; and though it terminated in things, yet it was for the most part so much by the intervention of words, that they seemed scarce separable from our general knowledge; at least they interpose themselves so much between our understandings and the truth which it would contemplate and apprehend, that, like the medium through which visible objects pass, their obscurity and disorder do not seldom cast a mist before our eyes, and impose upon our understandings. If we consider, in the fallacies men put upon themselves as well as others, and the mistakes in men's disputes and notions, how great a part is owing to words, and their uncertain and mistaken significations, we shall have reason to think this no small obstacle in the way to knowledge; which I conclude we are the more carefully to be warned of, because it has been so far from being taken notice of as an inconvenience, that the arts of improving it have been made the business of men's study, and obtained the reputation of learning and subtilty, as we shall see in the following chapter. But I am apt to imagine, that, were the imperfections of language, as

the instrument of knowledge, more thoroughly weighed, a great many of the controversies that make such a noise in the world, would of themselves cease; and the way to knowledge, and perhaps peace too, lie a great deal opener than it does.

22. *This should teach us Moderation in imposing our own Sense of old Authors.*—Sure I am that the signification of words in all languages depending very much on the thoughts, notions, and ideas of him that uses them, must unavoidably be of great uncertainty to men of the same language and country. This is so evident in the Greek authors, that he that shall peruse their writings will find in almost every one of them a distinct language, though the same words. But when to this natural difficulty in every country there shall be added different countries and remote ages, wherein the speakers and writers had very different notions, tempers, customs, ornaments, and figures of speech, &c., every one of which influenced the signification of their words then, though to us now they are lost and unknown; it would become us to be charitable one to another in our interpretations or misunderstanding of those ancient writings; which, though of great concernment to be understood, are liable to the unavoidable difficulties of speech, which (if we except the names of simple ideas, and some very obvious things) is not capable, without a constant defining the terms, of conveying the sense and intention of the speaker, without any manner of doubt and uncertainty to the hearer. And in discourses of religion, law, and morality, as they are matters of the highest concernment, so there will be the greatest difficulty.

23. The volumes of interpreters and commentators on the Old and New Testament are but too manifest proofs of this. Though everything said in the text be infallibly true, yet the reader may be—nay, cannot choose but be very fallible in the understanding of it. Nor is it to be wondered, that the will of God, when clothed in words, should be liable to that doubt and uncertainty which unavoidably attends that sort of conveyance; when even his Son, whilst clothed in flesh, was subject to all the frailties and inconveniences of human nature, sin excepted. And we ought to magnify his goodness that he hath spread before all the world such legible characters of his works and providence, and given all mankind so sufficient a light of reason, that they to whom this

written word never came, could not (whenever they set themselves to search) either doubt of the being of a God, or of the obedience due to him. Since, then, the precepts of natural religion are plain, and very intelligible to all mankind, and seldom come to be controverted; and other revealed truths which are conveyed to us by books and languages are liable to the common and natural obscurities and difficulties incident to words; methinks it would become us to be more careful and diligent in observing the former, and less magisterial, positive, and imperious, in imposing our own sense and interpretations of the latter.

CHAPTER X.

OF THE ABUSE OF WORDS.

1. *Abuse of Words.*—BESIDES the imperfection that is naturally in language, and the obscurity and confusion that is so hard to be avoided in the use of words, there are several wilful faults and neglects which men are guilty of in this way of communication, whereby they render these signs less clear and distinct in their signification than naturally they need to be.

2. *First, Words without any, or without clear Ideas.*—First, In this kind the first and most palpable abuse is, the using of words without clear and distinct ideas; or, which is worse, signs without anything signified. Of these there are two sorts.

1. One may observe in all languages certain words, that, if they be examined, will be found in their first original and their appropriated use not to stand for any clear and distinct ideas. These, for the most part, the several sects of philosophy and religion have introduced; for their authors or promoters, either affecting something singular and out of the way of common apprehensions, or to support some strange opinions, or cover some weakness of their hypothesis, seldom fail to coin new words, and such as, when they come to be examined, may justly be called insignificant terms. For having either had no determinate collection of ideas annexed to them when they were first invented; or at least such as, if well examined, will be found inconsistent; it is no wonder, if, after inward,

the vulgar use of the same party they remain empty sounds with little or no signification amongst those who think it enough to have them often in their mouths, as the distinguishing characters of their church or school, without much troubling their heads to examine what are the precise ideas they stand for. I shall not need here to heap up instances— every man's reading and conversation will sufficiently furnish him, or if he wants to be better stored, the great mint-masters of this kind of terms, I mean the schoolmen and metaphysicians (under which I think the disputing natural and moral philosophers of these latter ages may be comprehended) have wherewithal abundantly to content him.

3. II. Others there be who extend this abuse yet further, who take so little care to lay by words, which, in their primary notation have scarce any clear and distinct ideas which they are annexed to, that by an unpardonable negligence they familiarly use words which the propriety of language has affixed to very important ideas, without any distinct meaning at all. Wisdom, glory, grace, &c., are words frequent enough in every man's mouth; but if a great many of those who use them should be asked what they mean by them, they would be at a stand, and not know what to answer: a plain proof, that, though they have learned those sounds, and have them ready at their tongues' end, yet there are no determined ideas laid up in their minds, which are to be expressed to others by them.

4. *Occasioned by learning Names before the Ideas they belong to.*—Men having been accustomed from their cradles to learn words which are easily got and retained, before they knew or had framed the complex ideas to which they were annexed, or which were to be found in the things they were thought to stand for, they usually continue to do so all their lives; and without taking the pains necessary to settle in their minds determined ideas, they use their words for such unsteady and confused notions as they have; contenting themselves with the same words other people use: as if their very sound necessarily carried with it constantly the same meaning. This, though men make a shift with in the ordinary occurrences of life, where they find it necessary to be understood, and therefore they make signs till they are so; yet this insignificancy in their words, when they come to

reason concerning either their tenets or interest, manifestly fills their discourse with abundance of empty unintelligible noise and jargon, especially in moral matters, where the words for the most part standing for arbitrary and numerous collections of ideas, not regularly and permanently united in nature, their bare sounds are often only thought on, or at least very obscure and uncertain notions annexed to them. Men take the words they find in use amongst their neighbours; and that they may not seem ignorant what they stand for, use them confidently, without much troubling their heads about a certain fixed meaning; whereby, besides the ease of it, they obtain this advantage, that, as in such discourses they seldom are in the right, so they are as seldom to be convinced that they are in the wrong; it being all one to go about to draw those men out of their mistakes who have no settled notions, as to dispossess a vagrant of his habitation who has no settled abode. This I guess to be so, and every one may observe in himself and others whether it be so or not.

5. II. *Unsteady Application of them.*—Secondly, Another great abuse of words is inconstancy in the use of them. It is hard to find a discourse written on any subject, especially of controversy, wherein one shall not observe, if he read with attention, the same words (and those commonly the most material in the discourse, and upon which the argument turns) used sometimes for one collection of simple ideas, and sometimes for another; which is a perfect abuse of language: words being intended for signs of my ideas to make them known to others, not by any natural signification, but by a voluntary imposition, it is plain cheat and abuse, when I make them stand sometimes for one thing and sometimes for another; the wilful doing whereof can be imputed to nothing but great folly, or greater dishonesty. And a man in his accounts with another may, with as much fairness make the characters of numbers stand sometimes for one and sometimes for another collection of units (v. g., this character, 3, stands sometimes for three, sometimes for four, and sometimes for eight) as in his discourse or reasoning make the same words stand for different collections of simple ideas. If men should do so in their reckonings, I wonder who would have to do with them? One who would speak thus in the affairs and

business of the world, and call 8 sometimes seven, and sometimes nine, as best served his advantage, would presently have clapped upon him one of the two names men are commonly disgusted with. And yet in arguings and learned contests, the same sort of proceedings passes commonly for wit and learning; but to me it appears a greater dishonesty than the misplacing of counters in the casting up a debt; and the cheat the greater, by how much truth is of greater concernment and value than money.

6. III. *Affected Obscurity by wrong Application.*—Thirdly, Another abuse of language is an affected obscurity, by either applying old words to new and unusual significations, or introducing new and ambiguous terms, without defining either; or else putting them so together, as may confound their ordinary meaning. Though the Peripatetic philosophy has been most eminent in this way, yet other sects have not been wholly clear of it. There are scarce any of them that are not cumbered with some difficulties (such is the imperfection of human knowledge) which they have been fain to cover with obscurity of terms, and to confound the signification of words, which, like a mist before people's eyes, might hinder their weak parts from being discovered. That body and extension in common use stand for two distinct ideas, is plain to any one that will but reflect a little. For were their signification precisely the same, it would be proper, and as intelligible to say, the body of an extension, as the extension of a body; and yet there are those who find it necessary to confound their signification. To this abuse, and the mischiefs of confounding the signification of words, logic and the liberal sciences, as they have been handled in the schools, have given reputation; and the admired art of disputing hath added much to the natural imperfection of languages, whilst it has been made use of and fitted to perplex the signification of words, more than to discover the knowledge and truth of things; and he that will look into that sort of learned writings, will find the words there much more obscure, uncertain, and undetermined in their meaning, than they are in ordinary conversation.

7. *Logic and Dispute have much contributed to this.*—This is unavoidably to be so, where men's parts and learning are estimated by their skill in disputing. And if reputation and

reward shall attend these conquests, which depend mostly on the fineness and niceties of words, it is no wonder if the wit of man so employed, should perplex, involve, and subtilize the signification of sounds, so as never to want something to say in opposing or defending any question ; the victory being adjudged not to him who had truth on his side, but the last word in the dispute.

8. *Calling it Subtilty.*—This, though a very useless skill, and that which I think the direct opposite to the ways of knowledge, hath yet passed hitherto under the laudable and esteemed names of subtilty and acuteness, and has had the applause of the schools, and encouragement of one part of the learned men of the world.* And no wonder, since the philosophers of old, (the disputing and wrangling philosophers, I mean such as Lucian wittily and with reason taxes,) and the schoolmen since, aiming at glory and esteem for their great and universal knowledge, easier a great deal to be pretended to than really acquired, found this a good expedient to cover their ignorance with a curious and inexplicable web of perplexed words, and procure to themselves the admiration of others by unintelligible terms, the apter to produce wonder because they could not be understood ; whilst it appears in all history, that these profound doctors were no wiser nor more useful than their neighbours, and brought but small advantage to human life or the societies wherein they lived ; unless the coining of new words where they produced no new things to apply them to, or the perplexing or obscuring the signification of old ones, and so bringing all things into question and dispute, were a thing profitable to the life of man, or worthy commendation and reward.

9. *This Learning very little benefits Society.*—For, notwithstanding these learned disputants, these all-knowing doctors, it was to the unscholastic statesman that the governments of the world owed their peace, defence, and liberties ; and from the illiterate and contemned mechanic (a name of disgrace) that they received the improvements of useful arts. Nevertheless, this artificial ignorance and learned gibberish prevailed mightily in these last ages, by the interest and artifice of those who found no easier way to that pitch of authority

* For example, in his Hermotimus, Anglez, and Sale of the Philosophers.—ED.

and dominion they have attained, than by amusing the men of business and ignorant with hard words, or employing the ingenious and idle in intricate disputes about unintelligible terms, and holding them perpetually entangled in that endless labyrinth. Besides, there is no such way to gain admittance or give defence to strange and absurd doctrines, as to guard them round about with legions of obscure, doubtful, and undefined words, which yet make these retreats more like the dens of robbers, or holes of foxes, than the fortresses of fair warriors, which, if it be hard to get them out of, it is not for the strength that is in them, but the briars and thorns, and the obscurity of the thickets they are beset with. For untruth being unacceptable to the mind of man, there is no other defence left for absurdity but obscurity.

10. *But destroys the Instruments of Knowledge and Communication.*—Thus learned ignorance, and this art of keeping even inquisitive men from true knowledge hath been propagated in the world, and hath much perplexed whilst it pretended to inform the understanding. For we see that other well-meaning and wise men, whose education and parts had not acquired that acuteness, could intelligibly express themselves to one another, and in its plain use make a benefit of language. But though unlearned men well enough understood the words white and black, &c., and had constant notions of the ideas signified by those words, yet there were philosophers found who had learning and subtility enough to prove that snow was black; i. e., to prove that white was black. Whereby they had the advantage to destroy the instruments and means of discourse, conversation, instruction, and society, whilst with great art and subtilty they did no more but perplex and confound the signification of words, and thereby render language less useful than the real defects of it had made it; a gift which the illiterate had not attained to.

11. *As useful as to confound the Sound of the Letters.*— These learned men did equally instruct men's understandings and profit their lives, as he who should alter the signification of known characters, and by a subtle device of learning, far surpassing the capacity of the illiterate, dull, and vulgar, should in his writing show that he could put A for B, and

D for E, &c., to the no small admiration and benefit of his reader; it being as senseless to put black, which is a word agreed on to stand for one sensible idea, to put it, I say, for another, or the contrary idea; i. e., to call snow black, as to put this mark A, which is a character agreed on to stand for one modification of sound made by a certain motion of the organs of speech, for B, which is agreed on to stand for another modification of sound made by another certain mode of the organs of speech.

12. *This Art has perplexed Religion and Justice.*—Nor hath this mischief stopped in logical niceties, or curious empty speculations; it hath invaded the great concernments of human life and society—obscured and perplexed the material truths of law and divinity—brought confusion, disorder, and uncertainty into the affairs of mankind, and if not destroyed, yet in a great measure rendered useless these two great rules, religion and justice. What have the greatest part of the comments and disputes upon the laws of God and man served for, but to make the meaning more doubtful, and perplex the sense? What have been the effect of those multiplied curious distinctions and acute niceties but obscurity and uncertainty, leaving the words more unintelligible, and the reader more at a loss? How else comes it to pass that princes speaking or writing to their servants, in their ordinary commands are easily understood; speaking to their people in their laws, are not so? And, as I remarked before, doth it not often happen that a man of an ordinary capacity very well understands a text or a law that he reads, till he consults an expositor or goes to counsel, who, by that time he hath done explaining them, makes the words signify either nothing at all, or what he pleases.

13. *And ought not to pass for Learning.*—Whether any by-interests of these professions have occasioned this, I will not here examine; but I leave it to be considered whether it would not be well for mankind, whose concernment it is to know things as they are, and to do what they ought, and not to spend their lives in talking about them, or tossing words to and fro; whether it would not be well, I say, that the use of words were made plain and direct, and that language which was given us for the improvement of knowledge and bond of society, should not be employed to darken truth

and unsettle people's rights, to raise mists and render unintelligible both morality and religion? or that at least, if this will happen, it should not be thought learning or knowledge to do so?

14. IV. *Taking them for Things.* — Fourthly, Another great abuse of words is, the taking them for things. This, though it in some degree concerns all names in general, yet more particularly affects those of substances. To this abuse those men are most subject who most confine their thoughts to any one system, and give themselves up into a firm belief of the perfection of any received hypothesis; whereby they come to be persuaded that the terms of that sect are so suited to the nature of things, that they perfectly correspond with their real existence. Who is there that has been bred up in the Peripatetic philosophy, who does not think the ten names, under which are ranked the ten predicaments, to be exactly conformable to the nature of things? Who is there of that school that is not persuaded that substantial forms, vegetative souls, abhorrence of a vacuum, intentional species, &c., are something real? These words men have learned from their very entrance upon knowledge, and have found their masters and systems lay great stress upon them; and therefore they cannot quit the opinion, that they are conformable to nature, and are the representations of something that really exists. The Platonists have their soul of the world,* and the Epicureans their endeavour towards motion in their atoms, when at rest. There is scarce any sect in philosophy has not a distinct set of terms that others understand not; but yet this gibberish, which, in the weakness of human understanding, serves so well to palliate men's ignorance and cover their errors, comes, by familiar use amongst those of the same tribe, to seem the most important part of language, and of all other, the terms the most significant; and should aërial and ætherial vehicles come once, by the prevalency of that doctrine, to be generally received anywhere, no doubt those terms would make impressions on men's minds, so as to establish them in the persuasion of the reality of such things, as much as Peripatetic forms and intentional species have heretofore done.

15. *Instance, in Matter.* — How much names taken for

* See Tennemann's History of Philosophy, § 135; and Lipsius Physiologia Stoicorum, l. 7, diss 7 8. — ED.

things are apt to mislead the understanding, the attentive reading of philosophical writers would abundantly discover; and that, perhaps, in words little suspected of any such misuse. I shall instance in one only, and that a very familiar one: how many intricate disputes have there been about matter, as if there were some such thing really in nature, distinct from body, as it is evident the word matter stands for an idea distinct from the idea of body? For if the ideas these two terms stood for were precisely the same, they might indifferently, in all places, be put for one another. But we see, that, though it be proper to say there is one matter of all bodies, one cannot say there is one body of all matters: we familiarly say one body is bigger than another; but it sounds harsh (and I think is never used) to say one matter is bigger than another. Whence comes this, then? viz., from hence: that, though matter and body be not really distinct, but wherever there is the one there is the other; yet matter and body stand for two different conceptions, whereof the one is incomplete, and but a part of the other. For body stands for a solid extended figured substance, whereof matter is but a partial and more confused conception; it seeming to me to be used for the substance and solidity of body, without taking in its extension and figure; and therefore it is, that, speaking of matter, we speak of it always as one, because in truth it expressly contains nothing but the idea of a solid substance, which is everywhere the same, everywhere uniform. This being our idea of matter, we no more conceive or speak of different matters in the world than we do of different solidities; though we both conceive and speak of different bodies, because extension and figure are capable of variation. But since solidity cannot exist without extension and figure, the taking matter to be the name of something really existing under that precision, has no doubt produced those obscure and unintelligible discourses and disputes, which have filled the heads and books of philosophers concerning materia prima;* which imperfection or

* Among the number of these great philosophers was Hudibras, if we may rely upon that sage chronicler who celebrates his deeds:—

"As he professed,
He had first matter seen undressed;
He took her naked, all alone,
Before one rag of form was on."—ED.

abuse, how far it may concern a great many other general terms I leave to be considered. This, I think, I may at least say, that we should have a great many fewer disputes in the world if words were taken for what they are, the signs of our ideas only, and not for things themselves. For when we argue about matter or any the like term, we truly argue only about the idea we express by that sound, whether that precise idea agree to anything really existing in nature or no. And if men would tell what ideas they make their words stand for, there could not be half that obscurity or wrangling in the search or support of truth that there is.

16. *This makes Errors lasting.*—But whatever inconvenience follows from this mistake of words, this I am sure, that, by constant and familiar use they charm men into notions far remote from the truth of things. It would be a hard matter to persuade any one that the words which his father, or schoolmaster, the parson of the parish, or such a reverend doctor used, signified nothing that really existed in nature; which perhaps is none of the least causes that men are so hardly drawn to quit their mistakes, even in opinions purely philosophical, and where they have no other interest but truth. For the words they have a long time been used to, remaining firm in their minds, it is no wonder that the wrong notions annexed to them should not be removed.

17. V. *Setting them for what they cannot signify.*—Fifthly, Another abuse of words is, the setting them in the place of things which they do or can by no means signify. We may observe, that, in the general names of substances whereof the nominal essences are only known to us, when we put them into propositions, and affirm or deny anything about them, we do most commonly tacitly suppose or intend they should stand for the real essence of a certain sort of substances. For when a man says gold is malleable, he means and would insinuate something more than this, that what I call gold is malleable, (though truly it amounts to no more,) but would have this understood, viz., that gold, i. e., what has the real essence of gold, is malleable; which amounts to thus much, that malleableness depends on, and is inseparable from the real essence of gold. But a man not knowing wherein that real essence consists, the connexion in his mind of malleableness is not truly with an essence he knows not, but only

with the sound gold he puts for it. Thus, when we say that "animal rationale" is, and "animal implume bipes latis unguibus" is not a good definition of a man; it is plain we suppose the name man in this case to stand for the real essence of a species, and would signify that a rational animal better described that real essence than a two-legged animal with broad nails, and without feathers. For else, why might not Plato as properly make the word ἄνθρωπος, or man, stand for his complex idea, made up of the idea of a body, distinguished from others by a certain shape and other outward appearances, as Aristotle make the complex idea to which he gave the name ἄνθρωπος, or man, of body and the faculty of reasoning joined together; unless the name ἄνθρωπος, or man, were supposed to stand for something else than what it signifies, and to be put in the place of some other thing than the idea a man professes he would express by it?

18. *v. g., Putting them for the real Essences of Substances.*—It is true the names of substances would be much more useful, and propositions made in them much more certain, were the real essences of substances the ideas in our minds which those words signified. And it is for want of those real essences that our words convey so little knowledge or certainty in our discourses about them; and therefore the mind, to remove that imperfection as much as it can, makes them, by a secret supposition, to stand for a thing having that real essence, as if thereby it made some nearer approaches to it. For though the word man or gold signify nothing truly but a complex idea of properties united together in one sort of substances; yet there is scarce anybody, in the use of these words, but often supposes each of those names to stand for a thing having the real essence on which these properties depend. Which is so far from diminishing the imperfection of our words, that by a plain abuse it adds to it, when we would make them stand for something, which, not being in our complex idea, the name we use can no ways be the sign of.

19. *Hence we think every Change of our Idea in Substances not to change the Species.*—This shows us the reason why in mixed modes any of the ideas that make the composition of the complex one, being left out or changed, it is allowed to be another thing, i. e., to be of another species, it is plain in

chance-medley, manslaughter, murder, parricide, &c. The reason whereof is, because the complex idea signified by that name is the real as well as nominal essence; and there is no secret reference of that name to any other essence but that. But in substances, it is not so; for though in that called gold, one puts into his complex idea what another leaves out, and vice versâ; yet men do not usually think that therefore the species is changed; because they secretly in their minds refer that name, and suppose it annexed to a real immutable essence of a thing existing, on which those properties depend. He that adds to his complex idea of gold that of fixedness and solubility in aq. regia, which he put not in it before, is not thought to have changed the species, but only to have a more perfect idea, by adding another simple idea, which is always in fact joined with those other, of which his former complex idea consisted. But this reference of the name to a thing whereof we had not the idea is so far from helping at all, that it only serves the more to involve us in difficulties; for by this tacit reference to the real essence of that species of bodies, the word gold (which, by standing for a more or less perfect collection of simple ideas, serves to design that sort of body well enough in civil discourse) comes to have no signification at all, being put for somewhat whereof we have no idea at all, and so can signify nothing at all, when the body itself is away. For however it may be thought all one, yet, if well considered, it will be found a quite different thing to argue about gold in name, and about a parcel in the body itself, v. g., a piece of leaf-gold laid before us, though in discourse we are fain to substitute the name for the thing.

20. *The Cause of the Abuse, a Supposition of Nature's working always regularly.*—That which I think very much disposes men to substitute their names for the real essences of species, is the supposition before mentioned, that nature works regularly in the production of things, and sets the boundaries to each of those species, by giving exactly the same real internal constitution to each individual which we rank under one general name. Whereas any one who observes their different qualities can hardly doubt, that many of the individuals called by the same name are, in their internal constitution, as different one from another as several

of those which are ranked under different specific names. This supposition, however, that the same precise and internal constitution goes always with the same specific name, makes men forward to take those names for the representatives of those real essences, though indeed they signify nothing but the complex ideas they have in their minds when they use them. So that, if I may so say, signifying one thing, and being supposed for, or put in the place of another, they cannot but, in such a kind of use, cause a great deal of uncertainty in men's discourses; especially in those who have thoroughly imbibed the doctrine of substantial forms, whereby they firmly imagine the several species of things to be determined and distinguished.

21. *This Abuse contains two false Suppositions.*—But however preposterous and absurd it be to make our names stand for ideas we have not, or (which is all one) essences that we know not, it being in effect to make our words the signs of nothing; yet it is evident to any one who ever so little reflects on the use men make of their words, that there is nothing more familiar. When a man asks whether this or that thing he sees, let it be a drill, or a monstrous fœtus, be a man or no; it is evident the question is not whether that particular thing agree to his complex idea expressed by the name man; but whether it has in it the real essence of a species of things which he supposes his name man to stand for. In which way of using the names of substances, there are these false suppositions contained:—

First, that there are certain precise essences according to which nature makes all particular things, and by which they are distinguished into species. That everything has a real constitution, whereby it is what it is, and on which its sensible qualities depend, is past doubt; but I think it has been proved that this makes not the distinction of species as we rank them, nor the boundaries of their names.

Secondly, this tacitly also insinuates, as if we had ideas of these proposed essences. For to what purpose else is it to inquire whether this or that thing have the real essence of the species man, if we did not suppose that there were such a specific essence known? which yet is utterly false; and therefore, such application of names as would make them stand for ideas which we have not, must needs cause great disorder in discourses and reasonings about them, and be a great inconvenience in our communication by words.

22. VI. *A supposition that Words have a certain and evident Signification.*—Sixthly, there remains yet another more general, though perhaps less observed abuse of words; and that is, that men having by a long and familiar use annexed to them certain ideas, they are apt to imagine so near and necessary a connexion between the names and the signification they use them in, that they forwardly suppose one cannot but understand what their meaning is; and therefore one ought to acquiesce in the words delivered, as if it were past doubt that, in the use of those common received sounds, the speaker and hearer had necessarily the same precise ideas. Whence presuming, that when they have in discourse used any term, they have thereby, as it were, set before others the very thing they talked of; and so likewise taking the words of others, as naturally standing for just what they themselves have been accustomed to apply them to, they never trouble themselves to explain their own, or understand clearly others' meaning. From whence commonly proceed noise and wrangling, without improvement or information; whilst men take words to be the constant regular marks of agreed notions, which in truth are no more but the voluntary and unsteady signs of their own ideas. And yet men think it strange, if in discourse or (where it is often absolutely necessary) in dispute, one sometimes asks the meaning of their terms; though the arguings one may every day observe in conversation make it evident that there are few names of complex ideas which any two men use for the same just precise collection. It is hard to name a word which will not be a clear instance of this. Life is a term, none more familiar; any one almost would take it for an affront to be asked what he meant by it. And yet if it comes in question, whether a plant that lies ready formed in the seed have life; whether the embryo in an egg before incubation, or a man in a swoon without sense or motion, be alive or no; it is easy to perceive that a clear, distinct, settled idea does not always accompany the use of so known a word as that of life is. Some gross and confused conceptions men indeed ordinarily have, to which they apply the common words of their language; and such a loose use of their words serves them well enough in their ordinary discourses or affairs. But

this is not sufficient for philosophical inquiries; knowledge and reasoning require precise determinate ideas. And though men will not be so importunately dull, as not to understand what others say without demanding an explication of their terms, nor so troublesomely critical as to correct others in the use of the words they receive from them; yet, where truth and knowledge are concerned in the case, I know not what fault it can be to desire the explication of words whose sense seems dubious; or why a man should be ashamed to own his ignorance in what sense another man uses his words, since he has no other way of certainly knowing it but by being informed. This abuse of taking words upon trust has nowhere spread so far, nor with so ill effects, as amongst men of letters. The multiplication and obstinacy of disputes which have so laid waste the intellectual world, is owing to nothing more than to this ill use of words. For though it be generally believed that there is great diversity of opinions in the volumes and variety of controversies the world is distracted with, yet the most I can find that the contending learned men of different parties do, in their arguings one with another, is, that they speak different languages. For I am apt to imagine that when any of them, quitting terms, think upon things, and know what they think, they think all the same, though perhaps what they would have be different.

23. *The Ends of Language: First, To convey our Ideas.*— To conclude this consideration of the imperfection and abuse of language; the ends of language in our discourse with others being chiefly these three: first, to make known one man's thoughts or ideas to another; secondly, to do it with as much ease and quickness as possible; and, thirdly, thereby to convey the knowledge of things: language is either abused or deficient, when it fails of any of these three.

First, Words fail in the first of these ends, and lay not open one man's ideas to another's view: 1. When men have names in their mouths without any determinate ideas in their minds, whereof they are the signs; or, 2. When they apply the common received names of any language to ideas, to which the common use of that language does not apply them; or, 3. When they apply them very unsteadily, making them stand, now for one, and by and by for another idea.

24. *Secondly, To do it with Quickness.*—Secondly, Men fail of conveying their thoughts with all the quickness and ease that may be, when they have complex ideas without having any distinct names for them. This is sometimes the fault of the language itself, which has not in it a sound yet applied to such a signification; and sometimes the fault of the man, who has not yet learned the name for that idea he would show another.

25. *Thirdly, Therewith to convey the Knowledge of Things.* —Thirdly, There is no knowledge of things conveyed by men's words, when their ideas agree not to the reality of things. Though it be a defect that has its original in our ideas, which are not so conformable to the nature of things as attention, study, and application might make them, yet it fails not to extend itself to our words too, when we use them as signs of real beings, which yet never had any reality or existence.

26. *How Men's Words fail in all these.*—First, He that hath words of any language, without distinct ideas in his mind to which he applies them, does so far as he uses them in discourse, only make a noise without any sense or signification; and how learned soever he may seem by the use of hard words or learned terms, is not much more advanced thereby in knowledge, than he would be in learning, who had nothing in his study but the bare titles of books, without possessing the contents of them. For all such words, however put into discourse, according to the right construction of grammatical rules, or the harmony of well-turned periods, do yet amount to nothing but bare sounds, and nothing else.

27. Secondly, He that has complex ideas, without particular names for them, would be in no better case than a bookseller who had in his warehouse volumes that lay there unbound, and without titles, which he could therefore make known to others only by showing the loose sheets, and communicate them only by tale. This man is hindered in his discourse for want of words to communicate his complex ideas, which he is therefore forced to make known by an enumeration of the simple ones that compose them; and so is fain often to use twenty words to express what another man signifies in one.

28. Thirdly, He that puts not constantly the same sign for the same idea, but uses the same words sometimes in one and sometimes in another signification, ought to pass in the schools and conversation for as fair a man, as he does in the market and exchange, who sells several things under the same name.

29. Fourthly, He that applies the words of any language to ideas different from those to which the common use of that country applies them, however his own understanding may be filled with truth and light, will not by such words be able to convey much of it to others, without defining his terms. For however the sounds are such as are familiarly known, and easily enter the ears of those who are accustomed to them; yet standing for other ideas than those they usually are annexed to, and are wont to excite in the mind of the hearers, they cannot make known the thoughts of him who thus uses them.

30. Fifthly, He that imagined to himself substances such as never have been, and filled his head with ideas which have not any correspondence with the real nature of things, to which yet he gives settled and defined names, may fill his discourse, and perhaps another man's head, with the fantastical imaginations of his own brain, but will be very far from advancing thereby one jot in real and true knowledge.

31. He that hath names without ideas, wants meaning in his words, and speaks only empty sounds. He that hath complex ideas without names for them, wants liberty and dispatch in his expressions, and is necessitated to use periphrases. He that uses his words loosely and unsteadily will either be not minded or not understood. He that applies his names to ideas different from their common use, wants propriety in his language, and speaks gibberish. And he that hath the ideas of substances disagreeing with the real existence of things, so far wants the materials of true knowledge in his understanding, and hath instead thereof chimeras.

32. *How in Substances.*—In our notions concerning substances, we are liable to all the former inconveniences; v. g., he that uses the word tarantula, without having any imagination or idea of what it stands for, pronounces a good word; but so long means nothing at all by it. 2. He that in a new-discovered country shall see several sorts of animals

and vegetables unknown to him before, may have as true ideas of them, as of a horse or a stag; but can speak of them only by a description, till he shall either take the names the natives call them by, or give them names himself. 3. He that uses the word body sometimes for pure extension, and sometimes for extension and solidity together, will talk very fallaciously. 4. He that gives the name horse to that idea which common usage calls mule, talks improperly, and will not be understood. 5. He that thinks the name centaur stands for some real being, imposes on himself, and mistakes words for things.

33. *How in Modes and Relations.*—In modes and relations generally, we are liable only to the four first of these inconveniences; viz. 1. I may have in my memory the names of modes, as gratitude or charity, and yet not have any precise ideas annexed in my thoughts to those names. 2. I may have ideas, and not know the names that belong to them; v. g., I may have the idea of a man's drinking till his colour and humour be altered, till his tongue trips, and his eyes look red, and his feet fail him; and yet not know that it is to be called drunkenness. 3. I may have the ideas of virtues or vices, and names also, but apply them amiss; v. g., when I apply the name frugality to that idea which others call and signify by this sound, covetousness. 4. I may use any of those names with inconstancy. 5. But, in modes and relations, I cannot have ideas disagreeing to the existence of things; for modes being complex ideas, made by the mind at pleasure, and relation being but by way of considering or comparing two things together, and so also an idea of my own making, these ideas can scarce be found to disagree with anything existing, since they are not in the mind as the copies of things regularly made by nature, nor as properties inseparably flowing from the internal constitution or essence of any substance; but as it were patterns lodged in my memory, with names annexed to them, to denominate actions and relations by, as they come to exist. But the mistake is commonly in my giving a wrong name to my conceptions; and so using words in a different sense from other people; I am not understood, but am thought to have wrong ideas of them, when I give wrong names to them. Only if I put in my ideas of mixed modes or relations any inconsistent ideas

together, I fill my head also with chimeras; since such ideas, if well examined, cannot so much as exist in the mind, much less any real being ever be denominated from them.

34. VII. *Figurative Speech also and Abuse of Language.*—Since wit and fancy find easier entertainment in the world than dry truth and real knowledge, figurative speeches and allusion in language will hardly be admitted as an imperfection or abuse of it. I confess in discourses where we seek rather pleasure and delight than information and improvement, such ornaments as are borrowed from them can scarce pass for faults. But yet if we would speak of things as they are, we must allow that all the art of rhetoric, besides order and clearness, all the artificial and figurative application of words eloquence hath invented, are for nothing else but to insinuate wrong ideas, move the passions, and thereby mislead the judgment, and so indeed are perfect cheats; and therefore, however laudable or allowable oratory may render them in harangues and popular addresses, they are certainly, in all discourses that pretend to inform or instruct, wholly to be avoided; and where truth and knowledge are concerned, cannot but be thought a great fault, either of the language or person that makes use of them. What and how various they are, will be superfluous here to take notice: the books of rhetoric which abound in the world, will instruct those who want to be informed; only I cannot but observe how little the preservation and improvement of truth and knowledge is the care and concern of mankind; since the arts of fallacy are endowed and preferred. It is evident how much men love to deceive and be deceived, since rhetoric, that powerful instrument of error and deceit, has its established professors, is publicly taught, and has always been had in great reputation: and I doubt not but it will be thought great boldness, if not brutality in me, to have said thus much against it. Eloquence, like the fair sex, has too prevailing beauties in it to suffer itself ever to be spoken against; and it is in vain to find fault with those arts of deceiving, wherein men find pleasure to be deceived.*

* The notions which Locke here puts forward on the subject of rhetoric, and an ornate and figurative style, are as inconsistent with his own practice as they are with true philosophy. He himself constantly, both throughout this and every other of his works, makes use of a profusion

CHAPTER XI.
OF THE REMEDIES OF THE FOREGOING IMPERFECTIONS AND ABUSES.

1. *They are worth seeking.*—THE natural and improved imperfections of languages we have seen above at large; and of tropes and figures; nor, as will be evident to the reader, is his meaning thereby at all darkened, but placed in a broader, clearer, and more perfect light. It is, in fact, nearly impossible to convey truth from one mind to another without the abundant employment of metaphors; and the art of rhetoric, though it may sometimes be used to adorn and recommend falsehood, is no more to be rejected by truth on that account, than dress is to be laid aside by modest women because it also worn by courtezans. Plato, as is well known, has put forward on this subject crotchets similar to Locke's; and it is not at all improbable that the English philosopher may have been seduced into this diatribe against rhetoric by the eloquent and rhetorical master of the academy, who attempted to storm the citadel of eloquence with instruments supplied out of its own armoury. But if authority might be allowed any weight in this matter, I would venture to oppose to that of Plato and Locke, the deliberate conviction of Peter Melancthon, who, besides studying profoundly for his own use the art of rhetoric, composed for the service of others, a brief but admirable introduction to the larger works of Aristotle, Quintillian, and Cicero; and in the Epistola Nuncupatoria, addressed to the brothers Reifenstein, says: "Quanquam autem ipsa præcepta rhetorices levia et perquam puerilia videntur, tamen hoc sibi persuadeant adolescentes, et ad judicandum, et ad maximas caussas explicandas prorsus ea necessaria esse. Quare etiam adhortandi sunt ne his nostris libellis immorentur: sed cognitis his elementis, Ciceronem et Quintilianum legat nec degustent obiter, sed diu multumque legant auctores illos, non solum ad eloquentiam, sed etiam ad sapientiam profuturos, et discant ex eis eloquentiam metiri magnitudine sua. Videmus enim vulgo quosdam sciolos esse, qui somniat se in arce eloquentiæ sedere, postquam didicerunt epistolium scribere octo aut decem versuum, in quo duo aut tria insint hemistrichia aut proverbia, quasi emblemata. Hæc opinio juvenibus eximenda est, et ostendendum quibus in rebus eloquentia dominetur quod videlicet necessaria sit ad maximas ac difficillimas caussas omnes, in hac tota civili consuetudine vitæ explicandas, ad retinendas religiones, ad interpretandas ac defendendas leges, ad exercenda judicia, et consilium dandum reipublicæ in maximis periculis diligenter et hoc monendi sunt studiosi, rem unam esse omnium humanorum operum longe difficillima, bene dicere. Etenim qui magnitudinem eloquentiæ et rei difficultatem considerabit intelliget expetenti hanc laudem, acerrimum studium omnium maximarum artium adhibendum esse, et statuet ad magnarum et difficilium causarum tractationem in Ecclesia, et in Republica, non tantum hos rhetoricos libellos, sed perfectam doctrinam et magnam facultatem, longam exercitationem domesticam, et acerrimum judicium afferendum esse." (Edit. Antwerpiæ, 1573.) An example of Locke's own practice occurs in § 5 of the next chapter, where he speaks of "language being the great *conduit* whereby men convey their discoveries," etc.

VOL. II.

speech being the great bond that holds society together, and the common conduit whereby the improvements of knowledge are conveyed from one man and one generation to another, it would well deserve our most serious thoughts to consider what remedies are to be found for the inconveniences above mentioned.

2. *Are not easy.*—I am not so vain as to think that any one can pretend to attempt the perfect reforming the languages of the world, no, not so much as of his own country, without rendering himself ridiculous. To require that men should use their words constantly in the same sense, and for none but determined and uniform ideas, would be to think that all men should have the same notions, and should talk of nothing but what they have clear and distinct ideas of; which is not to be expected by any one who hath not vanity enough to imagine he can prevail with men to be very knowing or very silent. And he must be very little skilled in the world, who thinks that a voluble tongue shall accompany only a good understanding; or that men's talking much or little should hold proportion only to their knowledge.

3. *But yet necessary to Philosophy.*—But though the market and exchange must be left to their own ways of talking, and gossipings not be robbed of their ancient privilege; though the schools and men of argument would perhaps take it amiss to have anything offered to abate the length or lessen the number of their disputes; yet methinks those who pretend seriously to search after or maintain truth, should think themselves obliged to study how they might deliver themselves without obscurity, doubtfulness, or equivocation, to which men's words are naturally liable, if care be not taken.

4. *Misuse of Words the great Cause of Errors.*—For he that shall well consider the errors and obscurity, the mistakes and confusion, that are spread in the world by an ill use of words, will find some reason to doubt whether language, as it has been employed, has contributed more to the improvement or hindrance of knowledge amongst mankind. How many are there, that, when they would think on things, fix their thoughts only on words, especially when they would apply their minds to moral matters: and who then can wonder if the result of such contemplations and reasonings, about little more than sounds, whilst the ideas they annex

to them are very confused and very unsteady, or perhaps none at all; who can wonder, I say, that such thoughts and reasonings end in nothing but obscurity and mistake, without any clear judgment or knowledge?

5. *Obstinacy.*—This inconvenience in an ill use of words men suffer in their own private meditations; but much more manifest are the disorders which follow from it in conversation, discourse, and arguings with others. For language being the great conduit whereby men convey their discoveries, reasonings, and knowledge, from one to another; he that makes an ill use of it, though he does not corrupt the fountains of knowledge, which are in things themselves; yet he does as much as in him lies, break or stop the pipes whereby it is distributed to the public use and advantage of mankind. He that uses words without any clear and steady meaning, what does he but lead himself and others into errors? And he that designedly does it, ought to be looked on as an enemy to truth and knowledge. And yet who can wonder that all the sciences and parts of knowledge have been so overcharged with obscure and equivocal terms, and insignificant and doubtful expressions, capable to make the most attentive or quick-sighted very little or not at all the more knowing or orthodox? since subtilty, in those who make profession to teach or defend truth, hath passed so much for a virtue; a virtue, indeed, which, consisting for the most part in nothing but the fallacious and illusory use of obscure or deceitful terms, is only fit to make men more conceited in their ignorance and more obstinate in their errors.

6. *And Wrangling.*—Let us look into the books of controversy of any kind, there we shall see that the effect of obscure, unsteady, or equivocal terms, is nothing but noise and wrangling about sounds, without convincing or bettering a man's understanding. For if the idea be not agreed on betwixt the speaker and hearer, for which the words stand, the argument is not about things, but names. As often as such a word, whose signification is not ascertained betwixt them, comes in use, their understandings have no other object wherein they agree, but barely the sound; the things that they think on at that time, as expressed by that word, being quite different.

7. *Instance, Bat and Bird.*—Whether a bat be a bird or no, is not a question; whether a bat be another thing than indeed it is, or have other qualities than indeed it has, for that would be extremely absurd to doubt of: but the question is, 1. Either between those that acknowledged themselves to have but imperfect ideas of one or both of this sort of things, for which these names are supposed to stand; and then it is a real inquiry concerning the name of a bird or a bat, to make their yet imperfect ideas of it more complete, by examining whether all the simple ideas to which, combined together, they both give the name bird, be all to be found in a bat: but this is a question only of inquirers (not disputers) who neither affirm nor deny, but examine. Or, 2. It is a question between disputants, whereof the one affirms and the other denies that a bat is a bird; and then the question is barely about the signification of one or both these words; in that they not having both the same complex ideas to which they give these two names, one holds and the other denies, that these two names may be affirmed one of another. Were they agreed in the signification of these two names, it were impossible they should dispute about them; for they would presently and clearly see (were that adjusted between them) whether all the simple ideas of the more general name bird were found in the complex idea of a bat or no; and so there could be no doubt whether a bat were a bird or no. And here I desire it may be considered, and carefully examined, whether the greatest part of the disputes in the world are not merely verbal, and about the signification of words; and whether, if the terms they are made in were defined, and reduced in their signification (as they must be where they signify anything) to determined collections of the simple ideas they do or should stand for, those disputes would not end of themselves, and immediately vanish. I leave it, then, to be considered what the learning of disputation is, and how well they are employed for the advantage of themselves or others, whose business is only the vain ostentation of sounds; i. e., those who spend their lives in disputes and controversies. When I shall see any of those combatants strip all his terms of ambiguity and obscurity, (which every one may do in the words he uses himself,) I shall think him a champion for knowledge, truth, and peace, and not the slave of vain-glory, ambition, or a party.

8. To remedy the defects of speech before mentioned to some degree, and to prevent the inconveniences that follow from them, I imagine the observation of these following rules may be of use, till somebody better able shall judge it worth his while to think more maturely on this matter, and oblige the world with his thoughts on it.

First, Remedy; to use no Word without an Idea.—First, man shall take care to use no word without a signification, no name without an idea for which he makes it stand. This rule will not seem altogether needless to any one who shall take the pains to recollect how often he has met with such words as instinct, sympathy, and antipathy, &c., in the discourse of others, so made use of, as he might easily conclude that those that used them had no ideas in their minds to which they applied them, but spoke them only as sounds, which usually served instead of reasons on the like occasions. Not but that these words and the like have very proper significations in which they may be used; but there being no natural connexion between any words and any ideas, these and any other may be learned by rote, and pronounced or writ by men who have no ideas in their minds to which they have annexed them, and for which they make them stand; which is necessary they should, if men would speak intelligibly even to themselves alone.

9. *Secondly, To have distinct Ideas annexed to them in Modes.*—Secondly, It is not enough a man uses his words as signs of some ideas: those he annexes them to, if they be simple, must be clear and distinct; if complex, must be determinate, i. e., the precise collection of simple ideas settled in the mind, with that sound annexed to it, as the sign of that precise determined collection, and no other. This is very necessary in names of modes, and especially moral words; which, having no settled objects in nature, from whence their ideas are taken, as from their original, are apt to be very confused. Justice is a word in every man's mouth, but most commonly with a very undetermined, loose signification; which will always be so, unless a man has in his mind a distinct comprehension of the component parts that complex idea consists of: and if it

be decompounded, must be able to resolve it still on, till he at last comes to the simple ideas that make it up: and unless this be done, a man makes an ill use of the word, let it be justice, for example, or any other. I do not say, a man need stand to recollect and make this analysis at large every time the word justice comes in his way; but this at least is necessary, that he have so examined the signification of that name, and settled the idea of all its parts in his mind, that he can do it when he pleases. If any one who makes his complex idea of justice to be such a treatment of the person or goods of another as is according to law, hath not a clear and distinct idea what law is, which makes a part of his complex idea of justice, it is plain his idea of justice itself will be confused and imperfect. This exactness will, perhaps, be judged very troublesome, and therefore most men will think they may be excused from settling the complex ideas of mixed modes so precisely in their minds. But yet I must say, till this be done, it must not be wondered that they have a great deal of obscurity and confusion in their own minds, and a great deal of wrangling in their discourse with others.

10. *And distinct and conformable in Substances.*—In the names of substances, for a right use of them, something more is required than barely determined ideas. In these the names must also be conformable to things as they exist; but of this I shall have occasion to speak more at large by and by. This exactness is absolutely necessary in inquiries after philosophical knowledge, and in controversies about truth. And though it would be well, too, if it extended itself to common conversation and the ordinary affairs of life; yet I think that is scarce to be expected. Vulgar notions suit vulgar discourses; and both, though confused enough, yet serve pretty well the market and the wake. Merchants and lovers, cooks and tailors, have words wherewithal to dispatch their ordinary affairs; and so, I think, might philosophers and disputants too, if they had a mind to understand, and to be clearly understood.

11. *Thirdly, Propriety.*—Thirdly, It is not enough that men have ideas, determined ideas, for which they make these signs stand; but they must also take care to apply their words as near as may be to such ideas as common use

has annexed them to. For words, especially of languages already framed, being no man's private possession, but the common measure of commerce and communication, it is not for any one at pleasure to change the stamp they are current in, nor alter the ideas they are affixed to; or at least, when there is a necessity to do so, he is bound to give notice of it. Men's intentions in speaking are, or at least should be, to be understood; which cannot be without frequent explanations, demands, and other the like incommodious interruptions, where men do not follow common use. Propriety of speech is that which gives our thoughts entrance into other men's minds with the greatest ease and advantage; and therefore deserves some part of our care and study, especially in the names of moral words. The proper signification and use of terms is best to be learned from those who in their writings and discourses appear to have had the clearest notions, and applied to them their terms with the exactest choice and fitness. This way of using a man's words, according to the propriety of the language, though it have not always the good fortune to be understood; yet most commonly leaves the blame of it on him who is so unskilful in the language he speaks, as not to understand it when made use of as it ought to be.

12. *Fourthly, To make known their Meaning.*—Fourthly, But, because common use has not so visibly annexed any signification to words, as to make men know always certainly what they precisely stand for; and because men in the improvement of their knowledge, come to have ideas different from the vulgar and ordinary received ones, for which they must either make new words, (which men seldom venture to do, for fear of being thought guilty of affectation or novelty,) or else must use old ones in a new signification: therefore after the observation of the foregoing rules, it is sometimes necessary, for the ascertaining the signification of words, to declare their meaning; where either common use has left it uncertain and loose, (as it has in most names of very complex ideas,) or where the term, being very material in the discourse, and that upon which it chiefly turns, is liable to any doubtfulness or mistake.

13. *And that three Ways.*—As the ideas men's words stand for are of different sorts, so the way of making known the

ideas they stand for, when there is occasion, is also different. For though defining be thought the proper way to make known the proper signification of words, yet there are some words that will not be defined, as there are others whose precise meaning cannot be made known but by definition; and perhaps a third, which partake somewhat of both the other, as we shall see in the names of simple ideas, modes, and substances.

14. I. *In simple Ideas, by synonymous Terms, or showing.*—First, when a man makes use of the name of any simple idea which he perceives is not understood, or is in danger to be mistaken, he is obliged by the laws of ingenuity and the end of speech to declare his meaning, and make known what idea he makes it stand for. This, as has been shown, cannot be done by definition; and therefore, when a synonymous word fails to do it, there is but one of these ways left: First, sometimes the naming the subject wherein that simple idea is to be found, will make its name to be understood by those who are acquainted with that subject, and know it by that name. So to make a countryman understand what "feuillemorte" colour signifies, it may suffice to tell him it is the colour of withered leaves falling in autumn. Secondly, but the only sure way of making known the signification of the name of any simple idea, is by presenting to his senses that subject which may produce it in his mind, and make him actually have the idea that word stands for.

15. II. *In mixed Modes, by Definition.*—Secondly, Mixed modes, especially those belonging to morality, being most of them such combinations of ideas as the mind puts together of its own choice, and whereof there are not always standing patterns to be found existing, the signification of their names cannot be made known as those of simple ideas by any showing; but, in recompense thereof, may be perfectly and exactly defined. For they being combinations of several ideas that the mind of man has arbitrarily put together, without reference to any archetypes, men may, if they please, exactly know the ideas that go to each composition, and so both use these words in a certain and undoubted signification, and perfectly declare, when there is occasion, what they stand for. This, if well considered, would lay great blame on those who make not their discourses about moral things

very clear and distinct. For since the precise signification of the names of mixed modes, or, which is all one, the real essence of each species is to be known, they being not of nature's, but man's making, it is a great negligence and perverseness to discourse of moral things with uncertainty and obscurity; which is more pardonable in treating of natural substances, where doubtful terms are hardly to be avoided, for a quite contrary reason, as we shall see by and by.

16. *Morality capable of Demonstration.*—Upon this ground it is that I am bold to think that morality is capable of demonstration, as well as mathematics; since the precise real essence of the things moral words stand for may be perfectly known, and so the congruity and incongruity of the things themselves be certainly discovered, in which consists perfect knowledge. Nor let any one object, that the names of substances are often to be made use of in morality as well as those of modes, from which will arise obscurity. For as to substances, when concerned in moral discourses, their divers natures are not so much inquired into as supposed; v. g., when we say that man is subject to law, we mean nothing by man but a corporeal rational creature: what the real essence or other qualities of that creature are in this case is no way considered. And, therefore, whether a child or changeling be a man in a physical sense, may amongst the naturalists be as disputable as it will, it concerns not at all the moral man, as I may call him, which is this immovable, unchangeable idea, a corporeal rational being. For were there a monkey or any other creature to be found that has the use of reason to such a degree, as to be able to understand general signs, and to deduce consequences about general ideas, he would no doubt be subject to law, and in that sense be a man, how much soever he differed in shape from others of that name. The names of substances, if they be used in them as they should, can no more disturb moral than they do mathematical discourses; where, if the mathematician speaks of a cube or globe of gold, or of any other body, he has his clear, settled idea, which varies not, though it may by mistake be applied to a particular body to which it belongs not.

17. *Definitions can make moral Discourses clear.*—This I have here mentioned, by the by, to show of what consequence

it is for men, in their names of mixed modes, and consequently in all their moral discourses, to define their words when there is occasion; since thereby moral knowledge may be brought to so great clearness and certainty. And it must be great want of ingenuousness (to say no worse of it) to refuse to do it; since a definition is the only way whereby the precise meaning of moral words can be known; and yet a way whereby their meaning may be known certainly, and without leaving any room for any contest about it. And therefore the negligence or perverseness of mankind cannot be excused, if their discourses in morality be not much more clear than those in natural philosophy; since they are about ideas in the mind, which are none of them false or disproportionate, they having no external beings for the archetypes which they are referred to and must correspond with. It is far easier for men to frame in their minds an idea which shall be the standard to which they will give the name justice, with which pattern so made, all actions that agree shall pass under that denomination, than, having seen Aristides, to frame an idea that shall in all things be exactly like him; who is as he is, let men make what idea they please of him. For the one, they need but know the combination of ideas that are put together in their own minds; for the other, they must inquire into the whole nature, and abstruse hidden constitution, and various qualities of a thing existing without them.

18. *And is the only Way.*—Another reason that makes the defining of mixed modes so necessary, especially of moral words, is what I mentioned a little before, viz., that it is the only way whereby the signification of the most of them can be known with certainty. For the ideas they stand for being for the most part such whose component parts nowhere exist together, but scattered and mingled with others, it is the mind alone that collects them, and gives them the union of one idea; and it is only by words enumerating the several simple ideas which the mind has united, that we can make known to others what their names stand for; the assistance of the senses in this case not helping us by the proposal of sensible objects, to show the ideas which our names of this kind stand for, as it does often in the names of sensible simple ideas, and also to some degree in those of substances.

19. III. *In Substances, by showing and defining.*—Thirdly, for the explaining the signification of the names of substances, as they stand for the ideas we have of their distinct species, both the forementioned ways, viz., of showing and defining, are requisite in many cases to be made use of. For there being ordinarily in each sort some leading qualities, to which we suppose the other ideas which make up our complex idea of that species annexed, we forwardly give the specific name to that thing wherein that characteristical mark is found, which we take to be the most distinguishing idea of that species. These leading or characteristical (as I may call them) ideas in the sorts of animals and vegetables are (as has been before remarked, ch. vi. § 29, and ch. ix. § 15) mostly figure; and in inanimate bodies, colour; and in some, both together. Now,

20. *Ideas of the leading Qualities of Substances are best got by showing.*—These leading sensible qualities are those which make the chief ingredients of our specific ideas, and consequently the most observable and invariable part in the definitions of our specific names, as attributed to sorts of substances coming under our knowledge. For though the sound man, in its own nature, be as apt to signify a complex idea made up of animality and rationality, united in the same subject, as to signify any other combination; yet used as a mark to stand for a sort of creatures we count of our own kind, perhaps, the outward shape is as necessary to be taken into our complex idea, signified by the word man, as any other we find in it: and therefore, why Plato's " animal implume bipes latis unguibus" should not be a good definition of the name man, standing for that sort of creatures, will not be easy to show; for it is the shape, as the leading quality, that seems more to determine that species, than a faculty of reasoning, which appears not at first, and in some never. And if this be not allowed to be so, I do not know how they can be excused from murder who kill monstrous births, (as we call them,) because of an unordinary shape, without knowing whether they have a rational soul or no; which can be no more discerned in a well-formed than ill-shaped infant, as soon as born. And who is it has informed us that a rational soul can inhabit no tenement, unless it has just such a sort of frontispiece; or can join itself to,

and inform no sort of body but one that is just of such an outward structure?

21. Now these leading qualities are best made known by showing, and can hardly be made known otherwise. For the shape of a horse or cassowary will be but rudely and imperfectly imprinted on the mind by words; the sight of the animals doth it a thousand times better: and the idea of the particular colour of gold is not to be got by any description of it, but only by the frequent exercise of the eyes about it, as is evident in those who are used to this metal, who will frequently distinguish true from counterfeit, pure from adulterate, by the sight; where others (who have as good eyes, but yet by use have not got the precise nice idea of that peculiar yellow) shall not perceive any difference. The like may be said of those other simple ideas, peculiar in their kind to any substance; for which precise ideas there are no peculiar names. The particular ringing sound there is in gold, distinct from the sound of other bodies, has no particular name annexed to it, no more than the particular yellow that belongs to that metal.

22. *The Ideas of their Powers best known by Definition.*—But because many of the simple ideas that make up our specific ideas of substances are powers which lie not obvious to our senses in the things as they ordinarily appear; therefore, in the signification of our names of substances, some part of the signification will be better made known by enumerating those simple ideas, than by showing the substance itself. For he that to the yellow shining colour of gold, got by sight, shall, from my enumerating them, have the ideas of great ductility, fusibility, fixedness, and solubility, in aq. regia, will have a perfecter idea of gold than he can have by seeing a piece of gold, and thereby imprinting in his mind only its obvious qualities. But if the formal constitution of this shining, heavy, ductile thing, (from whence all these its properties flow,) lay open to our senses, as the formal constitution or essence of a triangle does, the signification of the word gold might as easily be ascertained as that of triangle.

23. *A Reflection on the Knowledge of Spirits.*—Hence we may take notice how much the foundation of all our knowledge of corporeal **things** lies in our senses. For how spirits

separate from bodies, (whose knowledge and ideas of these things are certainly much more perfect than ours,) know them, we have no notion, no idea at all. The whole extent of our knowledge or imagination reaches not beyond our own ideas limited to our ways of perception. Though yet it be not to be doubted that spirits of a higher rank than those immersed in flesh may have as clear ideas of the radical constitution of substances as we have of a triangle, and so perceive how all their properties and operations flow from thence, but the manner how they come by that knowledge exceeds our conceptions.

24. IV. *Ideas also of Substances must be conformable to Things.*—Fourthly, But though definitions will serve to explain the names of substances as they stand for our ideas, yet they leave them not without great imperfection as they stand for things. For our names of substances being not put barely for our ideas, but being made use of ultimately to represent things, and so are put in their place, their signification must agree with the truth of things as well as with men's ideas. And therefore, in substances, we are not always to rest in the ordinary complex idea commonly received as the signification of that word, but must go a little further, and inquire into the nature and properties of the things themselves, and thereby perfect, as much as we can, our ideas of their distinct species; or else learn them from such as are used to that sort of things, and are experienced in them. For since it is intended their names should stand for such collections of simple ideas as do really exist in things themselves, as well as for the complex idea in other men's minds, which in their ordinary acceptation they stand for, therefore, to define their names right, natural history is to be inquired into, and their properties are, with care and examination, to be found out. For it is not enough, for the avoiding inconveniencies in discourse and arguings about natural bodies and substantial things, to have learned, from the propriety of the language, the common, but confused, or very imperfect idea to which each word is applied, and to keep them to that idea in our use of them; but we must, by acquainting ourselves with the history of that sort of things, rectify and settle our complex idea belonging to each specific name; and in discourse with others, (if we find them mistake us,) we ought to tell what the complex idea is that we make such a name stand

for. This is the more necessary to be done by all those who search after knowledge and philosophical verity, in that children, being taught words, whilst they have but imperfect notions of things, apply them at random and without much thinking, and seldom frame determined ideas to be signified by them. Which custom (it being easy, and serving well enough for the ordinary affairs of life and conversation) they are apt to continue when they are men; and so begin at the wrong end, learning words first and perfectly, but make the notions to which they apply those words afterwards very overtly. By this means it comes to pass, that, men speaking the language of their country, i. e., according to grammar rules of that language, do yet speak very improperly of things themselves; and, by their arguing one with another, make but small progress in the discoveries of useful truths and the knowledge of things, as they are to be found in themselves, and not in our imaginations; and it matters not much for the improvement of our knowledge how they are called.

25. *Not easy to be made so.*—It were therefore to be wished that men versed in physical inquiries, and acquainted with the several sorts of natural bodies, would set down those simple ideas wherein they observe the individuals of each sort constantly to agree This would remedy a great deal of that confusion which comes from several persons applying the same name to a collection of a smaller or greater number of sensible qualities, proportionably as they have been more or less acquainted with, or accurate in examining the qualities of any sort of things which come under one denomination. But a dictionary of this sort, containing, as it were, a natural history, requires too many hands as well as too much time, cost, pains, and sagacity ever to be hoped for; and till that be done, we must content ourselves with such definitions of the names of substances as explain the sense men use them in. And it would be well, where there is occasion, if they would afford us so much. This yet is not usually done; but men talk to one another, and dispute in words whose meaning is not agreed between them, out of a mistake that the significations of common words are certainly established, and the precise ideas they stand for perfectly known; and that it is a shame to be ignorant of them. Both which suppositions are false: no names of complex ideas having so settled determined signi-

fications, that they are constantly used for the same precise ideas. Nor is it a shame for a man not to have a certain knowledge of anything, but by the necessary ways of attaining it; and so it is no discredit not to know what precise idea any sound stands for in another man's mind, without he declare it to me by some other way than barely using that sound; there being no other way, without such a declaration, certainly to know it. Indeed the necessity of communication by language brings men to an agreement in the signification of common words, within some tolerable latitude, that may serve for ordinary conversation: and so a man cannot be supposed wholly ignorant of the ideas which are annexed to words by common use, in a language familiar to him. But common use being but a very uncertain rule, which reduces itself at last to the ideas of particular men, proves often but a very variable standard. But though such a dictionary as I have above mentioned will require too much time, cost, and pains to be hoped for in this age; yet methinks it is not unreasonable to propose, that words standing for things which are known and distinguished by their outward shapes should be expressed by little draughts and prints made of them. A vocabulary made after this fashion would perhaps with more ease and in less time teach the true signification of many terms, especially in languages of remote countries or ages, and settle truer ideas in men's minds of several things whereof we read the names in ancient authors, than all the large and laborious comments of learned critics. Naturalists, that treat of plants and animals, have found the benefit of this way: and he that has had occasion to consult them will have reason to confess that he has a clearer idea of apium or ibex, from a little print of that herb or beast, than he could have from a long definition of the names of either of them. And so no doubt he would have of strigil and sistrum, if, instead of currycomb and cymbal, (which are the English names dictionaries render them by,) he could see stamped in the margin small pictures of these instruments, as they were in use amongst the ancients. "Toga, tunica, pallium," are words easily translated by gown, coat, and cloak; but we have thereby no more true ideas of the fashion of those habits amongst the Romans, than we have of the faces of the tailors who made them. Such things as these, which the eye distinguishes by their shapes, would be best let into the mind by draughts made of them, and more determine the signification of such words than any other words set for them, or made use of to define them. But this is only by the by.*

26. V. *By Constancy in their Signification.*—Fifthly, If men will not be at the pains to declare the meaning of their words, and definitions of their terms are not to be had, yet this is the least that can be expected, that, in all discourses wherein one man pretends to instruct or convince another, he should use the same word constantly in the same sense: if this were done, (which nobody can refuse without great disingenuity,) many of the books extant might be spared; many of the controversies in dispute would be at an end; several of those great volumes, swollen with ambiguous words, now used in one sense, and by and by in another, would shrink into a very narrow compass; and many of the philosophers' (to mention no other) as well as poets' works, might be contained in a nutshell.

27. *When the Variation is to be explained.*—But after all, the provision of words is so scanty in respect to that infinite variety of thoughts, that men, wanting terms to suit their precise notions, will, notwithstanding their utmost caution, be forced often to use the same word in somewhat different senses. And though in the continuation of a discourse, or the pursuit of an argument, there can be hardly room to digress into a particular definition as often as a man varies the signification of any term; yet the import of the discourse will, for the most part, if there be no designed fallacy, sufficiently lead candid and intelligent readers into the true meaning of it: but where there is not sufficient to guide the reader, there it concerns the writer to explain his meaning, and show in what sense he there uses that term.

* These suggestions of Locke have since been acted on in our encyclopœdias and dictionaries of natural science; in which the representation by engraving of objects spoken of in the text assists the descriptions in conveying clear ideas to the mind. The word strigil usually signifies an instrument used in the baths of the ancients for scraping off perspiration and dust from the skin. It was shaped like the crooked knife with which shoemakers hollow out the wood of ladies' high-heeled shoes. The sistrum had no resemblance to a pair of cymbals, but was in shape something like the jews' harp, with two or three cross-bars. The reader will find an exact engraved representation of it in Montfaucon and several other antiquarians.—ED.

BOOK IV.

CHAPTER I.

OF KNOWLEDGE IN GENERAL.

1. *Our Knowledge conversant about our Ideas.*—SINCE the mind, in all its thoughts and reasonings, hath no other immediate object but its own ideas, which it alone does or can contemplate, it is evident that our knowledge is only conversant about them.

2. *Knowledge is the Perception of the Agreement or Disagreement of two Ideas.*—Knowledge, then, seems to me to be nothing but the perception of the connexion and agreement, or disagreement and repugnancy of any of our ideas. In this alone it consists. Where this perception is, there is knowledge; and where it is not, there, though we may fancy, guess, or believe, yet we always come short of knowledge. For when we know that white is not black, what do we else but perceive that these two ideas do not agree? When we possess ourselves with the utmost security of the demonstration, that the three angles of a triangle are equal to two right ones, what do we more but perceive, that equality to two right ones does necessarily agree to, and is inseparable from the three angles of a triangle?*

3 *This Agreement fourfold.*—But to understand a little more distinctly wherein this agreement or disagreement consists, I think we may reduce it all to these four sorts:
 I. Identity, or diversity.
 II. Relation.
 III. Co-existence, or necessary connexion.
 IV. Real existence.

4. *First, Of Identity, or Diversity.*—First, As to the first sort of agreement or disagreement, viz., identity or diversity. It is the first act of the mind, when it has any sentiments or ideas at all, to perceive its ideas; and so far as it perceives them, to know each what it is, and thereby also to perceive

---

* See Appendix, No. VIII. at end of vol. ii.

their difference, and that one is not another. This is so absolutely necessary, that, without it, there could be no knowledge, no reasoning, no imagination, no distinct thoughts at all. By this the mind clearly and infallibly perceives each idea to agree with itself, and to be what it is; and all distinct ideas to disagree, i. e., the one not to be the other: and this it does without pains, labour, or deduction; but at first view, by its natural power of perception and distinction. And though men of art have reduced this into those general rules, "what is, is," and "it is impossible for the same thing to be and not to be," for ready application in all cases, wherein there may be occasion to reflect on it: yet it is certain, that the first exercise of this faculty is about particular ideas. A man infallibly knows, as soon as ever he has them in his mind, that the ideas he calls white and round are the very ideas they are, and that they are not other ideas which he calls red or square. Nor can any maxim or proposition in the world make him know it clearer or surer than he did before, and without any such general rule. This then, is the first agreement or disagreement which the mind perceives in its ideas, which it always perceives at first sight: and if there ever happen any doubt about it, it will always be found to be about the names, and not the ideas themselves, whose identity and diversity will always be perceived as soon and clearly as the ideas themselves are; nor can it possibly be otherwise.

5. *Secondly, Relative.*—Secondly, the next sort of agreement or disagreement the mind perceives in any of its ideas may, I think, be called relative, and is nothing but the perception of the relation between any two ideas, of what kind soever, whether substances, modes, or any other. For, since all distinct ideas must eternally be known not to be the same, and so be universally and constantly denied one of another, there could be no room for any positive knowledge at all, if we could not perceive any relation between our ideas, and find out the agreement or disagreement they have one with another, in several ways the mind takes of comparing them.

6. *Thirdly, Of Co-existence.*—Thirdly, The third sort of agreement or disagreement to be found in our ideas, which the perception of the mind is employed about, is co-existence or non-co-existence in the same subject; and this belongs

particularly to substances. Thus, when we pronounce concerning gold, that it is fixed, our knowledge of this truth amounts to no more but this, that fixedness, or a power to remain in the fire unconsumed, is an idea that always accompanies and is joined with that particular sort of yellowness, weight, fusibility, malleableness, and solubility in aq. regia, which make our complex idea, signified by the word gold.

7. *Fourthly. Of real Existence.*—Fourthly, The fourth and last sort is that of actual and real existence agreeing to any idea. Within these four sorts of agreement or disagreement is, I suppose, contained all the knowledge we have, or are capable of: for all the inquiries we can make concerning any of our ideas, all that we know or can affirm concerning any of them is, that it is, or is not, the same with some other ; that it does or does not always co-exist with some other idea in the same subject ; that it has this or that relation with some other idea ; or that it has a real existence without the mind. Thus, blue is not yellow, is of identity : two triangles upon equal bases between two parellels are equal, is of relation : iron is susceptible of magnetical impressions, is of co-existence : God is, is of real existence. Though identity and co-existence are truly nothing but relations, yet they are such peculiar ways of agreement or disagreement of our ideas, that they deserve well to be considered as distinct heads, and not under relation in general ; since they are so different grounds of affirmation and negation, as will easily appear to any one, who will but reflect on what is said in several places of this essay. I should not proceed to examine the several degrees of our knowledge, but that it is necessary first to consider the different acceptations of the word, knowledge.

8. *Knowledge actual or habitual.*—There are several ways wherein the mind is possessed of truth, each of which is called knowledge.

I. There is actual knowledge, which is the present view the mind has of the agreement or disagreement of any of its ideas, or of the relation they have one to another.

II. A man is said to know any proposition, which, having been once laid before his thoughts, he evidently perceived the agreement or disagreement of the ideas whereof it consists ; and so lodged it in his memory, that, whenever that proposition comes again to be reflected on, he, without doubt or hesitation, embraces the right side, assents to, and is certain of the truth of it. This, I think, one may call habitual knowledge: and thus a man may be said to know all those truths which are lodged in his memory, by a foregoing clear and full perception, whereof the mind is assured past doubt as often as it has occasion to reflect on them: for our finite understandings being able to think clearly and distinctly but on one thing at once, if men had no knowledge of any more than what they actually thought on, they would all be very ignorant; and he that knew most, would know but one truth—that being all he was able to think on at one time.

9. *Habitual Knowledge, twofold.*—Of habitual knowledge there are, also, vulgarly speaking, two degrees:

First, The one is of such truths laid up in the memory as, whenever they occur to the mind, it actually perceives the relation is between those ideas. And this is in all those truths whereof we have an intuitive knowledge; where the ideas themselves, by an immediate view, discover their agreement or disagreement one with another.

Secondly, the other is of such truths whereof the mind having been convinced, it retains the memory of the conviction, without the proofs. Thus, a man that remembers certainly that he once perceived the demonstration, that the three angles of a triangle are equal to two right ones, is certain that he knows it, because he cannot doubt the truth of it. In his adherence to a truth where the demonstration by which it was at first known, is forgot, though a man may be thought rather to believe his memory than really to know; and this way of entertaining a truth seemed formerly to me like something between opinion and knowledge; a sort of assurance which exceeds bare belief—for that relies on the testimony of another: yet upon a due examination I find it comes not short of perfect certainty, and is in effect true knowledge. That which is apt to mislead our first thoughts into a mistake in this matter, is, that the agreement or disagreement of the ideas in this case is not perceived, as it was at first, by an actual view of all the intermediate ideas whereby the agreement or disagreement of those in the proposition was at first perceived; but by other intermediate ideas, that show the agreement or disagreement of the ideas contained in the proposition whose certainty we remember.

For example: in this proposition, that the three angles of a triangle are equal to two right ones, one who has seen and clearly perceived the demonstration of this truth knows it to be true, when that demonstration is gone out of his mind; so that at present it is not actually in view, and possibly cannot be recollected: but he knows it in a different way from what he did before. The agreement of the two ideas joined in that proposition is perceived, but it is by the intervention of other ideas than those which at first produced that perception. He remembers, i. e., he knows (for remembrance is but the reviving of some past knowledge) that he was once certain of the truth of this proposition, that the three angles of a triangle are equal to two right ones. The immutability of the same relations between the same immutable things is now the idea that shows him, that, if the three angles of a triangle were once equal to two right ones, they will always be equal to two right ones. And hence he comes to be certain, that what was once true in the case, is always true; what ideas once agreed will always agree; and consequently what he once knew to be true, he will always know to be true, as long as he can remember that he once knew it. Upon this ground it is, that particular demonstrations in mathematics afford general knowledge. If then the perception that the same ideas will eternally have the same habitudes and relations, be not a sufficient ground of knowledge, there could be no knowledge of general propositions in mathematics; for no mathematical demonstration would be any other than particular: and when a man had demonstrated any proposition concerning one triangle or circle, his knowledge would not reach beyond that particular diagram. If he would extend it further, he must renew his demonstration in another instance, before he could know it to be true in another like triangle, and so on: by which means one could never come to the knowledge of any general propositions. Nobody, I think, can deny, that Mr. Newton certainly knows any proposition that he now at any time reads in his book to be true; though he has not in actual view that admirable chain of intermediate ideas whereby he at first discovered it to be true. Such a memory as that, able to retain such a train of particulars, may be well thought beyond the reach of human faculties; when the very discovery, perception, and laying together that wonderful connexion of ideas, is found to surpass most readers' comprehension. But yet it is evident the author himself knows the proposition to be true, remembering he once saw the connexion of those ideas, as certainly as he knows such a man wounded another, remembering that he saw him run him through. But because the memory is not always so clear as actual perception, and does in all men more or less decay in length of time, this amongst other differences is one, which shows that demonstrative knowledge is much more imperfect than intuitive, as we shall see in the following chapter.

CHAPTER II.
OF THE DEGREES OF OUR KNOWLEDGE.

1. *Intuitive.*—ALL our knowledge consisting, as I have said, in the view the mind has of its own ideas, which is the utmost light and greatest certainty we, with our faculties, and in our way of knowledge, are capable of; it may not be amiss to consider a little the degrees of its evidence. The different clearness of our knowledge seems to me to lie in the different way of perception the mind has of the agreement or disagreement of any of its ideas. For if we will reflect on our own ways of thinking, we shall find, that sometimes the mind perceives the agreement or disagreement of two ideas immediately by themselves, without the intervention of any other: and this I think we may call intuitive knowledge. For in this the mind is at no pains of proving or examining, but perceives the truth as the eye doth light, only by being directed towards it. Thus the mind perceives that white is not black, that a circle is not a triangle, that three are more than two, and equal to one and two. Such kinds of truths the mind perceives at the first sight of the ideas together, by bare intuition, without the intervention of any other idea; and this kind of knowledge is the clearest and most certain that human frailty is capable of. This part of knowledge is irresistible, and, like bright sunshine, forces itself immediately to be perceived, as soon as ever the mind turns its view that way, and leaves no room for hesita-

tion, doubt, or examination, but the mind is presently filled with the clear light of it. It is on this intuition that depends all the certainty and evidence of all our knowledge; which certainty every one finds to be so great, that he cannot imagine, and therefore not require a greater: for a man cannot conceive himself capable of a greater certainty than to know that any idea in his mind is such as he perceives it to be; and that two ideas wherein he perceives a difference, are different and not precisely the same. He that demands a greater certainty than this, demands he knows not what, and shows only that he has a mind to be a sceptic, without being able to be so. Certainty depends so wholly on this intuition, that, in the next degree of knowledge which I call demonstrative, this intuition is necessary in all the connexions of the intermediate ideas, without which we cannot attain knowledge and certainty.

2. *Demonstrative*—The next degree of knowledge is, where the mind perceives the agreement or disagreement of any ideas, but not immediately. Though wherever the mind perceives the agreement or disagreement of any of its ideas, there be certain knowledge; yet it does not always happen, that the mind sees that agreement or disagreement which there is between them, even where it is discoverable: and in that case remains in ignorance, and at most gets no further than a probable conjecture. The reason why the mind cannot always perceive presently the agreement or disagreement of two ideas, is, because those ideas, concerning whose agreement or disagreement the inquiry is made, cannot by the mind be so put together as to show it. In this case, then, when the mind cannot so bring its ideas together as by their immediate comparison, and as it were juxta-position or application one to another, to perceive their agreement or disagreement, it is fain, by the intervention of other ideas (one or more, as it happens) to discover the agreement or disagreement which it searches; and this is that which we call reasoning. Thus the mind being willing to know the agreement or disagreement in bigness between the three angles of a triangle and two right ones, cannot by an immediate view and comparing them do it: because the three angles of a triangle cannot be brought at once and be compared with any one or two angles; and so of this the mind has no im-

mediate, no intuitive knowledge. In this case the mind is fain to find out some other angles, to which the three angles of a triangle have an equality; and, finding those equal to two right ones, comes to know their equality to two right ones.

3. *Depends on Proofs.*—Those intervening ideas which serve to show the agreement of any two others, are called proofs; and where the agreement and disagreement is by this means plainly and clearly perceived, it is called demonstration; it being shown to the understanding, and the mind made to see that it is so. A quickness in the mind to find out these intermediate ideas (that shall discover the agreement or disagreement of any other) and to apply them right, is, I suppose, that which is called sagacity.*

4. *But not so easy.*—This knowledge by intervening proofs, though it be certain, yet the evidence of it is not altogether so clear and bright, nor the assent so ready as in intuitive knowledge. For though in demonstration the mind does at last perceive the agreement or disagreement of the ideas it considers, yet it is not without pains and attention: there must be more than one transient view to find it. A steady application and pursuit are required to this discovery; and there must be a progression by steps and degrees before the mind can in this way arrive at certainty, and come to perceive the agreement or repugnancy between two ideas that need proofs and the use of reason to show it.

5. *Not without precedent Doubt.*—Another difference between intuitive and demonstrative knowledge is, that, though in the latter all doubt be removed when, by the intervention of the intermediate ideas, the agreement or disagreement is perceived; yet before the demonstration there was a doubt, which in intuitive knowledge cannot happen to the mind that has its faculty of perception left to a degree capable of distinct ideas, no more than it can be a doubt to the eye

---

* Hobbes' account of this quality is as follows:—" Another sort of discussion is, when the appetite giveth a man his beginning; as in the example before, where honour, to which a man hath appetite, maketh him think upon the next means of attaining it, and that again to the next, &c. And this the Latins call *sagacitas*, and we call *hunting* or *tracing;* as dogs trace beasts by the smell, and men hunt them by their footsteps; or as men hunt after riches, place, or knowledge." (Hum. Nat. c. iv. § 4.)—ED.

(that can distinctly see white and black) whether this ink and this paper be all of a colour. If there be sight in the eyes, it will, at first glimpse, without hesitation, perceive the words printed on this paper different from the colour of the paper: and so if the mind have the faculty of distinct perceptions it will perceive the agreement or disagreement of those ideas that produce intuitive knowledge. If the eyes have lost the faculty of seeing, or the mind of perceiving, we in vain inquire after the quickness of sight in one, or clearness of perception in the other.

6. *Not so clear.*—It is true, the perception produced by demonstration is also very clear; yet it is often with a great abatement of that evident lustre and full assurance that always accompany that which I call intuitive; like a face reflected by several mirrors one to another, where, as long as it retains the similitude and agreement with the object, it produces a knowledge; but it is still in every successive reflection with a lessening of that perfect clearness and distinctness which is in the first, till at last, after many removes, it has a great mixture of dimness, and is not at first sight so knowable, especially to weak eyes. Thus it is with knowledge made out by a long train of proof.

7. *Each Step must have intuitive Evidence.*—Now, in every step reason makes in demonstrative knowledge, there is an intuitive knowledge of that agreement or disagreement it seeks with the next intermediate idea, which it uses as a proof: for if it were not so, that yet would need a proof; since without the perception of such agreement or disagreement there is no knowledge produced. If it be perceived by itself, it is intuitive knowledge: if it cannot be perceived by itself, there is need of some intervening idea, as a common measure, to show their agreement or disagreement. By which it is plain, that every step in reasoning that produces knowledge, has intuitive certainty; which when the mind perceives, there is no more required, but to remember it to make the agreement or disagreement of the ideas concerning which we inquire visible and certain. So that to make anything a demonstration, it is necessary to perceive the immediate agreement of the intervening ideas, whereby the agreement or disagreement of the two ideas under examination (whereof the one is always the first, and the other

the last in the account) is found. This intuitive perception of the agreement or disagreement of the intermediate ideas, in each step and progression of the demonstration, must also be carried exactly in the mind, and a man must be sure that no part is left out: which, because in long deductions, and the use of many proofs, the memory does not always so readily and exactly retain; therefore it comes to pass, that this is more imperfect than intuitive knowledge, and men embrace often falsehood for demonstrations.

8. *Hence the Mistake, " ex præcognitis, et præconcessis."*—The necessity of this intuitive knowledge in each step of scientifical or demonstrative reasoning gave occasion, I imagine, to that mistaken axiom, that all reasoning was " ex præcognitis et præconcessis;" which, how far it is mistaken I shall have occasion to show more at large when I come to consider propositions, and particularly those propositions which are called maxims; and to show that it is by a mistake that they are supposed to be the foundations of all our knowledge and reasonings.

9. *Demonstration not limited to Quantity.*—It has been generally taken for granted, that mathematics alone are capable of demonstrative certainty: but to have such an agreement or disagreement as may intuitively be perceived, being, as I imagine, not the privilege of the ideas of number, extension, and figure alone, it may possibly be the want of due method and application in us, and not of sufficient evidence in things, that demonstration has been thought to have so little to do in other parts of knowledge, and been scarce so much as aimed at by any but mathematicians. For whatever ideas we have wherein the mind can perceive the immediate agreement or disagreement that is between them, there the mind is capable of intuitive knowledge; and where it can perceive the agreement or disagreement of any two ideas, by an intuitive perception of the agreement or disagreement they have with any intermediate ideas, there the mind is capable of demonstration; which is not limited to ideas of extension, figure, number, and their modes.

10. *Why it has been so thought.*—The reason why it has been generally sought for, and supposed to be only in those, I imagine has been not only the general usefulness of those sciences; but because in comparing their equality or excess,

the modes of numbers have every the least difference very clear and perceivable; and though in extension every the least excess is not so perceptible, yet the mind has found out ways to examine and discover demonstratively the just equality of two angles, or extensions, or figures: and both these, i e., numbers and figures, can be set down by visible and lasting marks, wherein the ideas under consideration are perfectly determined; which for the most part they are not, where they are marked only by names and words.

11. But in other simple ideas whose modes and differences are made and counted by degrees, and not quantity, we have not so nice and accurate a distinction of their differences as to perceive and find ways to measure their just equality, or the least differences. For those other simple ideas being appearances of sensations produced in us by the size, figure, number, and motion of minute corpuscles singly insensible; their different degrees also depend upon the variation of some or of all those causes: which, since it cannot be observed by us in particles of matter, whereof each is too subtile to be perceived, it is impossible for us to have any exact measures of the different degrees of these simple ideas. For supposing the sensation or idea we name whiteness be produced in us by a certain number of globules, which, having a verticity about their own centres, strike upon the retina of the eye with a certain degree of rotation, as well as progressive swiftness; it will hence easily follow, that the more the superficial parts of any body are so ordered as to reflect the greater number of globules of light, and to give them the proper rotation, which is fit to produce this sensation of white in us, the more white will that body appear, that from an equal space sends to the retina the greater number of such corpuscles, with that peculiar sort of motion. I do not say that the nature of light consists in very small round globules, nor of whiteness in such a texture of parts as gives a certain rotation to these globules when it reflects them; for I am not now treating physically of light or colours. But this I think I may say, that I cannot (and I would be glad any one would make intelligible that he did) conceive how bodies without us can any ways affect our senses, but by the immediate contact of the sensible bodies themselves, as in tasting and feeling, or the impulse

of some sensible particles coming from them, as in seeing, hearing, and smelling; by the different impulse of which parts, caused by their different size, figure, and motion, the variety of sensations is produced in us.*

12. Whether then they be globules or no, or whether they have a verticity about their own centres that produces the idea of whiteness in us; this is certain, that the more particles of light are reflected from a body fitted to give them that peculiar motion which produces the sensation of whiteness in us; and possibly too, the quicker that peculiar motion is, the whiter does the body appear from which the greater number are reflected, as is evident in the same piece of paper put in the sunbeams, in the shade, and in a dark hole; in each of which it will produce in us the idea of whiteness in far different degrees.

13. Not knowing, therefore, what number of particles, nor what motion of them is fit to produce any precise degree of whiteness, we cannot demonstrate the certain equality of any two degrees of whiteness, because we have no certain standard to measure them by, nor means to distinguish every the least real difference—the only help we have being from our senses, which in this point fail us. But where the difference is so great as to produce in the mind clearly distinct ideas, whose differences can be perfectly retained, there these ideas or colours, as we see in different kinds, as blue and red, are as capable of demonstration as ideas of number and extension. What I have here said of whiteness and colours, I think holds true in all secondary qualities and their modes.

14. *Sensitive Knowledge of particular Existence.*—These two, viz., intuition and demonstration, are the degrees of our knowledge; whatever comes short of one of these, with what assurance soever embraced, is but faith or opinion, but not knowledge, at least in all general truths. There is, indeed, another perception of the mind employed about the particular existence of finite beings without us, which, going beyond bare probability, and yet not reaching perfectly to

* This whole theory is exceedingly unphilosophical; for thus a thing would wear out by being seen. Rather than countenance such wild notions it were better to admit at once that we comprehend nothing at all of the matter.--ED.

either of the foregoing degrees of certainty, passes under the name of knowledge. There can be nothing more certain than that the idea we receive from an external object is in our minds: this is intuitive knowledge. But whether there be anything more than barely that idea in our minds, whether we can thence certainly infer the existence of anything without us which corresponds to that idea, is that whereof some men think there may be a question made; because men may have such ideas in their minds when no such thing exists, no such object affects their senses. But yet here I think we are provided with an evidence that puts us past doubting: for I ask any one, whether he be not invincibly conscious to himself of a different perception when he looks on the sun by day, and thinks on it by night; when he actually tastes wormwood, or smells a rose, or only thinks on that savour or odour? We as plainly find the difference there is between an idea revived in our minds by our own memory, and actually coming into our minds by our senses, as we do between any two distinct ideas. If any one say, a dream may do the same thing, and all these ideas may be produced in us without any external objects; he may please to dream that I make him this answer:— 1. That it is no great matter, whether I remove this scruple or no: where all is but dream, reasoning and arguments are of no use, truth and knowledge nothing. 2. That I believe he will allow a very manifest difference between dreaming of being in the fire and being actually in it. But yet if he be resolved to appear so sceptical as to maintain that what I call being actually in the fire is nothing but a dream; and we cannot thereby certainly know that any such thing as fire actually exists without us: I answer, that we certainly finding that pleasure or pain follows upon the application of certain objects to us, whose existence we perceive, or dream that we perceive, by our senses; this certainty is as great as our happiness or misery, beyond which we have no concernment to know or to be. So that I think we may add to the two former sorts of knowledge this also of the existence of particular external objects, by that perception and consciousness we have of the actual entrance of ideas from them, and allow these three degrees of knowledge, viz., intuitive, demonstrative, and sensitive:

in each of which there are different degrees and ways of evidence and certainty.

15. *Knowledge not always clear, where the Ideas are so.*—But since our knowledge is founded on and employed about our ideas only, will it not follow from thence that it is conformable to our ideas; and that where our ideas are clear and distinct, or obscure and confused, our knowledge will be so too? To which I answer, No: for our knowledge consisting in the perception of the agreement or disagreement of any two ideas, its clearness or obscurity consists in the clearness or obscurity of that perception, and not in the clearness or obscurity of the ideas themselves; v. g., a man that has as clear ideas of the angles of a triangle, and of equality to two right ones, as any mathematician in the world, may yet have but a very obscure perception of their agreement, and so have but a very obscure knowledge of it. But ideas, which, by reason of their obscurity or otherwise, are confused, cannot produce any clear or distinct knowledge; because, as far as any ideas are confused, so far the mind cannot perceive clearly whether they agree or disagree: or, to express the same thing in a way less apt to be misunderstood, he that hath not determined ideas to the word he uses, cannot make propositions of them, of whose truth he can be certain.

CHAPTER III.

OF THE EXTENT OF HUMAN KNOWLEDGE.

1. KNOWLEDGE, as has been said, lying in the perception of the agreement or disagreement of any of our ideas, it follows from hence, that,

I. *No further than we have Ideas.*—First, we can have knowledge no further than we have ideas.

2. II. *No further than we can perceive their Agreement or Disagreement.*—Secondly, That we have no knowledge further than we can have perception of their agreement or disagreement. Which perception being: 1. Either by intuition, or the immediate comparing any two ideas; or, 2. By reason, examining the agreement or disagreement of two ideas, by the intervention of some others; or, 3. By sensation, per-

ceiving the existence of particular things; hence it also follows:

3. III. *Intuititive Knowledge extends itself not to all the Relations of all our Ideas.*—Thirdly, That we cannot have an intuitive knowledge that shall extend itself to all our ideas, and all that we would know about them; because we cannot examine and perceive all the relations they have one to another by juxta-position, or an immediate comparison one with another. Thus, having the ideas of an obtuse and an acute angled triangle, both drawn from equal bases, and between parallels, I can, by intuitive knowledge, perceive the one not to be the other, but cannot that way know whether they be equal or no; because their agreement or disagreement in equality can never be perceived by an immediate comparing them: the difference of figure makes their parts incapable of an exact immediate application, and therefore there is need of some intervening qualities to measure them by, which is demonstration, or rational knowledge.

4. IV. *Nor demonstrative Knowledge.*—Fourthly, It follows, also, from what is above observed, that our rational knowledge cannot reach to the whole extent of our ideas; because between two different ideas we would examine, we cannot always find such mediums as we can connect one to another with an intuitive knowledge in all the parts of the deduction; and wherever that fails, we come short of knowledge and demonstration.

5. V. *Sensitive Knowledge narrower than either.*—Fifthly Sensitive knowledge reaching no further than the existence of things actually present to our senses, is yet much narrower than either of the former.

6. VI. *Our Knowledge, therefore, narrower than our Ideas.* —From all which it is evident, that the extent of our knowledge comes not only short of the reality of things, but even of the extent of our own ideas. Though our knowledge be limited to our ideas, and cannot exceed them either in extent or perfection; and though these be very narrow bounds, in respect of the extent of all being, and far short of what we may justly imagine to be in some even created understandings, not tied down to the dull and narrow information which is to be received from some few, and not very acute ways of perception, such as are our senses; yet it would be

well with us if our knowledge were but as large as our ideas, and there were not many doubts and inquiries concerning the ideas we have, whereof we are not, nor I believe ever shall be in this world resolved. Nevertheless I do not question but that human knowledge, under the present circumstances of our beings and constitutions, may be carried much further than it has hitherto been, if men would sincerely, and with freedom of mind, employ all that industry and labour of thought in improving the means of discovering truth, which they do for the colouring or support of falsehood, to maintain a system, interest, or party they are once engaged in. But yet, after all, I think I may, without injury to human perfection, be confident, that our knowledge would never reach to all we might desire to know concerning those ideas we have; nor be able to surmount all the difficulties, and resolve all the questions that might arise concerning any of them. We have the ideas of a square, a circle, and equality; and yet, perhaps, shall never be able to find a circle equal to a square, and certainly know that it is so. We have the ideas of matter and thinking, but possibly shall never be able to know whether any mere material being thinks or no;* it being impossible for us, by the contemplation of our own ideas, without revelation, to discover whether Omnipotency has not given to some systems of matter fitly disposed, a power to perceive and think, or else joined and fixed to matter so disposed a thinking immaterial substance; it being, in respect of our notions, not much more remote from our comprehension to conceive that God can, if he pleases, superadd to matter a faculty of thinking, than that he should superadd to it another substance with a faculty of thinking; since we know not wherein thinking consists, nor to what sort of substances the Almighty has been pleased to give that power, which cannot be in any created being, but merely by the good pleasure and bounty of the Creator. For I see no contradiction in it, that the first eternal thinking being should, if he pleased, give to certain systems of created senseless matter, put together as he thinks fit, some degrees of sense, perception, and thought; though, as I think I have proved, lib. iv. ch 10, § 14, &c., it is no less than a contradiction to suppose

* See Appendix. No. IX. at the end of vol. ii.

matter (which is evidently in its own nature void of sense and thought) should be that eternal first-thinking being. What certainty of knowledge can any one have, that some perceptions, such as, v. g., pleasure and pain, should not be in some bodies themselves, after a certain manner modified and moved, as well as that they should be in an immaterial substance, upon the motion of the parts of body? Body, as far as we can conceive, being able only to strike and affect body; and motion, according to the utmost reach of our ideas, being able to produce nothing but motion; so that when we allow it to produce pleasure or pain, or the idea of a colour or sound, we are fain to quit our reason, go beyond our ideas, and attribute it wholly to the good pleasure of our Maker. For since we must allow he has annexed effects to motion, which we can no way conceive motion able to produce, what reason have we to conclude that he could not order them as well to be produced in a subject we cannot conceive capable of them, as well as in a subject we cannot conceive the motion of matter can any way operate upon? I say not this, that I would any way lessen the belief of the soul's immateriality: I am not here speaking of probability, but knowledge; and I think not only that it becomes the modesty of philosophy not to pronounce magisterially, where we want that evidence that can produce knowledge; but also, that it is of use to us to discern how far our knowledge does reach; for the state we are at present in, not being that of vision, we must in many things content ourselves with faith and probability; and in the present question, about the immateriality of the soul, if our faculties cannot arrive at demonstrative certainty, we need not think it strange. All the great ends of morality and religion are well enough secured, without philosophical proofs of the soul's immateriality; since it is evident, that he who made us at the beginning to subsist here, sensible, intelligent beings, and for several years continued us in such a state, can and will restore us to the like state of sensibility in another world, and make us capable there to receive the retribution he has designed to men, according to their doings in this life. And therefore it is not of such mighty necessity to determine one way or the other, as some, over-zealous for or against the immateriality of the soul, have been forward to make the world believe. Who, either on the one side indulging too much their thoughts immersed altogether in matter, can allow no existence to what is not material; or who, on the other side, finding not cogitation within the natural powers of matter, examined over and over again by the utmost intention of mind, have the confidence to conclude, that Omnipotency itself cannot give perception and thought to a substance which has the modification of solidity. He that considers how hardly sensation is, in our thoughts, reconcilable to extended matter; or existence to anything that has no existence at all, will confess that he is very far from certainly knowing what his soul is. It is a point which seems to me to be put out of the reach of our knowledge; and he who will give himself leave to consider freely, and look into the dark and intricate part of each hypothesis, will scarce find his reason able to determine him fixedly for or against the soul's materiality: since, on which side soever he views it, either as an unextended substance, or as a thinking extended matter, the difficulty to conceive either will, whilst either alone is in his thoughts, still drive him to the contrary side. An unfair way which some men take with themselves; who, because of the inconceivableness of something they find in one, throw themselves violently into the contrary hypothesis, though altogether as unintelligible to an unbiassed understanding. This serves not only to show the weakness and the scantiness of our knowledge, but the insignificant triumph of such sort of arguments, which, drawn from our own views, may satisfy us that we can find no certainty on one side of the question; but do not at all thereby help us to truth by running into the opposite opinion, which, on examination, will be found clogged with equal difficulties. For what safety, what advantage to any one is it, for the avoiding the seeming absurdities, and to him unsurmountable rubs he meets with in one opinion, to take refuge in the contrary, which is built on something altogether as inexplicable, and as far remote from his comprehension? It is past controversy, that we have in us something that thinks; our very doubts about what it is, confirm the certainty of its being, though we must content ourselves in the ignorance of what kind of being it is: and it is in vain to go about to be sceptical in this, as it is unreasonable in most other cases to be positive against the being of anything, because we cannot comprehend its nature. For I would fain know what substance exists, that has not something in it which manifestly baffles our understandings. Other spirits, who see and know the nature and inward constitution of things, how much must they exceed us in knowledge? To which, if we add larger comprehension, which enables them at one glance to see the connexion and agreement of very many ideas, and readily supplies to them the intermediate proofs, which we by single and slow steps, and long poring in the dark, hardly at last find out, and are often ready to forget one before we have hunted out another; we may guess at some part of the happiness of superior ranks of spirits, who have a quicker and more penetrating sight, as well as a larger field of knowledge.* But to return

* Baxter, than whom few men of purer mind or more undoubted piety have ever existed, appears to have contemplated this question in much the same light as Locke. He seems to have despaired of arriving at certainty on such matters in this world, and being passionately in love with knowledge, conceived that much of the happiness of a future life would consist in unravelling those mysteries, the bare skirts of which we can here discern through a glass darkly. "It will," he says, "be some addition to my future happiness that I shall then be much better acquainted with myself, both with my nature, and with my sin and grace. I shall then better know the nature of a soul, and its formal faculties, three in one. I shall know the nature and way of its operations, and how far its acts are simple, or compound, or organical. I shall know how far memory, phantasy, and sense internal and external belong to the rational soul, and whether the sensitive and rational are two or one, and what senses will perish, and what not. I shall know how the soul doth act upon itself, and what acts it hath that are not felt, in sleep, in apoplexies, and in the womb. I shall know whether the vegetative nature be anything else than fire, and whether it be of the same essence with the soul, sensitive or rational; and whether fire *eminenter* be a common fundamental substance of all spirits, diversely specified by the forms, mental, sensitive, and vegetative; or whether it be as a body, or vehicle to spirits, or rather a nature made for the copulation of spirits and bodies, and the operation of the former on the latter, as between both; and whether fire, and what sort, be the active *forma telluris*, and of other globes. I shall know how far souls are one and yet many, and how they are individuate; and whether their *quantitas discreta*, in being numerically many, do prove that they have any *quantitatem continuam*, and whether they are a purer sort of bodies, as the Greek fathers, Tertullian and others, thought, and what immateriality signifieth: and what substantiality of spirit; and how *substantia* and *materia* differ; and how far they are penetrable and indivisible; and whether a soul be properly *pars;* and whether individual souls are parts

to the argument in hand: our knowledge, I say, is not only limited to the paucity and imperfections of the ideas we have, and which we employ it about, but even comes short of that too. But how far it reaches, let us now inquire.

7. *How far our Knowledge reaches.*—The affirmations or negations we make concerning the ideas we have, may, as I have before intimated in general, be reduced to these four sorts, viz., identity, co-existence, relation, and real existence. I shall examine how far our knowledge extends in each of these.

8. I. *Our Knowledge of Identity and Diversity, as far as our Ideas.*—First, as to identity and diversity in this way of agreement or disagreement of our ideas, our intuitive knowledge is as far extended as our ideas themselves; and there can be no idea in the mind, which it does not presently, by an intuitive knowledge, perceive to be what it is, and to be different from any other.

9. II. *Of Co-existence, a very little Way.*—Secondly, as to the second sort, which is the agreement or disagreement of our ideas in co-existence, in this our knowledge is very short, though in this consists the greatest and most material part of our knowledge concerning substances. For our ideas of the species of substances being, as I have showed, nothing but certain collections of simple ideas united in one subject, and so co-existing together; v. g., our idea of flame is a body hot, luminous, and moving upward; of gold, a body heavy to a certain degree, yellow, malleable, and fusible; these, or some such complex ideas as these, in men's minds, do these two names of the different substances, flame and gold, stand for. When we would know anything further concerning these, or any other sort of substances, what do we inquire, but what other qualities or power these substances have or have not? Which is nothing else but to know what other

of any common soul; and how far the individuation doth continue. And whether separated from the body, they operate in and by any other vehicle, or without, and how; and whether they take with them any of their fiery nature as a vehicle or as a constitutive part. I shall know how God produceth souls; and how his production by emanation or creation, doth consist in generation; and how forms are multiplied; and what causality the parents' soul hath to the production of the child. Whether by communication of substance, or only by disposing the recipient matter." (Dying Thoughts, p. 183 et seq.)—ED.

simple ideas do or do not co-exist with those that make up that complex idea.

10. *Because the Connexion between most simple Ideas is unknown.*—This, how weighty and considerable a part soever of human science, is yet very narrow, and scarce any at all. The reason whereof is, that the simple ideas whereof our complex ideas of substances are made up are, for the most part, such as carry with them, in their own nature, no visible necessary connexion or inconsistency with any other simple ideas, whose co-existence with them we would inform ourselves about.

11. *Especially of secondary Qualities.*—The ideas that our complex ones of substances are made up of, and about which our knowledge concerning substances is most employed, are those of their secondary qualities; which depending all (as has been shown) upon the primary qualities of their minute and insensible parts; or, if not upon them, upon something yet more remote from our comprehension; it is impossible we should know which have a necessary union or inconsistency one with another: for not knowing the root they spring from, not knowing what size, figure, and texture of parts they are, on which depend and from which result those qualities which make our complex idea of gold, it is impossible we should know what other qualities result from or are incompatible with the same constitution of the insensible parts of gold, and so consequently must always co-exist with that complex idea we have of it, or else are inconsistent with it.

12. *Because all Connexion between any secondary and primary Qualities is undiscoverable.*—Besides this ignorance of the primary qualities of the insensible parts of bodies, on which depend all their secondary qualities, there is yet another and more incurable part of ignorance, which sets us more remote from a certain knowledge of the co-existence or inco-existence (if I may so say) of different ideas in the same subject; and that is, that there is no discoverable connexion between any secondary quality and those primary qualities which it depends on.

13. That the size, figure, and motion of one body should cause a change in the size, figure, and motion of another body, is not beyond our conception; the separation of the parts of one body upon the intrusion of another; and the

change from rest to motion upon impulse: these and the like seem to have some connexion one with another. And if we knew these primary qualities of bodies, we might have reason to hope we might be able to know a great deal more of these operations of them one with another; but our minds not being able to discover any connexion betwixt these primary qualities of bodies and the sensations that are produced in us by them, we can never be able to establish certain and undoubted rules of the consequences or co-existence of any secondary qualities, though we could discover the size, figure, or motion of those invisible parts which immediately produce them. We are so far from knowing what figure, size, or motion of parts produce a yellow colour, a sweet taste, or a sharp sound, that we can by no means conceive how any size, figure, or motion of any particles, can possibly produce in us the idea of any colour, taste or sound whatsover; there is no conceivable connexion betwixt the one and the other.

14. In vain, therefore, shall we endeavour to discover by our ideas (the only true way of certain and universal knowledge) what other ideas are to be found constantly joined with that of our complex idea of any substance: since we neither know the real constitution of the minute parts on which their qualities do depend; nor, did we know them, could we discover any necessary connexion between them and any of the secondary qualities; which is necessary to be done before we can certainly know their necessary co-existence. So, that, let our complex idea of any species of substances be what it will, we can hardly, from the simple ideas contained in it, certainly determine the necessary co-existence of any other quality whatsoever. Our knowledge in all these inquiries reaches very little further than our experience. Indeed some few of the primary qualities have a necessary dependence and visible connexion one with another, as figure necessarily supposes extension; receiving or communicating motion by impulse, supposes solidity. But though these and perhaps some other of our ideas have, yet there are so few of them that have a visible connexion one with another, that we can by intuition or demonstration discover the co-existence of very few of the qualities that are to be found united in substances; and we are left only to the assistance of our senses to make known to us what qualities they contain. For of all the qualities that are co-existent in any subject, with-

out this dependence and evident connexion of their ideas one with another, we cannot know certainly any two to co-exist any further than experience, by our senses, informs us. Thus, though we see the yellow colour, and upon trial, find the weight, malleableness, fusibility, and fixedness that are united in a piece of gold; yet because no one of these ideas has any evident dependence or necessary connexion with the other, we cannot certainly know that where any four of these are, the fifth will be there also, how highly probable soever it may be; because the highest probability amounts not to certainty, without which there can be no true knowledge. For this co-existence can be no further known than it is perceived; and it cannot be perceived but either in particular subjects, by the observation of our senses, or, in general, by the necessary connexion of the ideas themselves.

15. *Of Repugnancy to co-exist, larger.*—As to the incompatibility or repugnancy to co-existence, we may know, that any subject may have of each sort of primary qualities but one particular at once: v. g., each particular extension, figure, number of parts, motion, excludes all other of each kind. The like also is certain of all sensible ideas peculiar to each sense; for whatever of each kind is present in any subject, excludes all other of that sort: v. g., no one subject can have two smells or two colours at the same time. To this, perhaps will be said, Has not an opal, or the infusion of lignum nephriticum, two colours at the same time? To which I answer, that these bodies, to eyes differently placed, may at the same time afford different colours: but I take liberty also to say, that, to eyes differently placed, it is different parts of the object that reflect the particles of light: and therefore it is not the same part of the object, and so not the very same subject, which at the same time appears both yellow and azure. For it is as impossible that the very same particle of any body should at the same time differently modify or reflect the rays of light, as that it should have two different figures and textures at the same time.*

* Of this rare and beautiful stone Anselm Boetius de Boot, of Bruges, physician to the Emperor Rudolph II., gives the following description: —"Opalus gemma est omnium pulcherrima, meoque judicio omnibus aliis preferenda non solum propter summam ipsius e legantiam, dum omnis generis colores, lucis reflectione, in eadem parte ostentat (inest

16. *Of the Co-existence of Powers a very little Way.*—But as to the powers of substances to change the sensible qualities of other bodies, which make a great part of our inquiries about them, and is no inconsiderable branch of our knowledge; I doubt as to these, whether our knowledge reaches much further than our experience; or whether we can come to the discovery of most of these powers, and be certain that they are in any subject, by the connexion with any of those ideas which to us make its essence. Because the active and passive powers of bodies, and their ways of operating consisting in a texture and motion of parts, which we cannot by any means come to discover; it is but in very few cases we can be able to perceive their dependence on, or repugnance to, any of those ideas which make our complex one of that sort of things. I have here instanced in the corpuscularian hypothesis, as that which is thought to go furthest in an intelligible explication of those qualities of bodies; and I fear the weakness of human understanding is scarce able to substitute another, which will afford us a fuller and clearer

enim illi carbunculi tenuior ignis, Amethysti fulgens purpura, Smaragdi virens mare, et cuncta pariter incredibili mistura lucentia) verum etiam, quia ut aliæ gemme adulterari nulla ratione potest. Si subjeceris enim chrystallo varios colores illi in eodem loco herebunt, neque diversos pro radiorum reflectione edent. Apparet in opalo, ceruleus, purpureus, viridis, flavus, et ruber, interdum niger, et albus, id est, lacteus. Non videntur hi colores omnes inesse gemme: quia si frangatur opalus pereunt, ita ut tantum ex reflectione unius, aut duorum colorum colorum oriri, (ut in iride apparet, et in triangulo chrystallino, in quo ex sola lucis reflectione in angulos varii colores sese efferunt) putandum sit." (Gemmarum et Lapidum Historia, l. ii. c. 46.) No less elegant is the description which Mr. Mawe has given of this precious stone. "The colour of the opal is white or pearl grey; and when held between the eyes and the light is pale red or wine yellow, with a milky translucency. By reflected light it exhibits, as its position is varied, elegant and most irridescent colours, particularly emerald green, golden yellow, flame and fire red, violet purple, and celestial blue, so beautifully blended and so fascinating as to captivate the admirer. When the colour is arranged in small spangles it takes the name of harlequin opal. Sometimes it exhibits only one of the above colours; and of them the most esteemed are the civic emerald green, and the orange yellow. When the stone possesses the latter of these colours it is called the Golden opal." (Treatise on Diamonds, p. 123.) Hazelquist mentions an ancient opal, found in the ruins of Alexandria, which "was of the size of a hazel-nut in the form of a half-globe, and set in a ring; if it was held horizontally it had a very fine olive colour, but if it was held perpendicularly between the eye and the light it had the colour of the finest ruby." (Travels, &c. p. 273.)—ED.

discovery of the necessary connexion and co-existence of the powers which are to be observed united in several sorts of them. This at least is certain, that, whichever hypothesis be clearest and truest, (for of that it is not my business to determine,) our knowledge concerning corporeal substances will be very little advanced by any of them, till we are made to see what qualities and powers of bodies have a necessary connexion or repugnancy one with another; which in the present state of philosophy I think we know but to a very small degree: and I doubt whether, with those faculties we have, we shall ever be able to carry our general knowledge (I say not particular experience) in this part much further. Experience is that which in this part we must depend on. And it were to be wished that it were more improved. We find the advantages some men's generous pains have this way brought to the stock of natural knowledge. And if others, especially the philosophers by fire, who pretend to it, had been so wary in their observations, and sincere in their reports as those who call themselves philosophers ought to have been, our acquaintance with the bodies here about us, and our insight into their powers and operations had been yet much greater.*

17. *Of Spirits yet narrower.*—If we are at a loss in respect of the powers and operations of bodies, I think it is easy to conclude we are much more in the dark in reference to the spirits; whereof we naturally have no ideas but what we draw from that of our own, by reflecting on the operations of our own souls within us, as far as they can come within our observation. But how inconsiderable a rank the spirits that inhabit our bodies hold amongst those various and possibly innumerable kinds of nobler beings; and how far short they come of the endowments and perfections of cherubim and seraphim, and infinite sorts of spirits above us, is what by a transient hint in another place I have offered to my reader's consideration.

18. III. *Of other Relations it is not easy to say how far.*— Thirdly, As to the third sort of our knowledge, viz., the agreement or disagreement of any of our ideas in any other relation: this, as it is the largest field of our knowledge, so it is hard to determine how far it may extend; because the

* See Lord Bacon's New Atlantis, p 253, et seq.—ED.

advances that are made in this part of knowledge depending on our sagacity in finding intermediate ideas, that may show the relations and habitudes of ideas whose co-existence is not considered, it is a hard matter to tell when we are at an end of such discoveries; and when reason has all the helps it is capable of, for the finding of proofs, or examining the agreement or disagreement of remote ideas. They that are ignorant of algebra cannot imagine the wonders in this kind are to be done by it: and what further improvements and helps advantageous to other parts of knowledge the sagacious mind of man may yet find out, it is not easy to determine. This at least I believe, that the ideas of quantity are not those alone that are capable of demonstration and knowledge; and that other, and perhaps more useful parts of contemplation would afford us certainty, if vices, passions, and domineering interest did not oppose or menace such endeavours.

Morality capable of Demonstration.—The idea of a supreme Being, infinite in power, goodness, and wisdom, whose workmanship we are, and on whom we depend; and the idea of ourselves, as understanding rational beings; being such as are clear in us, would, I suppose, if duly considered and pursued, afford such foundations of our duty and rules of action as might place morality amongst the sciences capable of demonstration: wherein I doubt not but from self-evident propositions by necessary consequences, as incontestible as those in mathematics, the measures of right and wrong might be made out to any one that will apply himself with the same indifferency and attention to the one as he does to the other of these sciences. The relation of other modes may certainly be perceived, as well as those of number and extension: and I cannot see why they should not also be capable of demonstration if due methods were thought on to examine or pursue their agreement or disagreement. Where there is no property there is no injustice, is a proposition as certain as any demonstration in Euclid: for the idea of property being a right to anything, and the idea to which the name injustice is given being the invasion or violation of that right,* it is

* This is an exceedingly narrow and imperfect view of justice, the most complete theory of which is developed in the Republic of Plato. There prevailed, however, extremely false notions of this virtue among many ancient philosophers, one of whom defined it to be, obedience to

CHAP. III.]   EXTENT OF HUMAN KNOWLEDGE.   155

evident that these ideas being thus established, and these
names annexed to them, I can as certainly know this proposition to be true, as that a triangle has three angles equal
to two right ones. Again: No government allows absolute
liberty; The idea of government being the establishment of
society upon certain rules or laws which require conformity
to them, and the idea of absolute liberty being for any one
to do whatever he pleases, I am as capable of being certain of
the truth of this proposition as of any in the mathematics.

19. *Two things have made moral Ideas to be thought incapable of Demonstration: their Complexedness and Want of
sensible Representations.*—That which in this respect has given
the advantage to the ideas of quantity, and made them thought
more capable of certainty and demonstration, is,

First, That they can be set down and represented by sensible marks, which have a greater and nearer correspondence
with them than any words or sounds whatsoever. Diagrams
drawn on paper are copies of the ideas in the mind, and not
liable to the uncertainty that words carry in their signification. An angle, circle, or square, drawn in lines, lies open
to the view, and cannot be mistaken: it remains unchangeable, and may at leisure be considered and examined, and
the demonstration be revised, and all the parts of it may be
gone over more than once without any danger of the least
change in the ideas. This cannot be thus done in moral
ideas: we have no sensible marks that resemble them,
whereby we can set them down; we have nothing but words
to express them by; which, though when written they

rulers. "Δίκαιόν ἐστι ταῦτα ποιεῖν, ὃ οἱ ἄρχοντες προσέταξαν." But
if so, then certainly those philosophers were deluded dreamers, who sought
for eternal foundations for right and wrong. The government, according to this maxim, is the creator of justice, and can never possibly do
wrong; since, whatever it pleases to order or do, is just. The idea of
Pericles, however, respecting law, differed very little from the above.
"πάντες οὗτοι νόμοι εἰσίν, οὕς το πλῆθος συνελθὸν καὶ δοκιμάσαν
ἔγραφε φράζον ἅ τε δεῖ ποιεῖν καὶ ἅ μή." (Xen. Memor. l. I. c. 2, § 42.)
Upon this view Horace had framed his idea of a virtuous man.
    "Vir bonus est quis?
Qui consulta patrum, qui leges juraque servat," &c.
                        (Epist. b. i. 16, 40.)
The opinions of Democritus were somewhat loftier, though not perhaps
expressed with sufficient clearness:—Δίκη μέν ἐστιν, ἔρδειν τὰ χρὴ ἐόντα·
ἀδικίη δὲ μὴ ἔρδειν τὰ χρὴ ἐόντα, ἀλλὰ πάρα τρέποσθαι." (Stob. Gaisf.
XL. iv. 15.)—ED.

remain the same, yet the ideas they stand for may change in the same man, and it is very seldom that they are not different in different persons.

Secondly, Another thing that makes the greater difficulty in ethics is, that moral ideas are commonly more complex than those of the figures ordinarily considered in mathematics. From whence these two inconveniences follow:— First, that their names are of more uncertain signification; the precise collection of simple ideas they stand for not being so easily agreed on, and so the sign that is used for them in communication always, and in thinking often, does not steadily carry with it the same idea. Upon which the same disorder, confusion, and error follow, as would if a man, going to demonstrate something of an heptagon, should, in the diagram he took to do it, leave out one of the angles, or by oversight make the figure with one angle more than the name ordinarily imported, or he intended it should when at first he thought of his demonstration. This often happens, and is hardly avoidable in very complex moral ideas, where the same name being retained, one angle, i. e., one simple idea is left out or put in the complex one (still called by the same name) more at one time than another. Secondly, From the complexedness of these moral ideas there follows another inconvenience, viz., that the mind cannot easily retain those precise combinations so exactly and perfectly as is necessary in the examination of the habitudes and correspondences, agreements or disagreements of several of them one with another; especially where it is to be judged of by long deductions, and the intervention of several other complex ideas to show the agreement or disagreement of two remote ones.

The great help against this which mathematicians find in diagrams and figures, which remain unalterable in their draughts, is very apparent, and the memory would often have great difficulty otherwise to retain them so exactly, whilst the mind went over the parts of them step by step to examine their several correspondences. And though in casting up a long sum either in addition, multiplication, or division, every part be only a progression of the mind taking a view of its own ideas, and considering their agreement or disagreement, and the resolution of the question be nothing but the result of the whole, made up of such particulars, whereof the mind has a clear perception; yet, without setting down the several parts by marks, whose precise significations are known, and by marks that last and remain in view when the memory had let them go, it would be almost impossible to carry so many different ideas in the mind without confounding or letting slip some parts of the reckoning, and thereby making all our reasonings about it useless. In which case the cyphers or marks help not the mind at all to perceive the agreement of any two or more numbers, their equalities or proportions; that the mind has only by intuition of its own ideas of the numbers themselves. But the numerical characters are helps to the memory, to record and retain the several ideas about which the demonstration is made, whereby a man may know how far his intuitive knowledge in surveying several of the particulars has proceeded; that so he may without confusion go on to what is yet unknown, and at last have in one view before him the result of all his perceptions and reasonings.

20. *Remedies of those Difficulties.*—One part of these disadvantages in moral ideas which has made them be thought not capable of demonstration, may in a good measure be remedied by definitions, setting down that collection of simple ideas,* which every term shall stand for, and then using the terms steadily and constantly for that precise collection. And what methods algebra or something of that kind may hereafter suggest, to remove the other difficulties, it is not easy to foretel. Confident I am, that, if men would in the same method and with the same indifferency search after moral as they do mathematical truths, they would find them have a stronger connexion one with another, and a more necessary consequence from our clear and distinct ideas, and to come nearer perfect demonstration than is commonly imagined. But much of this is not to be expected whilst the desire of esteem, riches, or power makes men espouse the well-endowed opinions in fashion, and then seek arguments either to make good their beauty, or varnish over and cover their deformity: nothing being so beautiful to the eye as

* Cicero's notion of a definition, agreeing substantially with that of Locke, is very clear and precise. "Est definitio, earum, rerum, quæ sunt ejus rei propriæ, quam definire volumus, brevis et circumscripta quædam explicatio." (De Orat. l. I. c. xlii. n. 77.)—ED.

truth is to the mind, nothing so deformed and irreconcilable to the understanding as a lie. For though many a man can with satisfaction enough own a no very handsome wife in his bosom; yet who is bold enough openly to avow, that he has espoused a falsehood, and received into his breast so ugly a thing as a lie? Whilst the parties of men cram their tenets down all men's throats whom they can get into their power, without permitting them to examine their truth or falsehood, and will not let truth have fair play in the world, nor men the liberty to search after it; what improvements can be expected of this kind? What greater light can be hoped for in the moral sciences? The subject part of mankind in most places might, instead thereof, with Egyptian bondage expect Egyptian darkness, were not the candle of the Lord set up by himself in men's minds, which it is impossible for the breath or power of man wholly to extinguish.

21. *Fourthly, Of real Existence: we have an intuitive Knowledge of our own—demonstrative, of God's—sensitive, of some few other things.*—As to the fourth sort of our knowledge, viz., of the real actual existence of things, we have an intuitive knowledge of our own existence, and a demonstrative knowledge of the existence of a God; of the existence of anything else, we have no other but a sensitive knowledge, which extends not beyond the objects present to our senses.

22. *Our Ignorance great.*—Our knowledge being so narrow, as I have shown, it will perhaps give us some light into the present state of our minds if we look a little into the dark side, and take a view of our ignorance; which, being infinitely larger than our knowledge, may serve much to the quieting of disputes and improvement of useful knowledge; if discovering how far we have clear and distinct ideas, we confine our thoughts within the contemplation of those things that are within the reach of our understandings, and launch not out into that abyss of darkness, (where we have not eyes to see, nor faculties to perceive anything,) out of a presumption that nothing is beyond our comprehension. But to be satisfied of the folly of such a conceit, we need not go far. He that knows anything, knows this, in the first place, that he need not seek long for instances of his ignorance. The meanest and most obvious things that come in

our way have dark sides, that the quickest sight cannot penetrate into. The clearest and most enlarged understandings of thinking men find themselves puzzled and at a loss in every particle of matter. We shall the less wonder to find it so, when we consider the causes of our ignorance; which, from what has been said, I suppose will be found to be these three:—

First, Want of ideas.

Secondly, Want of a discoverable connexion between the ideas we have.

Thirdly, Want of tracing and examining our ideas.

23. *First, One Cause of it, Want of Ideas, either such as we have no Conception of, or such as particularly we have not.*— First, There are some things, and those not a few, that we are ignorant of, for want of ideas.

First, all the simple ideas we have, are confined (as I have shown) to those we receive from corporeal objects by sensation, and from the operations of our own minds as the objects of reflection. But how much these few and narrow inlets are disproportionate to the vast whole extent of all beings, will not be hard to persuade those who are not so foolish as to think their span the measure of all things. What other simple ideas it is possible the creatures in other parts of the universe may have, by the assistance of senses and faculties more or perfecter than we have, or different from ours, it is not for us to determine. But to say or think there are no such, because we conceive nothing of them, is no better an argument than if a blind man should be positive in it, that there was no such thing as sight and colours, because he had no manner of idea of any such thing, nor could by any means frame to himself any notions about seeing. The ignorance and darkness that is in us no more hinders nor confines the knowledge that is in others, than the blindness of a mole* is an argument against the quick-sightedness of an eagle. He that will consider the infinite

* This is a received error; but in point of fact, the common mole is not blind, though its eyes are small and dim, suited to the exigencies of its peculiar state of existence. Aristotle describes the mole as blind, for which he was long ridiculed by witty and unphilosophical naturalists, until it was at length discovered that the peculiar species of mole found in Greece is actually in the condition described by Aristotle and in the text. — ED.

power, wisdom, and goodness of the Creator of all things will find reason to think it was not all laid out upon so inconsiderable, mean, and impotent a creature as he will find man to be, who in all probability is one of the lowest of all intellectual beings. What faculties, therefore, other species of creatures have to penetrate into the nature and inmost constitutions of things, what ideas they may receive of them far different from ours, we know not. This we know and certainly find, that we want several other views of them besides those we have, to make discoveries of them more perfect. And we may be convinced that the ideas we can attain to by our faculties are very disproportionate to things themselves, when a positive, clear, distinct one of substance itself, which is the foundation of all the rest, is concealed from us. But want of ideas of this kind being a part as well as cause of our ignorance, cannot be described. Only this I think I may confidently say of it, that the intellectual and sensible world are in this perfectly alike; that that part which we see of either of them holds no proportion with what we see not; and whatsoever we can reach with our eyes or our thoughts of either of them is but a point, almost nothing in comparison of the rest.

24. *Because of their Remoteness; or,*—Secondly, Another great cause of ignorance is the want of ideas we are capable of. As the want of ideas, which our faculties are not able to give us, shuts us wholly from those views of things which it is reasonable to think other beings, perfecter than we, have, of which we know nothing; so the want of ideas I now speak of keeps us in ignorance of things we conceive capable of being known to us. Bulk, figure, and motion we have ideas of. But though we are not without ideas of these primary qualities of bodies in general, yet not knowing what is the particular bulk, figure, and motion, of the greatest part of the bodies of the universe, we are ignorant of the several powers, efficacies, and ways of operation, whereby the effects which we daily see are produced. These are hid from us in some things by being too remote, and in others by being too minute. When we consider the vast distance of the known and visible parts of the world, and the reasons we have to think that what lies within our ken is but a small part of the universe, we shall then discover a huge abyss of igno-

rance. What are the particular fabrics of the great masses of matter which make up the whole stupendous frame of corporeal beings, how far they are extended, what is their motion, and how continued or communicated, and what influence they have one upon another, are contemplations that at first glimpse our thoughts lose themselves in. If we narrow our contemplations and confine our thoughts to this little canton—I mean this system of our sun, and the grosser masses of matter that visibly move about it—what several sorts of vegetables, animals, and intellectual corporeal beings, infinitely different from those of our little spot of earth, may there probably be in the other planets, to the knowledge of which—even of their outward figures and parts—we can no way attain whilst we are confined to this earth; there being no natural means, either by sensation or reflection, to convey their certain ideas into our minds! They are out of the reach of those inlets of all our knowledge: and what sorts of furniture and inhabitants those mansions contain in them we cannot so much as guess, much less have clear and distinct ideas of them.

25. *Because of their Minuteness.*—If a great, nay, far the greatest part of the several ranks of bodies in the universe escape our notice by their remoteness, there are others that are no less concealed from us by their minuteness. These insensible corpuscles being the active parts of matter and the great instruments of nature, on which depend not only all their secondary qualities, but also most of their natural operations, our want of precise distinct ideas of their primary qualities keeps us in an incurable ignorance of what we desire to know about them. I doubt not but if we could discover the figure, size, texture, and motion of the minute constituent parts of any two bodies, we should know without trial several of their operations one upon another, as we do now the properties of a square or a triangle. Did we know the mechanical affections of the particles of rhubarb, hemlock, opium, and a man, as a watchmaker does those of a watch, whereby it performs its operations, and of a file, which by rubbing on them will alter the figure of any of the wheels, we should be able to tell beforehand that rhubarb will purge, hemlock kill, and opium make a man sleep; as well as a watchmaker can that a little piece of paper laid on the balance will keep the

watch from going, till it be removed; or that, some small part of it being rubbed by a file, the machine would quite lose its motion, and the watch go no more. The dissolving of silver in aqua fortis, and gold in aqua regia, and not vice versâ, would be then perhaps no more difficult to know than it is to a smith to understand why the turning of one key will open a lock, and not the turning of another. But whilst we are destitute of senses acute enough to discover the minute particles of bodies, and to give us ideas of their mechanical affections, we must be content to be ignorant of their properties and ways of operation; nor can we be assured about them any further than some few trials we make are able to reach. But whether they will succeed again another time, we cannot be certain.* This hinders our certain knowledge of universal truths concerning natural bodies: and our reason carries us herein very little beyond particular matter of fact.

26. *Hence no Science of Bodies.*—And therefore I am apt to doubt that, how far soever human industry may advance useful and experimental philosophy in physical things, scientifical will still be out of our reach; because we want perfect and adequate ideas of those very bodies which are nearest to us, and most under our command. Those which we have ranked into classes under names, and we think ourselves best acquainted with, we have but very imperfect and incomplete ideas of. Distinct ideas of the several sorts of bodies that fall under the examination of our senses perhaps we may have: but adequate ideas, I suspect, we have not of any one amongst them. And though the former of these will serve us for common use and discourse, yet whilst we want the latter, we are not capable of scientifical knowledge; nor shall ever be able to discover general, instructive, unquestionable truths concerning them. Certainty and demonstration are things we must not, in these matters, pretend to. By the colour, figure, taste, and smell, and other sensible qualities, we have as clear and distinct ideas of sage and hemlock, as we have of a circle and a triangle; but having no ideas of the particular primary qualities of the minute parts of either of these plants, nor of other bodies which we would apply them to, we cannot tell what effects they will

* See Hume's Essay on Necessary Connexion.—ED.

produce; nor when we see those effects can we so much as guess, much less know, their manner of production. Thus, having no ideas of the particular mechanical affections of the minute parts of bodies that are within our view and reach, we are ignorant of their constitutions, powers, and operations: and of bodies more remote we are yet more ignorant, not knowing so much as their very outward shapes, or the sensible and grosser parts of their constitutions.

27. *Much less of Spirits.*—This at first will show us how disproportionate our knowledge is to the whole extent even of material beings; to which if we add the consideration of that infinite number of spirits that may be, and probably are, which are yet more remote from our knowledge, whereof we have no cognizance, nor can frame to ourselves any distinct ideas of their several ranks and sorts, we shall find this cause of ignorance conceal from us, in an impenetrable obscurity, almost the whole intellectual world; a greater, certainly, and more beautiful world than the material. For, bating some very few, and those, if I may so call them, superficial ideas of spirit, which by reflection we get of our own, and from thence the best we can collect of the Father of all spirits, the eternal independent Author of them, and us, and all things, we have no certain information, so much as of the existence of other spirits, but by revelation. Angels of all sorts are naturally beyond our discovery; and all those intelligences, whereof it is likely there are more orders than of corporeal substances, are things whereof our natural faculties give us no certain account at all. That there are minds and thinking beings in other men as well as himself, every man has a reason, from their words and actions, to be satisfied: and the knowledge of his own mind cannot suffer a man that considers, to be ignorant that there is a God. But that there are degrees of spiritual beings between us and the great God, who is there, that, by his own search and ability, can come to know? Much less have we distinct ideas of their different natures, conditions, states, powers, and several constitutions wherein they agree or differ from one another and from us. And, therefore, in what concerns their different species and properties we are in absolute ignorance.*

* This is evidently directed against that part of the Cartesian system, which pretends to discuss the nature of angels. It even appears to have

28. *Secondly, Want of a discoverable Connexion between Ideas we have.*—Secondly, What a small part of the sub-been imagined by those bold speculators, that some approximation can be made towards ascertaining the numbers of the heavenly hosts, of which philosophical calculation take the following example from Antoine Le Grand:—"Talmudistæ Angelos ad certum quædam numerum redigunt, eos per turmas distribuendo, et cuique earum suos veluti milites assignando. Quippe secundum.R. P. Georgium Venetum ex ordine S. Francisci, distinguunt Talmudistæ Angelorum exercitus in Mazaloth, El, Ligion, Rihaton, Chirton, Gistera, Mazaloth autem dicunt esse duodecim, juxta duodecim signa Zodiaci. El verò dicunt esse cohortes triginta, pro quolibet illorum duodecim. Unde sunt in numero trecentæ sexginta Angelorum cohortes Legion autem multiplicat illum numerum trecentorum sexaginta per triginta. Unde resultat numerus decem millium et octingentorum. Et hunc numerum ipsi Talmudistæ multiplicant pariter per triginta: et sic fit Rihaton constans ex noningentis millium millibus et septuaginta duobus millibus. Et hunc numerum pari modo per triginta multiplicant, unde resultat Gistera, constans ex ducentis nonaginta et uno millium millibus, et sexcentis millibus. Quorum omnium summa, est trecenta et unum millium millia, sexcenta et quinquaginta quinque millia, centum et septuaginta duo; ut ex subjecta Tabella patet.

12 Mazaloth.
360 El.
10,800 Ligion.
324,000 Rihaton.
9,720,000 Chirton.
291,600,000 Gistera.
301,655,172 Angelorum Cohortes simul.

(Institut. Phil. Part III. art. vi. § 4.)

This is a part of philosophy which has been cultivated with singular perseverance by the Orientals, whose acquaintance with angels and devils has consequently been much more intimate than that of any nation in the West. Thus we find that, "Some of the Sabæans worshipped devils, believing they had the shapes of goats, and therefore called them Seirim. On the contrary, the Levitical law prohibited to offer sacrifices to Seirim and to goats, that is to say, devils, appearing in the form of goats. (Levit. xvii. 7.) Though they did abominate blood, as a thing exceedingly detestable, yet they did eat it, believing it to be the food of dæmons, and that he that did eat of it should become a brother, or intimate acquaintance of the dæmons, insomuch that they would come to him, and tell him future events, prohibited." (Lev. xvii. 10—23; Stanley's Hist. of Philosophy, c. ii.) Among the ancient magi of Persia, the orders, powers, and distributions of the inhabitants of the spiritual world constituted a favourite object of study; and even from the fragments of their system which have been transmitted to us, we perceive how great was their familiarity with the subjects of Ormuzd and Ahriman. "On y remarque trois ordres d'esprits, d'abord les sept Amschaspands, esprits doués d'immortalité, puis les vingt-huit Izeds, et en dernier lieu les innombrables Fervers. Ormuzd, maître du monde, est le créateur et le premier des Amschaspands; Bahman, chef des autres, est le second, et le roi de lumière; le troisième est Ardibehescht, l'esprit du feu, qui donne le feu

stantial beings that are in the universe the want of ideas leaves open to our knowledge, we have seen. In the next place, another cause of ignorance, of no less moment, is a want of a discoverable connexion between those ideas we have. For wherever we want that, we are utterly incapable of universal and certain knowledge; and are, in the former case, left only to observation and experiment: which, how narrow and confined it is, how far from general knowledge we need not be told. I shall give some few instances of this cause of our ignorance, and so leave it. It is evident

et la vie, le quatrième, Schahriver, roi des métaux; puis vient Sapandomad, fille d'Ormuzd, et mère des premiers êtres humains Meschia et Meschiane; ensuite Khordad, roi des saisons, des mois, des années, et des jours, qui donne au pur l'eau de pureté; et le dernier de tous, Amerdad, créateur et protecteur des arbres, des moissons, des troupeaux. Les Izeds, génies inférieures, ont été crées par Ormuzd pour verser les bénédictions sur le monde, et pour veiller sur le peuple des purs. Les mois, les jours, les divisions même du jour, et les elemens sont placés sous la protection et sous la garde des Amschaspands et des Izeds. Chacun des Amschaspands a son cortége d'Izeds, qui le servent comme les Amschaspands eux-mêmes servent Ormuzd. Les Izeds sont les uns mâles et les autres femelles. Parmi eux figurent Mithra, ou Meher, qui donne à la terre le bienfait du jour, et indépendamment de lui, Korschid, le soleil. Les Fervers sont les idées, les prototypes, les modèles de tous les êtres, formées de l'essence d'Ormuzd, et les plus pures emanations de cette essence. Ils existent par la parole vivante du créateur, aussi sont-ils immortels, et par eux tout vit dans la nature. Ils sont placées au ciel comme des sentinelles vigilantes contre Ahriman, et portent à Ormuzd les prières des hommes pieux, qu'ils protégent et punissent de tout mal. Sur la terre, unis à des corps, ils combattent sans cesse les mauvais esprits. Ils sont aussi nombreux et aussi diversifiés dans leurs espèce que les êtres eux-mêmes." Of the angels of darkness, who formed an exact counterpart to the above, we have the following account: "La royaume d'Ahriman corresponde en tout à celui d'Ormuzd. Là aussi se trouvent sept Devs supérieurs, Ahriman y compris, et à leur suite un nombre infini de Devs inférieurs. Ils ont été produits par Ahriman, après sa chute, et faits à son image pour la destruction du royaume d'Ormuzd. Celui-ci ayant créé le monde de lumière, Ahriman vint du sud, se mêla, aux planètes, pénétra dans les étoiles fixes, et créa le prince des devs, Eschem, le démon de l'envie, armé de sept têtes, et l'adversaire de Serosch, c'est-à-dire, d'Ormuzd, prince de la terre. Maintenant s'ouvre la lutte, et de même que, sur la terre, l'animal combat l'animal, de même, dans le monde des esprits, l'esprit combat l'esprit. Chacun des sept grands devs a son rival dans l'un des sept Amschaspands; chacun d'eux est l'auteur d'un mal ou d'un vice particulier.' (Creuzes. Relig. de l'Antiquité, l. ii. c. 2. Compare with the above the notes of Guigniaut, Part ii. p. 701, et seq.; and the account of Father Rhode, p. 178, et seq.)—ED.

that the bulk, figure, and motion of several bodies about us produce in us several sensations, as of colours, sounds, tastes, smells, pleasure, and pain, &c. These mechanical affections of bodies having no affinity at all with those ideas they produce in us, (there being no conceivable connexion between any impulse of any sort of body and any perception of a colour or smell which we find in our minds,) we can have no distinct knowledge of such operations beyond our experience; and can reason no otherwise about them, than as effects produced by the appointment of an infinitely wise Agent, which perfectly surpass our comprehensions. As the ideas of sensible secondary qualities which we have in our minds, can by us be no way deduced from bodily causes, nor any correspondence or connexion be found between them and those primary qualities which (experience shows us) produce them in us; so, on the other side, the operation of our minds upon our bodies is as inconceivable. How any thought should produce a motion in body is as remote from the nature of our ideas, as how any body should produce any thought in the mind. That it is so, if experience did not convince us, the consideration of the things themselves would never be able in the least to discover to us. These and the like, though they have a constant and regular connexion in the ordinary course of things; yet that connexion being not discoverable in the ideas themselves, which appearing to have no necessary dependence one on another, we can attribute their connexion to nothing else but the arbitrary determination of that all-wise Agent who has made them to be, and to operate as they do, in a way wholly above our weak understandings to conceive.

29. *Instances.*—In some of our ideas there are certain relations, habitudes, and connexions, so visibly included in the nature of the ideas themselves, that we cannot conceive them separable from them by any power whatsoever; and in these only we are capable of certain and universal knowledge. Thus the idea of a right-lined triangle necessarily carries with it an equality of its angles to two right ones. Nor can we conceive this relation, this connexion of these two ideas, to be possibly mutable, or to depend on any arbitrary power, which of choice made it thus, or could make it otherwise. But the coherence and continuity of the parts of

matter; the production of sensation in us of colours and sounds, &c., by impulse and motion; nay, the original rules and communication of motion being such, wherein we car discover no natural connexion with any ideas we have, we cannot but ascribe them to the arbitrary will and good pleasure of the wise Architect. I need not, I think, here mention the resurrection of the dead, the future state of this globe of earth, and such other things, which are by every one acknowledged to depend wholly on the determination of a free agent. The things that, as far as our observation reaches, we constantly find to proceed regularly, we may conclude do act by a law set them; but yet by a law that we know not: whereby, though causes work steadily, and effects constantly flow from them, yet their connexions and dependencies being not discoverable in our ideas, we can have but an experimental knowledge of them.* From all which it is easy to perceive what a darkness we are involved in, how little it is of being, and the things that are, that we are capable to know, and therefore we shall do no injury to our knowledge, when we modestly think with ourselves, that we are so far from being able to comprehend the whole nature of the universe, and all the things contained in it, that we are not capable of a philosophical knowledge of the bodies that are about us, and make a part of us: concerning their secondary qualities, powers, and operations, we can have no universal certainty. Several effects come every day within the notice of our senses, of which we have so far sensitive knowledge; but the causes, manner, and certainty of their production, for the two foregoing reasons, we must be content to be very ignorant of. In these we can go no further than particular experience informs us of matter of fact, and by analogy to guess what effects the like bodies are, upon other trials, like to produce. But as to a perfect science of natural bodies, (not to mention spiritual beings,) we are, I think, so far from being capable of any such thing, that I conclude it lost labour to seek after it.

30. III. *Want of Tracing our Ideas.*—Thirdly, Where we have adequate ideas, and where there is a certain and discoverable connexion between them, yet we are often ignorant, for want of tracing those ideas which we have or may have;

* See Hooker's Ecclesiastical Polity, l. 1, § 3.—Ed.

and for want of finding out those intermediate ideas, which may show us what habitude of agreement or disagreement they have one with another: and thus many are ignorant of mathematical truths, not out of any imperfection of their faculties, or uncertainty in the things themselves, but for want of application in acquiring, examining, and by due ways comparing those ideas. That which has most contributed to hinder the due tracing of our ideas, and finding out their relations, and agreements or disagreements one with another, has been, I suppose, the ill use of words. It is impossible that men should ever truly seek or certainly discover the agreement or disagreement of ideas themselves, whilst their thoughts flutter about, or stick only in sounds of doubtful and uncertain significations. Mathematicians abstracting their thoughts from names, and accustoming themselves to set before their minds the ideas themselves that they would consider, and not sounds instead of them, have avoided thereby a great part of that perplexity, puddering, and confusion, which has so much hindered men's progress in other parts of knowledge. For whilst they stick in words of undetermined and uncertain signification, they are unable to distinguish true from false, certain from probable, consistent from inconsistent, in their own opinions. This having been the fate or misfortune of a great part of men of letters, the increase brought into the stock of real knowledge has been very little, in proportion to the schools, disputes, and writings the world has been filled with; whilst students, being lost in the great wood of words, knew not whereabouts they were, how far their discoveries were advanced, or what was wanting in their own or the general stock of knowledge. Had men, in the discoveries of the material, done as they have in those of the intellectual world, involved all in the obscurity of uncertain and doubtful ways of talking, volumes writ of navigation and voyages, theories and stories of zones and tides, multiplied and disputed; nay, ships built, and fleets sent out, would never have taught us the way beyond the line; and the Antipodes would be still as much unknown, as when it was declared heresy to hold there were any.* But having spoken sufficiently of words,

* " Autrefois on se moquoit de quelques philosophes qui dissent qu'il y avoit des Antipodes ; quel est l'homme assez insensé, discit **Lactance,**

and the ill or careless use that is commonly made of them, I shall not say anything more of it here.

31. *Extent in respect to Universality.*—Hitherto we have examined the extent of our knowledge, in respect of the several sorts of beings that are. There is another extent of it, in respect of universality, which will also deserve to be considered; and in this regard, our knowledge follows the nature of our ideas. If the ideas are abstract, whose agreement or disagreement we perceive, our knowledge is universal. For what is known of such general ideas, will be true of every particular thing in whom that essence, i. e., that abstract idea, is to be found; and what is once known of such ideas, will be perpetually and for ever true. So that as to all general knowledge we must search and find it only in our minds, and it is only the examining of our own ideas that furnisheth us with that. Truths belonging to essences of things (that is, to abstract ideas) are eternal, and are to be found out by the contemplation only of those essences, as the existences of things are to be known only from experience. But having more to say of this in the chapters where I shall speak of general and real knowledge, this may here suffice as to the universality of our knowledge in general.

CHAPTER IV.

OF THE REALITY OF KNOWLEDGE.

1. *Objection. Knowledge placed in Ideas may be all bare Vision.*—I DOUBT not but my reader, by this time, may be apt to think that I have been all this while only building a castle in the air; and be ready to say to me, "To what purpose all this stir? Knowledge, say you, is only the perception of the agreement or disagreement of our own ideas: but who knows what those ideas may be? Is there anything so extravagant as the imaginations of men's brains? Where is the head that has no chimeras in it? Or if there be a sober and a wise man, what difference will there be, by

(l. 3, ch. 23,) pour croire qu'il y a des hommes dont les pieds sont plus elevés que la tête?" (Du Marsais Logique, Art. XIII. Soph. VI. p. 88.) —ED.

your rules, between his knowledge and that of the most extravagant fancy in the world? They both have their ideas, and perceive their agreement and disagreement one with another. If there be any difference between them, the advantage will be on the warm-headed man's side, as having the more ideas, and the more lively; and so, by your rules, he will be the more knowing. If it be true, that all knowledge lies only in the perception of the agreement or disagreement of our own ideas, the visions of an enthusiast and the reasonings of a sober man will be equally certain. It is no matter how things are, so a man observe but the agreement of his own imaginations, and talk conformably, it is all truth, all certainty. Such castles in the air will be as strongholds of truth, as the demonstrations of Euclid. That an harpy is not a centaur is by this way as certain knowledge, and as much a truth, as that a square is not a circle.

"But of what use is all this fine knowledge of men's own imaginations, to a man that inquires after the reality of things? It matters not what men's fancies are, it is the knowledge of things that is only to be prized; it is this alone gives a value to our reasonings, and preference to one man's knowledge over another's, that it is of things as they really are, and not of dreams and fancies."

2. *Answer. Not so, where Ideas agree with Things.*—To which I answer, that if our knowledge of our ideas terminate in them, and reach no further, where there is something further intended, our most serious thoughts will be of little more use than the reveries of a crazy brain; and the truths built thereon of no more weight than the discourses of a man, who sees things clearly in a dream, and with great assurance utters them. But I hope, before I have done, to make it evident that this way of certainty, by the knowledge of our own ideas, goes a little further than bare imagination; and I believe it will appear that all the certainty of general truths a man has lies in nothing else.

3. It is evident the mind knows not things immediately, but only by the intervention of the ideas it has of them. Our knowledge, therefore, is real only so far as there is a conformity between our ideas and the reality of things. But what shall be here the criterion? How shall the mind, when it perceives nothing but its own ideas, know that they

agree with things themselves? This, though it seems not to want difficulty, yet, I think, there be two sorts of ideas that we may be assured agree with things.

4. *As,* I. *All simple Ideas do.*—First, The first are simple ideas, which since the mind, as has been showed, can by no means make to itself, must necessarily be the product of things operating on the mind in a natural way, and producing therein those perceptions which by the wisdom and will of our Maker they are ordained and adapted to. From whence it follows, that simple ideas are not fictions of our fancies, but the natural and regular productions of things without us, really operating upon us, and so carry with them all the conformity which is intended, or which our state requires; for they represent to us things under those appearances which they are fitted to produce in us, whereby we are enabled to distinguish the sorts of particular substances, to discern the states they are in, and so to take them for our necessities, and to apply them to our uses. Thus the idea of whiteness or bitterness, as it is in the mind, exactly answering that power which is in any body to produce it there, has all the real conformity it can or ought to have, with things without us. And this conformity between our simple ideas and the existence of things, is sufficient for real knowledge.

5. II. *All complex Ideas, except of Substances.*—Secondly, All our complex ideas, except those of substances, being archetypes of the mind's own making, not intended to be the copies of anything, nor referred to the existence of anything, as to their originals, cannot want any conformity necessary to real knowledge. For that which is not designed to represent anything but itself, can never be capable of a wrong representation, nor mislead us from the true apprehension of anything by its dislikeness to it; and such, excepting those of substances, are all our complex ideas, which, as I have showed in another place, are combinations of ideas, which the mind, by its free choice, puts together, without considering any connexion they have in nature. And hence it is, that in all these sorts the ideas themselves are considered as the archetypes, and things no otherwise regarded, but as they are conformable to them. So that we cannot but be infallibly certain, that all the knowledge we attain con-

cerning these ideas is real, and reaches things themselves; because in all our thoughts, reasonings, and discourses of this kind, we intend things no further than as they are conformable to our ideas. So that in these we cannot miss of a certain and undoubted reality.

6. *Hence the Reality of Mathematical Knowledge.*—I doubt not but it will be easily granted, that the knowledge we have of mathematical truths is not only certain, but real knowledge; and not the bare empty vision of vain, insignificant chimeras of the brain; and yet, if we will consider, we shall find that it is only of our own ideas. The mathematician considers the truth and properties belonging to a rectangle or circle only as they are in idea in his own mind. For it is possible he never found either of them existing mathematically, i. e., precisely true, in his life. But yet the knowledge he has of any truths or properties belonging to a circle, or any other mathematical figure, are nevertheless true and certain, even of real things existing; because real things are no further concerned, nor intended to be meant by any such propositions, than as things really agree to those archetypes in his mind. Is it true of the idea of a triangle, that its three angles are equal to two right ones? It is true also of a triangle, wherever it really exists. Whatever other figure exists, that is not exactly answerable to the idea of a triangle in his mind, is not at all concerned in that proposition; and therefore he is certain all his knowledge concerning such ideas is real knowledge; because, intending things no further than they agree with those his ideas, he is sure what he knows concerning those figures, when they have barely an ideal existence in his mind, will hold true of them also when they have real existence in matter; his consideration being barely of those figures which are the same, wherever or however they exist.

7. *And of Moral.*—And hence it follows that moral knowledge is as capable of real certainty as mathematics; for certainty being but the perception of the agreement or disagreement of our ideas, and demonstration nothing but the perception of such agreement, by the intervention of other ideas or mediums; our moral ideas, as well as mathematical, being archetypes themselves, and so adequate and complete ideas, all the agreement or disagreement which we

shall find in them will produce real knowledge, as well as in mathematical figures.

8. *Existence not required to make it real.*—For the attaining of knowledge and certainty, it is requisite that we have determined ideas; and, to make our knowledge real, it is requisite that the ideas answer their archetypes. Nor let it be wondered, that I place the certainty of our knowledge in the consideration of our ideas, with so little care and regard (as it may seem) to the real existence of things; since most of those discourses which take up the thoughts and engage the disputes of those who pretend to make it their business to inquire after truth and certainty, will, I presume, upon examination, be found to be general propositions, and notions in which existence is not at all concerned. All the discourses of the mathematicians about the squaring of a circle, conic sections, or any other part of mathematics, concern not the existence of any of those figures; but their demonstrations, which depend on their ideas, are the same, whether there be any square or circle existing in the world or no. In the same manner, the truth and certainty of moral discourses abstracts from the lives of men, and the existence of those virtues in the world whereof they treat. Nor are Tully's Offices less true, because there is nobody in the world that exactly practises his rules, and lives up to that pattern of a virtuous man which he has given us, and which existed nowhere when he writ, but in idea. If it be true in speculation, i. e., in idea, that murder deserves death, it will also be true in reality of any action that exists conformable to that idea of murder. As for other actions, the truth of that proposition concerns them not. And thus it is of all other species of things, which have no other essences but those ideas which are in the minds of men.

9. *Nor will it be less true or certain, because moral Ideas are of our own making and naming.*—But it will here be said, that if moral knowledge be placed in the contemplation of our own moral ideas, and those, as other modes, be of our own making, what strange notions will there be of justice and temperance! What confusion of virtues and vices, if every one may make what ideas of them he pleases! No confusion or disorder in the things themselves, nor the reasonings about them; no more than (in mathematics) there would be

a disturbance in the demonstration, or a change in the properties of figures, and their relations one to another, if a man should make a triangle with four corners, or a trapezium with four right angles; that is, in plain English, change the names of the figures, and call that by one name, which mathematicians call ordinarily by another. For let a man man make to himself the idea of a figure with three angles, whereof one is a right one, and call it, if he please, equilaterum or trapezium, or anything else, the properties of and demonstrations about that idea will be the same, as if he called it a rectangular triangle. I confess the change of the name, by the impropriety of speech, will at first disturb him who knows not what idea it stands for; but as soon as the figure is drawn, the consequences and demonstrations are plain and clear. Just the same is it in moral knowledge: let a man have the idea of taking from others, without their consent, what their honest industry has possessed them of, and call this justice if he please. He that takes the name here without the idea put to it, will be mistaken by joining another idea of his own to that name: but strip the idea of that name, or take it such as it is in the speaker's mind, and the same things will agree to it, as if you called it injustice. Indeed, wrong names in moral discourses breed usually more disorder, because they are not so easily rectified as in mathematics, where the figure, once drawn and seen, makes the name useless and of no force. For what need of a sign, when the thing signified is present and in view? But in moral names that cannot be so easily and shortly done, because of the many decompositions that go to the making up the complex ideas of those modes. But yet for all this miscalling of any of those ideas, contrary to the usual signification of the words of that language, hinders not but that we may have certain and demonstrative knowledge of their several agreements and disagreements, if we will carefully, as in mathematics, keep to the same precise ideas, and trace them in their several relations one to another, without being led away by their names. If we but separate the idea under consideration from the sign that stands for it, our knowledge goes equally on in the discovery of real truth and certainty, whatever sounds we make use of.

10. *Misnaming disturbs not the Certainty of the Know-*

ledge.—One thing more we are to take notice of, that where God or any other law-maker hath defined any moral names, there they have made the essence of that species to which that name belongs; and there it is not safe to apply or use them otherwise: but in other cases it is bare impropriety of speech to apply them contrary to the common usage of the country. But yet even this too disturbs not the certainty of that knowledge which is still to be had by a due contemplation and comparing of those even nick-named ideas.

11. *Ideas of Substances have their Archetypes without us.*—Thirdly, There is another sort of complex ideas, which, being referred to archetypes without us, may differ from them, and so our knowledge about them may come short of being real. Such are our ideas of substances, which, consisting of a collection of simple ideas, supposed taken from the works of nature, may yet vary from them, by having more or different ideas united in them, than are to be found united in the things themselves. From whence it comes to pass, that they may, and often do fail of being exactly conformable to things themselves.

12. *So far as they agree with those, so far our Knowledge concerning them is real.*—I say, then, that to have ideas of substances, which, by being conformable to things, may afford us real knowledge, it is not enough, as in modes, to put together such ideas as have no inconsistence, though they did never before so exist; v. g., the ideas of sacrilege or perjury, &c., were as real and true ideas before, as after the existence of any such fact. But our ideas of substances being supposed copies, and referred to archetypes without us, must still be taken from something that does or has existed; they must not consist of ideas put together at the pleasure of our thoughts, without any real pattern they were taken from, though we can perceive no inconsistence in such a combination. The reason whereof is, because we, knowing not what real constitution it is of substances whereon our simple ideas depend, and which really is the cause of the strict union of some of them one with another, and the exclusion of others; there are very few of them that we can be sure are or are not inconsistent in nature, any further than experience and sensible observation reach. Herein, therefore, is founded the reality of our knowledge concerning substances, that all our

complex ideas of them must be such, and such only, as are made up of such simple ones as have been discovered to co-exist in nature. And our ideas being thus true, though not, perhaps, very exact copies, are yet the subjects of real (as far as we have any) knowledge of them; which (as has been already shown) will not be found to reach very far; but so far as it does, it will still be real knowledge. Whatever ideas we have, the agreement we find they have with others will still be knowledge. If those ideas be abstract, it will be general knowledge. But to make it real concerning substances, the ideas must be taken from the real existence of things. Whatever simple ideas have been found to co-exist in any substance, these we may with confidence join together again, and so make abstract ideas of substances. For whatever have once had an union in nature, may be united again.

13. *In our Inquiries about Substances, we must consider Ideas, and not confine our Thoughts to Names, or Species supposed set out by Names.*—This, if we rightly consider, and confine not our thoughts and abstract ideas to names, as if there were, or could be no other sorts of things than what known names had already determined, and, as it were, set out, we should think of things with greater freedom and less confusion than perhaps we do. It would possibly be thought a bold paradox, if not a very dangerous falsehood, if I should say that some changelings,* who have lived forty

* What changelings were by our superstitious ancestors supposed to be, may be learned from the following story.—"There lived once near Tir's lake two lonely people, who were sadly plagued with a changeling, given them by the underground people instead of their own child, which had not been baptised in time. This changeling behaved in a very strange and uncommon manner, for when there was no one in the place he was in great spirits, ran up the walls like a cat, sat under the roof, and shouted and bawled away lustily; but sat dozing at the end of the table when any one was in the room with him. He was able to eat as much as any four, and never cared what it was that was set before him; but, though he regarded not the quality of his food, in quantity he was never satisfied, and gave excessive annoyance to every one in the house. When they had tried for a long time in vain how they could best get rid of him, since there was no living in the house with him, a smart girl pledged herself that she would banish him from the house; who accordingly, while he was out in the fields, took a pig and killed it, and put it, hide, hair, and all, into a black pudding, and set it before him when he came home. He began, as was his custom,

years together without any appearance of reason, are something between a man and a beast; which prejudice is founded upon nothing else but a false supposition, that these two names, man and beast, stand for distinct species to set out by real essences, that there can come no other species between them: whereas, if we will abstract from those names, and the supposition of such specific essences made by nature, wherein all things of the same denominations did exactly and equally partake; if we would not fancy that there were a certain number of these essences, wherein all things, as in moulds, were cast and formed; we should find that the idea of the shape, motion, and life of a man without reason, is as much a distinct idea, and makes as much a distinct sort of things from man and beast, as the idea of the shape of an ass with reason would be different from either that of man or beast, and be a species of an animal between or distinct from both.

14. *Objection against a Changeling being something between a Man and Beast, answered.*—Here everybody will be ready to ask, If changelings may be supposed something between man and beast, pray what are they? I answer, Changelings; which is as good a word to signify something different from the signification of man or beast, as the names man and beast are to have significations different one from the other. This, well considered, would resolve this matter, and show my meaning without any more ado. But I am not so unacquainted with the zeal of some men, which enables them to spin consequences, and to see religion threatened whenever any one ventures to quit their forms of speaking, as not to foresee what names such a proposition as this is like to be charged with: and without doubt it will be asked, If changelings are something between man and beast, what will become of them in the other world? To which I answer,

---

to gobble it up; but when he had eaten for some time, he began to relax a little in his efforts, and at last he stood still, with his knife in his hand, looking at the pudding. At length, after sitting for some time in this manner, he began:—'A pudding with hide!—a pudding with hair!—a pudding with eyes!—and a pudding with legs in it! Well, three times have I seen a young wood by Tir's lake, but never yet did I see such a pudding! The devil himself may stay here now for me!' So saying, he ran off with himself, and never more came back again." (Keightley's Fairy Mythology, Bohn's edition.)—ED.

1. It concerns me not to know or inquire. To their own master they stand or fall. It will make their state neither better nor worse, whether we determine anything of it or no. They are in the hands of a faithful Creator and a bountiful Father, who disposes not of his creatures according to our narrow thoughts or opinions, nor distinguishes them according to names and species of our contrivance. And we that know so little of this present world we are in, may, I think, content ourselves without being peremptory in defining the different states which creatures shall come into when they go off this stage. It may suffice us, that he hath made known to all those who are capable of instruction, discoursing, and reasoning, that they shall come to an account, and receive according to what they have done in this body.

15. But, Secondly, I answer, The force of these men's question (viz., Will you deprive changelings of a future state?) is founded on one of these two suppositions, which are both false. The first is, that all things that have the outward shape and appearance of a man must necessarily be designed to an immortal future being after this life: or, secondly, that whatever is of human birth must be so. Take away these imaginations, and such questions will be groundless and ridiculous. I desire, then, those who think there is no more but an accidental difference between themselves and changelings, the essence in both being exactly the same, to consider, whether they can imagine immortality annexed to any outward shape of the body? the very proposing it is, I suppose, enough to make them disown it. No one yet, that ever I heard of, how much soever immersed in matter, allowed that excellency to any figure of the gross sensible outward parts, as to affirm eternal life due to it, or a necessary consequence of it;* or that any mass of matter should, after its dissolution here, be again restored hereafter to an everlasting state of sense, perception, and knowledge, only because it was moulded into this or that figure, and

* And yet who, by his feelings, is not led to think that beauty deserves immortality? The ancients, reasoning according to the principles of Paganism, imagined this quality to be of a godlike nature, and worthy of divine honours, which accordingly were in some places paid to it.—ED.

had such a particular frame of its visible parts. Such an opinion as this, placing immortality in a certain superficial figure, turns out of doors all consideration of soul or spirit, upon whose account alone some corporeal beings have hitherto been concluded immortal, and others not. This is to attribute more to the outside than inside of things; and to place the excellency of a man more in the external shape of his body, than internal perfections of his soul; which is but little better than to annex the great and inestimable advantage of immortality and life everlasting, which he has above other material beings, to annex it, I say, to the cut of his beard, or the fashion of his coat. For this or that outward mark of our bodies no more carries with it the hope of an eternal duration, than the fashion of a man's suit gives him reasonable grounds to imagine it will never wear out, or that it will make him immortal. It will perhaps be said, that nobody thinks that the shape makes anything immortal, but it is the shape is the sign of a rational soul within, which is immortal. I wonder who made it the sign of any such thing; for barely saying it, will not make it so; it would require some proofs to persuade one of it. No figure that I know speaks any such language. For it may as rationally be concluded, that the dead body of a man, wherein there is to be found no more appearance or action of life than there is in a statue, has yet nevertheless a living soul in it because of its shape; as that there is a rational soul in a changeling, because he has the outside of a rational creature, when his actions carry far less marks of reason with them, in the whole course of his life, than what are to be found in many a beast.

16. *Monsters.*—But it is the issue of rational parents, and must therefore be concluded to have a rational soul. I know not by what logic you must so conclude. I am sure this is a conclusion that men nowhere allow of. For if they did, they would not make bold, as everywhere they do, to destroy ill-formed and mis-shaped productions. Ay, but these are monsters. Let them be so: what will your drivelling, unintelligent, intractable changeling be? Shall a defect in the body make a monster; a defect in the mind (the far more noble, and, in the common phrase, the far more essential part) not? Shall the want of a nose, or a neck, make a

monster, and put such issue out of the rank of men; the want of reason and understanding, not? This is to bring all back again to what was exploded just now: this is to place all in the shape, and to take the measure of a man only by his outside. To show that, according to the ordinary way of reasoning in this matter, people do lay the whole stress on the figure, and resolve the whole essence of the species of man (as they make it) into the outward shape, how unreasonable soever it be, and how much soever they disown it; we need but trace their thoughts and practice a little further, and then it will plainly appear. The wellshaped changeling is a man, has a rational soul, though it appear not: this is past doubt, say you. Make the ears a little longer, and more pointed, and the nose a little flatter than ordinary, and then you begin to boggle: make the face yet narrower, flatter, and longer, and then you are at a stand: add still more and more of the likeness of a brute to it, and let the head be perfectly that of some other animal, then presently it is a monster; and it is demonstration with you that it hath no rational soul, and must be destroyed. Where now (I ask) shall be the just measure of the utmost bounds of that shape, that carries with it a rational soul? For since there have been human fœtuses produced, half beast and half man; and others three parts one, and one part the other; and so it is possible they may be in all the variety of approaches to the one or the other shape, and may have several degrees of mixture of the likeness of a man or a brute; I would gladly know what are those precise lineaments, which, according to this hypothesis, are or are not capable of a rational soul to be joined to them. What sort of outside is the certain sign that there is or is not such an inhabitant within? For till that be done, we talk at random of man; and shall always, I fear, do so, as long as we give ourselves up to certain sounds, and the imaginations of settled and fixed species in nature, we know not what. But, after all, I desire it may be considered, that those who think they have answered the difficulty by telling us, that a mis-shaped fœtus is a monster, run into the same fault they are arguing against, by constituting a species between man and beast. For what else, I pray, is their monster in the case, (if the word monster signifies anything at all,) but something neither man nor beast, but partaking somewhat of either? And just so is the changeling before mentioned. So necessary is it to quit the common notion of species and essences, if we will truly look into the nature of things, and examine them by what our faculties can discover in them as they exist, and not by groundless fancies that have been taken up about them.

17. *Words and Species.*—I have mentioned this here, because I think we cannot be too cautious that words and species, in the ordinary notions which we have been used to of them, impose not on us. For I am apt to think therein lies one great obstacle to our clear and distinct knowledge, especially in reference to substances: and from thence has rose a great part of the difficulties about truth and certainty. Would we accustom ourselves to separate our contemplations and reasonings from words, we might in a great measure remedy this inconvenience within our own thoughts; but yet it would still disturb us in our discourse with others, as long as we retained the opinion, that species and their essences were anything else but our abstract ideas (such as they are) with names annexed to them, to be the signs of them.

18. *Recapitulation.*—Wherever we perceive the agreement or disagreement of any of our ideas, there is certain knowledge; and wherever we are sure those ideas agree with the reality of things, there is certain real knowledge. Of which agreement of our ideas with the reality of things, having here given the marks, I think I have shown wherein it is that certainty, real certainty, consists, which, whatever it was to others, was, I confess, to me heretofore, one of those desiderata which I found great want of.

CHAPTER V.

OF TRUTH IN GENERAL.

1. *What Truth is.*—WHAT is truth? was an inquiry many ages since;* and it being that which all mankind either do,

* "What is truth? said jesting Pilate, and would not stay for an answer." (Bacon's Essays on Truth, p. 1.) The reader, it is probable, will in this place call to mind a passage of singular beauty and delicacy

or pretend to search after, it cannot but be worth our while carefully to examine wherein it consists, and so acquaint ourselves with the nature of it, as to observe how the mind distinguishes it from falsehood.

which occurs in Aristotle's Ethics, where, in a very few words, he draws a striking parallel between the claims of friendship and truth. Speaking of the supreme good, he says:—Τὸ δὲ καθόλου, βέλτιον ἴσως ἐπισκέψασθαί, καὶ διαπορῆσαι πῶς λέγεται, καίπερ προσάντους τῆς τοιαύτης γινομένης ζητήσεως, διὰ τὸ φίλους ἀνδρας εἰσαγαγεῖν τὰ εἴδη. Δόξειε δ' ἂν ἴσως βέλτιον εἶ ναι, καὶ δεῖν ἐπὶ σωτηρία γε τῆς ἀληθείας καὶ τὰ οἰκεῖα ἀναιρεῖν, ἄλλως τε καὶ φιλοσόφους ὄντας. Ἀμφοῖν γὰρ ὄντοιν, φίλοιν ὅσιον προτιμᾷν τὴν ἀλήθειαν. (Ethic. ad Nichom. L. I. c. vi. § 1.) "It were perhaps best to consider good universal, and examine how it is named; although this question be painful to me, because the doctrine of ideas was introduced by persons whom I sincerely love. Nevertheless, for truth's sake, it will perhaps be judged the best course for a philosopher to sacrifice even his own proper opinions. For though friendship and truth be both objects of love, I regard it as a sacred duty to prefer the latter." Hence the old saying:—"*Amicus Plato, amicus Socrates, sed majus amica veritas.*" Victor's remark upon this passage is worthy of being preserved:—" Purgat antem se primum, quod necessitate se cogente, adversaturus sit sententiæ sui doctoris: unde vocat hanc questionem arduam, quia amici ipsius homines, auctores fuerunt idearum: induxeruntque ipsas in disputationem de summo bono: dignum vero se ostendit esse, cui ignoscatur; ac fortasse etiam, qui laudetur cum officio fungatur: à philosopho enim veritas in primis amplexanda est, ceteris que rebus omnibus anteponenda, quare oportet etiam suas proprias opiniones confutare, cum cognitæ postea sunt alicui vitio, aut errori affines; id quod memoriæ proditum est, fecisse Hippocratem, qui non veritur est fateri, se in futura humani capitis aliquando deceptum fuisse." The search after truth, in the opinion of Montaigne, was so agreeable as to amount even to a luxury, which the Stoics abandoned as blamable. " Il ne faut pas trouver estrange, si gents desesperez de la prinse n'ont pas laissé d'avoir plaisir à la chasse, l'étude estant de soi une occupation plaisante, et si plaisante que parmi les voluptes, les Stoiciens defendent aussi celle qui vient de l'exercitation de l'esprit, y veulent de la bride, et trouvent de l'intemperance à trop scavoir." (Essais, l. XI. c. xii. t. v. p. 46.) Lord Bacon observes, that some persons love the lie for the lie's sake; and Montaigne confesses that something very similar had always been reproached to his countrymen. "Le premier traiet de la corruption des mœurs, c'est le bannissement de la Vérité: car comme disoit Pindare, l'estre veritable, est le commencement d'une grande vertu, et le premier article que Platon demande au Gouverneurs de sa Republique. Nostre vérité de maintenant, ce n'est pas ce qui est, mais ce qui se persuade à autruy ; comme nous appellons monnoye non celle qui est loyalle seulement, mais la fausse aussi, qui a mise. Nostre nation est de long temps reprochée de ce vice: car Salvianus Massiliensis, (De Gubernat Dei, L. 1. c. xiv. p. 87. Edit. 3, Baluz.) qui estoit du temps de l'Empereur Valentinian, dit, qu'*aux Francoys*

2. *A right joining or separating of Signs*, i. e., *Ideas or Words*.—Truth, then, seems to me, in the proper import of the word, to signify nothing but the joining or separating of signs, as the things signified by them do agree or disagree one with another. The joining or separating of signs here meant, is what by another name we call proposition. So that truth properly belongs only to propositions: whereof there are two sorts, viz., mental and verbal; as there are two sorts of signs commonly made use of, viz., ideas and words,

3. *Which make mental or verbal Propositions.*—To form a clear notion of truth, it is very necessary to consider truth of thought, and truth of words, distinctly one from another; but yet it is very difficult to treat of them asunder. Because it is unavoidable, in treating of mental propositions, to make use of words; and then the instances given of mental propositions cease immediately to be barely mental, and become verbal. For a mental proposition being nothing but a bare consideration of the ideas, as they are in our minds, stripped of names, they lose the nature of purely mental propositions as soon as they are put into words.

4. *Mental Propositions are very hard to be treated of.*—And that which makes it yet harder to treat of mental and verbal propositions separately is, that most men, if not all, in their thinking and reasonings within themselves, make use of words instead of ideas: at least when the subject of their meditation contains in it complex ideas. Which is a great evidence of the imperfection and uncertainty of our ideas of that kind, and may, if attentively made use of, serve for a mark to show us what are those things we have clear and perfect established ideas of, and what not. For if we will curiously observe the way our mind takes in thinking and reasoning, we shall find, I suppose, that when we make any propositions within our own thoughts about white or black, sweet or bitter, a triangle or a circle, we can and often do

le mentir et se parjurer n'est pas vice mais une facon de parler. Qui voudroit encheris sur ce tesmoignage, il pourroit dire qui ce leur est a present vertu. On s'y forme, on s'y faconne, comme à un exercise d'honneur: car la dissimulation est des plus notables qualités de ce siecle." (L. II. c. xviii. t. vi. p. 128 et seq. On Contemplative **Truth**, see **Hierocles**. In Carm. Pythag. pp. 219—276.)—ED.

frame in our minds the ideas themselves, without reflecting on the names. But when we would consider, or make propositions about the more complex ideas, as of a man, vitriol, fortitude, glory, we usually put the name for the idea; because the ideas these names stand for, being for the most part imperfect, confused, and undetermined, we reflect on the names themselves, because they are more clear, certain, and distinct, and readier occur to our thoughts than the pure ideas: and so we make use of these words instead of the ideas themselves, even when we would meditate and reason within ourselves, and make tacit mental propositions. In substances, as has been already noticed, this is occasioned by the imperfection of our ideas; we making the name stand for the real essence, of which we have no idea at all. In modes, it is occasioned by the great number of simple ideas that go to the making them up. For many of them being compound, the name occurs much easier than the complex idea itself, which requires time and attention to be recollected, and exactly represented to the mind, even in those men who have formerly been at the pains to do it; and is utterly impossible to be done by those who, though they have ready in their memory the greatest part of the common words of that language, yet perhaps never troubled themselves in all their lives to consider what precise ideas the most of them stood for. Some confused or obscure notions have served their turns, and many who talk very much of religion and conscience, of church and faith, of power and right, of obstructions and humours, melancholy and choler, would perhaps have little left in their thoughts and meditations, if one should desire them to think only of the things themselves, and lay by those words with which they so often confound others, and not seldom themselves also.

5. *Being nothing but the joining or separating Ideas without Words.*—But to return to the consideration of truth: we must, I say, observe two sorts of propositions that we are capable of making.

First, mental, wherein the ideas in our understandings are without the use of words put together, or separated by the mind, perceiving or judging of their agreement or disagreement.

Secondly, Verbal propositions, which are words, the signs

of our ideas, put together or separated in affirmative or negative sentences. By which way of affirming or denying, these signs, made by sounds, are, as it were, put together or separated one from another. So that proposition consists in joining or separating signs, and truth consists in the putting together or separating those signs, according as the things which they stand for agree or disagree.

6. *When mental Propositions contain real Truth, and when verbal.*—Every one's experience will satisfy him, that the mind, either by perceiving or supposing the agreement or disagreement of any of its ideas, does tacitly within itself put them into a kind of proposition affirmative or negative, which I have endeavoured to express by the terms putting together and separating. But this action of the mind, which is so familiar to every thinking and reasoning man, is easier to be conceived by reflecting on what passes in us when we affirm or deny, than to be explained by words. When a man has in his head the idea of two lines, viz., the side and diagonal of a square, whereof the diagonal is an inch long, he may have the idea also of the division of that line into a certain number of equal parts; v. g., into five, ten, a hundred, a thousand, or any other number, and may have the idea of that inch line being divisible, or not divisible, into such equal parts, as a certain number of them will be equal to the sideline. Now, whenever he perceives, believes, or supposes such a kind of divisibility to agree or disagree to his idea of that line, he, as it were, joins or separates those two ideas, viz., the idea of that line, and the idea of that kind of divisibility; and so makes a mental proposition, which is true or false, according as such a kind of divisibility, a divisibility into such aliquot parts, does really agree to that line or no. When ideas are so put together, or separated in the mind, as they or the things they stand for do agree or not, that is, as I may call it, mental truth. But truth of words is something more; and that is the affirming or denying of words one of another, as the ideas they stand for agree or disagree: and this again is two-fold; either purely verbal and trifling, which I shall speak of, (chap. viii.,) or real and instructive, which is the object of that real knowledge which we have spoken of already.

7. *Objection against verbal Truth, that thus it may all be chimerical.*—But here again will be apt to occur the same

doubt about truth, that did about knowledge: and it will be objected, that if truth be nothing but the joining and separating of words in propositions, as the ideas they stand for agree or disagree in men's minds, the knowledge of truth is not so valuable a thing as it is taken to be, nor worth the pains and time men employ in the search of it; since by this account it amounts to no more than the conformity of words to the chimeras of men's brains. Who knows not what odd notions many men's heads are filled with, and what strange ideas all men's brains are capable of? But if we rest here, we know the truth of nothing by this rule, but of the visionary words in our own imaginations: nor have other truth, but what as much concerns harpies and centaurs, as men and horses. For those, and the like, may be ideas in our heads, and have their agreement or disagreement there, as well as the ideas of real beings, and so have as true propositions made about them. And it will be altogether as true a proposition to say all centaurs are animals, as that all men are animals; and the certainty of one as great as the other. For in both the propositions, the words are put together according to the agreement of the ideas in our minds: and the agreement of the idea of animal with that of centaur is as clear and visible to the mind, as the agreement of the idea of animal with that of man; and so these two propositions are equally true, equally certain. But of what use is all such truth to us?

8. *Answered, Real Truth is about Ideas agreeing to things.*—Though what has been said in the foregoing chapter to distinguish real from imaginary knowledge, might suffice here, in answer to this doubt, to distinguish real truth from chimerical, or (if you please) barely nominal, they depending both on the same foundation; yet it may not be amiss here again to consider, that though our words signify nothing but our ideas, yet being designed by them to signify things, the truth they contain when put into propositions will be only verbal, when they stand for ideas in the mind that have not an agreement with the reality of things. And therefore truth as well as knowledge may well come under the distinction of verbal and real; that being only verbal truth. wherein terms are joined according to the agreement or disagreement of the ideas they stand for, without regarding

whether our ideas are such as really have, or are capable of having, an existence in nature. But then it is they contain real truth, when these signs are joined, as our ideas agree; and when our ideas are such as we know are capable of having an existence in nature; which in substances we cannot know, but by knowing that such have existed.

9. *Falsehood is the joining of Names otherwise than their Ideas agree.*—Truth is the marking down in words the agreement or disagreement of ideas as it is. Falsehood is the marking down in words the agreement or disagreement of ideas otherwise than it is. And so far as these ideas, thus marked by sounds, agree to their archetypes, so far only is the truth real. The knowledge of this truth consists in knowing what ideas the words stand for, and the perception of the agreement or disagreement of those ideas, according as it is marked by those words.

10. *General Propositions to be treated of more at large.*— But because words are looked on as the great conduits of truth and knowledge, and that in conveying and receiving of truth, and commonly in reasoning about it, we make use of words and propositions; I shall more at large inquire wherein the certainty of real truths contained in propositions consists, and where it is to be had; and endeavour to show in what sort of universal propositions we are capable of being certain of their real truth or falsehood.

I shall begin with general propositions, as those which most employ our thoughts, and exercise our contemplation. General truths are most looked after by the mind as those that most enlarge our knowledge; and by their comprehensiveness satisfying us at once of many particulars, enlarge our view, and shorten our way to knowledge.

11. *Moral and Metaphysical Truth.*—Besides truth taken in the strict sense before mentioned, there are other sorts of truth; as, 1. Moral truth, which is speaking of things according to the persuasion of our own minds, though the proposition we speak agree not to the reality of things. 2. Metaphysical truth, which is nothing but the real existence of things, conformable to the ideas to which we have annexed their names. This, though it seems to consist in the very beings of things, yet, when considered a little nearly, will appear to include a tacit proposition, whereby the mind joins

that particular thing to the idea it had before settled with the name to it. But these considerations of truth, either having been before taken notice of, or not being much to our present purpose, it may suffice here only to have mentioned them.

CHAPTER VI.

OF UNIVERSAL PROPOSITIONS, THEIR TRUTH AND CERTAINTY.

1. *Treating of Words necessary to Knowledge.*—THOUGH the examining and judging of ideas by themselves, their names being quite laid aside, be the best and surest way to clear and distinct knowledge; yet, through the prevailing custom of using sounds for ideas, I think it is very seldom practised. Every one may observe how common it is for names to be made use of, instead of the ideas themselves, even when men think and reason within their own breasts; especially if the ideas be very complex, and made up of a great collection of simple ones. This makes the consideration of words and propositions so necessary a part of the treatise of knowledge, that it is very hard to speak intelligibly of the one, without explaining the other.

2. *General Truths hardly to be understood, but in verbal Propositions.*—All the knowledge we have, being only of particular or general truths, it is evident that whatever may be done in the former of these, the latter, which is that which with reason is most sought after, can never be well made known, and is very seldom apprehended, but as conceived and expressed in words. It is not, therefore, out of our way in the examination of our knowledge, to inquire into the truth and certainty of universal propositions.

3. *Certainty twofold—of Truth and of Knowledge.*—But that we may not be misled in this case by that which is the danger everywhere, I mean by the doubtfulness of terms, it is fit to observe that certainty is twofold: certainty of truth and certainty of knowledge. Certainty of truth is, when words are so put together in propositions as exactly to express the agreement or disagreement of the ideas they stand for, as really it is. Certainty of knowledge is **to** per-

ceive the agreement or disagreement of ideas, as expressed in any proposition. This we usually call knowing, or being certain of the truth of any proposition.

4. *No Proposition can be known to be true, where the Essence of each Species mentioned is not known.*—Now, because we cannot be certain of the truth of any general proposition, unless we know the precise bounds and extent of the species its terms stand for, it is necessary we should know the essence of each species, which is that which constitutes and bounds it. This, in all simple ideas and modes, is not hard to do. For in these the real and nominal essence being the same, or, which is all one, the abstract idea which the general term stands for being the sole essence and boundary that is or can be supposed of the species, there can be no doubt how far the species extends, or what things are comprehended under each term; which, it is evident, are all that have an exact conformity with the idea it stands for, and no other. But in substances wherein a real essence distinct from the nominal is supposed to constitute, determine, and bound the species, the extent of the general word is very uncertain; because, not knowing this real essence, we cannot know what is, or what is not of that species; and, consequently, what may or may not with certainty be affirmed of it. And thus, speaking of a man, or gold, or any other species of natural substances, as supposed constituted by a precise and real essence which nature regularly imparts to every individual of that kind, whereby it is made to be of that species, we cannot be certain of the truth of any affirmation or negation made of it. For man or gold, taken in this sense, and used for species of things constituted by real essences, different from the complex idea in the mind of the speaker, stand for we know not what; and the extent of these species, with such boundaries, are so unknown and undetermined, that it is impossible with any certainty to affirm, that all men are rational, or that all gold is yellow. But where the nominal essence is kept to, as the boundary of each species, and men extend the application of any general term no further than to the particular things in which the complex idea it stands for is to be found, there they are in no danger to mistake the bounds of each species, nor can be in doubt, on this account, whether any proposition be true or not. I have chosen to

explain this uncertainty of propositions in this scholastic way, and have made use of the terms of essences, and species, on purpose to show the absurdity and inconvenience there is to think of them as of any other sort of realities, than barely abstract ideas with names to them. To suppose that the species of things are anything but the sorting of them under general names, according as they agree to several abstract ideas, of which we make those names the signs, is to confound truth, and introduce uncertainty into all general propositions that can be made about them. Though therefore these things might, to people not possessed with scholastic learning, be treated of in a better and clearer way; yet those wrong notions of essences or species having got root in most people's minds who have received any tincture from the learning which has prevailed in this part of the world, are to be discovered and removed, to make way for that use of words which should convey certainty with it.

5. *This more particularly concerns Substances.*—The names of substances, then, whenever made to stand for species which are supposed to be constituted by real essences which we know not, are not capable to convey certainty to the understanding: of the truth of general propositions made up of such terms we cannot be sure. The reason whereof is plain: for how can we be sure that this or that quality is in gold, when we know not what is or is not gold? Since in this way of speaking, nothing is gold but what partakes of an essence, which we not knowing, cannot know where it is or is not, and so cannot be sure that any parcel of matter in the world is or is not in this sense gold; being incurably ignorant whether it has or has not that which makes anything to be called gold; i. e., that real essence of gold whereof we have no idea at all: this being as impossible for us to know as it is for a blind man to tell in what flower the colour of a pansy is or is not to be found, whilst he has no idea of the colour of a pansy at all. Or if we could (which is impossible) certainly know where a real essence, which we know not, is; v. g., in what parcels of matter the real essence of gold is; yet could we not be sure that this or that quality could with truth be affirmed of gold; since it is impossible for us to know that this or that quality or idea has a necessary connexion with a real essence of which we have no idea at all.

whatever species that supposed real essence may be imagined to constitute.

6. *The Truth of few universal Propositions concerning Substances is to be known.*—On the other side, the names of substances, when made use of as they should be, for the ideas men have in their minds, though they carry a clear and determinate signification with them, will not yet serve us to make many universal propositions, of whose truth we can be certain. Not because in this use of them we are uncertain what things are signified by them, but because the complex ideas they stand for are such combinations of simple ones as carry not with them any discoverable connexion or repugnancy, but with a very few other ideas.

7. *Because Co-existence of Ideas in few Cases is to be known.*—The complex ideas that our names of the species of substances properly stand for, are collections of such qualities as have been observed to co-exist in an unknown substratum, which we call substance: but what other qualities necessarily co-exist with such combinations, we cannot certainly know, unless we can discover their natural dependence; which, in their primary qualities, we can go but a very little way in; and in all their secondary qualities we can discover no connexion at all, for the reasons mentioned, chap. iii., viz., 1. Because we know not the real constitutions of substances, on which each secondary quality particularly depends. 2. Did we know that it would serve us only for experimental (not universal) knowledge; and reach with certainty no further than that bare instance: because our understandings can discover no conceivable connexion between any secondary quality and any modification whatsoever of any of the primary ones. And therefore there are very few general propositions to be made concerning substances, which can carry with them undoubted certainty.

8. *Instance in Gold.*—All gold is fixed, is a proposition whose truth we cannot be certain of, how universally soever it be believed. For if, according to the useless imagination of the schools, any one supposes the term gold to stand for a species of things set out by nature, by a real essence belonging to it, it is evident he knows not what particular substances are of that species; and so cannot with certainty affirm anything universally of gold. But if he makes gold

stand for a species determined by its nominal essence, let the nominal essence, for example, be the complex idea of a body of a certain yellow colour, malleable, fusible, and heavier than any other known; in this proper use of the word gold, there is no difficulty to know what is or is not gold. But yet no other quality can with certainty be universally affirmed or denied of gold, but what hath a discoverable connexion or inconsistency with that nominal essence. Fixedness, for example, having no necessary connexion, that we can discover, with the colour, weight, or any other simple idea of our complex one, or with the whole combination together; it is impossible that we should certainly know the truth of this proposition, that all gold is fixed.

9. As there is no discoverable connexion between fixedness and the colour, weight, and other simple ideas of that nominal essence of gold; so if we make our complex idea of gold a body yellow, fusible, ductile, weighty, and fixed, we shall be at the same uncertainty concerning solubility in aq. regia, and for the same reason: since we can never, from consideration of the ideas themselves, with certainty affirm or deny of a body whose complex idea is made up of yellow, very weighty, ductile, fusible, and fixed, that it is soluble in aq. regia; and so on of the rest of its qualities. I would gladly meet with one general affirmation concerning any quality of gold, that any one can certainly know is true. It will, no doubt, be presently objected, Is not this an universal proposition, "all gold is malleable?" To which I answer, it is a very certain proposition, if malleableness be a part of the complex idea the word gold stands for. But then here is nothing affirmed of gold, but that that sound stands for an idea in which malleableness is contained: and such a sort of truth and certainty as this, it is to say a centaur is four-footed. But if malleableness make not a part of the specific essence the name of gold stands for, it is plain, "all gold is malleable," is not a certain proposition. Because, let the complex idea of gold be made up of whichsoever of its other qualities you please, malleableness will not appear to depend on that complex idea, nor follow from any simple one contained in it: the connexion that malleableness has (if it has any) with those other qualities being only by the intervention of the real constitution of its insensible parts; which,

since we know not, it is impossible we should perceive that connexion, unless we could discover that which ties them together.

10. *As far as any such Co-existence can be known, so far universal Propositions may be certain.—But this will go but a little Way, because*—The more, indeed, of these co-existing qualities we unite into one complex idea under one name, the more precise and determinate we make the signification of that word; but never yet make it thereby more capable of universal certainty, in respect of other qualities not contained in our complex idea; since we perceive not their connexion or dependence on one another, being ignorant both of that real constitution in which they are all founded, and also how they flow from it. For the chief part of our knowledge concerning substances is not, as in other things, barely of the relation of two ideas that may exist separately; but is of the necessary connexion and co-existence of several distinct ideas in the same subject, or of their repugnancy so to co-exist. Could we begin at the other end, and discover what it was wherein that colour consisted, what made a body lighter or heavier, what texture of parts made it malleable, fusible, and fixed, and fit to be dissolved in this sort of liquor, and not in another—if, I say, we had such an idea as this of bodies, and could perceive wherein all sensible qualities originally consist, and how they are produced; we might frame such ideas of them as would furnish us with matter of more general knowledge, and enable us to make universal propositions, that should carry general truth and certainty with them. But whilst our complex ideas of the sorts of substances are so remote from that internal real constitution on which their sensible qualities depend, and are made up of nothing but an imperfect collection of those apparent qualities our senses can discover, there can be few general propositions concerning substances of whose real truth we can be certainly assured; since there are but few simple ideas of whose connexion and necessary co-existence we can have certain and undoubted knowledge. I imagine, amongst all the secondary qualities of substances, and the powers relating to them, there cannot any two be named whose necessary co-existence or repugnance to co-exist can certainly be known, unless in those of the same sense, which neces-

sarily exclude one another, as I have elsewhere shewed. No one, I think, by the colour that is in any body, can certainly know what smell, taste, sound, or tangible qualities it has, nor what alterations it is capable to make or receive on or from other bodies. The same may be said of the sound or taste, &c. Our specific names of substances standing for any collections of such ideas, it is not to be wondered that we can with them make very few general propositions of undoubted real certainty. But yet so far as any complex idea of any sort of substances contains in it any simple idea, whose necessary co-existence with any other may be discovered, so far universal propositions may with certainty be made concerning it: v. g., could any one discover a necessary connexion between malleableness and the colour or weight of gold, or any other part of the complex idea signified by that name, he might make a certain universal proposition concerning gold in this respect; and the real truth of this proposition, "that all gold is malleable," would be as certain as of this, "the three angles of all right-lined triangles are all equal to two right ones."

11. *The Qualities which make our complex Ideas of Substances depend mostly on external, remote, and unperceived Causes.*—Had we such ideas of substances as to know what real constitutions produce those sensible qualities we find in them, and how those qualities flowed from thence, we could, by the specific ideas of their real essences in our own minds, more certainly find out their properties, and discover what qualities they had or had not, than we can now by our senses: and to know the properties of gold, it would be no more necessary that gold should exist, and that we should make experiments upon it, than it is necessary for the knowing the properties of a triangle, that a triangle should exist in any matter, the idea in our minds would serve for the one as well as the other. But we are so far from being admitted into the secrets of nature, that we scarce so much as ever approach the first entrance towards them. For we are wont to consider the substances we meet with, each of them as an entire thing by itself, having all its qualities in itself, and independent of other things; overlooking, for the most part, the operations of those invisible fluids they are encompassed with, and upon whose motions and

operations depend the greatest part of those qualities which are taken notice of in them, and are made by us the inherent marks of distinction whereby we know and denominate them. Put a piece of gold anywhere by itself, separate from the reach and influence of all other bodies, it will immediately lose all its colour and weight, and perhaps malleableness too; which, for aught I know, would be changed into a perfect friability. Water, in which to us fluidity is an essential quality, left to itself, would cease to be fluid. But if inanimate bodies owe so much of their present state to other bodies without them, that they would not be what they appear to us were those bodies that environ them removed; it is yet more so in vegetables, which are nourished, grow, and produce leaves, flowers, and seeds, in a constant succession. And if we look a little nearer into the state of animals, we shall find that their dependence, as to life, motion, and the most considerable qualities to be observed in them, is so wholly on extrinsical causes and qualities of other bodies that make no part of them, that they cannot subsist a moment without them: though yet those bodies on which they depend are little taken notice of, and make no part of the complex ideas we frame of those animals. Take the air but for a minute from the greatest part of living creatures, and they presently lose sense, life, and motion. This the necessity of breathing has forced into our knowledge. But how many other extrinsical and possibly very remote bodies do the springs of these admirable machines depend on, which are not vulgarly observed, or so much as thought on; and how many are there which the severest inquiry can never discover? The inhabitants of this spot of the universe, though removed so many millions of miles from the sun, yet depend so much on the duly tempered motion of particles coming from or agitated by it, that were this earth removed but a small part of the distance out of its present situation, and placed a little further or nearer that source of heat, it is more than probable that the greatest part of the animals in it would immediately perish: since we find them so often destroyed by an excess or defect of the sun's warmth, which an accidental position in some parts of this our little globe exposes them to. The qualities observed in a loadstone must needs have their source far beyond the confines of that body; and the ravage made often on several sorts of animals by invisible causes, the certain death (as we are told) of some of them, by barely passing the line, or, as it is certain of other, by being removed into a neighbouring country;* evidently show that the concurrence and operations

* Other animals, though not destroyed, lose many of their distinguishing properties. Thus, the scorpion, whose poison is fatal under the line, becomes less and less noxious as the race is propagated northward. Again: the shawl-goats of Thibet, transported to Northern India or Persia, lose their fine silky hair, and become covered with a rough shaggy coat, nearly resembling that of other animals of the same species. In Spain, too, the finest wool is produced by the sheep of the Mesta, which wander over nearly half the kingdom, from the plains of Estremadura to the mountains of Castile and Leon. Confined to any particular district, saving one small tract in the environs of Segovia, they degenerate, and produce a wool of coarser texture. Trees and plants also are visibly modified by climate: thus, such as are evergreens in Upper Egypt, transplanted to the north, become deciduous; and trees and shrubs which in our northern hemisphere flower in June, being conveyed south of the line, for the next few years make an attempt to flower at the same season, which happening to be midwinter in those regions, they gradually desist from their old habits, and learn to submit to the laws of the place. This fact was observed by Monsieur Barthelemy St. Hilaire, in his travels in Brazil, where, if I recollect rightly, it is regarded as a fact of recent discovery, though in truth it had been long ago noticed by Lord Bacon, who says: "Plants brought out of hot countries will endeavour to put forth at the same time that they usually do in their own climate; and therefore, to preserve them, there is no more required, than to keep them from the injury of putting back by cold." (Sylva Sylvarum, art. vi. no. 574.) Andrew Baccius, in his very curious and learned work, De Thermis, makes, on occult qualities, a remark very much in the spirit of Locke. "Dubium non est, quod quorumcunque effectuum, etiam singularium præter communes, et medias caussas, sunt suæ veræ, et propriæ causæ: hæ verò quoniam plerumque nobis notæ non sunt, utpote remotæ à sensibus (ubi enim nos deficit sensus, deficit et judicium) hinc est quòd singulares ac mirabiles appelluntur effectus, eventusque naturæ: nimirùm quia ignoramus caussam quam nos percipimus sensu." (l. VI. c. xxiii. p. 341.) He then proceeds to give examples of strange and seemingly miraculous qualities in the water of various fountains, springs, and lakes; such as the fountain-tree, in the Fortunate Islands; (See also Voy. de la Compagnie des Indes;) the lake in the mountains of Portugal which ebbs and flows simultaneously with the sea; a fountain in the same country, which absorbs whatever is thrown into it, even living creatures; a lake on the confines of Austria and Hungary, which, hiding itself in certain caverns during summer, leaves its bed a beautiful green valley, but, rushing forth in the autumn, fills up the hollows, and abounds with fish—he likewise celebrates fountains tinctured with milk and wine; but the most remarkable, perhaps, is that lake described by Cassiodorus,

of several bodies, with which they are seldom thought to have anything to do, is absolutely necessary to make them be what they appear to us, and to preserve those qualities by which we know and distinguish them. We are then quite out of the way, when we think that things contain within themselves the qualities that appear to us in them; and we in vain search for that constitution within the body of a fly or an elephant, upon which depend those qualities and powers we observe in them. For which perhaps, to understand them aright, we ought to look not only beyond this our earth and atmosphere, but even beyond the sun or remotest star our eyes have yet discovered. For how much the being and operation of particular substances in this our globe depends on causes utterly beyond our view, is impossible for us to determine. We see and perceive some of the motions and grosser operations of things here about us; but whence the streams come that keep all these curious machines in motion and repair, how conveyed and modified, is beyond our notice and apprehension: and the great parts and wheels, as I may so say, of this stupendous structure of the universe, may, for aught we know, have such a connexion and dependence in their influences and operations one upon another, that perhaps things in this our mansion would put on quite another face, and cease to be what they are, if some one of the stars or great bodies incomprehensibly remote from us, should cease to be or move as it does. This is certain: things, however absolute and entire they seem in themselves, are but retainers to other parts of nature, for that which they are most taken notice of by us. Their observable qualities, actions, and powers are owing to something without them; and there is not so complete and perfect a part that we know

(Epist. l. viii.) in Calabria. "Cum in coronæ speciem frequenti circum harundineto cingatur, ac placidus maneat, ut ne moveri quidem videatur: alioqui miranda res, ut adventante homine, quasi amore hominis percitus antiquæ illius Arethusæ instar, vel sibilo, vel voce edita, et quasi jussus excitatis sponte a quis fervere incipiat, ac subcensæ ollæ instar fragorem mittat. Unde stupescas cum silenti homini sileat, ad sonitum verò vocis a somno excitatus, et quasi respondens vocanti, ad sermonem hominis immurmeret: hæc scribit. In caussis quæro, an eundem hic fons referat sonitum cæteris animantibus, ut latratum canis, hinnitum equi? nam sic esset in aquis illis eadem quæ in echo caussa, an potius credam hinc veterem Midæ representari fabulam?" (Baccius. L VI. c. xxiii. p. 344.)—ED.

of nature, which does not owe the being it has, and the excellences of it, to its neighbours; and we must not confine our thoughts within the surface of any body, but look a great deal further, to comprehend perfectly those qualities that are in it.

12. If this be so, it is not to be wondered that we have very imperfect ideas of substances, and that the real essences, on which depend their properties and operations, are unknown to us. We cannot discover so much as that size, figure, and texture of their minute and active parts, which is really in them; much less the different motions and impulses made in and upon them by bodies from without, upon which depends, and by which is formed the greatest and most remarkable part of those qualities we observe in them, and of which our complex ideas of them are made up. This consideration alone is enough to put an end to all our hopes of ever having the ideas of their real essences; which whilst we want, the nominal essences we make use of instead of them, will be able to furnish us but very sparingly with any general knowledge or universal propositions capable of real certainty.

13. *Judgment may reach further, but that is not Knowledge.*—We are not therefore to wonder, if certainty be to be found in very few general propositions made concerning substances: our knowledge of their qualities and properties goes very seldom further than our senses reach and inform us. Possibly inquisitive and observing men may, by strength of judgment, penetrate further, and, on probabilities taken from wary observation, and hints well laid together, often guess right at what experience has not yet discovered to them. But this is but guessing still; it amounts only to opinion, and has not that certainty which is requisite to knowledge. For all general knowledge lies only in our own thoughts, and consists barely in the contemplation of our own abstract ideas. Wherever we perceive any agreement or disagreement amongst them, there we have general knowledge; and by putting the names of those ideas together accordingly in propositions, can with certainty pronounce general truths. But because the abstract ideas of substances, for which their specific names stand, whenever they have any distinct and determinate signification, have a discoverable connexion or inconsistency with but a very few other ideas, the certainty

of universal propositions concerning substances is very narrow and scanty in that part, which is our principal inquiry concerning them; and there are scarce any of the names of substances, let the idea it is applied to be what it will, of which we can generally and with certainty pronounce that it has or has not this or that other quality belonging to it, and constantly co-existing or inconsistent with that idea, wherever it is to be found.

14. *What is requisite for our Knowledge of Substances.*— Before we can have any tolerable knowledge of this kind, we must first know what changes the primary qualities of one body do regularly produce in the primary qualities of another, and how. Secondly, We must know what primary qualities of any body produce certain sensations or ideas in us. This is in truth no less than to know all the effects of matter, under its divers modifications of bulk, figure, cohesion of parts, motion and rest; which, I think every body will allow, is utterly impossible to be known by us without revelation. Nor if it were revealed to us what sort of figure, bulk, and motion of corpuscles would produce in us the sensation of a yellow colour, and what sort of figure, bulk, and texture of parts in the superfices of any body were fit to give such corpuscles their due motion to produce that colour; would that be enough to make universal propositions with certainty, concerning the several sorts of them, unless we had faculties acute enough to perceive the precise bulk, figure, texture, and motion of bodies in those minute parts, by which they operate on our senses, so that we might by those frame our abstract ideas of them. I have mentioned here only corporeal substances, whose operations seem to lie more level to our understandings: for as to the operations of spirits, both their thinking and moving of bodies, we at first sight find ourselves at a loss; though perhaps, when we have applied our thoughts a little nearer to the consideration of bodies and their operations, and examined how far our notions, even in these, reach with any clearness beyond sensible matter of fact, we shall be bound to confess that, even in these too, our discoveries amount to very little beyond perfect ignorance and incapacity.

15. *Whilst our Ideas of Substances contain not their real Constitutions, we can make but few general certain Propo-*

sitions concerning them.—This is evident, the abstract complex ideas of substances, for which their general names stand, not comprehending their real constitutions, can afford us very little universal certainty. Because our ideas of them are not made up of that on which those qualities we observe in them, and would inform ourselves about, do depend, or with which they have any certain connexion: v. g., let the ideas to which we give the name man be, as it commonly is, a body of the ordinary shape, with sense, voluntary motion, and reason joined to it. This being the abstract idea, and consequently the essence of our species, man, we can make but very few general certain propositions concerning man, standing for such an idea. Because not knowing the real constitution on which sensation, power of motion, and reasoning, with that peculiar shape, depend, and whereby they are united together in the same subject, there are very few other qualities with which we can perceive them to have a necessary connexion: and therefore we cannot with certainty affirm that all men sleep by intervals, that no man can be nourished by wood or stones, that all men will be poisoned by hemlock, because these ideas have no connexion nor repugnancy with this our nominal essence of man, with this abstract idea that name stands for; we must, in these and the like, appeal to trial in particular subjects, which can reach but a little way. We must content ourselves with probability in the rest; but can have no general certainty, whilst our specific idea of man contains not that real constitution which is the root wherein all his inseparable qualities are united, and from whence they flow. Whilst our idea the word man stands for is only an imperfect collection of some sensible qualities and powers in him, there is no discernible connexion or repugnance between our specific idea, and the operation of either the parts of hemlock or stones upon his constitution. There are animals that safely eat hemlock, and others that are nourished by wood and stones: but as long as we want ideas of those real constitutions of different sorts of animals whereon these and the like qualities and powers depend, we must not hope to reach certainty in universal propositions concerning them. Those few ideas only which have a discernible connexion with our nominal essence, or any part of it, can afford us such propositions. But these are so few, and of so little moment, that we may justly look on our certain general knowledge of substances as almost none at all.

16. *Wherein lies the general Certainty of Propositions.*—To conclude : general propositions, of what kind soever, are then only capable of certainty, when the terms used in them stand for such ideas, whose agreement or disagreement, as there expressed, is capable to be discovered by us. And we are then certain of their truth or falsehood, when we perceive the ideas the terms stand for to agree or not agree, according as they are affirmed or denied one of another. Whence we may take notice, that general certainty is never to be found but in our ideas. Whenever we go to seek it elsewhere, in experiment or observations without us, our knowledge goes not beyond particulars. It is the contemplation of our own abstract ideas that alone is able to afford us general knowledge.

CHAPTER VII.

OF MAXIMS.

1. *They are self-evident.*—There are a sort of propositions, which, under the name of maxims and axioms, have passed for principles of science ; and because they are self-evident, have been supposed innate, although nobody (that I know) ever went about to show the reason and foundation of their clearness or cogency. It may, however, be worth while to inquire into the reason of their evidence, and see whether it be peculiar to them alone, and also examine how far they influence and govern our other knowledge.

2. *Wherein that Self-evidence consists.*—Knowledge, as has been shown, consists in the perception of the agreement or disagreement of ideas ; now, where that agreement or disagreement is perceived immediately by itself, without the intervention or help of any other, there our knowledge is self-evident. This will appear to be so to any who will but consider any of those propositions, which, without any proof, he assents to at first sight ; for in all of them he will find that the reason of his assent is from that agreement or disa-

greement which the mind, by an immediate comparing them, finds in those ideas answering the affirmation or negation in the proposition.

3. *Self-evidence not peculiar to received Axioms.*—This being so, in the next place, let us consider whether this self-evidence be peculiar only to those propositions which commonly pass under the name of maxims, and have the dignity of axioms allowed them. And here it is plain, that several other truths, not allowed to be axioms, partake equally with them in this self-evidence. This we shall see, if we go over these several sorts of agreement or disagreement of ideas which I have above mentioned, viz., identity, relation, co-existence, and real existence; which will discover to us, that not only those few propositions which have had the credit of maxims are self-evident, but a great many, even almost an infinite number of other propositions are such.

4. I. *As to Identity and Diversity, all Propositions are equally self-evident.*—For, First, The immediate perception of the agreement or disagreement of identity being founded in the mind's having distinct ideas, that this affords us as many self-evident propositions as we have distinct ideas. Every one that has any knowledge at all, has, as the foundation of it, various and distinct ideas: and it is the first act of the mind (without which it can never be capable of any knowledge) to know every one of its ideas by itself, and distinguish it from others. Every one finds in himself, that he knows the ideas he has; that he knows also, when any one is in his understanding, and what it is; and that when more than one are there, he knows them distinctly and unconfusedly one from another; which always being so, (it being impossible but that he should perceive what he perceives,) he can never be in doubt when any idea is in his mind, that it is there, and is that idea it is; and that two distinct ideas, when they are in his mind, are there, and are not one and the same idea. So that all such affirmations and negations are made without any possibility of doubt, uncertainty, or hesitation, and must necessarily be assented to as soon as understood; that is, as soon as we have in our minds determined ideas, which the terms in the proposition stand for. And, therefore, whenever the mind with attention considers any proposition, so as to perceive the two ideas signified by

the terms, and affirmed or denied one of the other to be the same or different; it is presently and infallibly certain of the truth of such a proposition, and this equally whether these propositions be in terms standing for more general ideas, or such as are less so; v. g., whether the general idea of being be affirmed of itself, as in this proposition, whatsoever is, is; or a more particular idea be affirmed of itself, as a man is a man; or, whatsoever is white is white; or whether the idea of being in general be denied of not being, which is the only (if I may so call it) idea different from it, as in this other proposition, it is impossible for the same thing to be and not to be; or any idea of any particular being be denied of another different from it, as a man is not a horse; red is not blue. The difference of the ideas, as soon as the terms are understood, makes the truth of the proposition presently visible, and that with an equal certainty and easiness in the less as well as the more general propositions, and all for the same reason, viz., because the mind perceives, in any ideas that it has, the same idea to be the same with itself; and two different ideas to be different, and not the same; and this it is equally certain of, whether these ideas be more or less general, abstract, and comprehensive. It is not, therefore, alone to these two general propositions, whatsoever is, is; and it is impossible for the same thing to be and not to be; that this sort of self-evidence belongs by any peculiar right. The perception of being, or not being, belongs no more to these vague ideas, signified by the terms whatsoever, and thing, than it does to any other ideas. These two general maxims, amounting to no more, in short, but this, that the same is the same, and same is not different, are truths known in more particular instances, as well as in those general maxims, and known also in particular instances, before these general maxims are ever thought on, and draw all their force from the discernment of the mind employed about particular ideas. There is nothing more visible than that the mind, without the help of any proof, or reflection on either of these general propositions, perceives so clearly, and knows so certainly, that the idea of white is the idea of white, and not the idea of blue; and that the idea of white, when it is in the mind, is there, and is not absent; that the consideration of these axioms can add nothing to the evidence or certainty of its knowledge. Just so it is (as every one may experiment in himself) in all the ideas a man has in his mind : he knows each to be itself, and not to be another ; and to be in his mind, and not away when it is there, with a certainty that cannot be greater; and, therefore, the truth of no general proposition can be known with a greater certainty, nor add anything to this. So that, in respect of identity, our intuitive knowledge reaches as far as our ideas ; and we are capable of making as many self-evident propositions, as we have names for distinct ideas. And I appeal to every one's own mind, whether this proposition, a circle is a circle, be not as self-evident a proposition as that consisting of more general terms, whatsoever is, is ; and again, whether this proposition, blue is not red, be not a proposition that the mind can no more doubt of, as soon as it understands the words, than it does of that axiom, It is impossible for the same thing to be and not to be ; and so of all the like.

5. II. *In Co-existence we have few self-evident Propositions.*—Secondly, as to co-existence, or such necessary connexion between two ideas, that, in the subject where one of them is supposed, there the other must necessarily be also : of such agreement or disagreement as this, the mind has an immediate perception but in very few of them. And, therefore, in this sort we have but very little intuitive knowledge ; nor are there to be found very many propositions that are self-evident, though some there are ; v. g., the idea of filling a place equal to the contents of its superfices, being annexed to our idea of body, I think it is a self-evident proposition, that two bodies cannot be in the same place.

6. III. *In other-Relations we may have.*—Thirdly, As to the relations of modes, mathematicians have framed many axioms concerning that one relation of equality. As, equals taken from equals, the remainder will be equal ; which, with the rest of that kind, however they are received for maxims by the mathematicians, and are unquestionable truths ; yet, I think, that any one who considers them will not find that they have a clearer self-evidence than these, that one and one are equal to two ; that if you take from the five fingers of one hand two, and from the five fingers of the other hand two, the remaining numbers will be equal. These and a thousand other such propositions may be found in

numbers, which, at the very first hearing, force the assent, and carry with them an equal, if not greater clearness, than those mathematical axioms.

7. IV. *Concerning real Existence, we have none.*—Fourthly, as to real existence, since that has no connexion with any other of our ideas, but that of ourselves, and of a first being, we have in that, concerning the real existence of all other beings, not so much as demonstrative, much less a self-evident knowledge; and, therefore, concerning those there are no maxims.

8. *These Axioms do not much influence our other Knowledge.*—In the next place let us consider, what influence these received maxims have upon the other parts of our knowledge. The rules established in the schools, that all reasonings are "Ex præcognitis et præconcessis," seem to lay the foundation of all other knowledge in these maxims, and to suppose them to be præcognita; whereby, I think, are meant these two things: first, that these axioms are those truths that are first known to the mind. And, secondly, that upon them the other parts of our knowledge depend.

9. *Because they are not the Truths we first knew.*—First. That they are not the truths first known to the mind is evident to experience, as we have shown in another place. (Book I. chap. ii.) Who perceives not that a child certainly knows that a stranger is not its mother; that its sucking-bottle is not the rod, long before he knows that it is impossible for the same thing to be and not to be? And how many truths are there about numbers, which it is obvious to observe that the mind is perfectly acquainted with, and fully convinced of, before it ever thought on these general maxims, to which mathematicians, in their arguings, do sometimes refer them? Whereof the reason is very plain: for that which makes the mind assent to such propositions, being nothing else but the perception it has of the agreement or disagreement of its ideas, according as it finds them affirmed or denied one of another, in words it understands; and every idea being known to be what it is, and every two distinct ideas being known not to be the same; it must necessarily follow, that such self-evident truths must be first known which consist of ideas that are first in the mind: and the ideas first in the mind, it is evident, are those of particular things, from whence, by slow degrees, the understand

ing proceeds to some few general ones; which being taken from the ordinary and familiar objects of sense, are settled in the mind, with general names to them. Thus particular ideas are first received and distinguished, and so knowledge got about them; and next to them, the less general or specific, which are next to particular: for abstract ideas are not so obvious or easy to children, or the yet unexercised mind, as particular ones. If they seem so to grown men, it is only because by constant and familiar use they are made so. For when we nicely reflect upon them, we shall find that general ideas are fictions and contrivances of the mind, that carry difficulty with them, and do not so easily offer themselves as we are apt to imagine. For example, does it not require some pains and skill to form the general idea of a triangle, (which is yet none of the most abstract, comprehensive, and difficult,) for it must be neither oblique nor rectangle, neither equilateral, equicrural, nor scalenon; but all and none of these at once.* In effect, it is something imperfect, that cannot exist; an idea wherein some parts of several different and inconsistent ideas are put together. It is true, the mind, in this imperfect state, has need of such ideas, and makes all the haste to them it can, for the conveniency of communication and enlargement of knowledge, to both which it is naturally very much inclined. But yet one has reason to suspect such ideas are marks of our imperfection; at least, this is enough to show that the most abstract and general ideas are not those that the mind is first and most easily acquainted with, not such as its earliest knowledge is conversant about.

10. *Because on them the other Parts of our Knowledge do not depend.*—Secondly, from what has been said it plainly follows, that these magnified maxims are not the principles

* With this idea Bishop Berkeley makes himself particularly merry. "If any man," says he, "has the faculty of framing in his mind such an idea of a triangle as is here described, it is in vain to pretend to dispute him out of it, nor would I go about it. All I desire is, that the reader would fully and certainly inform himself, whether he has such an idea or not. And this, methinks, can be no hard task for any one to perform. What more easy than for any one to look a little into his own thoughts, and there try whether he has, or can attain to have, an idea that shall correspond with the description that is here given of the general idea of a triangle, which is, *neither oblique, nor rectangle, equilateral, equicrural, nor scalenon, but all and none of these at once?*" (Intr. to Prin. of Hum. Knowl., § 13.)

and foundations of all our other knowledge. For if there be a great many other truths, which have as much self-evidence as they, and a great many that we know before them, it is impossible they should be the principles from which we deduce all other truths. Is it impossible to know that one and two are equal to three, but by virtue of this, or some such axiom, viz., the whole is equal to all its parts taken together? Many a one knows that one and two are equal to three, without having heard or thought on that or any other axiom by which it might be proved; and knows it as certainly as any other man knows, that the whole is equal to all its parts, or any other maxim, and all from the same reason of self-evidence; the equality of those ideas being as visible and certain to him without that or any other axiom as with it, it needing no proof to make it perceived. Nor after the knowledge, that the whole is equal to all its parts, does he know that one and two are equal to three, better or more certainly than he did before. For if there be any odds in those ideas, the whole and parts are more obscure, or at least more difficult to be settled in the mind than those of one, two, and three. And indeed, I think, I may ask these men, who will needs have all knowledge, besides those general principles themselves, to depend on general, innate, and self-evident principles; what principle is requisite to prove that one and one are two, that two and two are four, that three times two are six? Which being known, without any proof, do evince, that either all knowledge does not depend on certain præcognita or general maxims, called principles, or else that these are principles; and if these are to be counted principles, a great part of numeration will be so. To which, if we add all the self-evident propositions which may be made about all our distinct ideas, principles will be almost infinite, at least innumerable, which men arrive to the knowledge of, at different ages; and a great many of these innate principles they never come to know all their lives. But whether they come in view of the mind earlier or later, this is true of them, that they are all known by their native evidence, are wholly independent, receive no light, nor are capable of any proof one from another; much less the more particular from the more general, or the more simple from the more compounded; the more simple and less abstract being the most familiar, and the easier and earlier apprehended. But whichever be the clearest ideas, the evidence and certainty of all such propositions is in this, that a man sees the same idea to be the same idea, and infallibly perceives two different ideas to be different ideas. For when a man has in his understanding the ideas of one and of two, the idea of yellow, and the idea of blue, he cannot but certainly know that the idea of one is the idea of one, and not the idea of two; and that the idea of yellow is the idea of yellow, and not the idea of blue. For a man cannot confound the ideas in his mind, which he has distinct: that would be to have them confused and distinct at the same time, which is a contradiction; and to have none distinct, is to have no use of our faculties, to have no knowlege at all. And, therefore, what idea soever is affirmed of itself, or whatsoever two entire distinct ideas are denied one of another, the mind cannot but assent to such a proposition as infallibly true, as soon as it understands the terms, without hesitation or need of proof, or regarding those made in more general terms, and called maxims.

11. *What use these general Maxims have.*—What shall we then say? Are these general maxims of no use? By no means; though perhaps their use is not that which it is commonly taken to be. But since doubting in the least of what hath been by some men ascribed to these maxims may be apt to be cried out against, as overturning the foundations of all the sciences; it may be worth while to consider them with respect to other parts of our knowledge, and examine more particularly to what purposes they serve, and to what not.

1. It is evident from what has been already said, that they are of no use to prove or confirm less general self-evident propositions.

2. It is as plain that they are not, nor have been the foundations whereon any science hath been built. There is, I know, a great deal of talk propagated from scholastic men, of sciences and the maxims on which they are built; but it has been my ill-luck never to meet with any such sciences, much less any one built upon these two maxims, what is, is; and it is impossible for the same thing to be and not to be. And I would be glad to be shown where any such science, erected upon these or any other general

axioms is to be found, and should be obliged to any one who would lay before me the frame and system of any science so built on these or any such like maxims, that could not be shown to stand as firm without any consideration of them. I ask, whether these general maxims have not the same use in the study of divinity, and in theological questions, that they have in other sciences? They serve here, too, to silence wranglers, and put an end to dispute. But I think that nobody will therefore say, that the Christian religion is built upon these maxims, or that the knowledge we have of it is derived from these principles. It is from revelation we have received it, and without revelation these maxims had never been able to help us to it. When we find out an idea by whose intervention we discover the connexion of two others, this is a revelation from God to us, by the voice of reason; for we then come to know a truth that we did not know before. When God declares any truth to us, this is a revelation to us by the voice of his Spirit, and we are advanced in our knowledge. But in neither of these do we receive our light or knowledge from maxims. But in the one, the things themselves afford it, and we see the truth in them by perceiving their agreement or disagreement: in the other, God himself affords it immediately to us, and we see the truth of what he says in his unerring veracity.

3. They are not of use to help men forward in the advancement of sciences, or new discoveries of yet unknown truths. Mr. Newton, in his never enough to be admired book, has demonstrated several propositions, which are so many new truths, before unknown to the world, and are further advances in mathematical knowledge: but, for the discovery of these, it was not the general maxims, what is, is; or, the whole is bigger than a part, or the like, that helped him. These were not the clues that led him into the discovery of the truth and certainty of those propositions. Nor was it by them that he got the knowledge of those demonstrations; but by finding out intermediate ideas that showed the agreement or disagreement of the ideas, as expressed in the propositions he demonstrated. This is the greatest exercise and improvement of human understanding in the enlarging of knowledge, and advancing the

sciences; wherein they are far enough from receiving any help from the contemplation of these or the like magnified maxims. Would those who have this traditional admiration of these propositions, that they think no step can be made in knowledge without the support of an axiom, no stone laid in the building of the sciences without a general maxim, but distinguish between the method of acquiring knowledge, and of communicating—between the method of raising any science and that of teaching it to others, as far as it is advanced—they would see that those general maxims were not the foundations on which the first discoverers raised their admirable structures, nor the keys that unlocked and opened those secrets of knowledge. Though afterwards, when schools were erected, and sciences had their professors to teach what others had found out, they often made use of maxims, i. e., laid down certain propositions which were self-evident, or to be received for true; which being settled in the minds of their scholars as unquestionable verities, they on occasion made use of, to convince them of truths in particular instances that were not so familiar to their minds as those general axioms which had before been inculcated to them, and carefully settled in their minds. Though these particular instances, when well reflected on, are no less self-evident to the understanding than the general maxims brought to confirm them: and it was in those particular instances that the first discoverer found the truth, without the help of the general maxims; and so may any one else do, who with attention considers them.

To come, therefore, to the use that is made of maxims.

1. They are of use, as has been observed, in the ordinary methods of teaching sciences as far as they are advanced but of little or none in advancing them further.

2. They are of use in disputes, for the silencing of obstinate wranglers, and bringing those contests to some conclusion. Whether a need of them to that end came not in the manner following, I crave leave to inquire. The schools having made disputation the touchstone of men's abilities, and the criterion of knowledge, adjudged victory to him that kept the field: and he that had the last word was concluded to have the better of the argument, if not of the cause. But because by this means there was like to be

no decision between skilful combatants, whilst one never failed of a medius terminus to prove any proposition; and the other could as constantly, without or with a distinction, deny the major or minor; to prevent, as much as could be, running out of disputes into an endless train of syllogisms, certain general propositions—most of them, indeed, self-evident—were introduced into the schools; which being such as all men allowed and agreed in, were looked on as general measures of truth, and served instead of principles (where the disputants had not lain down any other between them) beyond which there was no going, and which must not be receded from by either side. And thus these maxims getting the name of principles, beyond which men in dispute could not retreat, were by mistake taken to be originals and sources, from whence all knowledge began, and the foundations whereon the sciences were built. Because when in their disputes they came to any of these, they stopped there, and went no further, the matter was determined. But how much this is a mistake, hath been already shown.

This method of the schools, which have been thought the fountains of knowledge, introduced, as I suppose, the like use of these maxims into a great part of conversation out of the schools, to stop the mouths of cavillers, whom any one is excused from arguing any longer with, when they deny these general self-evident principles received by all reasonable men who have once thought of them: but yet their use herein is but to put an end to wrangling. They in truth, when urged in such cases, teach nothing: that is already done by the intermediate ideas made use of in the debate, whose connexion may be seen without the help of those maxims, and so the truth known before the maxim is produced, and the argument brought to a first principle. Men would give off a wrong argument before it came to that, if in their disputes they proposed to themselves the finding and embracing of truth, and not a contest for victory. And thus maxims have their use to put a stop to their perverseness, whose ingenuity should have yielded sooner. But the method of the schools having allowed and encouraged men to oppose and resist evident truth till they are baffled, i. e., till they are reduced to contradict themselves or some established principle; it is no wonder that they should not in civil conversation be ashamed of that which in the schools is counted a virtue and a glory, obstinately to maintain that side of the question they have chosen, whether true or false, to the last extremity, even after conviction. A strange way to attain truth and knowledge, and that which I think the rational part of mankind, not corrupted by education, could scarce believe should ever be admitted amongst the lovers of truth, and students of religion or nature, or introduced into the seminaries of those who are to propagate the truths of religion or philosophy amongst the ignorant and unconvinced. How much such a way of learning is like to turn young men's minds from the sincere search and love of truth;—nay, and to make them doubt whether there is any such thing—or, at least, worth the adhering to—I shall not now inquire. This I think, that, bating those places, which brought the peripatetic philosophy into their schools, where it continued many ages, without teaching the world anything but the art of wrangling, these maxims were nowhere thought the foundations on which the sciences were built, nor the great helps to the advancement of knowledge.

As to these general maxims, therefore, they are, as I have said, of great use in disputes, to stop the mouths of wranglers; but not of much use to the discovery of unknown truths, or to help the mind forwards in its search after knowledge. For who ever began to build his knowledge on this general proposition, what is, is; or, it is impossible for the same thing to be and not to be: and from either of these, as from a principle of science, deduced a system of useful knowledge? Wrong opinions often involving contradictions, one of these maxims, as a touchstone, may serve well to show whither they lead. But yet, however fit to lay open the absurdity or mistake of a man's reasoning or opinion, they are of very little use for enlightening the understanding: and it will not be found that the mind receives much help from them in its progress in knowledge, which would be neither less, nor less certain, were these two general propositions never thought on. It is true, as I have said, they sometimes serve in argumentation to stop a wrangler's mouth, by showing the absurdity of what he saith, and by exposing him to the shame of contradicting what all the world knows, and he himself cannot but own to be true. But it is one thing to show a man that he is in an error, and another to put him in possession of truth; and I would fain know what truths these two propositions are able to teach, and by their influence make us know, which we did not know before, or could not know without them. Let us reason from them as well as we can, they are only about identical predications, and influence, if any at all, none but such. Each particular proposition concerning identity or diversity is as clearly and certainly known in itself, if attended to, as either of these general ones; only these general ones, as serving in all cases, are therefore more inculcated and insisted on. As to other less general maxims, many of them are no more than bare verbal propositions, and teach us nothing but the respect and import of names one to another. "The whole is equal to all its parts:"— what real truth, I beseech you, does it teach us? What more is contained in that maxim, than what the signification of the word totum, or the whole, does of itself import? And he that knows that the word whole stands for what is made up of all its parts, knows very little less than that the whole is equal to all its parts. And, upon the same ground, I think that this propositon, "A hill is higher than a valley," and several the like, may also pass for maxims. But yet masters of mathematics, when they would, as teachers of what they know, initiate others in that science, do not without reason place this and some other such maxims at the entrance of their systems; that their scholars, having in the beginning perfectly acquainted their thoughts with these propositions made in such general terms, may be used to make such reflections, and have these more general propositions, as formed rules and sayings, ready to apply to all particular cases. Not that if they be equally weighed, they are more clear and evident than the particular instances they are brought to confirm; but that, being more familiar to the mind, the very naming them is enough to satisfy the understanding. But this, I say, is more from our custom of using them, and the establishment they have got in our minds by our often thinking of them, than from the different evidence of the things. But before custom has settled mcthods of thinking and reasoning in our minds, I am apt to imagine it is quite otherwise; and that the child, when a part of his apple is taken away, knows it better in that particular instance, than by this general proposition, "The whole is equal to all its parts;" and that, if one of these have need to be confirmed to him by the other, the general has more need to be let into his mind by the particular, than the particular by the general. For, in particulars, our knowledge begins, and so spreads itself, by degrees, to generals. Though afterwards the mind takes the quite contrary course, and having drawn its knowledge into as general propositions as it can, makes those familiar to its thoughts, and accustoms itself to have recourse to them, as to the standards of truth and falsehood. By which familiar use of them—as rules to measure the truth of other propositions—it comes in time to be thought, that more particular propositions have their truth and evidence from their conformity to these more general ones, which in discourse and argumentation are so frequently urged, and constantly admitted. And this I think to be the reason why amongst so many self-evident propositions, the most general only have had the title of maxims.

12. *Maxims, if Care be not taken in the Use of Words, may prove Contradictions.*—One thing further, I think, it may not be amiss to observe concerning these general maxims, that they are so far from improving or establishing our minds in true knowledge, that if our notions be wrong, loose, or unsteady, and we resign up our thoughts to the sound of words, rather than fix them on settled, determined ideas of things; I say, these general maxims will serve to confirm us in mistakes; and in such a way of use of words, which is most common, will serve to prove contradictions: v. g., he that with Descartes shall frame in his mind an idea of what he calls body to be nothing but extension,* may easily demonstrate that there is no vacuum, i. e., no space void of body, by this maxim, "What is, is." For the idea to which he annexes the name body, being bare extension, his knowledge that space cannot be without body, is certain. For he knows his own idea of extension clearly and distinctly, and knows that it is what it is, and not another idea, though it

---

* See note, Book II. ch xiii. p. 288.—Ed.

be called by these three names: extension, body, space. Which three words, standing for one and the same idea, may, no doubt, with the same evidence and certainty be affirmed one of another, as each of itself: and it is as certain, that, whilst I use them all to stand for one and the same idea, this predication is as true and identical in its signification, that space is body, as this predication is true and identical, that body is body, both in signification and sound.

13. *Instance in Vacuum.*—But if another should come and make to himself another idea, different from Descartes's, of the thing, which yet with Descartes he calls by the same name body, and make his idea, which he expresses by the word body, to be of a thing that hath both extension and solidity together; he will as easily demonstrate, that there may be a vacuum or space without a body, as Descartes demonstrated the contrary; because the idea to which he gives the name space being barely the simple one of extension, and the idea to which he gives the name body being the complex idea of extension and resistibility or solidity, together in the same subject, these two ideas are not exactly one and the same, but in the understanding as distinct as the ideas of one and two, white and black, or as of corporeity and humanity, if I may use those barbarous terms; and therefore the predication of them in our minds, or in words standing for them, is not identical, but the negation of them one of another; viz., this proposition: Extension or space is not body, is as true and evidently certain as this maxim, It is impossible for the same thing to be and not to be, can make any proposition.

14. *They prove not the Existence of Things without us.*—But yet, though both these propositions (as you see) may be equally demonstrated, viz., that there may be a vacuum, and that there cannot be a vacuum, by these two certain principles, viz., what is, is ; and the same thing cannot be and not be: yet neither of these principles will serve to prove to us, that any or what bodies do exist; for that we are left to our senses to discover to us as far as they can. Those universal and self-evident principles being only our constant, clear, and distinct knowledge of our own ideas, more general or comprehensive, can assure us of nothing that passes without the mind: their certainty is founded only upon the

knowledge we have of each idea by itself, and of its distinction from others; about which we cannot be mistaken whilst they are in our minds, though we may be and often are mistaken when we retain the names without the ideas; or use them confusedly, sometimes for one and sometimes for another idea. In which cases the force of these axioms, reaching only to the sound, and not the signification of the words, serves only to lead us into confusion, mistake, and error. It is to show men that these maxims, however cried up for the great guards of truth, will not secure them from error in a careless, loose use of their words, that I have made this remark. In all that is here suggested concerning their little use for the improvement of knowledge, or dangerous use in undetermined ideas, I have been far enough from saying or intending they should be laid aside, as some have been too forward to charge me. I affirm them to be truths, self-evident truths, and so cannot be laid aside. As far as their influence will reach, it is in vain to endeavour, nor will I attempt to abridge it. But yet, without any injury to truth or knowledge, I may have reason to think their use is not answerable to the great stress which seems to be laid on them; and I may warn men not to make an ill use of them, for the confirming themselves in errors.

15. *Their Application dangerous about complex Ideas.*— But let them be of what use they will in verbal propositions, they cannot discover or prove to us the least knowledge of the nature of substances, as they are found and exist without us, any further than grounded on experience. And though the consequence of these two propositions, called principles, be very clear, and their use not dangerous or hurtful, in the probation of such things, wherein there is no need at all of them for proof, but such as are clear by themselves without them, viz., where our ideas are determined, and known by the names that stand for them: yet when these principles, viz., what is, is, and it is impossible for the same thing to be and not to be, are made use of in the probation of propositions, wherein are words standing for complex ideas; v. g., man, horse, gold, virtue; there they are of infinite danger, and most commonly make men receive and retain falsehood for manifest truth, and uncertainty for demon-

stration; upon which follow error, obstinacy, and all the mischiefs that can happen from wrong reasoning. The reason whereof is not that these principles are less true, or of less force in proving propositions made of terms standing for complex ideas, than where the propositions are about simple ideas. But because men mistake generally, thinking that where the same terms are preserved, the propositions are about the same things, though the ideas they stand for are in truth different; therefore these maxims are made use of to support those which in sound and appearance are contradictory propositions; as is clear in the demonstrations above-mentioned about a vacuum: so that whilst men take words for things, as usually they do, these maxims may and do commonly serve to prove contradictory propositions; as shall yet be further made manifest.

16. *Instance in Man.*—For instance, let man be that concerning which you would by these first principles demonstrate anything, and we shall see, that so far as demonstration is by these principles, it is only verbal, and gives us no certain, universal, true proposition or knowledge of any being existing without us. First, a child having framed the idea of a man, it is probable that his idea is just like that picture which the painter makes of the visible appearances joined together; and such a complication of ideas together in his understanding, makes up the single complex idea which he calls man, whereof white or flesh-colour in England being one, the child can demonstrate to you that a negro is not a man, because white colour was one of the constant simple ideas of the complex idea he calls man; and therefore he can demonstrate by the principle, it is impossible for the same thing to be and not to be, that a negro is not a man; the foundation of his certainty being not that universal proposition, which perhaps he never heard nor thought of, but the clear, distinct perception he hath of his own simple ideas of black and white, which he cannot be persuaded to take, nor can ever mistake one for another, whether he knows that maxim or no: and to this child,- or any one who hath such an idea, which he calls man, can you never demonstrate that a man hath a soul, because his idea of man includes no such notion or idea in it; and therefore, to him, the principle of what is, is, proves not this matter, but it depends upon

collection and observation, by which he is to make his complex idea called man.

17. Secondly, Another that hath gone further in framing and collecting the idea he calls man, and to the outward shape adds laughter and rational discourse, may demonstrate that infants and changelings are no men: by this maxim, it is impossible for the same thing to be and not to be; and I have discoursed with very rational men, who have actually denied that they are men.

18. Thirdly, Perhaps another makes up the complex idea which he calls man, only out of the ideas of body in general, and the powers of language and reason, and leaves out the shape wholly; this man is able to demonstrate that a man may have no hands, but be quadrupes, neither of those being included in his idea of man: and in whatever body or shape he found speech and reason joined, that was a man; because, having a clear knowledge of such a complex idea, it is certain that what is, is.

19. *Little Use of these Maxims in Proofs where we have clear and distinct Ideas.*—So that, if rightly considered, I think we may say, that where our ideas are determined in our minds, and have annexed to them by us known and steady names under those settled determinations, there is little need, or no use at all of these maxims, to prove the agreement or disagreement of any of them. He that cannot discern the truth or falsehood of such propositions without the help of these and the like maxims, will not be helped by these maxims to do it; since he cannot be supposed to know the truth of these maxims themselves without proof, if he cannot know the truth of others without proof, which are as self-evident as these. Upon this ground it is, that intuitive knowledge neither requires nor admits any proof, one part of it more than another. He that will suppose it does, takes away the foundation of all knowledge and certainty; and he that needs any proof to make him certain, and give his assent to this proposition, that two are equal to two, will also have need of a proof to make him admit, that what is, is. He that needs a probation to convince him that two are not three, that white is not black, that a triangle is not a circle, &c., or any other two determined, distinct ideas are not one and the same, will need also a demonstration to

convince him that it is impossible for the same thing to be and not to be.

20. *Their Use dangerous, where our Ideas are confused.*—And as these maxims are of little use where we have determined ideas, so they are, as I have showed, of dangerous use where our ideas are not determined; and where we use words that are not annexed to determined ideas, but such as are of a loose and wandering signification, sometimes standing for one, and sometimes for another idea; from which follow mistake and error, which these maxims (brought as proofs to establish propositions, wherein the terms stand for undetermined ideas) do by their authority confirm and rivet.

CHAPTER VIII.

OF TRIFLING PROPOSITIONS.

1. *Some Propositions bring no Increase to our Knowledge.*—Whether the maxims treated of in the foregoing chapter be of that use to real knowledge as is generally supposed, I leave to be considered. This, I think, may confidently be affirmed, that there are universal propositions, which, though they be certainly true, yet they add no light to our understandings, bring no increase to our knowledge. Such are—

2. *As, First, identical Propositions.*—First, All purely identical propositions. These obviously and at first blush appear to contain no instruction in them; for when we affirm the said term of itself, whether it be barely verbal, or whether it contains any clear and real idea, it shows us nothing but what we must certainly know before, whether such a proposition be either made by or proposed to us. Indeed, that most general one, what is, is, may serve sometimes to show a man the absurdity he is guilty of, when, by circumlocution or equivocal terms, he would in particular instances deny the same thing of itself; because nobody will so openly bid defiance to common sense, as to affirm visible and direct contradictions in plain words; or, if he does, a man is excused if he breaks off any further discourse with him. But yet I think I may say, that neither that received maxim, nor any other identical proposition, teaches us any-

thing; and though in such kind of propositions this great and magnified maxim, boasted to be the foundation of demonstration, may be and often is made use of to confirm them, yet all it proves amounts to no more than this, that the same word may with great certainty be affirmed of itself, without any doubt of the truth of any such proposition; and let me add, also, without any real knowledge.

3. For at this rate, any very ignorant person, who can but make a proposition, and knows what he means when he says ay or no, may make a million of propositions of whose truth he may be infallibly certain, and yet not know one thing in the world thereby; v. g., what is a soul, is a soul; or, a soul is a soul; a spirit is a spirit; a fetiche is a fetiche, &c.* These all being equivalent to this proposition, viz., what is, is; i. e., what hath existence, hath existence, or, who hath a soul, hath a soul. What is this more than trifling with words? It is but like a monkey shifting his oyster from one hand to the other; and had he but words, might no doubt have said, "Oyster in right hand is subject, and oyster in left hand is predicate:" and so might have made a self-evident proposition of oyster, i. e., oyster is oyster; and yet, with all this, not have been one whit the wiser or more knowing: and that way of handling the matter would much at one have satisfied the monkey's hunger, or a man's understanding, and they would have improved in knowledge and bulk together.

I know there are some who, because identical propositions are self-evident, show a great concern for them, and think they do great service to philosophy by crying them up, as if in them was contained all knowledge, and the understanding were led into all truth by them only; I grant as forwardly as any one, that they are all true and self-evident. I

---

* The objects of worship among the people of Guinea, and the interior of Africa generally, except where the Mahommedan religion prevails, are denominated Fetishes, and consist of the first objects which, on issuing forth from their huts, they behold in the morning. Sometimes a permanent worship appears to be paid to particular animals, as the ox, the goat, with several kinds of birds. Rocks, too, lakes, trees, and fountains, share the indiscriminate adoration of those superstitious races. See Barbot's Travels in Nigritia, book i. c. 8; b. xi. c. 2—6. Cressyos conjectures, with much probability, that the animal worship of the Egyptians was of African origin, and derived from Fetishism. (Rel. de l'Antiquité, l. i. p. 500.)—ED.

grant further, that the foundation of all our knowledge lies in the faculty we have of perceiving the same idea to be the same, and of discerning it from those that are different, as I have shown in the foregoing chapter. But how that vindicates the making use of identical propositions, for the improvement of knowledge, from the imputation of trifling, I do not see. Let any one repeat, as often as he pleases, that the will is the will, or lay what stress on it he thinks fit; of what use is this, and an infinite the like propositions, for the enlarging our knowledge? Let a man abound, as much as the plenty of words which he has will permit, in such propositions as these: a law is a law, and obligation is obligation; right is right, and wrong is wrong; will these and the like ever help him to an acquaintance with ethics, or instruct him or others in the knowledge of morality? Those who know not, nor perhaps ever will know, what is right and what is wrong, nor the measures of them, can with as much assurance make, and infallibly know the truth of these and all such propositions, as he that is best instructed in morality can do. But what advance do such propositions give in the knowledge of anything necessary or useful for their conduct?

He would be thought to do little less than trifle, who, for the enlightening the understanding in any part of knowledge, should be busy with identical propositions, and insist on such maxims as these: substance is substance, and body is body; a vacuum is a vacuum, and a vortex is a vortex; a centaur is a centaur, and a chimera is a chimera, &c. For these and all such are equally true, equally certain, and equally self-evident. But yet they cannot but be counted trifling, when made use of as principles of instruction, and stress laid on them as helps to knowledge; since they teach nothing but what every one who is capable of discourse knows without being told, viz., that the same term is the same term, and the same idea the same idea. And upon this account it was that I formerly did and do still think the offering and inculcating such propositions, in order to give the understanding any new light or inlet into the knowledge of things, no better than trifling.

Instruction lies in something very different; and he that would enlarge his own or another's mind to truths he does not yet know, must find out intermediate ideas, and then lay them in such order one by another, that the understanding may see the agreement or disagreement of those in question. Propositions that do this are instructive; but they are far from such as affirm the same term of itself; which is no way to advance one's self or others in any sort of knowledge. It no more helps to that, than it would help any one in his learning to read, to have such propositions as these inculcated to him. An A is an A, and a B is a B; which a man may know as well as any schoolmaster, and yet never be able to read a word as long as he lives. Nor do these or any such identical propositions help him one jot forwards in the skill of reading, let him make what use of them he can.

If those who blame my calling them trifling propositions had but read and been at the pains to understand what I have above writ in very plain English, they could not but have seen that by identical propositions I mean only such, wherein the same term, importing the same idea, is affirmed of itself; which I take to be the proper signification of identical propositions: and concerning all such, I think I may continue safely to say, that to propose them as instructive is no better than trifling. For no one who has the use of reason can miss them, where it is necessary they should be taken notice of; nor doubt of their truth when he does take notice of them.

But if men will call propositions identical, wherein the same term is not affirmed of itself, whether they speak more properly than I, others must judge: this is certain, all that they say of propositions that are not identical in my sense, concerns not me nor what I have said; all that I have said relating to those propositions wherein the same term is affirmed of itself: and I would fain see an instance wherein any such can be made use of, to the advantage and improvement of any one's knowledge. Instances of other kinds, whatever use may be made of them, concern not me, as not being such as I call identical.

4. *Secondly, When a Part of any complex Idea is predicated of the Whole.*—II. Another sort of trifling propositions is, when a part of the complex idea is predicated of the name of the whole; a part of the definition of the word defined. Such are all propositions wherein the genus is predicated of

the species, or more comprehensive of less comprehensive terms; for what information, what knowledge carries this proposition in it, viz., Lead is a metal to a man who knows the complex idea the name lead stands for? all the simple ideas that go to the complex one signified by the term metal, being nothing but what he before comprehended and signified by the name lead. Indeed, to a man that knows the signification of the word metal, and not of the word lead, it is a shorter way to explain the signification of the word lead, by saying it is a metal, which at once expresses several of its simple ideas, than to enumerate them one by one, telling him it is a body very heavy, fusible, and malleable.

5. *As Part of the Definition of the Term defined.*—Alike trifling it is to predicate any other part of the definition of the term defined, or to affirm any one of the simple ideas of a complex one of the name of the whole complex idea; as, All gold is fusible. For fusibility being one of the simple ideas that goes to the making up the complex one the sound gold stands for, what can it be but playing with sounds, to affirm that of the name gold, which is comprehended in its received signification? It would be thought little better than ridiculous to affirm gravely, as a truth of moment, that gold is yellow; and I see not how it is any jot more material to say it is fusible, unless that quality be left out of the complex idea, of which the sound gold is the mark in ordinary speech. What instruction can it carry with it, to tell one that which he hath been told already, or he is supposed to know before? For I am supposed to know the signification of the word another uses to me, or else he is to tell me. And if I know that the name gold stands for this complex idea of body, yellow, heavy, fusible, malleable, it will not much instruct me to put it solemnly afterwards in a proposition, and gravely say, all gold is fusible. Such propositions can only serve to show the disingenuity of one who will go from the definition of his own terms, by reminding him sometimes of it; but carry no knowledge with them, but of the signification of words, however certain they be.

6. *Instance, Man and Palfrey.*—Every man is an animal, or living body, is as certain a proposition as can be; but no more conducing to the knowledge of things, than to say, a

palfrey is an ambling horse, or a neighing, ambling animal, both being only about the signification of words, and make me know but this: that body, sense, and motion, or power of sensation and moving, are three of those ideas that I always comprehend and signify by the word man: and where they are not to be found together, the name man belongs not to that thing: and so of the other, that body, sense, and a certain way of going, with a certain kind of voice, are some of those ideas which I always comprehend, and signify by the word palfrey; and when they are not to be found together, the name palfrey belongs not to that thing. It is just the same, and to the same purpose, when any term standing for any one or more of the simple ideas, that altogether make up that complex idea which is called man, is affirmed of the term man: v. g., suppose a Roman signified by the word homo all these distinct ideas united in one subject, " corporietas, sensibilitas, potentia se movendi rationalitas, risibilitas;" he might, no doubt, with great certainty, universally affirm one, more, or all of these together of the word homo, but did no more than say that the word homo, in his country, comprehended in its signification all these ideas. Much like a romance knight, who by the word palfrey signified these ideas: body of a certain figure, four-legged, with sense, motion, ambling, neighing, white, used to have a woman on his back, might with the same certainty universally affirm also any or all of these of the word palfrey: but did thereby teach no more, but that the word palfrey, in his or romance language, stood for all these, and was not to be applied to anything where any of these was wanting. But he that shall tell me, that in whatever thing sense, motion, reason, and laughter, were united, that thing had actually a notion of God, or would be cast into a sleep by opium, made indeed an instructive proposition; because neither having the notion of God, nor being cast into sleep by opium, being contained in the idea signified by the word man, we are by such propositions taught something more than barely what the word man stands for, and therefore the knowledge contained in it is more than verbal.

7. *For this teaches but the Signification of Words.*—Before a man makes any proposition, he is supposed to understand the terms he uses in it, or else he talks like a parrot, only

making a noise by imitation, and framing certain sounds, which he has learnt of others; but not as a rational creature, using them for signs of ideas which he has in his mind. The hearer also is supposed to understand the terms as the speaker uses them, or else he talks jargon, and makes an unintelligible noise. And therefore he trifles with words, who makes such a proposition, which, when it is made, contains no more than one of the terms does, and which a man was supposed to know before; v. g., a triangle hath three sides, or saffron is yellow. And this is no further tolerable, than where a man goes to explain his terms to one who is supposed or declares himself not to understand him; and then it teaches only the signification of that word, and the use of that sign.

8. *But no real Knowledge.*—We can know then the truth of two sorts of propositions with perfect certainty: the one is, of those trifling propositions which have a certainty in them, but it is only a verbal certainty, but not instructive. And, secondly, we can know the truth, and so may be certain in propositions, which affirm something of another, which is a necessary consequence of its precise complex idea, but not contained in it: as that the external angle of all triangles is bigger than either of the opposite internal angles; which relation of the outward angle to either of the opposite internal angles, making no part of the complex idea signified by the name triangle, this is a real truth, and conveys with it instructive real knowledge.

9. *General Propositions concerning Substances are often trifling.*—We having little or no knowledge of what combinations there be of simple ideas existing together in substances, but by our senses, we cannot make any universal certain propositions concerning them, any further than our nominal essences lead us; which being to a very few and inconsiderable truths, in respect of those which depend on their real constitutions, the general propositions that are made about substances, if they are certain, are for the most part but trifling; and if they are instructive, are uncertain, and such as we can have no knowledge of their real truth, how much soever constant observation and analogy may assist our judgment in guessing. Hence it comes to pass, that one may often meet with very clear and coherent discourses, that

amount yet to nothing. For it is plain, that names of substantial beings, as well as others, as far as they have relative significations affixed to them, may, with great truth, be joined negatively and affirmatively in propositions, as their relative definitions make them fit to be so joined; and propositions consisting of such terms, may, with the same clearness, be deduced one from another, as those that convey the most real truths; and all this without any knowledge of the nature or reality of things existing without us. By this method one may make demonstrations and undoubted propositions in words, and yet thereby advance not one jot in the knowledge of the truth of things; v. g., he that having learnt these following words, with their ordinary mutual relative acceptations annexed to them; v. g. substance, man, animal, form, soul, vegetative, sensitive, rational, may make several undoubted propositions about the soul, without knowing at all what the soul really is: and of this sort, a man may find an infinite number of propositions, reasonings, and conclusions, in books of metaphysics, school-divinity, and some sort of natural philosophy; and, after all, know as little of God, spirits, or bodies, as he did before he set out.

10. *And why.*—He that hath liberty to define, i. e., to determine the signification of his names of substances (as certainly every one does in effect, who makes them stand for his own ideas,) and makes their significations at a venture, taking them from his own or other men's fancies, and not from an examination or inquiry into the nature of things themselves; may with little trouble demonstrate them one of another, according to those several respects and mutual relations he has given them one to another; wherein, however things agree or disagree in their own nature, he needs mind nothing but his own notions, with the names he hath bestowed upon them; but thereby no more increases his own knowledge than he does his riches, who, taking a bag of counters, calls one in a certain place a pound, another in another place a shilling, and a third in a third place a penny; and so proceeding, may undoubtedly reckon right, and cast up a great sum, according to his counters so placed, and standing for. more or less as he pleases, without being one jot the richer, or without even knowing how much a pound, shilling, or penny is, but only that one is contained in the

other twenty times, and contains the other twelve: which a man may also do in the signification of words, by making them, in respect of one another, more or less, or equally comprehensive.

11. *Thirdly, Using Words variously is trifling with them.*——Though yet concerning most words used in discourses, equally argumentative and controversial, there is this more to be complained of, which is the worst sort of trifling, and which sets us yet further from the certainty of knowledge we hope to attain by them, or find in them; viz., that most writers are so far from instructing us in the nature and knowledge of things, that they use their words loosely and uncertainly, and do not, by using them constantly and steadily in the same significations, make plain and clear deductions of words one from another, and make their discourses coherent and clear, (how little soever they were instructive,) which were not difficult to do, did they not find it convenient to shelter their ignorance or obstinacy under the obscurity and perplexedness of their terms: to which, perhaps, inadvertency and ill custom do in many men much contribute.

12. *Marks of verbal Propositions.*—To conclude: Barely verbal propositions may be known by these following marks:

Predication in Abstract.—I. All propositions, wherein two abstract terms are affirmed one of another, are barely about the signification of sounds. For since no abstract idea can be the same with any other but itself, when its abstract name is affirmed of any other term, it can signify no more but this: that it may or ought to be called by that name, or that these two names signify the same idea. Thus, should any one say that parsimony is frugality, that gratitude is justice, that this or that action is or is not temperate; however specious these and the like propositions may at first sight seem, yet when we come to press them, and examine nicely what they contain, we shall find that it all amounts to nothing but the signification of those terms.

13. *Secondly, A Part of the Definition predicated of any Term.*—II. All propositions wherein a part of the complex idea which any term stands for is predicated of that term, are only verbal; v. g., to say that gold is a metal, or heavy

And thus all propositions wherein more comprehensive words, called genera, are affirmed of subordinate or less comprehensive, called species, or individuals, are barely verbal.

When by these two rules we have examined the propositions that make up the discourses we ordinarily meet with both in and out of books, we shall perhaps find that a greater part of them than is usually suspected are purely about the signification of words, and contain nothing in them but the use and application of these signs.

This I think I may lay down for an infallible rule, that, wherever the distinct idea any word stands for is not known and considered, and something not contained in the idea is not affirmed or denied of it; there our thoughts stick wholly in sounds, and are able to attain no real truth or falsehood. This, perhaps, if well heeded, might save us a great deal of useless amusement and dispute, and very much shorten our trouble and wandering in the search of real and true knowledge.

CHAPTER IX.

OF OUR KNOWLEDGE OF EXISTENCE.

1. *General certain Propositions concern not Existence.*—Hitherto we have only considered the essences of things, which being only abstract ideas, and thereby removed in our thoughts from particular existence, (that being the proper operation of the mind, in abstraction, to consider an idea under no other existence but what it has in the understanding,) gives us no knowledge of real existence at all. Where, by the way, we may take notice that universal propositions, of whose truth or falsehood we can have certain knowledge, concern not existence; and further, that all particular affirmations or negations that would not be certain if they were made general, are only concerning existence; they declaring only the accidental union or separation of ideas in things existing, which, in their abstract natures, have no known necessary union or repugnancy.

2. *A threefold Knowledge of Existence.*—But, leaving the nature of propositions and different ways of predication to be

considered more at large in another place, let us proceed now to inquire concerning our knowledge of the existence of things, and how we come by it. I say, then, that we have the knowledge of our own existence by intuition; of the existence of God by demonstration; and of other things by sensation.

3. *Our Knowledge of our own Existence is Intuitive.*—As for our own existence, we perceive it so plainly and so certainly, that it neither needs nor is capable of any proof. For nothing can be more evident to us than our own existence: I think, I reason, I feel pleasure and pain: can any of these be more evident to me than my own existence? If I doubt of all other things, that very doubt makes me perceive my own existence, and will not suffer me to doubt of that. For if I know I feel pain, it is evident I have as certain perception of my own existence, as of the existence of the pain I feel: or if I know I doubt, I have as certain perception of the existence of the thing doubting, as of that thought which I call doubt. Experience then convinces us that we have an intuitive knowledge of our own existence, and an internal infallible perception that we are. In every act of sensation, reasoning, or thinking, we are conscious to ourselves of our own being; and, in this matter, come not short of the highest degree of certainty.

CHAPTER X.

OF OUR KNOWLEDGE OF THE EXISTENCE OF A GOD.

1. *We are capable of knowing certainly that there is a God.*—Though God has given us no innate ideas of himself; though he has stamped no original characters on our minds, wherein we may read his being; yet having furnished us with those faculties our minds are endowed with, he hath not left himself without witness: since we have sense, perception, and reason, and cannot want a clear proof of him, as long as we carry ourselves about us. Nor can we justly complain of our ignorance in this great point, since he has so plentifully provided us with the means to discover and know him, so far as is necessary to the end of our being, and the great concernment of our happiness. But though this be

the most obvious truth that reason discovers, and though its evidence be (if I mistake not) equal to mathematical certainty; yet it requires thought and attention, and the mind must apply itself to a regular deduction of it from some part of our intuitive knowledge, or else we shall be as uncertain and ignorant of this as of other propositions, which are in themselves capable of clear demonstration. To show, therefore, that we are capable of knowing, i. e., being certain that there is a God, and how we may come by this certainty, I think we need go no further than ourselves, and that undoubted knowledge we have of our own existence.

2. *Man knows that he himself is.*—I think it is beyond question, that man has a clear idea of his own being; he knows certainly he exists, and that he is something. He that can doubt whether he be anything or no, I speak not to; no more than I would argue with pure nothing, or endeavour to convince nonentity that it were something. If any one pretends to be so sceptical as to deny his own existence, (for really to doubt of it is manifestly impossible,) let him for me enjoy his beloved happiness of being nothing, until hunger or some other pain convince him of the contrary. This, then, I think I may take for a truth, which every one's certain knowledge assures him of, beyond the liberty of doubting, viz., that he is something that actually exists.

3. *He knows also that Nothing cannot produce a Being, therefore Something eternal.*—In the next place, man knows by an intuitive certainty, that bare nothing can no more produce any real being, than it can be equal to two right angles. If a man knows not that nonentity, or the absence of all being, cannot be equal to two right angles, it is impossible he should know any demonstration in Euclid. If, therefore, we know there is some real being, and that nonentity cannot produce any real being, it is an evident demonstration, that from eternity there has been something; since what was not from eternity had a beginning; and what had a beginning must be produced by something else.

4. *That eternal Being must be most powerful.*—Next, it is evident, that what had its being and beginning from another, must also have all that which is in and belongs to its being from another too. All the powers it has must be owing to and received from the same source. This eternal source, then,

of all being, must also be the source and original of all power; and so this eternal being must be also the most powerful.

5. *And most knowing.*—Again, a man finds in himself perception and knowledge. We have then got one step further; and we are certain now that there is not only some being, but some knowing, intelligent being in the world. There was a time, then, when there was no knowing being, and when knowledge began to be; or else there has been also a knowing being from eternity. If it be said, there was a time when no being had any knowledge, when that eternal being was void of all understanding; I reply, that, then it was impossible there should ever have been any knowledge; it being as impossible that things wholly void of knowledge, and operating blindly, and without any perception, should produce a knowing being, as it is impossible that a triangle should make itself three angles bigger than two right ones. For it is as repugnant to the idea of senseless matter, that it should put into itself sense, perception, and knowledge, as it is repugnant to the idea of a triangle, that it should put into itself greater angles than two right ones.

6. *And therefore God.*—Thus, from the consideration of ourselves, and what we infallibly find in our own constitutions, our reason leads us to the knowledge of this certain and evident truth, that there is an eternal, most powerful, and most knowing being, which whether any one will please to call God, it matters not; the thing is evident, and from this idea duly considered, will easily be deduced all those other attributes, which we ought to ascribe to this eternal being. If, nevertheless, any one should be found so senselessly arrogant, as to suppose man alone knowing and wise, but yet the product of mere ignorance and chance; and that all the rest of the universe acted only by that blind haphazard; I shall leave with him that very rational and emphatical rebuke of Tully, (l. ii. De Leg.) to be considered at his leisure: "What can be more sillily arrogant and misbecoming, than for a man to think that he has a mind and understanding in him, but yet in all the universe beside there is no such thing? Or that those things, which with the utmost stretch of his reason he can scarce comprehend, should be moved and managed without any reason at all?" " Quid est enim verius, quam neminem esse oportere tam stulte arrogantem,

ut in se mentem et rationem putet inesse, in cœlo mundoque non putet? Aut ea quæ vix summa ingenii ratione comprehendat, nulla ratione moveri putet?"

From what has been said, it is plain to me we have a more certain knowledge of the existence of a God, than of anything our senses have not immediately discovered to us. Nay, I presume I may say, that we more certainly know that there is a God, than that there is anything else without us. When I say we know, I mean there is such a knowledge within our reach which we cannot miss, if we will but apply our minds to that, as we do to several other inquiries.*

7. *Our idea of a most perfect Being, not the sole Proof of a God.*—How far the idea of a most perfect being, which a man may frame in his mind, does or does not prove the existence of a God, I will not here examine. For in the different make of men's tempers and application of their thoughts, some arguments prevail more on one, and some on another, for the confirmation of the same truth. But yet, I think, this I may say, that it is an ill way of establishing this

* Nor is there need of very great application, since there appears in reality to be no nation upon the surface of the earth which has not rendered itself master of this knowledge. Travellers, I know, have sometimes formed a different opinion; but their rash, hasty, and almost random conclusions, are, in matters of this kind, worthy of little credit. Thus we find Le Vaillant, a writer of great talent and curious observation, contradicting himself flatly upon this point; first affirming that the Kabobiquois are the only African nation known to him, who believed in the existence of a God; whereas he, in another place, relates that the Caffres not only believed in God, but in the immortality of the soul). "De toutes les nations Africaines, calle-ci (des Kabobiquois) est la seule chez laquelle j'aie trouvé quelque ideé confuse d'un Dieu. J'ignore si c'est à ses seules réflexions ou à ces communications avec d'autres peuples, qu'elle doit cette connaissance sublime, qui seule la rapprocherait des nations policées, mais elle croit (autant que j'ai pu m'en assurer par mes gens) qu'au dessous des astres il existe un être puissant lequel a fait et gouverne toutes choses. Au reste, je dois à la vérité d'ajouter ici que ce n'est là pour elle qu'une idée vague, stérile et sans suite; qu'elle ne soupçonne ne l'existence de l'ame ni par consequent les peines et les récompenses d'une autre vie." (l. viii. p. 95 et seq.) When writing this, however, he had clearly forgotten what he elsewhere says of the Caffres:—"Ces peuples ont une très-haute idée de l'auteur des êtres et de sa puissance; ils croient à une autre vie, à la punition des méchans, à la récompense des bons, mais ils n'ont point d'idée de la création; ils pensent que le monde a toujours existé, qu'il sera toujours ce qu'il est." (L. iv. p. 40.)

truth, and silencing atheists, to lay the whole stress of so important a point as this upon that sole foundation; and take some men's having that idea of God in their minds, (for it is evident some men have none, and some worse than none, and the most very different,) for the only proof of a Deity: and out of an over fondness of that darling invention, cashier, or at least endeavour to invalidate all other arguments, and forbid us to hearken to those proofs, as being weak or fallacious, which our own existence and the sensible parts of the universe offer so clearly and cogently to our thoughts, that I deem it impossible for a considering man to withstand them. For I judge it as certain and clear a truth as can anywhere be delivered, that the invisible things of God are clearly seen from the creation of the world, being understood by the things that are made, even his eternal power and Godhead. Though our own being furnishes us, as I have shown, with an evident and incontestible proof of a Deity; and I believe nobody can avoid the cogency of it, who will but as carefully attend to it, as to any other demonstration of so many parts: yet this being so fundamental a truth, and of that consequence, that all religion and genuine morality depend thereon, I doubt not but I shall be forgiven by my reader if I go over some parts of this argument again, and enlarge a little more upon them.

8. *Something from Eternity.*—There is no truth more evident than that something must be from eternity. I never yet heard of any one so unreasonable, or that could suppose so manifest a contradiction, as a time wherein there was perfectly nothing; this being of all absurdities the greatest, to imagine that pure nothing, the perfect negation and absence of all beings, should ever produce any real existence.*

---

* The nature of the arguments by which Hobbes conceived the existence of a Deity to be proved, though briefly delivered, and perhaps somewhat imperfectly stated, are yet upon the whole similar to those now put forward by Locke. "Forasmuch," he says, "as God Almighty is incomprehensible, it followeth, that we can have no conception or image of the Deity: and, consequently, all his attributes signify our inability and defect of power to conceive anything concerning his nature, and not any conception of the same, excepting only this, that there is a God. For the effects we acknowledge naturally, do exclude a power of their producing, before they were produced; and that power presupposeth something existent that hath such a power: and the thing so existing with power to produce, if it were not eternal, must needs have been pro-

It being, then, unavoidable for all rational creatures to conclude, that something has existed from eternity; let us next see what kind of thing that must be.

duced by somewhat before it, and that again by something else before that, till we come to an eternal (that is to say the first) Power of all powers, and first Cause of all causes: and this it is which all men conceive by the name of God, implying eternity, incomprehensibility, and omnipotency. And thus all that will consider may know that God is, though not *what* he is: even a man born blind, though it be not possible for him to have any imagination what kind of thing fire is, yet he cannot but know that something there is that men call fire, because it warmeth him." (Hum. Nat. c. xi. § 2.) The ancient Egyptians sought to express their opinion of the unsearchable nature of God by an extraordinary hieroglyphic:—" A lion wiping out with his tail the impressions his feet had made on the sand, was the emblem of the Demiourgos, or supreme architect, covering over the marks of his divinity by the works of nature, and hiding his immediate power by the visible agony of inferior beings." (Galtruchio.) It has nevertheless been doubted whether the Egyptians believed in one supreme God; and many distinguished scholars are found ranged on both sides of the question. The writers of greatest authority, however, are of opinion that originally the Egyptians, like the Hindoos, believed in the existence of one supreme divinity, from which pure faith they lapsed by degrees into Polytheism and idolatry. Their Phtha is sometimes supposed to be the Hephaistos of the Greeks; that is, the subtile fire which pervades the universe. (Jablonski. Panth. Egypt. t. i. pp. 30—49.) Like the Chinese, (La Croye. Thess Epist. l. iii. p. 194,) the ancient Egyptians have by certain writers been suspected of Atheism, a charge opposed by the pious and learned Cudworth, who conceives, that, under the name of Nox, they worshipped the invisible God. Jablonski, though he cannot see any foundation for this opinion, contends that the Egyptians—that is, the philosophical part of the nation, were not polytheists. (L. I. c. i. p. 2.) With a pardonable partiality he regards Egypt as the inventress of theology, and all the other sciences. (ib. et. Proleg. p. 4.) They had, according to his views, elevated their minds to a clear idea of God; but proceeding to the polytneistic period, he places Athor, or Aphrodite, at the head of all their divinities, as the Brahmins do Bhavani. (2.) The grammarian Orion, cited by the author of the Etymologicum Magnum, observes, that Athys was, among the Egyptians, the name of a month, and that they denominated Venus, Athor. (In voce, 'Aθύρ) Hezychius corroborates the testimony of Orion, adding, that the name Athor was likewise applied to the cow; but this is not to be understood of the animal, but of the symbolical cow, by which Athor was represented. (Jab. i. 4.) It may be noticed *en passant*, that the word is always written Athor in the books of the Copts. (Hezych. in v. Orion in Etym. Magn. ut sup.) But Jablonski maintains that this goddess and the Grecian Aphrodite were greatly dissimilar, and that in many respects she rather resembles Hera, or Venus Urania. (6.) Herodotus, however, observes that Hera was unknown to the Egyptians. (L. xi. c. 50.) Some of the ancients confounded the goddess with the moon

CHAP. X.] KNOWLEDGE OF THE EXISTENCE OF A GOD. 235

9. *Two Sorts of Beings, cogitative and incogitative.*—There are but two sorts of beings in the world that man knows or conceives.

First, such as are purely material, without sense, percep-

(Seld. de Diss. Syris. Synt. II. c. ii. iv. et Voss. de Idolol. L xi. c. 21, 22.) Others, again, suppose her to have been the planet Venus, so highly venerated by the Arabs. (Jabl. i. 7.) But in reality the Orientals meant nothing by the name, but the plastic power of nature, (Plut. vit. Crassi. Jab. 8.)—the mother of gods and men. (Apul. Met. 1. ix.; Ovid. Fast. IV. 99. et seq.) Jablonski himself thinks the word Athor is synonymous with Nox, Night, (l. 10,) which was also one of the deities of the Phœnicians. (Euseb. Præp. Evan. l. I. c. 10.) There were in Greece, also, temples to Night, by Hesiod called the mother of the Gods. (Theog. v. 123, conf. Paus. on Abb. et Phœn.) Night, in fact, as suspected by Cudworth, was among the Egyptians accounted the first principle of all things. (Jab. 18, 19, conf. to 27.) According to Herodotus, (l. xi. c. 46 and 145,) the eight great gods of the Egyptians were the four elements, the sun, the moon, day, and night. They, however, degenerated by degrees into mere Pantheism. (Diog. Laert. Pr. vii. 10 :) and Jablonski inquires whether one would not suppose that Spinoza had borrowed his system from the Egyptians?" (l. 36.) The learned mythologist is of opinion, however, that the more ancient philosophers of Egypt believed in one God, (p. 38,) who was called Phtha, (44,) and included both the sexes. This is identical, or perfectly agrees with the doctrine of the Brahmins, (p. 47,) yet the worship of this god, like that of Brahma in India, gradually died away, and he honoured but one temple, which was in Memphis. (52.) The solitary fane in honour of the supreme God exists likewise in Hindustan. (Todd. Annal. of Bojart, I. p. 774.) The primitive conception which the Hindus had framed of the divinity, we may collect from a sublime hymn in the Lajus-Veda, "in which a yearning to inculcate the unity of God is clearly distinguishable, in the midst of ideas of a pantheistical tendency." (Hindoos. I. p. 146.) "Fire is that original cause; the sun is *that;* so is air; so is the moon; such, too, is that pure Brahmin, and those waters, and that lord of creatures. Moments, and other measures of time, proceeded from the effulgent person, whom none can apprehend as an object of perception, above, around, or in the midst. Of him whose glory is so great there is no image; he it is who is celebrated in various holy strains. Even he is the God, who pervades all regions; he is the first-born; it is he who is in the womb; he who is born; and he who will be produced: he severally and universally remains with all persons. He, prior to whom nothing was born, and who became all things; himself the lord of creatures with a body composed of sixteen members, being delighted by creation, produced the three luminaries, the sun, the moon, and fire. To what God should we offer oblations, but to him who made the fluid sky and solid earth; who fixed the solar orb and celestial abode: and who formed drops of rain in the atmosphere? To what God should we offer oblation, but to him whom heaven and earth mentally contemplate, while they are strengthened and embellished by offerings, and illuminated by the sun rising above them? The wise man views that mysterious

tion, or thought, as the clippings of our beards, and parings of our nails.

Secondly, sensible, thinking, perceiving beings, such as we find ourselves to be, which, if you please, we will hereafter call cogitative and incogitative beings; which to our present purpose, if for nothing else, are perhaps better terms than material and immaterial.

10. *Incogitative Beings cannot produce a cogitative.*—If, then, there must be something eternal, let us see what sort of being it must be. And to that it is very obvious to reason, that it must necessarily be a cogitative being. For it is as impossible to conceive that ever bare incogitative matter should produce a thinking intelligent being, as that nothing should of itself produce matter. Let us suppose any parcel of matter eternal—great or small—we shall find it, in itself, able to produce nothing. For example: let us suppose the matter of the next pebble we meet with eternal, closely united, and the parts firmly at rest together; if there were no other being in the world, must it not eternally remain so—a dead inactive lump? Is it possible to conceive it can add motion to itself—being purely matter—or produce anything? Matter, then, by its own strength, cannot produce in itself so much as motion: the motion it has must also be from eternity, or else be produced, and added to matter by some other being more powerful than matter; matter, as is evident, having not power to produce motion in itself. But let us suppose motion eternal too: yet matter —incogitative matter and motion—whatever changes it might produce of figure and bulk, could never produce thought: knowledge will still be as far beyond the power of motion and matter to produce, as matter is beyond the power of nothing or nonentity to produce. And I appeal to every one's own thoughts, whether he cannot as easily conceive

Being in whom the universe perpetually exists, resting on that sole support. In him this world is absorbed; from him it comes; in creatures he is twined and wove with various forms of existence. Let the wise man who is conversant with the import of revelation, promptly celebrate that immortal Being, the mysteriously existing and various abode: he who knows its three states, (its creation, continuance, and destruction,) which are involved in mystery, is father of the father. That Brahma in whom the gods attain immortality, while they abide in the third or celestial region, is our venerable parent, and the Providence which governs all worlds." (Asiatic Researches. VIII. pp. 431—433.)—ED.

matter produced by nothing, as thought to be produced by pure matter, when, before, there was no such thing as thought or an intelligent being existing? Divide matter into as many parts as you will, (which we are apt to imagine a sort of spiritualizing, or making a thinking thing of it,) vary the figure and motion of it as much as you please—a globe, cube, cone, prism, cylinder, &c., whose diameters are but 100,000th part of a gry,* will operate no otherwise upon other bodies of proportionable bulk, than those of an inch or foot diameter; and you may as rationally expect to produce sense, thought, and knowledge, by putting together, in a certain figure and motion, gross particles of matter, as by those that are the very minutest that do anywhere exist. They knock, impel, and resist one another, just as the greater do, and that is all they can do. So that, if we will suppose nothing first or eternal, matter can never begin to be: if we suppose bare matter without motion, eternal; motion can never begin to be: if we suppose only matter and motion first, or eternal, thought can never begin to be. For it is impossible to conceive that matter, either with or without motion, could have originally in and from itself sense, perception, and knowledge; as is evident from hence, that then sense, perception, and knowledge, must be a property eternally inseparable from matter and every particle of it. Not to add, that, though our general or specific conception of matter makes us speak of it as one thing, yet really all matter is not one individual thing, neither is there any such thing existing as one material being, or one single body that we know or can conceive. And therefore, if matter were the eternal first cogitative being, there would not be one eternal, infinite, cogitative being, but an infinite number of eternal, finite, cogitative beings, independent one of another, of limited force, and distinct thoughts, which could never produce that order, harmony, and beauty which are to be found

* A gry is one-tenth of a line, a line one-tenth of an inch, an inch one-tenth of a philosophical foot, a philosophical foot one-third of a pendulum, whose diadroms, in the latitude of forty-five degrees, are each equal to one second of time, or one-sixtieth of a minute. I have affectedly made use of this measure here, and the parts of it, under a decimal division, with names to them; because I think it would be of general convenience that this should be the common measure in the commonwealth of letters.

in nature. Since, therefore, whatsoever is the first eternal being must necessarily be cogitative; and whatsoever is first of all things must necessarily contain in it, and actually have, at least, all the perfections that can ever after exist; nor can it ever give to another any perfection that it hath not either actually in itself, or, at least, in a higher degree; it necessarily follows, that the first eternal being cannot be matter.

11. *Therefore, there has been an eternal Wisdom.*—If, therefore, it be evident that something necessarily must exist from eternity, it is also as evident that that something must necessarily be a cogitative being: for it is as impossible that incogitative matter should produce a cogitative being, as that nothing, or the negation of all being should produce a positive being or matter.

12. Though this discovery of the necessary existence of an eternal mind does sufficiently lead us into the knowledge of God; since it will hence follow, that all other knowing beings that have a beginning must depend on him, and have no other ways of knowledge or extent of power than what he gives them; and therefore, if he made those, he made also the less excellent pieces of this universe, all inanimate beings, whereby his omniscience, power, and providence will be established, and all his other attributes necessarily follow: yet, to clear up this a little further, we will see what doubts can be raised against it.

13. *Whether material or no.*—First, Perhaps it will be said, that, though it be as clear as demonstration can make it, that there must be an eternal being, and that being must also be knowing: yet it does not follow, but that thinking being may also be material. Let it be so: it equally still follows that there is a God. For if there be an eternal, omniscient, omnipotent being, it is certain that there is a God, whether you imagine that being to be material or no. But herein, I suppose, lies the danger and deceit of that supposition: there being no way to avoid the demonstration, that there is an eternal knowing being, men devoted to matter would willingly have it granted, that this knowing being is material; and then, letting slide out of their minds, or the discourse, the demonstration whereby an eternal knowing being was proved necessarily to exist, would argue all to be

matter, and so deny a God—that is, an eternal cogitative being; whereby they are so far from establishing, that they destroy their own hypothesis. For if there can be, in their opinion, eternal matter, without any eternal cogitative being, they manifestly separate matter and thinking, and suppose no necessary connexion of the one with the other, and so establish the necessity of an eternal spirit, but not of matter; since it has been proved already, that an eternal cogitative being is unavoidably to be granted. Now, if thinking and matter may be separated, the eternal existence of matter will not follow from the eternal existence of a cogitative being, and they suppose it to no purpose.

14. *Not material*, I. *Because every Particle of Matter is not cogitative.*—But now let us suppose that can satisfy themselves or others, that this eternal thinking being is material.

First, I would ask them, whether they imagine that all matter—every particle of matter—thinks? This, I suppose, they will scarce say; since then there would be as many eternal thinking beings as there are particles of matter, and so an infinity of gods. And yet, if they will not allow matter as matter—that is, every particle of matter to be as well cogitative as extended, they will have as hard a task to make out to their own reasons a cogitative being out of incogitative particles, as an extended being out of unextended parts, if I may so speak.

15. II. *One Particle alone of Matter cannot be cogitative.*—Secondly, If all matter does not think, I next ask, Whether it be only one atom that does so? This has as many absurdities as the other; for then this atom of matter must be alone eternal or not. If this alone be eternal, then this alone, by its powerful thought or will, made all the rest of matter. And so we have the creation of matter by a powerful thought, which is that the materialists stick at; for if they suppose one single thinking atom to have produced all the rest of matter, they cannot ascribe that pre-eminence to it upon any other account than that of its thinking, the only supposed difference. But allow it to be by some other way, which is above our conception, it must still be creation, and these men must give up their great maxim, "Ex nihilo nil fit." If it be said, that all the rest of matter is equally eternal as that thinking atom, it will be to say anything at

pleasure, though ever so absurd: for to suppose all matter eternal, and yet one small particle in knowledge and power infinitely above all the rest, is without any the least appearance of reason to frame an hypothesis. Every particle of matter, as matter, is capable of all the same figures and motions of any other; and I challenge any one, in his thoughts, to add anything else to one above another.

16. III. *A System of incogitative Matter cannot be cogitative.*—If, then, neither one peculiar atom alone can be this eternal thinking being; nor all matter, as matter, i. e., every particle of matter, can be it; it only remains, that it is some certain system of matter duly put together, that is this thinking eternal being. This is that which, I imagine, is that notion which men are aptest to have of God; who would have him a material being, as most readily suggested to them by the ordinary conceit they have of themselves, and other men, which they take to be material thinking beings. But this imagination, however more natural, is no less absurd than the other: for to suppose the eternal thinking being to be nothing else but a composition of particles of matter, each whereof is cogitative, is to ascribe all the wisdom and knowledge of that eternal being only to the juxta-position of parts; than which nothing can be more absurd. For unthinking particles of matter, however put together, can have nothing thereby added to them, but a new relation of position, which it is impossible should give thought and knowledge to them.

17. *Whether in Motion or at Rest.*—But further: this corporeal system either has all its parts at rest, or it is a certain motion of the parts wherein its thinking consists. If it be perfectly at rest, it is but one lump, and so can have no privileges above one atom.

If it be the motion of its parts, on which its thinking depends, all the thoughts there must be unavoidably accidental and limited; since all the particles that by motion cause thought, being each of them in itself without any thought, cannot regulate its own motions, much less be regulated by the thought of the whole: since that thought is not the cause of motion, (for then it must be antecedent to it, and so without it,) but the consequence of it, whereby freedom, power, choice, and all rational and wise thinking or acting, will be quite taken away: so that such a thinking being will be no better nor wiser than pure blind matter; since to resolve all into the accidental unguided motions of blind matter, or into thought depending on unguided motions of blind matter, is the same thing: not to mention the narrowness of such thoughts and knowledge that must depend on the motion of such parts. But there needs no enumeration of any more absurdities and impossibilities in this hypothesis (however full of them it be) than that before mentioned; since, let this thinking system be all or a part of the matter of the universe, it is impossible that any one particle should either know its own or the motion of any other particle, or the whole know the motion of every particle; and so regulate its own thoughts or motions, or indeed have any thought resulting from such motion.

18. *Matter not co-eternal with an eternal Mind.*—Others would have matter to be eternal, notwithstanding that they allow an eternal, cogitative, immaterial being. This, though it take not away the being of a God, yet, since it denies one and the first great piece of his workmanship, the creation, let us consider it a little. Matter must be allowed eternal: why? because you cannot conceive how it can be made out of nothing: why do you not also think yourself eternal? You will answer, perhaps, because, about twenty or forty years since, you began to be. But if I ask you, what that you is which began then to be, you can scarce tell me. The matter whereof you are made began not then to be; for if it did, then it is not eternal: but it began to be put together in such a fashion and frame as makes up your body; but yet that frame of particles is not you, it makes not that thinking thing you are; (for I have now to do with one who allows an eternal, immaterial, thinking being, but would have unthinking matter eternal too;) therefore, when did that thinking thing begin to be? If it did never begin to be, then have you always been a thinking thing from eternity; the absurdity whereof I need not confute, till I meet with one who is so void of understanding as to own it. If, therefore, you can allow a thinking thing to be made out of nothing, (as all things that are not eternal must be,) why also can you not allow it possible for a material being to be made out of nothing by an equal power, but that you have

the experience of the one in view, and not of the other? though when well considered, creation of a spirit will be found to require no less power than the creation of matter. Nay, possibly, if we would emancipate ourselves from vulgar notions, and raise our thoughts as far as they would reach, to a closer contemplation of things, we might be able to aim at some dim and seeming conception how matter might at first be made, and begin to exist by the power of that eternal first being: but to give beginning and being to a spirit, would be found a more inconceivable effect of omnipotent power. But, this being what would perhaps lead us too far from the notions on which the philosophy now in the world is built, it would not be pardonable to deviate so far from them; or to inquire, so far as grammar itself would authorize, if the common settled opinion opposes it: especially in this place, where the received doctrine serves well enough to our present purpose, and leaves this past doubt, that the creation or beginning of any one substance out of nothing being once admitted, the creation of all other but the Creator himself, may, with the same ease, be supposed.

19. But you will say, Is it not impossible to admit of the making anything out of nothing, since we cannot possibly conceive it? I answer, No: 1. Because it is not reasonable to deny the power of an infinite being, because we cannot comprehend its operations. We do not deny other effects upon this ground, because we cannot possibly conceive the manner of their production. We cannot conceive how anything but impulse of body can move body; and yet that is not a reason sufficient to make us deny it possible,* against the constant experience we have of it in ourselves, in all our voluntary motions, which are produced in us only by the free action or thought of our own minds; and are not, nor can be, the effects of the impulse or determination of the motion of blind matter in or upon our own bodies; for then it could not be in our power or choice to alter it. For example: my right hand writes, whilst my left hand is still: what causes rest in one, and motion in the other? Nothing but my will—a thought of my mind; my thought only

---

* So in the fol. 1714. But in the modern editions it is usually printed "deny it impossible." (See following page.)—ED.

changing, the right hand rests, and the left hand moves. This is matter of fact, which cannot be denied: explain this and make it intelligible, and then the next step will be to understand creation. For the giving a new determination to the motion of the animal spirits (which some make use of to explain voluntary motion) clears not the difficulty one jot: to alter the determination of motion, being in this case no easier nor less, than to give motion itself; since the new determination given to the animal spirits must be either immediately by thought, or by some other body put in their way by thought, which was not in their way before, and so must owe its motion to thought: either of which leaves voluntary motion as unintelligible as it was before. In the meantime, it is an overvaluing ourselves to reduce all to the narrow measure of our capacities; and to conclude all things impossible to be done, whose manner of doing exceeds our comprehension. This is to make our comprehension infinite, or God finite, when what we can do is limited to what we can conceive of it. If you do not understand the operations of your own finite mind—that thinking thing within you, do not deem it strange that you cannot comprehend the operations of that eternal infinite mind, who made and governs all things, and whom the heaven of heavens cannot contain.*

CHAPTER XI.

OF OUR KNOWLEDGE OF THE EXISTENCE OF OTHER THINGS.

1. *It is to be had only by Sensation.*—THE knowledge of our own being we have by intuition. The existence of a God, reason clearly makes known to us, as has been shown.

† In the philosophical system of the Hindoos, God is regarded as pure spirit, divested of all attributes. Matter, which comprehends everything that is not God, is inert. Here are two principles clearly taught. This Being is individuated in every form of life, vegetable as well as animal; but may also be contemplated as dwelling in his own eternal solitude. From the union of spirit with matter arise vice and misery: to dissolve this union, and return the divine particle to its pure source, which is to be effected only by complete abstraction, and perpetual meditation on the Divine Nature, is the great business of life. The Hindoo philosophers, therefore endeavour, by performing the most fearful austerities, and, by annihilating as far as possible all wants, affections

The knowledge of the existence of any other thing we can have only by sensation: for there being no necessary connexion of real existence with any idea a man hath in his memory, nor of any other existence but that of God, with the existence of any particular man; no particular man can know the existence of any other being, but only when, by actual operating upon him, it makes itself perceived by him. For the having the idea of anything in our mind, no more proves the existence of that thing, than the picture of a man evidences his being in the world, or the visions of a dream make thereby a true history.

2. *Instance: Whiteness of this Paper.*—It is therefore the actual receiving of ideas from without that gives us notice of the existence of other things, and makes us know that something doth exist at that time without us, which causes that idea in us, though perhaps we neither know nor consider how it does it: for it takes not from the certainty of our senses, and the ideas we receive by them, that we know not the manner wherein they are produced: v. g., whilst I write this, I have, by the paper affecting my eyes, that idea produced in my mind, which, whatever object causes, I call white; by which I know that that quality or accident (i. e., whose appearance before my eyes always causes that idea) doth really exist, and hath a being without me. And of this the greatest assurance I can possibly have, and to which my faculties can attain, is the testimony of my eyes, which are the proper and sole judges of this thing, whose testimony I have reason to rely on as so certain, that I can no more doubt, whilst I write this, that I see white and black, and that something really exists that causes that sensation in me, than that I write or move my hand: which is a certainty as great as human nature is capable of, concerning the existence of anything, but a man's self alone, and of God.

3. *This, though not so certain as Demonstration, yet may be called Knowledge, and proves the Existence of Things without us.*—The notice we have by our senses of the existing of

and desires, to elevate themselves to that spiritual life, or absorption, in the Deity, in which they expect to be plunged after death, and lost in ineffable beatitude, as the air contained in a vessel mingles, when this vessel is broken, with the great body of atmospheric air, or as a drop is lost in the ocean. (Ward. pref. p. 20—21.)—ED.

things without us, though it be not altogether so certain as our intuitive knowledge, or the deductions of our reason, employed about the clear abstract ideas of our own minds; yet it is an assurance that deserves the name of knowledge. If we persuade ourselves that our faculties act and inform us right concerning the existence of those objects that affect them, it cannot pass for an ill-grounded confidence: for I think nobody can, in earnest, be so sceptical as to be uncertain of the existence of those things which he sees and feels. At least, he that can doubt so far, (whatever he may have with his own thoughts,) will never have any controversy with me; since he can never be sure I say anything contrary to his own opinion. As to myself, I think God has given me assurance enough of the existence of things without me; since, by their different application, I can produce in myself both pleasure and pain, which is one great concernment of my present state. This is certain, the confidence that our faculties do not herein deceive us, is the greatest assurance we are capable of concerning the existence of material beings. For we cannot act anything but by our faculties; nor talk of knowledge itself, but by the helps of those faculties which are fitted to apprehend even what knowledge is. But besides the assurance we have from our senses themselves, that they do not err in the information they give us of the existence of things without us, when they are affected by them, we are further confirmed in this assurance by other concurrent reasons.

4. I. *Because we cannot have them but by the Inlet of the Senses.*—First, It is plain those perceptions are produced in us by exterior causes affecting our senses; because those that want the organs of any sense, never can have the ideas belonging to that sense produced in their minds. This is too evident to be doubted: and therefore we cannot but be assured that they come in by the organs of that sense, and no other way. The organs themselves, it is plain, do not produce them; for then the eyes of a man in the dark would produce colours, and his nose smell roses in the winter: but we see nobody gets the relish of a pineapple, till he goes to the Indies, where it is, and tastes it.*

* It would seem from this, that the pineapple had not then been introduced into Europe.—ED.

5. II. *Because an Idea from actual Sensation, and another from Memory, are very distinct Perceptions.*—Secondly, Because sometimes I find, that I cannot avoid the having those ideas produced in my mind. For though, when my eyes are shut, or windows fast, I can at pleasure recal to my mind the ideas of light, or the sun, which former sensations had lodged in my memory; so I can at pleasure lay by that idea, and take into my view that of the smell of a rose, or taste of sugar. But, if I turn my eyes at noon towards the sun, I cannot avoid the ideas which the light or sun then produces in me. So that there is a manifest difference between the ideas laid up in my memory, (over which, if they were there only, I should have constantly the same power to dispose of them, and lay them by at pleasure,) and those which force themselves upon me, and I cannot avoid having. And therefore it must needs be some exterior cause, and the brisk acting of some objects without me, whose efficacy I cannot resist, that produces those ideas in my mind, whether I will or no. Besides, there is nobody who doth not perceive the difference in himself between contemplating the sun, as he hath the idea of it in his memory, and actually looking upon it: of which two, his perception is so distinct, that few of his ideas are more distinguishable one from another. And therefore he hath certain knowledge, that they are not both memory, or the actions of his mind, and fancies only within him; but that actual seeing hath a cause without.

6. III. *Pleasure or Pain which accompanies actual Sensation, accompanies not the returning of those Ideas without the external Objects.*—Thirdly, Add to this, that many of those ideas are produced in us with pain, which afterwards we remember without the least offence. Thus, the pain of heat or cold, when the idea of it is revived in our minds, gives us no disturbance; which, when felt, was very troublesome, and is again, when actually repeated; which is occasioned by the disorder the external object causes in our bodies when applied to it. And we remember the pains of hunger, thirst, or the headache, without any pain at all; which would either never disturb us, or else constantly do it, as often as we thought of it, were there nothing more but ideas floating in our minds, and appearances entertaining our fancies, without the

real existence of things affecting us from abroad. The same may be said of pleasure, accompanying several actual sensations: and though mathematical demonstrations depend not upon sense, yet the examining them by diagrams gives great credit to the evidence of our sight, and seems to give it a certainty approaching to that of demonstration itself. For it would be very strange, that a man should allow it for an undeniable truth, that two angles of a figure, which he measures by lines and angles of a diagram, should be bigger one than the other, and yet doubt of the existence of those lines and angles, which by looking on he makes use of to measure that by.

7. IV. *Our Senses assist one another's Testimony of the Existence of outward Things.*—Fourthly, Our senses in many cases bear witness to the truth of each other's report, concerning the existence of sensible things without us. He that sees a fire, may, if he doubt whether it be anything more than a bare fancy, feel it too; and be convinced, by putting his hand in it; which certainly could never be put into such exquisite pain by a bare idea or phantom, unless that the pain be a fancy too, which yet he cannot, when the burn is well, by raising the idea of it, bring upon himself again.

Thus I see, whilst I write this, I can change the appearance of the paper, and by designing the letters tell beforehand what new idea it shall exhibit the very next moment, by barely drawing my pen over it: which will neither appear (let me fancy as much as I will) if my hands stand still; or though I move my pen, if my eyes be shut: nor when those characters are once made on the paper, can I choose afterwards but see them as they are; that is, have the ideas of such letters as I have made. Whence it is manifest, that they are not barely the sport and play of my own imagination, when I find that the characters that were made at the pleasure of my own thoughts, do not obey them; nor yet cease to be, whenever I shall fancy it; but continue to affect the senses constantly and regularly, according to the figures I made them. To which if we will add, that the sight of those shall, from another man, draw such sounds as I beforehand design they shall stand for, there will be little reason left to doubt that those words I write do **really** exist without me, when they cause a long series of regular sounds to affect my ears, which could not be the effect of my imagination, nor could my memory retain them in that order.

8. *This Certainty is as great as our Condition needs.*—But yet, if after all this, any one will be so sceptical as to distrust his senses, and to affirm that all we see and hear, feel and taste, think and do, during our whole being, is but the series and deluding appearances of a long dream, whereof there is no reality; and therefore will question the existence of all things, or our knowledge of anything; I must desire him to consider, that, if all be a dream, then he doth but dream that he makes the question, and so it is not much matter that a waking man should answer him. But yet, if he pleases, he may dream that I make him this answer, that the certainty of things existing in rerum natura, when we have the testimony of our senses for it, is not only as great as our frame can attain, but as our condition needs. For our faculties being suited not to the full extent of being, nor to a perfect, clear, comprehensive knowledge of things free from all doubt and scruple; but to the preservation of us, in whom they are, and accommodated to the use of life, they serve to our purpose well enough, if they will but give us certain notice of those things, which are convenient or inconvenient to us. For he that sees a candle burning, and hath experimented the force of its flame by putting his finger in it, will little doubt that this is something existing without him, which does him harm, and puts him to great pain; which is assurance enough when no man requires greater certainty to govern his actions by, than what is as certain as his actions themselves. And if our dreamer pleases to try whether the glowing heat of a glass furnace be barely a wandering imagination in a drowsy man's fancy, by putting his hand into it, he may perhaps be wakened into a certainty greater than he could wish, that it is something more than bare imagination; so that this evidence is as great as we can desire, being as certain to us as our pleasure or pain, i. e., happiness or misery; beyond which we have no concernment, either of knowing or being. Such an assurance of the existence of things without us is sufficient to direct us in the attaining the good and avoiding the **evil** which is caused by them, which is the import and concernment we have of being made acquainted with them.

2. *But reaches no further than actual Sensation.*—In fine, then, when our senses do actually convey into our understandings any idea, we cannot but be satisfied that there doth something at that time really exist without us, which doth affect our senses, and by them give notice of itself to our apprehensive faculties, and actually produce that idea which we then perceive : and we cannot so far distrust their testimony, as to doubt that such collections of simple ideas as we have observed by our senses to be united together, do really exist together. But this knowledge extends as far as the present testimony of our senses, employed about particular objects that do then affect them, and no further. For if I saw such a collection of simple ideas as is wont to be called man, existing together one minute since, and am now alone, I cannot be certain that the same man exists now, since there is no necessary connexion of his existence a minute since with his existence now: by a thousand ways he may cease to be, since I had the testimony of my senses for his existence. And if I cannot be certain that the man I saw last to-day is now in being, I can less be certain that he is so who hath been longer removed from my senses, and I have not seen since yesterday, or since the last year ; and much less can I be certain of the existence of men that I never saw. And, therefore, though it be highly probable that millions of men do now exist, yet, whilst I am alone writing this, I have not that certainty of it which we strictly call knowledge; though the great likelihood of it puts me past doubt, and it be reasonable for me to do several things upon the confidence that there are men (and men also of my acquaintance, with whom I have to do) now in the world : but this is but probability, not knowledge.

10. *Folly to expect Demonstration in everything.*—Whereby yet we may observe how foolish and vain a thing it is for a man of a narrow knowledge, who having reason given him to judge of the different evidence and probability of things, and to be swayed accordingly ; how vain, I say, it is to expect demonstration and certainty in things not capable of it ; and refuse assent to very rational propositions, and act contrary to very plain and clear truths, because they cannot be made out so evident, as to surmount every the least (I will not say reason, but) pretence of doubting. He that, in the ordinary affairs of life, would admit of nothing but direct plain de-

monstration, would be sure of nothing in this world, but of perishing quickly. The wholesomeness of his meat or drink would not give him reason to venture on it: and I would fain know what it is he could do upon such grounds, as are capable of no doubt, no objection.

11. *Past Existence is known by Memory.*—As when our senses are actually employed about any object, we do know that it does exist; so by our memory we may be assured, that heretofore things that affected our senses have existed. And thus we have knowledge of the past existence of several things, whereof our senses having informed us, our memories still retain the ideas; and of this we are past all doubt, so long as we remember well. But this knowledge also reaches no further than our senses have formerly assured us. Thus, seeing water at this instant, it is an unquestionable truth to me that water doth exist; and remembering that I saw it yesterday, it will also be always true, and as long as my memory retains it always an undoubted proposition to me, that water did exist the 10th of July, 1688, as it will also be equally true that a certain number of very fine colours did exist, which at the same time I saw upon a bubble of that water; but, being now quite out of the sight both of the water and bubbles too, it is no more certainly known to me that the water doth now exist, than that the bubbles or colours therein do so: it being no more necessary that water should exist to-day, because it existed yesterday, than that the colours or bubbles exist to-day, because they existed yesterday; though it be exceedingly much more probable, because water hath been observed to continue long in existence, but bubbles, and the colours on them, quickly cease to be.

12. *The Existence of Spirits not knowable.*—What ideas we have of spirits, and how we come by them, I have already shown. But though we have those ideas in our minds, and know we have them there, the having the ideas of spirits does not make us know that any such things do exist without us, or that there are any finite spirits, or any other spiritual beings but the eternal God. We have ground from revelation, and several other reasons, to believe with assurance that there are such creatures: but our senses not being able to discover them, we want the means of knowing their particular existences. For we can no more know that

there are finite spirits really existing by the idea we have of such beings in our minds, than by the ideas any one has of fairies or centaurs, he can come to know that things answering those ideas do really exist.

And therefore concerning the existence of finite spirits, as well as several other things, we must content ourselves with the evidence of faith; but universal, certain propositions concerning this matter are beyond our reach. For however true it may be—v. g., that all the intelligent spirits that God ever created, do still exist: yet it can never make a part of our certain knowledge. These and the like propositions we may assent to, as highly probable, but are not, I fear, in this state capable of knowing. We are not, then, to put others upon demonstrating, nor ourselves upon search of universal certainty in all those matters, wherein we are not capable of any other knowledge, but what our senses give us in this or that particular.

13. *Particular Propositions concerning Existence are knowable.*—By which it appears that there are two sorts of propositions. 1. There is one sort of propositions concerning the existence of anything answerable to such an idea: as having the idea of an elephant, phœnix, motion, or an angel, in my mind, the first and natural inquiry is, whether such a thing does anywhere exist? And this knowledge is only of particulars. No existence of anything without us, but only of God, can certainly be known further than our senses inform us. 2. There is another sort of propositions, wherein is expressed the agreement or disagreement of our abstract ideas, and their dependence on one another. Such propositions may be universal and certain. So, having the idea of God and myself, of fear and obedience, I cannot but be sure that God is to be feared and obeyed by me: and this proposition will be certain, concerning man in general, if I have made an abstract idea of such a species, whereof I am one particular. But yet this proposition, how certain soever, that men ought to fear and obey God, proves not to me the existence of men in the world, but will be true of all such creatures, whenever they do exist: which certainty of such general propositions depends on the agreement or disagreement to be discovered in those abstract ideas.

14. *And general Propositions concerning abstract Ideas.*—

In the former case, our knowledge is the consequence of the existence of things producing ideas in our minds by our senses: in the latter, knowledge is the consequence of the ideas (be they what they will) that are in our minds producing there general certain propositions. Many of these are called æternæ veritates, and all of them indeed are so; not from being written all or any of them in the minds of all men, or that they were any of them propositions in any one's mind, till he, having got the abstract ideas, joined or separated them by affirmation or negation. But wheresoever we can suppose such a creature as man is, endowed with such faculties, and thereby furnished with such ideas as we have, we must conclude, he must needs, when he applies his thoughts to the consideration of his ideas, know the truth of certain propositions that will arise from the agreement or disagreement which he will perceive in his own ideas. Such propositions are therefore called eternal truths, not because they are eternal propositions actually formed, and antecedent to the understanding, that at any time makes them; nor because they are imprinted on the mind from any patterns that are anywhere out of the mind, and existed before; but because being once made about abstract ideas, so as to be true, they will, whenever they can be supposed to be made again at any time past or to come, by a mind having those ideas, always actually be true. For names being supposed to stand perpetually for the same ideas, and the same ideas having immutably the same habitudes one to another; propositions concerning any abstract ideas that are once true must needs be eternal verities.

CHAPTER XII.

OF THE IMPROVEMENT OF OUR KNOWLEDGE.

1. *Knowledge is not from Maxims.*—It having been the common received opinion amongst men of letters, that maxims were the foundation of all knowledge; and that the sciences were each of them built upon certain præcognita, from whence the understanding was to take its rise, and by which it was to conduct itself in its inquiries into the matters belonging to that science, the beaten road of the schools has been to lay down in the beginning one or more general propositions

as foundations whereon to build the knowledge that was to be had of that subject. These doctrines, thus laid down for foundations of any science, were called principles, as the beginnings from which we must set out, and look no further backwards in our inquiries, as we have already observed.

2. *(The Occasion of that Opinion.)*—One thing which might probably give an occasion to this way of proceeding in other sciences, was (as I suppose) the good success it seemed to have in mathematics, wherein men, being observed to attain a great certainty of knowledge, these sciences came by pre-eminence to be called Μαθήματα, and Μάθησις, learning, or things learned, thoroughly learned, as having of all others the greatest certainty, clearness, and evidence in them.

3. *But from the comparing clear and distinct Ideas.*—But if any one will consider, he will (I guess) find that the great advancement and certainty of real knowledge which men arrived to in these sciences, was not owing to the influence of these principles, nor derived from any peculiar advantage they received from two or three general maxims, laid down in the beginning; but from the clear, distinct, complete ideas their thoughts were employed about, and the relation of equality and excess so clear between some of them, that they had an intuitive knowledge, and by that a way to discover it in others, and this without the help of those maxims. For I ask, is it not possible for a young lad to know that his whole body is bigger than his little finger, but by virtue of this axiom, that the whole is bigger than a part; nor be assured of it, till he has learned that maxim? Or cannot a country wench know that, having received a shilling from one that owes her three, and a shilling also from another that owes her three, the remaining debts in each of their hands are equal? Cannot she know this, I say, unless she fetch the certainty of it from this maxim, that if you take equals from equals, the remainder will be equals, a maxim which possibly she never heard or thought of? I desire any one to consider, from what has been elsewhere said, which is known first and clearest by most people, the particular instance, or the general rule; and which it is that gives life and birth to the other. These general rules are but the comparing our more general and abstract ideas, which are the workmanship of the mind, made, and names given to

them for the easier dispatch in its reasonings, and drawing into comprehensive terms and short rules its various and multiplied observations. But knowledge began in the mind, and was founded on particulars; though afterwards, perhaps, no notice was taken thereof: it being natural for the mind (forward still to enlarge its knowledge) most attentively to lay up those general notions, and make the proper use of them, which is to disburden the memory of the cumbersome load of particulars. For I desire it may be considered, what more certainty there is to a child, or any one, that his body, little finger, and all, is bigger than his little finger alone, after you have given to his body the name whole, and to his little finger the name part, than he could have had before; or what new knowledge concerning his body can these two relative terms give him, which he could not have without them? Could he not know that his body was bigger than his little finger, if his language were yet so imperfect, that he had no such relative terms as whole and part? I ask, further, when he has got these names, how is he more certain that his body is a whole, and his little finger a part, than he was or might be certain before he learnt those terms, that his body was bigger than his little finger? Any one may as reasonably doubt or deny that his little finger is a part of his body, as that it is less than his body. And he that can doubt whether it be less, will as certainly doubt whether it be a part. So that the maxim, the whole is bigger than a part, can never be made use of to prove the little finger less than the body, but when it is useless, by being brought to convince one of a truth which he knows already. For he that does not certainly know that any parcel of matter, with another parcel of matter joined to it, is bigger than either of them alone, will never be able to know it by the help of these two relative terms, whole and part, make of them what maxim you please.

4. *Dangerous to build upon precarious Principles.*—But be it in the mathematics as it will, whether it be clearer, that, taking an inch from a black line of two inches, and an inch from a red line of two inches, the remaining parts of the two lines will be equal, or that if you take equals from equals, the remainder will be equals; which, I say, of these

two is the clearer and first known, I leave to any one to determine, it not being material to my present occasion. That which I have here to do, is to inquire, whether if it be the readiest way to knowledge to begin with general maxims, and build upon them, it be yet a safe way to take the principles, which are laid down in any other science as unquestionable truths; and so receive them without examination, and adhere to them without suffering them to be doubted of, because mathematicians have been so happy, or so fair, to use none but self-evident and undeniable. If this be so, I know not what may not pass for truth in morality, what may not be introduced and proved in natural philosophy.

Let that principle of some of the philosophers, that all is matter, and that there is nothing else, be received for certain and indubitable, and it will be easy to be seen by the writings of some that have revived it again in our days, what consequences it will lead us into.* Let any one, with Polemo, take the world; or with the Stoics, the æther, or the sun;† or with Anaximenes, the air, to be God; and what a divinity, religion, and worship must we needs have! Nothing can be so dangerous as principles thus taken up without questioning or examination; especially if they be such as concern morality, which influence men's lives, and give a bias to all their actions. Who might not justly expect another kind of life in Aristippus, who placed happiness in bodily pleasure; and in Antisthenes, who made virtue

---

* See Lipsius Physiolog. Stoic. l. 1. Diss. VII. Op. t. iv. p. 846. On the Divinity of the sun, see l. ii. Diss. 13. "Ἥλιος θεὸς μέγιστος τῶν κατ' οὐρανόν θεῶν, ᾧ πάντες ἕκουσιν οἱ οὐράνιοι θεοί, ὡσανεὶ βασιλεῖ καὶ δυνάστῃ." (Trismegistus ap. Lips. ub. sup.)—ED.

† Anaximenes maintained, according to Diogenes Laertius, that the air and the infinite were the first principles of all things:—" Οὗτος ἀρχὴν ἀὴρα εἶπε, καὶ τὸ ἄπειρον." (L. II. c. 11, § 1.) Tennemann, therefore, is wrong, where he says, that, " instead of the indeterminate ἄπειρον of the latter, (Anaximandros,) certain observations, though partial and limited, on the origin of things, and the nature of the soul, led him to regard the air (ἀὴρ,) as the primitive element." (Hist. of Phil. § 87.) Cicero, however, (De Nat. Deor. I. 10,) and Aristotle, (Met. I. 3,) omit to mention the τὸ ἄπειρον. On the general opinions of Anaximenes, Menage refers to the notes of Casaubon, Euseb. Præp. Evan. l. x. c. ult.; Nemesius, c. v.; and the Adversaries of Deselerius. Heraldus, l. ii. c. 12.—ED.

sufficient to felicity? And he who, with Plato, shall place beatitude in the knowledge of God, will have his thoughts raised to other contemplations than those who look not beyond this spot of earth, and those perishing things which are to be had in it. He that, with Archelaus,* shall lay it down as a principle, that right and wrong, honest and dishonest, are defined only by laws, and not by nature, will have other measures of moral rectitude and pravity, than those who take it for granted that we are under obligations antecedent to all human constitutions.

5. *This is no certain Way to Truth.*—If, therefore, those that pass for principles are not certain, (which we must have some way to know, that we may be able to distinguish them from those that are doubtful,) but are only made so to us by our blind assent, we are liable to be misled by them; and instead of being guided into truth, we shall, by principles, be only confirmed in mistake and error.

6. *But to compare clear, complete Ideas, under steady Names.*—But since the knowledge of the certainty of principles, as well as of all other truths, depends only upon the perception we have of the agreement or disagreement of our ideas, the way to improve our knowledge is not, I am sure, blindly, and with an implicit faith, to receive and swallow principles; but is, I think, to get and fix in our minds clear, distinct, and complete ideas, as far as they are to be had, and annex to them proper and constant names. And thus, perhaps, without any other principles, but barely considering those ideas, and by comparing them one with another, finding their agreement and disagreement, and their several relations and habitudes; we shall get more true and clear knowledge by the conduct of this one rule, than by taking up principles, and thereby putting our minds into the disposal of others.

7. *The true Method of advancing Knowledge is by considering our abstract Ideas.*—We must, therefore, if we will proceed as reason advises, adapt our methods of inquiry to the nature of the ideas we examine, and the truth we search after. General and certain truths are only founded in the habitudes and relations of abstract ideas. A sagacious and methodical application of our thoughts, for the finding out

* On the opinions of Archelaus, see Diog. Laert. II. 16. Tennemann, Hist. of Phil. § 107.—Ed.

these relations, is the only way to discover all that can be put with truth and certainty concerning them into general propositions. By what steps we are to proceed in these, is to be learned in the schools of the mathematicians, who, from very plain and easy beginnings, by gentle degrees, and a continued chain of reasonings, proceed to the discovery and demonstration of truths, that appear at first sight beyond human capacity. The art of finding proofs, and the admirable methods they have invented for the singling out and laying in order those intermediate ideas that demonstratively show the equality or inequality of unapplicable quantities, is that which has carried them so far, and produced such wonderful and unexpected discoveries; but whether something like this, in respect of other ideas, as well as those of magnitude, may not in time be found out, I will not determine. This, I think, I may say, that if other ideas that are the real as well as nominal essences of their species, were pursued in the way familiar to mathematicians, they would carry our thoughts further, and with greater evidence and clearness than possibly we are apt to imagine.

8. *By which Morality also may be made clearer.*—This gave me the confidence to advance that conjecture, which I suggest, (chap. iii.) viz., that morality is capable of demonstration as well as mathematics. For the ideas that ethics are conversant about, being all real essences, and such as I imagine have a discoverable connexion and agreement one with another; so far as we can find their habitudes and relations, so far we shall be possessed of certain, real, and general truths; and I doubt not, but if a right method were taken, a great part of morality might be made out with that clearness, that could leave, to a considering man, no more reason to doubt, than he could have to doubt of the truth of propositions in mathematics, which have been demonstrated to him.

9. *But Knowledge of Bodies is to be improved only by Experience.*—In our search after the knowledge of substances, our want of ideas that are suitable to such a way of proceeding obliges us to a quite different method. We advance not here, as in the other, (where our abstract ideas are real as well as nominal essences,) by contemplating our ideas, and considering their relations and correspondences; that

helps us very little, for the reasons, that in another place we have at large set down. By which I think it is evident, that substances afford matter of very little general knowledge; and the bare contemplation of their abstract ideas will carry us but a very little way in the search of truth and certainty. What, then, are we to do for the improvement of our knowledge in substantial beings? Here we are to take a quite contrary course; the want of ideas of their real essences sends us from our own thoughts to the things themselves, as they exist. Experience here must teach me what reason cannot; and it is by trying alone, that I can certainly know, what other qualities co-exist with those of my complex idea, v. g., whether that yellow, heavy, fusible body I call gold, be malleable, or no; which experience (which way ever it prove in that particular body I examine) makes me not certain, that it is so in all, or any other yellow, heavy, fusible bodies, but that which I have tried. Because it is no consequence one way or the other from my complex idea; the necessity or inconsistence of malleability hath no visible connexion with the combination of that colour, weight, and fusibility in any body. What I have said here of the nominal essence of gold, supposed to consist of a body of such a determinate colour, weight, and fusibility, will hold true, if malleableness, fixedness, and solubility in aqua regia be added to it. Our reasonings from these ideas will carry us but a little way in the certain discovery of the other properties in those masses of matter wherein all these are to be found. Because the other properties of such bodies, depending not on these, but on that unknown real essence on which these also depend, we cannot by them discover the rest; we can go no further than the simple ideas of our nominal essence will carry us, which is very little beyond themselves; and so afford us but very sparingly any certain, universal, and useful truths. For upon trial having found that particular piece (and all others of that colour, weight, and fusibility, that I ever tried) malleable, that also makes now, perhaps, a part of my complex idea, part of my nominal essence of gold: whereby though I make my complex idea to which I affix the name gold, to consist of more simple ideas than before; yet still, it not containing the real essence of any species of bodies, it helps me not certainly to know (I say to know, perhaps it may be to conjecture) the other remaining properties of that body, further than they have a visible connexion with some or all of the simple ideas that make up my nominal essence. For example, I cannot be certain from this complex idea, whether gold be fixed or no; because, as before, there is no necessary connexion or inconsistence to be discovered betwixt a complex idea of a body yellow, heavy, fusible, malleable; betwixt these, I say, and fixedness; so that I may certainly know, that in whatsoever body these are found, there fixedness is sure to be. Here, again, for assurance, I must apply myself to experience; as far as that reaches, I may have certain knowledge, but no further.

10. *This may procure us Convenience, not Science.*—I deny not but a man, accustomed to rational and regular experiments, shall be able to see further into the nature of bodies, and guess righter at their yet unknown properties, than one that is a stranger to them: but yet, as I have said, this is but judgment and opinion, not knowledge and certainty. This way of getting and improving our knowledge in substances only by experience and history, which is all that the weakness of our faculties in this state of mediocrity which we are in in this world can attain to, makes me suspect that natural philosophy is not capable of being made a science. We are able, I imagine, to reach very little general knowledge concerning the species of bodies, and their several properties. Experiments and historical observations we may have, from which we may draw advantages of ease and health, and thereby increase our stock of conveniences for this life; but beyond this I fear our talents reach not, nor are our faculties, as I guess, able to advance.

11. *We are fitted for moral Knowledge and natural Improvements.*—From whence it is obvious to conclude, that, since our faculties are not fitted to penetrate into the internal fabric and real essences of bodies; but yet plainly discover to us the being of a God, and the knowledge of ourselves, enough to lead us into a full and clear discovery of our duty and great concernment; it will become us, as rational creatures, to employ those faculties we have about what they are most adapted to, and follow the direction of nature, where it seems to point us out the way. For it is rational to con-

clude, that our proper employment lies in those inquiries, and in that sort of knowledge which is most suited to our natural capacities, and carries in it our greatest interest, i. e., the condition of our eternal estate. Hence I think I may conclude, that morality is the proper science and business of mankind in general, (who are both concerned and fitted to search out their summum bonum,) as several arts, conversant about several parts of nature, are the lot and private talent of particular men, for the common use of human life, and their own particular subsistence in this world. Of what consequence the discovery of one natural body and its properties may be to human life, the whole great continent of America is a convincing instance: whose ignorance in useful arts, and want of the greatest part of the conveniences of life, in a country that abounded with all sorts of natural plenty, I think may be attributed to their ignorance of what was to be found in a very ordinary, despicable stone; I mean the mineral of iron. And whatever we think of our parts or improvements in this part of the world, where knowledge and plenty seem to vie with each other; yet to any one that will seriously reflect on it, I suppose it will appear past doubt, that, were the use of iron lost among us, we should in a few ages be unavoidably reduced to the wants and ignorance of the ancient savage Americans, whose natural endowments and provisions come no way short of those of the most flourishing and polite nations. So that he who first made known the use of that contemptible mineral, may be truly styled the father of arts, and author of plenty.

12. *But must beware of Hypotheses and wrong Principles.—* I would not, therefore, be thought to disesteem or dissuade the study of nature. I readily agree the contemplation of his works gives us occasion to admire, revere, and glorify their Author; and, if rightly directed, may be of greater benefit to mankind than the monuments of exemplary charity, that have at so great charge been raised by the founders of hospitals and almshouses. He that first invented printing, discovered the use of the compass, or made public the virtue and right use of kin kina, did more for the propagation of knowledge, for the supply and increase of useful commodities, and saved more from the grave, than those who built colleges, workhouses, and hospitals. All that I would say is, that we

should not be too forwardly possessed with the opinion or expectation of knowledge, where it is not to be had, or by ways that will not attain to it: that we should not take doubtful systems for complete sciences, nor unintelligible notions for scientifical demonstrations. In the knowledge of bodies, we must be content to glean what we can from particular experiments; since we cannot, from a discovery of their real essences, grasp at a time whole sheaves, and in bundles comprehend the nature and properties of whole species together. Where our inquiry is concerning co-existence, or repugnancy to co-exist, which by contemplation of our ideas we cannot discover; there experience, observation, and natural history, must give us, by our senses and by retail, an insight into corporeal substances. The knowledge of bodies we must get by our senses, warily employed in taking notice of their qualities and operations on one another; and what we hope to know of separate spirits in this world, we must, I think, expect only from revelation. He that shall consider how little general maxims, precarious principles, and hypotheses laid down at pleasure, have promoted true knowledge, or helped to satisfy the inquiries of rational men after real improvements: how little, I say, the setting out at that end has, for many ages together, advanced men's progress towards the knowledge of natural philosophy, will think we have reason to thank those who in this latter age have taken another course, and have trod out to us, though not an easier way to learned ignorance, yet a surer way to profitable knowledge.

13. *The true Use of Hypotheses.*—Not that we may not, to explain any phenomena of nature, make use of any probable hypothesis whatsoever; hypotheses, if they are well made, are at least great helps to the memory, and often direct us to new discoveries. But my meaning is, that we should not take up any one too hastily (which the mind, that would always penetrate into the causes of things, and have principles to rest on, is very apt to do,) till we have very well examined particulars, and made several experiments, in that thing which we would explain by our hypothesis, and see whether it will agree to them all; whether our principles will carry us quite through, and not be as inconsistent with one phenomenon of nature, as they seem to accommodate

and explain another. And at least that we take care that the name of principles deceive us not, nor impose on us, by making us receive that for an unquestionable truth, which is really at best but a very doubtful conjecture, such as are most (I had almost said all) of the hypotheses in natural philosophy.

14. *Clear and distinct Ideas with settled Names, and the finding of those which show their Agreement or Disagreement, are the Ways to enlarge our Knowledge.*—But whether natural philosophy be capable of certainty or no, the ways to enlarge our knowledge, as far as we are capable, seem to me, in short, to be these two:

First, The first is to get and settle in our minds determined ideas of those things whereof we have general or specific names; at least, so many of them as we would consider and improve our knowledge in, or reason about. And if they be specific ideas of substances, we should endeavour also to make them as complete as we can, whereby I mean, that we should put together as many simple ideas as, being constantly observed to co-exist, may perfectly determine the species; and each of those simple ideas which are the ingredients of our complex ones, should be clear and distinct in our minds. For it being evident that our knowledge cannot exceed our ideas; as far as they are either imperfect, confused, or obscure, we cannot expect to have certain, perfect, or clear knowledge.

Secondly, The other is the art of finding out those intermediate ideas, which may show us the agreement or repugnancy of other ideas, which cannot be immediately compared.

15. *Mathematics an Instance of it.*—That these two (and not the relying on maxims, and drawing consequences from some general propositions) are the right methods of improving our knowledge in the ideas of other modes besides those of quantity, the consideration of mathematical knowledge will easily inform us. Where first we shall find that he that has not a perfect and clear idea of those angles or figures of which he desires to know anything, is utterly thereby incapable of any knowledge about them. Suppose but a man not to have a perfect exact idea of a right angle, a scalenum, or trapezium, and there is nothing more certain than that he will in vain seek any demonstration about them. Fur-

ther, it is evident, that it was not the influence of those maxims which are taken for principles in mathematics, that hath led the masters of that science into those wonderful discoveries they have made. Let a man of good parts know all the maxims generally made use of in mathematics ever so perfectly, and contemplate their extent and consequences as much as he pleases, he will, by their assistance, I suppose, scarce ever come to know that the square of the hypothenuse in a right-angled triangle is equal to the squares of the two other sides. The knowledge that the whole is equal to all its parts, and if you take equals from equals, the remainder will be equal, &c., helped him not, I presume, to this demonstration: and a man may, I think, pore long enough on those axioms, without ever seeing one jot the more of mathematical truths. They have been discovered by the thoughts otherwise applied: the mind had other objects, other views before it, far different from those maxims, when it first got the knowledge of such truths in mathematics, which men well enough acquainted with those received axioms, but ignorant of their method who first made these demonstrations, can never sufficiently admire. And who knows what methods to enlarge our knowledge in other parts of science may hereafter be invented, answering that of algebra in mathematics, which so readily finds out the ideas of quantities to measure others by; whose equality or proportion we could otherwise very hardly, or, perhaps, never come to know?

CHAPTER XIII.

SOME FURTHER CONSIDERATIONS CONCERNING OUR KNOWLEDGE.

1. *Our Knowledge partly necessary, partly voluntary.*—OUR knowledge, as in other things, so in this, has so great a conformity with our sight, that it is neither wholly unnecessary, nor wholly voluntary. If our knowledge were altogether necessary, all men's knowledge would not only be alike, but every man would know all that is knowable; and if it were wholly voluntary, some men so little regard or value it, that they would have extreme little, or none at all. Men that have senses cannot choose but receive some ideas by them; and if

they have memory, they cannot but retain some of them; and if they have any distinguishing faculty, cannot but perceive the agreement or disagreement of some of them one with another; as he that has eyes, if he will open them by day, cannot but see some objects, and perceive a difference in them. But though a man with his eyes open in the light, cannot but see, yet there be certain objects which he may choose whether he will turn his eyes to; there may be in his reach a book containing pictures and discourses, capable to delight or instruct him, which yet he may never have the will to open, never take the pains to look into.

2. *The Application voluntary; but we know as things are, not as we please.*—There is also another thing in a man's power, and that is, though he turns his eyes sometimes towards an object, yet he may choose whether he will curiously survey it, and with an intent application endeavour to observe accurately all that is visible in it; but yet, what he does see, he cannot see otherwise than he does. It depends not on his will to see that black which appears yellow; nor to persuade himself, that what actually scalds him, feels cold. The earth will not appear painted with flowers, nor the fields covered with verdure, whenever he has a mind to it: in the cold winter, he cannot help seeing it white and hoary, if he will look abroad. Just thus is it with our understanding: all that is voluntary in our knowledge is the employing or withholding any of our faculties, from this or that sort of objects, and a more or less accurate survey of them: but, they being employed, our will hath no power to determine the knowledge of the mind one way or another; that is done only by the objects themselves, as far as they are clearly discovered. And therefore, as far as men's senses are conversant about external objects, the mind cannot but receive those ideas which are presented by them, and be informed of the existence of things without; and so far as men's thoughts converse with their own determined ideas, they cannot but in some measure observe the agreement or disagreement that is to be found amongst some of them, which is so far knowledge: and if they have names for those ideas which they have thus considered, they must needs be assured of the truth of those propositions which express that agreement or disagreement they perceive in them, and be undoubtedly

convinced of those truths. For what a man sees, he cannot but see; and what he perceives, he cannot but know that he perceives.

3. *Instance in Numbers.*—Thus, he that has got the ideas of numbers, and hath taken the pains to compare one, two, and three, to six, cannot choose but know that they are equal: he that hath got the idea of a triangle, and found the ways to measure its angles and their magnitudes, is certain that its three angles are equal to two right ones; and can as little doubt of that, as of this truth, that, It is impossible for the same thing to be, and not to be.

4. *In Natural Religion.*—He also that hath the idea of an intelligent, but frail and weak being, made by and depending on another, who is eternal, omnipotent, perfectly wise and good, will as certainly know that man is to honour, fear, and obey God, as that the sun shines when he sees it. For if he hath but the ideas of two such beings in his mind, and will turn his thoughts that way, and consider them, he will as certainly find that the inferior, finite, and dependent, is under an obligation to obey the supreme and infinite, as he is certain to find that three, four, and seven are less than fifteen, if he will consider and compute those numbers; nor can he be surer in a clear morning that the sun is risen, if he will but open his eyes, and turn them that way. But yet these truths, being ever so certain, ever so clear, he may be ignorant of either, or all of them, who will never take the pains to employ his faculties, as he should, to inform himself about them.

CHAPTER XIV.
OF JUDGMENT.

1. *Our Knowledge being short, we want something else.*— THE understanding faculties being given to man, not barely for speculation, but also for the conduct of his life, man would be at a great loss if he had nothing to direct him but what has the certainty of true knowledge. For that being very short and scanty, as we have seen, he would be often utterly in the dark, and in most of the actions of his life, perfectly at a stand, had he nothing to guide him in the absence of clear and certain knowledge. He that will

not eat till he has demonstration that it will nourish him; he that will not stir till he infallibly knows the business he goes about will succeed, will have little else to do but to sit still and perish.

2. *What Use to be made of this twilight State.*—Therefore, as God has set some things in broad daylight; as he has given us some certain knowledge, though limited to a few things in comparison, probably as a taste of what intellectual creatures are capable of to excite in us a desire and endeavour after a better state: so, in the greatest part of our concernments, he has afforded us only the twilight, as I may so say, of probability; suitable, I presume, to that state of mediocrity and probationership he has been pleased to place us in here; wherein, to check our over-confidence and presumption, we might, by every day's experience, be made sensible of our short-sightedness and liableness to error;* the sense whereof might be a constant admonition to us, to spend the days of this our pilgrimage with industry and care, in the search and following of that way which might lead us to a state of greater perfection: it being highly rational to think, even were revelation silent in the case, that, as men employ those talents God has given them here, they shall accordingly receive their rewards at the close of the day, when their sun shall set, and night shall put an end to their labours.

3. *Judgment supplies the Want of Knowledge.*—The faculty which God has given man to supply the want of clear and certain knowledge, in cases where that cannot be had, is judgment: whereby the mind takes its ideas to agree or disagree; or, which is the same, any proposition to be true or false, without perceiving a demonstrative evidence in the proofs. The mind sometimes exercises this judgment out of necessity, where demonstrative proofs and certain knowledge are not to be had; and sometimes out of laziness, unskilfulness, or haste, even where demonstrative and certain proofs are to be had. Men often stay not warily to examine the agreement or disagreement of two ideas, which they are desirous or concerned

---

* See, for a picture of the quick-judging man of the world, who seizes on the fittest occasions for action, and is able at a glance to distinguish the expedient from the inexpedient, Cardan's curious and valuable treatise, De Prudentia Civile, c. xxii. p. 67.—ED.

to know; but, either incapable of such attention as is requisite in a long train of gradations, or impatient of delay. lightly cast their eyes on, or wholly pass by the proofs; and so, without making out the demonstration, determine of the agreement or disagreement of two ideas, as it were by a view of them as they are at a distance, and take it to be the one or the other, as seems most likely to them upon such a loose survey. This faculty of the mind, when it is exercised immediately about things, is called judgment; when about truths delivered in words, is most commonly called assent or dissent: which being the most usual way, wherein the mind has occasion to employ this faculty, I shall, under these terms, treat of it, as least liable in our language to equivocation.

4. *Judgment is the presuming Things to be so, without perceiving it.*—Thus the mind has two faculties conversant about truth and falsehood.

First, Knowledge, whereby it certainly perceives, and is undoubtedly satisfied of the agreement or disagreement of any ideas.

Secondly, Judgment, which is the putting ideas together, or separating them from one another in the mind, when their certain agreement or disagreement is not perceived, but presumed to be so; which is, as the word imports, taken to be so before it certainly appears. And if it so unites or separates them, as in reality things are, it is right judgment.

CHAPTER XV.
OF PROBABILITY.

1. *Probability is the Appearance of Agreement upon fallible Proofs.*—As demonstration is the showing the agreement or disagreement of two ideas, by the intervention of one or more proofs, which have a constant, immutable, and visible connexion one with another; so probability is nothing but the appearance of such an agreement or disagreement, by the intervention of proofs, whose connexion is not constant and immutable, or at least is not perceived to be so, but is, or appears for the most part to be so, and is enough to induce the mind to judge the proposition to be true or false, rather

than the contrary. For example: in the demonstration of it a man perceives the certain, immutable connexion there is of equality between the three angles of a triangle, and those intermediate ones which are made use of to show their equality to two right ones; and so, by an intuitive knowledge of the agreement or disagreement of the intermediate ideas in each step of the progress, the whole series is continued with an evidence, which clearly shows the agreement or disagreement of those three angles in equality to two right ones: and thus he has certain knowledge that it is so. But another man, who never took the pains to observe the demonstration, hearing a mathematician, a man of credit, affirm the three angles of a triangle to be equal to two right ones, assents to it, i. e., receives it for true: in which case the foundation of his assent is the probability of the thing; the proof being such as for the most part carries truth with it: the man on whose testimony he receives it, not being wont to affirm anything contrary to or besides his knowledge, especially in matters of this kind: so that that which causes his assent to this proposition, that the three angles of a triangle are equal to two right ones, that which makes him take these ideas to agree, without knowing them to do so, is the wonted veracity of the speaker in other cases, or his supposed veracity in this.

2. *It is to supply the Want of Knowledge.*—Our knowledge, as has been shown, being very narrow, and we not happy enough to find certain truth in everything which we have occasion to consider; most of the propositions we think, reason, discourse—nay, act upon, are such as we cannot have undoubted knowledge of their truth: yet some of them border so near upon certainty, that we make no doubt at all about them; but assent to them as firmly, and act, according to that assent, as resolutely as if they were infallibly demonstrated, and that our knowledge of them was perfect and certain. But there being degrees herein, from the very neighbourhood of certainty and demonstration, quite down to improbability and unlikeness, even to the confines of impossibility; and also degrees of assent from full assurance and confidence, quite down to conjecture, doubt, and distrust: I shall come now, (having, as I think, found out the bounds of human knowledge and certainty,) in the next place, to

consider the several degrees and grounds of probability, and assent or faith.

3. *Being that which makes us presume Things to be true before we know them to be so.*—Probability is likeliness to be true, the very notation of the word signifying such a proposition, for which there be arguments or proofs to make it pass or be received for true. The entertainment the mind gives this sort of propositions is called belief, assent, or opinion, which is the admitting or receiving any proposition for true, upon arguments or proofs that are found to persuade us to receive it as true, without certain knowledge that it is so. And herein lies the difference between probability and certainty, faith and knowledge, that in all the parts of knowledge there is intuition; each immediate idea, each step has its visible and certain connexion: in belief, not so. That which makes me believe, is something extraneous to the thing I believe; something not evidently joined on both sides to, and so not manifestly showing the agreement or disagreement of those ideas that are under consideration.

4. *The Grounds of Probability are two: Conformity with our own experience, or the Testimony of others' Experience.*—Probability, then, being to supply the defect of our knowledge and to guide us where that fails, is always conversant about propositions, whereof we have no certainty, but only some inducements to receive them for true. The grounds of it are, in short, these two following:

First, The conformity of anything with our own knowledge, observation, and experience.

Secondly, The testimony of others, vouching their observation and experience. In the testimony of others, is to be considered, 1. The number. 2. The integrity. 3. The skill of the witnesses. 4. The design of the author, where it is a testimony out of a book cited. 5. The consistency of the parts, and circumstances of the relation. 6. Contrary testimonies.

5. *In this, all the Arguments pro and con ought to be examined before we come to a Judgment.*—Probability wanting that intuitive evidence which infallibly determines the understanding, and produces certain knowledge, the mind, if it would proceed rationally, ought to examine all the grounds of probability, and see how they make more or less for or against

any proposition, before it assents to or dissents from it; and, upon a due balancing the whole, reject or receive it, with a more or less firm assent, proportionably to the preponderancy of the greater grounds of probability on one side or the other. For example:

If I myself see a man walk on the ice, it is past probability, it is knowledge: but if another tells me he saw a man in England, in the midst of a sharp winter, walk upon water, hardened with cold, this has so great conformity with what is usually observed to happen, that I am disposed by the nature of the thing itself to assent to it, unless some manifest suspicion attend the relation of that matter of fact. But if the same thing be told to one born between the tropics, who never saw nor heard of any such thing before, there the whole probability relies on testimony: and as the relators are more in number, and of more credit and have no interest to speak contrary to the truth, so that matter of fact is like to find more or less belief. Though to a man whose experience has always been quite contrary, and who has never heard of anything like it, the most unattainted credit of a witness will scarce be able to find belief. As it happened to a Dutch ambassador, who entertaining the king of Siam with the particularities of Holland, which he was inquisitive after, amongst other things told him, that the water in his country would sometimes, in cold weather, be so hard, that men walked upon it, and that it would bear an elephant, if he were there. To which the king replied, "Hitherto I have believed the strange things you have told me, because I look upon you as a sober fair man, but now I am sure you lie."

6. *They being capable of great Variety.* — Upon these grounds depends the probability of any proposition: and as the conformity of our knowledge, as the certainty of observations, as the frequency and constancy of experience, and the number and credibility of testimonies do more or less agree or disagree with it, so is any proposition in itself more or less probable. There is another, I confess, which, though by itself it be no true ground of probability, yet is often made use of for one, by which men most commonly regulate their assent, and upon which they pin their faith more than anything else, and that is, the opinion of others: though

there cannot be a more dangerous thing to rely on, nor more likely to mislead one; since there is much more falsehood and error among men, than truth and knowledge. And if the opinions and persuasions of others, whom we know and think well of, be a ground of assent, men have reason to be Heathens in Japan, Mahometans in Turkey, Papists in Spain, Protestants in England, and Lutherans in Sweden. But of this wrong ground of assent I shall have occasion to speak more at large in another place.

CHAPTER XVI.
OF THE DEGREES OF ASSENT.

1. *Our Assent ought to be regulated by the Grounds of Probability.*—The grounds of probability we have laid down in the foregoing chapter; as they are the foundations on which our assent is built, so are they also the measure whereby its several degrees are, or ought to be regulated: only we are to take notice, that, whatever grounds of probability there may be, they yet operate no further on the mind which searches after truth, and endeavours to judge right, than they appear; at least, in the first judgment or search that the mind makes. I confess, in the opinions men have, and firmly stick to in the world, their assent is not always from an actual view of the reasons that at first prevailed with them: it being in many cases almost impossible, and in most, very hard, even for those who have very admirable memories, to retain all the proofs which, upon a due examination, made them embrace that side of the question. It suffices that they have once with care and fairness sifted the matter as far as they could; and that they have searched into all the particulars, that they could imagine to give any light to the question; and, with the best of their skill, cast up the account upon the whole evidence: and thus, having once found on which side the probability appeared to them, after as full and exact an inquiry as they can make, they lay up the conclusion in their memories, as a truth they have discovered; and for the future they remain satisfied with the testimony of their memories, that this is the opinion that,

by the proofs they have once seen of it, deserves such a degree of their assent as they afford it.

2. *These cannot always be actually in View, and then we must content ourselves with the Remembrance that we once saw Ground for such a Degree of Assent.*—This is all that the greatest part of men are capable of doing, in regulating their opinions and judgments; unless a man will exact of them, either to retain distinctly in their memories all the proofs concerning any probable truth, and that too, in the same order, and regular deduction of consequences in which they have formerly placed or seen them; which sometimes is enough to fill a large volume on one single question: or else they must require a man, for every opinion that he embraces, every day to examine the proofs: both which are impossible. It is unavoidable, therefore, that the memory be relied on in the case, and that men be persuaded of several opinions, whereof the proofs are not actually in their thoughts: nay, which perhaps they are not able actually to recal. Without this, the greatest part of men must be either very sceptics, or change every moment, and yield themselves up to whoever, having lately studied the question, offers them arguments; which, for want of memory, they are not able presently to answer.

3. *The ill Consequence of this, if our former Judgments were not rightly made.*—I cannot but own, that men's sticking to their past judgment, and adhering firmly to conclusions formerly made, is often the cause of great obstinacy in error and mistake. But the fault is not that they rely on their memories for what they have before well judged, but because they judged before they had well examined. May we not find a great number (not to say the greatest part) of men that think they have formed right judgments of several matters; and that for no other reason, but because they never thought otherwise? who imagine themselves to have judged right, only because they never questioned, never examined their own opinions? Which is indeed to think they judged right, because they never judged at all: and yet these, of all men, hold their opinions with the greatest stiffness; those being generally the most fierce and firm in their tenets, who have least examined them. What we once know, we are certain is so: and we may be secure, that there are

no latent proofs undiscovered, which may overturn our knowledge, or bring it in doubt. But, in matters of probability, it is not in every case we can be sure that we have all the particulars before us, that any way concern the question; and that there is no evidence behind, and yet unseen, which may cast the probability on the other side, and outweigh all that at present seems to preponderate with us. Who almost is there that hath the leisure, patience, and means to collect together all the proofs concerning most of the opinions he has, so as safely to conclude that he hath a clear and full view; and that there is no more to be alleged for his better information? And yet we are forced to determine ourselves on the one side or other. The conduct of our lives, and the management of our great concerns, will not bear delay: for those depend, for the most part, on the determination of our judgment in points wherein we are not capable of certain and demonstrative knowledge, and wherein it is necessary for us to embrace the one side or the other.

4. *The right Use of it, mutual Charity and Forbearance.*—Since, therefore, it is unavoidable to the greatest part of men, if not all, to have several opinions, without certain and indubitable proofs of their truth; and it carries too great an imputation of ignorance, lightness, or folly for men to quit and renounce their former tenets presently upon the offer of an argument which they cannot immediately answer, and show the insufficiency of: it would, methinks, become all men to maintain peace, and the common offices of humanity and friendship, in the diversity of opinions; since we cannot reasonably expect that any one should readily and obsequiously quit his own opinion, and embrace ours with a blind resignation to an authority which the understanding of man acknowledges not.* For however it may

---

* In exactly the same spirit, Jeremy Taylor writes as follows, speaking of the heresies and schisms which formerly rose in the Christian world, and the attempts which were made to introduce uniformity of opinion:—" Few men in the mean time considered, that, so long as men had such variety of principles, such several constitutions, educations, tempers, and distempers, hopes, interests, and weaknesses, degrees of light, and degrees of understanding, it was impossible all should be of one mind. And what is impossible to be done is not necessary it should be done; and therefore, although variety of opinions was im-

often mistake, it can own no other guide but reason, nor blindly submit to the will and dictates of another. If he you would bring over to your sentiments be one that examines before he assents, you must give him leave at his leisure to go over the account again, and, recalling what is out of his mind, examine all the particulars, to see on which side the advantage lies: and if he will not think our arguments of weight enough to engage him anew in so much pains, it is but what we often do ourselves in the like case; and we should take it amiss if others should prescribe to us what points we should study. And if he be one who takes his opinions upon trust, how can we imagine that he should renounce those tenets which time and custom have so settled in his mind, that he thinks them self-evident, and of an unquestionable certainty; or which he takes to be impressions he has received from God himself, or from men sent by him? How can we expect, I say, that opinions thus settled should be given up to the arguments or authority of a stranger or adversary, especially if there be any suspicion of interest or design, as there never fails to be, where men find themselves ill treated? We should do well to commiserate our mutual ignorance, and endeavour to remove it in all the gentle and fair ways of information; and not instantly treat others ill, as obstinate and perverse, because they will not renounce their own, and receive our opinions, or at least those we would force upon them, when it is more than probable that we are no less obstinate in not embracing some of theirs. For where is the man that has incontestible evidence of the truth of all that he holds, or of the falsehood of all he condemns; or can say that he has examined to the bottom all his own, or other men's opinions? The necessity of believing without knowledge, nay often upon very slight grounds, in this fleeting state of action and blindness we are in, should make us more busy and careful to inform ourselves than constrain others. At least, those who have not thoroughly

possible to be cured, (and they who attempted it, did like him who claps his shoulder to the ground to stop an earthquake,) yet the inconveniences arising from it might possibly be cured, not by uniting their beliefs—that was to be despaired of—but by curing that which caused these mischiefs, and accidental inconveniences of their disagreeings." (Int. to Lib. of Proph. p. 2.)—ED.

examined to the bottom all their own tenets, must confess they are unfit to prescribe to others; and are unreasonable in imposing that as truth on other men's belief, which they themselves have not searched into, nor weighed the arguments of probability, on which they should receive or reject it. Those who have fairly and truly examined, and are thereby got past doubt in all the doctrines they profess and govern themselves by, would have a juster pretence to require others to follow them: but these are so few in number, and find so little reason to be magisterial in their opinions, that nothing insolent and imperious is to be expected from them: and there is reason to think, that, if men were better instructed themselves, they would be less imposing on others.

5. *Probability is either of Matter of Fact or Speculation.*—But to return to the grounds of assent, and the several degrees of it, we are to take notice, that the propositions we receive upon inducements of probability are of two sorts; either concerning some particular existence, or, as it is usually termed, matter of fact, which, falling under observation, is capable of human testimony; or else concerning things, which, being beyond the discovery of our senses, are not capable of any such testimony.

6. *The concurrent Experience of all other Men with ours, produces Assurance approaching to Knowledge.*—Concerning the first of these, viz., particular matter of fact.

First, Where any particular thing, consonant to the constant observation of ourselves and others in the like case, comes attested by the concurrent reports of all that mention it, we receive it as easily, and build as firmly upon it, as if it were certain knowledge; and we reason and act thereupon with as little doubt as if it were perfect demonstration. Thus, if all Englishmen who have occasion to mention it, should affirm that it froze in England the last winter, or that there were swallows seen there in the summer, I think a man could almost as little doubt of it as that seven and four are eleven. The first, therefore, and highest degree of probability, is, when the general consent of all men, in all ages, as far as it can be known, concurs with a man's constant and never-failing experience in like cases, to confirm the truth of any particular matter of fact attested by fair witnesses: such are all the stated constitutions and properties of bodies, and the regular proceedings of causes and effects in the ordinary course of nature. This we call an argument from the nature of things themselves. For what our own and other men's constant observation has found always to be after the same manner, that we with reason conclude to be the effect of steady and regular causes, though they come not within the reach of our knowledge. Thus, that fire warmed a man, made lead fluid, and changed the colour or consistency in wood or charcoal; that iron sunk in water, and swam in quicksilver; these and the like propositions about particular facts, being agreeable to our constant experience, as often as we have to do with these matters; and being generally spoke of (when mentioned by others) as things found constantly to be so, and therefore not so much as controverted by anybody, we are put past doubt that a relation affirming any such thing to have been, or any predication that it will happen again in the same manner, is very true. These probabilities rise so near to certainty, that they govern our thoughts as absolutely, and influence all our actions as fully, as the most evident demonstration; and in what concerns us we make little or no difference between them and certain knowledge. Our belief, thus grounded, rises to assurance.

7. *Unquestionable Testimony and Experience for the most part produce Confidence.*—Secondly, The next degree of probability is, when I find by my own experience, and the agreement of all others that mention it, a thing to be for the most part so, and that the particular instance of it is attested by many and undoubted witnesses, v. g., history giving us such an account of men in all ages, and my own experience, as far as I had an opportunity to observe, confirming it, that most men prefer their private advantage to the public: if all historians that write of Tiberius, say that Tiberius did so, it is extremely probable. And in this case, our assent has a sufficient foundation to raise itself to a degree which we may call confidence.

8. *Fair Testimony, and the Nature of the Thing indifferent, produce also confident Belief.*—Thirdly, In things that happen indifferently, as that a bird should fly this or that way; that it should thunder on a man's right or left hand, &c., when

any particular matter of fact is vouched by the concurrent testimony of unsuspected witnesses, there our assent is also unavoidable. Thus, that there is such a city in Italy as Rome; that about one thousand seven hundred years ago, there lived in it a man, called Julius Cæsar; that he was a general, and that he won a battle against another, called Pompey: this, though in the nature of the thing there be nothing for nor against it, yet being related by historians of credit, and contradicted by no one writer, a man cannot avoid believing it, and can as little doubt of it as he does of the being and actions of his own acquaintance, whereof he himself is a witness.

9. *Experience and Testimonies clashing, infinitely vary the Degrees of Probability.*—Thus far the matter goes easy enough. Probability upon such grounds carries so much evidence with it, that it naturally determines the judgment, and leaves us as little liberty to believe or disbelieve, as a demonstration does, whether we will know, or be ignorant. The difficulty is, when testimonies contradict common experience, and the reports of history and witnesses clash with the ordinary course of nature or with one another; there it is, where diligence, attention, and exactness are required, to form a right judgment, and to proportion the assent to the different evidence and probability of the thing; which rises and falls, according as those two foundations of credibility, viz., common observation in like cases, and particular testimonies in that particular instance, favour or contradict it. These are liable to so great variety of contrary observations, circumstances, reports, different qualifications, tempers, designs, oversights, &c., of the reporters, that it is impossible to reduce to precise rules the various degrees wherein men give their assent. This only may be said in general, that as the arguments and proofs pro and con, upon due examination, nicely weighing every particular circumstance, shall to any one appear, upon the whole matter in a greater or less degree to preponderate on either side; so they are fitted to produce in the mind such different entertainments, as we call belief, conjecture, guess, doubt, wavering, distrust, disbelief, &c.

10. *Traditional Testimonies, the further removed the less their Proof.*—This is what concerns assent in matters wherein testimony is made use of; concerning which, I think, it may

not be amiss to take notice of a rule observed in the law of England; which is, that though the attested copy of a record be good proof, yet the copy of a copy ever so well attested, and by ever so credible witnesses, will not be admitted as a proof in judicature. This is so generally approved as reasonable, and suited to the wisdom and caution to be used in our inquiry after material truths, that I never yet heard of any one that blamed it. This practice, if it be allowable in the decisions of right and wrong, carries this observation along with it, viz., that any testimony, the further off it is from the original truth, the less force and proof it has. The being and existence of the thing itself, is what I call the original truth. A credible man vouching his knowledge of it is a good proof; but if another equally credible do witness t from his report, the testimony is weaker; and a third that attests the hearsay of an hearsay is yet less considerable. So that in traditional truths, each remove weakens the force of the proof; and the more hands the tradition has successively passed through, the less strength and evidence does it receive from them. This I thought necessary to be taken notice of, because I find amongst some men the quite contrary commonly practised, who look on opinions to gain force by growing older; and what a thousand years since would not to a rational man contemporary with the first voucher have appeared at all probable, is now urged as certain beyond all question, only because several have since from him said it one after another. Upon this ground propositions, evidently false or doubtful enough in their first beginning, come, by an inverted rule of probability, to pass for authentic truths; and those which found or deserved little credit from the mouths of their first authors, are thought to grow venerable by age, and are urged as undeniable.

11. *Yet History is of great Use.*—I would not be thought here to lessen the credit and use of history; it is all the light we have in many cases, and we receive from it a great part of the useful truths we have, with a convincing evidence. I think nothing more valuable than the records of antiquity: I wish we had more of them, and more uncorrupted. But this truth itself forces me to say, that no probability can rise higher than its first original. What has no other evidence than the single testimony of one only witness must stand or

fall by his only testimony, whether good, bad, or indifferent; and though cited afterwards by hundreds of others, one after another, is so far from receiving any strength thereby, that it is only the weaker. Passion, interest, inadvertency, mistake of his meaning, and a thousand odd reasons, or capricios, men's minds are acted by, (impossible to be discovered,) may make one man quote another man's words or meaning wrong. He that has but ever so little examined the citations of writers, cannot doubt how little credit the quotations deserve, where the originals are wanting; and consequently how much less quotations of quotations can be relied on. This is certain, that what in one age was affirmed upon slight grounds, can never after come to be more valid in future ages by being often repeated. But the further still it is from the original, the less valid it is, and has always less force in the mouth or writing of him that last made use of it, than in his from whom he received it.

12. *In Things which Sense cannot discover, Analogy is the great Rule of Probability.*—The probabilities we have hitherto mentioned are only such as concern matter of fact, and such things as are capable of observation and testimony. There remains that other sort, concerning which men entertain opinions with variety of assent, though the things be such, that falling not under the reach of our senses, they are not capable of testimony. Such are, 1. The existence, nature, and operations of finite immaterial beings without us; as, spirits, angels, devils, &c., or the existence of material beings; which, either for their smallness in themselves, or remoteness from us, our senses cannot take notice of; as, whether there be any plants, animals, and intelligent inhabitants in the planets and other mansions of the vast universe. 2. Concerning the manner of operation in most parts of the works of nature: wherein though we see the sensible effects, yet their causes are unknown, and we perceive not the ways and manner how they are produced. We see animals are generated, nourished, and move; the loadstone draws iron; and the parts of a candle, successively melting, turn into flame, and give us both light and heat. These and the like effects we see and know: but the causes that operate, and the manner they are produced in, we can only guess and probably conjecture. For these and the like, coming not within the

scrutiny of human senses, cannot be examined by them, or be attested by anybody; and therefore can appear more or less probable, only as they more or less agree to truths that are established in our minds, and as they hold proportion to other parts of our knowledge and observation. Analogy in these matters is the only help we have, and it is from that alone we draw all our grounds of probability. Thus, observing that the bare rubbing of two bodies violently one upon another, produces heat, and very often fire itself, we have reason to think, that what we call heat and fire consists in a violent agitation of the imperceptible minute parts of the burning matter; observing likewise that the different refractions of pellucid bodies produce in our eyes the different appearances of several colours; and also, that the different ranging and laying the superficial parts of several bodies, as of velvet, watered silk, &c., does the like, we think it probable that the colour and shining of bodies is in them nothing but the different arrangement and refraction of their minute and insensible parts. Thus, finding in all parts of the creation that fall under human observation, that there is a gradual connexion of one with another, without any great or discernible gaps between, in all that great variety of things we see in the world, which are so closely linked together, that, in the several ranks of beings, it is not easy to discover the bounds betwixt them; we have reason to be persuaded that, by such gentle steps, things ascend upwards in degrees of perfection. It is a hard matter to say where sensible and rational begin, and where insensible and irrational end: and who is there quick-sighted enough to determine precisely which is the lowest species of living things, and which the first of those which have no life? Things, as far as we can observe, lessen and augment, as the quantity does in a regular cone; where, though there be a manifest odds betwixt the bigness of the diameter at a remote distance, yet the difference between the upper and under, where they touch one another, is hardly discernible. The difference is exceeding great between some men and some animals; but if we will compare the understanding and abilities of some men and some brutes, we shall find so little difference, that it will be hard to say, that that of the man is either clearer or larger. Observing, I say, such gradual and gentle descents downwards in those parts of the creation that are beneath man, the rule of analogy may make it probable, that it is so also in things above us and our observation; and that there are several ranks of intelligent beings, excelling us in several degrees of perfection, ascending upwards towards the infinite perfection of the Creator, by gentle steps and differences, that are every one at no great distance from the next to it. This sort of probability, which is the best conduct of rational experiments, and the rise of hypothesis, has also its use and influence; and a wary reasoning from analogy leads us often into the discovery of truths and useful productions, which would otherwise lie concealed.

13. *One Case where contrary Experience lessens not the Testimony.*—Though the common experience and the ordinary course of things have justly a mighty influence on the minds of men, to make them give or refuse credit to anything proposed to their belief; yet there is one case, wherein the strangeness of the fact lessens not the assent to a fair testimony given of it. For where such supernatural events are suitable to ends aimed at by him who has the power to change the course of nature, there, under such circumstances, they may be the fitter to procure belief, by how much the more they are beyond or contrary to ordinary observation. This is the proper case of miracles, which, well attested, do not only find credit themselves, but give it also to other truths, which need such confirmation.*

14. *The bare Testimony of Revelation is the highest Certainty.*—Besides those we have hitherto mentioned, there is one sort of propositions that challenge the highest degree of our assent upon bare testimony, whether the thing proposed agree or disagree with common experience, and the ordinary course of things, or no. The reason whereof is, because the testimony is of such an one as cannot deceive nor be deceived, and that is of God himself. This carries with it an assurance beyond doubt, evidence beyond exception. This is called by a peculiar name, revelation; and our assent to it, faith: which as absolutely determines our minds, and

---

* In his discourse on the subject, Locke defines a miracle to be, "A sensible operation, which, being above the comprehension of the spectator, and, in his opinion, contrary to the established course of nature, is taken by him to be divine." (p. 275.)—ED.

as perfectly excludes all wavering, as our knowledge itself; and we may as well doubt of our own being, as we can whether any revelation from God be true. So that faith is a settled and sure principle of assent and assurance, and leaves no manner of room for doubt or hesitation. Only we must be sure that it be a divine revelation, and that we understand it right: else we shall expose ourselves to all the extravagancy of enthusiasm, and all the error of wrong principles, if we have faith and assurance in what is not divine revelation. And therefore in those cases, our assent can be rationally no higher than the evidence of its being a revelation, and that this is the meaning of the expressions it is delivered in. If the evidence of its being a revelation, or that this is its true sense, be only on probable proofs; our assent can reach no higher than an assurance or diffidence, arising from the more or less apparent probability of the proofs. But of faith, and the precedency it ought to have before other arguments of persuasion, I shall speak more hereafter; where I treat of it as it is ordinarily placed, in contradistinction to reason; though in truth it be nothing else but an assent founded on the highest reason.

CHAPTER XVII.

OF REASON.

1. *Various Significations of the Word Reason.*—The word reason in the English language has different significations: sometimes it is taken for true and clear principles; sometimes for clear and fair deductions from those principles; and sometimes for the cause, and particularly the final cause. But the consideration I shall have of it here is in a signification different from all these; and that is, as it stands for a faculty in man, that faculty whereby man is supposed to be distinguished from beasts, and wherein it is evident he much surpasses them.

2. *Wherein Reasoning consists.*—If general knowledge, as has been shown, consists in a perception of the agreement or disagreement of our own ideas, and the knowledge of the existence of all things without us (except only of a God, whose existence every man may certainly know and demonstrate to himself from his own existence) be had only by our

senses, what room is there for the exercise of any other faculty, but outward sense and inward perception? What need is there of reason? Very much: both for the enlargement of our knowledge, and regulating our assent: for it hath to do both in knowledge and opinion, and is necessary and assisting to all our other intellectual faculties, and indeed contains two of them, viz., sagacity and illation. By the one, it finds out; and by the other, it so orders the intermediate ideas, as to discover what connexion there is in each link of the chain, whereby the extremes are held together; and thereby, as it were, to draw into view the truth sought for, which is that which we call illation or inference, and consists in nothing but the perception of the connexion there is between the ideas, in each step of the deduction, whereby the mind comes to see either the certain agreement or disagreement of any two ideas, as in demonstration, in which it arrives at knowledge; or their probable connexion, on which it gives or withholds its assent, as in opinion. Sense and intuition reach but a very little way. The greatest part of our knowledge depends upon deductions and intermediate ideas: and in those cases where we are fain to substitute assent instead of knowledge, and take propositions for true, without being certain they are so, we have need to find out, examine, and compare the grounds of their probability. In both these cases, the faculty which finds out the means, and rightly applies them to discover certainty in the one, and probability in the other, is that which we call reason. For as reason perceives the necessary and indubitable connexion of all the ideas or proofs one to another, in each step of any demonstration that produces knowledge; so it likewise perceives the probable connexion of all the ideas or proofs one to another, in every step of a discourse, to which it will think assent due. This is the lowest degree of that which can be truly called reason. For where the mind does not perceive this probable connexion, where it does not discern whether there be any such connexion or no; there men's opinions are not the product of judgment, or the consequence of reason, but the effects of chance and hazard, of a mind floating at all adventures, without choice and without direction.

3. *Its four Parts.*—So that we may in reason consider these four degrees: the first and highest is the discovering

and finding out of truths; the second, the regular and methodical disposition of them, and laying them in a clear and fit order, to make their connexion and force be plainly and easily perceived; the third is the perceiving their connexion; and the fourth, a making a right conclusion. These several degrees may be observed in any mathematical demonstration; it being one thing to perceive the connexion of each part, as the demonstration is made by another; another to perceive the dependence of the conclusion on all the parts; a third, to make out a demonstration clearly and neatly one's self; and something different from all these, to have first found out these intermediate ideas or proofs by which it is made.

4. *Syllogism not the great Instrument of Reason.*—There is one thing more which I shall desire to be considered concerning reason; and that is, whether syllogism, as is generally thought, be the proper instrument of it, and the usefullest way of exercising this faculty. The causes I have to doubt are these:—

First, Because syllogism serves our reason but in one only of the forementioned parts of it; and that is, to show the connexion of the proofs in any one instance, and no more; but in this it is of no great use, since the mind can perceive such connexion where it really is, as easily—nay, perhaps better—without it.

If we will observe the actings of our own minds, we shall find that we reason best and clearest, when we only observe the connexion of the proof, without reducing our thoughts to any rule of syllogism. And therefore we may take notice, that there are many men that reason exceeding clear and rightly, who know not how to make a syllogism. He that will look into many parts of Asia and America, will find men reason there perhaps as acutely as himself, who yet never heard of a syllogism, nor can reduce any one argument to those forms: and I believe scarce any one makes syllogisms in reasoning within himself. Indeed syllogism is made use of on occasion to discover a fallacy hid in a rhetorical flourish, or cunningly wrapt up in a smooth period; and, stripping an absurdity of the cover of wit and good language, show it in its naked deformity. But the weakness or fallacy of such a loose discourse it shows, by the artificial form it is put into, only to those who have thoroughly studied mode and figure, and have so examined the many ways that three propositions may be put together, as to know which of them does certainly conclude right, and which not, and upon what grounds it is that they do so. All who have so far considered syllogism, as to see the reason why in three propositions laid together in one form, the conclusion will be certainly right, but in another not certainly so, I grant are certain of the conclusion they draw from the premises in the allowed modes and figures. But they who have not so far looked into those forms, are not sure by virtue of syllogism, that the conclusion certainly follows from the premises; they only take it to be so by an implicit faith in their teachers and a confidence in those forms of argumentation; but this is still but believing, not being certain. Now, if, of all mankind those who can make syllogisms are extremely few in comparison of those who cannot; and if, of those few who have been taught logic, there is but a very small number who do any more than believe that syllogisms, in the allowed modes and figures do conclude right, without knowing certainly that they do so, if syllogisms must be taken for the only proper instrument of reason and means of knowledge, it will follow, that, before Aristotle, there was not one man that did or could know anything by reason; and that, since the invention of syllogisms, there is not one of ten thousand that doth.

But God has not been so sparing to men to make them barely two-legged creatures, and left it to Aristotle to make them rational, i. e., those few of them that he could get so to examine the grounds of syllogisms, as to see that, in above three score ways, that three propositions may be laid together, there are but about fourteen wherein one may be sure that the conclusion is right; and upon what grounds it is, that, in these few, the conclusion is certain, and in the other not. God has been more bountiful to mankind than so. He has given them a mind that can reason, without being instructed in methods of syllogizing: the understanding is not taught to reason by these rules; it has a native faculty to perceive the coherence or incoherence of its ideas, and can range them right, without any such perplexing repetitions. I say not this any way to lessen Aristotle, whom I look on as one of the greatest men amongst the ancients; whose large views, acuteness, and penetration of thought and strength of judgment, few have equalled; and who, in this very invention of forms of argumentation, wherein the conclusion may be shown to be rightly inferred, did great service against those who were not ashamed to deny anything. And I readily own, that all right reasoning may be reduced to his forms of syllogism. But yet I think, without any diminution to him, I may truly say, that they are not the only, nor the best way of reasoning, for the leading of those into truth who are willing to find it, and desire to make the best use they may of their reason, for the attainment of knowledge. And he himself, it is plain, found out some forms to be conclusive, and others not, not by the forms themselves, but by the original way of knowledge, i. e., by the visible agreement of ideas. Tell a country gentlewoman that the wind is south-west, and the weather lowering, and like to rain, and she will easily understand it is not safe for her to go abroad thin clad in such a day, after a fever; she clearly sees the probable connexion of all these, viz., south-west wind, and clouds, rain, wetting, taking cold, relapse, and danger of death, without tying them together in those artificial and cumbersome fetters of several syllogisms, that clog and hinder the mind, which proceeds from one part to another quicker and clearer without them; and the probability which she easily perceives in things thus in their native state would be quite lost, if this argument were managed learnedly and proposed in mode and figure. For it very often confounds the connexion; and, I think, every one will perceive in mathematical demonstrations, that the knowledge gained thereby comes shortest and clearest without syllogisms.

Inference is looked on as the great act of the rational faculty, and so it is when it is rightly made; but the mind, either very desirous to enlarge its knowledge, or very apt to favour the sentiments it has once imbibed, is very forward to make inferences, and therefore often makes too much haste, before it perceives the connexion of the ideas that must hold the extremes together.

To infer, is nothing but by virtue of one proposition laid down as true, to draw in another as true, i. e., to see or suppose such a connexion of the two ideas of the inferred proposition: v. g., let this be the proposition laid down, "Men shall be punished in another world," and from thence be inferred this other, "Then men can determine themselves." The question now is, to know whether the mind has made this inference right or no; if it has made it by finding out the intermediate ideas, and taking a view of the connexion of them, placed in a due order, it has proceeded rationally, and made a right inference. If it has done it without such a view, it has not so much made an inference that will hold, or an inference of right reason, as shown a willingness to have it be, or be taken for such. But in neither case is it syllogism that discovered those ideas, or showed the connexion of them, for they must be both found out, and the connexion everywhere perceived, before they can rationally be made use of in syllogism; unless it can be said, that any idea, without considering what connexion it hath with the two other, whose agreement should be shown by it, will do well enough in a syllogism, and may be taken at a venture for the medius terminus, to prove any conclusion. But this nobody will say, because it is by virtue of the perceived agreement of the intermediate idea with the extremes, that the extremes are concluded to agree; and therefore each intermediate idea must be such as in the whole chain hath a visible connexion with those two it has been placed between, or else thereby the conclusion cannot be inferred or drawn in: for wherever any link of the chain is loose and without connexion, there the whole strength of it is lost, and it hath no force to infer or draw in anything. In the instance above mentioned, what is it shows the force of the inference, and consequently the reasonableness of it, but a view of the connexion of all the intermediate ideas that draw in the conclusion or proposition inferred? v. g., "Men shall be punished;" "God the punisher;" "Just punishment;" "The punished guilty;" "Could have done otherwise;" "Freedom;" "Self-determination;" by which chain of ideas thus visibly linked together in train, i. e., each intermediate idea agreeing on each side with those two it is immediately placed between, the ideas of men and self-determination appear to be connected, i. e., this proposition men can determine themselves is drawn in or inferred from this, that they shall be punished in the other world. For here the mind seeing the connexion there is between the idea of men's punishment in the other world and the idea of God punishing; between God punishing and the justice of the punishment; between justice of the punishment and guilt; between guilt and a power to do otherwise; between a power to do otherwise and freedom; and between freedom and self-determination, sees the connexion between men and self-determination.

Now I ask, whether the connexion of the extremes be not more clearly seen in this simple and natural disposition, than in the perplexed repetitions, and jumble of five or six syllogisms.* I must beg pardon for calling it jumble, till somebody shall put these ideas into so many syllogisms, and then say that they are less jumbled, and their connexion more visible, when they are transposed and repeated, and spun out to a greater length in artificial forms, than in that short and natural plain order they are laid down in here, wherein everyone may see it, and wherein they must be seen before they can be put into a train of syllogisms. For the natural order of the connecting ideas must direct the order of the syllogisms, and a man must see the connexion of each intermediate idea with those that it connects, before he can with reason make use of it in a syllogism. And when all those syllogisms are made, neither those that are nor those that are

* In my appendix to the Reasonableness of Christianity, I have on this subject made the following remark:—"Between the publication of the several editions of the "Essay on the Human Understanding," which appeared during his lifetime, Locke changed his opinion on more than one point, and, like an honest and independent thinker, he was always careful to acknowledge this change. This, among other things, was the case with the use of syllogisms. For in Book IV. ch. 17, "I grant," says he, "that mood and figure is commonly made use of in such cases, (in the discovery of fallacies,) as if the detection of the incoherence of such loose discourses were wholly owing to the syllogistical form; and so I myself formerly thought, till upon a stricter examination I now find, that laying the intermediate ideas naked, in their due order, shows the incoherence of the argumentation better than syllogism." His opinions, however, on this point were fluctuating; for in his "Second Vindication," speaking of the fallacies and incoherence of his antagonist, he has these words:—"Nay, if he or anybody, in the 112 pages of his 'Socinianism Unmasked,' can find but ten arguments that will bear *the test of syllogism, the true touchstone of right arguing*, I will grant that that treatise deserves all those commendations he has bestowed upon it; though it be made up more of his own panegyric than a confutation of me." (p. 239.)—ED.

not logicians will see the force of the argumentation, i. e., the connexion of the extremes, one jot the better. [For those that are not men of art, not knowing the true forms of syllogism, nor the reasons of them, cannot know whether they are made in right and conclusive modes and figures or no, and so are not at all helped by the forms they are put into; though by them the natural order, wherein the mind could judge of their respective connexion, being disturbed, renders the illation much more uncertain than without them.] And as for the logicians themselves, they see the connexion of each intermediate idea with those it stands between, (on which the force of the inference depends,) as well before as after the syllogism is made, or else they do not see it at all. For a syllogism neither shows nor strengthens the connexion of any two ideas immediately put together, but only by the connexion seen in them shows what connexion the extremes have one with another. But what connexion the intermediate has with either of the extremes in the syllogism, that no syllogism does or can show. That the mind only doth or can perceive as they stand there in that juxta-position only by its own view, to which the syllogistical form it happens to be in gives no help or light at all; it only shows that if the intermediate idea agrees with those it is on both sides immediately applied to; then those two remote ones, or, as they are called, extremes, do certainly agree, and therefore the immediate connexion of each idea to that which it is applied to on each side, on which the force of the reasoning depends, is as well seen before as after the syllogism is made, or else he that makes the syllogism could never see it at all. This, as has been already observed, is seen only by the eye, or the perceptive faculty of the mind, taking a view of them laid together, in a juxta-position; which view of any two it has equally, whenever they are laid together in any proposition, whether that proposition be placed as a major or a minor, in a syllogism or no.

Of what use, then, are syllogisms? I answer, their chief and main use is in the schools, where men are allowed without shame to deny the agreement of ideas that do manifestly agree; or out of the schools, to those who from thence have learned without shame to deny the connexion of ideas, which even to themselves is visible. But to an ingenuous searcher after truth, who has no other aim but to find it, there is no need of any such form to force the allowing of the inference: the truth and reasonableness of it is better seen in ranging of the ideas in a simple and plain order; and hence it is that men, in their own inquiries after truth, never use syllogisms to convince themselves [or in teaching others to instruct willing learners.] Because, before they can put them into a syllogism, they must see the connexion that is between the intermediate idea and the two other ideas it is set between and applied to, to show their agreement; and when they see that, they see whether the inference be good or no, and so syllogism comes too late to settle it. For to make use again of the former instance, I ask whether the mind, considering the idea of justice, placed as an intermediate idea between the punishment of men and the guilt of the punished, (and till it does so consider it, the mind cannot make use of it as a medius terminus,) does not as plainly see the force and strength of the inference as when it is formed into a syllogism. To show it in a very plain and easy example; let animal be the intermediate idea or medius terminus that the mind makes use of to show the connexion of homo and vivens; I ask whether the mind does not more readily and plainly see that connexion in the simple and proper position of the connnecting idea in the middle? thus:

   Homo   Animal   Vivens,
than in this perplexed one,—
    Animal   Vivens   Homo   Animal:
which is the position these ideas have in a syllogism, to show the connexion between homo and vivens by the intervention of animal.

Indeed syllogism is thought to be of necessary use, even to the lovers of truth, to show them the fallacies that are often concealed in florid, witty, or involved discourses. But that this is a mistake will appear, if we consider, that the reason why sometimes men who sincerely aim at truth are imposed upon by such loose, and, as they are called, rhetorical discourses, is, that their fancies being struck with some lively metaphorical representations, they neglect to observe, or do not easily perceive what are the true ideas upon which the inference depends. Now, to show such men the weakness of such an argumentation, there needs no more but to strip it of the superfluous ideas, which, blended and confounded with those on which the inference depends, seem to show a connexion where there is none; or at least to hinder the discovery of the want of it; and then to lay the naked ideas on which the force of the argumentation depends in their due order, in which position the mind, taking a view of them, sees what connexion they have, and so is able to judge of the inference without any need of a syllogism at all.

I grant that mode and figure is commonly made use of in such cases, as if the detection of the incoherence of such loose discourses were wholly owing to the syllogistical form; and so I myself formerly thought, till upon a stricter examination I now find, that, laying the intermediate ideas naked in their due order, shows the incoherence of the argumentation better than syllogism; not only as subjecting each link of the chain to the immediate view of the mind in its proper place, whereby its connexion is best observed; but also because syllogism shows the incoherence only to those (who are not one of ten thousand) who perfectly understand mode and figure, and the reason upon which those forms are established; whereas a due and orderly placing of the ideas upon which the inference is made, makes every one, whether logician or not logician, who understands the terms, and hath the faculty to perceive the agreement or disagreement of such ideas, (without which, in or out of syllogism, he cannot perceive the strength or weakness, coherence or incoherence of the discourse) see the want of connexion in the argumentation, and the absurdity of the inference.

And thus I have known a man unskilful in syllogism, who at first hearing could perceive the weakness and inconclusiveness of a long artificial and plausible discourse, wherewith others better skilled in syllogism have been misled: and I believe there are few of my readers who do not know such. And indeed, if it were not so, the debates of most princes' councils, and the business of assemblies, would be in danger to be mismanaged, since those who are relied upon, and have usually a great stroke in them, are not always such who have the good luck to be perfectly knowing in the forms of syllogism, or expert in mode and figure. And if syllogism were the only, or so much as the surest way to detect the fallacies of artificial discourses; I do not think that all mankind, even princes in matters that concern their crowns and dignities, are so much in love with falsehood and mistake, that they would everywhere have neglected to bring syllogism into the debates of moment; or thought it ridiculous so much as to offer them in affairs of consequence; a plain evidence to me, that men of parts and penetration, who were not idly to dispute at their ease, but were to act according to the result of their debates, and often pay for their mistakes with their heads or fortunes, found those scholastic forms were of little use to discover truth or fallacy, whilst both the one and the other might be shown, and better shown without them, to those who would not refuse to see what was visibly shown them.

Secondly, Another reason that makes me doubt whether syllogism be the only proper instrument of reason in the discovery of truth, is, that of whatever use, mode, and figure, is pretended to be in the laying open of fallacy, (which has been above considered,) those scholastic forms of discourse are not less liable to fallacies than the plainer ways of argumentation; and for this I appeal to common observation, which has always found these artificial methods of reasoning more adapted to catch and entangle the mind, than to instruct and inform the understanding. And hence it is that men, even when they are baffled and silenced in this scholastic way, are seldom or never convinced, and so brought over to the conquering side: they perhaps acknowledge their adversary to be the more skilful disputant, but rest nevertheless persuaded of the truth on their side, and go away worsted as they are, with the same opinion they brought with them, which they could not do if this way of argumentation carried light and conviction with it, and made men see where the truth lay; and therefore syllogism has been thought more proper for the attaining victory in dispute, than for the discovery or confirmation of truth in fair inquiries. And if it be certain, that fallacies can be couched in syllogism, as it cannot be denied; it must be something else, and not syllogism, that must discover them.

I have had experience how ready some men are, when all

the use which they have been wont to ascribe to anything is not allowed, to cry out, that I am for laying it wholly aside. But to prevent such unjust and groundless imputations, I tell them, that I am not for taking away any helps to the understanding in the attainment of knowledge. And if men skilled in and used to syllogisms, find them assisting to their reason in the discovery of truth, I think they ought to make use of them. All that I aim at, is, that they should not ascribe more to these forms than belongs to them, and think that men have no use, or not so full an use of their reasoning faculties without them. Some eyes want spectacles to see things clearly and distinctly; but let not those that use them therefore say nobody can see clearly without them: those who do so will be thought in favour of art, (which, perhaps, they are beholden to,) a little too much to depress and discredit nature. Reason, by its own penetration, where it is strong and exercised, usually sees quicker and clearer without syllogism. If use of those spectacles has so dimmed its sight, that it cannot without them see consequences or inconsequences in argumentation, I am not so unreasonable as to be against the using them. Every one knows what best fits his own sight; but let him not thence conclude all in the dark, who use not just the same helps that he finds a need of.*

5. *Helps little in Demonstration, less in Probability.*—But however it be in knowledge, I think I may truly say, it is of far less, or no use at all in probabilities. For the assent there being to be determined by the preponderancy, after due weighing of all the proofs, with all circumstances on both sides, nothing is so unfit to assist the mind in that as syllogism; which, running away with one assumed probability, or one topical argument, pursues that till it has led the mind quite out of sight of the thing under consideration; and, forcing it upon some remote difficulty, holds it fast there, entangled, perhaps, as it were, manacled, in the chain of syllogisms, without allowing it the liberty, much less affording it the helps, requisite to show on which side, all things considered, is the greater probability.

* On the subject of syllogism, see the smaller "Logic" of Christian Wolf, c. vi. p. 74, where it is perhaps treated of more satisfactorily than by any other modern writer.—ED.

6. *Serves not to increase our Knowledge, but fence with it.*—But let it help us (as perhaps may be said) in convincing men of their errors and mistakes, (and yet I would fain see the man that was forced out of his opinion by dint of syllogism,) yet still it fails our reason in that part, which, if not its highest perfection, is yet certainly its hardest task, and that which we most need its help in: and that is the finding out of proofs, and making new discoveries. The rules of syllogism serve not to furnish the mind with those intermediate ideas that may show the connexion of remote ones. This way of reasoning discovers no new proofs, but is the art of marshalling and ranging the old ones we have already. The forty-seventh proposition of the first book of Euclid is very true; but the discovery of it, I think, not owing to any rules of common logic. A man knows first, and then he is able to prove syllogistically; so that syllogism comes after knowledge, and then a man has little or no need of it. But it is chiefly by the finding out those ideas that show the connexion of distant ones, that our stock of knowledge is increased, and that useful arts and sciences are advanced. Syllogism, at best, is but the art of fencing with the little knowledge we have, without making any addition to it; and if a man should employ his reason all this way, he will not do much otherwise than he who, having got some iron out of the bowels of the earth, should have it beaten up all into swords, and put it into his servants' hands to fence with and bang one another. Had the King of Spain employed the hands of his people, and his Spanish iron so, he had brought to light but little of that treasure that lay so long hid in the entrails of America. And I am apt to think, that he who shall employ all the force of his reason only in brandishing of syllogisms, will discover very little of that mass of knowledge which lies yet concealed in the secret recesses of nature, and which, I am apt to think, native rustic reason (as it formerly has done) is likelier to open a way to, and add to the common stock of mankind, rather than any scholastic proceeding by the strict rule of mode and figure.

7. *Other Helps should be sought.*—I doubt not, nevertheless, but there are ways to be found to assist our reason in this most useful part; and this the judicious Hooker encourages me to say, who in his Eccl. Pol. l. i. § 6, speaks thus:

"If there might be added the right helps of true art and learning, (which helps, I must plainly confess, this age of the world, carrying the name of a learned age, doth neither much know nor generally regard,) there would undoubtedly be almost as much difference in maturity of judgment between men therewith inured, and that which men now are, as between men that are now, and innocents."* I do not pretend to have found or discovered here any of those right helps of art, this great man of deep thought mentions; but this is plain, that syllogism, and the logic now in use, which were as well known in his days, can be none of those he means. It is sufficient for me, if by a discourse, perhaps something out of the way, I am sure, as to me, wholly new and unborrowed, I shall have given occasion to others to cast about for new discoveries, and to seek in their own thoughts for those right helps of art, which will scarce be found, I fear, by those who servilely confine themselves to the rules and dictates of others. For beaten tracks lead this sort of cattle, (as an observing Roman calls them,) whose thoughts reach only to imitation, "non quo eundum est, sed quo itur." But I can be bold to say, that this age is adorned with some men of that strength of judgment and largeness of comprehension, that, if they would employ their thoughts on this subject, could open new and undiscovered ways to the advancement of knowledge.

8. *We reason about Particulars.* — Having here had an occasion to speak of syllogism in general, and the use of it in reasoning, and the improvement of our knowledge, it is fit, before I leave this subject, to take notice of one manifest mistake in the rules of syllogism, viz., that no syllogistical reasoning can be right and conclusive, but what has at least one general proposition in it. As if we could not reason, and have knowledge about particulars; whereas, in truth, the matter rightly considered, the immediate object of all our reasoning and knowledge, is nothing but particulars. Every man's reasoning and knowledge is only about the ideas existing in his own mind, which are truly, everyone of them, particular exist-

---

* Plato has a similar idea in speaking of Isocrates:—"ὥστε οὐδὲν ἂν γένοιτο θαυμαστὸν προϊούσης τῆς ἡλικίας εἰ περὶ αὐτούς τε τοὺς λόγους, οἷς νῦν ἐπιχειρεῖ, πλέον ἢ παίδων διενέγκοι τῶν πώποτ' ἁψαμένων, λόγων, ἔτι τε εἰ αὐτῷ μὴ ἀποχρήσαι ταῦτα, ἐπὶ μείζω δὲ τις αὐτὸν ἄγοι ὁρμὴ θειοτέρα." (Phædrus, t. I. p. 105 seq. Bekk.)—ED

ences; and our knowledge and reason about other things, is only as they correspond with those of our particular ideas. So that the perception of the agreement or disagreement of our particular ideas, is the whole and utmost of all our knowledge. Universality is but accidental to it, and consists only in this, that the particular ideas about which it is, are such as more than one particular thing can correspond with and be represented by. But the perception of the agreement or disagreement of any two ideas, and consequently our knowledge, is equally clear and certain, whether either, or both, or neither of those ideas, be capable of representing more real beings than one or no. One thing more I crave leave to offer about syllogism, before I leave it, viz., may one not upon just ground inquire whether the form syllogism now has, is that which in reason it ought to have? For the medius terminus being to join the extremes, i. e., the intermediate idea by its intervention, to show the agreement or diagreement of the two in question, would not the position of the medius terminus be more natural, and show the agreement or disagreement of the extremes clearer and better, if it were placed in the middle between them? Which might be easily done by transposing the propositions, and making the medius terminus the predicate of the first, and the subject of the second. As thus:

"Omnis homo est animal. Omne animal est vivens. Ergo, omnis homo est vivens.

"Omne corpus est extensum et solidum. Nullum extensum et solidum est pura extensio. Ergo, corpus non est pura extensio."

I need not trouble my reader with instances in syllogisms whose conclusions are particular. The same reason holds for the same form in them, as well as in the general.

9. *First, Reason fails us for Want of Ideas.*—Reason, though it penetrates into the depths of the sea and earth, elevates our thoughts as high as the stars, and leads us through the vast spaces and large rooms of this mighty fabric, yet it comes far short of the real extent of even corporeal being; and there are many instances wherein it fails us: as,

First, It perfectly fails us, where our ideas fail.—It neither does nor can extend itself further than they do; and therefore, wherever we have no ideas, our reasoning stops, and we are at an end of our reckoning; and if at any time we reason about words which do not stand for any ideas, it is only about those sounds, and nothing else.

10. *Secondly, Because of obscure and imperfect Ideas.*—II. Our reason is often puzzled and at a loss, because of the obscurity, confusion, or imperfection of the ideas it is employed about; and there we are involved in difficulties and contradictions. Thus, not having any perfect idea of the least extension of matter, nor of infinity, we are at a loss about the divisibility of matter; but having perfect, clear, and distinct ideas of number, our reason meets with none of those inextricable difficulties in numbers, nor finds itself involved in any contradictions about them. Thus, we having but imperfect ideas of the operations of our minds, and of the beginning of motion, or thought, how the mind produces either of them in us, and much imperfecter yet of the operation of God, run into great difficulties about free created agents, which reason cannot well extricate itself out of.

11. *Thirdly, For Want of Intermediate Ideas.*—III. Our reason is often at a stand, because it perceives not those ideas, which could serve to show the certain or probable agreement or disagreement of any other two ideas; and in this some men's faculties far outgo others. Till algebra, that great instrument and instance of human sagacity, was discovered, men with amazement looked on several of the demonstrations of ancient mathematicians, and could scarce forbear to think the finding several of those proofs to be something more than human.

12. *Fourthly, Because of wrong Principles.*—IV. The mind, by proceeding upon false principles, is often engaged in absurdities and difficulties, brought into straits and contradictions, without knowing how to free itself; and in that case it is in vain to implore the help of reason, unless it be to discover the falsehood and reject the influence of those wrong principles. Reason is so far from clearing the difficulties which the building upon false foundations brings a man into, that if he will pursue it, it entangles him the more, and engages him deeper in perplexities.

13. *Fifthly, Because of doubtful Terms.*—V. As obscure and imperfect ideas often involve our reason, so, upon the

same ground, do dubious words and uncertain signs often in discourses and arguings, when not warily attended to, puzzle men's reason, and bring them to a nonplus. But these two latter are our fault, and not the fault of reason. But yet the consequences of them are nevertheless obvious; and the perplexities or errors they fill men's minds with are everywhere observable.

14. *Our highest Degreee of Knowledge is intuitive, without Reasoning.*—Some of the ideas that are in the mind, are so there, that they can be by themselves immediately compared one with another; and in these the mind is able to perceive that they agree or disagree as clearly as that it has them. Thus the mind perceives, that an arch of a circle is less than the whole circle, as clearly as it does the idea of a circle; and this, therefore, as has been said, I call intuitive knowledge; which is certain, beyond all doubt, and needs no probation, nor can have any, this being the highest of all human certainty. In this consists the evidence of all those maxims which nobody has any doubt about, but every man (does not, as is said, only assent to, but) knows to be true, as soon as ever they are proposed to his understanding. In the discovery of and assent to these truths, there is no use of the discursive faculty, no need of reasoning, but they are known by a superior and higher degree of evidence. And such, if I may guess at things unknown, I am apt to think that angels have now, and the spirits of just men made perfect shall have in a future state, of thousands of things which now either wholly escape our apprehensions, or which our short-sighted reason having got some faint glimpse of, we, in the dark, grope after.

15. *The next is Demonstration by Reasoning.*—But though we have, here and there, a little of this clear light, some sparks of bright knowledge, yet the greatest part of our ideas are such, that we cannot discern their agreement or disagreement by an immediate comparing them. And in all these we have need of reasoning, and must, by discourse and inference, make our discoveries. Now of these there are two sorts, which I shall take the liberty to mention here again.

First, Those whose agreement or disagreement, though it cannot be seen by an immediate putting them together, yet may be examined by the intervention of other ideas which can be compared with them. In this case, when the agreement or disagreement of the intermediate idea, on both sides with those which we would compare, is plainly discerned, there it amounts to a demonstration, whereby knowledge is produced; which, though it be certain, yet it is not so easy, nor altogether so clear as intuitive knowledge. Because in that there is barely one simple intuition, wherein there is no room for any the least mistake or doubt; the truth is seen all perfectly at once. In demonstration, it is true, there is intuition too, but not altogether at once; for there must be a remembrance of the intuition of the agreement of the medium, or intermediate idea, with that we compared it with before, when we compare it with the other; and where there be many mediums, there the danger of the mistake is the greater. For each agreement or disagreement of the ideas must be observed and seen in each step of the whole train, and retained in the memory, just as it is; and the mind must be sure that no part of what is necessary to make up the demonstration is omitted or overlooked. This makes some demonstrations long and perplexed, and too hard for those who have not strength of parts distinctly to perceive, and exactly carry so many particulars orderly in their heads. And even those who are able to master such intricate speculations, are fain sometimes to go over them again, and there is need of more than one review before they can arrive at certainty. But yet where the mind clearly retains the intuition it had of the agreement of any idea with another, and that with a third, and that with a fourth, &c., there the agreement of the first and the fourth is a demonstration, and produces certain knowledge, which may be called rational knowledge, as the other is intuitive.

16. *To supply the Narrowness of this, we have Nothing but Judgment upon probable Reasoning.* — Secondly, There are other ideas, whose agreement or disagreement can no otherwise be judged of, but by the intervention of others which have not a certain agreement with the extremes, but an usual or likely one: and in these it is that the judgment is properly exercised, which is the acquiescing of the mind, that any ideas do agree, by comparing them with such probable mediums. This, though it never amounts to knowledge, no, not to that which is the lowest degree of it; yet

sometimes the intermediate ideas tie the extremes so firmly together, and the probability is so clear and strong, that assent as necessarily follows it, as knowledge does demonstration. The great excellency and use of the judgment is to observe right, and take a true estimate of the force and weight of each probability; and then casting them up all right together, choose that side which has the overbalance.

17. *Intuition, Demonstration, Judgment.*—Intuitive knowledge is the perception of the certain agreement or disagreement of two ideas immediately compared together.

Rational knowledge is the perception of the certain agreement or disagreement of any two ideas, by the intervention of one or more other ideas.

Judgment is the thinking or taking two ideas to agree or disagree, by the intervention of one or more ideas, whose certain agreement or disagreement with them it does not perceive, but hath observed to be frequent and usual.

18. *Consequences of Words, and Consequences of Ideas.*—Though the deducing one proposition from another, or making inferences in words, be a great part of reason, and that which it is usually employed about; yet the principal act of ratiocination is the finding the agreement or disagreement of two ideas one with another, by the intervention of a third. As a man, by a yard, finds two houses to be of the same length, which could not be brought together to measure their equality by juxta-position. Words have their consequences, as the signs of such ideas; and things agree or disagree, as really they are; but we observe it only by our ideas.

19. *Four Sorts of Arguments.*—Before we quit this subject, it may be worth our while a little to reflect on four sorts of arguments, that men, in their reasonings with others, do ordinarily make use of to prevail on their assent; or at least so to awe them as to silence their opposition.

1. *Ad verecundiam.*—First, The first is to allege the opinions of men, whose parts, learning, eminency, power, or some other cause has gained a name, and settled their reputation in the common esteem with some kind of authority. When men are established in any kind of dignity, it is thought a breach of modesty for others to derogate any way from it, and question the authority of men who are in possession of it. This is apt to be censured, as carrying with it

too much pride, when a man does not readily yield to the determination of approved authors, which is wont to be received with respect and submission by others; and it is looked upon as insolence for a man to set up and adhere to his own opinion against the current stream of antiquity; or to put it in the balance against that of some learned doctor, or otherwise approved writer. Whoever backs his tenets with such authorities, thinks he ought thereby to carry the cause, and is ready to style it impudence in any one who shall stand out against them. This I think may be called argumentum ad verecundiam.

20. II. *Ad Ignorantiam.*—Secondly, Another way that men ordinarily use to drive others, and force them to submit their judgments, and receive the opinion in debate, is to require the adversary to admit what they allege as a proof, or to assign a better. And this I call argumentum ad ignorantiam.

21. III. *Ad hominem.*—Thirdly, A third way is to press a man with consequences drawn from his own principles or concessions. This is already known under the name of argumentum ad hominem.

22. IV. *Fourthly, Ad judicium.*—The fourth is the using of proofs drawn from any of the foundations of knowledge or probability. This I call argumentum ad judicium. This alone, of all the four, brings true instruction with it, and advances us in our way to knowledge. For, 1. It argues not another man's opinion to be right, because I, out of respect, or any other consideration but that of conviction, will not contradict him. 2. It proves not another man to be in the right way, nor that I ought to take the same with him, because I know not a better. 3. Nor does it follow that another man is in the right way, because he has shown me that I am in the wrong. I may be modest, and therefore not oppose another man's persuasion: I may be ignorant, and not be able to produce a better; I may be in an error, and another may show me that I am so. This may dispose me, perhaps, for the reception of truth, but helps me not to it; that must come from proofs and arguments, and light arising from the nature of things themselves, and not from my shame-facedness, ignorance, or error.

23. *Above, contrary, and according to Reason.*—By what

has been before said of reason, we may be able to make some guess at the distinction of things, into those that are according to, above, and contrary to reason. 1. According to reason are such propositions whose truth we can discover by examining and tracing those ideas we have from sensation and reflection; and by natural deduction find to be true or probable. 2. Above reason are such propositions whose truth or probability we cannot by reason derive from those principles. 3. Contrary to reason are such propositions as are inconsistent with or irreconcilable to our clear and distinct ideas. Thus the existence of one God is according to reason; the existence of more than one God, contrary to reason; the resurrection of the dead, above reason. Further, as above, reason may be taken in a double sense, viz., either as signifying above probability, or above certainty; so in that large sense also, contrary to reason, is, I suppose, sometimes taken.

24. *Reason and Faith not opposite.*—There is another use of the word reason, wherein it is opposed to faith; which, though it be in itself a very improper way of speaking, yet common use has so authorized it, that it would be folly either to oppose or hope to remedy it; only I think it may not be amiss to take notice, that, however faith be opposed to reason, faith is nothing but a firm assent of the mind; which, if it be regulated, as is our duty, cannot be afforded to anything but upon good reason, and so cannot be opposite to it. He that believes without having any reason for believing, may be in love with his own fancies, but neither seeks truth as he ought, nor pays the obedience due to his Maker, who would have him use those discerning faculties he has given him, to keep him out of mistake and error. He that does not this to the best of his power, however he sometimes lights on truth, is in the right but by chance; and I know not whether the luckiness of the accident will excuse the irregularity of his proceeding. This at least is certain, that he must be accountable for whatever mistakes he runs into; whereas he that makes use of the light and faculties God has given him, and seeks sincerely to discover truth by those helps and abilities he has, may have this satisfaction in doing his duty as a rational creature, that, though he should miss truth, he will not miss the reward of it; for he governs his

assent right, and places it as he should, who, in any case or matter whatsoever, believes or disbelieves according as reason directs him. He that doth otherwise, transgresses against his own light, and misuses those faculties which were given him to no other end, but to search and follow the clearer evidence and greater probability. But since reason and faith are by some men opposed, we will so consider them in the following chapter.

CHAPTER XVIII.

OF FAITH AND REASON, AND THEIR DISTINCT PROVINCES.

1. *Necessary to know their Boundaries.*—It has been above shown, 1. That we are of necessity ignorant, and want knowledge of all sorts, where we want ideas. 2. That we are ignorant, and want rational knowledge, where we want proofs. 3. That we want certain knowledge and certainty, as far as we want clear and determined specific ideas. 4. That we want probability to direct our assent in matters where we have neither knowledge of our own nor testimony of other men to bottom our reason upon.

From these things thus premised, I think we may come to lay down the measures and boundaries between faith and reason; the want whereof may possibly have been the cause, if not of great disorders, yet at least of great disputes, and perhaps mistakes in the world. For till it be resolved how far we are to be guided by reason, and how far by faith, we shall in vain dispute, and endeavour to convince one another in matters of religion.

2. *Faith and Reason, what, as contradistinguished.*—I find every sect, as far as reason will help them, make use of it gladly; and where it fails them, they cry out, It is matter of faith, and above reason. And I do not see how they can argue with any one, or ever convince a gainsayer who makes use of the same plea, without setting down strict boundaries between faith and reason, which ought to be the first point established in all questions, where faith has anything to do.

Reason, therefore, here, as contradistinguished to faith, I take to be the discovery of the certainty or probability of such propositions or truths, which the mind arrives at by deduction made from such ideas, which it has got by the use of its natural faculties; viz., by sensation or reflection.

Faith, on the other side, is the assent to any proposition not thus made out by the deductions of reason, but upon the credit of the proposer, as coming from God, in some extraordinary way of communication. This way of discovering truths to men, we call revelation.

3. *No new simple Idea can be conveyed by traditional Revelation.*—First, Then I say, that no man inspired by God can by any revelation communicate to others any new simple ideas, which they had not before from sensation or reflection. For whatsoever impressions he himself may have from the immediate hand of God, this revelation, if it be of new simple ideas, cannot be conveyed to another, either by words or any other signs; because words, by their immediate operation on us, cause no other ideas but of their natural sounds; and it is by the custom of using them for signs, that they excite and revive in our minds latent ideas; but yet only such ideas as were there before. For words seen or heard, recal to our thoughts those ideas only, which to us they have been wont to be signs of, but cannot introduce any perfectly new, and formerly unknown simple ideas. The same holds in all other signs, which cannot signify to us things of which we have before never had any idea at all.

Thus, whatever things were discovered to St. Paul, when he was rapt up into the third heaven, whatever new ideas his mind there received, all the description he can make to others of that place, is only this, that there are such things, "as eye hath not seen, nor ear heard, nor hath it entered into the heart of man to conceive." And supposing God should discover to any one, supernaturally, a species of creatures inhabiting, for example, Jupiter or Saturn, (for that it is possible there may be such, nobody can deny,) which had six senses, and imprint on his mind the ideas conveyed to theirs by that sixth sense; he could no more, by words, produce in the minds of other men those ideas imprinted by that sixth sense, than one of us could convey the idea of any colour by the sounds of words into a man, who, having the other four senses perfect, had always totally wanted the fifth, of seeing. For our simple ideas, then, which are the foundation and sole matter of all our notions and knowledge, we must depend wholly on our reason, I mean our natural faculties; and can by no means receive them, or any of them from traditional revelation; I say, traditional revelation, in distinction to original revelation. By the one, I mean that first impression which is made immediately by God on the mind of any man, to which we cannot set any bounds; and by the other, those impressions delivered over to others in words, and the ordinary ways of conveying our conceptions one to another.

4. *Traditional Revelation may make us know Propositions knowable also by Reason, but not with the same Certainty that Reason doth.*—Secondly, I say that the same truths may be discovered and conveyed down from revelation, which are discoverable to us by reason, and by those ideas we naturally may have. So God might by revelation discover the truth of any proposition in Euclid; as well as men, by the natural use of their faculties, come to make the discovery themselves. In all things of this kind there is little need or use of revelation, God having furnished us with natural and surer means to arrive at the knowledge of them. For whatsoever truth we come to the clear discovery of, from the knowledge and contemplation of our own ideas, will always be certainer to us than those which are conveyed to us by traditional revelation. For the knowledge we have that this revelation came at first from God, can never be so sure as the knowledge we have from the clear and distinct perception of the agreement or disagreement of our own ideas; v. g., if it were revealed some ages since, that the three angles of a triangle were equal to two right ones, I might assent to the truth of that proposition, upon the credit of the tradition, that it was revealed; but that would never amount to so great a certainty as the knowledge of it, upon the comparing and measuring my own ideas of two right angles, and the three angles of a triangle. The like holds in matter of fact knowable by our senses; v. g., the history of the deluge is conveyed to us by writings which had their original from revelation: and yet nobody, I think, will say he has as certain and clear a knowledge of the flood as Noah, that saw it; or that he himself would have had, had he then been alive and seen it. For he has no greater an assurance than that of his senses, that it is writ

in the book supposed writ by Moses inspired; but he has not so great an assurance that Moses wrote that book as if he had seen Moses write it. So that the assurance of its being a revelation is less still than the assurance of his senses.

5. *Revelation cannot be admitted against the clear Evidence of Reason.*—In propositions, then, whose certainty is built upon the clear perception of the agreement or disagreement of our ideas, attained either by immediate intuition, as in self-evident propositions or by evident deductions of reason in demonstrations, we need not the assistance of revelation, as necessary to gain our assent, and introduce them into our minds. Because the natural ways of knowledge could settle them there, or had done it already, which is the greatest assurance we can possibly have of anything, unless where God immediately reveals it to us; and there too our assurance can be no greater than our knowledge is, that it is a revelation from God. But yet nothing, I think, can, under that title, shake or overrule plain knowledge, or rationally prevail with any man to admit it for true, in a direct contradiction to the clear evidence of his own understanding. For since no evidence of our faculties, by which we receive such revelations, can exceed, if equal, the certainty of our intuitive knowledge, we can never receive for a truth anything that is directly contrary to our clear and distinct knowledge; v. g., the ideas of one body and one place do so clearly agree, and the mind has so evident a perception of their agreement, that we can never assent to a proposition that affirms the same body to be in two distant places at once, however it should pretend to the authority of a divine revelation : since the evidence, first, that we deceive not ourselves, in ascribing it to God; secondly, that we understand it right; can never be so great as the evidence of our own intuitive knowledge, whereby we discern it impossible for the same body to be in two places at once. And therefore no proposition can be received for divine revelation, or obtain the assent due to all such, if it be contradictory to our clear intuitive knowledge. Because this would be to subvert the principles and foundations of all knowledge, evidence, and assent whatsoever : and there would be left no difference between truth and falsehood, no measures of credible and incredible in the world, if doubtful propositions shall take

place before self-evident, and what we certainly know give way to what we may possibly be mistaken in. In propositions, therefore, contrary to the clear perception of the agreement or disagreement of any of our ideas, it will be in vain to urge them as matters of faith: they cannot move our assent under that or any other title whatsoever; for faith can never convince us of anything that contradicts our knowledge. Because, though faith be founded on the testimony of God (who cannot lie) revealing any proposition to us; yet we cannot have an assurance of the truth of its being a divine revelation greater than our own knowledge: since the whole strength of the certainty depends upon our knowledge that God revealed it, which, in this case, where the proposition supposed revealed contradicts our knowledge or reason, will always have this objection hanging to it, viz., that we cannot tell how to conceive that to come from God, the bountiful Author of our being, which, if received for true, must overturn all the principles and foundations of knowledge he has given us; render all our faculties useless; wholly destroy the most excellent part of his workmanship, our understandings, and put a man in a condition wherein he will have less light, less conduct than the beast that perisheth. For if the mind of man can never have a clearer (and perhaps not so clear) evidence of anything to be a divine revelation, as it has of the principles of its own reason, it can never have a ground to quit the clear evidence of its reason, to give a place to a proposition, whose revelation has not a greater evidence than those principles have.

6. *Traditional Revelation much less.*—Thus far a man has use of reason, and ought to hearken to it, even in immediate and original revelation, where it is supposed to be made to himself: but to all those who pretend not to immediate revelation, but are required to pay obedience, and to receive the truths revealed to others, which, by the tradition of writings, or word of mouth, are conveyed down to them, reason has a great deal more to do, and is that only which can induce us to receive them. For matter of faith being only divine revelation, and nothing else, faith, as we use the word, (called commonly divine faith,) has to do with no propositions, but those which are supposed to be divinely revealed. So that I do not see how those who make revelation alone the sole

object of faith can say, that it is a matter of faith, and not of reason, to believe that such or such a proposition, to be found in such or such a book, is of divine inspiration, unless it be revealed that that proposition, or all in that book, was communicated by divine inspiration. Without such a revelation, the believing or not believing that proposition or book to be of divine authority, can never be matter of faith, but matter of reason; and such as I must come to an assent to only by the use of my reason, which can never require or enable me to believe that which is contrary to itself: it being impossible for reason ever to procure any assent to that which to itself appears unreasonable.

In all things, therefore, where we have clear evidence from our ideas, and those principles of knowledge I have above mentioned, reason is the proper judge; and revelation, though it may, in consenting with it, confirm its dictates, yet cannot in such cases invalidate its decrees: nor can we be obliged, where we have the clear and evident sentence of reason to quit it for the contrary opinion, under a pretence that it is matter of faith, which can have no authority against the plain and clear dictates of reason.

7. *Things above Reason.*—But, Thirdly, There being many things wherein we have very imperfect notions, or none at all; and other things, of whose past, present, or future existence, by the natural use of our faculties, we can have no knowledge at all; these, as being beyond the discovery of our natural faculties, and above reason, are, when revealed, the proper matter of faith. Thus, that part of the angels rebelled against God, and thereby lost their first happy state; and that the dead shall rise, and live again: these and the like, being beyond the discovery of reason, are purely matters of faith, with which reason has directly nothing to do.

8. *Or not contrary to Reason, if revealed, are Matter of Faith.*—But since God, in giving us the light of reason, has not thereby tied up his own hands from affording us, when he thinks fit, the light of revelation in any of those matters wherein our natural faculties are able to give a probable determination; revelation, where God has been pleased to give it, must carry it against the probable conjectures of reason. Because the mind not being certain of the truth of that it does not evidently know, but only yielding to the

probability that appears in it, is bound to give up its assent to such a testimony; which, it is satisfied, comes from one who cannot err, and will not deceive. But yet it still belongs to reason to judge of the truth of its being a revelation, and of the signification of the words wherein it is delivered. Indeed, if anything shall be thought revelation which is contrary to the plain principles of reason, and the evident knowledge the mind has of its own clear and distinct ideas; there reason must be hearkened to, as to a matter within its province: since a man can never have so certain a knowledge, that a proposition which contradicts the clear principles and evidence of his own knowledge was divinely revealed, or that he understands the words rightly wherein it is delivered, as he has that the contrary is true: and so is bound to consider and judge of it as a matter of reason, and not swallow it, without examination, as a matter of faith.

9. *Revelation in Matters where Reason cannot judge, or but probably, ought to be hearkened to.*—First, Whatever proposition is revealed, of whose truth our mind, by its natural faculties and notions, cannot judge; that is purely matter of faith, and above reason.

Secondly, All propositions whereof the mind, by the use of its natural faculties, can come to determine and judge, from naturally acquired ideas, are matter of reason, with this difference still, that, in those concerning which it has but an uncertain evidence, and so is persuaded of their truth only upon probable grounds, which still admit a possibility of the contrary to be true, without doing violence to the certain evidence of its own knowledge, and overturning the principles of all reason; in such probable propositions, I say, an evident revelation ought to determine our assent, even against probability. For where the principles of reason have not evidenced a proposition to be certainly true or false, there clear revelation, as another principle of truth and ground of assent, may determine; and so it may be matter of faith, and be also above reason. Because reason, in that particular matter, being able to reach no higher than probability, faith gave the determination where reason came short; and revelation discovered on which side the truth lay.

10. *In Matters where Reason can afford certain Knowledge, that is to be hearkened to.*—Thus far the dominion of faith

reaches, and that without any violence or hindrance to reason, which is not injured or disturbed, but assisted and improved by new discoveries of truth, coming from the eternal fountain of all knowledge. Whatever God hath revealed is certainly true: no doubt can be made of it. This is the proper object of faith; but whether it be a divine revelation or no, reason must judge, which can never permit the mind to reject a greater evidence to embrace what is less evident, nor allow it to entertain probability in opposition to knowledge and certainty. There can be no evidence that any traditional revelation is of divine original, in the words we receive it, and in the sense we understand it, so clear and so certain as that of the principles of reason: and therefore nothing that is contrary to, and inconsistent with, the clear and self-evident dictates of reason, has a right to be urged or assented to as a matter of faith, wherein reason hath nothing to do. Whatsoever is divine revelation, ought to overrule all our opinions, prejudices, and interest, and hath a right to be received with full assent. Such a submission as this, of our reason to faith, takes not away the landmarks of knowledge: this shakes not the foundations of reason, but leaves us that use of our faculties for which they were given us.

11. *If the Boundaries be not set between Faith and Reason, no Enthusiasm or Extravagancy in Religion can be contradicted.*—If the provinces of faith and reason are not kept distinct by these boundaries, there will, in matters of religion, be no room for reason at all; and those extravagant opinions and ceremonies that are to be found in the several religions of the world will not deserve to be blamed. For to this crying up of faith in opposition to reason, we may, I think, in good measure ascribe those absurdities that fill almost all the religions which possess and divide mankind. For men having been principled with an opinion, that they must not consult reason in the things of religion, however apparently contradictory to common sense and the very principles of all their knowledge, have let loose their fancies and natural superstition; and have been by them led into so strange opinions and extravagant practices in religion, that a considerate man cannot but stand amazed at their follies, and judge them so far from being acceptable to the great and wise God, that he cannot avoid thinking them ridiculous and

offensive to a sober good man. So that, in effect, religion, which should most distinguish us from beasts, and ought most peculiarly to elevate us, as rational creatures, above brutes, is that wherein men often appear most irrational and more senseless than beasts themselves. "Credo, quia impossibile est;" I believe, because it is impossible, might in a good man pass for a sally of zeal; but would prove a very ill rule for men to choose their opinions or religion by.

CHAPTER XIX.

OF ENTHUSIASM.

1. *Love of Truth necessary.*—HE that would seriously set upon the search of truth,[*] ought in the first place to prepare his mind with a love of it. For he that loves it not, will not take much pains to get it, nor be much concerned when he misses it. There is nobody in the commonwealth of learning who does not profess himself a lover of truth; and there is not a rational creature that would not take it amiss to be thought otherwise of. And yet, for all this, one may truly say, that there are very few lovers of truth, for truth's sake, even amongst those who persuade themselves that they are so. How a man may know whether he be so in earnest,

[*] In Milton's Areopagitica there occurs a passage on the love and beauty of truth so fervid, nervous, and worthy of admiration, that I am tempted to introduce it as a note upon this passage, which yet, I confess, stands in little need of illustration. "Truth indeed came once into the world with her Divine Master, and was a perfect shape most glorious to look on: but when he ascended, and his apostles after him were laid asleep, then straight arose a wicked race of deceivers, who, as that story goes of the Egyptian Typhon with his conspirators, how they dealt with the god Osiris, took the virgin Truth, hewed her lovely form into a thousand pieces, and scattered them to the four winds. From that time ever since, the sad friends of Truth, such as durst appear, imitating the careful search that Isis made for the mangled body of Osiris, went up and down, gathering up limb by limb still as they could find them. We have not yet found them all—lords and commons —nor ever shall do, till her Master's second coming; he shall bring together every joint and member, and shall mould them into an immortal feature of loveliness and perfection. Suffer not these licensing prohibitions to stand at every place of opportunity, forbidding and disturbing them that continue seeking—that continue to do our obsequies to the torn body of our martyred saint." (§ 61.)—ED.

is worth inquiry: and I think there is one unerring mark of it, viz., the not entertaining any proposition with greater assurance than the proofs it is built upon will warrant. Whoever goes beyond this measure of assent, it is plain receives not the truth in the love of it; loves not truth for truth's sake, but for some other bye-end.* For the evidence that any proposition is true (except such as are self-evident) lying only in the proofs a man has of it, whatsoever degrees of assent he affords it beyond the degrees of that evidence, it is plain that all the surplusage of assurance is owing to some other affection, and not to the love of truth: it being as impossible that the love of truth should carry my assent above the evidence there is to me that it is true, as that the love of truth should make me assent to any proposition for the sake of that evidence, which it has not that it is true; which is in effect to love it as a truth, because it is possible or probable that it may not be true. In any truth that gets not possession of our minds by the irresistible light of self-evidence, or by the force of demonstration, the arguments that gain it assent are the vouchers and gage of its probability to us; and we can receive it for no other than such as they deliver it to our understandings. Whatsoever credit or authority we give to any proposition more than it receives from the principles and proofs it supports itself upon, is owing to our inclinations that way, and is so far a derogation from the love of truth as such: which, as it can receive no evidence from our passions or interests, so it should receive no tincture from them.

2. *A Forwardness to dictate, from whence.*—The assuming an authority of dictating to others, and a forwardness to prescribe to their opinions, is a constant concomitant of this bias and corruption of our judgments. For how almost can it be otherwise, but that he should be ready to impose on another's belief, who has already imposed on his own? Who can reasonably expect arguments and conviction from him in dealing with others, whose understanding is not accustomed

* In the same spirit Milton remarks, that, "A man may be a heretic in the truth; and if he believe things only because his pastor says so, or the assembly so determines, without knowing other reason, though his belief be true, yet the very truth he holds becomes his heresy." (Areopag. § 54.)—Ed.

to them in his dealing with himself? Who does violence to his own faculties, tyrannizes over his own mind, and usurps the prerogative that belongs to truth alone, which is to command assent by only its own authority, i. e., by and in proportion to that evidence which it carries with it.

3. *Force of Enthusiasm.*—Upon this occasion I shall take the liberty to consider a third ground of assent, which with some men has the same authority, and is as confidently relied on as either faith or reason; I mean enthusiasm: which, laying by reason, would set up revelation without it. Whereby in effect it takes away both reason and revelation, and substitutes in the room of it the ungrounded fancies of a man's own brain, and assumes them for a foundation both of opinion and conduct.

4. *Reason and Revelation.*—Reason is natural revelation, whereby the eternal Father of light and fountain of all knowledge, communicates to mankind that portion of truth which he has laid within the reach of their natural faculties: revelation is natural reason enlarged by a new set of discoveries communicated by God immediately, which reason vouches the truth of, by the testimony and proofs it gives that they come from God. So that he that takes away reason to make way for revelation, puts out the light of both; and does muchwhat the same as if he would persuade a man to put out his eyes, the better to receive the remote light of an invisible star by a telescope.

5. *Rise of Enthusiasm.*—Immediate revelation being a much easier way for men to establish their opinions and regulate their conduct, than the tedious and not always successful labour of strict reasoning, it is no wonder that some have been very apt to pretend to revelation, and to persuade themselves that they are under the peculiar guidance of heaven in their actions and opinions, especially in those of them which they cannot account for by the ordinary methods of knowledge and principles of reason. Hence we see, that, in all ages, men in whom melancholy has mixed with devotion, or whose conceit of themselves has raised them into an opinion of a greater familiarity with God, and a nearer admittance to his favour than is afforded to others, have often flattered themselves with a persuasion of an immediate intercourse with the Deity, and frequent communications from

the Divine Spirit. God, I own, cannot be denied to be able to enlighten the understanding by a ray darted into the mind immediately from the fountain of light: this they understand he has promised to do, and who then has so good a title to expect it as those who are his peculiar people chosen by him, and depending on him?

6. *Enthusiasm.*—Their minds being thus prepared, whatever groundless opinion comes to settle itself strongly upon their fancies, is an illumination from the Spirit of God, and presently of divine authority: and whatsoever odd action they find in themselves a strong inclination to do, that impulse is concluded to be a call or direction from heaven, and must be obeyed; it is a commission from above, and they cannot err in executing it.

7. This I take to be properly enthusiasm,[*] which, though founded neither on reason nor divine revelation, but rising from the conceits of a warmed or overweening brain, works yet, where it once gets footing, more powerfully on the persuasions and actions of men than either of those two, or both together: men being most forwardly obedient to the impulses they receive from themselves; and the whole man is sure to act more vigorously where the whole man is carried by a natural motion. For strong conceit, like a new prin-

[*] This chapter did not appear in the first edition, but was planned afterwards, and the idea communicated by letter to the author's friend, Mr. Molyneux; who at first thought it unnecessary, yet, upon reconsideration, recommended it to be introduced, but in a very different shape. "I must freely confess," he writes, "that if my notion of enthusiasm agrees with yours, there is no necessity of adding anything concerning it, more than by the by, and in a single section in chap. 18, lib. iv. I conceive it to be no other than a religious sort of madness, and comprises not in it any mode of thinking, or operation of the mind different from what you have treated of in your essay. 'T is true, indeed, the absurdities men embrace on account of religion are most astonishing; and if, in a chapter of Enthusiasm, you endeavour to give an account of them, it would be very acceptable. So that, (on second thought,) I do very well approve of what you propose therein, being very desirous of having your sentiments on any subject." (Works, III. 533.) To which Locke replies, "What I shall add concerning enthusiasm, I guess, will very much agree with your thoughts, since yours jump so right with mine. About the place where it is to come in, I have designed it for chap. 18, lib. iv. as a false principle of reasoning often made use of. But, to give an historical account of the various ravings men have embraced for religion, would, I fear, be beside my purpose, and be enough to make a huge volume." (p. 535.)

ciple, carries all easily with it, when got above common sense and freed from all restraint of reason and check of reflection, it is heightened into a divine authority, in concurrence with our own temper and inclination.

8. *Enthusiasm mistaken for Seeing and Feeling.*—Though the odd opinions and extravagant actions enthusiasm has run men into were enough to warn them against this wrong principle, so apt to misguide them both in their belief and conduct, yet the love of something extraordinary, the ease and glory it is to be inspired, and be above the common and natural ways of knowledge, so flatters many men's laziness, ignorance, and vanity, that, when once they are got into this way of immediate revelation, of illumination without search, and of certainty without proof and without examination, it is a hard matter to get them out of it. Reason is lost upon them, they are above it: they see the light infused into their understandings, and cannot be mistaken; it is clear and visible there, like the light of bright sunshine; shows itself, and needs no other proof but its own evidence: they feel the hand of God moving them within, and the impulses of the Spirit, and cannot be mistaken in what they feel. Thus they support themselves, and are sure reason hath nothing to do with what they see and feel in themselves: what they have a sensible experience of admits no doubt, needs no probation. Would he not be ridiculous, who should require to have it proved to him that the light shines, and that he sees it? It is its own proof, and can have no other. When the Spirit brings light into our minds, it dispels darkness. We see it as we do that of the sun at noon, and need not the twilight of reason to show it us. This light from heaven is strong, clear, and pure; carries its own demonstration with it: and we may as naturally take a glow-worm to assist us to discover the sun, as to examine the celestial ray by our dim candle, reason.

9. *Enthusiasm how to be discovered.*—This is the way of talking of these men: they are sure, because they are sure: and their persuasions are right, because they are strong in them. For, when what they say is stripped of the metaphor of seeing and feeling, this is all it amounts to: and yet these similies so impose on them, that they serve them for certainty in themselves, and demonstration to others.

10. But to examine a little soberly this internal light, and this feeling on which they build so much. These men have, they say, clear light, and they see; they have awakened sense, and they feel: this cannot, they are sure, be disputed them. For when a man says he sees or feels, nobody can deny him that he does so. But here let me ask:—this seeing, is it the perception of the truth of the proposition, or of this, that it is a revelation from God?—this feeling, is it a perception of an inclination or fancy to do something, or of the Spirit of God moving that inclination? These are two very different perceptions, and must be carefully distinguished, if we would not impose upon ourselves. I may perceive the truth of a proposition, and yet not perceive that it is an immediate revelation from God. I may perceive the truth of a proposition in Euclid, without its being or my perceiving it to be a revelation: nay, I may perceive I came not by this knowledge in a natural way, and so may conclude it revealed, without perceiving that it is a revelation of God; because there be spirits which, without being divinely commissioned, may excite those ideas in me, and lay them in such order before my mind, that I may perceive their connexion. So that the knowledge of any proposition coming into my mind, I know not how, is not a perception that it is from God. Much less is a strong persuasion that it is true, a perception that it is from God, or so much as true. But however it be called light and seeing, I suppose it is at most but belief and assurance: and the proposition taken for a revelation, is not such as they know to be true, but take to be true. For where a proposition is known to be true, revelation is needless: and it is hard to conceive how there can be a revelation to any one of what he knows already. If therefore it be a proposition which they are persuaded, but do not know, to be true, whatever they may call it, it is not seeing, but believing. For these are two ways whereby truth comes into the mind, wholly distinct, so that one is not the other. What I see, I know to be so, by the evidence of the thing itself: what I believe, I take to be so upon the testimony of another: but this testimony I must know to be given, or else what ground have I of believing? I must see that it is God that reveals this to me, or else I see nothing. The question then here is, how do I know that

God is the revealer of this to me; that this impression is made upon my mind by his Holy Spirit, and that therefore I ought to obey it? If I know not this, how great soever the assurance is that I am possessed with, it is groundless; whatever light I pretend to, it is but enthusiasm. For whether the proposition supposed to be revealed, be in itself evidently true, or visibly probable, or by the natural ways of knowledge uncertain, the proposition that must be well grounded and manifested to be true, is this, that God is the revealer of it, and that what I take to be a revelation is certainly put into my mind by him, and is not an illusion dropped in by some other spirit or raised by my own fancy. For, if I mistake not, these men receive it for true, because they presume God revealed it. Does it not, then, stand them upon to examine on what grounds they presume it to be a revelation from God? or else all their confidence is mere presumption: and this light they are so dazzled with is nothing but an ignis fatuus, that leads them constantly round in this circle;* it is a revelation, because they firmly believe it, and they believe it, because it is a revelation.

11. *Enthusiasm fails of Evidence, that the Proposition is from God.*—In all that is of divine revelation, there is need of no other proof but that it is an inspiration from God; for he can neither deceive nor be deceived. But how shall it be known that any proposition in our minds is a truth infused by God; a truth that is revealed to us by him, which he declares to us, and therefore we ought to believe? Here it is that enthusiasm fails of the evidence it pretends to. For men thus possessed, boast of a light whereby they say they are enlightened, and brought into the knowledge of this or that truth. But if they know it to be a truth, they must know it to be so, either by its own self-evidence to natural reason, or by the rational proofs that make it out to be so. If they see and know it to be a truth, either of these two ways, they in vain suppose it to be a revelation. For they know it to be true the same way that any other man naturally may know that it is so, without the help of revelation. For thus, all the truths, of what kind soever, that men uninspired are enlightened with, came into their minds,

---

* An ignis fatuus that bewitches,
And leads them into pools and ditches.—HUDIBRAS.—ED.

and are established there. If they say they know it to be true, because it is a revelation from God, the reason is good; but then it will be demanded how they know it to be a revelation from God. If they say, by the light it brings with it which shines bright in their minds, and they cannot resist: I beseech them to consider whether this be any more than what we have taken notice of already, viz., that it is a revelation, because they strongly believe it to be true. For all the light they speak of is but a strong, though ungrounded persuasion of their own minds, that it is a truth. For rational grounds from proofs that it is a truth, they must acknowledge to have none; for then it is not received as a revelation, but upon the ordinary grounds that other truths are received: and if they believe it to be true because it is a revelation, and have no other reason for its being a revelation, but because they are fully persuaded without any other reason that it is true; they believe it to be a revelation only because they strongly believe it to be a revelation; which is a very unsafe ground to proceed on, either in our tenets or actions. And what readier way can there be to run ourselves into the most extravagant errors and miscarriages, than thus to set up fancy for our supreme and sole guide, and to believe any proposition to be true, any action to be right, only because we believe it to be so? The strength of our persuasions is no evidence at all of their own rectitude: crooked things may be as stiff and inflexible as straight: and men may be as positive and peremptory in error as in truth. How come else the untractable zealots in different and opposite parties? For if the light, which every one thinks he has in his mind, which in this case is nothing but the strength of his own persuasion, be an evidence that it is from God, contrary opinions have the same title to inspirations; and God will be not only the Father of lights, but of opposite and contradictory lights, leading men contrary ways; and contradictory propositions will be divine truths, if an ungrounded strength of assurance be an evidence that any proposition is a divine revelation.

12. *Firmness of Persuasion no Proof that any Proposition is from God.*—This cannot be otherwise, whilst firmness of persuasion is made the cause of believing, and confidence of being in the right is made an argument of truth. St. Paul

himself believed he did well, and that he had a call to it when he persecuted the Christians, whom he confidently thought to be in the wrong; but yet it was he, and not they, who were mistaken. Good men are men still, liable to mistakes; and are sometimes warmly engaged in errors, which they take for divine truths, shining in their minds with the clearest light.

13. *Light in the Mind, what.*—Light, true light, in the mind is, or can be nothing else but the evidence of the truth of any proposition; and if it be not a self-evident proposition, all the light it has or can have is from the clearness and validity of those proofs upon which it is received. To talk of any other light in the understanding, is to put ourselves in the dark, or in the power of the Prince of Darkness, and by our own consent to give ourselves up to delusion to believe a lie. For if strength of persuasion be the light which must guide us; I ask how shall any one distinguish between the delusions of Satan, and the inspirations of the Holy Ghost? He can transform himself into an angel of light. And they who are led by this son of the morning, are as fully satisfied of the illumination, i. e., are as strongly persuaded that they are enlightend by the Spirit of God as any one who is so: they acquiesce and rejoice in it, are actuated by it, and nobody can be more sure, nor more in the right (if their own strong belief may be judge) than they.

14. *Revelation must be judged of by Reason.*—He, therefore, that will not give himself up to all the extravagances of delusion and error, must bring this guide of his light within to the trial. God, when he makes the prophet, does not unmake the man. He leaves all his faculties in the natural state, to enable him to judge of his inspirations, whether they be of divine original or no. When he illuminates the mind with supernatural light, he does not extinguish that which is natural. If he would have us assent to the truth of any proposition, he either evidences that truth by the usual methods of natural reason, or else makes it known to be a truth which he would have us assent to by his authority, and convinces us that it is from him, by some marks which reason cannot be mistaken in. Reason must be our last judge and guide in everything. I do not mean that we must consult reason, and examine whether a proposition revealed from God can be made out by natural principles,

and if it cannot, that then we may reject it; but consult it we must, and by it examine whether it be a revelation from God or no. And if reason finds it to be revealed from God, reason then declares for it as much as for any other truth, and makes it one of her dictates. Every conceit that thoroughly warms our fancies must pass for an inspiration, if there be nothing but the strength of our persuasions, whereby to judge of our persuasions: if reason must not examine their truth by something extrinsical to the persuasions themselves, inspirations and delusions, truth and falsehood, will have the same measure, and will not be possible to be distinguished.

15. *Belief no Proof of Revelation.*—If this internal light, or any proposition which under that title we take for inspired, be conformable to the principles of reason, or to the word of God, which is attested revelation, reason warrants it, and we may safely receive it for true, and be guided by it in our belief and actions: if it receive no testimony nor evidence from either of these rules, we cannot take it for a revelation, or so much as for true, till we have some other mark that it is a revelation, besides our believing that it is so. Thus we see the holy men of old, who had revelations from God, had something else besides that internal light of assurance in their own minds, to testify to them that it was from God. They were not left to their own persuasions alone, that those persuasions were from God, but had outward signs to convince them of the author of those revelations. And when they were to convince others, they had a power given them to justify the truth of their commission from heaven, and by visible signs to assert the divine authority of a message they were sent with. Moses saw the bush burn without being consumed, and heard a voice out of it. This was something besides finding an impulse upon his mind to go to Pharaoh, that he might bring his brethren out of Egypt: and yet he thought not this enough to authorize him to go with that message, till God, by another miracle of his rod turned into a serpent, had assured him of a power to testify his mission, by the same miracle repeated before them, whom he was sent to. Gideon was sent by an angel to deliver Israel from the Midianites, and yet he desired a sign to convince him that this commission was from God. These, and several the like

instances to be found among the prophets of old, are enough to show that they thought not an inward seeing or persuasion of their own minds, without any other proof, a sufficient evidence that it was from God; though the Scripture does not everywhere mention their demanding or having such proofs.

16. In what I have said I am far from denying, that God can or doth sometimes enlighten men's minds in the apprehending of certain truths, or excite them to good actions by the immediate influence and assistance of the Holy Spirit, without any extraordinary signs accompanying it. But in such cases too we have reason and Scripture, unerring rules to know whether it be from God or no. Where the truth embraced is consonant to the revelation in the written word of God, or the action conformable to the dictates of right reason or holy writ, we may be assured that we run no risk in entertaining it as such; because, though perhaps it be not an immediate revelation from God, extraordinarily operating on our minds, yet we are sure it is warranted by that revelation which he has given us of truth. But it is not the strength of our private persuasion within ourselves, that can warrant it to be a light or motion from heaven; nothing can do that but the written Word of God without us, or that standard of reason which is common to us with all men. Where reason or Scripture is express for any opinion or action, we may receive it as of divine authority; but it is not the strength of our own persuasions which can by itself give it that stamp. The bent of our own minds may favour it as much as we please; that may show it to be a fondling of our own, but will by no means prove it to be an offspring of heaven, and of divine original.

CHAPTER XX.

OF WRONG ASSENT, OR ERROR.

1. *Causes of Error.*—KNOWLEDGE being to be had only of visible and certain truth, error is not a fault of our knowledge, but a mistake of our judgment, giving assent to that which is not true.

But if assent be grounded on likelihood, if the proper object and motive of our assent be probability, and that probability consists in what is laid down in the foregoing chapters, it will be demanded how men come to give their assents contrary to probability. For there is nothing more common than contrariety of opinions; nothing more obvious than that one man wholly disbelieves what another only doubts of, and a third stedfastly believes and firmly adheres to. The reasons whereof, though they may be very various, yet, I suppose may all be reduced to these four:

    I. Want of proofs.
    II. Want of ability to use them.
    III. Want of will to use them.
    IV. Wrong measures of probability.

2. I. *Want of Proofs.*—First, By want of proofs, I do not mean only the want of those proofs which are nowhere extant, and so are nowhere to be had; but the want even of those proofs which are in being, or might be procured. And thus men want proofs, who have not the convenience or opportunity to make experiments and observations themselves tending to the proof of any proposition; nor likewise the convenience to inquire into and collect the testimonies of others: and in this state are the greatest part of mankind, who are given up to labour, and enslaved to the necessity of their mean condition, whose lives are worn out only in the provisions for living. These men's opportunities of knowledge and inquiry are commonly as narrow as their fortunes; and their understandings are but little instructed, when all their whole time and pains is laid out to still the croaking of their own bellies, or the cries of their children. It is not to be expected that a man who drudges on all his life in a laborious trade, should be more knowing in the variety of things done in the world than a packhorse, who is driven constantly forwards and backwards in a narrow lane and dirty road, only to market, should be skilled in the geography of the country. Nor is it at all more possible, that he who wants leisure, books, and languages, and the opportunity of conversing with variety of men, should be in a condition to collect those testimonies and observations which are in being, and are necessary to make out many, nay, most of the propositions that, in the societies of men, are judged of the greatest moment; or to find out grounds of assurance so great as the belief of the points he would build on them

thought necessary. So that a great part of mankind are, by the natural and unalterable state of things in this world, and the constitution of human affairs, unavoidably given over to invincible ignorance of those proofs on which others build, and which are necessary to establish those opinions; the greatest part of men, having much to do to get the means of living, are not in a condition to look after those of learned and laborious inquiries.

3. *Obj. What shall become of those who want them? answered.*—What shall we say, then? Are the greatest part of mankind, by the necessity of their condition, subjected to unavoidable ignorance in those things which are of greatest importance to them? (for of these it is obvious to inquire.) Have the bulk of mankind no other guide but accident and blind chance to conduct them to their happiness or misery? Are the current opinions and licensed guides of every country, sufficient evidence and security to every man to venture his great concernments on; nay, his everlasting happiness or misery? Or can those be the certain and infallible oracles and standards of truth, which teach one thing in Christendom and another in Turkey? Or shall a poor countryman be eternally happy for having the chance to be born in Italy; or a day-labourer be unavoidably lost because he had the ill-luck to be born in England?* How ready some men may

* Thus that charitable Dominican, Navarrete, by wholesale damns the Chinese for not being born in Spain. "They dress him (the dead man) in his best clothes, which they keep carefully while they are living, against they are dead; the devil takes them very richly and warmly clad." (l. II. c. viii. § 7.) But the good father is perfectly impartial, for not the Chinese only, but all Mahometans, Lutherans, and Calvinists go the same broad way to destruction. "Here we might discuss a point of great moment, which is, whether those sectaries we have mentioned were saved, or whether we may doubt of their salvation? In the second tome, which is the proper place, what was said to this point in China, shall be declared, I never made any difficulty to maintain they were damned, as I affirm of Mahomet, Calvin, Luther, and others of the same leaven. I know those of the contrary opinion all hang by one another, and say the same of those we have mentioned as they do of Fo and others. But I follow the opinion of S. Peter Marimenus Martyr, mentioned in the Martyrology, on the twenty-first of February. He lying sick at Damascus, some Mahometans came in to visit him. The saint told them that those who did not profess the law of God went to hell as Mahomet had done. The infidels killed him for these words, and he was a glorious martyr. Why might not he be so, who should say the same of Fo and others?' (L. II. c. xii. § 8,) -Ed.

be to say some of these things, I will not here examine; but this I am sure, that men must allow one or other of these to be true, (let them choose which they please,) or else grant that God has furnished men with faculties sufficient to direct them in the way they should take, if they will but seriously employ them that way, when their ordinary vocations allow them the leisure. No man is so wholly taken up with the attendance on the means of living, as to have no spare time at at all to think of his soul, and inform himself in matters of religion. Were men as intent upon this, as they are on things of lower concernment, there are none so enslaved to the necessities of life, who might not find many vacancies that might be husbanded to this advantage of their knowledge.

4. *People hindered from Inquiry.*—Besides those whose improvements and informations are straitened by the narrowness of their fortunes, there are others whose largeness of fortune would plentifully enough supply books and other requisites for clearing of doubts and discovering of truth; but they are cooped in close, by the laws of their countries, and the strict guards of those whose interest it is to keep them ignorant, lest, knowing more, they should believe the less in them. These are as far, nay further, from the liberty and opportunities of a fair inquiry, than these poor and wretched labourers we before spoke of; and however they may seem high and great, are confined to narrowness of thought, and enslaved in that which should be the freest part of man: their understandings. This is generally the case of all those who live in places where care is taken to propagate truth without knowledge; where men are forced, at a venture, to be of the religion of the country; and must therefore swallow down opinions, as silly people do empiric's pills, without knowing what they are made of, or how they will work, and having nothing to do but believe that they will do the cure; but in this are much more miserable than they, in that they are not at liberty to refuse swallowing what perhaps they had rather let alone; or to choose the physician, to whose conduct they would trust themselves.

5. II. *Want of Skill to use them.*—Secondly, Those who want skill to use those evidences they have of probabilities; who cannot carry a train of consequences in their heads; nor weigh exactly the preponderancy of contrary proofs and tes

timonies, making every circumstance its due allowance; may be easily misled to assent to positions that are not probable. There are some men of one, some but of two syllogisms, and no more; and others that can but advance one step further. These cannot always discern that side on which the strongest proofs lie, cannot constantly follow that which in itself is the more probable opinion. Now that there is such a difference between men, in respect of their understandings, I think nobody, who has had any conversation with his neighbours, will question: though he never was at Westminster-Hall or the Exchange on the one hand, or at Alms-houses or Bedlam on the other. Which great difference in men's intellectuals, whether it rises from any defect in the organs of the body, particularly adapted to thinking; or in the dulness or untractableness of those faculties for want of use; or, as some think, in the natural differences of men's souls themselves; or some, or all of these together; it matters not here to examine: only this is evident, that there is a difference of degrees in men's understandings, apprehensions, and reasonings, to so great a latitude, that one may, without doing injury to mankind, affirm, that there is a greater distance between some men and others in this respect, than between some men and some beasts. But how this comes about is a speculation, though of great consequence, yet not necessary to our present purpose.

6. III. *Want of Will to use them.*—Thirdly, There are another sort of people that want proofs, not because they are out of their reach, but because they will not use them; who, though they have riches and leisure enough, and want neither parts nor other helps, are yet never the better for them. Their hot pursuit of pleasure, or constant drudgery in business, engages some men's thoughts elsewhere: laziness and oscitancy in general, or a particular aversion for books, study, and meditation, keep others from any serious thoughts at all; and some out of fear that an impartial inquiry would not favour those opinions which best suit their prejudices, lives, and designs, content themselves, without examination, to take upon trust what they find convenient and in fashion. Thus, most men, even of those that might do otherwise, pass their lives without an acquaintance with, much less a rational assent to, probabilities they are concerned to know, though

they lie so much within their view, that, to be convinced of them, they need but turn their eyes that way. We know some men will not read a letter which is supposed to bring ill news; and many men forbear to cast up their accounts, or so much as think upon their estates, who have reason to fear their affairs are in no very good posture. How men, whose plentiful fortunes allow them leisure to improve their understandings, can satisfy themselves with a lazy ignorance, I cannot tell: but methinks they have a low opinion of their souls, who lay out all their incomes in provisions for the body, and employ none of it to procure the means and helps of knowledge; who take great care to appear always in a neat and splendid outside, and would think themselves miserable in coarse clothes, or a patched coat, and yet contentedly suffer their minds to appear abroad in a piebald livery of coarse patches and borrowed shreds, such as it has pleased chance or their country tailor (I mean the common opinion of those they have conversed with) to clothe them in. I will not here mention how unreasonable this is for men that ever think of a future state and their concernment in it, which no rational man can avoid to do sometimes: nor shall I take notice what a shame and confusion it is to the greatest contemners of knowledge, to be found ignorant in things they are concerned to know. But this at least is worth the consideration of those who call themselves gentlemen, that, however they may think credit, respect, power, and authority the concomitants of their birth and fortune, yet they will find all these still carried away from them by men of lower condition, who surpass them in knowledge. They who are blind will always be led by those that see, or else fall into the ditch: and he is certainly the most subjected, the most enslaved, who is so in his understanding. In the foregoing instances some of the causes have been shown of wrong assent, and how it comes to pass, that probable doctrines are not always received with an assent proportionable to the reasons which are to be had for their probability: but hitherto we have considered only such probabilities whose proofs do exist, but do not appear to him who embraces the error.

7. IV. *Wrong Measures of Probability; whereof:*—Fourthly There remains yet the last sort. who, even where the real pro-

babilities appear, and are plainly laid before them, do not admit of the conviction, nor yield unto manifest reasons, but do either ἐπέχειν, suspend their assent, or give it to the less probable opinion. And to this danger are those exposed who have taken up wrong measures of probability; which are,

I. Propositions that are not in themselves certain and evident, but doubtful and false, taken up for principles.

II. Received hypothesis.

III. Predominant passions or inclinations

IV. Authority.

8. I. *Doubtful Propositions taken for Principles.*—First, The first and firmest ground of probability is the conformity anything has to our own knowledge, especially that part of our knowledge which we have embraced, and continue to look on as principles. These have so great an influence upon our opinions, that it is usually by them we judge of truth, and measure probability to that degree, that what is inconsistent with our principles, is so far from passing for probable with us, that it will not be allowed possible. The reverence borne to these principles is so great, and their authority so paramount to all other, that the testimony, not only of other men, but the evidence of our own senses are often rejected, when they offer to vouch anything contrary to these established rules. How much the doctrine of innate principles, and that principles are not to be proved or questioned, has contributed to this, I will not here examine. This I readily grant, that one truth cannot contradict another: but withal I take leave also to say, that every one ought very carefully to beware what he admits for a principle, to examine it strictly, and see whether he certainly knows it to be true of itself by its own evidence, or whether he does only with assurance believe it to be so upon the authority of others. For he hath a strong bias put into his understanding, which will unavoidably misguide his assent, who hath imbibed wrong principles, and has blindly given himself up to the authority of any opinion in itself not evidently true.

9. There is nothing more ordinary than children's receiving into their minds propositions (especially about matters of religion) from their parents, nurses, or those about them; which being insinuated into their unwary as well as unbiassed understandings, and fastened by degrees, are at last

(equally whether true or false) riveted there by long custom and education, beyond all possibility of being pulled out again. For men, when they are grown up, reflecting upon their opinions, and finding those of this sort to be as ancient in their minds as their very memories, not having observed their early insinuation, nor by what means they got them, they are apt to reverence them as sacred things, and not to suffer them to be profaned, touched, or questioned: they look on them as the Urim and Thummim set up in their minds immediately by God himself, to be the great and unerring deciders of truth and falsehood, and the judges to which they are to appeal in all manner of controversies.

10. This opinion of his principles (let them be what they will) being once established in any one's mind, it is easy to be imagined what reception any proposition shall find—how clearly soever proved—that shall invalidate their authority, or at all thwart with these internal oracles; whereas the grossest absurdities and improbabilities, being but agreeable to such principles, go down glibly, and are easily digested. The great obstinacy that is to be found in men firmly believing quite contrary opinions, though many times equally absurd, in the various religions of mankind, are as evident a proof as they are an unavoidable consequence of this way of reasoning from received traditional principles. So that men will disbelieve their own eyes, renounce the evidence of their senses, and give their own experience the lie, rather than admit of anything disagreeing with these sacred tenets. Take an intelligent Romanist that, from the first dawning of any notions in his understanding, hath had this principle constantly inculcated, viz., that he must believe as the church (i. e., those of his communion) believes, or that the pope is infallible; and this he never so much as heard questioned, till at forty or fifty years old he met with one of other principles: how is he prepared easily to swallow, not only against all probability, but even the clear evidence of his senses, the doctrine of transubstantiation? This principle has such an influence on his mind, that he will believe that to be flesh which he sees to be bread. And what way will you take to convince a man of any improbable opinion he holds, who, with some philosophers, hath laid down this as a foundation of reasoning, that he must believe his reason (for so men in-

properly call arguments drawn from their principles) against his senses? Let an enthusiast be principled that he or his teacher is inspired, and acted* by an immediate communication of the Divine Spirit, and you in vain bring the evidence of clear reasons against his doctrine. Whoever, therefore, have imbibed wrong principles, are not, in things inconsistent with these principles, to be moved by the most apparent and convincing probabilities, till they are so candid and ingenuous to themselves, as to be persuaded to examine even those very principles, which many never suffer themselves to do.

11. II. *Received Hypothesis.*—Secondly, Next to these are men whose understandings are cast into a mould, and fashioned just to the size of a received hypothesis. The difference between these and the former, is, that they will admit of matter of fact, and agree with dissenters in that; but differ only in assigning of reasons and explaining the manner of operation. These are not at that open defiance with their senses, with the former: they can endure to hearken to their information a little more patiently; but will by no means admit of their reports in the explanation of things; nor be prevailed on by probabilities, which would convince them that things are not brought about just after the same manner that they have decreed within themselves that they are. Would it not be an insufferable thing for a learned professor, and that which his scarlet would blush at, to have his authority of forty years standing, wrought out of hard rock, Greek and Latin, with no small expense of time and candle, and confirmed by general tradition and a reverend beard, in an instant overturned by an upstart novelist? Can any one expect that he should be made to confess, that what he taught his scholars thirty years ago was all error and mistake; and that he sold them hard words and ignorance at a very dear rate.† What probabilities, I say, are sufficient

---

* That is, actuated.—ED.

† The reader who is acquainted with that very philosophical work, the Adventures of Gil Blas, of Santillane, will doubtless recollect a practical illustration of the reluctance which men usually feel to give up any opinions which they have once acknowledged to be their own, even though their adhering to them should cost the lives and happiness of half their neighbours. But in case any one should have forgotten it, and not have the volume at hand, he may not be displeased to find it here. " 'Sir,

to prevail in such a case? And whoever, by the most cogent arguments, will be prevailed with to disrobe himself at once of all his old opinions, and pretences to knowledge and learning, which with hard study he hath all his time been labouring for; and turn himself out stark naked, in quest afresh of new notions? All the arguments that can be used will be as little able to prevail, as the wind did with the traveller to part with his cloak, which he held only the faster.†

(said I, one evening to Dr. Sangrado,) I take heaven to witness that I follow your method with the utmost exactness: yet, every one of my patients leave me in the lurch. It looks as if they took a pleasure in dying, merely to bring our practice into discredit. This very day I met two of them going to their long home.' 'Why, truly, child,' answered he, 'I have reason to make pretty much the same observation: I have not often the satisfaction of curing those who fall into my hands; and if I was not so sure as I am of the principles on which I proceed, I should think my principles were pernicious in almost all the cases that come under my care.' 'If you will take my advice, sir,' said I, 'we will change our method, and give chemical preparations to our patients, through curiosity: the worst that can happen will only be, that they produce the same effect that follows our bleedings and warm water.' 'I would willingly make the experiment,' he replied, 'provided it could have no bad consequence; but I have published a book, in which I have extolled the use of frequent bleeding and aqueous draughts: and wouldst thou have me go and deny my own work?' 'Oh! you are certainly in the right,' said I, 'you must not give your enemies such a triumph over you; they would say you are at last disabused; and therefore ruin your reputation; perish rather the nobility, clergy, and people! and let us continue in our old path. After all, our brother doctors, notwithstanding their aversion for bleeding, perform as few miracles as we do; and I believe their drugs are no better than our specifics. We went to work, therefore, afresh, and proceeded in such a manner, that, in less than six weeks, we made more widows and orphans than the seige of Troy." (t. ii. c. 5.)—ED.

* This will doubtless bring to the reader's mind that exquisite fable of La Fontaine's, in which, while relating "une conte d'une vielle femme," he presents us with two charming pictures of external nature, full of as true poetry as is to be found in any language.

"Notre souffleur à gage
    Se gorge de vapeurs, s'enfle comme un balon,
        Fait un vacarme de démon
    Siffle, souffle, tempête, et brise en son passage
    Maint toit qui n'en peut mais, peur fait maint bateau
        Le tout au sujet d'un manteau.
Le cavalier eut soin d'empêcher que l'orage,
    Ne se pût engouffler dedans.
Cela le preserva. Le vent perdit son temps;
Plus il se tourmentois, plus il tenois ferme,
Il eut beau faire agir le collet et les plis.

To this of wrong hypothesis may be reduced the errors that may be occasioned by a true hypothesis, or right principles, but not rightly understood. There is nothing more familiar than this. The instances of men contending for different opinions, which they all derive from the infallible truth of the Scripture, are an undeniable proof of it. All that call themselves Christians, allow the text that says, μετανοεῖτε, to carry in it the obligation to a very weighty duty. But yet how very erroneous will one of their practices be, who, understanding nothing but the French, take this rule with one translation to be, " Repentez-vous," repent; or with the other, " Faitiez penitence," do penance.

12. III. *Predominant Passions.*—Thirdly, Probabilities which cross men's appetites and prevailing passions, run the same fate. Let ever so much probability hang on one side of a covetous man's reasoning, and money on the other; it is easy to foresee which will outweigh. Earthly minds, like mud walls, resist the strongest batteries: and though, perhaps, sometimes the force of a clear argument may make some impression, yet they nevertheless stand firm, and keep out the enemy, truth, that would captivate or disturb them. Tell a man passionately in love, that he is jilted; bring a score of witnesses of the falsehood of his mistress, it is ten to one but three kind words of hers shall invalidate all their testimonies. " Quod volumus, facile credimus;" what suits our wishes, is forwardly believed; is, I suppose, what every one hath more than once experimented: and though men cannot always openly gainsay or resist the force of manifest probabilities that make against them, yet yield they not to the argument. Not but that it is the nature of the understanding constantly to close with the more probable side; but yet a man hath a power to suspend and restrain its inquiries, and not permit a full and satisfactory examination, as far as the matter in question is capable, and will bear it to be made. Until that

> Sitot qu'il fut au bout du terme
> Qu'à la gageure on avoit mis,
> Le soleil dissipe la nue,
> Recrée et puis penetre enfin le cavalier,
> Sous son balandras fait qu'il sue
> Le contraint de s'en dépouiller:
> Encore n'usa-t il pas de toute sa puissance,
> Plus fait douceur que violence." (L. vi. fab. 3.)—ED.

be done, there will be always these two ways left of evading the most apparent probabilities.

13. *The Means of evading Probabilities:* I. *Supposed Fallacy.*—First, That the arguments being (as for the most part they are) brought in words, there may be a fallacy latent in them: and the consequences being, perhaps, many in train, they may be some of them incoherent. There are very few discourses so short, clear, and consistent, to which most men may not, with satisfaction enough to themselves, raise this doubt; and from whose conviction they may not, without reproach of disingenuity or unreasonableness, set themselves free with the old reply, "Non persuadebis, etiamsi persuaseris;" though I cannot answer, I will not yield.

14. II. *Supposed Arguments for the contrary.*—Secondly, Manifest probabilities may be evaded, and the assent withheld upon this suggestion, that I know not yet all that may be said on the contrary side. And therefore, though I be beaten, it is not necessary I should yield, not knowing what forces there are in reserve behind. This is a refuge against conviction so open and so wide, that it is hard to determine when a man is quite out of the verge of it.

15. *What Probabilities determine the Assent.*—But yet there is some end of it; and a man having carefully inquired into all the grounds of probability and unlikeliness, done his utmost to inform himself in all particulars fairly, and cast up the sum total on both sides; may, in most cases, come to acknowledge, upon the whole matter, on which side the probability rests: wherein some proofs in matter of reason, being suppositions upon universal experience, are so cogent and clear, and some testimonies in matter of fact so universal, that he cannot refuse his assent. So that I think we may conclude, that, in propositions, where though the proofs in view are of most moment, yet there are sufficient grounds to suspect that there is either fallacy in words, or certain proofs as considerable to be produced on the contrary side; there assent, suspense, or dissent, are often voluntary actions: but where the proofs are such as make it highly probable, and there is not sufficient ground to suspect that there is either fallacy of words (which sober and serious consideration may discover) nor equally valid proofs yet undiscovered, latent on the other side; (which also the nature of the thing

may, in some cases, make plain to a considerate man;) there, I think, a man who has weighed them can scarce refuse his assent to the side on which the greater probability appears. Whether it be probable that a promiscuous jumble of printing letters should often fall into a method and order, which should stamp on paper a coherent discourse;* or that a blind fortuitous concourse of atoms, not guided by an understanding agent, should frequently constitute the bodies of any species of animals; in these and the like cases, I think, nobody that considers them can be one jot at a stand which side to take, nor at all waver in his assent. Lastly, when there can be no supposition (the thing in its own nature indifferent, and wholly depending upon the testimony of witnesses) that there is as fair testimony against, as for the matter of fact attested; which by inquiry is to be learned, v. g., whether there was one thousand seven hundred years ago such a man at Rome as Julius Cæsar: in all such cases, I say, I think it is not in any rational man's power to refuse his assent; but that it necessarily follows, and closes with such probabilities. In other less clear cases, I think it is in man's power to suspend his assent; and perhaps content himself with the proofs he has, if they favour the opinion that suits with his inclination or interest, and so stop from

* When Locke wrote the above sentence he had probably in his mind a very eloquent and curious passage in Cicero, where he makes use of much the same illustration in treating of the same subject. "Hic ego non mirer esse quemquam, qui sibi persuadeat, corpora quædam solida, atque individua, vi et gravitate ferri, mundumque effici ornatissimum et pulcherrimum ex eorum corporum concursione fortuitâ? Hoc qui existimat fieri potuisse, non intelligo, cur non idem putet, si innumerabiles unius et viginti formæ litterarum vel aureæ, vel quales libet, aliquò conjiciantur, posse ex his in terram excussis annales Ennii, ut deinceps legi possint, effici: quod nescio an ne in uno quidem versu possit tantum valere fortuna. Isti autem quemadmodum asseverant ex corpusculis non colore, non qualitate aliquâ quam ποιότητα Græci vocant, non sensu præditis sed concurrentibus temerè atque casu, mundum esse perfectum? vel innumerabiles potius in omni puncto temporis alios nasci, alios interire? Quòd si mundum efficere potest concursus atomorum, cur porticum, cur templum, cur domum, cur urbem non potest? quæ sunt minus operosa et multo quidem faciliora." (De Nat. Deo. ii. 37.) It has been thought, as the Abbé d'Olivet observes on this passage, that it must have led to the discovery of the art of printing; and certainly if they were altogether ignorant of the invention, they had at least approached the very brink of it.—ED.

further search. But that a man should afford his assent to that side on which the less probability appears to him, seems to me utterly impracticable, and as impossible as it is to believe the same thing probable and improbable at the same time.

16. *Where it is in our Power to suspend it.*—As knowledge is no more arbitrary than perception; so, I think, assent is no more in our power than knowledge. When the agreement of any two ideas appears to our minds, whether immediately or by the assistance of reason, I can no more refuse to perceive, no more avoid knowing it, than I can avoid seeing those objects which I turn my eyes to, and look on in daylight; and what upon full examination I find the most probable, I cannot deny my assent to. But though we cannot hinder our knowledge, where the agreement is once perceived, nor our assent, where the probability manifestly appears upon due consideration of all the measures of it; yet we can hinder both knowledge and assent, by stopping our inquiry, and not employing our faculties in the search of any truth. If it were not so, ignorance, error, or infidelity, could not in any case be a fault. Thus, in some cases we can prevent or suspend our assent; but can a man versed in modern or ancient history doubt whether there is such a place as Rome, or whether there was such a man as Julius Cæsar? Indeed, there are millions of truths that a man is not, or may not think himself concerned to know; as whether our king Richard the Third was crooked or no; or whether Roger Bacon was a mathematician or a magician. In these and such like cases, where the assent one way or other is of no importance to the interest of any one; no action, no concernment of his following or depending thereon; there it is not strange that the mind should give itself up to the common opinion, or render itself to the first comer. These and the like opinions are of so little weight and moment, that, like motes in the sun, their tendencies are very rarely taken notice of. They are there, as it were, by chance, and the mind lets them float at liberty. But where the mind judges that the proposition has concernment in it: where the assent or not assenting is thought to draw consequences of moment after it, and good and evil to depend on choosing or refusing the right side; and the mind sets itself seriously to inquire and examine the probability; ther

I think it is not in our choice to take which side we please, if manifest odds appear on either. The greater probability, I think, in that case will determine the assent; and a man can no more avoid assenting, or taking it to be true, where he perceives the greater probability, than he can avoid knowing it to be true, where he perceives the agreement or disagreement of any two ideas.

If this be so, the foundation of error will lie in wrong measures of probability; as the foundation of vice in wrong measures of good.

17. IV. *Authority.*—Fourthly, The fourth and last wrong measure of probability I shall take notice of, and which keeps in ignorance or error more people than all the other together, is that which I have mentioned in the foregoing chapter; I mean the giving up our assent to the common received opinions, either of our friends or party, neighbourhood or country. How many men have no other ground for their tenets, than the supposed honesty, or learning, or number of those of the same profession? As if honest or bookish men could not err, or truth were to be established by the vote of the multitude; yet this with most men serves the turn. The tenet has had the attestation of reverend antiquity; it comes to me with the passport of former ages, and therefore I am secure in the reception I give it; other men have been and are of the same opinion, (for that is all is said,) and therefore it is reasonable for me to embrace it. A man may more justifiably throw up cross and pile for his opinions, than take them up by such measures. All men are liable to error, and most men are in many points, by passion or interest, under temptation to it. If we could but see the secret motives that influenced the men of name and learning in the world, and the leaders of parties, we should not always find that it was the embracing of truth for its own sake, that made them espouse the doctrines they owned and maintained. This at least is certain, there is not an opinion so absurd, which a man may not receive upon this ground; there is no error to be named, which has not had its professors: and a man shall never want crooked paths to walk in, if he thinks that he is in the right way, wherever he has the footsteps of others to follow.

18. *Men not in so many Errors as imagined.*—But, notwithstanding the great noise is made in the world about

errors and opinions, I must do mankind that right, as to say there are not so many men in errors and wrong opinions as is commonly supposed. Not that I think they embrace the truth; but indeed, because concerning those doctrines they keep such a stir about, they have no thought, no opinion at all. For if any one should a little catechise the greatest part of the partizans of most of the sects in the world, he would not find, concerning those matters they are so zealous for, that they have any opinions of their own; much less would he have reason to think that they took them upon the examination of arguments and appearance of probability. They are resolved to stick to a party that education or interest has engaged them in; and there, like the common soldiers of an army, show their courage and warmth as their leaders direct, without ever examining or so much as knowing the cause they contend for. If a man's life shows that he has no serious regard for religion; for what reason should we think that he beats his head about the opinions of his church, and troubles himself to examine the grounds of this or that doctrine? It is enough for him to obey his leaders, to have his hand and his tongue ready for the support of the common cause, and thereby approve himself to those who can give him credit, preferment, or protection in that society.* Thus men become professors of, and combatants for, those opinions they were never convinced of nor proselytes to; no, nor ever had so much as floating in their heads; and though one cannot say there are fewer improbable or erroneous opinions in the world than there are, yet it is certain there are fewer that actually assent to them and mistake them for truth than is imagined.

CHAPTER XXI.
OF THE DIVISION OF THE SCIENCES.

1. *Three Sorts.*—ALL that can fall within the compass of human understanding, being either, First, the nature of things,

* Milton has drawn a lively and admirable picture of a character of this kind, in which he is, if possible, still more sarcastic than Locke. "A wealthy man," he says, "addicted to his pleasure and to his profits, finds religion to be a traffic, so entangled, and of so many piddling accounts, that of all mysteries he cannot skill to keep a stock going upon that trade. What should he do? Fain he would have the name to be religious, fain he would bear up with his neighbour in that. What does he, therefore, but resolves to give over toiling, and to find himself out

as they are in themselves, their relations, and their manner of operation; or, Secondly, that which man himself ought to do, as a rational and voluntary agent, for the attainment of any end, especially happiness; or, Thirdly, the ways and means whereby the knowledge of both the one and the other of these is attained and communicated: I think science may be divided properly into these three sorts.

2. I. *Physica.*—First, The knowledge of things, as they are in their own proper beings, their constitution, properties, and operations; whereby I mean not only matter and body, but spirits also, which have their proper natures, constitutions, and operations, as well as bodies. This, in a little more enlarged sense of the word, I call Φυσική, or natural philosophy. The end of this is bare speculative truth; and whatsoever can afford the mind of man any such, falls under this branch, whether it be God himself, angels, spirits, bodies, or any of their affections, as number, and figure, &c.

3. II. *Practica.*—Secondly, Ηρακτική, the skill of right applying our own powers and actions, for the attainment of things good and useful. The most considerable under this head is ethics, which is the seeking out those rules and measures of human actions, which lead to happiness, and the means to practise them. The end of this is not bare speculation and the knowledge of truth, but right, and a conduct suitable to it.

4. III. Σημειωτική.—Thirdly, The third branch may be called Σημείωτική, or the doctrine of signs; the most usual whereof being words, it is aptly enough termed also Λογική, logic; the business whereof is to consider the nature of signs,

some factor, to whose care and credit he may commit the whole managing of his religious affairs; some divine of note and estimation that must be. To him he adheres, resigns the whole warehouse of his religion, with all the locks and keys into his custody; and indeed makes the very person of that man his religion; esteems his associating with him a sufficient evidence and commendatory of his own piety. So that a man may say his religion is now no more within himself, but is become a dividual movable, and goes and comes near him, according as that good man frequents the house. He entertains him, gives him gifts, feasts him, lodges him; his religion comes home at night, prays, is liberally supped, and sumptuously laid to sleep; rises, is saluted, and after the malmsey, or some well-spiced beverage, and better breakfasted than he whoso morning appetite would have gladly fed on green figs between Bethany and Jerusalem; his religion walks abroad at eight, and leaves his kind entertainer in the shop, trading all day without his religion." (Areopag. § 55.)—ED.

the mind makes use of for the understanding of things, or conveying its knowledge to others. For since the things the mind contemplates are none of them, besides itself, present to the understanding, it is necessary that something else, as a sign or representation of the thing it considers, should be present to it; and these are ideas. And because the scene of ideas that makes one man's thoughts cannot be laid open to the immediate view of another, nor laid up anywhere but in the memory, a no very sure repository; therefore to communicate our thoughts to one another, as well as record them for our own use, signs of our ideas are also necessary. Those which men have found most convenient, and therefore generally make use of, are articulate sounds. The consideration, then, of ideas and words, as the great instruments of knowledge, makes no despicable part of their contemplation who would take a view of human knowledge in the whole extent of it. And perhaps if they were distinctly weighed, and duly considered, they would afford us another sort of logic and critic,* than what we have been hitherto acquainted with.

5. *This is the first Division of the Objects of Knowledge.*—This seems to me the first and most general, as well as natural division of the objects of our understanding. For a man can employ his thoughts about nothing, but either the contemplation of things themselves for the discovery of truth; or about the things in his own power, which are his own actions, for the attainment of his own ends; or the signs the mind makes use of both in the one and the other, and the right ordering of them for its clearer information. All which three, viz., things, as they are in themselves knowable; actions as they depend on us, in order to happiness; and the right use of signs in order to knowledge, being toto cœlo different, they seemed to me to be the three great provinces of the intellectual world, wholly separate and distinct one from another.

* Criticism.—ED.

END OF ESSAY ON HUMAN UNDERSTANDING

APPENDIX.

CONTROVERSY WITH THE BISHOP OF WORCESTER.

[It was originally my intention to reprint the whole of those Letters of Locke which were addressed to the Bishop of Worcester, on the subject of the Essay on the Human Understanding. But upon a more diligent examination of those compositions, I found there was much in them which could scarcely be denominated philosophical, containing matter merely of temporary interest, or turning upon points appertaining solely to the disputants themselves. There are, nevertheless, several passages in those letters, which, because they throw some light on topics discussed in the Essay on the Human Understanding, have usually been subjoined as notes to that work. It has been judged more advisable in the present edition, to introduce them by way of Appendix; first, that they might not interfere with the New Notes; and secondly, because they will probably be read with more advantage where they now stand.

I would not, by what has been said above, be understood to detract from the merit of the Letters to the Bishop of Worcester, which may in themselves be regarded as models of controversial writing; but the very nature of the dispute often led Locke over the ground which he had previously trodden in his Essay, and compelled him to repeat diffusely and hurriedly, what he had there stated in a briefer and more masterly manner. In itself, moreover, his style of correspondence is too voluminous; not, perhaps, through any aversion of his for brevity, but because of his earnest anxiety not to betray the cause of truth from the apprehension of growing tedious. But the taste of the present age is intolerant, at least in what relates to truth and philosophy. We read no page of a book with so much pleasure as the last, because too frequently we read to boast of it as an achievement rather than to profit by it as an exercise. For this reason, most persons will probably be content with those portions of Locke's correspondence with the Bishop of Worcester which are here given. They will perceive with how great dexterity he defends himself from the assaults of his adversary, and how triumphantly he establishes the important truths laid down with modest dogmatism in his great system of philosophy. Should any one, from these specimens, desire to read more, he may congratulate himself upon his own taste and judgment, which will at least incite him to a careful perusal of the minor treatises bequeathed us by the great philosopher.—ED.]

No. I.—Vol. I. p. 134, par. 8.

This modest apology of our author could not procure him the free use of the word *idea:* but great offence has been taken at it, and it has been censured as of dangerous consequence: to which you may see what he answers. "The world,"* saith the Bishop of Worcester. "hath been strangely amused with *ideas* of late; and we have been told that strange things might be done by the help of *ideas*, and yet these *ideas*, at last, come to be only common notions of things, which we must make use of in our reasoning. You (*i.e.*, the author of the Essay concerning Human Understanding) say in that chapter about the existence of God, you thought it most proper to express yourself in the most usual and familiar way, by common words and expressions. I would you had done so quite through your book; for then you had never given that occasion to the enemies of our faith, to take up your new way of *ideas*, as an effectual battery (as they imagined) against the mysteries of the Christian faith. But you might have enjoyed the satisfaction of your *ideas* long enough before I had taken notice of them, unless I had found them employed about doing mischief."

To which our author replies:† "It is plain that that which your lordship apprehends in my book may be of dangerous consequence to the article which your lordship has endeavoured to defend, is my introducing new terms: and that which your lordship instances in, is that of *ideas*. And the reason that your lordship gives in every of these places why your lordship has such an apprehension of *ideas*, that they may be of dangerous consequence to that article of faith which your lordship has endeavoured to defend, is, because they have been applied to such purposes. And I might (your lordship says) have enjoyed the satisfaction of my *ideas* long enough, before you had taken notice of them, unless your lordship had found them employed in doing mischief. Which, at last, as I humbly conceive, amounts to thus much, and no more, viz., that your lordship fears *ideas*, *i. e.*, the term *ideas*, may some time or other prove of very dangerous consequence to what your lordship has endeavoured to defend, because they have been made use of in arguing against it. For I am sure your lordship does not mean, that you apprehend the things signified by *ideas*, may be of dangerous consequence to the article of faith your lordship endeavours to defend, because they have been made use of against it: for (besides that your lordship mentions *terms*) that would be to expect that those who oppose that article should oppose it without any thoughts; for the things signified by *ideas*, are nothing but the immediate objects of our minds in thinking: so that unless any one can oppose the article your lordship defends, without thinking on something, he must use the thing signified by *ideas*; for he that thinks, must have some immediate object of his mind in thinking: *i. e.*, must have *ideas*.

"But whether it be the name or the thing; *ideas* in sound, or *ideas* in signification; that your lordship apprehends may be of dangerous consequence to that article of faith which your lordship endeavours to defend; it seems to me, I will not say a new way of reasoning, (for that belongs to me,) but were it not your lordship's, I should think it a very extraordinary way of reasoning to write against a book wherein your lordship acknowledges they are not used to bad purposes nor employed to do mischief; only because you find that *ideas* are, by those who

* Answer to Mr. Locke's First Letter.
† In his Second Letter to the Bishop of Worcester.

oppose your lordship, employed to do mischief; and to apprehend they may be of dangerous consequence to the article your lordship has engaged in the defence of. For whether *ideas* as terms, or *ideas* as the immediate objects of the mind, signified by those terms, may be, in your lordship's apprehension, of dangerous consequence to that article; I do not see how your lordship's writing against the notions of *ideas*, as stated in my book, will at all hinder your opposers from employing them in doing mischief, as before.

"However, be that as it will, so it is, that your lordship apprehends these new terms, these *ideas*, with which the world hath of late been so strangely amused, (though at last they come to be only common notions of things, as your lordship owns,) may be of dangerous consequence to that article.

"My lord, if any, in answer to your lordship's sermons, and in other pamphlets, wherein your lordship complains they have talked so much of *ideas*, have been troublesome to your lordship with that term; it is not strange that your lordship should be tired with that sound; but how natural soever it be to our weak constitutions, to be offended with any sound wherewith an importunate din hath been made about our ears; yet, my lord, I know your lordship has a better opinion of the articles of our faith, than to think any of them can be overturned, or so much as shaken, with a breath formed into any sound or term whatsoever.

"Names are the arbitrary marks of conception; and so they be sufficiently appropriated to them in their use, I know no other difference any of them have in particular but as they are of easy or difficult pronunciation, and of a more or less pleasant sound; and what particular antipathies there may be in men, to some of them upon that account, it is not easy to be foreseen. This I am sure, no term whatsoever, in itself, bears, one more than another, any opposition to the truth of any kind; they are only propositions that do or can oppose the truth of any article or doctrine: and thus no term is privileged from being set in opposition to truth.

"There is no word to be found, which may not be brought into a proposition, wherein the most sacred and most evident truths may be opposed: but that is not a fault in the term, but him that uses it. And therefore I cannot easily persuade myself (whatever your lordship hath said in the heat of your concern) that you have bestowed so much pains upon my book because the word *idea* is so much used there. For though upon my saying, in my chapter about the existence of God, 'that I scarce use the word *idea* in that chapter,' your lordship wishes that I had done so quite through my book. Yet I must rather look upon that as a compliment to me, wherein your lordship wished that my book had been all through suited to vulgar readers, not used to that and the like terms, than that your lordship has such an apprehension of the word *idea*; or that there is any such harm in the use of it, instead of the word *notion*, (with which your lordship seems to take it to agree in signification,) that your lordship would think it worth your while to spend any part of your valuable time and thoughts about my book, for having the word *idea* so often in it, for this would be to make your lordship to write only against an impropriety of speech. I own to your lordship, it is a great condescension in your lordship to have done it, if that word have such a share in what your lordship has writ against my book, as some expressions would persuade one; and I would, for the satisfaction of your lordship, change the term of *idea* for a better, if your lordship, or any one, could help me to it. For, that *notion* will not so well stand for every immediate object of the mind in thinking, as *idea* does, I have (as I guess) somewhere given a reason in my book, by showing that the term *notion* is more peculiarly appropriated to a certain sort of those objects, which I call mixed modes; and I think it would not sound altogether so well to say, the *notion* of red, and the *notion* of a horse; as the *idea* of red, and the *idea* of a horse. But if any one thinks it will, I contend not: for I have no fondness for, no antipathy to, any particular articulate sounds: nor do I think there is any spell or fascination in any of them.

"But be the word *idea* proper or improper, I do not see how it is the better or the worse, because all men have made use of it, or because it has been made use of to bad purposes; for if that be a reason to condemn or lay it by, we must lay by the terms *scripture, reason, perception, distinct, clear,* &c. Nay, the name of *God* himself will not escape; for I do not think any of these, or any other term, can be produced, which hath not been made use of by such men, and to such purposes. And therefore, if the Unitarians, in their late pamphlets, have talked very much of, and strangely amused the world with *ideas;* I cannot believe your lordship will think that word one jot the worse, or the more dangerous, because they use it; any more than, for the use of them, you will think *reason* or *scripture* terms ill or dangerous. And therefore, what your lordship says in the bottom of this 93rd page, that 'I might have enjoyed the satisfaction of my *ideas* long enough before your lordship had taken notice of them, unless you had found them employed in doing mischief,' will, I presume, when your lordship has considered again of this matter, prevail with your lordship to let me enjoy still the satisfaction I take in my *ideas, i. e.,* as much satisfaction as I can take in so small a matter, as is the using of a proper term, notwithstanding it should be employed by others in doing mischief.

"For, my lord, if I should leave it wholly out of my book, and substitute the word *notion* everywhere in the room of it; and everybody else should do so too (though your lordship does not, I suppose, suspect that I have the vanity to think they would follow my example) my book would, it seems, be the more to your lordship's liking; but I do not see how this would one jot abate the mischief your lordship complains of. For the Unitarians might as much employ *notions,* as they do now *ideas,* to do mischief; unless they are such fools to think they can conjure with this notable word *idea;* and that the force of what they say, lies in the sound, and not in the signification of their terms.

"This I am sure of, that the truths of the Christian religion can be no more battered by one word than another; nor can they be beaten down or endangered by any sound whatsoever. And I am apt to flatter myself, that your lordship is satisfied that there is no harm in the word *ideas,* because you say you should not have taken notice of my *ideas,* if the enemies of our faith had not taken up my new way of *ideas,* as an effectual battery against the mysteries of the Christian faith. In which place, by new way of *ideas,* nothing, I think, can be construed to be meant, but my expressing myself by that of *ideas*, and not by other more common words, and of ancienter standing in the English language."

As to the objection of the author's way by *ideas* being a new way, he thus answers: "My *new way by ideas*, or *my way by ideas*, which often occurs in your lordship's letter, is, I confess, a very large and doubtful expression, and may, in the full latitude, comprehend my whole Essay; because, treating in it of the understanding, which is nothing but the faculty of thinking, I could not well treat of that faculty of the mind which consists in thinking, without considering the immediate objects of the mind in thinking, which I call *ideas;* and therefore, in treating of the understanding, I guess it will not be thought strange, that the greatest part of my book has been taken up in considering what these objects of the mind in thinking are; whence they come; what use the mind makes of them, in its several ways of thinking; and what are the outward marks whereby it signifies them to others, or records them for its own use. And this, in short, is my way by *ideas*, that which your lordship calls my *new way by ideas;* which, my lord, if it be new, it is but a new history of an old thing. For I think it will not be doubted that men always performed the actions of thinking, reasoning, believing, and knowing, just after the same manner that they do now; though whether the same account has heretofore been given of the way how they performed these actions, or wherein they consisted, I do not know. Were I as well read as your lordship, I should have been safe from that gentle reprimand of your lordship's, for thinking my way of *ideas* new, for want of looking into other men's thoughts, which appear in their books.

"Your lordship's words, as an acknowledgment of your instructions in the case, and as a warning to others, who will be so bold adventurers as to spin anything barely out of their own thoughts, I shall set down at large; and they run thus: 'Whether you took this way of *ideas* from the modern philosopher, mentioned by you, is not at all material; but I intended no reflection upon you in it; (for that you mean by my commending you as a scholar of so great a master;) I never meant to take from you the honour of your own inventions; and I do believe you, when you say that you wrote from your own thoughts, and the *ideas* you had there. But many things may seem new to one that converses only with his own thoughts, which really are not so; as he may find, when he looks into the thoughts of other men, which appear in their books. And therefore, although I have a just esteem for the invention of such, who can spin volumes barely out of their own thoughts; yet I am apt to think they would oblige the world more, if, after they have thought so much themselves, they would examine what thoughts others have had before them concerning the same things; that so those may not be thought their own inventions, which are common to themselves and others If a man should try all the magnetical experiments himself, and publish them as his own thoughts, he might take himself to be the inventor of them. But he that examines and compares them with what Gilbert and others have done before him, will not diminish the praise of his diligence, but may wish he had compared his thoughts with other men's; by which the world would receive greater advantage, though he lost the honour of being an original.'

"To alleviate my fault herein, I agree with your lordship, that many things may seem new to one that converses only with his own thoughts, which really are not so: but I must crave leave to suggest to your lordship, that if, in spinning of them out of his own thoughts, they seem new to him, he is certainly the inventor of them; and they may as justly be thought his own invention as any one's; and he is as certainly the inventor of them, as any one who thought on them before him: the distinction of invention, or not invention, lying not in thinking first, or not first, but in the borrowing, or not borrowing, our thoughts from another; and he to whom, spinning them out of his own thoughts, they seem new, could not certainly borrow them from another. So he truly invented printing in Europe, who, without any communication with the Chinese, spun it out of his own thoughts; though it was never so true, that the Chinese had the use of printing, nay, of printing in the very same way, among them, many ages before him. So that he that spins anything out of his own thoughts, that seems new to him, cannot cease to think it is his own invention, should he examine ever so far, what thoughts others have had before him concerning the same thing, and should find, by examining, that they had the same thoughts too.

" But what great obligation this would be to the world, or weighty cause of turning over and looking into books, I confess I do not see. The great end to me, in conversing with my own or other men's thoughts, in matters of speculation, is to find truth, without being much concerned whether my own spinning of it out of mine, or their spinning of it out of their own thoughts, helps me to it. And how little I affect the honour of an original, may be seen in that place of my book, where, if anywhere, that itch of vain-glory was likeliest to have shown itself, had I been so overrun with it as to need a cure. It is where I speak of certainty, in these following words, taken notice of by your lordship in another place: 'I think I have shown wherein it is that certainty, real certainty, consists, which, whatever it was to others, was, I confess, to me, heretofore, one of those *desiderata* which I found great want of.'

"Here, my lord, however new this seemed to me, and the more so because possibly I had in vain hunted for it in the books of others; yet I spoke of it as new only to myself; leaving others in the undisturbed possession of what, either by invention or reading, was theirs before; without assuming to myself any other honour but that of my own ignorance, until that time, if others before had shown wherein certainty lay. And yet, my lord, if I had upon this occasion been forward to assume to myself the honour of an original, I think I had been pretty safe in it; since I should have had your lordship for my guarantee and vindicator on that point, who are pleased to call it new, and, as such, to write against it.

"And truly, my lord, in this respect my book has had very unlucky stars, since it hath had the misfortune to displease your lordship, with many things in it, for their novelty; as *new way of reasoning; new hypothesis about reason; new sort of certainty; new terms; new way of ideas; new method of certainty,* &c. And yet, in other places, your lordship seems to think it worthy in me of your lordship's reflection, for saying, but what others have said before; as where I say, 'In the different make of men's tempers, and application of their thoughts, some arguments prevail more on one and some on another, for the confirmation of the same truth;' your lordship asks, 'What is this different from what all men of understanding have said?' Again, I take it, your lordship meant not these words for a commendation of my book, where you say, But if no more be meant by 'The simple *ideas* that come in by sensation or reflection, and their being the foundation of our knowledge,' but that our notions of things come in either from our senses or the exercise of our minds: as there is nothing extraordinary in the discovery, so your lordship is far enough from opposing that wherein you think all mankind are agreed.

"And again: 'But what need all this great noise about *ideas* and certainty, true and real *certainty* by *ideas;* if, after all, it comes only to this, that our *ideas* only represent to us such things, from whence we bring arguments to prove the truth of things.

"'But the world hath been strangely amused with *ideas* of late: and we have been told, that strange things might be done by the help of *ideas;* yet these *ideas*, at last, come to be only common notions of things, which we must make use of in our reasoning.' And to the like purpose in other places.

"Whether, therefore, at last, your lordship will resolve that it is new or no; or more faulty by its being new, must be left to your lordship. This I find by it, that my book cannot avoid being condemned on the one side or the other; nor do I see a possibility to help it. If there be readers that like only new thoughts; or, on the other side, others that can bear nothing but what can be justified by received authorities in print, I must desire them to make themselves amends in that part which they like, for the displeasure they receive in the other; but if any should be so exact as to find fault with both, truly I know not what to say to them. The case is a plain case: the book is all over naught; and there is not a sentence in it that is not, either from its antiquity or novelty, to be condemned; and so there is a short end of it. From your lordship, indeed, in particular, I can hope for something better; for your lordship thinks the general design of it so good, that that, I flatter myself, would prevail on your lordship to preserve it from the fire.

"But as to the way your lordship thinks I should have taken to prevent the having it thought my invention, when it was common to me with others, it unluckily so fell out, in the subject of my Essay of Human Understanding, that I could not look into the thoughts of other men to inform myself. For my design being, as well as I could, to copy nature, and to give an account of the operations of the mind in thinking, I could look into nobody's understanding but my own, to see how it wrought; nor have a prospect into other men's minds, to view their thoughts there, and observe what steps and motions they took, and by what gradations they proceeded in their acquainting themselves with truth, and their advance in knowledge; what we find of their thoughts in books, is but the result of this, and not the progress and working of their minds, in coming to the opinions or conclusions they set down and published.

"All, therefore, that I can say of my book is, that it is a copy of my own mind, in its several ways of operation. And all that I can say for the publishing of it is, that I think the intellectual faculties are made, and operate alike in most men; and that some that I showed it to before I published it, liked it so well, that I was confirmed in that opinion. And, therefore, if it should happen that it should not be so, but that some men should have ways of thinking, reasoning, or arriving at certainty, different from others, and above those that I find my mind to use and acquiesce in, I do not see of what use my book can be to them. I can only make it my humble request, in my own name, and in the name of those that are of my size, who find their minds work, reason, and know in the same low way that mine does, that those men of a more happy genius would show us the way of their nobler flights; and particularly would discover to us their shorter or surer way to certainty, than by *ideas*, and the observing their agreement or disagreement."

" Your lordship adds : ' But now, it seems, nothing is intelligible but what suits with the new way of *ideas*.' My lord, the new way of *ideas*, and the old way of speaking intelligibly,* was always, and ever will be the same; and, if I may take the liberty to declare my sense of it, herein it consists: 1. That a man use no words but such as he makes the sign of certain determined objects of his mind in thinking, which he can make known to another. 2. Next, That he use the same word steadily for the sign of the same immediate object of his mind in thinking. 3. That he join those words together in propositions, according to the grammatical rules of that language he speaks in. 4. That he unite those sentences into a coherent discourse. Thus, and thus only, I humbly conceive, any one may preserve himself from the confines and suspicion of jargon, whether he pleases to call those immediate objects of his mind, which his words do or should stand for, *ideas* or no."

No. II.—Vol. I. p. 87, par. 8.

On this reasoning of the author against innate ideas, great blame hath been laid, because it seems to invalidate an argument commonly used to prove the being of a God, viz., universal consent. To which our author answers :† " I think that the universal consent of mankind as to the being of a God, amounts to thus much, that the vastly greater majority of mankind have, in all ages of the world, actually believed in a God ; that the majority of the remaining part have not actually disbelieved it; and, consequently, those who have actually opposed the belief of a God, have truly been very few. So that comparing those that have actually disbelieved, with those who have actually believed in a God, their number is so inconsiderable, that in respect of this incomparably greater majority of those who have owned the belief of a God, it may be said to be the universal consent of mankind.

" This is all the universal consent which truth or matter of fact will a_low, and, therefore, all that can be made use of to prove a God. But if any one would extend it further, and speak deceitfully for God; if this universality should be urged in a strict sense, not for much the majority, but for a general consent of every one, even to a man, in all ages and countries, this would make it either no argument, or a perfectly useless and unnecessary one. For if any one deny a God, such an

* Mr. Locke's Third Letter to the Bishop of Worcester. † Ibid.

universality of consent is destroyed: and if nobody does deny a God, what need of arguments to convince Atheists?

"I would crave leave to ask your lordship, were there ever in the world any Atheists or not? If there were not, what need is there of raising a question about the being of a God, when nobody questions it? What need of provisional arguments against a fault from which mankind are so wholly free; and which, by an universal consent, they may be presumed to be secure from? If you say (as I doubt not but you will) that there have been Atheists in the world, then your lordship's universal consent reduces itself to only a great majority; and then make that majority as great as you will, what I have said in the place quoted by your lordship leaves it in its full force: and I have not said one word that does in the least invalidate this argument for a God. The argument I was upon there was to show, that the idea of God was not innate; and to my purpose it was sufficient, if there were but a less number found in the world who had no idea of God, than your lordship will allow there have been of professed Atheists; for whatsoever is innate must be universal in the strictest sense. One exception is a sufficient proof against it. So that all that I said, and which was quite to another purpose, did not at all tend, nor can be made use of, to invalidate the argument for a Deity, grounded on such an universal consent, as your lordship, and all that build on it, must own: which is only a very disproportioned majority: such an universal consent, my argument there neither affirms nor requires to be less than you will be pleased to allow it. Your lordship, therefore, might without any prejudice to those declarations of goodwill and favour you have for the author of the Essay of Human Understanding, have spared the mentioning his quoting authors that are in print, for matters of fact to quite another purpose, 'as going about to invalidate the argument for a Deity from the universal consent of mankind,' since he leaves that universal consent as entire and as large as you yourself do, or can own or suppose it. But here I have no reason to be sorry that your lordship has given me this occasion for the vindication of this passage of my book; if there should be any one besides your lordship, who should so far mistake it as to think it in the least invalidates the argument for a God, from the universal consent of mankind.

"But because you question the credibility of those authors I have quoted, which you say were very ill chosen, I will crave leave to say, that he whom I relied on for his testimony concerning the Hottentots of Soldania, was no less a man than an ambassador from the King of England to the great Mogul, of whose relation M. Thevenot, no ill judge in the case, had so great an esteem, that he was at the pains to translate it into French, and publish it in his (which is counted no injudicious) Collection of Travels. But to intercede with your lordship for a little more favourable allowance of credit to Sir Thomas Roe's relation: Coore, an inhabitant of the country, who could speak English, assured Mr. Terry,* that they of Soldania had no God. But if he, too, have the ill luck to find no credit with you, I hope you will be a little more favourable to a divine of the Church of England now living, and admit of his

* Terry's Voyage, p. 17, 23.

testimony in confirmation of Sir Thomas Roe's. This worthy gentleman, in the relation of his voyage to Surat, printed but two years since, speaking of the same people, has these words:* 'They are sunk even below idolatry, are destitute of both priest and temple; and, saving a little show of rejoicing which is made at the full and new moon, have lost all kind of religious devotion. Nature has so richly provided for their convenience in this life, that they have drowned all sense of the God of it, and are grown quite careless of the next.'

"But to provide against the clearest evidence of Atheism in these people, you say, 'That the account given of them makes them not fit to be a standard for the sense of mankind.' This, I think, may pass for nothing, till somebody be found that makes them to be a standard for the sense of mankind. All the use I made of them was to show that there were men in the world that had no innate idea of God. But to keep something like an argument going, (for what will not that do?) you go near to deny those Caffres to be men. What else do these words signify? 'A people so strangely bereft of common sense, that they can hardly be reckoned among mankind, as appears by the best accounts of the Caffres of Soldania,' &c. I hope if any of them were called Peter, James, or John, it would be past scruple that they were men: however, Courwee, Wewena, and Cowsheda, and those others who had names, that had no places in your nomenclature, would hardly pass muster with your lordship.

"My lord, I should not mention this, but that what you yourself say here, may be a motive to you to consider, that what you have laid such stress on concerning the general nature of man, as a real being, and the subject of properties, amounts to nothing for the distinguishing of species; since you yourself own, that there may be individuals, wherein there is a common nature with a particular subsistence proper to each of them; whereby you are so little able to know of which of the ranks or sorts they are, into which you say God has ordered beings, and which he hath distinguished by essential properties, that you are in doubt whether they ought to be reckoned among mankind or not."

No. III.—Vol. I. p. 224, par. 2.

Against this, that the materials of all our knowledge are suggested and furnished to the mind only by sensation and reflection, the Bishop of Worcester makes use of the idea of substance in these words: "If the idea of substance be grounded upon plain and evident reason, then we must allow an idea of substance, which comes not in by sensation or reflection; and so we may be certain of something which we have not by these ideas."

To which our author answers: † "These words of your lordship contain nothing, as I see, in them, against me; for I never said that the general idea of substance comes in by sensation and reflection; or that it is a simple idea of sensation or reflection, though it be ultimately founded in them; for it is a complex idea, made up of the general idea of some-

* Mr. Ovington, p. 489.
† In his First Letter to the Bishop of Worcester.

APPENDIX. 349

thing, or being, with the relation of a support to accidents. For general ideas come not into the mind by sensation or reflection; but are the creatures or inventions of the understanding, as I think I have shown;* and also how the mind makes them from ideas which it has got by sensation and reflection; and as to the ideas of relation, how the mind forms them, and how they are derived from, and ultimately terminate in, ideas of sensation and reflection, I have likewise shown.

"But that I may not be mistaken in what I mean, when I speak of ideas of sensation and reflection, as the materials of all our knowledge; give me leave, my lord, to set down here a place or two, out of my book, to explain myself; as I thus speak of ideas of sensation and reflection:

"'That these, when we have taken a full survey of them, and their several modes, and the compositions made out of them, we shall find to contain our whole stock of ideas, and we have nothing in our minds which did not come in one of these two ways.'† This thought, in another place, I express thus:

"'These are the most considerable of these simple ideas which the mind has, and out of which is made all its other knowledge; all which it receives by the two fore-mentioned ways of sensation and reflection.' ‡ And,

"'Thus I have in a short draught given a view of our original ideas, from whence all the rest are derived, and of which they are made up. §

"This, and the like, said in other places, is what I have thought concerning ideas of sensation and reflection, as the foundation and materials of all our ideas, and consequently of all our knowledge: I have set down these particulars out of my book, that the reader, having a full view of my opinion herein, may the better see what in it is liable to your lordship's reprehension. For that your lordship is not very well satisfied with it, appears not only by the words under consideration, but by these also: 'But we are still told, that our understanding can have no other ideas, but either from sensation or reflection.'

"Your lordship's argument in the passage we are upon, stands thus: 'If the general idea of substance be grounded upon plain and evident reason, then we must allow an idea of substance, which comes not in by sensation or reflection.' This is a consequence which, with submission, I think will not hold, because it is founded upon a supposition which I think will not hold, viz., 'That reason and ideas are inconsistent:' for if that supposition be not true, then the general idea of substance may be grounded on plain and evident reason; and yet it will not follow from thence, that it is not ultimately grounded on and derived from ideas which come in by sensation or reflection, and so cannot be said to come in by sensation or reflection.'

"To explain myself, and clear my meaning in this matter: all the ideas of all the sensible qualities of a cherry come into my mind by sensation: the ideas of perceiving, thinking, reasoning, knowing, &c., come into my mind by reflection. The ideas of these qualities and actions, or powers, are perceived by the mind, to be by themselves inconsistent with existence; or,

* B. 3. c. 3.   B. 2. par. 25, and c. 28. par. 18.
† B. 2. c. 1. par. 5.   ‡ B. 2. c. 7. par. 10.   § B. 2. c. 21. par. 73.

as your lordship well expresses it, 'we find that we can have no true conception of any modes or accidents, but we must conceive a substratum, or subject, wherein they are, *i. e.*, that they cannot exist or subsist of themselves.' Hence the mind perceives their necessary connexion with inherence, or being supported, which being a relative idea, superadded to the red colour in a cherry, or to thinking in a man, the mind frames the correlative idea of a support. For I never denied, that the mind could frame to itself ideas of relation, but have shown the quite contrary in my chapters about relation. But because a relation cannot be founded in nothing, or be the relation of nothing, and the thing here related as the supporter, or a support, is not represented to the mind by any clear and distinct idea; therefore, the obscure and indistinct vague idea of thing, or something, is all that is left to be the positive idea, which has the relation of a support, or substratum, to modes or accidents; and that general indetermined idea of something is, by the abstraction of the mind, derived also from the simple ideas of sensation and reflection; and thus the mind, from the positive simple ideas got by sensation and reflection; comes to the general relative idea of substance, which, without these positive simple ideas it would never have.

"This your lordship (without giving by detail all the particular steps of the mind in this business) has well expressed in this more familiar way: 'We find we can have no true conception of any modes or accidents, but we must conceive a substratum, or subject, wherein they are; since it is a repugnancy to our conception of things, that modes or accidents should subsist by themselves.'

"Hence your lordship calls it the rational idea of substance. And say, 'I grant, that by sensation and reflection we come to know the powers and properties of things; but our reason is satisfied that there must be something beyond these, because it is impossible that they should subsist by themselves;' so that if this be what your lordship means by rational ideas of substances, I see nothing there is in it against what I have said, that it is founded on simple ideas of sensation or reflection, and that it is a very obscure idea.

"Your lordship's conclusion from your foregoing words, is, 'And so we may be certain of some things which we have not by those ideas:' which is a proposition, whose precise meaning your lordship will forgive me, if I profess, as it stands there, I do not understand. For it is uncertain to me, whether your lordship means, we may certainly know the existence of something which we have not by those ideas; or certainly know the distinct properties of something which we have not by those ideas; or certainly know the truth of some propositions, which we have not by those ideas; for to be certain of something, may signify either of these: but in which soever of these it be meant, I do not see how I am concerned in it.

No. IV.—Vol. I. p. 423, par. 1.

This section, which was intended only to show how the individuals of distinct species of substances came to be looked upon as simple ideas, and so to have simple names, viz., from the supposed substratum or substance, which was looked upon as the thing itself in which inhered, and from which resulted that complication of ideas, by which it was represented to us, hath been mistaken for an account of the idea of substance in general; and as such, hath been represented in these words: But how comes the general idea of substance to be framed in our minds? Is this by abstracting and enlarging simple ideas? No: 'But it is by a complication of many simple ideas together: because, not imagining how these simple ideas can subsist by themselves, we accustom ourselves to suppose some substratum, wherein they do subsist, and from whence they do result; which, therefore, we call substance.' 'And is this all, indeed, that is to be said for the being of substance, that we accustom ourselves to suppose a substratum? Is that custom grounded upon true reason, or not? If not, then accidents or modes must subsist of themselves; and these simple ideas need no tortoise to support them; for figures and colours, &c., would do well enough of themselves, but for some fancies men have accustomed themselves to.'

To which objection of the Bishop of Worcester, our author answers thus:* "Herein your lordship seems to charge me with two faults: one, that I make the general idea of substance to be framed, not by abstracting and enlarging simple ideas, but by a complication of many simple ideas together; the other, as if I had said, the being of substance had no other foundation but the fancies of men.

"As to the first of these, I beg leave to remind your lordship, that I say in more places than one, and particularly Book 3, Chap. 3, par. 6, and Book 1, Chap. 11, par. 9, where, *ex professo*, I treat of abstraction and general ideas, that they are all made by abstracting, and, therefore, could not be understood to mean, that that of substance was made any other way; however my pen might have slipped, or the negligence of expression, where I might have something else than the general idea of substance in view, might make me seem to say so.

"That I was not speaking of the general idea of substance, in the passage your lordship quotes, is manifest from the title of that chapter, which is, 'Of the complex ideas of substances;' and the first paragraph of it, which your lordship cites for those words you have set down.

"In which words I do not observe any that deny the general idea of substance to be made by abstraction, nor any that say it is made by a complication of many simple ideas together. But speaking in that place of the ideas of distinct substances, such as man, horse, gold, &c., I say they are made up of certain combinations of simple ideas, which combinations are looked upon, each of them, as one simple idea, though they are many; and we call it by one name of substance, though made up of modes, from the custom of supposing a substratum, wherein that combination does subsist. So that in this paragraph I only give an account of the idea of distinct substances, such as oak, elephant, iron, &c., how, though they are made up of distinct complications of modes, yet they are looked on as one idea, called by one name, as making distinct sorts of substances.

"But that my notion of substance in general is quite different from these, and has no such combination of simple ideas in it, is evident fro

---

* In his First Letter to the Bishop of Worcester.

the immediate following words, where I say,* 'The idea of pure substance in general, is only a supposition of we know not what support of such qualities as are capable of producing simple ideas in us.' And these too I plainly distinguish all along, particularly where I say, 'whatever, therefore, be the secret and abstract nature of substance in general, all the ideas we have of particular distinct substances are nothing but several combinations of simple ideas, co-existing in such, though unknown cause of their union, as makes the whole subsist of itself'

"The other thing laid to my charge is, as if I took the being of substance to be doubtful, or rendered it so by the imperfect and ill-grounded idea I have given of it. To which I beg leave to say, that I ground not the being, but the idea of substance, on our accustoming ourselves to suppose some subtratum: for it is of the idea alone I speak there, and not of the being of substance. And having everywhere affirmed, and built upon it, that a man is a substance, I cannot be supposed to question or doubt of the being of substance, till I can question or doubt of my own being. Further, I say,† 'Sensation convinces us that there are solid, extended substances; and reflection, that there are thinking ones.' So that, I think, the being of substance is not shaken by what I have said; and if the idea of it should be, yet (the being of things depending not on our ideas) the being of substance would not be at all shaken by my saying, we had but an obscure imperfect idea of it, and that that idea came from our accustoming ourselves to suppose some substratum; or indeed, if I should say, we had no idea of substance at all. For a great many things may be, and are granted to have a being, and be in nature, of which we have no ideas. For example: it cannot be doubted but there are distinct species of separate spirits, of which yet we have no distinct ideas at all; it cannot be questioned but spirits have ways of communicating their thoughts, and yet we have no idea of it at all.

"The being then of substance being safe and secure, notwithstanding anything I have said, let us see whether the idea of it be not so too. Your lordship asks, with concern, 'And is this all, indeed, that is to be said, for the being (if your lordship please, let it be the idea) of substance, that we accustom ourselves to suppose a substratum? Is that custom grounded upon true reason or not?' I have said that it is grounded upon this,‡ 'That we cannot conceive how simple ideas of sensible qualities should subsist alone, and, therefore, we suppose them to exist in, and to be supported by, some common subject; which support we denote by the same substance.' Which, I think, is a true reason, because it is the same your lordship grounds the supposition of a substratum on, in this very page: even on the repugnancy to our conceptions, that modes and accidents should subsist by themselves. So that I have the good luck to agree here with your lordship: and consequently conclude I have your approbation in this, that the substratum to modes or accidents, which is our idea of substance in general, is founded in this, 'that we cannot conceive how modes or accidents can subsist by themselves.'"

* B. 2. c. 23. par. 2. † Ibid. par. 29. ‡ Ibid. par. 4.

APPENDIX.

No. V.—Vol. I. page 424, par. 2.

From this paragraph, there hath been raised an objection by the Bishop of Worcester, as if our author's doctrine here, concerning ideas, had almost discarded substance out of the world: his words in this second paragraph being brought to prove, that he is one of the gentlemen of this new way of reasoning, that have almost discarded substance out of the reasonable part of the world. To which our author replies:* "This, my lord, is an accusation which your lordship will pardon me, if I do not readily know what to plead to, because I do not understand what is almost to discard substance out of the reasonable part of the world. If your lordship means by it, that I deny or doubt, that there is in the world any such thing as substance, that your lordship will acquit me of, when your lordship looks again into the 23rd chapter of the second book, which you have cited more than once; where you will find these words, par. 4: 'When we talk or think of any particular sort of corporeal substances, as horse, stone, &c., though the idea we have of either of them be but the complication or collection of those several simple ideas of sensible qualities which we used to find united in the thing called horse, or stone; yet, because we cannot conceive how they should subsist alone, nor one in another, we suppose them existing in and supported by some common subject, which support we denote by the name substance; though it be certain, we have no clear and distinct idea of that thing we suppose a support.' And again, par. 5: 'The same happens concerning the operations of the mind, viz., thinking, reasoning, fearing, &c., which we considering not to subsist of themselves, nor apprehending how they can belong to body, or be produced by it, we are apt to think these the actions of some other substance, which we call spirit; whereby yet it is evident, that having no other idea or notion of matter, but something wherein those many sensible qualities which affect our senses do subsist, by supposing a substance, wherein thinking, knowing, doubting, and a power of moving, &c., do subsist, we have as clear a notion of the nature or substance of spirit, as we have of body; the one being supposed to be (without knowing what it is) the substratum to those simple ideas we have from without: and the others supposed (with a like ignorance of what it is) to be the substratum to those operations, which we experiment in ourselves within.' And again, par. 6: 'Whatever, therefore, be the secret nature of substance in general, all the ideas we have of particular distinct substances, are nothing but several combinations of simple ideas co-existing in such, though unknown, cause of their union, as makes the whole subsist of itself.' And I further say, in the same paragraph, 'that we suppose these combinations to rest in, and to be adherent to, that unknown common subject, which inheres not in anything else.' And, par. 3: 'That our complex ideas of substances, besides all those simple ideas they are made up of, have always the confused idea of something to which they belong, and in which they subsist; and, therefore, when we speak of any sort of substance, we say it is a thing having such and

* In his First Letter to that Bishop.

such qualities; a body is a thing that is extended, figured, and capable of motion; a spirit, a thing capable of thinking, &c. These and the like fashions of speaking, intimate that the substance is supposed always something besides the extension, figure, solidity, motion, thinking, or other observable idea, though we know not what it is.'

"'Our idea of body,' I say,* 'is an extended solid substance; and our idea of soul, is of a substance that thinks.' So that as long as there is any such thing as body or spirit in the world, I have done nothing towards the discarding substance out of the reasonable part of the world. Nay, as long as there is any simple idea or sensible quality left, according to my way of arguing, substance cannot be discarded; because all simple ideas, all sensible qualities, carry with them a supposition of a substratum to exist in, and of a substance wherein they inhere: and of this, that whole chapter is so full, that I challenge any one who reads it, to think I have almost, or one jot, discarded substance out of the reasonable part of the world. And of this, man, horse, sun, water, iron, diamond, &c., which I have mentioned of distinct sorts of substances, will be my witnesses, as long as any such thing remains in being; of which I say,† 'That the ideas of substances are such combinations of simple ideas, as are taken to represent distinct particular things subsisting by themselves, in which the supposed or confused idea of substance is always the first and chief.'

"If by almost discarding substance out of the reasonable part of the world, your lordship means, that I have destroyed and almost discarded the true idea we have of it, by calling it 'a substratum,‡ a supposition of we know not what support of such qualities as are capable of producing simple ideas in us; an obscure and relative idea : § that without knowing what it is, it is that which supports accidents; so that of substance we have no idea of what it is, but only a confused and obscure one, of what it does:' I must confess, this and the like I have said of our idea of substance; and should be very glad to be convinced by your lordship, or anybody else, that I have spoken too meanly of it. He that would show me a more clear and distinct idea of substance, would do me a kindness I should thank him for. But this is the best I can hitherto find, either in my own thoughts, or in the books of logicians; for their account or idea of it is, that it is *ens,* or *res per se subsistens, et substans accidentibus;* which in effect is no more, but that substance is a being or thing; or, in short, something, they know not what, or of which they have no clearer idea, than that it is something which supports accidents, or other simple ideas or modes, and is not supported itself, as a mode, or an accident. So that I do not see but Burgersdicius, Sanderson, and the whole tribe of logicians, must be reckoned with 'the gentlemen of this new way of reasoning, who have almost discarded substance out of the reasonable part of the world.'

"But supposing, my lord, that I, or these gentlemen, logicians of note in the schools, should own that we have a very imperfect, obscure, inadequate idea of substance, would it not be a little too hard to charge us with discarding substance out of the world? For what almost do

* B. 2. c. 23. par. 22. † B. 2. c. 12. par. 6.
‡ B. 2. c. 23. pars. 1, 2, 3. § B. 2 c. 13. par. 19.

carding, and reasonable part of the world, signify, I must confess I do not clearly comprehend; but let, almost, and, reasonable part, signify here what they will, for I dare say your lordship meant something by them; would not your lordship think you were a little too hardly dealt with, if, for acknowledging yourself to have a very imperfect and inadequate idea of God, or of several other things, which in this very treatise you confess our understandings come short in, and cannot comprehend, you should be accused to be one of these gentlemen that have almost discarded God, or those other mysterious things, whereof you contend we have very imperfect and inadequate ideas out of the reasonable world? For I suppose your lordship means by almost discarding out of the reasonable world, something that is blamable, for it seems not to be inserted for a commendation; and yet I think he deserves no blame, who owns the having imperfect, inadequate, obscure ideas, where he has no better: however, if it be inferred from thence, that either he almost excludes those things out of being, or out of rational discourse, if that be meant by the reasonable world; for the first of these will not hold, because the being of things in the world depends not on our ideas: the latter, indeed, is true in some degree, but is no fault; for it is certain, that where we have imperfect, inadequate, confused, obscure ideas, we cannot discourse and reason about those things so well, fully, and clearly, as if we had perfect, adequate, clear, and distinct ideas.

Other objections are made against the following parts of this paragraph, by that reverend prelate, viz., "The repetition of the story of the Indian philosopher, and the talking like children about substance:" to which our author replies:—

"Your lordship, I must own, with great reason, takes notice, that I paralleled, more than once, our idea of substance with the Indian philosopher's Ho-knew-not-what, which supported the tortoise, &c.

"This repetition, is, I confess a fault in exact writing; but I have acknowledged and excused it in these words, in my preface: 'I am not ignorant how little I herein consult my own reputation, when I knowingly let my Essay go with a fault so apt to disgust the most judicious, who are always the nicest readers.' And there further add, 'That I did not publish my Essay for such great masters of knowledge as your lordship: but fitted it to men of my own size, to whom repetitions might be sometimes useful.' It would not, therefore, have been beside your lordship's generosity, (who were not intended to be provoked by the repetition,) to have passed by such a fault as this, in one who pretends not beyond the lower rank of writers. But I see your lordship would have me exact, and without any faults: and I wish I could be so, the better to deserve your lordship's approbation.

' My saying, 'That when we talk of substance, we talk like children who, being asked a question about something which they know not, readily give this satisfactory answer, That it is something;' your lordship seems mightily to lay to heart in these words that follow: 'If this be the truth of the case, we must still talk like children, and I know not how it can be remedied. For if we cannot come at a rational idea of substance, we can have no principle of certainty to go upon in this debate.'

"If your lordship has any better and distincter idea of substance than mine is, which I have given an account of, your lordship is not at all concerned in what I have there said. But those whose idea of substance, whether a rational or not rational idea, is like mine, something, they know not what, must in that, with me, talk like children, when they speak of something, they know not what. For a philosopher that says, that which supports accidents is something he knows not what, and a countryman that says, the foundation of the great church at Haarlem is supported by something, he knows not what; and a child that stands in the dark, upon his mother's muff, and says he stands upon something, he knows not what; in this respect talk all three alike. But if the countryman knows that the foundation of the church at Haarlem is supported by a rock, as the houses about Bristol are; or by gravel, as the houses about London are; or by wooden piles, as the houses in Amsterdam are; it is plain, that, then having a clear and distinct idea of the thing that supports the church, he does not talk of this matter as a child; nor will he of the support of accidents, when he has a clearer and more distinct idea of it, than that it is barely something. But as long as we think like children, in cases where our ideas are no clearer nor distincter than theirs, I agree with your lordship, that I know not how it can be remedied, but that we must talk like them."

Further, the bishop asks, "Whether there be no difference between the bare being of a thing, and its subsistence by itself?" To which our author answers: "Yes.* But what will that do to prove, that, upon my principles, we can come to no certainty of reason, that there is any such thing as substance? You seem by this question to conclude, that the idea of a thing that subsists by itself, is a clear and distinct idea of substance; but I beg leave to ask, Is the idea of the manner of subsistence of a thing, the idea of the thing itself? If it be not, we may have a clear and distinct idea of the manner, and yet have none but a very obscure and confused one of the thing. For example: I tell your lordship, that I know a thing that cannot subsist without a support, and I know another thing that does subsist without a support, and say no more of them; can you, by having the clear and distinct ideas of having a support, and not having a support, say, that you have a clear and distinct idea of the thing, that I know which has, and of the thing that I know which has not a support? If your lordship can, I beseech you to give me the clear and distinct ideas of these, which I only call by the general name, things, that have or have not supports: for such there are, and such I shall give your lordship clear and distinct ideas of, when you shall please to call upon me for them; though I think your lordship will scarcely find them by the general and confused idea of things, nor in the clearer and more distinct idea of having or not having a support.

"To show a blind man that he has no clear and distinct idea of scarlet, I tell him, that his notion of it, that it is a thing or being, does not prove that he has any clear or distinct idea of it; but barely that he takes it to be something, he knows not what. He replies, That he knows more than that, v. g., he knows that it subsists, or inheres in another thing; and is there no difference, says he, in your lordship's words, between the bare being of a thing, and its subsistence in an-

* Mr. Locke's Third Letter.

other? Yes, say I to him, a great deal; they are very different ideas. But for all that, you have no clear and distinct idea of scarlet, nor such a one as I have, who see and know it, and have another kind of idea of it, besides that of inherence,

"Your lordship has the idea of subsisting by itself, and therefore, you conclude, you have a clear and distinct idea of the thing that subsists by itself; which, methinks, is all one, as if your countryman should say, he hath an idea of a cedar of Lebanon, that it is a tree of a nature to need no prop to lean on for its support; therefore, he hath a clear and distinct idea of a cedar of Lebanon; which clear and distinct idea, when he comes to examine, is nothing but a general one of a tree, with which his indetermined idea of a cedar is confounded. Just so is the idea of substance; which, however, called clear and distinct, is confounded with the general indetermined idea of something. But suppose that the manner of subsisting by itself, gives us a clear and distinct idea of substance, how does that prove, that upon my principles, we can come to no certainty of reason, that there is any such thing as substance in the world? Which is the proposition to be proved.

No. VI.—Vol. I. p. 482, par. 29.

"Give me leave, my lord," says Mr. Locke, in his answer to the Bishop of Worcester, "to say, that the reason of believing any article of the Christian faith (such as your lordship is here speaking of) to me, and upon my grounds, is its being a part of divine revelation: upon this ground I believed it, before I either wrote that chapter on identity and diversity, and before I ever thought of those propositions which your lordship quotes out of that chapter; and upon the same ground I believe it still; and not from my idea of identity. This saying of your lordship's, therefore, being a proposition neither self-evident, nor allowed by me to be true, remains to be proved. So that your foundation failing, all your large superstructure built thereon comes to nothing.

"But, my lord, before we go any further, I crave leave humbly to represent to your lordship, that I thought you undertook to make out, that my notion of ideas was inconsistent with the articles of the Christian faith. But that which your lordship instances in here, is not, that I yet know, an article of the Christian faith. The resurrection of the dead, I acknowledge to be an article of the Christian faith; but that the resurrection of the same body, in your lordship's sense of the same body, is an article of the Christian faith, is what, I confess, I do not yet know.

"In the New Testament (wherein I think are contained all the articles of the Christian faith) I find our Saviour and the apostles, to preach the resurrection of the dead, and the resurrection from the dead, in many places: but I do not remember any place where the resurrection of the same body is so much as mentioned. Nay, which is very remarkable in the case, I do not remember in any place of the New Testament (where the general resurrection of the last day is spoken of) any such expression as the resurrection of the body, much less of the same body.

"I say the general resurrection at the last day; because where the resurrection of some particular persons, presently upon our Saviour's resurrection, is mentioned, the words are,* 'The graves were opened, and many bodies of saints, which slept, arose, and came out of the graves, after his resurrection, and went into the Holy City, and appeared to many:' of which peculiar way of speaking of this resurrection, the passage itself gives a reason in these words, appeared to many, *i. e.*, those who slept appeared, so as to be known to be risen. But this could not be known, unless they brought with them the evidence that they were those who had been dead; whereof there were these two proofs, their graves were opened, and their bodies not only gone out of them, but appeared to be the same to those who had known them formerly alive, and knew them to be dead and buried. For if they had been those who had been dead so long, that all who knew them once alive, were now gone, those to whom they appeared might have known them to be men; but could not have known they were risen from the dead, because they never knew they had been dead. All that by their appearing they could have known was, that they were so many living strangers, of whose resurrection they knew nothing. It was necessary, therefore, that they should come in such bodies as might, in make and size, &c., appear to be the same they had before, that they might be known to those of their acquaintance whom they appeared to. And it is probable they were such as were newly dead, whose bodies were not yet dissolved and dissipated; and, therefore, it is particularly said here (differently from what is said of the general resurrection) that their bodies arose ; because they were the same that were then lying in their graves, the moment before they arose.

"But your lordship endeavours to prove it must be the same body; and let us grant that your lordship, nay, and others too, think you have proved it must be the same body; will you therefore say, that he holds what is inconsistent with an article of faith who, having never seen this your lordship's interpretation of the Scripture, nor your reasons for the same body, in your sense of same body; or, if he has seen them, yet not understanding them, or not perceiving the force of them, believes what the Scripture proposes to him, viz., 'That at the last day, the dead shall be raised,' without determining whether it shall be with the very same bodies or not?

"I know your lordship pretends not to erect your particular interpretations of Scripture into articles of faith. And if you do not, he that believes the dead shall be raised, believes that article of faith that the Scripture proposes; and cannot be accused of holding anything inconsistent with it, if it should happen, that what he holds is inconsistent with another proposition, viz., 'That the dead shall be raised with the same bodies,' in your lordship's sense, which I do not find proposed in Holy Writ as an article of faith.

"But your lordship argues, It must be the same body; which, as you explain same body,† is not the same individual particles of matter which were united at the point of death; nor the same particles of matter that the sinner had at the time of the commission of his sins: but that it must be the same material substance which was vitally united to the soul here ; *i. e.*, as I understand it, the same individual

* Matt. xxvii. 52, 53.   † Second Answer.

particles of matter which were some time or other, during his life here, vitally united to his soul.

"Your first argument to prove that it must be the same body, in this sense of the same body, is taken from these words of our Saviour,* 'All that are in the graves shall hear his voice, and shall come forth:† from whence your lordship argues, that these words, 'All that are in their graves,' relate to no other substance than what was united to the soul in life; because, 'a different substance cannot be said to be in the graves and to come out of them.' Which words of your lordship's, if they prove anything, prove that the soul too is lodged in the grave, and raised out of it at the last day. For your lordship says, 'Can a different substance be said to be in the graves, and come out of them?' so that, according to this interpretation of these words of our Saviour, 'no other substance being raised but what hears his voice; and no other substance hearing his voice but what, being called, comes out of the grave; and no other substance coming out of the grave, but what was in the grave;' any one must conclude, that the soul, unless it be in the grave, will make no part of the person that is raised, unless as your lordship argues against me,‡ you can make it out, that a substance which never was in the grave, may come out of it, or that the soul is no substance.

"But, setting aside the substance of the soul, another thing that will make any one doubt whether this your interpretation of our Saviour's words be necessary to be received as their true sense, is, that it will not be very easily reconciled to your saying,‖ you do not mean by the same body, the same individual particles which were united at the point of death. And yet by this interpretation of our Saviour's words, you can mean no other particles but such as were united at the point of death; because you mean no other substance but what comes out of the grave; and no substance, no particles come out, you say, but what were in the grave; and I think your lordship will not say that the particles that were separate from the body by perspiration before the point of death, were laid up in the grave.

"But your lordship, I find, has an answer to this, viz.,§ That, by comparing this with other places, you find that the words (of our Saviour above quoted) are to be understood of the substance of the body to which the soul was united, and not to (I suppose your lordship wrote, of) those individual particles, *i. e.,* those individual particles that are in the grave at the resurrection. For so they must be read, to make your lordship's sense entire and to the purpose of your answer here; and then, methinks, this last sense of our Saviour's words, given by your lordship, wholly overturns the sense which we have given of them above, where, from those words, you press the belief of the resurrection of the same body, by this strong argument, that a substance could not, upon hearing the voice of Christ, come out of the grave, which was never in the grave. There (as far as I can understand your words) your lordship argues, that our Saviour's words are to be understood of the particles in the grave, unless, as your lordship says, one can make it out, that a substance which never was in the grave may come out of it. And here,

* John, v. 28, 29. † Second Answer. ‡ Ibid. ‖ Ibid. § Ibid.

your lordship expressly says, 'That our Saviour's words are to be understood of the substance of that body, to which the soul was (at any time) united, and not to those individual particles that are in the grave.' Which, put together, seems to me to say, That our Saviour's words are to be understood of those particles only which are in the grave, and not of those particles only which are in the grave, but of others also, which have at any time been vitally united to the soul, but never were in the grave.

"The next text your lordship brings to make the resurrection of the same body in your sense, an article of faith, are these words of St. Paul:* 'For we must all appear before the judgment-seat of Christ, that every one may receive the things done in his body, according to that he hath done, whether it be good or bad' To which your lordship subjoins this question:† 'Can these words be understood of any other material substance, but that body in which these things were done?' Answer: A man may suspend his determining the meaning of the apostle to be, that a sinner shall suffer for his sins, in the very same body wherein he committed them; because St. Paul does not say he shall have the very same body when he suffers, that he had when he sinned. The apostle says, indeed, done in his body. The body he had, and did things in at five or fifteen, was, no doubt, his body, as much as that which he did things in at fifty was his body, though his body were not the very same body at those different ages; and so will the body which he shall have after the resurrection be his body, though it be not the very same with that which he had at five, or fifteen, or fifty. He that at threescore is broken on the wheel for a murder he committed at twenty, is punished for what he did in his body though the body he has, *i.e.*, his body at threescore, be not the same, *i.e.*, made up of the same individual particles of matter that that body was which he had forty years before. When your lordship has resolved with yourself, what that same immutable he is which, at the last judgment, shall receive the things done in his body, your lordship will easily see, that the body he had when an embryo in the womb, when a child playing in petticoats, when a man marrying a wife, and when bed-rid dying of a consumption, and at last, which he shall have after his resurrection, are each of them his body, though neither of them be the same body the one with the other.

"But further, to your lordship's question, 'Can these words be understood of any other material substance, but that body in which these things were done?' I answer, These words of St. Paul may be understood of another material substance than that body in which these things were done, because your lordship teaches me, and gives me a strong reason so to understand them. Your lordship says,‡ 'That you do not say the same particles of matter which the sinner had at the very time of the commission of his sins, shall be raised at the last day.' And your lordship gives this reason for it;§ 'For then a long sinner must have a vast body, considering the continued spending of particles by perspiration.' Now, my lord, if the apostle's words, as your lordship would argue, cannot be understood of any other material substance but that

* 2 Cor. v. 10.   † Second Answer.   ‡ Ibid.   § Ibid.

body in which these things were done: and no body, upon the removal or change of some of the particles that at any time make it up, is the same material substance, or the same body, it will, I think, thence follow that either the sinner must have all the same individual particles vitally united to his soul when he is raised, that he had vitally united to his soul when he sinned; or else St. Paul's words here cannot be understood to mean the same body in which the things were done. For if there were other particles of matter in the body, wherein the things were done, than in that which is raised, that which is raised cannot be the same body in which they were done; unless that alone, which has just all the same individual particles, when any action is done, being the same body wherein it was done, that also, which has not the same individual particles wherein that action was done, can be the same body wherein it was done; which is, in effect, to make the same body sometimes to be the same, and sometimes not the same.

"Your lordship thinks it suffices to make the same body to have not all, but no other particles of matter, but such as were some time or other vitally united to the soul before; but such a body made up of part of the particles some time or other vitally united to the soul, is no more the same body, wherein the actions were done in the distant parts of the long sinner's life, than that is the same body in which a quarter, or half, or three quarters of the same particles, that made it up, are wanting. For example: A sinner has acted here in his body a hundred years; he is raised at the last day, but with what body? The same, says your lordship, that he acted in; because St. Paul says, he must receive the things done in his body. What, therefore, must his body at the resurrection consist of? Must it consist of all the particles of matter that have ever been vitally united to his soul? For they, in succession, have all of them made up his body, wherein he did these things: 'No,' says your lordship,[*] 'that would make his body too vast; it suffices to make the same body in which the things were done, that it consists of some of the particles and no other, but such as were, some time during his life, vitally united to his soul.' But, according to this account, his body at the resurrection being, as your lordship seems to limit it, near the same size it was in some part of his life; it will be no more the same body in which the things were done in the distant parts of his life, than that is the same body in which half, or three quarters, or more, of the individual matter that then made it up, is now wanting. For example, let his body at fifty years old, consist of a million of parts; five hundred thousand at least of those parts will be different from those which made up his body at ten years, and at a hundred. So that to take the numerical particles that made up his body at fifty, or any other season of his life, or to gather them promiscuously out of those which at different times have successively been vitally united to his soul, they will no more make the same body, which was his, wherein some of his actions were done, than that is the same body, which has but half the same particles: and yet all your lordship's argument here for the same body is, because St. Paul says, it must be his body in which these things were done; which it could not be if any other substance were joined to

[*] Second Answer.

it, *i. e.*, if any other particles of matter made up the body, which were not vitally united to the soul when the action was done.

"Again, your lordship, says:* 'That you do not say the same individual particles [shall make up the body at the resurrection] which were united at the point of death, for there must be a great alteration in them in a lingering disease, as if a fat man falls into a consumption.' Because, it is likely, your lordship thinks, these particles of a decrepit, wasted, withered body, would be too few, or unfit to make such a plump, strong, vigorous, well-sized body, as it has pleased your lordship to proportion out in your thoughts to men, at the resurrection; and, therefore, some small portion of the particles formerly united vitally to that man's soul, shall be reassumed to make up his body to the bulk your lordship judges convenient; but the greatest part of them shall be left out, to avoid the making his body more vast than your lordship thinks will be fit, as appears by these, your lordship's words immediately following, viz.:† 'That you do not say the same particles the sinner had at the very time of the commission of his sins; for then a long sinner must have a vast body.'

"But then, pray, my lord, what must an embryo do, who, dying within a few hours after his body was vitally united to his soul, has no particles of matter which were formerly vitally united to it, to make up his body of that size and proportion, which your lordship seems to require in bodies at the resurrection? Or, must we believe he shall remain content with that small pittance of matter, and that yet imperfect body to eternity, because it is an article of faith to believe the resurrection of the very same body, *i. e.*, made up of only such particles as have been vitally united to the soul? For if it be so, as your lordship says,‡ 'That life is the result of the union of soul and body,' it will follow, that the body of an embryo, dying in the womb, may be very little, not the thousandth part of any ordinary man. For since, from the first conception and beginning of formation it has life, and 'life is the result of the union of the soul with the body;' an embryo that shall die either by the untimely death of the mother, or by any other accident, presently after it has life, must, according to your lordship's doctrine, remain a man, not an inch long, to eternity; because there are not particles of matter formerly united to his soul, to make him larger, and no other can be made use of to that purpose: though what greater congruity the soul hath with any particles of matter which were once vitally united to it, but are now so no longer, than it hath with particles of matter which it was never united to, would be hard to determine, if that should be demanded.

"By these, and not a few other the like consequences, one may see what service they do to religion and the Christian doctrine, who raise questions, and make articles of faith, about the resurrection of the same body, where the Scripture says nothing of the same body; or, if it does, it is with no small reprimand § to those who make such an inquiry, 'But some man will say, How are the dead raised up? and with what body do they come? Thou fool, that which thou sowest, is not quickened, except it die. And that which thou sowest, thou sowest not that body

* Second Answer.   † Ibid.   ‡ Ibid.   § 1 Cor. xv. 35, &c.

that shall be, but bare grain; it may chance of wheat, or some other grain. But God giveth it a body, as it hath pleased him.' Words, I should think, sufficient to deter us from determining anything for or against the same body's being raised at the last day. It suffices, that all the dead shall be raised, and every one appear and answer for the things done in this life, and receive according to the things he hath done in his body, whether good or bad. He that believes this, and has said nothing inconsistent herewith, I presume may, and must be acquitted from being guilty of anything inconsistent with the article of the resurrection of the dead.

"But your lordship, to prove the resurrection of the same body to be an article of faith, further asks,* 'How could it be said, if any other substance be joined to the soul at the resurrection, as its body, that they were the things done in or by the body?' Answer. Just as it may be said of a man at a hundred years old, that hath then another substance joined to his soul, than he had at twenty; that the murder or drunkenness he was guilty of at twenty, were things done in the body: how 'by the body,' comes in here I do not see.

"Your lordship adds, 'and St. Paul's dispute about the manner of raising the body, might soon have ended, if there were no necessity of the same body.' Answer. When I understand what argument there is in these words to prove the resurrection of the same body, without the mixture of one new atom of matter, I shall know what to say to it. In the meantime, this I understand, that St. Paul would have put as short an end to all disputes about this matter, if he had said, that there was a necessity of the same body, or that it should be the same body.

"The next text of Scripture you bring for the same body is,† 'If there be no resurrection of the dead, then is not Christ raised.' From which your lordship argues,‡ 'It seems, then, other bodies are to be raised as his was.' I grant other dead, as certainly raised as Christ was; for else his resurrection would be of no use to mankind. But I do not see how it follows, that they shall be raised with the same body, as Christ was raised with the same body as your lordship infers, in these words annexed: 'And can there be any doubt, whether his body was the same material substance which was united to his soul before? I answer, None at all; nor that it had just the same distinguishing lineaments and marks, yea, and the same wounds, that it had at the time or his death. If, therefore, your lordship will argue from other bodies being raised as his was, That they must keep proportion with his in sameness; then we must believe that every man shall be raised with the same lineaments and other notes of distinction he had at the time of his death, even with his wounds yet open, if he had any, because our Saviour was so raised, which seems to me scarcely reconcilable with what your lordship says,§ of a fat man falling into a consumption and dying.

"But whether it will consist or not with your lordship's meaning in that place, this to me seems a consequence that will need to be better proved, viz., That our bodies must be raised the same, just as our Saviour's was: because St. Paul says, 'if there be no resurrection of the dead, then is not Christ risen.' For it may be a good consequence,

* Second Answer.   † 2 Cor. xv. 16.   ‡ Second Answer.   § Ibid.

Christ is risen, and therefore there shall be a resurrection of the dead: and yet this may not be a good consequence. Christ was raised with the same body he had at his death, therefore, all men shall be raised with the same bodies they had at their death, contrary to what your lordship says concerning a fat man dying of a consumption. But the case I think far different betwixt our Saviour and those to be raised at the last day.

"1. His body saw not corruption, and, therefore, to give him another body, new moulded, mixed with other particles, which were not contained in it, as it lay in the grave, whole and entire as it was laid there, had been to destroy his body to frame him a new one, without any need. But why, with the remaining particles of a man's body, long since dissolved and moulded into dust, and atoms, (whereof possibly, a great part may have undergone variety of changes, and entered into other concretions; even in the bodies of other men,) other new particles of matter mixed with them, may not serve to make his body again, as well as the mixture of new and different particles of matter with the old, did in the compass of his life make his body, I think no reason can be given.

"This may serve to show, why, though the materials of our Saviour's body were not changed at his resurrection; yet it does not follow, but that the body of a man dead and rotten in his grave, or burnt, may, at the last day have several new particles in it, and that without any inconvenience: since whatever matter is vitally united to his soul, is his body, as much as is that which was united with it when he was born, or in any other part of his life.

"2. In the next place, the size, shape, figure, and lineaments of our Saviour's body, even to his wounds, into which doubting Thomas put his fingers, and his hand, were to be kept in the raised body of our Saviour, the same they were at his death, to be a conviction to his disciples, to whom he showed himself, and who were to be witnesses of his resurrection, that their Master, the very same man, was crucified, dead, and buried, and raised again; and, therefore, he was handled by them, and eat before them, after he was risen, to give them in all points full satisfaction that it was really he, the same and not another, not a spectre, or apparition of him; though I do not think your lordship will thence argue, that, because others are to be raised as he was, therefore, it is necessary to believe, that because he eat after his resurrection, others, at the last day, shall eat and drink after they are raised from the dead; which seems to me as good an argument, as, because his undissolved body was raised out of the grave, just as it there lay entire, without the mixture of any new particles; therefore, the corrupted and consumed bodies of the dead at the resurrection, shall be new framed only out of those scattered particles which were once vitally united to their souls, without the least mixture of any one single atom of new matter. But at the last day when all men are raised, there will be no need to be assured of any one particular man's resurrection. It is enough that every one shall appear before the judgment-seat of Christ, to receive according to what he had done in his former life; but in what sort of body he shall appear, or of what particles made up, the Scripture having said nothing, but that it shall be a spiritual body raised in incorruption, it is not for me to determine.

APPENDIX. 365

"Your lordship asks,* 'Were they (who saw our Saviour after his resurrection) witnesses only of some material substance then united to his soul?' In answer, I beg your lordship to consider, whether you suppose our Saviour was to be known to be the same man (to the witnesses that were to see him, and testify his resurrection) by his soul, that could neither be seen or known to be the same: or by his body, that could be seen, and by the discernible structure and marks of it, be known to be the same? When your lordship has resolved that, all that you say in that page will answer itself. But because one man cannot know another to be the same, but by the outward visible lineaments, and sensible marks he has been wont to be known and distinguished by, will your lordship, therefore, argue that the Great Judge, at the last day, who gives to each man whom he raises his new body, shall not be able to know who is who, unless he gives to every one of them a body, just of the same figure, size, and features, and made up of the very same individual particles he had in his former life? Whether such a way of arguing for the resurrection of the same body, to be an article of faith, contributes much to the strengthening the credibility of the article of the resurrection of the dead, I shall leave to the judgment of others.

"Further, for the proving the resurrection of the same body, to be an article of faith, your lordship says,† 'But the apostle insists upon the resurrection of Christ, not merely as an argument of the possibility of ours, but of the certainty of it,‡ because he rose as the first-fruits; Christ the first-fruits, afterwards they that are Christ's at his coming.' Answer. No doubt the resurrection of Christ is a proof of the certainty of our resurrection. But is it therefore a proof of the resurrection of the same body consisting of the same individual particles, which concurred to the making up of our body here, without the mixture of any other particle of matter? I confess I see no such consequence.

"But your lordship goes on:§ 'St. Paul was aware of the objections in men's minds about the resurrection of the same body; and it is of great consequence as to this article, to show upon what grounds he proceeds: 'But some men will say, how are the dead raised up, and with what body do they come?' First, he shows, that the seminal parts of plants are wonderfully improved by the ordinary providence of God, in the manner of their vegetation.' Answer. I do not perfectly understand, what it is 'for the seminal parts of plants to be wonderfully improved by the ordinary providence of God, in the manner of their vegetation;' or else, perhaps, I should better see how this here tends to the proof of the resurrection of the same body in your lordship's sense.

"It continues, ‖ 'They sow bare grain of wheat, or of some other grain, but God giveth it a body, as it hath pleased him, and to every seed his own body. Here,' says your lordship, 'is an identity of the material substance supposed.' It may be so. But to me a diversity of the material substance, *i. e.*, of the component particles, is here supposed, or in direct words said. For the words of St. Paul taken altogether run thus: ¶ 'That which thou sowest, thou sowest not that body that shall be, but bare grain:' and so on, as your lordship has set down in the remainder of them. From which words of St. Paul, the natura

* Second Answer.   † Ibid.   ‡ 1 Cor. xv. 20. 23.
§ Second Answer.   ‖ Ibid.   ¶ V. 37.

argument seems to me to stand thus: If the body that is put in the earth in sowing, is not that body which shall be, then the body that is put in the grave, is not that, *i. e.*, the same body that shall be.

"But your lordship proves it to be the same body, by these three Greek words of the text, τὸ ἴδιον σῶμα, which your lordship interprets thus:* 'that proper body which belongs to it.' Answer. Indeed by those Greek words, τὸ ἴδιον σῶμα, whether our translators have rightly rendered them 'his own body,' or your lordship more rightly, 'that proper body which belongs to it,' I formerly understood no more but this, that in the production of wheat, and other grain from seed, God continued every species distinct; so that from grains of wheat sown, root, stalk, blade, ear, grains of wheat were produced, and not those of barley, and so of the rest, which I took to be the meaning of, to every seed his own body. 'No,' says your lordship, 'these words prove, that to every plant of wheat, and to every grain of wheat produced in it, is given the proper body that belongs to it, which is the same body with the grain that was sown.' Answer. This I confess, I do not understand: because I do not understand how one individual grain can be the same with twenty, fifty, or a hundred individual grains; for such sometimes is the increase.

"But your lordship proves it. 'For,' says your lordship,† 'every seed having that body in little, which is afterwards so much enlarged; and in grain, the seed is corrupted before its germination; but it hath its proper organical parts, which make it the same body with that which it grows up to. For, although grain be not divided into lobes, as other seeds are, yet it hath been found, by the most accurate observations, that upon separating the membranes, these seminal parts are discerned in them; which afterwards grow up to that body which we call corn.' In which words I beg leave to observe, that your lordship supposes that a body may be enlarged by the addition of a hundred or a thousand times as much in bulk as its own matter, and yet continue the same body; which I confess I cannot understand.

"But, in the next place, if that could be so, and that the plant in its full growth at harvest, increased by a thousand or million of times as much new matter added to it, as it had when it lay a little concealed in the grain that was sown, was the very same body; yet I do not think that your lordship will say that every minute, insensible, and inconceivably small grain of the hundred grains, contained in that little organized seminal plant, is every one of them the very same with that grain which contains that whole little seminal plant, and all those invisible grains in it. For, then, it will follow, that one grain is the same with a hundred, and a hundred distinct grains the same with one; which I shall be able to assent to, when I can conceive, that all the wheat in the world is but one grain.

"For I beseech you, my lord, consider what it is St. Paul here speaks of: it is plain he speaks of that which is sown and dies, *i. e.*, the grain that the husbandman takes out of his barn to sow in his field, and of this grain St. Paul says, 'that it is not that body that shall be.' These two, viz., 'that which is sown, and that body that shall be,' are all the

* Second Answer.   † Ibid.

bodies that St. Paul here speaks of, to represent the agreement or difference of men's bodies after the resurrection, with those they had before they died. Now, I crave leave to ask your lordship, which of these two is that little invisible seminal plant which your lordship here speaks of? Does your lordship mean by it the grain that is sown? But that is not what St. Paul speaks of; he could not mean this embryonated little plant, for he could not denote it by these words, 'that which thou sowest,' for that, he says, must die: but this little embryonated plant, contained in the seed that is sown, dies not: or does your lordship mean by it, 'the body that shall be?' But neither by these words, "the body that shall be,' can St. Paul be supposed to denote this insensible little embryonated plant; for that is already in being, contained in the seed that is sown, and therefore, could not be spoken of under the name of 'the body that shall be.' And, therefore, I confess I cannot see of what use it is to your lordship to introduce here this third body, which St. Paul mentions not, and to make that the same, or not the same, with any other, when those which St. Paul speaks of are, as I humbly conceive, these two visible sensible bodies, the grain sown, and the corn grown up to ear: with neither of which this insensible embryonated plant can be the same body, unless an insensible body can be the same body with a sensible body, and a little body can be the same body with one ten thousand, or a hundred thousand times as big as itself. So that yet, I confess, I see not the resurrection of the same body proved, from these words of St. Paul, to be an article of faith.

"Your lordship goes on:* 'St. Paul indeed saith, 'That we sow not that body that shall be;' but he speaks not of the identity, but the perfection of it. Here my understanding fails me again: for I cannot understand St. Paul to say, That the same identical sensible grain of wheat, which was sown at seed-time, is the very same with every grain of wheat in the ear at harvest, that sprang from it: yet, so I must understand it, to make it prove that the same sensible body that is laid in the grave, shall be the very same with that which shall be raised at the resurrection. For I do not know of any seminal body in little, contained in the dead carcass of any man or woman, which, as your lordship says, in seeds, having its proper organical parts, shall afterwards be enlarged, and at the resurrection grow up into the same man. For I never thought of any seed or seminal parts, either of plant or animal, 'so wonderfully improved by the providence of God,' whereby the same plant or animal should beget itself; nor ever heard that it was by Divine Providence designed to produce the same individual, but for the producing of future and distinct individuals, for the continuation of the same species.

"Your lordship's next words are,† 'And although there be such a difference from the grain itself, when it comes up to be perfect corn, with root, stalk, blade, and ear, that it may be said to outward appearance not to be the same body; yet with regard to the seminal and organical parts, it is as much the same, as a man grown up is the same with the embryo in the womb.' Answer. It does not appear, by anything I can find in the text, that St. Paul here compared the body produced,

* Second Answer.   † Ibid.

with the seminal and organical parts contained in the grain it sprang from, but with the whole sensible grain that was sown. Microscopes had not then discovered the little embryo plant in the seed: and supposing it should have been revealed to St. Paul, (though in the Scripture we find little revelation of natural philosophy,) yet an argument taken from a thing perfectly unknown to the Corinthians, whom he wrote to, could be of no manner of use to them: nor serve at all either to instruct or convince them. But granting that those St. Paul wrote to, knew it as well as Mr. Lewenhoek; yet your lordship thereby proves not the raising of the same body: your lordship says: 'It is as much the same' (I crave leave to add body) 'as a man grown up is the same' (same what, I beseech your lordship?) 'with the embryo in the womb.' For that the body of the embryo in the womb, and body of the man grown up, is the same body, I think no one will say; unless he can persuade himself, that a body that is not the hundredth part of another, is the same with that other; which I think no one will do, till, having renounced this dangerous way by ideas of thinking and reasoning, he has learned to say, that a part and the whole are the same.

"Your lordship goes on:* 'And although many arguments may be used to prove that a man is not the same, because life, which depends upon the course of the blood and the manner of respiration and nutrition, is so different in both states: yet that man would be thought ridiculous, that should seriously affirm, that it was not the same man.' And your lordship says, 'I grant, that the variation of great particles of matter in plants, alters not the identity: and that the organization of the parts in one coherent body, partaking of one common life, makes the identity of a plant.' Answer. My lord, I think the question is not about the same man, but the same body. For, though I do say,† (somewhat differently from what your lordship sets down as my words here,) 'That that which has such an organization, as is fit to receive and distribute nourishment, so as to continue and frame the wood, bark, and leaves, &c., of a plant in which consists the vegetable life, continues to be the same plant, as long as it partakes of the same life, though that life be communicated to new particles of matter, vitally united to the living plant:' yet, I do not remember that I anywhere say, 'That a plant, which was once no larger than an oaten straw, and afterwards grows to be above a fathom about, is the same body, though it be still the same plant.'

"The well-known tree in Epping Forest, called the King's Oak, which, from not weighing an ounce at first, grew to have many tons of timber in it, was all along the same oak, the very same plant; but nobody, I think, will say that it was the same body, when it weighed a ton, as it was when it weighed but an ounce; unless he has a mind to signalize himself by saying, That that is the same body which has a thousand particles of different matter in it, for one particle that is the same; which is no better than to say, That a thousand different particles are but one and the same particle, and one and the same particle is a thousand different particles; a thousand times a greater absurdity, than

* Second Answer.   † Essay, B. 2. c. 27. par. 4.

to say half is the whole, or the whole is the same with the half; which will be improved ten thousand times yet further, if a man shall say, (as your lordship seems to me to argue here,) that that great oak is the very same body with the acorn it sprang from, because there was in that acorn an oak in little, which was afterwards (as your lordship expresses it) so much enlarged as to make that mighty tree. For this embryo, if I may so call it, or oak in little, being not the hundredth, or perhaps, the thousandth part of the acorn, and the acorn being not the thousandth part of the grown oak, it will be very extraordinary to prove the acorn and the grown oak to be the same body, by a way wherein it cannot be pretended, that above one particle of a hundred thousand, or a million, is the same in the one body that it was in the other. From which way of reasoning it will follow, that a nurse and her sucking child have the same body; and be past doubt, that a mother and her infant have the same body. But this is a way of certainty, found out to establish the articles of faith, and to overturn the new method of certainty that your lordship says I have started, which is apt to leave men's minds more doubtful than before.

"And now I desire your lordship to consider of what use it is to you, in the present case, to quote out of my Essay these words: 'That partaking of one common life, makes the identity of a plant;' since the question is not about the identity of a plant, but about the identity of a body. It being a very different thing to be the same plant, and to be the same body. For that which makes the same plant does not make the same body; the one being the partaking in the same continued vegetable life; the other, the consisting of the same numerical particles of matter. And, therefore, your lordship's inference from my words above quoted, in these which you subjoin,* seems to me a very strange one, viz., 'So that in things capable of any sort of life, the identity is consistent with a continued succession of parts: and so the wheat grown up is the same body with the grain that was sown.' For I believe, if my words, from which you infer, 'and so the wheat grown up is the same body with the grain that was sown,' were put into a syllogism, this would hardly be brought to be the conclusion.

"But your lordship goes on with consequence upon consequence, though I have not eyes acute enough everywhere to see the connexion, till you bring it to the resurrection of the same body. The connexion of your lordship's words † is as followeth: 'And thus the alteration of the parts of the body at the resurrection, is consistent with its identity, if its organization and life be the same; and this is a real identity of the body, which depends not upon consciousness. From whence it follows, that to make the same body, no more is required, but restoring life to the organized parts of it.' If the question were about raising the same plant, I do not say but there might be some appearance for making such an inference from my words as this, 'Whence it follows, that to make the same plant, no more is required but to restore life to the organized parts of it.' But this deduction, wherein from those words of mine, that speak only of the identity of a plant, your lordship infers, there is no more required to make the same body, than to

Second Answer.   † Ibid.

make the same plant, being too subtle for me, I leave to my reader to find out.

"Your lordship goes on and says,* 'That I grant likewise, that the identity of the same man consists in a participation of the same continued life, by constantly fleeting particles of matter in succession, vitally united to the same organized body.' Answer. I speak in these words of the identity of the same man, and your lordship thence roundly concludes; 'so that there is no difficulty of the sameness of the body.' But your lordship knows, that I do not take these two sounds, man and body, to stand for the same thing; nor the identity of the man to be the same with the identity of the body.

"But let us read out your lordship's words.† 'So that there is no difficulty as to the sameness of the body, if life were continued: and if, by Divine Power, life be restored to that material substance, which was before united by a reunion of the soul to it, there is no reason to deny the identity of the body, not from the consciousness of the soul, but from that life which is the result of the union of the soul and body.'

"If I understand your lordship right, you, in these words, from the passages above quoted out of my book, argue, that from those words of mine it will follow, 'That it is or may be the same body that is raised at the resurrection.' If so, my lord, your lordship has then proved, That my book is not inconsistent with, but conformable to, this article of the resurrection of the same body, which your lordship contends for, and will have to be an article of faith: for though I do by no means deny that the same bodies shall be raised at the last day, yet I see nothing your lordship has said to prove it to be an article of faith.

"But your lordship goes on with your proofs, and says,‡ 'But St. Paul still supposes, that it must be that material substance to which the soul was before united. 'For,' saith he, 'it is sown in corruption, it is raised in incorruption: it is sown in dishonour, it is raised in glory: it is sown in weakness, it is raised in power: it is sown a natural body, it is raised a spiritual body. Can such a material substance, which was never united to the body, be said to be sown in corruption, and weakness, and dishonour? either, therefore, he must speak of the same body, or his meaning cannot be comprehended.' I answer, 'Can such a material substance, which was never laid in the grave, be said to be sown?' &c. For your lordship says,§ 'You do not say the same individual particles, which were united at the point of death, shall be raised at the last day;' and no other particles are laid in the grave, but such as are united at the point of death; either, therefore, your lordship must speak of another body, different from that which was sown, which shall be raised, or else your meaning, I think, cannot be comprehended.

"But whatever be your meaning, your lordship proves it to be St. Paul's meaning, that the same body shall be raised, which was sown, in these following words: ‖ 'For what does all this relate to a conscious principle?' Answer. The Scripture being express, That the same person should be raised and appear before the judgment seat of Christ, that every one may receive according to what he had done in his body; it was very well suited to common apprehensions, (which refined not about

* Second Answer.   † Ibid.   ‡ Ibid.   § Ibid.   ‖ Ibid.

'particles that had been vitally united to the soul,') to speak of the body, which each one was to have after the resurrection, as he would be apt to speak of it himself. For it being his body both before and after the resurrection, every one ordinarily speaks of his body as the same, though in a strict and philosophical sense, as your lordship speaks, it be not the very same. Thus it is no impropriety of speech to say, This body of mine, which was formerly strong and plump, is now weak and wasted, though, in such a sense as you are speaking here, it be not the same body. Revelation declares nothing anywhere concerning the same body, in your lordship's sense of the same body, which appears not to have been thought of. The apostle directly proposes nothing for or against the same body, as necessary to be believed; that which he is plain and direct in, is, his opposing and condemning such curious questions about the body, which could serve only to perplex, not to confirm, what was material and necessary for them to believe, viz., a day of judgment and retribution to men in a future state; and, therefore, it is no wonder that, mentioning their bodies, he should use a way of speaking, suited to vulgar notions, from which it would be hard positively to conclude anything for the determining of this question (especially against expressions in the same discourse that plainly incline to the other side) in a matter which, as it appears, the apostle thought not necessary to determine; and the Spirit of God thought not fit to gratify any one's curiosity in.

"But your lordship says,* 'The apostle speaks plainly of that body which was once quickened, and afterwards falls to corruption, and is to be restored with more noble qualities.' I wish your lordship had quoted the words of St. Paul, wherein he speaks plainly of that numerical body that was once quickened, they would presently decide this question. But your lordship proves it by these following words of St. Paul: 'For this corruption must put on incorruption, and this mortal must put on immortality;' to which your lordship adds, that 'you do not see how he could more expressly affirm the identity of this corruptible body, with that after the resurrection.' How expressly it is affirmed by the apostle, shall be considered by and by. In the meantime, it is past doubt that your lordship best knows what you do or do not see. But this I would be bold to say, that if St. Paul had anywhere in this chapter (where there are so many occasions for it, if it had been necessary to have been believed,) but said in express words, that the same bodies should be raised, every one else, who thinks of it, will see he had more expressly affirmed the identity of the bodies which men now have, with those they shall have after the resurrection.

"The remainder of your lordship's period is:† 'And that without any respect to the principle of self-consciousness.' Answer. These words, I doubt not, have some meaning, but I must own I know not what; either towards the proof of the resurrection of the same body, or to show that anything I have said concerning self-consciousness is inconsistent; for I do not remember that I have anywhere said that the identity of body consisted in self-consciousness.

"From your preceding words, your lordship concludes thus:‡ 'And

* Second Answer.   † Ibid.   ‡ Ibid.

so if the Scripture be the sole foundation of our faith, this is an article of it.' My lord, to make the conclusion unquestionable, I humbly conceive the words must run thus: And so if the Scripture, and your lordship's interpretation of it, be the sole foundation of our faith, the resurrection of the same body is an article of it. For, with submission, your lordship has neither produced express words of Scripture for it, nor so proved that to be the meaning of any of those words of Scripture which you have produced for it, that a man who reads and sincerely endeavours to understand the Scripture, cannot but find himself obliged to believe as expressly, that the same bodies of the dead, in your lordship's sense, shall be raised, as that the dead shall be raised. And I crave leave to give your lordship this one reason for it. He who reads with attention this discourse of St. Paul,* where he discourses of the resurrection, will see that he plainly distinguishes between the dead that shall be raised, and the bodies of the dead. For it is νεκροὶ, ὦάντες, οἳ, are the nominative cases to † ἐγείρονται, ζωοποιηθήσονται, ἐγερθήσονται, all along, and not σώματα, bodies; which one may with reason think would somewhere or other have been expressed, if all this had been said to propose it as an article of faith, that the very same bodies should be raised. The same manner of speaking the Spirit of God observes all through the New Testament, where it is said, ‡ raise the dead, quicken or make alive the dead, the resurrection of the dead. Nay, these very words of our Saviour, ∥ urged by your lordship, for the resurrection of the same body, run thus: Παντες οἱ ἐν τοῖς μνημείοις ἀκούσονται τῆς φωνῆς αὐτοῦ. καὶ ἐκπορεύσονται, οἱ τὰ ἀγαθὰ ποιήσαντες εἰς ἀνάστασιν ζωῆς, οἱ δὲ τὰ φαῦλα πράξαντες εἰς ἀνάστασιν κρίσεως. Would not a well-meaning searcher of the Scriptures be apt to think, that if the thing here intended by our Saviour were to teach and propose it as an article of faith, necessary to be believed by every one, that the very same bodies of the dead should be raised; would not, I say, any one be apt to think, that if our Saviour meant so, the words should rather have been, πάντα τὰ σώματα ἃ ἐν τοῖς μνημείοις, i. e., all the bodies that are in the graves, rather than all who are in the graves; which must denote persons, and not precisely bodies?

"Another evidence that St. Paul makes a distinction between the dead, and the bodies of the dead, so that the dead cannot be taken in this, 1 Cor. xv., to stand precisely for the bodies of the dead, are these words of the apostle:§ 'But some man will say, how are the dead raised? and with what bodies do they come?' Which words, dead and they, if supposed to stand precisely for the bodies of the dead, the question will run thus: How are the dead bodies raised? and with what bodies do the dead bodies come? Which seems to have no very agreeable sense.

"This therefore being so, that the Spirit of God keeps so expressly to this phrase or form of speaking, in the New Testament, 'of raising, quickening, rising, resurrection, &c., of the dead,' where the resurrection of the last day is spoken of; and that the body is not mentioned, but

---

* 1 Cor. xv. † Ver. 15. 22. 23. 29. 32. 35. 52.
‡ Matt. xxii. 31. Mark xii. 26. John v. 21. Acts xvi. 7. Rom. iv. 17. 2 Cor. i. 9. 1 Thess. iv. 14. 16. ∥ John v. 28.-29. § Ver. 35.

in answer to this question, 'With what bodies shall those dead, who are raised, come?' so that by the dead cannot precisely be meant the dead bodies; I do not see but a good Christian, who reads the Scripture with an intention to believe all that is there revealed to him, concerning the resurrection, may acquit himself of his duty therein, without entering into the inquiry, whether the dead shall have the very same bodies or not? which sort of inquiry, the apostle, by the appellation he bestows here on him that makes it, seems not much to encourage. Nor, if he shall think himself bound to determine concerning the identity of the bodies of the dead, raised at the last day; will he, by the remainder of St. Paul's answer, find the determination of the apostle to be much in favour of the very same body, unless the being told, that the body sown is not that body that shall be; that the body raised is as different from that which was laid down, as the flesh of man is from the flesh of beasts, fishes, and birds; or as the sun, moon, and stars, are different one from another; or as different as a corruptible, weak, natural, mortal body, is from an incorruptible, powerful, spiritual, immortal body; and, lastly, as different as a body that is flesh and blood, is from a body that is not flesh and blood.' 'For flesh and blood cannot,' says St. Paul, in this very place,* 'inherit the kingdom of God:' unless, I say, all this, which is contained in St. Paul's words, can be supposed to be the way to deliver this as an article of faith, which is required to be believed by every one, viz., That the dead should be raised with the very same bodies that they had before in this life; which article proposed in these or the like plain and express words, could have left no room for doubt in the meanest capacities, nor for contest in the most perverse minds.

Your lordship adds in the next words,† 'And so it hath been always understood by the Christian church,' viz., That the resurrection of the same body, in your lordship's sense of the same body, is an article of faith. Answer. What the Christian church has always understood, is beyond my knowledge. But for those who, coming short of your lordship's great learning, cannot gather their articles of faith from the understanding of all the whole Christian church, ever since the preaching of the Gospel, (who make the far greater part of Christians, I think I may say nine hundred and ninety and nine of a thousand,) but are forced to have recourse to the Scripture, to find them there, I do not see that they will easily find there this proposed as an article of faith, that there shall be a resurrection of the same body; but that there shall be a resurrection of the dead, without explicitly determining, That they shall be raised with bodies made up wholly of the same particles which were once vitally united to their souls, in their former life, without the mixture of any one other particle of matter; which is that which your lordship means by the same body.

"But supposing your lordship to have demonstrated this to be an article of faith, though I crave leave to own that I do not see that all that your lordship has said here, makes it so much as probable: What is all this to me? 'Yes,' says your lordship in the following words,‡ 'my idea of personal identity is inconsistent with it, for it makes the same body which was here united to the soul, not to be necessary to the

* John v. 50. † Second Answer. ‡ Ibid.

doctrine of the resurrection. But any material substance united to the same principle of consciousness, makes the same body.

"This is an argument of your lordship's, which I am obliged to answer to. But is it not fit I should first understand it, before I answer it? Now, here, I do not well know, what it is to make a thing not to be necessary to the doctrine of the resurrection. But to help myself out the best I can, with a guess, I will conjecture (which, in disputing with learned men, is not very safe) your lordship's meaning is, That 'my idea of personal identity makes it not necessary, that for the raising the same person, the body should be the same.'

"Your lordship's next word is, 'but;' to which I am ready to reply, but what? what does my idea of personal identity do? for something of that kind, the adversative particle 'but' should, in the ordinary construction of our language, introduce to make the proposition clear and intelligible: but here is no such thing. 'But,' is one of your lordship's privileged particles, which I must not meddle with; for fear your lordship complain of me again, 'as so severe a critic, that for the least ambiguity in any particle, fill up pages in my answer, to make my book look considerable for the bulk of it.' But since this proposition here, 'my idea of personal identity, makes the same body which was here united to the soul, not necessary to the doctrine of the resurrection; but any material substance being united to the same principle of consciousness, makes the same body,' is brought to prove my idea of personal identity inconsistent with the article of the resurrection; I must make it out in some direct sense or other, that I may see whether it be both true and conclusive. I, therefore, venture to read it thus: 'my idea of personal identity makes the same body which was here united to the soul, not to be necessary at the resurrection, but allows, that any material substance being united to the same principle of consciousness, makes the same body. *Ergo*, my idea of personal identity, is inconsistent with the article of the resurrection of the same body.'

"If this be your lordship's sense in this passage, as I here have guessed it to be, or else I know not what it is, I answer,

"1. That my idea of personal identity does not allow that any material substance, being united to the same principle of consciousness, makes the same body. I say no such thing in my book, nor anything from whence it may be inferred; and your lordship would have done me a favour to have set down the words where I say so, or those from which you infer so, and showed how it follows from anything I have said.

"2. Granting, that it were a consequence from my idea of personal identity, that 'any material substance being united to the same principle of consciousness, makes the same body;' this would not prove that my idea of personal identity was inconsistent with this proposition, 'that the same body shall be raised;' but, on the contrary, affirms it: since, if I affirm, as I do, that the same persons shall be raised, and it be a consequence of my idea of personal identity, that 'any material substance being united to the same principle of consciousness, makes the same body;' it follows, that if the same person be raised, the same body must be raised: and so I have herein not only said nothing inconsistent with the resurrection of the same body, but have said more for it than your lordship. For there can be nothing plainer, than that in the Scripture it is revealed, that the same persons shall be raised, and appear before the judgment-seat of Christ, to answer for what they have done in their bodies. If, therefore, whatever matter be joined to the same principle of consciousness makes the same body, it is demonstration, that if the same persons are raised, they have the same bodies.

"How then your lordship makes this an inconsistency with the resurrection is beyond my conception. 'Yes,' says your lordship,* 'it is inconsistent with it, for it makes the same body, which was here united to the soul, not to be necessary.'

"3. I answer, therefore, *Thirdly*, That this is the first time I ever learned, that 'not necessary,' was the same with 'inconsistent.' I say that a body made up of the same numerical parts of matter, is not necessary to the making of the same person; from whence it will indeed follow, that to the resurrection of the same person, the same numerical particles of matter are not required. What does your lordship infer from hence? to wit, this: therefore, he who thinks that the same particles of matter are not necessary to the making of the same person, cannot believe that the same persons shall be raised with bodies made of the very same particles of matter, if God should reveal that it shall be so, viz., that the same persons shall be raised with the same bodies they had before. Which is all one as to say, that he who thought the blowing of rams' horns was not necessary in itself to the falling down of the walls of Jericho, could not believe that they should fall upon the blowing of rams' horns, when God had declared it should be so.

"Your lordship says, 'my idea of personal identity is inconsistent with the article of the resurrection;' the reason you ground it on is this, because it makes not the same body necessary to the making the same person. Let us grant your lordship's consequence to be good, what will follow from it? No less than this, that your lordship's notion (for I dare not say your lordship has any so dangerous things as ideas) of personal identity, is inconsistent with the article of the resurrection. The demonstration of it is thus; your lordship says,† 'It is not necessary that the body to be raised at the last day, should consist of the same particles of matter which were united at the point of death; for there must be a great alteration in them in a lingering disease; as if a fat man falls into a consumption: you do not say the same particles which the sinner had at the very time of commission of his sins: for then a long sinner must have a vast body, considering the continual spending of particles by perspiration.' And again, here your lordship says, ‡ 'you allow the notion of personal identity to belong to the same man under several changes of matter.' From which words it is evident, that your lordship supposes a person in this world may be continued and preserved the same in a body not consisting of the same individual particles of matter; and hence it demonstratively follows, that let your lordship's notion of personal identity be what it will, it makes the same body not to be necessary to the same person; and, therefore, it is by your lordship's rule, inconsistent with the article of the resurrection. When your lordship shall think fit to clear your own notion of personal identity from

---

* Second Answer.   † Ibid.   ‡ Ibid.

this inconsistency with the article of the resurrection, I do not doubt but my idea of personal identity will be thereby cleared too. Till then, all inconsistency with that article, which your lordship has here charged on mine, will unavoidably fall upon your lordship's too.

"But for the clearing of both, give me leave to say, my lord, that whatsoever is not necessary, does not, thereby, become inconsistent. It is not necessary to the same person, that his body should always consist of the same numerical particles; this is demonstration, because the particles of the bodies of the same persons, in this life, change every moment, and your lordship cannot deny it; and yet this makes it not inconsistent with God's preserving, if he thinks fit, to the same persons, bodies consisting of the same numerical particles always, from the resurrection to eternity. And so, likewise, though I say anything that supposes it not necessary, that the same numerical particles, which were vitally united to the soul in this life, should be reunited to it at the resurrection, and constitute the body it shall then have; yet it is not inconsistent with this, that God may, if he pleases, give to everyone a body consisting only of such particles as were before vitally united to his soul. And thus, I think, I have cleared my book from all that inconsistency which your lordship charges on it, and would persuade the world it has with the article of the resurrection of the dead.

"Only before I leave it, I will set down the remainder of what your lordship says upon this head, that though I see not the coherence nor tendency of it, nor the force of any argument in it against me; yet that nothing may be omitted that your lordship has thought fit to entertain your reader with, on this new point, nor any one have reason to suspect, that I have passed by any word of your lordship's (on this now first introduced subject) wherein he might find your lordship had proved what you had promised in your title-page. Your remaining words are these:*
'The dispute is not how far personal identity in itself may consist in the very same material substance; for we allow the notion of personal identity to belong to the same man under several changes of matter; but whether it doth not depend upon a vital union between the soul and body, and the life which is consequent upon it; and therefore in the resurrection, the same material substance must be reunited, or else it cannot be called a resurrection, but a renovation, $i.\ e.$, it may be a new life, but not a raising the body from the dead.' I confess I do not see how what is here ushered in by the words, 'and therefore,' is a consequence from the preceding words; but as to the propriety of the name, I think it will not be much questioned, that if the same man rise who was dead, it may very properly be called the resurrection of the dead; which is the language of the Scripture.

"I must not part with this article of the resurrection, without returning my thanks to your lordship for making me † take notice of a fault in my Essay. When I wrote that book, I took it for granted, as I doubt not but many others have done, that the Scripture had mentioned, in express terms, 'the resurrection of the body.' But upon the occasion your lordship has given me in your last letter, to look a little more narrowly into what revelation has declared concerning the resurrection,

* Second Answer. † Ibid.

and finding no such express words in the Scripture, as that 'the body snall rise, or be raised, or the resurrection of the body;' I shall, in the next edition of it, change these words of my book,* 'The dead bodies of men shall rise,' into these of the Scripture, 'the dead shall rise.' Not that I question that the dead shall be raised with bodies; but in matters of revelation I think it not only safest, but our duty, as far as any one delivers it for revelation, to keep close to the words of the Scripture, unless he will assume to himself the authority of one inspired, or make himself wiser than the Holy Spirit himself. If I had spoken of the resurrection in precisely Scripture terms, I had avoided giving your lordship the occasion of making† here such a verbal reflection on my words; What! not if there be an idea of identity as to the body?'"

No. VII.—Vol. II. page 14, par. 11.

"This, as I understand," replies Mr. Locke to the Bishop of Worcester's objection, "is to prove that the abstract general essence of any sort of things, or things of the same denomination, $v. g.$, of man or marigold, hath a real being out of the understanding; which, I confess, I am not able to conceive. Your lordship's proof here brought out of my Essay, concerning the sun, I humbly conceive will not reach it; because what is said there, does not at all concern the real, but nominal essence, as is evident from hence, that the idea I speak of there is a complex idea; but we have no complex idea of the internal constitution, or real essence of the sun. Besides, I say expressly, That our distinguishing substances into species by names, is not at all founded on their real essences. So that the sun being one of these substances, I cannot, in the place quoted by your lordship, be supposed to mean by essence of the sun, the real essence of the sun, unless I had so expressed it. But all this argument will be at an end, when your lordship shall have explained what you mean by these words, 'true sun.' In my sense of them, anything will be a true sun, to which the name sun may be truly and properly applied; and to that substance or thing the name sun may be truly and properly applied, which has united in it that combination of sensible qualities, by which anything else that is called sun, is distinguished from other substances, $i. e.$, by the nominal essence; and thus our sun is denominated and distinguished from a fixed star, not by a real essence that we do not know, (for if we did, it is possible we should find the real essence or constitution of one of the fixed stars to be the same with that of our sun,) but by a complex idea of sensible qualities co-existing, which, wherever they are found, make a true sun. And thus I crave leave to answer your lordship's question: 'For what is it makes the second sun to be a true sun, but having the same real essence with the first? If it were but a nominal essence, then the second would have nothing but the name.'

"I humbly conceive, if it had the nominal essence, it would have something besides the name, viz., That nominal essence which is sufficient to denominate it truly a sun, or to make it to be a true sun, though we know nothing of that real essence whereon that nominal one depends. Your lordship will then argue, that that real essence is in the

* Essay, B. 4, c. 18, par. 7.   † Second Answer.

second sun, and makes the second sun. I grant it when the second sun comes to exist, so as to be perceived by us to have all the ideas contained in our complex idea, *i.e.*, in our nominal essence of the sun. For should it be true, (as is now believed by astronomers,) that the real essence of the sun were in any of the fixed stars, yet such a star could not for that be by us called a sun, whilst it answers not our complex idea, or nominal essence of a sun. But how far that will prove, that the essences of things, as they are knowable by us, have a reality in them distinct from that of abstract ideas in the mind, which are merely creatures of the mind, I do not see; and we shall further inquire, in considering your lordship's following words: 'Therefore,' say you, 'there must be a real essence in every individual of the same kind.' Yes, and I beg leave of your lordship to say, of a different kind too. For that alone is it which makes it to be what it is.

"That every individual substance has a real, internal, individual constitution, *i.e.*, a real essence, that makes it to be what it is, I readily grant. Upon this, your lordship says, 'Peter, James, and John, are all true and real men.' Answer. Without doubt, supposing them to be men, they are true and real men, *i.e.*, supposing the name of that species belongs to them. And so three bobaques are all true and real bobaques, supposing the name of that species of animals belongs to them.

" For I beseech your lordship to consider, whether in your way of arguing, by naming them Peter, James, and John, names familiar to us as appropriated to individuals of the species man, your lordship does not first suppose them men, and then very safely ask, whether they be not all true and real men? But if I should ask your lordship whether Weweena, Chuckery, and Cousheda, were true and real men or not? your lordship would not be able to tell me, till I have pointed out to your lordship the individuals called by those names, your lordship, by examining whether they had in them those sensible qualities which your lordship has combined into that complex idea to which you give the specific name man, determined them all, or some of them, to be the species which you call man, and so to be true and real man; which, when your lordship has determined, it is plain you did it by that which is only the nominal essence, as not knowing the real one. But your lordship further asks, 'What is it makes Peter, James, and John, real men? Is it the attributing the general name to them? No, certainly; but that the true and real essence of a man is in every one of them.'

" If when your lordship asks, 'What makes them men?' your lordship used the word *making* in the proper sense for the efficient cause, and in that sense it were true, that the essence of a man, *i.e.*, the specific essence of that species made a man; it would undoubtedly follow, that this specific essence had a reality beyond that of being only a general abstract idea in the mind. But when it is said, that it is the true and real essence of a man in every one of them, that makes Peter, James, and John, true and real men, the true and real meaning of these words is no more, but that the essence of that species, *i.e.*, the properties answering the complex abstract idea to which the specific name is given, being found in them, that makes them be properly and truly called men, or is the reason why they are called men. Your lordship adds, 'And we must be as certain of this, as we are that they are men.'

"How, I beseech your lordship, are we certain that they are men, but only by our senses finding those properties in them which answer the abstract complex idea which is in our minds, of the specific idea to which we have annexed the specific name man? This I take to be the true meaning of what your lordship says in the next words, viz., 'They take their denomination of being men from that common nature or essence which is in them;' and I am apt to think these words will not hold true in any other sense.

"Your lordship's fourth inference begins thus: 'That the general idea is not made from the simple ideas by the mere act of the mind abstracting from circumstances, but from reason and consideration of the nature of things.'

"I thought, my lord, that reason and consideration had been acts of the mind, mere acts of the mind, when anything was done by them. Your lordship gives a reason for it, viz., 'For when we see several individuals that have the same powers and properties, we thence infer, that there must be something common to all, which makes them of one kind.'

"I grant the inference to be true; but must beg leave to deny that this proves that the general idea the name is annexed to, is not made by the mind. I have said, and it agrees with what your lordship here says,* That 'the mind in making its complex ideas of substances, only follows nature, and puts no ideas together, which are not supposed to have a union in nature. Nobody joins the voice of a sheep with the shape of a horse; nor the colour of lead with the weight and fixedness of gold to be the complex ideas of any real substances; unless he has a mind to fill his head with chimeras, and his discourses with unintelligible words. Men observing certain qualities, always joined and existing together, therein copied nature, and of ideas so united, made their complex ones of substance, &c.' Which is very little different from what your lordship here says, 'that it is from our observation of individuals, that we come to infer, ' that there is something common to them all.' But I do not see how it will thence follow, that the general or specific idea is not made by the mere act of the mind. 'No,' says your lordship, 'there is something common to them all, which makes them of one kind; and if the difference of kinds be real, that which makes them all of one kind, must not be a nominal, but real essence.'

"This may be some objection to the name of nominal essence; but is, as I humbly conceive, none to the thing designed by it. There is an internal constitution of things, on which their properties depend. This your lordship and I are agreed of, and this we call the real essence. There are also certain complex ideas, or combinations of these properties in men's minds to which they commonly annex specific names, or names of sorts or kinds of things. This, I believe, your lordship does not deny. These complex ideas, for want of a better name, I have called nominal essences; how properly, I will not dispute. But if any one will help me to a better name for them, I am ready to receive it: till then, I must, to express myself, use this. Now, my lord, body, life, and the power of reasoning, being not the real essence of a man, as I believe

* B. 3, c. 6, par. 28, 29.

your lordship will agree, will your lordship say, that they are not enough to make the thing wherein they are found, of the kind called man, and not of the kind called baboon, because the difference of these kinds is real? If this be not real enough to make the thing of one kind, and not of another, I do not see how *animal rationale* can be enough really to distinguish a man from a horse: for that is but the nominal, not real essence of that kind, designed by the name man. And yet I suppose every one thinks it real enough to make a real difference between that and other kinds. And if nothing will serve the turn, to make things of one kind, and not of another, (which, as I have shown, signifies no more but ranking of them under different specific names,) but their real unknown constitutions, which are the real essences we are speaking of, I fear it would be a long while before we should have really different kinds of substances, or distinct names for them, unless we could distinguish them by these differences, of which we have no distinct conceptions. For I think it would not be readily answered me, if I should demand, wherein lies the real difference in the internal constitution of a stag from that of a buck, which are each of them very well known to be of one kind, and not of the other; and nobody questions but that the kinds whereof each of them is, are really different.

"Your lordship further says, And this difference doth not depend upon the complex ideas of substances, whereby men arbitrarily join modes together in their minds. I confess, my lord, I know not what to say to this, because I do not know what these complex ideas of substances are, whereby men arbitrarily join modes together in their minds. But I am apt to think there is a mistake in the matter, by the words that follow, which are these: 'For let them mistake in their complication of ideas, either in leaving out or putting in what doth not belong to them; and let their ideas be what they please, the real essence of a man, and a horse, and a tree, are just what they were.'

"The mistake I spoke of, I humbly suppose, is this, that things are here taken to be distinguished by their real essences; when, by the very way of speaking of them, it is clear that they are already distinguished by their nominal essences, and are so taken to be. For what, I beseech your lordship, does your lordship mean, when you say, 'The real essence of a man, and a horse, and a tree,' but that there are such kinds already set out by the signification of these names, 'man, horse, tree?' And what, I beseech your lordship, is the signification of each of these specific names, but the complex idea it stands for? And that complex idea is the nominal essence, and nothing else. So that taking man, as your lordship does here, to stand for a kind or sort of individuals, all which agree in that common complex idea, which that specific name stands for, it is certain that the real essence of all the individuals comprehended under the specific name man, in your use of it, would be just the same; let others leave out or put into their complex idea of man what they please; because the real essence on which that unaltered complex idea, *i. e.*, those properties depend, must necessarily be concluded to be the same.

"For I take it for granted, that in using the name man, in this place, your lordship uses it for that complex idea which is in your lordship's mind of that species. So that your lordship, by putting it for, or substituting it in the place of, that complex idea where you say the real essence of it is just as it was, or the very same as it was, does suppose the idea it stands for to be steadily the same. For if I change the signification of the word man, whereby it may not comprehend just the same individuals which in your lordship's sense it does, but shut out some of those that to your lordship are men in your signification of the word man, or take in others, to which your lordship does not allow the name man; I do not think you will say, that the real essence of man in both these senses is the same. And yet your lordship seems to say so, when you say, 'Let men mistake in the complication of their ideas, either in leaving out or putting in what doth not belong to them;' and let their ideas be what they please, the real essence of the individuals comprehended under the names annexed to these ideas will be the same; for so I humbly conceive, it must be put to make out what your lordship aims at. For as your lordship puts it by the name of man, or any other specific name, your lordship seems to me to suppose, that that name stands for, and not for, the same idea, at the same time.

"For example, my lord, let your lordship's idea to which you annex the sign man, be a rational animal: let another man's idea be a rational animal of such a shape; let a third man's idea be of an animal of such a size and shape, leaving out rationality; let a fourth's be an animal with a body of such a size and shape, and an immaterial substance, with a power of reasoning; let a fifth leave out of his idea, an immaterial substance: it is plain every one of these will call his a man, as well as your lordship; and yet it is as plain that man, as standing for all these distinct complex ideas, cannot be supposed to have the same internal constitution, *i. e.*, the same real essence. The truth is, every distinct abstract idea with a name to it, makes a real distinct kind, whatever the real essence (which we know not of any of them) be.

"And therefore I grant it true what your lordship says in the next words: 'And let the nominal essences differ never so much, the real common essence or nature of the several kinds are not at all altered by them;' *i. e.*, that our thoughts or ideas cannot alter the real constitutions that are in things that exist, there is nothing more certain. But yet it is true, that the change of ideas to which we annex them, can and does alter the signification of their names, and thereby alter the kinds, which by these names we rank and sort them into. Your lordship further adds, 'And these real essences are unchangeable; *i. e.*, the internal constitutions are unchangeable. Of what, I beseech your lordship, are the internal constitutions unchangeable? Not of anything that exists, but of God alone; for they may be changed all as easily by that hand that made them, as the internal frame of a watch. What then is it that is unchangeable? the internal constitution or real essence of a species: which, in plain English, is no more but this, whilst the same specific name, *v. g.*, of man, horse, or tree, is annexed to, or made the sign of the same abstract complex idea under which I rank several individuals; it is impossible but the real constitution on which that unaltered complex idea or nominal essence depends, must be the same; *i. e.*, in other words, where we find all the same properties, we have reason to conclude there is the same real internal constitution from which those properties flow.

"But your lordship proves the real essences to be unchangeable, because God makes them, in these following words: 'For, however there may happen some variety in individuals by particular accidents, yet the essences of men, and horses, and trees, remain always the same; because they do not depend on the ideas of men, but on the will of the Creator, who hath made several sorts of beings.'

"It is true, the real constitutions or essences of particular things existing do not depend on the ideas of men, but on the will of the Creator; but their being ranked into sorts, under such and such names, does depend, and wholly depend on the ideas of men."

No. VIII.—Vol. II. p. 129, par. 2.

The placing of certainty, as Mr. Locke does, in the perception of the agreement or disagreement of our ideas, the Bishop of Worcester suspects may be of dangerous consequence to that article of faith which he has endeavoured to defend: to which Mr. Locke answers:* "Since your lordship hath not, as I remember, shown, or gone about to show, how this proposition, viz., that certainty consists in the perception of the agreement or disagreement of two ideas, is opposite or inconsistent with that article of faith which your lordship has endeavoured to defend: it is plain, it is but your lordship's fear that it may be of dangerous consequence to it, which, as I humbly conceive, is no proof that it is any way inconsistent with that article.

"Nobody, I think, can blame your lordship, or any one else, for being concerned for any article of the Christian faith; but if that concern (as it may, and as we know it has done) makes any one apprehend danger, where no danger is, are we, therefore, to give up and condemn any proposition, because any one, though of the first rank and magnitude, fears it may be of dangerous consequence to any truth of religion, without showing that it is so? If such fears be the measures whereby to judge of truth and falsehood, the affirming that there are antipodes would be still a heresy; and the doctrine of the motion of the earth must be rejected as overthrowing the truth of the Scripture, for of that dangerous consequence it has been apprehended to be, by many learned and pious divines, out of their great concern for religion. And yet, notwithstanding those great apprehensions of what dangerous consequence it might be, it is now universally received by learned men as an undoubted truth; and written for by some, whose belief of the Scripture is not at all questioned; and particularly, very lately, by a divine of the Church of England, with great strength of reason, in his wonderfully ingenious New Theory of the Earth.

"The reason your lordship gives of your fears, that it may be of such dangerous consequence to that article of faith, which your lordship endeavours to defend, though it occur in more places than one, is only this: viz., that it is made use of by ill men to do mischief, *i. e.*, to oppose that article of faith, which your lordship hath endeavoured to defend. But, my lord, if it be a reason to lay by anything as bad, because it is, or may be used to an ill purpose, I know not what will be innocent enough to be kept. Arms, which were made for our defence,

---

* In his Second Letter to the Bishop of Worcester.

are sometimes made use of to do mischief; and yet they are not thought of dangerous consequence for all that. Nobody lays by his sword and pistols, or thinks them of such dangerous consequence as to be neglected, or thrown away, because robbers, and the worst of men, sometimes make use of them to take away honest men's lives or goods. And the reason is, because they were designed, and will serve to preserve them. And who knows but this may be the present case? If your lordship thinks that placing of certainty in the perception of the agreement or disagreement of ideas, be to be rejected as false, because you apprehend it may be of dangerous consequence to that article of faith: on the other side, perhaps others, with me, may think it a defence against error, and so (as being of good use) to be received and adhered to.

"I would not, my lord, be hereby thought to set up my own, or any one's judgment against your lordship's. But I have said this only to show, whilst the argument lies for or against the truth of any proposition, barely in an imagination that it may be of consequence to the supporting or overthrowing of any remote truth; it will be impossible, that way, to determine of the truth or falsehood of that proposition. For imagination will be set up against imagination, and the stronger probably will be against your lordship; the strongest imaginations being usually in the weakest heads. The only way, in this case, to put it past doubt, is to show the inconsistency of the two propositions; and then it will be seen that one overthrows the other, the true the false one.

'Your lordship says, indeed, this is a new method of certainty. I will not say so myself, for fear of deserving a second reproof from your lordship, for being too forward to assume to myself the honour of being an original. But this, I think, gives me occasion, and will excuse me from being thought impertinent, if I ask your lordship whether there be any other, or older method of certainty? and what it is? For if there be no other, nor older than this, either this was always the method of certainty, and so mine is no new one; or else the world is obliged to me for this new one, after having been so long in the want of so necessary a thing as a method of certainty. If there be an older, I am sure your lordship cannot but know it: your condemning mine as new, as well as your thorough insight into antiquity, cannot but satisfy everybody that you do. And therefore, to set the world right in a thing of that great concernment, and to overthrow mine, and thereby prevent the dangerous consequence there is in my having unreasonably started it, will not, I humbly conceive, misbecome your lordship's care of that article you have endeavoured to defend, nor the goodwill you bear to truth in general. For I will be answerable for myself that I shall; and I think I may be for all others, that they all will give off the placing of certainty in the perception of the agreement or disagreement of ideas, if your lordship will be pleased to show, that it lies in anything else.

"But truly, not to ascribe to myself an invention of what has been as old as knowledge is in the world, I must own I am not guilty of what your lordship is pleased to call starting new methods of certainty. Knowledge, ever since there has been any in the world, has consisted in one particular action in the mind; and so, I conceive, will continue to do to the end of it. And to start new methods of knowledge or certainty, (for they are to me the same thing,) *i. e.*, to find out and propose new methods of attaining knowledge, either with more ease and quickness, or in things yet unknown, is what I think nobody could blame; but this is not that which your lordship here means by new methods of certainty. Your lordship, I think, means by it, the placing of certainty in something, wherein either it does not consist, or else wherein it was not placed before now; if this be to be called a new method of certainty. As to the latter of these, I shall know whether I am guilty or not, when your lordship will do me the favour to tell me wherein it was placed before; which your lordship knows I professed myself ignorant of when I wrote my book; and so I am still. But if starting new methods of certainty be the placing of certainty in something wherein it does not consist, whether I have done that or not, I must appeal to the experience of mankind.

"There are several actions of men's minds, that they are conscious to themselves of performing, as willing, believing, knowing, &c., which they have so particular a sense of, that they can distinguish them one from another; or else they could not say when they willed, when they believed, and when they knew anything. But though these actions were different enough from one another, not to be confounded by those who spoke of them, yet nobody that I have met with had in their writings particularly set down wherein the act of knowing precisely consisted.

"To this reflection upon the actions of my own mind, the subject of my Essay concerning Human Understanding naturally led me; wherein if I have done anything new, it has been to describe to others, more particularly than had been done before, what it is their minds do when they perform that action which they call knowing; and if, upon examination, they observe I have given a true account of that action of their minds in all the parts of it, I suppose it will be in vain to dispute against what they find and feel in themselves; and if I have not told them right, and exactly what they find and feel in themselves, when their minds perform the act of knowing, what I have said will be all in vain, men will not be persuaded against their senses. Knowledge is an internal perception of their minds; and if, when they reflect on it, they find that it is not what I have said it is, my groundless conceit will not be hearkened to, but be exploded by everybody, and die of itself, and nobody need to be at any pains to drive it out of the world. So impossible is it to find out or start new methods of certainty, or to have them received, if any one places it in anything but in that wherein it really consists; much less can any one be in danger to be misled into error by any such new, and to every one, visibly senseless project. Can it be supposed that any one could start a new method of seeing and persuade men thereby that they do not see what they do see? Is it to be feared that any one can cast such a mist over their eyes, that they should not know when they see, and so be led out of their way by it?

"Knowledge, I find in myself, and I conceive in others, consists in the perception of the agreement or disagreement of the immediate objects of the mind in thinking, which I call ideas; but whether it does so in others or not, must be determined by their own experience, reflecting upon the action of their minds in knowing; for that I cannot alter, nor, I think, they themselves. But whether they will call those immediate objects of their minds in thinking, ideas or not, is perfectly in their own choice. If they dislike that name, they may call them notions or conceptions, or how they please; it matters not, if they use them so as to avoid obscurity and confusion. If they are constantly used in the same and a known sense, every one has the liberty to please himself in his terms; there lies neither truth, nor error, nor science in that; though those that take them for things, and not for what they are, bare arbitrary signs of our ideas, make a great deal ado often about them; as if some great matter lay in the use of this or that sound. All that I know or can imagine of difference about them is, that those words are always best whose significations are best known in the sense they are used, and so are least apt to breed confusion.

"My lord, your lordship hath been pleased to find fault with my use of the new term ideas, without telling me a better name for the immediate objects of the mind in thinking. Your lordship also has been pleased to find fault with my definition of knowledge, without doing me the favour to give me a better. For it is only about my definition of knowledge, that all this stir concerning certainty is made: for, with me, to know and to be certain is the same thing: what I know, that I am certain of, and what I am certain of, that I know. What reaches to knowledge, I think may be called certainty; and what comes short of certainty, I think cannot be called knowledge, as your lordship could not but observe in the 18th par. of chap. iv. of my fourth Book, which you have quoted.

"My definition of knowledge stands thus: 'Knowledge seems to me to be nothing but the perception of the connexion and agreement or disagreement and repugnancy of any of our ideas.' This definition your lordship dislikes, and apprehends it may be of dangerous consequence as to that article of Christian faith which your lordship hath endeavoured to defend. For this there is a very easy remedy; it is but for your lordship to set aside this definition of knowledge by giving us a better, and this danger is over. But your lordship chooses rather to have a controversy with my book for having it in it, and to put me upon the defence of it; for which I must acknowledge myself obliged to your lordship for affording me so much of your time, and for allowing me the honour of conversing so much with one so far above me in all respects.

"Your lordship says, it may be of dangerous consequence to that article of Christian faith which you have endeavoured to defend. Though the laws of disputing allow bare denial as a sufficient answer to sayings, without any offer of a proof; yet, my lord, to show how willing I am to give your lordship all satisfaction, in what you apprehend may be of dangerous consequence in my book, as to that article, I shall not stand still sullenly, and put your lordship upon the difficulty of showing wherein that danger lies; but shall, on the other side, endeavour to show your lordship that that definition of mine, whether true or false, right or wrong, can be of no dangerous consequence to that article of faith. The reason which I shall offer for it is this, because it can be of no consequence to it at all.

"That which your lordship is afraid it may be dangerous to, is an article of faith: that which your lordship labours and is concerned for, is the certainty of faith. Now, my lord, I humbly conceive the certainty of faith, if your lordship thinks fit to call it so, has nothing to do with the certainty of knowledge. And to talk of the certainty of faith, seems all one to me as to talk of the knowledge of believing, a way of speaking not easy to me to understand.

"Place knowledge in what you will; start what new methods of certainty you please, that are apt to leave men's minds more doubtful than before; place certainty on such grounds as will leave little or no knowledge in the world, (for these are the arguments your lordship uses against my definition of knowledge,) this shakes not at all, nor in the least concerns the assurance of faith; that is quite distinct from it, neither stands nor falls with knowledge.

"Faith stands by itself, and upon grounds of its own; nor can be removed from them, and placed on those of knowledge. Their grounds are so far from being the same, or having anything common, that when it is brought to certainty, faith is destroyed; it is knowledge then, and faith no longer.

"With what assurance soever of believing I assent to any article of faith, so that I stedfastly venture my all upon it, it is still but believing. Bring it to certainty, and it ceases to be faith. 'I believe that Jesus Christ was crucified, dead, and buried, rose again the third day from the dead, and ascended into heaven:' let now such methods of knowledge or certainty be started, as leave men's minds more doubtful than before; let the grounds of knowledge be resolved into what any one pleases, it touches not my faith; the foundation of that stands as sure as before, and cannot be at all shaken by it; and one may as well say, that anything that weakens the sight, or casts a mist before the eyes, endangers the hearing; as that anything which alters the nature of knowledge (if that could be done) should be of dangerous consequence to an article of faith.

"Whether, then, I am or am not mistaken, in the placing certainty in the perception of the agreement or disagreement of ideas; whether this account of knowledge be true or false, enlarges or straitens the bounds of it more than it should, faith still stands upon its own basis, which is not at all altered by it; and every article of that has just the same unmoved foundation, and the very same credibility that it had before. So that, my lord, whatever I have said about certainty, and how much soever I may be out in it, if I am mistaken, your lordship has no reason to apprehend any danger to any article of faith from thence; every one of them stands upon the same bottom it did before, out of the reach of what belongs to knowledge and certainty. And thus much of my way of certainty by ideas; which I hope will satisfy your lordship how far it is from being dangerous to any article of the Christian faith whatsoever."

No. IX.—Vol. II. p. 144, par. 6.

Against that assertion of Mr. Locke, that "possibly we shall never be able to know whether any mere material being thinks or not," &c., the Bishop of Worcester argues thus: "If this be true, then, for all that we can know by our ideas of matter and thinking, matter may have a power of thinking; and if this hold, then it is impossible to prove a spiritual substance in us from the idea of thinking; for how can we be assured by our ideas, that God hath not given such a power of thinking to matter so disposed as our bodies are? Especially since it is said,* 'That, in respect of our notions, it is not much more remote from our comprehension to conceive that God can, if he pleases, superadd to our idea of matter a faculty of thinking, than that he should superadd to it another substance, with a faculty of thinking.' Whoever asserts this, can never prove a spiritual substance in us from a faculty of thinking, because he cannot know from the idea of matter and thinking, that matter so disposed cannot think; and he cannot be certain, that God hath not framed the matter of our bodies so as to be capable of it."

To which Mr. Locke answers thus:† "Here your lordship argues, that upon my principles, it cannot be proved that there is a spiritual substance in us. To which, give me leave, with submission, to say, that I think it may be proved from my principles, and I think I have done it; and the proof in my book stands thus: First, We experiment in ourselves thinking. The idea of this action, or mode of thinking, is inconsistent with the idea of self-subsistence, and therefore has a necessary connexion with a support or subject of inhesion: the idea of that support is what we call substance; and so from thinking experimented in us, we have a proof of a thinking substance in us, which in my sense is a spirit. Against this your lordship will argue, that, by what I have said of the possibility that God may, if he pleases, superadd to matter a faculty of thinking, it can never be proved that there is a spiritual substance in us, because, upon that supposition, it is possible it may be a material substance that thinks in us. I grant it; but add, that the general idea of substance being the same everywhere, the modification of thinking, or the power of thinking, joined to it, makes it a spirit, without considering what other modifications it has, as whether it has the modification of solidity or not. As, on the other side, substance that has the modification of solidity, is matter, whether it has the modification of thinking or not. And therefore, if your lordship means by a spiritual, an immaterial substance, I grant I have not proved, nor upon my principles can it be proved, (your lordship meaning, as I think you do, demonstratively proved,) that there is an immaterial substance in us that thinks. Though I presume, from what I have said about this supposition of a system of matter, thinking ‡ (which there demonstrates that God is immaterial) will prove it in the highest degree probable, that the thinking substance in us is immaterial. But your lordship thinks not probability enough, and by charging the want of demonstration upon my principle, that the thinking thing in us is immaterial, your lordship seems to conclude it demonstrable from principles of philosophy. That demonstration I should with joy receive from your lordship or any one. For though all the great ends of morality and religion are well enough secured without it, as I have shown,§ yet it would be a great advance of our knowledge in nature and philosophy.

"To what I have said in my book, to show that all the great ends of

---

* Essay on Human Understanding, B. 4, c. 3, p. 6.
† In his First Letter to the Bishop of Worcester.
‡ B. 4, c. 10, par. 16. § Ibid. c. 3, par. 6.

religion and morality are secured barely by the immortality of the soul, without a necessary supposition that the soul is immaterial, I crave leave to add, that immortality may, and shall be, annexed to that which in its own nature is neither immaterial nor immortal, as the apostle expressly declares in these words:* 'For this corruptible must put on incorruption, and this mortal must put on immortality.'

"Perhaps my using the word spirit for a thinking substance, without excluding materiality out of it, will be thought too great a liberty, and such as deserves censure, because I leave immateriality out of the idea I make it a sign of. I readily own, that words should be sparingly ventured on in a sense wholly new, and nothing but absolute necessity can excuse the boldness of using any term in a sense whereof we can produce no example. But in the present case I think I have great authorities to justify me. The soul is agreed, on all hands, to be that in us which thinks. And he that will look into the first book of Cicero's Tusculan Questions, and into the sixth book of Virgil's Æneid, will find that these two great men, who, of all the Romans, best understood philosophy, thought, or at least did not deny, the soul to be a subtile matter, which might come under the name of *aura*, or *ignis*, or *æther*, and this soul they both of them called *spiritus:* in the notion of which, it is plain, they included only thought and active motion, without the total exclusion of matter. Whether they thought right in this I do not say— that is not the question; but whether they spoke properly, when they called an active, thinking, subtile substance, out of which they excluded only gross and palpable matter, *spiritus*, spirit? I think that nobody will deny, that if any among the Romans can be allowed to speak properly, Tully and Virgil are the two who may most securely be depended on for it; and one of them, speaking of the soul, says, *Dum spiritus hos reget artus:* and the other *Vita continetur corpore et spiritu.* Where it is plain by *corpus* he means (as generally everywhere) only gross matter that may be felt and handled, as appears by these words: *Si cor, aut sanguis, aut cerebrum est animus: certe, quoniam est corpus, interibit cum reliquo corpore: si anima est forte dissipabitur: si ignis, extinguetur.* Tusc. Quæst. l. I. c. 11. Here Cicero opposes *corpus* to *ignis* and *anima*, i. e., *aura*, or breath. And the foundation of that his distinction of the soul, from that which he calls *corpus*, or body, he gives a little lower in these words: *Tanta ejus tenuitas ut fugiat aciem.* Ibid. c. 22. Nor was it the heathen world alone that had this notion of spirit; the most enlightened of all the ancient people of God, Solomon himself, speaks after the same manner:† 'That which befalleth the sons of men, befalleth beasts: even one thing befalleth them: as the one dieth, so dieth the other; yea, they have all one spirit.' So I translate the Hebrew word רוּחַ here, for so I find it translated the very next verse but one:‡ 'Who knoweth the spirit of man that goeth upward, and the spirit of the beast that goeth downward to the earth?' In which places it is plain that Solomon applies the word רוּחַ, and our translators of him the word spirit, to a substance out of which materiality was not wholly excluded, unless the spirit of a beast that goeth downwards to the earth be immaterial. Nor did the way of speaking in our Saviour's time vary

* 1 Cor. xv. 53. † Eccl. iii. 19. ‡ Ibid. 21.

APPENDIX. 389

from this; St. Luke tells us,* 'That when our Saviour, after his resurrection, stood in the midst of them, they were affrighted, and supposed that they had seen πνεῦμα,' the Greek word which always answers spirit in English: and so the translators of the Bible render it here; they supposed that they had seen a spirit. But our Saviour says to them, 'Behold my hands and my feet, that it is I myself; handle me, and see, for a spirit hath not flesh and bones, as you see me have.' Which words of our Saviour put the same distinction between body and spirit, that Cicero did in the place above cited, viz., That the one was a gross compages that could be felt and handled; and the other such as Virgil describes the ghost or soul of Anchises:

> 'Ter conatus ibi collo dare brachia circum:
> Ter frustra comprensa manus effugit imago,
> Par levibus ventis, volucrique simillima somno.'†

"I would not be thought hereby to say, that spirit never does signify a purely immaterial substance. In that sense the Scripture, I take it, speaks, when it says God is a spirit; and in that sense I have used it; and in that sense I have proved from my principles that there is a spiritual substance, and am certain that there is a spiritual immaterial substance; which is, I humbly conceive, a direct answer to your lordship's question in the beginning of this argument: viz., 'How we come to be certain that there are spiritual substances, supposing this principle to be true, that the simple ideas by sensation and reflection are the sole matter and foundation of all our reasoning?' But this hinders not, but that if God, that infinite, omnipotent, and perfectly immaterial Spirit, should please to give to a system of very subtile matter, sense and motion, it might with propriety of speech be called spirit, though materiality were not excluded out of its complex idea. Your lordship proceeds: 'It is said, indeed, elsewhere,‡ that it is repugnant to the idea of senseless matter, that it should put into itself sense, perception, and knowledge. But this doth not reach the present case, which is not what matter can do of itself, but what matter prepared by an omnipotent hand can do. And what certainty can we have that he hath not done it? We can have none from the ideas, for those are given up in this case, and consequently we can have no certainty, upon these principles, whether we have any spiritual substance within us or not.'

"Your lordship in this paragraph proves, that from what I say, we can have no certainty whether we have any spiritual substance in us or not. If by spiritual substance, your lordship means an immaterial substance in us, as you speak, I grant what your lordship says is true, that it cannot upon these principles be demonstrated. But I must crave leave to say, at the same time, that upon these principles it can be proved, to the highest degree of probability. If by spiritual substance, your lordship means a thinking substance, I must dissent from your lordship, and say, that we can have a certainty, upon my principles, that there is a spiritual substance in us. In short, my lord, upon my principles, i. e., from the idea of thinking, we can have a certainty that

* Chap. xxiv. 37.   † Æneid. lib. vi.   ‡ Essay, B. 4, c. 10, par. 5

there is a thinking substance in us; from hence we have a certainty that there is an eternal thinking substance. This thinking substance, which has been from eternity, I have proved to be immaterial. This eternal, immaterial, thinking substance, has put into us a thinking substance, which, whether it be a material or immaterial substance, cannot be infallibly demonstrated from our ideas; though from them it may be proved that it is to the highest degree probable that it is immaterial."

Again, the Bishop of Worcester undertakes to prove, from Mr. Locke's principles, that we may be certain, "That the first eternal thinking Being, or omnipotent Spirit, cannot, if he would, give to certain systems of created sensible matter, put together as he sees fit, some degrees of sense, perception, and thought."

To which Mr. Locke has made the following answer in his Third Letter:

"Your first argument I take to be this: that according to me, the knowledge we have being by our ideas, and our ideas of matter in general being a solid substance, and our idea of body a solid extended figured substance; if I admit matter to be capable of thinking, I confound the idea of matter with the idea of a spirit: to which I answer, No; no more than I confound the idea of matter with the idea of a horse, when I say that matter in general is a solid extended substance, and that a horse is a material animal, or an extended solid substance, with sense and spontaneous motion.

"The idea of matter is an extended solid substance; wherever there is such a substance, there is matter, and the essence of matter, whatever other qualities, not contained in that essence, it shall please God to superadd to it For example: God creates an extended solid substance, without the superadding anything else to it, and so we may consider it at rest: to some parts of it he superadds motion, but it has still the essence of matter; other parts of it he frames into plants, with all the excellences of vegetation, life, and beauty, which is to be found in a rose or peach tree, &c., above the essence of matter in general, but it is still but matter: to other parts he adds sense and spontaneous motion, and those other properties that are to be found in an elephant. Hitherto it is not doubted but the power of God may go, and that the properties of a rose, a peach, or an elephant, superadded to matter, change not the properties of matter; but matter is in these things matter still. But if one venture to go one step further, and say, God may give to matter thought, reason, and volition, as well as sense and spontaneous motion, there are men ready presently to limit the power of the omnipotent Creator, and tell us he cannot do it, because it destroys the essence, or changes the essential properties of matter. To make good which assertion, they have no more to say, but that thought and reason are not included in the essence of matter. I grant it; but whatever excellency, not contained in its essence, be superadded to matter, it does not destroy the essence of matter, if it leaves it an extended solid substance; wherever that is, there is the essence of matter; and if everything of greater perfection, superadded to such a substance, destroys the essence of matter, what will become of the essence of matter in a plant or an animal, whose properties far exceed those of a mere extended solid substance?

APPENDIX. 391

"But it is further urged, that we cannot conceive how matter can think. I grant it: but to argue from thence, that God, therefore, cannot give to matter a faculty of thinking, is to say, God's omnipotency is limited to a narrow compass, because man's understanding is so, and brings down God's infinite power to the size of our capacities. If God can give no power to any parts of matter, but what men can account for from the essence of matter in general; if all such qualities and properties must destroy the essence, or change the essential properties of matter, which are to our conceptions above it, and we cannot conceive to be the natural consequence of that essence; it is plain that the essence of matter is destroyed, and its essential properties changed, in most of the sensible parts of this our system. For it is visible, that all the planets have revolutions about certain remote centres, which I would have any one explain, or make conceivable by the bare essence, or natural powers depending on the essence of matter in general, without something added to that essence, which we cannot conceive; for the moving of matter in a crooked line, or the attraction of matter by matter, is all that can be said in the case; either of which it is above our reach to derive from the essence of matter or body in general; though one of these two must unavoidably be allowed to be superadded in this instance to the essence of matter in general. The omnipotent Creator advised not with us in the making of the world, and his ways are not the less excellent because they are past our finding out.

"In the next place, the vegetable part of the creation is not doubted to be wholly material; and yet he that will look into it will observe excellences and operations in this part of matter, which he will not find contained in the essence of matter in general, nor be able to conceive how they can be produced by it. And will he therefore say, that the essence of matter is destroyed in them, because they have properties and operations not contained in the essential properties of matter as matter, nor explicable by the essence of matter in general?

"Let us advance one step further, and we shall in the animal world meet with yet greater perfections and properties, no ways explicable by the essence of matter in general. If the omnipotent Creator had not superadded to the earth, which produced the irrational animals, qualities far surpassing those of the dull dead earth out of which they were made, life, sense, and spontaneous motion, nobler qualities than were before in it, it had still remained rude, senseless matter; and if to the individuals of each species he had not superadded a power of propagation, the species had perished with those individuals; but by these essences or properties of each species, superadded to the matter which they were made of, the essence or properties of matter in general were not destroyed or changed, any more than anything that was in the individual before, was destroyed or changed by the power of generation, superadded to them by the first benediction of the Almighty.

"In all such cases, the superinducement of greater perfections and nobler qualities destroys nothing of the essence or perfections that were there before; unless there can be showed a manifest repugnancy between them: but all the proof offered for that, is only that we cannot conceive how matter, without such superadded perfections, can produce such effects; which is, in truth, no more than to say, matter in general, or every part of matter, as matter, has them not; but it is no reason to prove that God, if he pleases, cannot superadd them to some parts of matter, unless it can be proved to be a contradiction, that God should give to some parts of matter qualities and perfections which matter in general has not; though we cannot conceive how matter is invested with them, or how it operates by virtue of those new endowments; nor is it to be wondered that we cannot, whilst we limit all its operations to those qualities it had before, and would explain them by the known properties of matter in general, without any such superinduced perfections. For if this be a right rule of reasoning, to deny a thing to be, because we cannot conceive the manner how it comes to be; I shall desire them who use it, to stick to this rule, and see what work it will make both in divinity as well as philosophy; and whether they can advance anything more in favour of scepticism.

"For to keep within the present subject of the power of thinking and self-motion, bestowed by omnipotent Power in some parts of matter: the objection to this is, I cannot conceive how matter should think. What is the consequence? *ergo*, God cannot give it a power to think. Let this stand for a good reason, and then proceed in other cases by the same. You cannot conceive how matter can attract matter at any distance, much less at the distance of 1,000,000 of miles; *ergo*, God cannot give it such a power; you cannot conceive how matter should feel, or move itself, or affect an immaterial being, or be moved by it; *ergo*, God cannot give it such powers; which is, in effect, to deny gravity, and the revolution of the planets about the sun; to make brutes mere machines, without sense or spontaneous motion; and to allow man neither sense nor voluntary motion.

"Let us apply this rule one degree further. You cannot conceive how an extended solid substance should think; therefore God cannot make it think: can you conceive how your own soul, or any substance, thinks? You find indeed that you do think, and so do I; but I want to be told how the action of thinking is performed; this, I confess, is beyond my conception, and I would be glad any one who conceives it would explain it to me. God, I find, has given me this faculty; and since I cannot but be convinced of his power in this instance, which though I every moment experiment in myself, yet I cannot conceive the manner of; what would it be less than an insolent absurdity, to deny his power in other like cases, only for this reason, because I cannot conceive the manner how?

"To explain this matter a little further: God has created a substance; let it be, for example, a solid extended substance. Is God bound to give it, besides being, a power of action? That, I think, nobody will say: he therefore may leave it in a state of inactivity, and it will be nevertheless a substance; for action is not necessary to the being of any substance that God does create. God has likewise created and made to exist, *de novo*, an immaterial substance, which will not lose its being of a substance, though God should bestow on it nothing more but this bare being, without giving it any activity at all. Here are now two distinct substances, the one material, the other immaterial, both in a state of perfect inactivity. Now I ask what power God can give to one of these substances (supposing them to retain the same distinct natures that they

APPENDIX.

bad as substances in their state of inactivity) which he cannot give to the other? In that state it is plain neither of them thinks; for thinking being an action, it cannot be denied that God can put an end to any action of any created substance, without annihilating of the substance whereof it is an action; and if it be so, he can also create or give existence to such a substance, without giving that substance any action at all. By the same reason it is plain that neither of them can move itself: now I would ask why Omnipotency cannot give to either of these substances, which are equally in a state of perfect inactivity, the same power that it can give to the other? Let it be for example, that of spontaneous or self-motion, which is a power that is supposed God can give to an unsolid substance, but denied that he can give to a solid substance.

"If it be asked why they limit the omnipotency of God in reference to the one rather than the other of these substances? all that can be said to it is, that they cannot conceive how the solid substance should ever be able to move itself. And as little, say I, are they able to conceive, how a created unsolid substance should move itself. But there may be something in an immaterial substance that you do not know. I grant it; and in a material one too; for example, gravitation of matter towards matter, and in the several proportions observable, inevitably shows that there is something in matter that we do not understand, unless we can conceive self-motion in matter; or an inexplicable and inconceivable attraction in matter, at immense, almost incomprehensible distances; it must, therefore, be confessed that there is something in solid as well as unsolid substances that we do not understand. But this we know, that they may each of them have their distinct beings, without any activity superadded to them, unless you will deny that God can take from any being its power of acting, which it is probable will be thought too presumptuous for any one to do; and I say it is as hard to conceive self-motion in a created immaterial, as in a material being, consider it how you will; and therefore this is no reason to deny Omnipotency to be able to give a power of self-motion to a material substance, if he pleases, as well as to an immaterial, since neither of them can have it from themselves, nor can we conceive how it can be in either of them.

The same is visible in the other operation of thinking: both these substances may be made and exist without thought; neither of them has or can have the power of thinking from itself; God may give it to either of them, according to the good pleasure of his omnipotency; and in whichever of them it is, it is equally beyond our capacity to conceive how either of these substances thinks. But for that reason to deny that God, who had power enough to give them both a being out of nothing, can by the same omnipotency give them what other powers and perfections he pleases, has no better foundation than to deny his power of creation because we cannot conceive how it is performed: and there, at last, this way of reasoning must terminate.

"That Omnipotency cannot make a substance to be solid and not solid at the same time, I think, with due reverence, we may say; but that a solid substance may not have qualities, perfections, and powers, which have no natural or visibly necessary connexion with solidity and extension, is too much for us (who are but of yesterday, and know nothing) to be positive in. If God cannot join things together by connexions inconceivable to us, we must deny even the consistency and being of matter itself; since every particle of it having some bulk, has its parts connected by ways inconceivable to us. So that all the difficulties that are raised against the thinking of matter, from our ignorance, or narrow conceptions, stand not at all in the way of the power of God, if he pleases to ordain it so; nor prove anything against his having actually endued some parcels of matter, so disposed as he thinks fit, with a faculty of thinking, till it can be shown that it contains a contradiction to suppose it.

"Though to me sensation be comprehended under thinking in general, yet in the foregoing discourse I have spoken of sense in brutes, as distinct from thinking; because your lordship, as I remember, speaks of sense in brutes. But here I take liberty to observe, that if your lordship allows brutes to have sensation, it will follow, either that God can and doth give to some parcels of matter a power of perception and thinking, or that all animals have immaterial, and consequently, according to your lordship, immortal souls, as well as men, and to say that fleas and mites, &c., have immortal souls as well as men, will possibly be looked on as going a great way to serve an hypothesis.

"I have been pretty large in making this matter plain, that they who are so forward to bestow hard censures or names on the opinions of those who differ from them, may consider whether sometimes they are not more due to their own; and that they may be persuaded a little to temper that heat, which, supposing the truth in their current opinions, gives them (as they think) a right to lay what imputations they please on those who would fairly examine the grounds they stand upon. For talking with a supposition and insinuations, that truth and knowledge, nay, and religion too, stand and fall with their systems, is at best but an imperious way of begging the question, and assuming to themselves, under the pretence of zeal for the cause of God, a title to infallibility. It is very becoming that men's zeal for truth should go as far as their proofs, but not go for proofs themselves. He that attacks received opinions with anything but fair arguments, may, I own, be justly suspected not to mean well, nor to be led by the love of truth; but the same may be said of him too, who so defends them. An error is not the better for being common, nor truth the worse for having lain neglected; and if it were put to the vote anywhere in the world, I doubt, as things are managed, whether truth would have the majority, at least whilst the authority of men, and not the examination of things, must be its measure. The imputation of scepticism, and those broad insinuations to render what I have written suspected, so frequent, as if that were the great business of all this pains you have been at about me, has made me say thus much, my lord, rather as my sense of the way to establish truth in its full force and beauty, than that I think the world will need to have anything said to it, to make it distinguish between your lordship's and my design in writing, which, therefore, I securely leave to the judgment of the reader, and return to the argument in hand.

"What I have above said, I take to be a full answer to all that your lordship would infer from my idea of matter, of liberty, of identity, and from the power of abstracting. You ask,* 'How can my idea of liberty

---

* First Answer.

agree with the idea that bodies can operate only by motion and impulse?' Answer. By the omnipotency of God, who can make all things agree, that involve not a contradiction. It is true, I say,* That bodies operate by impulse, and nothing else. And so I thought when I wrote it, and can yet conceive no other way of their operation. But I am since convinced by the judicious Mr. Newton's incomparable book, that it is too bold a presumption to limit God's power in this point by my narrow conceptions. The gravitation of matter towards matter, by ways inconceivable to me, is not only a demonstration that God can, if he pleases, put into bodies powers and ways of operation, above what can be derived from our idea of body, or can be explained by what we know of matter; but also an unquestionable, and everywhere visible instance that he has done so. And, therefore, in the next edition of my book I will take care to have that passage rectified.

"As to self-consciousness, your lordship asks,† 'What is there like self-consciousness in matter?' Nothing at all in matter, as matter. But that God cannot bestow on some parcels of matter a power of thinking, and with it self-consciousness, will never be proved by asking,‡ How is it possible to apprehend that mere body should perceive that it doth perceive? The weakness of our apprehension, I grant in the case: I confess as much as you please, that we cannot conceive how a solid, no, nor how an unsolid, created substance thinks; but this weakness of our apprehensions reaches not the power of God, whose weakness is stronger than anything in men.

"Your argument from abstraction, we have in this question: || 'If it may be in the power of matter to think, how comes it to be so impossible for such organized bodies as the brutes have, to enlarge their ideas by abstraction?' Ans. This seems to suppose that I place thinking within the natural power of matter. If that be your meaning, my lord, I never say nor suppose that all matter has naturally in it a faculty of thinking, but the direct contrary. But if you mean that certain parcels of matter, ordered by the Divine Power, as seems fit to him, may be made capable of receiving from his omnipotency the faculty of thinking; that, indeed, I say: and that being granted, the answer to your question is easy; since, if Omnipotency can give thought to any solid substance, it is not hard to conceive that God may give that faculty in a higher or lower degree, as it pleases him, who knows what disposition of the subject is suited to such a particular way or degree of thinking.

"Another argument to prove that God cannot endue any parcel of matter with the faculty of thinking, is taken from those words of mine,§ where I show by what connexion of ideas we may come to know that God is an immaterial substance. They are these: 'The idea of an eternal actual knowing being, with the idea of immateriality, by the intervention of the idea of matter, and of its actual division, divisibility, and want of perception, &c. From whence your lordship thus argues:¶ 'Here the want of perception is owned to be so essential to matter, that God is therefore concluded to be immaterial.' Ans. Perception and knowledge in that one Eternal Being, where it has its

---

* Essay, B. 2, c. 8, par. 11.   † First Answer.   ‡ Ibid. || Ibid.
§ First Letter.   ¶ Ibid.

source, it is visible must be essentially inseparable from it; therefore the actual want of perception in so great a part of the particular parcels of matter, is a demonstration, that the first Being, from whom perception and knowledge are inseparable, is not matter: how far this makes the want of perception an essential property of matter, I will not dispute; it suffices that it shows that perception is not an essential property of matter, and therefore matter cannot be that eternal original being to which perception and knowledge are essential. Matter, I say, naturally is without perception: *Ergo*, says your lordship, 'want of perception is an essential property of matter, and God does not change the essential properties of things, their nature remaining.' From whence you infer, that God cannot bestow on any parcel of matter (the nature of matter remaining) a faculty of thinking. If the rules of logic, since my days, be not changed, I may safely deny this consequence. For an argument that runs thus, God does not, *ergo*, he cannot, I was taught when I first came to the university, would not hold. For I never said God did; but,* 'That I see no contradiction in it, that he should, if he pleased, give to some systems of senseless matter a faculty of thinking;' and I know nobody before Descartes that ever pretended to show that there was any contradiction in it. So that at worst, my not being able to see in matter any such incapacity as makes it impossible for Omnipotency to bestow on it a faculty of thinking, makes me opposite only to the Cartesians. For as far as I have seen or heard, the Fathers of the Christian church never pretended to demonstrate that matter was incapable to receive a power of sensation, perception, and thinking, from the hand of the omnipotent Creator. Let us, therefore, if you please, suppose the form of your argumentation right, and that your lordship means, 'God cannot:' and then if your argument be good, it proves, 'That God could not give to Balaam's ass a power to speak to his master, as he did, for the want of rational discourse being natural to that species;' it is but for your lordship to call it an essential property, and then God cannot change the essential properties of things, their nature remaining: whereby it is proved, 'That God cannot, with all his omnipotency, give to an ass a power to speak, as Balaam's did.'

"You say, † my lord, you 'do not set bounds to God's omnipotency. For he may, if he please, change a body into an immaterial substance,' *i. e.*, take away from a substance the solidity which it had before, and which made it matter, and then give it a faculty of thinking which it had not before, and which makes it a spirit, the same substance remaining. For if the substance remains not, body is not changed into an immaterial substance. But the solid substance, and all belonging to it, is annihilated, and an immaterial substance created, which is not a change of one thing into another, but the destroying of one and making another *de novo*. In this change, therefore, of a body or material substance, into an immaterial, let us observe these distinct considerations.

"First, you say, 'God may, if he please, take away from a solid substance, solidity, which is that which makes a material substance or body; and may make it an immaterial substance, *i. e.*, a substance without solidity. But this privation of one quality gives it not another; the bare

* B 4, c. 3, par. 6.   † First Answer.

APPENDIX.   397

taking away a lower or less noble quality, does not give it a higher or nobler; that must be the gift of God. For the bare privation of one, and a meaner quality, cannot be the position of a higher and better: unless any one will say that cogitation, or the power of thinking, results from the nature of substance itself; which if it do, then, wherever there is substance, there must be cogitation, or a power of thinking. Here, then, upon your lordship's own principles, is an immaterial substance without the faculty of thinking.

"In the next place, you will not deny that God may give to this substance, thus deprived of solidity, a faculty of thinking: for you suppose it made capable of that by being made immaterial; whereby you allow that the same numerical substance may be sometimes wholly incogitative, or without a power of thinking, and at other times perfectly cogitative, or endued with a power of thinking.

"Further, you will not deny but God can give it solidity, and make it material again. For I conlcude it will not be denied that God can make it again what it was before. Now I crave leave to ask your lordship, why God, having given to this substance the faculty of thinking, after solidity was taken from it, cannot restore to it solidity again, without taking away the faculty of thinking? When you have resolved this, my lord, you will have proved it impossible for God's omnipotence to give to a solid substance a faculty of thinking; but till then, not having proved it impossible, and yet denying that God can do it, is to deny that he can do what is in itself possible; which, as I humbly conceive, is visibly to set bounds to God's omnipotency, though you say here,* you do not set bounds to God's omnipotency.'

"If I should imitate your lordship's way of writing, I should not omit to bring in Epicurus here, and take notice that this was his way, *Deum verbis ponere, re tollere;* and then add, that I am certain you do not think he promoted the great ends of religion and morality. For it is with such candid and kind insinuations as these that you bring in both Hobbes† and Spinosa‡ into your discourse here about God's being able, if he please, to give to some parcels of matter, ordered as he thinks fit, a faculty of thinking; neither of those authors having, as appears by any passages you bring out of them, said anything to this question; nor having, as it seems, any other business here, but by their names, skilfully to give that character to my book with which you would recommend it to the world.

"I pretend not to inquire what measure of zeal, nor for what, guides your lordship's pen in such a way of writing, as yours has all along been with me; only I cannot but consider, what reputation it would give to the writings of the fathers of the church, if they should think truth required, or religion allowed them to imitate such patterns. But God be thanked, there be those amongst them who do not admire such ways of managing the cause of truth or religion; they being sensible, that if every one who believes, or can pretend he hath truth on his side, is thereby authorized, without proof, to insinuate whatever may serve to prejudice men's minds against the other side, there will be great ravage made on charity and practice, without any gain to truth or know-

* First Answer.   † Ibid.   ‡ Ibid.

ledge; and that the liberties frequently taken by disputants to do so, may have been the cause that the world in all ages has received so much harm, and so little advantage, from controversies in religion.

"These are the arguments which your lordship has brought to confute one saying in my book, by other passages in it; which, therefore, being all but *argumenta ad hominem*, if they did prove what they do not, are of no other use than to gain a victory over me; a thing, methinks, so much beneath your lordship, that it does not deserve one of your pages. The question is, whether God can, if he please, bestow on any parcel of matter, ordered as he thinks fit, a faculty of perception and thinking. You say,* you 'look upon a mistake herein to be of dangerous consequence as to the great ends of religion and morality.' If this be so, my lord, I think one may well wonder why your lordship has brought no arguments to establish the truth itself, which you look on to be of such dangerous consequence to be mistaken in; but have spent so many pages only in a personal matter, in endeavouring to show that I had inconsistencies in my book; which if any such thing had been shown, the question would be still as far from being decided, and the danger of mistaking about it as little prevented, as if nothing of all this had been said. If, therefore, your lordship's care of the great ends of religion and morality have made you think it necessary to clear this question, the world has reason to conclude there is little to be said against that proposition which is to be found in my book, concerning the possibility that some parcels of matter might be so ordered by Omnipotence, as to be endued with a faculty of thinking, if God so pleased; since your lordship's concern for the promoting the great ends of religion and morality has not enabled you to produce one argument against a proposition that you think of so dangerous consequence to them.

"And here I crave leave to observe, that though in your title page you promise to prove that my notion of ideas is inconsistent with itself, (which if it were, it could hardly be proved to be inconsistent with anything else,) and with the articles of the Christian faith; yet your attempts all along have been to prove me, in some passages of my book, inconsistent with myself, without having shown any proposition in my book inconsistent with any article of the Christian faith.

"I think your lordship has, indeed, made use of one argument of your own: but it is such an one, that I confess I do not see how it is apt much to promote religion, especially the Christian religion, founded on revelation. I shall set down your lordship's words that they may be considered; you say,† ' that you are of opinion that the great ends of religion and morality are best secured by the proofs of the immortality of the soul, from its nature, and properties; and which you think prove it immaterial,' Your lordship does not question whether God can give immortality to a material substance: but you say it takes off very much from the evidence of immortality, if it depend wholly upon God's giving that which of its own nature it is not capable of, &c. So likewise you say,‡ 'If a man cannot be certain but that matter may think, (as I affirm,) then what becomes of the soul's immateriality (and consequently immortality) from its operations?' But for all this, say I, his assurance

---

* First Answer. † Ibid. ‡ Second Answer.

of faith remains on its own basis. Now, you appeal to any man of sense, whether the finding the uncertainty of his own principles which he went upon, in point of reason, doth not weaken the credibility of these fundamental articles, when they are considered purely as matters of faith? For before, there was a natural credibility in them on account of reason; but by going on wrong grounds of certainty, all that is lost; and instead of being certain, he is more doubtful than ever. And if the evidence of faith fall so much short of that of reason, it must needs have less effect upon men's minds when the subserviency of reason is taken away; as it must be, when the grounds of certainty by reason are vanished. Is it at all probable, that he who finds his reason deceive him in such fundamental points, shall have his faith stand firm and immovable on the account of revelation? For in matters of revelation, there must be some antecedent principles supposed, before we can believe anything on the account of it.'

"More to the same purpose we have some pages further, where, from some of my words, your lordship says,* 'You cannot but observe, that we have no certainty upon my grounds, that self-consciousness depends upon an individual immaterial substance, and, consequently, that a material substance may, according to my principles, have self-consciousness in it; at least, that I am not certain of the contrary.' Whereupon your lordship bids me consider, whether this does not a little affect the whole article of the resurrection? What does all this tend to, but to make the world believe that I have lessened the credibility of the immortality of the soul, and the resurrection, by saying, that though it be most highly probable that the soul is immaterial, yet upon my principles it cannot be demonstrated; because it is not impossible to God's omnipotency, if he pleases to bestow upon some parcels of matter, disposed as he sees fit, a faculty of thinking?

"This, your accusation of my lessening the credibility of these articles of faith, is founded on this: that the article of the immortality of the soul abates of its credibility, if it be allowed, that its immateriality (which is the supposed proof from reason and philosophy of its immortality) cannot be demonstrated from natural reason: which argument of your lordship's bottoms, as I humbly conceive, on this: that divine revelation abates of its credibility in all those articles it proposes, proportionably as human reason fails to support the testimony of God. And all that your lordship in those passages has said, when examined, will, I suppose, be found to import thus much: viz., Does God propose anything to mankind to be believed? It is very fit and credible to be believed, if reason can demonstrate it to be true. But if human reason comes short in the case, and cannot make it out, its credibility is thereby lessened; which is, in effect, to say, that the veracity of God is not a firm and sure foundation of faith to rely upon, without the concurrent testimony of reason, *i. e.*, with reverence be it spoken, God is not to be believed on his own word, unless what he reveals be in itself credible, and might be believed without him.

"If this be a way to promote religion, the Christian religion, in all its articles, I am not sorry that it is not a way to be found in any of my

* Second Answer.

writings; for I imagine anything like this would (and I should think deserve to) have other titles than bare scepticism bestowed upon it, and would have raised no small outcry against any one who is not to be supposed to be in the right in all that he says, and so may securely say what he pleases. Such as I, the *profanum vulgus*, who take too much upon us, if we would examine, have nothing to do but to hearken and believe, though what he said should subvert the very foundations of the Christian faith.

"What I have above observed, is so visibly contained in your lordship's argument, that when I met with it in your answer to my first letter, it seemed so strange for a man of your lordship's character, and in a dispute in defence of the doctrine of the Trinity, that I could hardly persuade myself but it was a slip of your pen; but when I found it in your second letter* made use of again, and seriously enlarged as an argument of weight to be insisted upon, I was convinced that it was a principle that you heartily embraced, how little favourable soever it was to the articles of the Christian religion, and particularly those which you undertook to defend.

"I desire my reader to peruse the passages as they stand in your letters themselves, and see whether what you say in them does not amount to this, that a revelation from God is more or less credible, according as it has a stronger or weaker confirmation from human reason. For,

"1. Your lordship says,† 'You do not question whether God can give immortality to a material substance; but you say it takes off very much from the evidence of immortality, if it depends wholly upon God's giving that, which of its own nature it is not capable of.'

"To which I reply, any one not being able to demonstrate the soul to be immaterial, takes off not very much, nor at all, from the evidence of its immortality, if God has revealed that it shall be immortal; because the veracity of God is a demonstration of the truth of what he has revealed and the want of another demonstration of a proposition, that is demonstratively true, takes not off from the evidence of it. For where there is a clear demonstration, there is as much evidence as any truth can have, that is not self-evident. God has revealed that the souls of men shall live for ever. 'But,' says your lordship, 'from this evidence it takes off very much, if it depends wholly upon God's giving that which of its own nature it is not capable of,' *i. e.*, the revelation and testimony of God loses much of its evidence, if this depends wholly upon the good pleasure of God, and cannot be demonstratively made out by natural reason, that the soul is immaterial, and consequently, in its own nature, immortal. For that is all that here is or can be meant by these words, 'which of its own nature it is not capable of,' to make them to the purpose. For the whole of your lordship's discourse here is to prove, that the soul cannot be material, because, then, the evidence of its being immortal would be very much lessened. Which is to say, that it is not as credible upon divine revelation, that a material substance should be immortal, as an immaterial; or, which is all one, that God is not equally to be believed when he declares, that a material sub

* Second Answer.   † First Answer.

stance shall be immortal, as when he declares, that an immaterial shall be so, because the immortality of a material substance cannot be demonstrated from natural reason.

"Let us try this rule of your lordship's a little further: God hath revealed that the bodies men shall have after the resurrection, as well as their souls, shall live to eternity. Does your lordship believe the eternal life of the one of these more than of the other, because you think you can prove it of one of them by natural reason, and of the other not? or can any one who admits of divine revelation in the case, doubt of one of them more than the other? or think this proposition less credible, that the bodies of men after the resurrection shall live for ever; than this, that the souls of men, shall, after the resurrection, live for ever? For that he must do, if he thinks either of them is less credible than the other. If this be so, reason is to be consulted how far God is to be believed, and the credit of divine testimony must receive its force from the evidence of reason; which is evidently to take away the credibility of divine revelation in all supernatural truths wherein the evidence of reason fails. And how much such a principle as this tends to the support of the doctrine of the Trinity, or the promoting the Christian religion, I shall leave it to your lordship to consider.

"I am not so well read in Hobbes or Spinosa, as to be able to say what were their opinions in this matter. But, possibly, there be those who will think your lordship's authority of more use to them in the case than those justly decried names; and be glad to find your lordship a patron of the oracles of reason, so little to the advantage of the oracles of divine revelation. This, at least, I think, may be subjoined to the words at the bottom of the next page,* That those who have gone about to lessen the credibility of the articles of faith, which evidently they do who say they are less credible, because they cannot be made out demonstratively by natural reason, have not been thought to secure several of the articles of the Christian faith, especially those of the Trinity, incarnation, and resurrection of the body, which are those upon the account of which I am brought by your lordship into this dispute.

"I shall not trouble the reader with your lordship's endeavours in the following words, to prove, 'That if the soul be not an immaterial substance, it can be nothing but life;' your very first words visibly confuting all that you allege to that purpose. They are,† 'If the soul be a material substance, it is really nothing but life;' which is to say, that if the soul be really a substance, it is not really a substance, but really nothing else but an affection of a substance; for the life, whether of a material or immaterial substance, is not the substance itself, but an affection of it.

"2. You say,‡ 'Although we think the separate state of the soul after death, is sufficiently revealed in the Scripture; yet it creates a great difficulty in understanding it, if the soul be nothing but life, or a material substance, which must be dissolved when life is ended. For if the soul be a material substance, it must be made up, as others are, of the cohesion of solid and separate parts, how minute and invisible soever they be. And what is it which should keep them together, when life is

* First Answer.   † Ibid.   ‡ Ibid.

gone? So that it is no easy matter to give an account, how the soul should be capable of immortality, unless it be an immaterial substance; and then we know the solution and texture of bodies cannot reach the soul, being of a different nature.'

"Let it be as hard a matter as it will to give an account what it is that should keep the parts of a material soul together, after it is separated from the body, yet it will be always as easy to give an account of it, as to give an account what it is that shall keep together a material and immaterial substance. And yet the difficulty that there is to give an account of that, I hope does not, with your lordship, weaken the credibility of the inseparable union of soul and body to eternity: and I persuade myself that the men of sense, to whom your lordship appeals in the case, do not find their belief of this fundamental point much weakened by that difficulty. I thought heretofore, (and by your lordship's permission, would think so still,) that the union of the parts of matter, one with another, is as much in the hands of God, as the union of a material and immaterial substance; and that it does not take off very much, or at all, from the evidence of immortality, which depends on that union, that it is no easy matter to give an account what it is that should keep them together: though its depending wholly upon the gift and good pleasure of God, where the manner creates great difficulty in the understanding, and our reason cannot discover in the nature of things how it is, be that which your lordship so positively says, lessens the credibility of the fundamental articles of the resurrection and immortality.

"But, my lord, to remove this objection a little, and to show of how small force it is even with yourself; give me leave to presume, that your lordship as firmly believes the immortality of the body after the resurrection, as any other article of faith: if so, then it being no easy matter to give an account, what it is that shall keep together the parts of a material soul, to one that believes it is material, can no more weaken the credibility of its immortality, than the like difficulty weakens the credibility of the immortality of the body. For when your lordship shall find it an easy matter to give an account what it is, besides the good pleasure of God, which shall keep together the parts of our material bodies to eternity, or even soul and body; I doubt not but any one, who shall think the soul material, will also find it as easy to give an account what it is that shall keep those parts of matter also together to eternity.

"Were it not that the warmth of controversy is apt to make men so far forget, as to take up those principles themselves (when they will serve their turn) which they have highly condemned in others, I should wonder to find your lordship to argue, that because it is a difficulty to understand what shall keep together the minute parts of a material soul, when life is gone; and because it is not an easy matter to give an account how the soul shall be capable of immortality, unless it be an immaterial substance: therefore it is not so credible, as if it were easy to give an account by natural reason, how it could be. For to this it is, that all this your discourse tends, as is evident by what is already set down; and will be more fully made out by what your lordship says in other places, though there needs no such proof, since it would all be nothing against me in any other sense.

"I thought your lordship had in other places asserted, and insisted on this truth, that no part of divine revelation was the less to be believed, because the thing itself created great difficulty in the understanding, and the manner of it was hard to be explained; and it was no easy matter to give an account how it was. This, as I take it, your lordship condemned in others, as a very unreasonable principle, and such as would subvert all the articles of the Christian religion, that were mere matters of faith, as I think it will: and is it possible, that you should make use of it here yourself, against the article of life and immortality, that Christ hath brought to light through the gospel, and neither was nor could be made out by natural reason without revelation? But you will say, you speak only of the soul; and your words are, 'That it is no easy matter to give an account how the soul should be capable of immortality, unless it be an immaterial substance.' I grant it; but crave leave to say, that there is not any one of those difficulties, that are or can be raised about the manner how a material soul can be immortal, which do not as well reach the immortality of the body.

"But if it were not so, I am sure this principle of your lordship's would reach other articles of faith, wherein our natural reason finds it not so easy to give an account how those mysteries are: and which, therefore, according to your principles, must be less credible than other articles, that create less difficulty to the understanding. For your lordship says,* 'That you appeal to any man of sense, whether to a man who thought by his principles, he could from natural grounds demonstrate the immortality of the soul, the finding the uncertainty of those principles he went upon in point of reason,' *i. e.*, the finding he could not certainly prove it by natural reason, doth not weaken the credibility of that fundamental article, when it is considered purely as a matter of faith? Which, in effect, I humbly conceive, amounts to this, that a proposition divinely revealed that cannot be proved by natural reason, is less credible than one that can: which seems to me to come very little short of this, with due reverence be it spoken, that God is less to be believed when he affirms a proposition that cannot be proved by natural reason, than when he proposes what can be proved by it. The direct contrary to which is my opinion, though you endeavour to make it good by these following words: † 'If the evidence of faith fall so much short of that of reason, it must needs have less effect upon men's minds, when the subserviency of reason is taken away; as it must be, when the grounds of certainty by reason are vanished. Is it at all probable, that he who finds his reason deceive him in such fundamental points, should have his faith stand firm and immovable on the account of revelation?' Than which I think there are hardly plainer words to be found out to declare, that the credibility of God's testimony depends on the natural evidence of probability of the things we receive from revelation; and rises and falls with it; and that the truths of God, or the articles of mere faith, lose so much of their credibility as they want proof from reason; which, if true, revelation may come to have no credibility at all. For if in this present case, the credibility of this proposition, 'the souls of men shall live for ever,' revealed in the Scripture, be lessened by con-

* Second Answer. † Ibid.

fessing it cannot be demonstratively proved from reason, though it be asserted to be most highly probable; must not, by the same rule, its credibility dwindle away to nothing, if natural reason should not be able to make it out to be so much as probable, or should place the probability from natural principles on the other side? For if mere want of demonstration lessens the credibility of any proposition divinely revealed, must not want of probability, or contrary probability from natural reason, quite take away its credibility? Here at last it must end, if in any one case the veracity of God, and the credibility of the truths we receive from him by revelation, be subjected to the verdicts of human reason, and be allowed to receive any accession or diminution from other proofs, or want of other proofs of its certainty or probability.

"If this be your lordship's way to promote religion, or defend its articles, I know not what argument the greatest enemies of it could use more effectually for the subversion of those you have undertaken to defend; this being to resolve all revelation perfectly and purely into natural reason, to bound its credibility by that, and leave no room for faith in other things, than what can be accounted for by natural reason without revelation.

"Your lordship * insists much upon it, as if I had contradicted what I have said in my Essay,† by saying, 'that upon my principles it cannot be demonstratively proved, that it is an immaterial substance in us that thinks, however probable it be.' He that will be at the pains to read that chapter of mine, and consider it, will find that my business there was to show, that it was no harder to conceive an immaterial than a material substance; and that from the ideas of thought, and a power of moving of matter, which we experienced in ourselves, (ideas originally not belonging to matter as matter,) there was no more difficulty to conclude there was an immaterial substance in us, than that we had material parts. These ideas of thinking and power of moving of matter, I, in another place, showed, did demonstratively lead us to the certain knowledge of the existence of an immaterial thinking being, in whom we have the idea of spirit in the strictest sense; in which sense I also applied it to the soul, in the 23rd chapter of my Essay; the easily conceivable possibility, nay, great probability, that the thinking substance in us is immaterial, giving me sufficient ground for it. In which sense I shall think I may safely attribute it to the thinking substance in us, till your lordship shall have better proved from my words, that it is impossible it should be immaterial. For I only say, that it is possible, *i. e.*, involves no contradiction, that God, the omnipotent, immaterial Spirit, should, if he please, give to some parcels of matter, disposed as he thinks fit, a power of thinking and moving; which parcels of matter so endued with a power of thinking and motion, might properly be called spirits, in contradistinction to unthinking matter: in all which, I presume, there is no manner of contradiction.

"I justified my use of the word spirit, in that sense, from the authorities of Cicero and Virgil, applying the Latin word *spiritus*, from whence spirit is derived, to the soul, as a thinking thing, without excluding materiality out of it. To which your lordship replies,‡ 'that Cicero, in his

* First Answer.   † B. 2. c. 23.   ‡ First Answer.

APPENDIX. 405

Tusculan Questions, supposes the soul not to be a finer sort of body, but of a different nature from the body—that he calls the body, the prison of the soul—and says, that 'a wise man's business is to draw off his soul from his body.' And then your lordship concludes, as is usual, with a question: 'Is it possible not to think so great a man looked on the soul but as a modification of the body, which must be at an end with life?' Answer, No; it is impossible that a man of so good sense as Tully, when he uses the word *corpus*, or body, for the gross and visible parts of a man, which he acknowledges to be mortal, should look on the soul to be a modification of that body, in a discourse wherein he was endeavouring to persuade another that it was immortal. It is to be acknowledged, that truly great men, such as he was, are not wont so manifestly to contradict themselves. He had therefore no thought concerning the modification of the body of a man in the case: he was not such a trifler as to examine whether the modification of the body of a man was immortal, when that body itself was mortal. And therefore, that which he reports as Dicæarchus's opinion, he dismisses in the beginning without any more ado, c. 11. But Cicero's was a direct, plain, and sensible inquiry, viz., What the soul was? to see whether from thence he could discover its immortality. But in all that discourse in his first book of Tusculan questions, where he lays out so much of his reading and reason, there is not one syllable showing the least thought that the soul was an immaterial substance; but many things directly to the contrary.

Indeed, (1.) he shuts out the body, taken in the sense he uses * *corpus* all along, for the sensible organical parts of a man; and is positive that it is not the soul: and body in this sense, taken for the human body, he calls the prison of the soul; and says, a wise man, instancing in Socrates and Cato, is glad of a fair opportunity to get out of it. But he nowhere says any such thing of matter: he calls not matter in general the prison of the soul, nor talks a word of being separate from it.

'2. He concludes that the soul is not, like other things here below, made up of a composition of the elements, c. 27.

'3. He excludes the two gross elements, earth and water, from being the soul, c. 26.

'So far he is clear and positive; but beyond this he is uncertain, beyond this he could not get. For in some places he speaks doubtfully, whether the soul be not air or fire, *Anima sit animus, ignisve, nescio*, c. 25, And therefore he agrees with Panætius, that if it be at all elementary, it is, as he calls it, *inflammata anima*, inflamed air; and for this he gives several reasons, c. 18, 19. And though he thinks it to be of a peculiar nature of its own, yet he is so far from thinking it immaterial, that he says, c. 19, that the admitting it to be of an aërial or igneous nature will not be inconsistent with anything he had said.

'That which he seems most to incline to, is, that the soul was not at all elementary, but was of the same substance with the heavens; which Aristotle, to distinguish from the four elements, and the changeable bodies here below, which he supposed made up of them, called *quinta essentia*. That this was Tully's opinion, is plain, from these words:

* Ch. 19, 22, 30, 31, &c.

Ergo animus (qui, ut ego dico, divinus) est, ut Euripides audet dicere Deus; et quidem si Deus aut anima aut ignis est, idem est animus hominis. Nam ut illa natura cœlestis et terrâ vacat et humore; sic utriusque harum rerum humanus animus est expers. Sin autem est quinta quædam natura ab Aristotele inducta; primum hæc et deorum, est et animorum. Hanc nos sententiam secuti, his ipsis verbis in consolatione hæc expressimus, c. 26. And then he goes on, c. 27, to repeat those his own words, which your lordship has quoted out of him, wherein he had affirmed, in his treatise *De Consolatione*, the soul not to have its original from the earth, or to be mixed or made of anything earthly; but had said, *Singularis est igitur quædam natura et vis animi, sejuncta ab his usitatis notisque naturis;* whereby, he tells us, he meant nothing but Aristotle's *quinta essentia;* which being unmixed, being that of which the gods and souls consisted, he calls it *divinum cœleste,* and concludes it eternal; it being as he speaks, *sejuncta ab omni mortali concretione.* From which it is clear, that in all his inquiry about the substance of the soul, his thoughts went not beyond the four elements, or Aristotle's *quinta essentia,* to look for it. In all which, there is nothing of immateriality, but quite the contrary.

"He was willing to believe (as good and wise men have always been) that the soul was immortal; but for that it is plain he never thought of its immateriality, but as the eastern people do, who believe the soul to be immortal, but have nevertheless no thought, no conception of its immateriality. It is remarkable what a very considerable and judicious author says in this case.* 'No opinion,' says he, 'has been so universally received as that of the immortality of the soul; but its immateriality is a truth, the knowledge whereof has not spread so far. And indeed it is extremely difficult to let into the mind of a Siamite the idea of a pure spirit. This the missionaries, who have been longest amongst them, are positive in. All the Pagans of the East do truly believe that there remains something of a man after his death, which subsists independently and separately from his body. But they give extension and figure to that which remains, and attribute to it all the same members, all the same substances, both solid and liquid, which our bodies are composed of. They only suppose that the souls are of a matter subtile enough to escape being seen or handled. Such were the shades and the manes of the Greeks and the Romans. And it is by these figures of the souls, answerable to those of the bodies, that Virgil supposed Æneas knew Palinurus, Dido, and Anchises in the other world.'

"This gentleman was not a man that travelled into those parts for his pleasure, and to have the opportunity to tell strange stories collected by chance, when he returned; but one chosen on purpose (and he seems well chosen for the purpose) to inquire into the singularities of Siam. And he has so well acquitted himself of the commission which his Epistle Dedicatory tells us he had, to inform himself exactly of what was most remarkable there, that had we but such an account of other countries of the East as he has given us of this kingdom, which he was an envoy to, we should be much better acquainted than we are with the manners, notions, and religions of that part of the world in-

* Loubère du Royaume de Siam, t. i. c. 19, § 4.

habited by civilized nations, who want neither good sense nor acuteness of reason, though not cast into the mould of the logic and philosophy of our schools.

"But to return to Cicero: it is plain that, in his inquiries about the soul, his thoughts went not at all beyond matter. This the expressions that drop from him in several places of this book evidently show. For example, 'That the souls of excellent men and women ascended into heaven; of others, that they remained here on earth,' c. 12. 'That the soul is hot, and warms the body; that on its leaving the body, it penetrates and divides, and breaks through our thick, cloudy, moist air; that it stops in the region of fire, and ascends no further, the equality of warmth and weight making that its proper place, where it is nourished and sustained with the same things wherewith the stars are nourished and sustained, and that by the convenience of its neighbourhood it shall there have a clearer view and fuller knowledge of the heavenly bodies,' c. 19. 'That the soul also, from this height, shall have a pleasant and fairer prospect of the globe of the earth, the disposition of whose parts will then lie before it in one view,' c. 20. 'That it is hard to determine what conformation, size, and place the soul has in the body: that it is too subtile to be seen; that it is in the human body, as in a house or a vessel, or a receptacle,' c. 22. All which are expressions that sufficiently evidence that he who used them had not in his mind separated materiality from the idea of the soul.

"It may perhaps be replied, that a great part of this which we find in c. 19, is said upon the principles of those who would have the soul to be *anima inflammata*, inflamed air. I grant it. But it is also to be observed, that in this 19th and the two following chapters, he does not only not deny, but even admits, that so material a thing as inflamed air may think.

"The truth of the case, in short, is this: Cicero was willing to believe the soul immortal; but when he sought in the nature of the soul itself something to establish this his belief into a certainty of it, he found himself at a loss. He confessed he knew not what the soul was; but the not knowing what it was, he argues, c. 22, was no reason to conclude it was not. And thereupon he proceeds to the repetition of what he had said in his 6th book, *de Repub.*, concerning the soul. The argument which, borrowed from Plato, he there makes use of, if it have any force in it, not only proves the soul to be immortal, but more than, I think, your lordship will allow to be true; for it proves it to be eternal, and without beginning, as well as without end: *Neque nata certe est, et æterna est*, says he.

"Indeed, from the faculties of the soul, he concludes right, 'that it is of divine original.' But as to the substance of the soul, he at the end of this discourse concerning its faculties, c. 25, as well as at the beginning of it, c. 22, is not ashamed to own his ignorance of what it is: *Anima sit animus, ignisve, nescio; nec me pudet ut istos, fateri nescire quod nesciam. Illud, si ulla alia de re obscura affirmare possem, sive anima, sive ignis sit animus, eum jurarem esse divinum*, c. 25. So that all the certainty he could attain to about the soul was, that he was confident there was something divine in it, *i. e.*, there were faculties in the soul that could not result from the nature of matter, but must have their original from a divine power; but yet those qualities, divine as they were, he acknowledged might be placed in breath or fire, which I think your lordship will not deny to be material substances. So that all those divine qualities, which he so much and so justly extols in the soul, led him not, as appears, so much as to any the least thought of immateriality. This is demonstration that he built them not upon an exclusion of materiality out of the soul; for he avowedly professes he does not know but breath or fire might be this thinking thing in us: and in all his considerations about the substance of the soul itself, he stuck in air or fire, or Aristotle's *quinta essentia;* for beyond those it is evident he went not.

"But with all his proofs out of Plato, to whose authority he defers so much, with all the arguments his vast reading and great parts could furnish him with for the immortality of the soul, he was so little satisfied, so far from being certain, so far from any thought that he had or could prove it, that he over and over again professes his ignorance and doubt of it. In the beginning, he enumerates the several opinions of the philosophers, which he had well studied, about it. And then, full of uncertainty, says, *Harum sententiarum quæ vera sit, Deus aliquis viderit; quæ verisimillima magna quæstio,* c. 11. And towards the latter end, having gone them all over again, and one after another examined them, he professes himself still at a loss, not knowing on which to pitch, nor what to determine. *Mentis acies,* says he, *seipsam intuens, nonnunquam hebescit, ob eamque causam contemplandi diligentiam omittimus. Itaque dubitans, circumspectans, hæsitans, multa adversa revertens, tanquam in rate in mari immenso, nostra vehitur oratio,* c. 30. And to conclude this argument, when the person he introduces as discoursing with him tells him he is resolved to keep firm to the belief of immortality, Tully answers, c. 32, *Laudo id quidem, et si nihil animis oportet considere: movemur enim sæpe aliquo acute concluso; labamus, mutamusque sententiam clarioribus etiam in rebus; in his est enim aliqua obscuritas.*

"So immovable is that truth delivered by the Spirit of Truth, that though the light of nature gave some obscure glimmering, some uncertain hopes of a future state; yet human reason could attain to no clearness, no certainty about it, but that it was JESUS CHRIST alone who had brought life and immortality to light, through the gospel.* Though we are now told, that to own the inability of natural reason to bring immortality to light, or, which passes for the same, to own principles upon which the immateriality of the soul (and, as it is urged, consequently, its immortality) cannot be demonstratively proved, does lessen the belief of this article of revelation, which JESUS CHRIST alone has brought to light, and which, consequently, the scripture assures us is established and made certain only by revelation. This would not perhaps have seemed strange from those who are justly complained of, for slighting the revelation of the gospel, and therefore would not be much regarded, if they should contradict so plain a text of scripture, in favour of their all-sufficient reason. But what use the promoters of scepticism and infidelity, in an age so much suspected by your lordship, may make of

* 2 Tim. i. 10.

what comes from one of your great authority and learning, may deserve your consideration.

"And thus, my lord, I hope I have satisfied you concerning Cicero's opinion about the soul, in his first book of Tusculan Questions; which, though I easily believe, as your lordship says, you are no stranger to, yet I humbly conceive you have not shown (and upon a careful perusal of that treatise again, I think I may boldly say you cannot show) one word in it that expresses anything like a notion in Tully of the soul's immateriality, or its being an immaterial substance.

"From what you bring out of Virgil, your lordship concludes,* 'that he, no more than Cicero, does me any kindness in this matter, being both asserters of the soul's immortality.' My lord, were not the question of the soul's immateriality, according to custom, changed here into that of its immortality, which I am no less an asserter of than either of them, Cicero and Virgil do me all the kindness I desired of them in this matter; and that was to show that they attributed the word *spiritus* to the soul of man, without any thought of its immateriality; and this the verses you yourself bring out of Virgil,†

'Et cum frigida mors animæ seduxerit artus,
Omnibus umbra locis adero; dabis, improbe, poenas'

confirm, as well as those I quoted out of his sixth Book; and for this M. de la Loubère shall be my witness, in the words above set down out of him; where he shows that there be those amongst the heathens of our days, as well as Virgil and others amongst the ancient Greeks and Romans, who thought the souls or ghosts of men departed did not die with the body, without thinking them to be perfectly immaterial; the latter being much more incomprehensible to them than the former. And what Virgil's notion of the soul is, and that *corpus*, when put in contradistinction to the soul, signifies nothing but the gross tenement of flesh and bones, is evident from this verse of his Æneid, 6, where he calls the souls which yet were visible,

——— 'Tenues sine corpore vitæ.'

"Your lordship's answer ‡ concerning what is said, Eccles. xii., turns wholly upon Solomon's taking the soul to be immortal, which was not what I question; all that I quoted that place for, was to show that spirit in English might properly be applied to the soul, without any notion of its immateriality, as רוח was by Solomon, which, whether he thought the souls of men to be immaterial, does little appear in that passage where he speaks of the souls of men and beasts together, as he does. But further, what I contended for is evident from that place, in that the word spirit is there applied by our translators to the souls of beasts, which your lordship, I think, does not rank amongst the immaterial, and consequently immortal spirits, though they have sense and spontaneous motion.

"But you say, § 'if the soul be not of itself a free, thinking substance, you do not see what foundation there is in nature for a day of judgment.' Answer. Though the heathen world did not of old, nor do to this day,

* First Answer.   † Æneid. 4. 385.   ‡ First Answer.   § Ibid.

see a foundation in nature for a day of judgment; yet in revelation, if that will satisfy your lordship, every one may see a foundation for a day of judgment, because God has positively declared it; though God has not by that revelation taught us what the substance of the soul is; nor has anywhere said, that the soul of itself is a free agent. Whatsoever any created substance is, it is not of itself, but is by the good pleasure of its Creator: whatever degrees of perfection it has, it has from the bountiful hand of its Maker. For it is true in a natural, as well as a spiritual sense, what St. Paul says,* 'Not that we are sufficient of ourselves to think anything as of ourselves, but our sufficiency is of God.'

"But your lordship, as I guess by your following words, would argue, that a material substance cannot be a free agent; whereby I suppose you only mean, that you cannot see or conceive how a solid substance should begin, stop, or change its own motion. To which give me leave to answer, that when you can make it conceivable how any created, finite, dependent substance can move itself, or alter or stop its own motion, which it must to be a free agent, I suppose you will find it no harder for God to bestow this power on a solid than an unsolid created substance. Tully, in the place above quoted,† could not conceive this power to be in anything but what was from eternity: *Cum pateat igitur æternum id esse quod seipsum moveat quis est qui hanc naturam animis esse tributam neget?* But though you cannot see how any created substance, solid or not solid, can be a free agent, (pardon me, my lord, if I put in both, till your lordship please to explain it of either, and show the manner how either of them can of itself move itself or anything else,) yet I do not think you will so deny men to be free agents, from the difficulty there is to see how they are free agents, as to doubt whether there be foundation enough for a day of judgment.

"It is not for me to judge how far your lordship's speculations reach; but finding in myself nothing to be truer than what the wise Solomon tells me, ‡ 'As thou knowest not what is the way of the spirit, nor how the bones do grow in the womb of her that is with child; even so thou knowest not the works of God, who maketh all things;' I gratefully receive and rejoice in the light of revelation, which sets me at rest in many things, the manner whereof my poor reason can by no means make out to me. Omnipotency, I know, can do anything that contains in it no contradiction; so that I readily believe whatever God has declared, though my reason find difficulties in it, which it cannot master. As in the present case, God having revealed that there shall be a day of judgment, I think that foundation enough to conclude men are free enough to be made answerable for their actions, and to receive according to what they have done; though how man is a free agent, surpasses my explication or comprehension.

"In answer to the place I brought out of St. Luke,§ your lordship asks, ‖ 'Whether from these words of our Saviour it follows that a spirit is only an appearance? I answer, No; nor do I know who drew such an inference from them: but it follows, that in apparitions there is

* 2 Cor. iii. 5.   † Tus. Quæst. l. i. c. 23.   ‡ Eccles. xi. 5.
§ Luke xxiv. 39.   ‖ First Answer.

something that appears, and that that which appears is not wholly immaterial; and yet this was properly called πνεῦμα, and was often looked upon by those who called it πνεῦμα in Greek, and now call it spirit in English, to be the ghost or soul of one departed; which, I humbly conceive, justifies my use of the word spirit, for a thinking, voluntary agent, whether material or immaterial.

"Your lordship says,* 'that I grant, that it cannot upon these principles be demonstrated, that the spiritual substance in us is immaterial:' from whence you conclude, 'that then my grounds of certainty from ideas are plainly given up.' This being a way of arguing that you often make use of, I have often had occasion to consider it, and cannot after all see the force of this argument. I acknowledge that this or that proposition cannot upon my principles be demonstrated; *ergo*, I grant this proposition to be false, that certainty consists in the perception of the agreement or disagreement of ideas. For that is my ground of certainty, and till that be given up, my grounds of certainty are not given up."

* First Answer.

AN EXAMINATION
OF
P. MALEBRANCHE'S OPINION
OF
SEEING ALL THINGS IN GOD.

[IT would here be altogether out of place to attempt an outline of Malebranche's whole philosophy, since only a very small portion of it is attacked in the following treatise by Locke. Besides, the merit of Malebranche lies not, I think, in the invention of a system, but in the criticism of such other systems as still preserved some credit in his time. Tennemann (Manual of the History of Philosophy, § 341,) gives an account of the doctrines of this writer. Buhle (Histoire de la Philosophie Moderne, t. iii. p. 367—425) supplies a tolerably correct and intelligible abridgment of his general views. But, stated in any other language than his own, it is to be feared that his method of reasoning will appear unsatisfactory, since the whole vitality of the Recherche de la Vérité is, in my humble opinion, to be found in the rich, polished, and flexible style in which it is written. Here it is not to be denied he possesses considerable superiority over Locke; but however ably he may write, and however subtly he may reason, it soon becomes evident, upon a diligent perusal, that his mind was too much clouded by mysticism to permit of his seeing his way clearly through the labyrinth of metaphysics. He falls perpetually into contradictions; often appears to confound the soul with its material organ, the brain; now verges towards the loftiest idealism; now adopts the tone and language of a Pantheist; and in the favourite, and perhaps the only new, part of his system, viz., that which teaches that we behold all things in God, he grows so mystical, so confused, so irreconcilable with common sense and experience, that we at length dismiss the whole speculation as a mere dream. In this light it is quite clear Locke considered it. He was no doubt restrained by the widely-extended reputation of Malebranche, as well as by his own natural politeness, from speaking of it so plainly as now becomes our duty; but yet he manages to show, in the course of his arguments, that the worthy father of the Oratory is very frequently at variance with common sense. Undeterred by this exposure, by anticipation, of his principles, Bishop Berkeley very shortly afterwards spun his famous system on Malebranche's distaff; for it is almost capable of demonstration, that the Bishop of Cloyne's idealism was hatched in the cloisters of the Oratory. I am far from desiring to undervalue the contributions which any philosopher has made towards the more complete understanding of the origin and nature of our ideas, of the powers of our mind, our relations to the First Cause of ideas, of sensations, and of knowledge; but it must be owned that the frank and earnest student of philosophy frequently finds himself called upon to exercise all his patience and forbearance, in making his way through the writings of Malebranche. Even the refutation of his errors by Locke may be said to furnish a proof of this fact, since the utter groundlessness of his suppositions now appears so self-evident, as to stand in need of no refutation. But the case was very different in Locke's time, and perhaps would be so still, had not the public mind been long ago weaned from pursuits purely speculative, in order to apply itself with undivided earnestness to the sciences which are the more immediate ministers of the progress and happiness to mankind.—ED.]

1. THE acute and ingenious author of the Recherche de la Vérité,* among a great many very fine thoughts, judicious reasonings, and uncommon reflections, has in that treatise started the notion of Seeing all Things in God, as the best way to explain the nature and manner of the ideas in our understanding. The desire I had to have my unaffected ignorance removed, has made it necessary for me to see whether this hypothesis, when examined, and the parts of it put together, can be thought to cure our ignorance, or is intelligible and satisfactory to one who would not deceive himself take words for things, and think he knows what he knows not.

2. This I observe at the entrance, that P. Malebranche having enumerated, and in the following chapters showed the difficulties of the other ways, whereby he thinks human understanding may be attempted to be explained, and how insufficient they are to give a satisfactory account of the ideas we have, erects this of Seeing all Things in God upon their ruin, as the true, because it is impossible to find a better; which argument, so far from being only argumentum ad ignorantiam, loses all its force as soon as we consider the weakness of our minds and the narrowness of our capacities, and have but humility enough to allow, that there may be many things which we cannot fully comprehend, and that God is not bound in all he does to subject his ways of operation to the scrutiny of our thoughts, and confine himself to do no

* The edition of the Recherche de la Vérité which Locke used, was that in quarto, printed at Paris, in 1678; and when he had occasion to compare it with any other, he seems always to have made use of the small octavo, printed at the same place, and in the same year. By chance it happens that this second edition is the one we have now before us, and to which we shall refer in the notes.—ED.

thing but what we must comprehend. And it will very little help to cure my ignorance, that this is the best of four or five hypotheses proposed, which are all defective; if this too has in it what is inconsistent with itself, or unintelligible to me.

3. The P. Malebranche's Recherche de la Vérité, l. 3, p. 2, c. 1, tells us, that, whatever the mind perceives, "must be actually present and intimately united to it."* That the things that the mind perceives are its own sensations, imaginations, or notions; which being in the soul, the modifications of it need no ideas to represent them. But all things exterior to the soul we cannot perceive but by the intervention of ideas, supposing that the things themselves cannot be intimately united to the soul. But because spiritual things may possibly be united to the soul, therefore he thinks it probable that they can discover themselves immediately without ideas;† though of this he doubts, because he believes not there is any substance purely intelligible, but that of God; and that though spirits can possibly unite themselves to our minds, yet, at present, we cannot entirely know them. But he speaks here principally of material things, which he says certainly cannot unite themselves to our souls in such a manner as is necessary that it should perceive them; because, being extended, the soul not being so, there is no proportion between them.

4. This is the sum of his doctrine contained in the first chapter of the second part of the third book, as far as I can comprehend it. Wherein, I confess, there are many expressions which, carrying with them, to my mind, no clear ideas,

* The words of Malebranche are—"Il faut bien remarquer qu'afin que l'esprit appercoive quelque chose, il est absolument necessaire que l'idée de cette chose lui soit actuellement présente." (Recherche de la Vérité, l. III. p. ii. c. 1.)

† On this part of his system Malebranche evidently entertained no very clear or distinct ideas. "De sorte," says he, "qu'il ne semble pas absolument necessaire d'admettre des idées pour representer à l'ame des choses spirituelles parce qu'l se peut faire qu'on les voye par elles mêmes, quoique d'une manière fort imparfaite." (t. p. 346.) In the notes on the Essay on the Human Understanding, the reader will have observed that Bishop Berkeley, who may be regarded as the Malebranche of Great Britain, entertained as nearly as possible the same opinion, with respect to the knowledge we can have of spirits. (See Book II. c. xxi. p. 210.)—Ed

are like to remove but little of my ignorance by their sounds; v. g., "What it is to be intimately united to the soul." What it is for two souls or spirits to be intimately united; for intimate union being an idea taken from bodies when the parts of one get within the surface of the other, and touch their inward parts; what is the idea of intimate union I must have between two beings that have neither of them any extension or surface? And if it be not so explained as to give me a clear idea of that union, it will make me understand very little more of the nature of the ideas in my mind, when it is said I see them in God, who, being *intimately united to the soul*, exhibits them to it; than when it is only said they are, by the appointment of God, produced in the mind by certain motions of our bodies, to which our minds are united: which, however imperfect a way of explaining this matter, will still be as good as any other that does not by clear ideas remove my ignorance of the manner of my perception.

5. But he says that "certainly material things cannot unite themselves to our souls." Our bodies are united to our souls, yes; but, says he, "not after a manner which is necessary that the soul may perceive them."* Explain this manner of union, and show wherein the difference consists between the union necessary and not necessary to perception, and then I shall confess this difficulty removed.

The reason that he gives why material things cannot be united to our souls after a manner that is necessary to the soul's perceiving them, is this, viz., "That material things being extended, and the soul not, there is no proportion between them." This, if it shows anything, shows only that a soul and a body cannot be united, because one has surface to be united by, and the other none. But it shows not why a

† To reasoning like that of Malebranche, no other answer perhaps could properly be made, but that which is here given by Locke. Having promised to explain, in a future chapter, the manner in which we obtain a knowledge of spirits, Malebranche goes on to remark of material substances, that they cannot be united to our souls in the way necessary to enable us to perceive them; and he subjoins his reason, such as it is, for this opinion. "Je parle," says he, "principallement ici des choses materielles lesquelles certainement ne peuvent s'unir à nôtre ame de la manière qu'il est necessaire afin qu'elle les appercoive, parce qu' etant étendue et l'ame ne l'etant pas il n'y a point de proportion entre-elles." (t. i. p. 340.)—ED.

soul united to a body, as ours is, cannot, by that body, have the idea of a triangle excited in it, as well as by being united to God (between whom and the soul there is as little proportion, as between any creature immaterial or material, and the soul) see in God the idea of a triangle that is in him, since we cannot conceive a triangle, whether seen in matter or in God, to be without extension.

6. He says, "There is no substance purely intelligible but that of God."* Here again I must confess myself in the dark, having no notion at all of the *substance of God;* nor being able to conceive how his is more intelligible than any other substance.

7. One thing more there is, which, I confess, stumbles me in the very foundation of this hypothesis, which stands thus: "We cannot *perceive* anything but what is *intimately united to the soul.* The reason why some things, (viz., material,) cannot be intimately united to the soul, is, because there is no proportion between the soul and them." If this be a good reason, it follows that the greater the proportion there is between the soul and any other being, the better and more intimately they can be united. Now, then, I ask, whether there be a greater proportion between God, an infinite Being, and the soul, or between finite created spirit and the soul? And yet the author says, that " he believes that there is no substance purely intelligible, but that of God," and that " we cannot entirely know created spirits

* The passage in which Malebranche states this opinion is the following:—" Il n'y a que Dieu que l'on connoisse par lui même; car encore qu'il y ait, d'autres êtres Spirituels que lui, et qui semblent être intelligible par leur nature, il n'y a présentement que lui seul, qui penetre l'esprit et se decouvre a lui. Nous ne voyons que Dieu d'une vue immediate et directe. Peut être même qu'il n'y a que lui, qui puisse éclairer l'esprit par se propre substance. Enfin dans cette vie ce n'est que par l'union que nous avons avec lui, que nous sommes capable de connoitre ce que nous connoissons." (t. i. p. 374.) The error of this philosopher appears to have originated in the pious desire to exalt the greatness of God, by dwelling on the weakness and insignificance of man; but, like many other writers equally well-meaning, he fell into what, written with other intentions, would have been mere impiety. For since it is God who created the human understanding, who has bestowed on us all our faculties, who, in short, has made us what we are, it cannot be consistent with true piety to depreciate our own intellects, or to seek to degrade and vilify the powers with which we have been gifted by Omnipotence.—ED.

at present." Make this out upon your principles of intimate union and proportion, and then they will be of some use to the clearing of your hypothesis, otherwise intimate union and proportion are only sounds serving to amuse, not instruct us.

8. In the close of this chapter he enumerates the several ways whereby he thinks we come by ideas, and compares them severally with his own way; which, how much more intelligible it is than either of those, the following chapters will show; to which I shall proceed, when I have observed that it seems a bold determination, when he says, that it must be one of these ways, and we can see objects no other.* Which assertion must be built on this good opinion of our capacities that God cannot make the creatures operate but in ways conceivable to us. That we cannot discourse and reason about them further than we conceive, is a great truth; and it would be well if we would not, but would ingenuously own the shortness of our sight where we do not see. To say there can be no other, because we conceive no other, does not, I confess, much instruct. And if I should say, that it is possible God has made our souls so, and so united them to our bodies that, upon certain motions made in our bodies by external objects, the soul should have such or such perceptions or ideas, though in a way inconceivable to us; this perhaps would appear as true and as instructive a proposition as what is so positively laid down.

9. Though the Peripatetic Doctrine of the Species† does

* It was, no doubt, very far from being the intention of Malebranche to set up his own understanding as the measure of the Infinite; but yet, without appearing to have any such design, he contrives to make it felt that God can furnish us with ideas by no other means, and in no other ways, than such as he ventures to enumerate. "Nous assurons donc qu'il est absolument necessaire, que les idées que nous avons des corps, et de tous les autres objets que nous n'appercevons point par eux-mêmes, viennent de ces mêmes corps, ou de ces objets; ou bien que nôtre ame, ait la puissance de produire ces idées : ou que Dieu les ait produites avec elle en la creant, ou qu'il les produire toutes les fois qu'on pense à quelque objet: ou que l'ame ait en elle même toutes les perfections qu'elle voit dans ces corps: ou enfin qu'elle soit unie avec un être tout parfait, et qui renferme généralement toutes les perfections des êtres éréez." (L. III. Pt. II. c. i. f. i. p. 346.)—Ed.

† The passage in which Malebranche ridicules the doctrine of species visible, maintained by the Peripatetics, is witty enough; but when the reader has considered it carefully, I very much question whether he will allow it to be a correct representation of the ancient system, or in any

not at all satisfy me, yet I think it were not hard to show, that it is as easy to account for the difficulties he charges on it, as for those his own hypothesis is laden with. But t being not my business to defend what I do not understand, nor to prefer the learned gibberish of the schools to what way conclusive against it. "On assure donc qu'il n'y a aucune vraisemblance, que les objets envoyent des images, ou des espèces qui leur resemblent; de quoi voici quelques raisons. La premiere se tire de l'impenétrabilité des corps. Tous les objets, comme le soliel, les etoiles, et tous ceux qui sont proche de nos yeux, ne peuvent pas envoyer des espèces qui soient d'autre nature qu'eux: c'est pourquoi les philosophes disent ordinairement, que ces espèces sont grossieres et materielles, à la difference des espèces expresses qui sont spiritualisées. Ces espèces impresses des objets sont donc de petits corps: elles ne peuvent donc pas se penetrer ni tous les espaces qui sont depuis la terre jusqu'au ciel, lesquels en doivent être tous remplis. D'ou il est facile de conclure qu'elles devroient se froisser, et se briser, les unes allant d'un côté et les autres de l'autre, si l'on voyoit les objets par leur moyen." (L. III. Pt. II. c. 2, b. i. p. 348.) Hobbes, also, (Human Nature, chap. ii. § 4,) makes himself merry with the Peripatetic visible species; but when he comes in his turn to explain the act of sight, he proposes an hypothesis very little more intelligible. "I have shown," says he, "that no motion is generated but by a body contiguous and moved: from whence it is manifest, that the immediate cause of sense or perception consists in this—that the first organ of sense is touched and pressed. For when the uttermost part of the organ is pressed, it no sooner yields, but the part next within it is pressed also; and in this manner the pressure or motion is propagated through all the parts of the organ, to the innermost. And thus also the pressure of the uttermost part proceeds from the pressure of some more remote body, and so continually, till we come to that from which, as from its fountain, we derive the phantasm or idea that is made in us by our sense. And this, whatsoever it be, is that we commonly call the object. Sense, therefore, is some internal motion in the sentient, generated by some internal motion of the parts of the object, and propagated through all the medium to the innermost part of the organ. By which words I have almost defined what sense is." (Elements of Philosophy, Pt. IV. c. xxv. § 2.) Descartes, with great good sense, regarded the manner by which images are conveyed to the mind as wholly inexplicable. Antoine Le Grand, however, the best expositor of his philosophy, has a passage which may be worth introducing here. "Nulla est necessitas tales *imagines* ad visiones, aut alius sensus explicandos admittendi, cum videamus multa posse in animis nostris affectiones, et commotiones producere, quæ cum objectis, quæ significant, similitudines non habent: ut cum *verba* ore pronuntiata, aut papyro mandata strages hominum, urbrum eversiones, maris procellas repræsentant; aut amoris odiive effectûs excitant; quæ tamen *representationes*, seu cogitationes nullam prorsus similitudinem habent, cum illis rebus, quas significant. Deinde explicari nos potest, quomodò tales imagines ab objectis effluere possuit." (Instit. Philosoph. Pt. VIII. art. x. p. 431)—ED.

is yet unintelligible to me in P. M., I shall only take notice of so much of his objections, as concerns what I guess to be the truth. Though I do not think any material species, carrying the resemblance of things by a continual flux from the body we perceive, bring the perception of them to our senses; yet I think the perception we have of bodies at a distance from ours may be accounted for, as far as we are capable of understanding it, by the motion of particles of matter coming from them and striking on our organs.* In feeling and tasting there is immediate contact. Sound is not unintelligibly explained by a vibrating motion communicated to the medium, and the effluviums of odorous bodies will, without any great difficulties, account for smells. And therefore P. M. makes his objections only against visible species, as the most difficult to be explained by material causes, as indeed they are. But he that shall allow extreme smallness in the particles of light, and exceeding swiftness in their motion; and the great porosity that must be granted in bodies, if we compare gold, which wants them not, with air, the medium wherein the rays of light come to our eyes, and that of a million of rays that rebound from any visible area of any body, perhaps the thousandth or ten thousandth part coming to the eye, are enough to move the retina sufficiently to cause a sensation in the mind, will not find any great difficulty in the objections which are orought from the impenetrability of matter; and these rays ruffling and breaking one another in the medium which is full of them. As to what is said, that from one point we can see a great number of objects, that is no objection against the species, or visible appearances of bodies, being brought into the eye by the rays of light; for the bottom of the eye or retina, which, in regard of these rays, is the place of vision, is far from being a point. Nor is it true, that, though the eye be in any one place, yet that the sight is performed in one point; i. e., that the rays that bring those visible species do all meet in a point; for they cause their distinct sensations, by striking on distinct parts of the retina, as is plain in optics; and

* This notion appears to me as completely unfounded, to say the least of it, as that of the Peripatetics; for if particles of matter may thus travel from the dog-star to us, why may not the image or visible species of the star? I am apt to think that the hostility waged against visible species was founded on a misunderstanding.—ED.

the figure they paint there must be of some considerable bigness, since it takes up on the retina an area whose diameter is at least thirty seconds of a circle, whereof the circumference is in the retina, and the centre somewhere in the crystalline, as a little skill in optics will manifest to any one that considers, that few eyes can perceive an object less than thirty minutes of a circle, whereof the eye is the centre. And he that will but reflect on that seeming odd experiment, of seeing only the two outward ones of three bits of paper stuck up against a wall, at about half a foot, or a foot one from another, without seeing the middle one at all, whilst his eye remains fixed in the same posture, must confess that vision is not made in a point, when it is plain, that looking with one eye, there is always one part between the extremes of the area that we see, which is not seen at the same time that we perceive the extremes of it; though the looking with two eyes, or the quick turning of the axis of the eye to the part we would distinctly view, when we look but with one, does not let us take notice of it.

10. What I have here said, I think sufficient to make intelligible how by material rays of light, visible species may be brought into the eye, notwithstanding any of P. M.'s objections against so much of material causes as my hypothesis is concerned in. But when by this means an image is made on the retina, how we see it, I conceive no more than when I am told we see it in God. How we see it is, I confess, what I understand not in the one or in the other; only it appears to me more difficult to conceive a distinct visible image in the uniform, unvariable essence of God, that in variously modifiable matter; but the manner how I see either, still escapes my comprehension. Impressions made on the retina by rays of light, I think I understand; and motions from thence continued to the brain may be conceived, and that these produce ideas in our minds, I am persuaded, but in a manner to me incomprehensible. This I can resolve only into the good pleasure of God, whose ways are past finding out. And, I think, I know it as well when I am told these are ideas that the motion of the animal spirits, by a law established by God, produces in me, as when I am told they are ideas I see in God. The ideas it is certain I have, and God both ways is the original cause of my hav

ing them; but the manner how I come by them, how it is that I perceive, I confess I understand not;* though it be plain motion has to do in the producing of them: and motion, so modified, is appointed to be the cause of our having of them; as appears by the curious and artificial structure of the eye, accommodated to all the rules of refraction and dioptrics, that so visible objects might be exactly and regularly painted on the bottom of the eye.

11. The change of bigness in the ideas of visible objects, by distance and optic-glasses, which is the next argument he uses against visible species, is a good argument against them, as supposed by the Peripatetics, but when considered, would persuade one that we see the figures and magnitudes of things rather in the bottom of our eyes than in God; the idea we have of them and their grandeur being still proportioned to the bigness of the area, on the bottom of our eyes, that is affected by the rays which paint the image there, and we may be said to see the picture in the retina, as, when it is pricked, we are truly said to feel the pain in our finger.

12. In the next place, where he says, that when we look on a cube "we see all its sides equal." This, I think, is a mistake; and I have in another place shown how the idea we have from a regular solid, is not the true idea of that solid, but such an one as by custom (as the name of it does) serves to excite our judgment to form such an one.

13. What he says of seeing an object several millions of leagues, the very same instant that it is uncovered, I think may be shown to be a mistake in matter of fact. For by observations made on the satellites of Jupiter, it is discovered that light is successively propagated, and is about ten minutes coming from the sun to us.†

14. By what I have said, I think it may be understood how we may conceive, that from remote objects material causes may reach our senses, and therein produce several

* The same caution, forbearance, and good sense, which constitute the characteristics of the Essay on the Human Understanding are visible here, where, in the particular instance before him, Locke accurately marks the limits between the knowable and unknowable.—ED.

† Recent experiments, I believe, have rendered it extremely probable that light makes its passage from the sun to the earth in seven minutes and a half.—ED.

motions that may be the causes of ideas in us; notwithstanding what P. M. has said in this second chapter against material species. I confess his arguments are good against those species as usually understood by the Peripatetics. But, since my principles have been said to be conformable to the Aristotelian philosophy, I have endeavoured to remove the difficulties it is charged with, as far as my opinion is concerned in them.

15. His third chapter is to confute the "opinion of those who think our minds have a power to produce the ideas of things on which they would think, and that they are excited to produce them by the impressions which objects make on the body." One who thinks ideas are nothing but perceptions of the mind annexed to certain motions of the body by the will of God, who hath ordered such perceptions always to accompany such motions, though we know not how they are produced, does in effect conceive those ideas or peceptions to be only passions of the mind, when produced in it, whether we will or no, by external objects. But he conceives them to be a mixture of action and passion when the mind attends to them or revives them in the memory. Whether the soul has such a power as this we shall perhaps have occasion to consider hereafter; and this power our author does not deny, since in this very chapter he says, "When we conceive a square by pure understanding, we can yet imagine it; i. e., perceive it in ourselves by tracing an image of it on the brain." Here, then, he allows the soul power to trace images on the brain, and perceive them. This, to me, is matter of new perplexity in this hypothesis; for if the soul be so united to the brain as to trace images on it, and perceive them, I do not see how this consists with what he says a little before in the first chapter, viz., "That certainly material things cannot be united to our souls after a manner necessary to its perceiving them."

16. That which is said about objects exciting ideas in us by motion; and our reviving the ideas we have once got in our memories, does not, I confess, fully explain the manner how it is done. In this I frankly avow my ignorance, and should be glad to find in him anything that would clear it to me; but in his explications I find these difficulties which I cannot get over.

17. The mind cannot produce ideas, says he, because they are "real spiritual beings,"* i. e., substances; for so is the conclusion of that paragraph, where he mentions it as an absurdity to think they are "annihilated when they are not present to the mind." And the whole force of this argument would persuade one to understand him so; though I do not remember that he anywhere speaks it out, or in direct terms calls them substances.

18. I shall here only take notice how inconceivable it is to me, that a spiritual, i. e., an unextended, substance should represent to the mind an extended figure, v. g., a triangle of unequal sides, or two triangles of different magnitudes. Next, supposing I could conceive an unextended substance to represent a figure, or be the idea of a figure, the difficulty still remains to conceive how it is my soul sees it. Let this substantial being be ever so sure, and the picture never so clear; yet how we see it is to me inconceivable. Intimate union, were it as intelligible of two unextended substances, as of two bodies, would not yet reach perception, which is something beyond union. But yet a little lower he agrees, that an idea "is not a substance," but yet affirms it is "a spiritual thing." This spiritual thing, therefore, must either be a spiritual substance, or a mode of a spiritual substance, or a relation; for besides these I have no conception of any thing. And if any shall tell me it is a mode, it must be a mode of the substance of God; which, besides that it will be strange to mention any modes in the simple essence of God; whosoever shall propose any such modes as a way to explain the nature of our ideas, proposes to me something inconceivable, as a means to conceive what I do not yet know; and so, bating a new phrase, teaches me nothing, but leaves me as much in the dark as one can be where he conceives nothing. So that supposing ideas real spiritual things never so much, if they are neither substances nor modes, let them be what they will, I am no more instructed in their nature than when I am told they are perceptions, such as I find them. And I appeal to my reader, whether that hypothesis be to be preferred for its easiness to be understood, which

* On the nature of ideas, see Plato, on the Parmenides, and Diogenes Laertius, iii. 1. 12; x. 1. 20. Aristotle appears to have thought that the whole doctrine of ideas arose from the misemployment of poetical metaphors. (Metaphys. xii. 5.)—ED.

is explained by real beings, that are neither substances nor modes.

19. In the fourth chapter he proves, that we do not see objects by ideas that are created with us; because the ideas we have even of one very simple figure, v. g., a triangle, are not infinite, though there may be infinite triangles. What this proves I will not here examine; but the reason he gives being built on his hypotheses, I cannot get over, and that is, that "it is not for want of ideas, or that infinite is not present to us, but it is only for want of capacity and extension of our souls, because the extension of our spirits is very narrow and limited." To have a limited extension, is to have some extension, which agrees but ill with what is before said of our souls, that they "have no extension." By what he says here and in other places, one would think he were to be understood as if the soul, being but a small extension, could not at once receive all the ideas conceivable in infinite space, because but a little part of that infinite space can be applied to the soul at once. To conceive thus of the soul's intimate union with an infinite being, and by that union receiving of ideas, leads one as naturally into as gross thoughts, as a country maid would have of an infinite butter-print, in which was engraven figures of all sorts and sizes, the several parts whereof being, as there was occasion, applied to her lump of butter, left on it the figure or idea there was present need of. But whether any one would thus explain our ideas I will not say, only I know not well how to understand what he says here, with what he says before of *union* in a better sense.

20. He further says, that had we a magazine of all ideas that are necessary for seeing things, they would be of no use, since the mind could not know which to choose, and set before itself to see the sun. What he here means by the sun is hard to conceive; and, according to his hypothesis of Seeing all Things in God, how can he know that there is any such real being in the world as the sun? Did he ever see the sun? No; but on occasion of the presence of the sun to his eyes, he has seen the idea of the sun in God, which God has exhibited to him; but the sun, because it cannot be united to his soul, he cannot see. How then does he know that there is a sun which he never saw? And since God

does all things by the most compendious ways, what need is there that God should make a sun that we might see its idea in him when he pleased to exhibit it, when this might as well be done without any real sun at all.*

21. He further says, that God does not actually produce in us as many new ideas as we every moment perceive different things. Whether he has proved this or no, I will not examine.

22. But he says, that "we have at all times actually in ourselves the ideas of all things." Then we have always actually in ourselves the ideas of all triangles, which was but now denied, "but we have them confusedly." If we see them in God, and they are not in him confusedly, I do not understand how we can see them in God confusedly.

23. In the fifth chapter he tells us, "all things are in God, even the most corporeal and earthly, but after a manner altogether spiritual, and which we cannot comprehend." Here, therefore, he and I are alike ignorant of these good words; "material things are in God after a spiritual manner," signify nothing to either of us; and "spiritual manner" signifies no more but this, that material things are in God immaterially. This and the like are ways of speaking which our vanity has found out to cover, not remove, our ignorance. But "material things are in God," because "their ideas are in God, and those ideas which God had of them before the world was created, are not at all different from himself." This seems to me to come very near saying, not only that there is variety in God, since we see variety in what "is not different from himself," but that material things are God, or

* This doctrine Berkeley maintained in good earnest; as also did honest Arthur Collier, who, whether he had met with the works of Berkeley or not, had completely imbibed his spirit of philosophising. The following is the manner in which he blots the sun and moon out of the external universe, and reduces them to creatures of the imagination. "Let a man," says he, "whilst he looks upon any object, as suppose the moon, press or distort one of his eyes with his finger. This done, he will perceive or see two moons, at some distance from each other; one, as it were, proceeding or sliding off from the other. Now both these moons are equally external, or seen by us as external; and yet one *at least* of these is not external, there being but one moon supposed to be in the heavens, or without us. Therefore an object is *seen* by us as external, which is *not indeed* external, which is again the thing to be shown." (Clavus Universalis, p. 17.)

a part of him;* which, though I do not think to be what our author designs; yet thus I fear he must be forced to talk, who thinks he knows God's understanding so much better than his own, that he will make use of the divine intellect to explain the human.

24. In the sixth chapter he comes more particularly to explain his own doctrine, where first he says, "the ideas of all beings are in God." Let it be so, God has the idea of a triangle, of a horse, of a river, just as we have; for hitherto this signifies no more, for we see them as they are in him; and so the ideas that are in him, are the ideas we perceive: Thus far I then understand God hath the same ideas we have. This tells us, indeed, that there are ideas, which was agreed before, and I think nobody denies, but tells me not yet what they are.

25. Having said that they are in God, the next thing he tells us is, that we "can see them in God." His proof, that "our souls can see them in God," is, because God is most straitly united to our souls by his presence, insomuch, that one may say, God is the place of spirits, as spaces are the places of bodies;" in which there is not, I confess, one word that I can understand.† For, first, in what sense can he

* Locke's charity here induces him to put an interpretation on Malebranche's theory, which, upon examination, may perhaps be found to be somewhat too lenient. Whatever he may have intended, he taught Pantheism: piously, no doubt, but not the less certainly.

† This talking about the place of spirits is nothing but a fragment of the ancient jargon of the schools; and probably means nothing more than that all existence being upheld by God, must necessarily be surrounded by the power of God, or be comprehended within his sphere. But then it will inevitably follow that God is as much the place of bodies as of spirits, since both equally derive their existence from him. The original passages, which the reader may desire to compare with Locke's translation, are as follows:—"Il faut sçavoir que Dieu est tres-etroitement mie à nos ames par sa presence, ensorte qu'on peut dire qu'il est le lieu des esprits, de même que les espaces sont le lieu des corps." (L. III. pt. 2, chap. vii. t. i. p. 363.) In the next place where this doctrine is asserted, Malebranche adds, that God *is the intelligible world:* "Demeurons donc dans ce sentiment, que Dieu est le monde intelligible, ou le lieu des esprits, de même que le monde matériel est le lieu des corps. (p. 372.) Here, as the reader will perceive, there is a prodigious confusion of ideas. First, God is the intelligible world; which means, if it mean anything, that God is alone intelligible, or that everything which is intelligible forms a part of God; which, when thoroughly sifted, is the real doctrine of Malebranche, and can by no degree of ingenuity be dis-

say that "spaces are the places of bodies," when he makes body and space, or extension, to be the same thing? So that I do no more understand what he means, when he says "spaces are the places of bodies," than if he had said, bodies are the places of bodies. But when this simile is applied to God and spirits, it makes this saying, that "God is the place of spirits," either to be merely metaphorical, and so signifies literally nothing; or else, being literal, makes us conceive that spirits move up and down, and have their distances and intervals in God, as bodies have in space. When I am told in which of these senses he is to be understood, I shall be able to see how far it helps us to understand the nature of ideas. But is not God as straitly united to bodies as to spirits? For he is also present, even where they are, but yet they see not these ideas in him. He therefore adds, "that the soul can see in God the works of God, supposing God would discover to it what there is in him to represent them," viz., the ideas that are in him. Union, therefore, is not the cause of this seeing; for the soul may be united to God, and yet not see the ideas are in him, till he *discover* them to it; so that after all I am but where I was. I have ideas, that I know; but I would know what they are, and to that I am yet only told, that *I see them in God.* I ask, how *I see them in God?* And it is answered, by my *intimate union* with God, for he is everywhere present. I answer, if that were enough, bodies are also intimately united with God, for he is everywhere present; besides, if that were enough, I should see all the ideas that are in God. No, but only those that he pleases to *discover*. Tell me wherein this discovery lies, besides barely making me see them, and you explain the manner of my having ideas: otherwise, all that has been said amounts to no more but this, that I have those ideas that it pleases God I should have, but by ways that I know not; and of this mind I was before, and am not got one jot further.

tinguished from Pantheism. Again, the material world is the place of bodies: but it is these bodies that constitute the material world; and if we must make use of the scholastic jargon, at all, we ought to say that space is the place of the material world, otherwise we affirm that a thing is its own place, which it requires all the politeness of Locke to denominate anything but nonsense.

26. In the next paragraph he calls them "beings, representative beings." But whether these beings are substances, modes, or relations, I am not told; and so by being told they are spiritual beings, I know no more but that they are something, I know not what, and that I knew before.

27. To explain this matter a little further, he adds: "It must be observed, that it cannot be concluded that souls see the essence of God in that they see all things in God; because what they see is very imperfect, and God is very perfect. They see matter divisible, figured, &c., and in God there is nothing divisible and figured: for God is all being, because he is infinite and comprehends all things; but he is not any being in particular. Whereas what we see is but some one or more beings in particular; and we do not at all comprehend that perfect simplicity of God which contains all beings. Moreover, one may say, that we do not so much see the ideas of things as the things themselves, which the ideas represent. For when, for example, one sees a square, one says not that one sees the idea of a square which is united to the soul, but only the square that is without." I do not pretend not to be short-sighted; but if I am not duller than ordinary, this paragraph shows that P. M. himself is at a stand in this matter, and comprehends not what it is wee in God, or how. In the fourth chapter he says, in express words, that "it is necessary that at all times we should have actually in ourselves the ideas of all things."* And in this very chapter, a little lower, he says, that "all beings are present to our minds," and that we have "general ideas antecedent to particular." And in the eighth chapter, that we are never without the "general idea of being;" and yet here he says, "that which we see is but one or more beings in particular." And after having taken a great deal

* This strange hypothesis is thus stated by Malebranche:—"Il est necessaire qu'en tout tems nous ayons actuellement dans nous mêmes les idées de toutes choses, puisqu'en tout tems nous pouvons penser à toutes choses: ce que nous ne pourrions pas, si nous ne les appercevions déja confusément, c'est à-dire si un nombre infini d'idées n'étoit present à notre esprit." (L. III. pt. 2, chap. iv. t. i. p. 357.) To this notion he again alludes in chap. vi. p. 366, where he says: "Il est constant, et tout le monde le sçait par expérience, que lors que nous voulons penser à quelque chose en particulier, nous envisageons d'abourd tous les être, et nous nous appliquons ensuite à la consideration de l'objet

of pains to prove, that "we cannot possibly see things themselves, but only ideas," here he tells us "we do not so much see the ideas of things as the things themselves." In this uncertainty of the author what it is we see, I am to be excused if my eyes see not more clearly in his hypothesis than he himself does.

28. He further tells us in this sixth chapter, that "we see all beings, because God wills that that which is in him that represents them should be discovered to us." This tells us only, that there are ideas of things in God, and that we see them when he pleases to discover them; but what does this show us more of the nature of those ideas, or of the discovery of them, wherein that consists, than he that says, without pretending to know what they are, or how they are made, that ideas are in our minds when God pleases to produce them there, by such motions as he has appointed to do it? The next argument for our "Seeing all things in God," is in these words: "But the strongest of all the reasons is the manner in which the mind perceives all things. It is evident, and all the world knows it by experience, that when we would think of anything in particular, we at first cast our view upon all beings, and afterwards we apply ourselves to the consideration of the object which we desire to think on." This argument has no other effect on me, but to make me doubt the more of the truth of this doctrine. First, Because this, which he calls the *strongest reason of all*, is built upon matter of fact, which I connot find to be so in myself. I do not observe, that when I would think of a triangle I first think of *all beings;* whether these words *all beings* be to be taken here in their proper sense, or very improperly for *being* in general. Nor do I think my country neighbours do so, when they first wake in the morning, who, I imagine, do not find it impossible to think of a lame horse

que nous souhaitons de voir." It would not be easy to exceed the cool hardihood of this assertion, though the object of Malebranche in making it is perfectly intelligible; for since he maintains that the substance of God is intimately united with our souls; and since the ideas, or archetypes of all things, past, present, and to come, are unquestionably in God, it follows as a necessary consequence of his theory, that, as the mind of God is open to our contemplation, like an infinite mirror, we must be able to perceive, however dimly and obscurely, whatever images, so to speak, are painted there.

they have, or their blighted corn, till they have run over in their minds *all beings* that are, and then pitch on Dapple; or else begin to think of *being* in general, which is *being* abstracted from all its inferior species, before they come to think of the fly in their sheep, or the tares in their corn. For I am apt to think that the greatest part of mankind very seldom, if ever at all, think of *being* in general, i.e., abstracted from all its inferior species and individuals. But taking it to be so, that a carrier when he would think of a remedy for his galled horse, or a footboy for an excuse for some fault he has committed, begins with casting his eye upon all things;* how does this make out the conclusion? Therefore "we can desire to see all objects, whence it follows, that all beings are present to our minds." Which presence signifies that we see them, or else it signifies nothing at all. They are all actually always seen by us; which, how true, let every one judge.

29. The words wherein he pursues this argument stand thus: "Now it is indubitable that we cannot desire to see any particular object without seeing it already, although confusedly, and in general. So that being able to desire to see all beings, sometimes one, sometimes another, it is certain that all beings are present to our spirits; and it seems all beings could not be present to our spirits but because God is present to them, i.e., he that contains all things in the simplicity of his being." I must leave it to others to judge how far it is blamable in me, but so it is, that I cannot make to myself the links of this chain to hang together; and methinks if a man would have studied obscurity, he could not have writ more unintelligible than this. "We can desire to see all beings, sometimes one, sometimes another; therefore we do already see all things, because we cannot desire to see any particular object, but what we see already confusedly and in general." The discourse here is about ideas, which he says are real things, and we see in God. In taking this along with me, to make it prove anything to his purpose, the argument must, as it seems to me stand thus: We can desire to have all ideas, sometimes one, sometimes

* This humorous way of illustrating the philosophy of Malebranche though it may not be thought a sufficient refutation, helps nevertheless to show its absurdity.

another; therefore we have already all ideas, because we cannot desire to have any particular idea, but what we have already *confusedly* and *in general*. What can be meant here by having any *particular* idea *confusedly and in general*, I confess I cannot conceive, unless it be a capacity in us to have them; and in that sense the whole argument amounts to no more but this: We have all ideas, because we are capable of having all ideas, and so proves not at all that we actually have them, by being united to God, who *contains them all in the simplicity of his being*. That anything else is, or can be meant by it, I do not see; for that which we desire to see, being nothing but what we see already, (for if it can be anything else, the argument falls, and proves nothing,) and that which we desire to see being, as we are told here, something particular, *sometimes one thing, sometimes another;* that which we do see must be particular too; but how to see a particular thing in general, is past my comprehension. I cannot conceive how a blind man has the particular idea of scarlet confusedly or in general, when he has it not at all; and yet that he might desire to have it I cannot doubt, no more than I doubt that I can desire to perceive, or to have the ideas of those things that God has prepared for those that love him, though they be such as eye hath not seen, nor ear hath heard, nor hath it entered into the heart of man to conceive, such as I have yet no idea of. He who desires to know what creatures are in Jupiter, or what God hath prepared for them that love him, hath, it is true, a supposition that there is something in Jupiter, or in the place of the blessed; but if that be to have the particular ideas of things there, enough to say that we see them already, nobody can be ignorant of anything. He that hath seen one thing hath seen all things; for he has got the general idea of something. But this is not, I confess, sufficient to convince me, that hereby we see all things *in the simplicity of God's being, which comprehends all things.* For if the ideas I see are all, as our author tells us, real beings in him, it is plain they must be so many real distinct beings in him; and if we see them in him, we must see them as they are, distinct particular things, and so shall not see them confusedly and in general. And what is it to see any idea (to which I do not give a name) confusedly, is what

I do not well understand. What I see, I see, and the idea I see is distinct from all others that are not the same with it: besides, I see them as they are in God, and as he shows them me. Are they in God confusedly—or does he show them to me confusedly?

30. Secondly, This *seeing of all things*, because we *can desire to see all things*, he makes a proof that *they are present* to our minds; and if they *be present, they can no ways be present but by the presence of God, who contains them in all the simplicity of his being.* This reasoning seems to be founded on this, that the reason of seeing all things is their being present to our minds; because God, in whom they are, is present. This, though the foundation he seems to build on, is liable to a very natural objection, which is, that then we should actually always see all things, because in God, who is present, they are all actually present to the mind. This he has endeavoured to obviate, by saying we see all the ideas in God which he is pleased *to discover to us;* which indeed is an answer to this objection;-but such an one as overturns his whole hypothesis, and renders it useless and as unintelligible as any of those he has for that reason laid aside. He pretends to explain to us how we come to perceive anything, and that is, by having the ideas of them present in our minds; for the soul cannot perceive things at a distance, or remote from it; and those ideas are present to the mind only because God, in whom they are, is present to the mind. This so far hangs together, and is of a piece; but when after this I am told, that their presence is not enough to make them be seen, but God must do something further to discover them to me, I am as much in the dark as I was at first; and all this talk of their presence in my mind explains nothing of the way wherein I perceive them, nor ever will, till he also makes me understand what God does more than make them present to my mind, when he discovers them to me. For I think nobody denies, I am sure I affirm, that the ideas we have, are in our minds by the will and power of God, though in a way that we conceive not, nor are able to comprehend. God, says our author, is strictly united to the soul, and so the ideas of things too. But yet that presence or union of theirs is not enough to make them seen, but God must show or exhibit them; and what does God do more than make

them present to the mind when he shows them? Of that there is nothing said to help me over this difficulty, but that when God shows them, we see them; which, in short, seems to me to say only thus much, that when we have these ideas we have them, and we owe the having of them to our Maker, which is to say no more than I do with my ignorance. We have the ideas of figures and colours by the operation of exterior objects on our senses, when the sun shows them us; but how the sun shows them us, or how the light of the sun produces them in us; what, and how the alteration is made in our souls, I know not, nor does it appear, by anything our author says, that he knows any more what God does when he shows them us, or what it is that is done upon our minds, since the presence of them to our minds, he confesses, does it not.

31. Thirdly, One thing more is incomprehensible to me in this matter, and that is how the *simplicity of God's being* should contain in it a variety of real beings, so that the soul can discern them in him distinctly one from another; it being said in the fifth chapter, that the ideas in God *are not different from God himself.* This seems to me to express a simplicity made up of variety, a thing I cannot understand. God I believe to be a simple being, that by his wisdom knows all things, and by his power can do all things; but how he does it I think myself less able to comprehend, than to contain the ocean in my hand, or grasp the universe with my span. *Ideas are real beings,* you say; if so, it is evident they must be distinct *real beings;* for there is nothing more certain than that there are distinct ideas; and they are in God, in whom we see them. There they are, then, actually distinct, or else we could not see them distinct in him. Now these distinct real beings that are in God, are they either parts or modifications of the Deity, or comprehended in him as things in a place? For besides these three, I think we can scarce think of another way wherein we can conceive them to be in him, so that we can see them. For to say they are in him *eminenter,* is to say they are not in him actually and really to be seen; but only if they are in him *eminenter,* and we see them only in him, we can be said to see them only *eminenter* too. So that though it cannot be denied that God sees and knows all things, yet when we say

we see all things in him, it is but a metaphorical expression to cover our ignorance, in a way that pretends to explain our knowledge; seeing things in God signifying no more than that we perceive them we know not how.

32. He further adds, that he "does not believe that one can well give an account of the manner wherein the mind knows many abstract and general truths, but by the presence of him who can enlighten the mind after a thousand different fashions." It is not to be denied that God can enlighten our minds after a thousand different fashions; and it cannot also be denied that those thousand different fashions may be such as we comprehend not one of them. The question is, whether this talk of seeing all things in God does make us clearly, or at all, comprehend one of them; if it did so to me I should gratefully acknowledge that then I was ignorant of nine hundred and ninety-nine of the thousand, whereas I must yet confess myself ignorant of them all.

33. The next paragraph, if it prove anything, seems to me to prove that the idea we have of God is God himself, it being something, as he says, *uncreated.* The ideas that men have of God are so very different, that it would be very hard to say it was God himself. Nor does it avail to say they would all have the same, if they would apply their minds to the contemplation of him; for this being brought here to prove that God is present in all men's minds, and that therefore they see him, it must also, in my apprehension, prove that he being immutably the same, and they seeing him, must needs see him all alike.

34. In the next section we are told that we have "not only the idea of infinite, but before that of finite." This being a thing of experience every one must examine himself; and it being my misfortune to find it otherwise in myself, this argument, of course, is like to have the less effect on me, who therefore cannot so easily admit the inference, viz., "Thus the mind perceives not one thing, but in the idea it has of infinite." And I cannot but believe many a child can tell twenty, have the idea of a square trencher, or a round plate, and have the distinct clear ideas of two and three, long before he has any idea of *infinite* at all.

35. The last argument which he tells us is a demonstration that we see all things in God, is this: "God has made all

things for himself; but if God made a spirit or mind, and gave it the sun for its idea, or the immediate object of its knowledge, God would have made that spirit or mind for the sun, and not for himself." The natural inference from this argument seems to me to be this: therefore God has given himself for the idea, or immediate object of the knowledge of all human minds. But experience too manifestly contradicting this, our author hath made another conclusion, and says thus: "It is necessary, then, that the light which he gives the mind, should make us know something that is in him;" v. g., because "all things that come from God cannot be but for God." Therefore a covetous man sees in God the money, and a Persian the sun that he worships; and thus God is the *immediate object* of the mind, both of the one and the other. I confess this demonstration is lost on me, and I cannot see the force of it. All things, it is true, are made for God, i. e., for his glory; and he will be glorified even by those rational beings who would not apply their faculties to the knowledge of him.

36. But the next paragraph explains this: "God could not then make a soul for to know his works, were it not that that soul sees God after a fashion in seeing his works;" just *after such a fashion* that if he never saw more of him he would never know anything of a God, nor oelieve there was any such being. A child, as soon as he is born, sees a candle, or before he can speak, the ball he plays with; these he *sees in God*, whom he has yet no notion of. Whether this be enough to make us say that the mind is made for God, and this be the proof of it, other people must judge for themselves. I must own, that if this were the knowledge of God, which intelligent beings were made for, I do not see but they might be made for the knowledge of God without knowing anything of him; and those that deny him were made for the knowledge of him. Therefore I am not convinced of the truth of what follows, that "we do not see any one thing but by the natural knowledge which we have of God." Which seems to me a quite contrary way of arguing to what the apostle uses, where he says, that "the invisible things of God are seen by the visible things that he has made." For it seems to me a quite contrary way of arguing, to say, we see the Creator in or by the creatures, and we see the creatures

in the Creator. The apostle begins our knowledge in the creatures, which leads us to the knowledge of God, if we will make use of our reason: our author begins our knowledge in God, and by that leads us to the creatures.

37. But to confirm his argument he says: "All the particular ideas we have of the creatures are but limitations of the idea of the Creator." As for example, I have the idea of the solidity of matter, and of the motion of body, what is the idea of God that either of these limits? And when I think of the number ten, I do not see how that any way concerns or limits the idea of God.

38. The distinction he makes a little lower between *sentiment* and *idea*, does not at all clear to me, but cloud his doctrine. His words are: "It must be observed that I do not say that we have the sentiment of material things in God, but that it is from God that acts in us; for God knows sensible things, but feels them not. When we perceive any sensible thing, there is in our perception sentiment and pure idea." If by *sentiment*, which is the word he uses in French, he means the act of sensation, or the operation of the soul in perceiving; and by *pure idea* the immediate object of that perception, which is the definition of ideas he gives us here in the first chapter, there is some foundation for it, taking ideas for real beings or substances. But taken thus, I cannot see how it can be avoided, but that we must be said to smell a rose in God, as well as to see a rose in God; and the scent of the rose that we smell, as well as the colour and figure of the rose that we see, must be in God; which seems not to be his sense here, and does not well agree with what he says concerning the ideas we see in God, which I shall consider in its due place. If by *sentiment* here he means something that is neither the act of perception nor the idea perceived, I confess I know not what it is, nor have any conception at all of it. When we see and smell a violet, we perceive the figure, colour, and scent of that flower. Here I cannot but ask whether all these three are *pure ideas*, or all *sentiments?* If they are all *ideas*, then, according to his doctrine, they are all in God; and then it will follow that, as I see the figure of the violet in God, so also I see the colour of it, and smell the scent of it in God, which way of speaking he does not allow, nor can I blame him. For it shows a

little too plainly the absurdity of that doctrine, if he should say we smell a violet, taste wormwood, or feel cold in God, and yet I can find no reason why the action of one of our senses is applied only to God, when we use them all as well as our eyes in receiving ideas. If the figure, colour, and smell are all of them *sentiments*, then they are none of them in God, and so this whole business of seeing in God is out of doors. If (as, by what he says in his *Eclaircissements*, it appears to me to be his meaning) the figure of the violet be to be taken for an *idea*, but its *colour* and *smell* for *sentiments*, I confess it puzzles me to know by what rule it is that in a violet the purple colour, whereof whilst I write this I seem to have as clear an idea in my mind as of its figure, is not as much an idea as the figure of it; especially, since he tells me in the first chapter here, which is concerning the nature of ideas, that by this word idea he understands here nothing else but what is the immediate or nearest object of the mind when it perceives anything.

39. The "sentiment," says he, in the next words, "is a modification of our soul." This word *modification* here, that comes in for explication, seems to me to signify nothing more than the word to be explained by it; v. g., I see the purple colour of a violet; this, says he, is a *sentiment:* I desire to know what *sentiment* is; that, says he, is a *modification of the soul*. I take the word, and desire to see what I can conceive by it concerning my soul; and here, I confess, I can conceive nothing more, but that I have the idea of purple in my mind, which I had not before, without being able to apprehend anything the mind does or suffers in this, besides barely having the idea of purple; and so the good word *modification* signifies nothing to me more than I knew before; v. g., that I have now the idea of purple in it, which I had not some minutes since. So that though they say sensations are modifications of the mind; yet, having no manner of idea what that modification of the mind is, distinct from that very sensation, v. g., the sensation of a red colour or a bitter taste, it is plain this explication amounts to no more than that a sensation is a sensation, and the sensation of red or bitter is the sensation of *red* or *bitter;* for if I have no other idea when I say it is a modification of the mind than when I say it is the sensation of *red* or *bitter*, it is plain sen-

sation and modification stand both for the same idea, and so are but two names of one and the same thing. But to examine their doctrine of modification a little further. Different sentiments are different modifications of the mind. The mind or soul that perceives is one immaterial indivisible substance. Now I see the white and black on this paper, I hear one singing in the next room, I feel the warmth of the fire I sit by, and I taste an apple I am eating, and all this at the same time. Now I ask, take *modification* for what you please, can the same unextended indivisible substance have different, nay, inconsistent and opposite (as these of white and black must be) modifications at the same time? Or must we suppose distinct parts in an indivisible substance, one for black, another for white, and another for red ideas, and so of the rest of those infinite sensations which we have in sorts and degrees; all which we can distinctly perceive, and so are distinct ideas, some whereof are opposite, as heat and cold, which yet a man may feel at the same time? I was ignorant before how sensation was performed in us; this they call an explanation of it. Must I say now I understand it better? If this be to cure one's ignorance, it is a very slight disease, and the charm of two or three insignificant words will at any time remove it, *probatum est*. But let it signify what it will when I recollect the figure of one of the leaves of a violet, is not that a new modification of my soul, as well as when I think of its purple colour? Does my mind do or suffer nothing anew when I see that figure in God?

40. The idea of that figure, you say, is in God. Let it be so; but it may be there and I not see it; that is allowed; when I come to see it, which I did not before, is there no new modification, as you call it, of my mind? If there be, then, seeing of figure in God, as well as having the idea of purple, is *a modification of the mind*, and this distinction signifies nothing. If seeing that figure in God now, which a minute or two since I did not see at all, be no new modification or alteration in my mind, no different action or passion from what was before, there is no difference made, in my apprehension, between seeing and not seeing. The ideas of figures, our author says, are in God, and are real beings in God; and God being united to the mind, these are also united to it. This all seems to me to have something very

obscure and unconceivable in it, when I come to examine particulars; but let it be granted to be as clear as any one would suppose it, yet it reaches not the main difficulty, which is in *seeing*. How, after all, do I see? The ideas are in God, they are real things, they are intimately united to my mind, because God is so, but yet I do not see them. How at last, after all this preparation, which hitherto is ineffectual, do I come to see them? And to that I am told, "when God is pleased to discover them to me." This in good earnest seems to me to be nothing but going a great way about to come to the same place; and this learned circuit, thus set out, brings me at last no further than this: that I see, or perceive, or have ideas, when it pleases God I should, but in a way I cannot comprehend; and this I thought without all this ado.

41. This *sentiment*, he tells us in the next words, "it is God causes in us, and he can cause it in us although he has it not, because he sees in the idea that he has of our soul that it is capable of them." This I take to be said to show the difference between *sentiments* and *ideas* in us: v. g., *figures* and *numbers* are ideas, and they are in God. *Colours* and *smells*, &c., are *sentiments* in us, and not ideas in God. First, As to ourselves, I ask, why, when I recollect in my memory a violet, the purple colour as well as figure is not an idea in me? The making, then, the picture of any visible thing in my mind, as of a landscape I have seen, composed of figure and colour, the colour is not an idea, but the figure is an idea, and the colour a *sentiment*. Every one, I allow, may use his words as he pleases; but if it be to instruct others, he must, when he uses two words where others use but one, show some ground of the distinction. And I do not find but the colour of the marigold I now think of is as much *the immediate object of my mind* as its figure; and so, according to his definition, is an *idea*. Next, as to God, I ask whether before the creation of the world the idea of the whole marigold, colour as well as figure, was not in God? "God," says he, "can cause those sentiments in us, because he sees, in the idea that he has of our soul, that it is capable of them." God, before he created any soul, knew all that he would make it capable of. He resolved to make it capable of having the perception of the colour as well

as figure of a marigold; he had then the idea of that colour that he resolved to make it capable of, or else he made it capable (with reverence let it be spoken) of he knew not what: and if he knew what it should be capable of, he had the idea of what he knew; for before the creation there was nothing but God, and the ideas he had. It is true the colour of that flower is not actually in God, no more is its figure actually in God; but we that can consider no other understanding, but in analogy to our own, cannot conceive otherwise but as the ideas of the figure, colour, and situation of the leaves of a marigold is in our minds, when we think of that flower in the night when we see it not; so it was in the thoughts of God before he made that flower. And thus we conceive him to have the idea of the smell of a violet, of the taste of sugar, the sound of a lute or trumpet and of the pain and pleasure that accompanies any of these or other sensations which he designed we should feel, though he never felt any of them, as we have the ideas of the taste of a cherry in winter, or of the pain of a burn when it is over. This is what I think we conceive of the ideas in God, which we must allow to have distinctly represented to him all that was to be in time, and consequently the colours, odours, and other ideas they were to produce in us. I cannot be so bold as to pretend to say what those ideas are in God, or to determine that they are real beings; but this I think I may say, that the idea of the colour of a marigold or the motion of a stone are as much real beings in God as the idea of the figure or number of its leaves.

42. The reader must not blame me for making use here all along of the word *sentiment*, which is our author's own, and I understood it so little, that I knew not how to translate it into any other. He concludes, "that he believes there is no appearance of truth in any other ways of explaining these things, and that this of seeing all things in God is more than probable." I have considered, with as much indifferency and attention as possible, and I must own it appears to me as little or less intelligible than any of the rest; and the summary of his doctrine, which he here subjoins, is to me wholly incomprehensible. His words are: "Thus our souls depend on God all manner of ways: for as

it is he which makes them feel pleasure and pain, and all other sensations, by the natural union which he has made between them and our bodies, which is nothing else but his decree and general will; so it is he, who, by the natural union which he has made betwixt the will of man and the representation of ideas, which the immensity of the Divine Being contains, makes them know all that they know; and this natural union is also nothing but his general will." This phrase, of the union of our wills to the ideas contained in God's immensity, seems to me a very strange one, and what light it gives to his doctrine I truly cannot find. It seemed so unintelligible to me, that I guessed it an error in the print of the edition I used, which was the quarto printed at Paris, 78, and therefore consulted the octavo, printed also at Paris, and found it *will* in both of them. Here again the *immensity of the Divine Being* being mentioned as that which *contains* in it the *ideas* to which our *wills* are united; which ideas being only those of quantity, as I shall show hereafter, seems to me to carry with it a very gross notion of this matter, as we have above remarked. But that which I take notice of principally here, is, that this union of our *wills* to the ideas contained in God's immensity, does not at all explain our seeing of them. This union of our *wills* to the ideas, or, as in other places, of our souls to God, is, says he, nothing but the will of God. And after this union, our seeing them is only when God discovers them; i. e., our having them in our minds is nothing but the will of God; all which is brought about in a way we comprehend not. And what, then, does this explain more than when one says our souls are united to our bodies by the will of God, and by the motion of some parts of our bodies?—v. g., the nerves or animal spirits have ideas or perceptions produced in them, and this is the will of God. Why is not this as intelligible and as clear as the other? Here is the will of God giving union and perception in both cases; but how that perception is made, in both ways seems to me equally imcomprehensible. In one, God discovers ideas in himself to the soul united to him when he pleases; and in the other he discovers ideas to the soul, or produces perception in the soul united to the body by motion, according to laws established by the good pleasure of his will; but how it is done in the one or the other I confess my incapacity to comprehend. So that I agree perfectly with him in his conclusion, that "there is nothing but God that can enlighten us; but a clear comprehension of the manner how he does it I doubt I shall not have, until I know a great deal more of him and myself than in this state of darkness and ignorance our souls are capable of.

43. In the next chapter (VII.) he tells us, " there are four ways of knowing;* the first is to know things by themselves;" and thus, he says, " we know God alone;" and the reason he gives of it is this, because "at present he alone penetrates the mind, and discovers himself to it."

First, I would know what it is to penetrate a thing that is unextended. These are ways of speaking, which taken from body, when they are applied to spirit, signify nothing, nor show us anything but our ignorance. To God's penetrating our spirits, he joins his *discovering himself ;* as if one were the cause of the other, and explained it: but I not conceiving anything of the penetration of an unextended thing, it is lost upon me. But next God penetrates our souls, and therefore we *see him by a direct and immediate view*, as he says in the following words. The ideas of all things which are in God, he elsewhere tells us, are not at all different from God himself; and if God's penetrating our minds be the cause of our direct and immediate seeing God, we have a direct and immediate view of all that we see; for we see nothing but God and ideas; and it is impossible for us to know that there is anything else in the universe; for since we see, and can see nothing but God and ideas, how can we know there is anything else which we neither do nor can see? But if there be anything to be understood by this *penetration* of our souls, and we have a direct view of God by this *penetration*, why have we not also a *direct and*

---

* On this subject Malebranche states his views briefly and distinctly. "Afin d'abreger et d'éclaircir le sentiment que je viens d'établir touchant la manière, dont l'esprit aperçoit tous les différens objets de sa connoissance, il est nécessaire que je distingue en lui quatre manières de connoître. La première est de connoître les choses par elles-mêmes. La seconde de les connoître par leurs idées, c'est-à-dire, comme je l'entens ici, par quelque chose qui soit différent d'elles. La troisiéme de les connoître par *conscience*, on par sentiment intérieur. La quatrième de les connoître par conjecture. (T. i. p. 373.)—ED.

immediate view of other separate spirits besides God? To this he says, that there is none but God alone who at *present* penetrates our spirits. This he says, but I do not see for what reason, but because it suits with his hypothesis: but he proves it not, nor goes about to do it, unless the *direct and immediate view*, he says, we have of God, be to be taken as a proof of it. But what is *that direct and immediate view* we have of God that we have not of a cherubim?* The ideas of being, power, knowledge, goodness, duration, make up the complex idea we have of one and of the other; but only that in the one we join the idea of infinite to each simple idea, that makes our complex one, but to the other, that of finite. But how have we a more *direct or immediate view* of the idea of power, knowledge, or duration, when we consider them in God than when we consider them in an angel? The view of these ideas seems to be the same. Indeed we have a clearer proof of the existence of God than of a cherubim; but the idea of either, when we have it in our minds, seems to me to be there by an equally *direct and immediate view*. And it is about the ideas which are in our minds that I think our author's inquiry here is, and not about the real existence of those things whereof we have ideas, which are two very remote things.

44. "Perhaps it is God alone," says our author, "who can enlighten our minds by his substance." When I know what the *substance* of God is, and what it is to be *enlightened by that substance*, I shall know what I also shall think of it; but at present I confess myself in the dark as to this matter; nor do these good words of *substance* and *enlightening*, in the way they are here used, help me one jot out of it.

45. He goes on—"One cannot conceive," says he, "that anything created can represent what is infinite." And I cannot conceive that there is any positive comprehensive idea in any finite mind that does represent it fully and clearly as it is. I do not find that the mind of man has infinity, positively and fully represented to it, or comprehended by it; which must be, if his argument were true, that therefore God enlightens our minds by his proper substance; because no created thing is big enough to represent what is infinite;

† It should have been *cherub*; *cherubim* in the plural.—ED.

and therefore what makes us conceive his infinity, is the presence of his own infinite substance in our minds; which to me manifestly supposes that we comprehend in our minds God's infinite substance, which is present to our minds; for if this be not the force of his argument, where he says, "Nothing created can represent what is infinite; the Being that is without bounds, the Being immense, the Being universal, cannot be perceived by an idea, i. e., by a particular being, by a being different from the universal infinite Being itself." It seems to me that this argument is founded on a supposition of our comprehending the infinite substance of God in our minds, or else I see not any force in it, as I have already said. I shall take notice of one or two things in it that confound me, and that is, that he calls God here *the universal Being;* which must either signify that Being which contains, and is made up as one comprehensive aggregate of all the rest, in which sense the universe may be called *the universal Being;* or else it must mean being in general, which is nothing but the idea of *Being* abstracted from all inferior divisions of that general notion, and from all particular existence. But in neither of these senses can I conceive God to *be the universal Being,* since I cannot think the creatures either to be a part or a species of him. Next he calls the ideas that are in God, *particular Beings.* I grant whatever exists is particular; it cannot be otherwise; but that which is particular in existence may be universal in representation, which I take to be all the universal beings we know, or can conceive to be. But let *universal* and *particular beings* be what they will, I do not see how our author can say that God is an *universal Being,* and the ideas we see in him *particular beings;* since he in another place tells us, that the ideas we see in God are not at all different from God. "But," says he, "as to particular beings, it is not hard to conceive that they can be represented by the infinite Being which contains them, and contains them after a very spiritual manner, and consequently very intelligible." It seems as impossible to me, that an infinite simple Being, in whom there is no variety, nor shadow of variety, should represent a finite thing, as that a finite thing should represent an infinite; nor do I see how its "containing all things in it after a very spiritual manner makes it so very intelligible;" since I understand not what it is to contain a material thing *spiritually*, nor the manner how God contains anything in himself, but either as an aggregate contains all things which it is made up of; and so indeed that part of him may be seen which comes within the reach of our view. But this way of *containing all things* can by no means belong to God; and to make things thus visible in him is to make the material world a part of him, or else as having a power to produce all things; and in this way, it is true, God *contains all things* in himself, but in a way not proper to make the *Being* of God a representative of those things to us; for then his *Being*, being the representative of the effects of that power, it must represent to us all that he is capable of producing, which I do not find in myself that it does.

46. Secondly. "The second way of knowing things," he tells us, "is by ideas, that is, by something that is different from them;" and thus we "know things when they are not intelligible by themselves, either because they are corporeal, or because they cannot penetrate the mind, or discover themselves to it;" and this is the way "we know corporeal things." This reasoning I do not understand: First, Because I do not understand why a line or a triangle is not as *intelligible* as anything that can be named; for we must still carry along with us that the discourse here is about our perception, or what we have any idea or conception of in our own minds. Secondly, Because I do not understand what is meant by the *penetrating* a spirit; and till I can comprehend these, upon which this reasoning is built, this reasoning cannot work on me. But from these reasons he concludes, "thus it is in God, and by their ideas that we see bodies and their properties; and it is for this reason that the knowledge we have of them is most perfect." Whether others will think that what we see of bodies is seen in God, by seeing the ideas of them that are in God, must be left to them. Why I cannot think so I have shown; but the inference he makes here from it I think few will assent to, that we know bodies and their properties most perfectly.* For who is

* On the imperfection of our knowledge of bodies it is unnecessary to dwell, the fresh discoveries which are continually made by natural philosophers being, in some sort, a demonstration of it. Malebranche's notions, however, were not built upon experience, but fashioned to suit

there that can say he knows the properties either of body in general, or of any one particular body perfectly? One property of body in general is to have parts cohering and united together, for wherever there is body there is cohesion of parts; but who is there that perfectly understands that cohesion? And as for particular bodies, who can say that he perfectly understands gold, or a loadstone, and all its properties? But to explain himself, he says, that "the idea we have of extension suffices to make us know all the properties whereof extension is capable, and that we cannot desire to have an idea more distinct, and more fruitful of extension, of figures, and of motions, than that which God has given us of them." This seems to me a strange proof that we see *bodies and their properties in God*, and *know them perfectly*, because God has given us distinct and fruitful ideas of extension, figure, and motion: for this had been the same, whether God had given these ideas, by showing them in himself or by any other way; and his saying, that God *has given us* as *distinct and fruitful ideas* of them as we can *desire*, seems as if our author himself had some other thoughts of them. If he thought we see them in God, he must think we see them as they are in themselves, and there would be no room for saying, God had given them us as *distinct* as we could desire: the calling them *fruitful* shows this yet more; for one that thinks he sees the ideas of figures in God, and can see no idea of a figure but in God, with what thought can he call any one of them *feconde*, which is said only of such things as produce others? which expres-

the rest of his theory. He maintains that it is our ideas of bodies, and not bodies themselves, that are the proper objects of this branch of our knowledge: "On connoit les choses par leurs idées, lorsqu'elles ne sont point intelligibles par elles-mêmes, soit parce qu'elles sont corporelles, soit parce qu'elles ne peuvent pénétrer l'esprit ou se découvrir a lui." (t. i. p. 373.) Nevertheless, though we come to the knowledge of bodies not immediately, but through the medium of ideas, and owe the knowledge of our own minds to consciousness and direct study, he supposes us to understand the nature of bodies much better than that of our own minds. "On peut conclure," says he, "qu'encore que nous connoissons plus distinctement l'existence de nôtre ame que l'existence de nôtre corps, et de ceux qui nous environnent: cependant nous n'avons pas une connoissance si parfaite de la nature de l'ame que de la nature des corps ; et cela peut servir à accorder les différens sentimens de ceux qui disent qu'il n'y a rien qu'on connoisse mieux que l'ame, et de ceux qui assurent qu'il n'y a rien qu'ils connoissent moins." (p. 376.)—ED.

sion of his seems to proceed only from this thought in him, that when I have once got the idea of extension, I can frame the ideas of what figures, and of what bigness I please. And in this I agree with him, as appears in what I have said, l. ii. c. 1 . But then this can by no means proceed from a supposition that I see these figures only in God; for there they do not produce one another, but are there, as it were, in their first pattern to be seen, just such and so many as God is pleased to show them to us. But it will be said, our desire to see them is the occasional cause of God's showing them us, and so we see whatever figure we desire. Let it be so, this does not make any idea *feconde*, for here is no production of one out of another; but as to the occasional cause, can any one say that is so? I, or our author, desire to see an angle next in greatness to a right angle; did, upon this, God ever show him or me such an angle? That God knows, or has in himself the idea of such an angle, I think will not be denied; but that he ever showed it to any man, how much soever he desired it, I think may be doubted. But after all, how comes it by this means that we have a *perfect knowledge of bodies and their properties*, when several men in the world have not the same idea of body, and this very author and I differ in it? He thinks bare extension to be body, and I think extension alone makes not body, but extension and solidity;* thus either he or I, one of us, has a wrong and imperfect knowledge of bodies and their properties. For if bodies be extension alone, and nothing else, I cannot conceive how they can move and hit one against another, or what can make distinct surfaces in an uniform simple extension. A solid extended thing I can conceive movable; but then, if I have a clear view of bodies and their properties in God, I must see the idea of solidity in God, which yet I think, by what our author has said in his Eclaircissements, he does not allow that we do. He says further: "That, whereas the ideas of things that are in God contain all their properties, he that sees their ideas may see successively all their properties." This seems to me not to concern our ideas more, whether we see them in God, or have them otherwise. Any idea that we have, whencesoever we have it, contains in it all the proper-

* See Antoine Le Grand, Instit. Philosoph. IV. iii. p. 150; Hobbes, Elements of Philosophy, Pt. II. chap. viii.—ED.

ties it has, which are nothing but the relations it has to other ideas, which are always the same. What he says concerning the *properties*, that we may *successively know them*, is equally true, whether we see them in God or have them by any other means. They that apply them as they ought to the consideration of their ideas, may successively come to the knowledge of some of their properties; but that they may *know all their properties* is more than I think the reason proves, which he subjoins in these words: "For when one sees the things as they are in God, one sees them always in a most perfect manner." We see, for example, in God, the idea of a triangle or a circle; does it hence follow that we *can know all the properties* of either of them? He adds, that the manner of seeing them "would be infinitely perfect, if the mind which sees them in God was infinite." I confess myself here not well to comprehend his distinction between seeing after a manner [*tres-parfait*] *most perfect* and *infinitely perfect*. He adds: "That which is wanting to the knowledge that we have of extension, figures, and motion is not a defect of the idea which represents it, but of our mind which considers it." If by *ideas* be meant here the real objects of our knowledge, I easily agree that the want of knowledge in us is a defect in our minds, and not in the things to be known. But if by *ideas* be here meant the perception or representation of things in the mind, that I cannot but observe in myself to be very imperfect and defective, as when I desire to perceive what is the substance of body or spirit the idea thereof fails me. To conclude, I see not what there is in this paragraph that makes anything for the doctrine of "seeing all things in God."

47. "The third way of knowing is by consciousness,* or interior sentiments; and thus," he says, "we know our souls, and it is for this reason that the knowledge we have of them is imperfect; we know nothing of our souls but what we feel within ourselves." This confession of our author brings me back, do what I can, to that original of all our ideas which my thoughts led me to when I writ my book, viz., sensation and reflection; and therefore I am forced to ask any one who

---

* According to Condillac, all knowledge is based on consciousness. (Essai sur l'Origine du Connoissances humaines, § 2, chap. i. p. 26.)—ED.

is of our author's principles, whether God had not the idea of mine, or of a human soul, before he created it? Next, whether that idea of a human soul be not as much a *real being* in God as the idea of a triangle? If so, why does not my soul, being intimately united to God, as well see the idea of my soul which is in him, as the idea of a triangle which is in him? And what reason can there be given why God shows the idea of a triangle to us, and not the idea of our souls, but this, that God has given us external sensation to perceive the one and none to perceive the other, but only internal sensation to perceive the operation of the latter? He that pleases may read what our author says in the remainder of this and the two or three next paragraphs, and see whether it carries him beyond where my ignorance stopped; I must own that me it does not.

48. "This," [i. e., the ignorance we are in of our own souls,] says he, "may serve to prove that the ideas that represent anything to us that is without us, are not modifications of our souls; for if the soul saw all things by considering its own proper modifications, it should know more clearly its own essence, or its own nature, than that of bodies, and all the sensations or modifications whereof it is capable, than the figures or modifications of which bodies are capable. In the meantime it knows not that it is capable of any such sensation by sight as it has of itself, but only by experience; instead that it knows that extension is capable of an infinite number of figures by the idea that it has of extension. There are, moreover, certain sensations, as colours and sounds, which the greatest part of men cannot discover whether they are modifications of the soul; and there are figures which all men do not discover by the idea of extension to be modifications of bodies." This paragraph is, as he tells us, to prove, "that the ideas that represent to us something without us are not modifications of the soul;" but instead of that, it seems to prove that figure is the modification of space, and not of our souls. For if this argument had tended to prove "that the ideas that represent anything without us were not modifications of the soul," he should not have put the mind's not knowing what modifications itself was capable of, and knowing what figures space was capable of, in opposition one to another; but the antithesis must have lain in this, that

the mind knew it was capable of the perception of figure or motion without any modification of itself, but was not capable of the perception of sound or colour without a modification of itself. For the question here is not whether space be capable of figure, and the soul not; but whether the soul be capable of perceiving, or having the idea of figure, without a modification of itself, and not capable of having the idea of colour without a modification of itself. I think now of the figure, colour, and hardness of a diamond that I saw some time since: in this case, I desire to be informed how my mind knows that the thinking on, or the idea of the figure, is not a modification of the mind; but the thinking on, or having an idea of the colour or hardness is a modification of the mind. It is certain there is some alteration in my mind when I think of a figure which I did not think of before, as well as when I think of a colour that I did not think of before. But one I am told is seeing it in God, and the other a modification of my mind. But supposing one is seeing in God, is there no alteration in my mind between seeing and not seeing? And is that to be called a modification or no? For when he says seeing a colour, and hearing a sound, is a modification of the mind, what does it signify but an alteration of the mind from not perceiving to perceiving that sound or colour? And so when the mind sees a triangle, which it did not see before, what is this but an alteration of the mind from not seeing to seeing, whether that figure be seen in God or no? And why is not this alteration of the mind to be called a modification, as well as the other? Or, indeed, what service does that word do us in the one case or the other, when it is only a new sound brought in without any new conception at all? For my mind, when it sees a colour or figure is altered, I know, from the not having such or such a perception to the having it; but when, to explain this, I am told that either of these perceptions is a modification of the mind, what do I conceive more, than that from not having such a perception my mind is come to have such a perception? which is what I as well knew before the word *modification* was made use of, which by its use has made me conceive nothing more than what I conceived before.

49. One thing I cannot but take notice of here by the by,

that he says, that "the soul knows that extension is capable of an infinite number of figures by the idea it has of extension," which is true. And afterwards he says, that "there are no figures which all men do not discover, by the idea they have of extension, to be modifications of body." One would wonder why he did not say *modifications* of extension, rather than, as he does, the *modifications of body*, they being *discovered by the idea of extension;* but the truth would not bear such an expression. For it is certain that in pure space or extension, which is not terminated, there is truly no distinction of figures, but in distinct bodies that are terminated there are distinct figures, because simple space or extension, being in itself uniform, inseparable, immovable, has in it no such modification or distinction of figures. But it is *capable*, as he says, but of what? Of bodies of all sorts of figures and magnitudes, without which there is no distinction of figures in space. Bodies that are solid, separable, terminated, and movable, have all sorts of figures, and they are bodies alone that have them: and so figures are properly modifications of bodies, for pure space is not anywhere terminated, nor can be, whether there be or be not body in it, it is uniformly continued on. This that he plainly said here, to me plainly shows that body and extension are two things, though much of our author's doctrine be built upon their being one and the same.

50. The next paragraph is to show us the difference between ideas and sentiments in this: that "sentiments are not tied to words; so that he that never had seen a colour or felt heat could never be made to have those sensations by all the definitions one could give him of them." This is true of what he calls *sentiments*, and as true also of what he calls *ideas*. Show me one who has not got by experience, i. e., by seeing or feeling the idea of space or motion, and I will as soon by words make one who never felt what heat is, have a conception of heat, as he that has not by his senses perceived what space or motion is, can by words be made to conceive either of them. The reason why we are apt to think these ideas belonging to extension got another way than other ideas, is because our bodies being extended, we cannot avoid the distinction of parts in ourselves; and all that is for the support of our lives being by motion applied to us, it is im-

possible to find any one who has not by experience got those
ideas; and so by the use of language learned what words
stand for them, which by custom came to excite them in his
mind, as the names of heat and pleasure do excite, in the
mind of those who have by experience got them, the ideas
they are by use annexed to. Not that words or definitions
can teach or bring into the mind one more than another of
those I call simple ideas; but can by use excite them in
those, who having got them by experience, know certain
sounds to be by use annexed to them as the signs of them.

51. Fourthly. "The fourth way of knowing," he tells us,
"is by conjecture, and thus only we know the souls of other
men and pure intelligences:" i. e., we know them not at all;
but we probably think there are such beings really existing
in *rerum natura.** But this looks to me beside our author's
business here, which seems to be to examine what ideas we
have, and how we came by them. So that the thing here
considered should, in my opinion, be, not whether there were
any souls of men or pure intelligences anywhere existing,
but what ideas we have of them, and how we came by them.
For when he says, we know not angels, either *in themselves*,
or *by their ideas*, or *by consciousness*, what in that place does
angel signify? What idea in him does it stand for? Or is
it the sign of no idea at all, and so a bare sound without
signification? He that reads this seventh chapter of his
with attention, will find that we have simple ideas as far as
our experience reaches, and no further. And beyond that
we know nothing at all, no, not even what those ideas are
that are in us, but only that they are perceptions in the mind,
but how made we cannot comprehend.

52. In his Eclaircissements on the Nature of Ideas, p. 535,

* "De tous les objets de nôtre connoissance, il ne nous reste plus
que les ames des autres hommes, et que les pures intelligences; et il est
manifeste que nous ne les connoissons que par conjecture nous ne les
connoissons presentement ni en elles-mêmes ni par leurs idées, et comme
elles sont différentes de nous, il n'est pas possible que nous les connoissons par conscience. Nous conjecturons que les ames des autres hommes
sont comme la nôtre. Ce que nous sentons en nous-mêmes, nous pré-
tendons qu'ils le sentent, et même lorsque ces sentimens n'ont point de
rapport au corps, nous sommes assurez que nous ne nous trompons
point: parce que nous voyons en Dieu certaines idées et certaines loix
immuable, selon lesquelles nous sçavons avec certitude, que Dieu agit
également dans tous les esprits." (p. 378 seq.)—

of the 4to edition, he says, that "he is certain that the ideas of things are unchangeable." This I cannot comprehend; for how can I know that the picture of anything is like that thing, when I never see that which it represents? For if these words do not mean that ideas are true unchangeable representations of things, I know not to what purpose they are. And if that be not their meaning, then they can only signify, that the idea I have once had will be unchangeably the same as long as it recurs the same in my memory; but when another different from that comes into my mind, it will not be that. Thus the idea of a horse, and the idea of a centaur, will, as often as they recur in my mind, be unchangeably the same; which is no more than this, the same idea will be always the same idea; but whether the one or the other be the true representation of anything that exists, that, upon his principles, neither our author nor anybody else can know.

53. What he says here of *universal reason*, which *enlightens* every one, *whereof all men* partake, seems to me nothing else but the power men have to consider the ideas they have one with another, and by thus comparing them, find out the relations that are between them; and therefore if an intelligent being at one end of the world, and another at the other end of the world, will consider twice two and four together, he cannot but find them to be equal, i. e., to be the same number. These relations, it is true, are *infinite*, and God, who knows all things, and their relations as they are, knows them all, and so his knowledge is infinite. But men are able to discover more or less of these relations, only as they apply their minds to consider any sort of ideas, and to find out intermediate ones, which can show the relation of those ideas, which cannot be immediately compared by juxta-position. But then what he means by that *infinite reason* which men consult, I confess myself not well to understand. For if he means that they consider a part of those relations of things which are infinite, that is true; but then, this is a very improper way of speaking, and I cannot think that a man of his parts would use it to mean nothing else by it. If he means, as he says, p. 536, that this infinite and universal reason, whereof men partake, and which they consult, is the reason of God himself, I can by no means

assent to it. First, Because I think we cannot say God reasons at all; for he has at once a view of all things. But reason is very far from such an intuition; it is a laborious and gradual progress in the knowledge of things, by comparing one idea with a second, and a second with a third, and that with a fourth, &c., to find the relation between the first and the last of these in this train, and in search for such intermediate ideas as may show us the relation we desire to know, which sometimes we find, and sometimes not. This way, therefore, of finding truth, so painful, uncertain, and limited, is proper only to men or finite understandings, but can by no means be supposed in God; it is, therefore, in God, understanding or knowledge. But then, to say, that we partake in the knowledge of God, or consult his understanding, is what I cannot receive for true. God has given me an understanding of my own; and I should think it presumption in me to suppose I apprehended anything by God's understanding, saw with his eyes, or shared of his knowledge. I think it more possible for me to see with other men's eyes, and understand with another man's understanding, than with God's; there being some proportion between mine and another man's understanding, but none between mine and God's. But if this "infinite reason which we consult," be at last nothing but those infinite unchangeable relations which are in things, some of which we make a shift to discover, this indeed is true, but seems to me to make little to our author's purpose, of seeing all things in God; and that " if we see not all things by the natural union of our minds with the universal and infinite reason, we should not have the liberty to think on all things," as he expresses it, p. 538. To explain himself further concerning this universal *reason*, or as he there calls it by another name, *order*, p. 539, he says, that " God contains in himself the perfections of all the creatures that he has created, or can create, after an intelligible manner." *Intelligible* to himself, that is true; but intelligible to men, at least to me, that I do not find, unless " by containing in himself the perfections of all the creatures," be meant, that there is no perfection in any creature but there is a greater in God, or that there is in God greater perfection than all the perfection in the creatures taken together. And therefore, though it be true what follows in the next words, "that it is by these intelligible perfections that God knows the essence of everything," yet it will not follow from hence, or from anything else that he has said, that those *perfections in God* which contain in them the perfections of all the creatures, are *the immediate objects of the mind of man*, or that they are so the objects of the mind of man that he can in them see the essences of the creatures. For I ask in which of the perfections of God does a man see the essence of a horse or an ass, of a serpent or a dove, of hemlock or parsley? I, for my part, I confess, see not the essence of any of these things in any of the perfections of God which I have any notion of. For indeed I see not the distinct essence either of these things at all, or know wherein it consists. And therefore I cannot comprehend the force of the inference, which follows in these words: "Then the intelligible ideas or perfections that are in God, which represent to us what is out of God, are absolutely necessary and unchangeable." That the perfections that are in God are necessary and unchangeable, I readily grant; but that the *ideas* that are *intelligible* to God, or are in the understanding of God, (for so we must speak of him whilst we conceive of him after the manner of men,) can be seen by us; or that the perfections that are in God represent to us the essences of things that are out of God, that I cannot conceive. The essence of matter, as much as I can see of it, is extension, solidity, divisibility, and mobility; but in which of the perfections of God do I see this essence? To another man, as to our author, perhaps, the essence of body is quite another thing; and when he has told us what to him is the essence of body, it will be then to be considered in which of the perfections of God he sees it. For example, let it be pure extension alone, the idea then that God had in himself of the essence of body before body was created, was the idea of pure extension; when God then created body he created extension, and then space, which existed not before, began to exist. This, I confess, I cannot conceive; but we see in the perfections of God the *necessary* and *unchangeable* essences of things. He sees one essence of body in God, and I another; which is that *necessary* and *unchangeable* essence of body which is contained in the perfections of God, his or mine? Or, indeed, how do or can we know there is any such thing existing as body at all? For we see nothing but the ideas that are in God; but body itself, we neither do nor can possibly see at all; and how then can we know that there is any such thing existing as body, since we can by no means see or perceive it by our senses, which is all the way we can have of knowing any corporeal thing to exist? But it is said, God shows us the ideas in himself, on occasion of the presence of those bodies to our senses. This is *gratis dictum*, and begs the thing in question; and therefore I desire to have it proved to me that they are present. I see the sun, or a horse; no, says our author, that is impossible; they cannot be seen, because being bodies they cannot be united to my mind, and be present to it. But the sun being risen, and the horse brought within convenient distance, and so being present to my eyes, God shows me their ideas in himself; and I say God shows me these ideas when he pleases, without the presence of any such bodies to my eyes. For when I think I see a star at such a distance from me, which truly I do not see, but the idea of it which God shows me, I would have it proved to me that there is such a star existing a million of million of miles from me when I think I see it, more than when I dream of such a star. For until it be proved that there is a candle in the room by which I write this, the supposition of my seeing in God the pyramidical idea of its flame upon occasion of the candle's being there, is begging what is in question. And to prove to me that God exhibits to me that idea upon occasion of the presence of the candle, it must first be proved to me that there is a candle there, which upon these principles can never be done.

Further, We see the *necessary and unchangeable essences of things* in the perfections of God. Water, a rose, and a lion, have their distinct essences one from another, and all other things; what I desire to know are these distinct essences. I confess I neither see them in nor out of God, and in which of the perfections of God do we see each of them?

Page 504, I find these words: "It is evident that the perfections that are in God, which represent created or possible beings, are not at all equal: that those, for example, that represent bodies, are not so noble as those, for example, that represent spirits; and amongst those themselves, which represent nothing but body, or nothing but spirits, there are more perfect one than another to infinity. This is conceivable clearly, and without pain, though one finds some difficulty to reconcile the simplicity of the Divine Being with this variety of intelligible ideas which he contains in his wisdom." This difficulty is to me insurmountable, and I conclude it always shall be so till I can find a way to make simplicity and variety the same. And this difficulty must always cumber this doctrine, which supposes that the perfections of God are the representatives to us of whatever we perceive of the creatures; for then those perfections must be many, and diverse, and distinct one from another, as those ideas are that represent the different creatures to us. And this seems to me to make God formally to contain in him all the distinct ideas of all the creatures, and that so that they might be seen one after another: which seems to me, after all the talk of abstraction, to be but a little less gross conception than of the sketches of all the pictures that ever a painter draws, kept by him in his closet, which are there all to be seen one after another, as he pleases to show them. But whilst these abstract thoughts produce nothing better than this, I the easier content myself with my ignorance, which roundly thinks thus: God is a simple Being, omniscient, that knows all things possible; and omnipotent, that can do or make all things possible. But how he knows, or how he makes, I do not conceive: his ways of knowing, as well as his ways of creating, are to me incomprehensible; and if they were not so, I should not think him to be God, or to be perfecter in knowledge than I am. To which our author's thoughts seem, in the close of what is above cited, somewhat to incline, when he says, "The variety of intelligible ideas which God contains in his wisdom;" whereby he seems to place this variety of ideas in the mind or thoughts of God, as we may so say, whereby it is hard to conceive how we can see them, and not in the being of God, where they are to be seen as so many distinct things in it.

REMARKS
UPON
SOME OF MR. NORRIS'S BOOKS,
WHEREIN HE ASSERTS
P. MALEBRANCHE'S OPINION, OF OUR SEEING ALL THINGS IN GOD.

[As this little treatise is merely a continuation of the preceding, it is unnecessary to give a separate account of it. Of Norris it may be observed, that about the year 1704 he published a second attack on Locke's philosophy, which I have never met with. The fact, however, is mentioned by Tennemann, (Manual of the History of Philosophy, § 337,) though the work is now probably of rare occurrence.—ED.]

THERE are some who think they have given an account of the nature of ideas, by telling us "we see them in God,"* as if we understood what ideas in the understanding of God are, better than when they are in our own understandings; or their nature were better known when it is said that "the immediate object of our understandings" are "the divine ideas, the omniform essence of God, partially represented or exhibited."† So that this now has made the matter clear, there can be no difficulty left, when we are told that our ideas are the *divine ideas,* and the *divine ideas* the *omniform essence of God.* For what the *divine ideas* are we know as plainly as we know what one, two, and three is: and it is a satisfactory explication of what our ideas are to tell us, they are no other than the *divine ideas;* and the *divine essence* is more familiar and level to our knowledge than anything we think of. Besides, there can be no difficulty in understanding how the *divine ideas* are *God's essence.*

* See Cursory Reflections upon a Book called "An Essay concerning Human Understanding," written by John Norris, M.A., rector of Newton St. Loe, in Somersetshire, and late Fellow of All-Souls' College, in a Letter to a Friend: printed at the end of his Christian Blessedness, or Discourses upon the Beatitudes of our Lord and Saviour Jesus Christ, page 30. London, 1690, 8vo.
† Ibid. p. 31.

2. I am complained of for not having "given an account of," or "defined the nature of our ideas."* By "giving an account of the nature of ideas," is not meant that I should make known to men their ideas; for I think nobody can imagine that any articulate sounds of mine, or anybody else, can make known to another what his ideas, that is, what his perceptions, are, better than what he himself knows and perceives them to be; which is enough for affirmations or negations about them. By the "nature of ideas," therefore, is meant here their causes and manner of production in the mind, i. e., in what alteration of the mind this perception consists: and as to that, I answer, no man can tell; for which I not only appeal to experience, which were enough, but shall add this reason, viz., because no man can give any account of any alteration made in any simple substance whatsoever: all the alteration we can conceive being only of the alteration of compounded substances, and that only by a transposition of parts. Our ideas, say these men, are the *divine ideas*, or the *omniform essence of God*,† which the mind sometimes sees and sometimes not. Now I ask these men, what alteration is made in the mind upon *seeing?* for there lies the difficulty which occasions the inquiry.

For what difference a man finds in himself when he sees a marigold and sees not a marigold has no difficulty, and needs not be inquired after; he has the idea now, which he had not before. The difficulty is, what alteration is made in his mind; what changes that has in itself, when it sees what it did not see before, either the "divine idea" in the understanding of God, or, as the ignorant think, the marigold in the garden. Either supposition, as to this matter, is all one; for they are both things extrinsical to the mind, till it has that perception; and when it has it, I desire them to explain to me what the alteration in the mind is, besides saying, as we vulgar do, it is having a perception which it had not the moment before; which is only the difference between perceiving and not perceiving; a difference in matter of fact agreed on all hands; which wherein it consists is, for aught I see, unknown to one side as well as the other: only the one

* See Cursory Reflections, &c., p. 3.
† See "Man in Search of Himself," by Cuthbert, Comment, p. 190, 183.

have the ingenuity to confess their ignorance, and the other pretend to be knowing.

3. P. Malebranche says, "God does all things by the simplest and shortest ways," i. e., as it is interpreted in Mr. Norris's Reason and Religion, "God never does anything in vain."* This will easily be granted them; but how will they reconcile to this principle of theirs, on which their whole system is built, the curious structure of the eye and ear, not to mention the other parts of the body? For if the perception of colours and sounds depended on nothing but the presence of the object affording an *occasional cause* to God Almighty to exhibit to the mind the ideas of figures, colours, and sounds, all that nice and curious structure of those organs is wholly in vain; since the sun by day, and the stars by night, and the visible objects that surround us, and the beating of a drum, the talk of people, and the change made in the air by thunder, are as much present to a blind and deaf man, as to those who have their eyes and ears in the greatest perfection. He that understands optics ever so little, must needs admire the wonderful make of the eye, not only for the variety and neatness of the parts, but as suited to the nature of refraction, so as to paint the image of the object in the retina; which these men must confess to be all lost labour, if it contributes nothing at all, in the ordinary way of causes and effects, to the producing that idea in the mind. But that only the presence of the object *gave occasion* to God to show to the mind that idea in himself, which certainly is as present to one that has a gutta serena, as to the quickest-sighted man living. But we do not know how by any natural operation this can produce an idea in the mind: and therefore (a good conclusion!) God, the author of nature, cannot this way produce it. As if it were impossible for the Almighty to produce anything but by ways we must conceive, and are able to comprehend; when he that is best satisfied of his omniscient understanding, and knows so well how God perceives and man thinks, cannot explain the cohe-

* Reason and Religion; or the Grounds and Measures of Devotion, considered from the Nature of God and the Nature of Man. In several Contemplations. With Exercises of Devotion applied to every Contemplation. By John Norris, M.A., and Fellow of All-Souls' College, in Oxford, Part II. Contemplation II. § 17, p 195. London, 1689, 8vo

sion of parts in the lowest degree of created beings, unorganized bodies.

4. The "perception of universals," also proves that all beings are present to our minds; and that can only be by the presence of God, because all created things are individuals.* Are not all things that exist *individuals?*† If so, then say not all created, but all existing things are individuals; and if so, then the having any general idea proves not that we have all objects present to our minds; but this is for want of considering wherein universality consists; which is only in representation abstracting from particulars. An idea of a circle of an inch diameter will represent, where or whensoever existing, all the circles of an inch diameter; and that by abstracting from time and place. And it will also represent all circles of any bigness, by abstracting also from that particular bigness, and by retaining only the relation of equi-distance of the circumference from the centre, in all the parts of it.

5. We have a "distinct idea of God,"‡ whereby we clearly enough distinguish him from the creatures; but I fear it would be presumption for us to say we have a clear idea of him, as he is in himself.

6. The argument, that "we have the idea of infinite, before the idea of finite," because "we conceive infinite being barely by conceiving being, without considering whether it be finite or infinite,"¶ I shall leave to be considered, whether it is not a mistake of priority of nature for priority of conception.

7. "God made all things for himself;" || therefore we "see all things in him." This is called demonstration. As if *all things* were not as well *made for God*, and mankind had not as much reason to magnify him, if their perception of things were any other way than such an one of *seeing them in him;* as shows *not* God more than the other, and wherein not one

---

* Reason and Religion, &c. Part II., Contemp. II. § 19, p. 191.
† See, on the subject of Universals, Hobbes' Universal Nature, chap. v. § 6; where he does but reproduce, in reality, the notions of the Peripatetics, since Aristotle maintains precisely the same doctrines. See Barthélemy Saint-Hilaire, De la Logique d'Aristotle, t. i. pp. 283, 292, 302.
‡ Reason and Religion, Part II., Contemp. II., § 20, p. 198.
¶ Ibid. § 21, p. 198. || Ibid. § 22, p. 199.

of a million takes more notice of him than those who think they perceive things where they are, by their senses.

8. "If God should create a mind, and give it the sun, suppose, for its idea, or immediate object of knowledge, God would then make that mind for the sun, and not for himself."* This supposes, that those that see things in God, see at the same time God also, and thereby show that their minds are made for God, having him for "the immediate object of their knowledge." But for this I must appeal to common experience, whether every one, as often as he sees anything else, sees and perceives God in the case; or whether it be not true of men, who see other things every moment, that God is not in all their thoughts? "Yet," says he, " when the mind sees his works, it sees him in some manner."† This *some manner* is no manner at all to the purpose of being *made* only *for God*, for his idea, or for his immediate object of knowledge. A man bred up in the obscurity of a dungeon,‡ where by a dim and almost no light he perceives the objects about him, it is true he owes this idea to the light of the sun; but having never heard nor thought of the sun, can one say that the idea of the sun is "his immediate object of knowledge," or that therefore "his mind was made for the sun?" This is the case of a great part of mankind; and how many can we imagine of those who have got some notion of a God, either from tradition or reason, have an idea of him present in their minds as often as they think of anything else?

9. But if our being "made for God," necessarily demonstrates that we should "see all things in him," this at last will demonstrate that we are not half made for him; since it is confessed by our author that we see no other ideas in God but those of number, extension, and essences, which are not half the ideas that take up men's minds.

10. "The simple essences of things are nothing else but the divine essence itself considered with his connotation, as variously representative or exhibitive of things, and as variously imitable or participable by them;§ and this he tells us are ideas.|| The meaning, I take it, of all this put into plain

---

* Ibid. † Ibid. § 23. p. 200.
‡ Plato has a similar thought in the beginning of the seventh book of his Republic, Opera, t. vi. p. 327.
§ Reason and Religion, Part I. Contemp. V. § 19, p. 82.
|| Ibid. § 20.

intelligible words, is this: God has always a power to produce anything that involves not a contradiction. He also knows what we can do. But what is all this to ideas in him, as real beings visible by us? God knew from eternity he could produce a pebble, a mushroom, and a man. Were these, which are distinct ideas, part of his simple essence? It seems then, we know very well the essence of God, and use the word *simple*, which comprehends all sorts of variety in a very proper way. But God knew he could produce such creatures; therefore where shall we place those ideas he saw of them, but in his own *essence?* There these ideas existed *eminentér;* and so they are the *essence of God.* There the things themselves existed too, *eminentér*, and therefore all the creatures as they really exist are the *essence of God.* For if finite real beings of one kind, as ideas are said to be, are the essence of the infinite God; other finite beings, as the creatures, may be also the essence of God. But after this rate we must talk when we will allow ourselves to be ignorant of nothing, but will know even the knowledge of God and the way of his understanding!

11. The "essences of things, or ideas existing in God."* There are many of them that *exist in God:* and so the simple essence of God has actually existing in it as great a variety of ideas as there are of creatures; all of them real beings, and distinct one from another. If it be said, this means God can and knows he can produce them, what doth this say more than every one says? If it doth say more, and shows us not this infinite number of real distinct beings in God, so as to be his very essence, what is this better than what those say who make God to be nothing but the universe;† though

---

* Ibid. § 21, p. 83.

† It has been already observed, that the philosophy of Malebranche, which Norris appears to have adopted, lies open to the suspicion of Pantheism. Among the numerous passages in the Recherche de la Vérité, which might be adduced in support of this view, is the following:—
"Il faut bien remarquer qu'on ne peut pas conclure que les esprits voyent l'essence de Dieu, de ce qu'ils voyent toutes choses en Dieu, de ce qu'ils voyent toutes choses en Dieu de cette manière. Parce que ce qu'ils voyent est tres-imparfait, et que Dieu est tres-parfait. Ils voyent de la matiere divisible, figurée, &c., et il n'y a rien en Dieu qui soit divisible, ou figuré; car Dieu est tout être, parce qu'il est infini et qu'il comprend tout; mais il n'est aucun être en particulier. Cependant ce que nous voyons n'est qu'un ou plusieurs êtres en particulier, et nous ne comprenons point cette simplicité parfaite de Dieu qui renferme tous les êtres."

it be covered under unintelligible expressions of *simplicity* and *variety* at the same time, in the *essence of God?* But those who would not be thought ignorant of anything, to attain it, make God like themselves; or else they could not talk as they do, of "the mind of God," and the ideas in the mind of God, exhibitive of all the whole possibility of being."*

12. "It is in the divine nature that these universal natures, which are the proper object of science, are to be found; and consequently it is in God that we know all the truth which we know."† Doth any *universal nature*, therefore, exist? Or can anything that exists anywhere, or anyhow, be any other than singular? I think it cannot be denied that God having a power to produce ideas in us, can give that power to another; or, to express it otherwise, make any idea the effect of any operation on our bodies. This has no contradiction in it, and therefore is possible. But you will say, you conceive not the way how this is done. If you stand to that rule, that it cannot be done because you conceive not the manner how it is brought to pass, you must deny that God can do this, because you cannot conceive the manner how he produces any idea in us. If visible objects are seen only by God's exhibiting their ideas to our minds, *on occasion* of the presence of those objects, what hinders the Almighty from exhibiting their ideas to a blind man, to whom, being set before his face, and as near his eyes, and in as good a light as to one not blind, they are, according to this supposition, as much the occasional cause to one as to the other? But yet under this equality of occasional causes, one has the idea, and the other not, and this constantly; which would give one reason to suspect something more than a presential *occasional cause* in the object.

13. Further, if light striking upon the eyes be but the *occasional cause* of seeing, God, in making the eyes of so

---

(t. i. p. 365.) The system of Pantheism has always been in great favour with a certain class of philosopers, from the earliest dawn of speculation. Thus we find the ancient Egyptians had anticipated the fundamental doctrine of Spinoza, so that, after carefully reviewing their theology, Jablonski exclaims:—"Would you not imagine that Spinoza had borrowed his system from the Egyptians?" (Pantheon Ægyptiorum, t. i p. 36.)

* Reason and Religion, Part I. Contemp. V. § 30, p. 92, 93.
† Ibid. Part II. Contemp. II. § 30. p. 206.

curious a structure, operates not by the simplest ways; for God could have produced visible ideas upon the occasion of light striking upon the eyelids or forehead.

14. Outward objects are not, when present, always *occasional causes*. He that has long continued in a room perfumed with sweet odours, ceases to smell, though the room be filled with those flowers; though as often as after a little absence he returns again, he smells them afresh. He that comes out of bright sunshine into a room where the curtains are drawn, at first sees nothing in the room; though those who have been there some time see him and everything plainly. It is hard to account for either of these phenomena, by God's producing these ideas upon the account of *occasional causes*. But by the production of ideas in the mind, by the operation of the object on the organs of sense, this difference is easy to be explained.

15. Whether the ideas of light and colours come in by the eyes or no, it is all one as if they did; for those who have no eyes never have them. And whether or no God has appointed that a certain modified motion of the fibres, or spirits in the optic nerve, should excite, or produce, or cause them in us, call it what you please, it is all one as if it did; since where there is no such motion there is no such perception or idea. For I hope they will not deny God the privilege to give such a power to motion if he pleases. Yes, say they, they be the *occasional*, but not the *efficient cause;* for that they cannot be, because that is in effect to say, he has given this motion in the optic nerve a power to operate on himself, but cannot give it a power to operate on the mind of man: it may by this appointment operate on himself, the impassable infinite Spirit, and put him in mind when he is to operate on the mind of man, and exhibit to it the idea which is in himself of any colour. The infinite eternal God is certainly the cause of all things, the fountain of all being and power. But because all being was from him, can there be nothing but God himself? or because all power was originally in him, can there be nothing of it communicated to his creatures? This is to set very narrow bounds to the power of God, and, by pretending to extend it, takes it away. For which (I beseech you, as we can comprehend) is the perfectest power, to make a machine—a watch, for example—

that, when the watchmaker has withdrawn his hands, shall go and strike by the fit contrivance of the parts; or else requires that whenever the hand, by pointing to the hour, minds him of it, he should strike twelve upon the bell? No machine of God's making can go of itself. Why? because the creatures have no power; can neither move themselves, nor anything else. How then comes about all that we see! Do they do nothing? Yes, they are the *occasional causes* to God, why he should produce certain thoughts and motions in them. The creatures cannot produce any idea, any thought in man. How then comes he to perceive or think? God, upon the *occasion* of some motion in the optic nerve, exhibits the colour of a marigold or a rose to his mind. How came that motion in his optic nerve? *On occasion* of the motion of some particles of light striking on the retina, God producing it, and so on. And so, whatever a man thinks, God produces the thought; let it be infidelity, murmuring, or blasphemy. The mind doth nothing; his mind is only the mirror that receives the ideas that God exhibits to it, and just as God exhibits them: the man is altogether passive in the whole business of thinking.*

* This doctrine, scarcely at all modified, has been preached in our own day under the name of Socialism. Malebranche's exposition of it is most explicit, eloquent, and persuasive. "Je sçai bien que l'ame est capable de penser; mais je sçai aussi que l'étendue est capable de figures; l'ame est capable de volonté, comme la matière de mouvement. Mais de même qu'il est faux que la matière, quoique capable de figure et de mouvement, ait en elle-même une *force*, une *faculté*, une *nature*, par laquelle elle se puisse mouvoir, ou se donner tantôt une figure ronde, et tantôt une quarrée: quoique l'ame soit naturellement et essentiellement capable de connoissance et de volonté, il est faux qu'elle ait des *facultés* par lesquelles elle puisse produire en elle ses idées, on son mouvement vers le bien. Il y a bien de la différence entre être mobile et se mouvoir: la matière de sa nature est mobile et capable de figures: elle ne peut même subsister sans figure. Mais elle ne se meut pas; elle ne se figure pas; elle n'a point de faculté pour cela. L'esprit de sa nature est capable de mouvement et d'idées; j'en conviens. Mais il ne se meut pas; il ne s'éclaire pas: c'est Dieu qui fait tout dans les esprits aussi-bien que dans les corps. Peut-on dire que Dieu fait les changemens qui arrivent dans la matière, et qu'il ne fait pas ceux qui arrivent dans l'esprit? Est-ce rendre à Dieu ce qui lui appartient, que d'abandonner à sa disposition les derniers des êtres? N'est-il pas également le maître de toutes choses? N'est-il pas le créateur, le conservateur, le seul véritable moteur des esprits aussi bien que des corps? Certainement il fait tout, substances, accidens, êtres, manières. Car

16. A man cannot move his arm or his tongue; he has no power; only upon *occasion*, the man willing it, God moves it. Then man *wills*, he doth something; or else God, upon the *occasion* of something which he himself did before, pro-

enfin il connoît tout; mais il ne connoît que ce qu'il fait. On lui ôte donc sa connaissance, si on borne son action." (Éclaircissement sur le troisieme livre, t. iii. p. 124.) This doctrine Mr. Robert Owen, in his Book of the New Moral World, also teaches, with the characteristic omission of certain terms. "The feelings and convictions experienced by man are not produced or regulated by his will, but are the necessary effects of the action of circumstances upon his physical and mental nature. Hitherto the world has been governed under the supposition that the feelings and convictions have been produced by the *choice* of the individual, and that they are under the control of what is called *free-will*. The languages of all nations are filled with the terms, that you must love or hate, believe or disbelieve certain qualities and creeds, or if you disobey, you will be punished here and hereafter; and for so loving, hating, believing, or disbelieving, men are now praised and rewarded, as though there were great merit in so doing. Yet, from an investigation of the facts connected with this subject, it appears that the feelings and convictions are *instincts of human nature*,—instincts which every one is compelled to possess or receive,—and for which no man can have merit or demerit, or deserve reward or punishment" (chap. iii. p. 7.) The doctrine of Hobbes, from whom the philosophers of Mr. Owen's school appear to have borrowed so much, does not quite square with the modern hypothesis on the subject of human laws. Hobbes maintains, indeed, that man acts under the impulse of dire necessity; but argues, pleasantly enough, that he may, notwithstanding, be very justly punished for what he does: first, because all laws are just; and second, because his example may deter others, though they also be of course obnoxious to the force of necessity. Let us, however, hear his own exposition, which places the absurdity of his reasoning in a more striking light than almost any other language could do. "The necessity," he says, "of an action, doth not make the laws which prohibit it unjust. To let pass, that not the necessity, but the will, to break the law, maketh the action unjust; because the law regardeth the will, and no other precedent causes of action. And to let pass, that no law can possibly be unjust; inasmuch as every man maketh (by his consent) the law he is bound to keep; and which consequently must be just, unless a man can be unjust to himself. I say, what necessary cause soever precede an action, yet if the action be forbidden, he that doth it willingly may be justly punished. For instance, suppose the law, on pain of death, prohibit stealing; and that there be a man who by the strength of temptation is necessitated to steal, and is thereupon put to death; does not this punishment deter others from theft? Is it not a cause that others steal not? Doth it not frame and make their wills to justice? To make the law is, therefore, to make a cause of justice, and to necessitate justice: and consequently, 'tis no injustice to make such a law." (Of Liberty and Necessity, English Works, vol. iv. p. 252, Molesworth's edition.)— ED.

duced this will and this action in him. This is the hypothesis that clears doubts, and brings us at last to the religion of Hobbes and Spinoza; by resolving all, even the thoughts and will of men, into an irresistible fatal necessity. For whether the original of it be from the continued motion of eternal all-doing matter, or from an omnipotent immaterial Being, which having begun matter and motion, continues it by the direction of *occasions*, which he himself has also made: as to religion and morality, it is just the same thing. But we must know how everything is brought to pass, and thus we have it resolved without leaving any difficulty to perplex us. But perhaps it would better become us to acknowledge our ignorance, than to talk such things boldly of the Holy One of Israel, and condemn others for not daring to be as unmannerly as ourselves.

17. Ideas may be real beings, though not substances; as motion is a real being, though not a substance; and it seems probable that, in us, ideas depend on, and are some way or other the effect of motion; since they are so fleeting, it being, as I have elsewhere observed, so hard and almost impossible to keep in our minds the same unvaried idea long together, unless when the object that produces it is present to the senses; from which the same motion that first produced it, being continued, the idea itself may continue.

18. To excuse, therefore, the ignorance I have owned of what our ideas are, any further than as they are perceptions we experiment in ourselves; and the dull, unphilosophical way I have taken of examining their production, only so far as experience and observation lead me, wherein my dim sight went not beyond *sensation* and *reflection*.

19. *Truth** lies only in propositions. The foundation of this truth is the relation that is between our ideas. The knowledge of truth is that perception of the relation between our ideas to be as it is expressed.

20. The *immutability* of *essences* lies in the same sounds, supposed to stand for the same ideas. These things considered, would have saved this learned discourse.

21. Whatever exists, whether in God or out of God, is *singular*.†

22. If no propositions should be made, there would be no

---

* See Reason and Religion, &c. Part II. Contemp. II. § 29, p. 204.
† Ibid., 30, p. 206.

truth nor falsehood; though the same relations still between the same ideas, is a foundation of the *immutability* of *truth** in the same propositions, whenever made.

23. What wonder is it that the same idea† should always be the same idea? For if the word *triangle* be supposed to have the same signification always, that is all this amounts to.

24. I "desire to know‡ what things they are that God has prepared for them that love him?" Therefore I have some knowledge of them already, though they be such as "eye hath not seen, nor ear heard, nor have entered into the heart of man to conceive."

25. If I "have all things actually present to my mind," why do I not know all things distinctly?

26. He that considers|| the force of such ways of speaking as these: "I desire it—pray give it me—She was afraid of the snake, and ran away trembling"—will easily conceive how the meaning of the words *desire* and *fear*, and so all those which stand for intellectual notions, may be taught by words of *sensible* significations.

27. This, however otherwise in experience, should be so on this hypothesis: v. g., the uniformity of the ideas that different men have when they use such words as these, *glory, worship, religion,* are clear proofs that "God exhibited to their minds that part of the ideal world as is signified by that sign."

28. Strange! that *truth,* being in any question but one, the more we discover of it the more *uniform* our *judgments* should be *about it!* ¶

29. This argues that the ground of it is the always immutable relations of the same ideas. Several ideas that we have once got acquainted with, we can revive, and so they are present to us when we please; but the knowledge of their relations, so as to know what we may affirm or deny of them, is not always present to our minds; but we often miss truth, even after study. But in many, and possibly not the fewest, we have neither the ideas nor the truth *constantly,* or so much as at all *present* to our minds.

And I think, I may, without any disparagement to the author, doubt whether he ever had, or with all his applica-

* See Reason and Religion, &c. Part II. Contemp. II. § 32, p. 207.
† Ibid. § 33 p. 208, 209.   ‡ Ibid. § 34, p. 210.
|| Ibid. § 35, p. 211—213.   ¶ Ibid. § 36, p. 214.

tion ever would have, the ideas or truths present to the mind, that Mr. Newton had in writing his book.

30. This section* supposes we are better acquainted with *God's understanding* than our own. But this pretty argument would perhaps look as smilingly thus: We are *like* God in our understandings; he sees what he sees by ideas in his own mind: therefore we see what we see by ideas that are in our own minds.

31. These texts† do not prove that we shall "hereafter see all things in God." There will be objects in a future state, and we shall have bodies and senses.

32. Is he, whilst we see through the *veil* of our mortal flesh here, intimately present to our minds?

33. To think of anything,‡ is to contemplate that precise idea. The idea of *being in general*, is the idea of being abstracted from whatever may limit or determine it to any inferior species; so that he that thinks always of *being in general*, thinks never of any *particular* species of being; unless he can think of it with and without precision at the same time. But if he means that he *thinks* of *being in general*, whenever he thinks of this or that particular being, or sort of being; then it is certain he may always think of *being in general*, till he can find out a way of thinking on nothing.

34. *Being in general*, is being ‖ abstracted from wisdom, goodness, power, and any particular sort of duration; and I have as true an idea of being, when these are excluded out of it, as when extension, place, solidity, and mobility are excluded out of my idea. And therefore, if *being in general*, and *God*, be *the same*, I have a true idea of God when I exclude out of it power, goodness, wisdom, and eternity.

35. As if there was no difference ¶ between "man's being his own light," and "not seeing things in God." Man may be enlightened by God, though it be not by "seeing all things in God."

The finishing of these hasty thoughts must be deferred to another season.

Oates, 1693.   JOHN LOCKE.

* See Reason and Religion, &c. Part II. Contemp. II. § 37, p. 215
† Ibid. § 38, p. 216, 217.   ‡ Ibid. § 39, p. 217, 213.
‖ Ibid. § 40, p. 219.   ¶ Ibid. § 43, p. 223.

ELEMENTS OF
NATURAL PHILOSOPHY.

[I AM not acquainted with a better compendium of natural philosophy than this. The science, no doubt, has received very great improvements since the time of Locke, but his exposition of it is still sufficiently exact for all practical purposes. The explanations of terms are brief, correct, and intelligible; and the accounts of the grander phenomena of the universe, though designed only as incentives to inquiry, are such as to open up very magnificent prospects before the mind. As it would be preposterous to render that long by annotation which the author expressly made short and simple, that it might be the more easily comprehended and the substance of it lodged firmly in the memory, I shall trouble the reader with very few notes.—ED.]

CHAPTER I.

OF MATTER AND MOTION.

MATTER is an extended solid substance; which being comprehended under distinct surfaces, makes so many particular distinct bodies.

Motion is so well known by the sight and touch, that to use words to give a clearer idea of it would be in vain.

Matter, or body, is indifferent to motion or rest.

There is as much force required to put a body, which is in motion, at rest; as there is to set a body, which is at rest, into motion.

No parcel of matter can give itself either motion or rest, and therefore a body at rest will remain so eternally, except some external cause puts it in motion; and a body in motion will move eternally, unless some external cause stops it.

A body in motion will always move on in a straight line, unless it be turned out of it by some external cause, because a body can no more alter the determination of its motion than it can begin, alter, or stop, its motion itself.

The swiftness of motion is measured by distance of place and length of time wherein it is performed. For instance, if A and B, bodies of equal or different bigness, move each of them an inch in the same time, their motions are equally swift; but if A moves two inches in the time whilst B is moving one inch, the motion of A is twice as swift as that of B.

The quantity of motion is measured by the swiftness of the motion,* and the quantity of the matter moved, taken together. For instance, if A, a body equal to B, moves as swift as B, then it hath an equal quantity of motion. If A hath twice as much matter as B, and moves equally as swift, it hath double the quantity of motion, and so in proportion.

It appears, as far as human observation reaches, to be a settled law of nature, that all bodies have a tendency, attraction, or gravitation towards one another.

The same force, applied to two different bodies, produces always the same quantity of motion in each of them. For instance, let a boat which with its lading is one ton, be tied at a distance to another vessel, which with its lading is twenty-six tons; if the rope that ties them together be pulled, either in the less or bigger of these vessels, the less of the two, in their approach one to another, will move twenty-six feet, while the other moves but one foot.

Wherefore the quantity of matter in the earth being twenty-six times more than in the moon, the motion in the moon towards the earth, by the common force of attraction, by which they are impelled towards one another, will be twenty six times as fast as in the earth; that is, the moon will move twenty-six miles towards the earth, for every mile the earth moves towards the moon.

Hence it is, that, in this natural tendency of bodies towards one another, that in the lesser is considered as gravitation, and that in the bigger as attraction,† because the motion

* Whether this be consistent with the received theory of motion is more than I can say, but it appears to me to be a fallacy; for motion having reference to the space traversed, and the time in which the transit is performed, there is as much motion in an ounce ball which traverses five hundred yards in a given number of seconds as in a pound ball which traverses the same distance in the same time, though the motive power which set the matter in motion must be evidently greater than that which imparted motion to the former. Locke, therefore, appears here to confound motion with the motive power; that is, if I apprehend his meaning exactly.—ED.

† Besides the works of Sir Isaac Newton and the more modern phi-

of the lesser body (by reason of its much greater swiftness) is alone taken notice of.

This attraction is the strongest the nearer the attracting bodies are to each other; and, in different distances of the same bodies, is reciprocally in the duplicate proportion of those distances. For instance, if two bodies, at a given distance, attract each other with a certain force, at half the distance they will attract each other with four times that force; at one third of the distance, with nine times that force; and so on.

Two bodies at a distance will put one another into motion by the force of attraction; which is inexplicable by us, though made evident to us by experience, and so to be taken as a principle in natural philosophy.

Supposing then the earth the sole body in the universe, and at rest; if God should create the moon, at the same distance that it is now from the earth, the earth and the moon would presently begin to move one towards another in a straight line by this motion of attraction or gravitation.

If a body, that by the attraction of another would move in a straight line towards it, receives a new motion any ways oblique to the first, it will no longer move in a straight line, according to either of those directions, but in a curve that will partake of both. And this curve will differ, according to the nature and quantity of the forces that concurred to produce it; as, for instance, in many cases it will be such a curve as ends where it began, or recurs into itself: that is, makes up a circle, or an ellipsis * or oval very little differing from a circle.

losophers, to which the reader will refer on this subject, it may be worth while to examine the previous speculation of Hobbes, in which the same theory is developed, though with less method and completeness. (Elements of Philosophy, Part IV. c. xxx. § 2. See also Lord Bacon, Sylva Sylvarum, 703-4.)—ED.

* Kepler seems to have been the first who observed that the planets may move in ellipses; but it was reserved for Sir Isaac Newton to demonstrate the truth of this observation. The reader will find this demonstration in Lord King's Life of Locke, vol. i. p. 389, et seq., "where," in the opinion of his Lordship, "the lemmas which are prefixed are expressed in a more explanatory form than those of the Principia usually are."—ED.

CHAPTER II.
OF THE UNIVERSE.

To any one, who looks about him in the world, there are obvious several distinct masses of matter, separate from one another; some whereof have discernible motions. These are the sun, the fixed stars, the comets and the planets, amongst which this earth, which we inhabit, is one. All these are visible to our naked eyes.

Besides these, telescopes have discovered several fixed stars, invisible to the naked eye; and several other bodies moving about some of the planets; all which were invisible and unknown, before the use of perspective glasses were found.

The vast distances between these great bodies are called intermundane spaces; in which though there may be some fluid matter, yet it is so thin and subtile, and there is so little of that in respect of the great masses that move in those spaces, that it is as much as nothing.

These masses of matter are either luminous, or opaque or dark.

Luminous bodies, are such as give light of themselves; and such are the sun and the fixed stars.

Dark or opaque bodies are such as emit no light of themselves, though they are capable of reflecting of it, when it is cast upon them from other bodies; and such are the planets.

There are some opaque bodies, as for instance the comets, which, besides the light that they may have from the sun, seem to shine with a light that is nothing else but an accension, which they receive from the sun, in their near approaches to it, in their respective revolutions.

The fixed stars are called fixed, because they always keep the same distance one from another.

The sun, at the same distance from us that the fixed stars are, would have the appearance of one of the fixed stars.

CHAPTER III.
OF OUR SOLAR SYSTEM.

Our solar system consists of the sun, and the planets and comets moving about it.

The planets are bodies. which appear to us like stars; not that they are luminous bodies, that is, have light in themselves; but they shine by reflecting the light of the sun.

They are called planets from a Greek word, which signifies wandering; because they change their places, and do not always keep the same distance with one another, nor with the fixed stars, as the fixed stars do.

The planets are either primary, or secondary.

There are six primary planets,* viz., Mercury, Venus, the Earth, Mars, Jupiter, and Saturn.

All these move round the sun, which is, as it were, the centre of their motions.

The secondary planets move round about other planets. Besides the moon, which moves about the earth, four moons move about Jupiter, and five about Saturn,† which are called their satellites.

The middle distances of the primary planets from the sun are as follows:—

Mercury		32,000,000	
Venus	Is distant	59,000,000	Statute miles, each 5280 English and 4943 French feet.
The Earth	from the	81,000,000	
Mars	sun's centre, about	123,000,000	
Jupiter		424,000,000	
Saturn		777,000,000	

The orbits of the planets, and their respective distances from the sun and from one another, together with the orbit of a comet, may be seen in the figure of the solar system hereunto annexed.‡

The periodical times of each planet's revolution about the sun are as follows:—

---

* The number now discovered amounts to twenty-three. Of these, twelve have been discovered since the year 1845, eleven of them rotating between the orbits of Mars and Jupiter; the remaining one is the planet Neptune, exterior to all the rest, and whose discovery is one of the greatest intellectual triumphs of the present age.—ED.

† Saturn has been found by modern astronomers to possess eight moons, besides his luminous belts; and Uranus certainly has four moons, if not more.—ED.

‡ The engraving alluded to, being now commonly found in all elementary treatises on the subject, has been omitted.—-ED.

		Y.	D.	H.	M.
Mercury	Revolves	0	88	0	0
Venus	about the	0	225	0	0
The Earth	Sun, in	0	365	5	49
Mars	the space	1	322	0	0
Jupiter	of	11	319	0	0
Saturn		29	138	0	0

The planets move round about the sun from west to east in the zodiac, or, to speak plainer, are always found amongst some of the stars of those constellations, which make the twelve signs of the zodiac.

The motion of the planets about the sun is not perfectly circular, but rather elliptical.

The reason of their motions in curve lines is the attraction of the sun, or their gravitations towards the sun, (call it which you please,) and an oblique or sidelong impulse or motion.

These two motions or tendencies, the one always endeavouring to carry them in a straight line from the circle they move in, and the other endeavouring to draw them in a straight line to the sun, makes that curve line they revolve in.

The motion of the comets about the sun is in a very long slender oval; whereof one of the focuses is the centre of the sun, and the other very much beyond the sphere of Saturn.

The moon moves about the earth, as the earth doth about the sun; so that it hath the centre of its motion in the earth; as the earth hath the centre of its revolution in the sun, about which it moves.

The moon makes its synodical motion about the earth, in twenty-nine days, twelve hours, and about forty-four minutes.

It is full moon, when, the earth being between the sun and the moon, we see all the enlightened part of the moon; new moon, when, the moon being between us and the sun, its enlightened part is turned from us; and half moon, when the moon being in the quadratures, as the astronomers call it, we see but half the enlightened part.

An eclipse of the moon is, when the earth, being between the sun and the moon, hinders the light of the sun from falling upon, and being reflected by the moon. If the light of the sun is kept off from the whole body of the moon, it is a total eclipse; if from a part only, it is a partial one.

An eclipse of the sun is, when the moon, being between the sun and the earth, hinders the light of the sun from coming to us. If the moon hides from us the whole body of the sun, it is a total eclipse; if not, a partial one.

Our solar system is distant from the fixed stars 20,000,000,000 semi-diameters of the earth; or, as Mr. Huygens expresses this distance, in his Cosmotheoros:* the fixed stars are so remote from the earth, that, if a cannon-bullet should come from one of the fixed stars with as swift a motion as it hath when it is shot out of the mouth of a cannon, it would be 700,000 years in coming to the earth.

This vast distance so much abates the attraction of those remote bodies, that its operation upon those of our system is not at all sensible, nor would draw away or hinder the return of any of our solar comets; though some of them should go so far from the sun, as not to make the revolution about it in less than 1000 years.

It is more suitable to the wisdom, power, and greatness of God, to think that the fixed stars are all of them suns, with systems of inhabitable planets moving about them, to whose inhabitants he displays the marks of his goodness, as well as to us; rather than to imagine that those very remote bodies, so little useful to us, were made only for our sake.

CHAPTER IV
OF THE EARTH, CONSIDERED AS A PLANET.

The earth, by its revolution about the sun in three hundred and sixty-five days, five hours, forty-nine minutes, akes that space of time we call a year.

The line, which the centre of the earth describes in its annual revolution about the sun, is called ecliptic.

The annual motion of the earth about the sun, is in the order of the signs of the zodiac; that is, speaking vulgarly, from west to east.

Besides this annual revolution of the earth about the sun

* Christiani Hugenii ΚΟΣΜΟΘΕΩΡΟΣ, sive de Terris Cœlestibus earumque ornatu conjecturæ, &c., p. m. 137

in the ecliptic, the earth turns round upon its own axis in twenty-four hours.

The turning of the earth upon its own axis every twenty-four hours, whilst it moves round the sun in a year, we may conceive by the running of a bowl on a bowling-green; in which not only the centre of the bowl hath a progressive motion on the green; but the bowl in its going forward from one part of the green to another, turns round about its own axis.

The turning of the earth upon its own axis, makes the difference of day and night; it being day in those parts of the earth which are turned towards the sun, and night in those parts which are in the shade, or turned from the sun.

The annual revolution of the earth in the ecliptic is the cause of the different seasons, and of the several lengths of days and nights, in every part of the world, in the course of the year.

The reason of it is the earth's going round its own axis in the ecliptic, but at the same time keeping everywhere its axis equally inclined to the plane of the ecliptic, and parallel to itself. For the plane of the ecliptic inclining to the plane of the equator twenty-three degrees and a half, makes that the earth, moving round in the ecliptic, hath sometimes one of its poles, and sometimes the other, nearer the sun.

If the diameter of the sun be to the diameter of the earth as forty-eight to one, as by some it is accounted, then the disk of the sun, speaking *numero rotundo*, is above 2000 times bigger than the disk of the earth; and the globe of the sun above 100,000 times bigger than the globe of the earth.

The distance of the earth's orbit from the sun is above 20,000 semi-diameters of the earth.

If a cannon bullet should come from the sun with the same velocity it hath when it is shot out of the mouth of a cannon, it would be twenty-five years in coming to the earth.

CHAPTER V.

OF THE AIR AND ATMOSPHERE.

WE have already considered the earth as a planet, or one of the great masses of matter moving about the sun; we shall now consider it as it is made up of its several parts, abstractedly from its diurnal and annual motions.

The exterior part of this our habitable world is the air or atmosphere; a light, thin fluid, or springy body, that encompasses the solid earth on all sides.

The height of the atmosphere, above the surface of the solid earth, is not certainly known; but that it doth reach but to a very small part of the distance betwixt the earth and the moon, may be concluded from the refraction of the rays coming from the sun, moon, and other luminous bodies.

Though considering that the air we are in, being near 1000 times lighter than water, and that the higher it is, the less it is compressed by the superior incumbent air, and so consequently being a springy body the thinner it is; and considering also that a pillar of air of any diameter is equal in weight to a pillar of quicksilver of the same diameter of between twenty-nine and thirty inches height; we may infer that the top of the atmosphere is not very near the surface of the solid earth.

It may be concluded, that the utmost extent of the atmosphere reaches upwards from the surface of the solid earth that we walk on, to a good distance above us; first, if we consider that a column of air of any given diameter is equiponderant to a column of quicksilver of between twenty-nine and thirty inches height. Now, quicksilver being near fourteen times heavier than water, if air was as heavy as water, the atmosphere would be about fourteen times higher than the column of quicksilver, i. e., about thirty-five feet.

Secondly, if we consider that air is 1000 times lighter than water, then a pillar of air equal in weight to a pillar of quicksilver of thirty inches high will be 35,000 feet; whereby we come to know that the air or atmosphere is 35,000 feet, i. e., near seven miles high.

Thirdly, if we consider that the air is a springy body, and that that which is nearest the earth is compressed by the weight of all the atmosphere that is above it, and rests perpendicularly upon it, we shall find that the air here, near the surface of the earth, is much denser and thicker than it is in the upper parts. For example, if upon a fleece of wool you lay another, the under one will be a little compressed by the weight of that which lies upon it; and so both of them by a third, and so on; so that if 10,000 were piled one upon another, the under one would, by the weight of all the rest, be very much compressed, and all the parts of it be brought abundantly closer together than when there was no other upon it, and the next to that a little less compressed, the third a little less than the second, and so on till it came to the uppermost, which would be in its full expansion, and not compressed at all. Just so it is in the air, the higher you go in it, the less it is compressed, and consequently the less dense it is; and so the upper part being exceedingly thinner than the lower part, which we breathe in, (which is that that is 1000 times lighter than water,) the top of the atmosphere is probably much higher than the distance above assigned.

That the air near the surface of the earth will mightily expand itself, when the pressure of the incumbent atmosphere is taken off, may be abundantly seen in the experiments made by Mr. Boyle in his pneumatic engine. In his "Physico-mechanical Experiments," concerning the air, he declares[*] it probable that the atmosphere may be several hundred miles high; which is easy to be admitted, when we consider what he proves in another part of the same treatise, viz., that the air here about the surface of the earth, when the pressure is taken from it, will dilate itself about one hundred and fifty-two times.

The atmosphere is the scene of the meteors; and therein is collected the matter of rain, hail, snow, thunder, and lightning; and a great many other things observable in the air.

CHAPTER VI.

OF METEORS IN GENERAL.

Besides the springy particles of pure air, the atmosphere is made up of several steams or minute particles of several sorts, rising from the earth and the waters, and floating in the air, which is a fluid body, and though much finer and thinner, may be considered in respect of its fluidity to be

---

[*] New Experiments Physico-mechanical, touching the Spring of the Air, and its effects; (made for the most part in a new Pneumatical Engine;) written by the Honourable Robert Boyle. Experiment xxxvi. p. 155. Oxford, 1662. 4to.

like water, and so capable, like other liquors, of having heterogeneous particles floating in it.

The most remarkable of them are: first, the particles of water raised into the atmosphere, chiefly by the heat of the sun, out of the sea and other waters, and the surface of the earth, from whence it falls in dew,* rain, hail, and snow.

Out of the vapours rising from moisture, the clouds are principally made.

Clouds do not consist wholly of watery parts; for, besides the aqueous vapours that are raised into the air, there are also sulphureous and saline particles that are raised up, and in the clouds mixed with the aqueous particles, the effects whereof are sometimes very sensible; as particularly in lightning and thunder, when the sulphureous and nitrous particles firing, break out with that violence of light and noise, which is observable in thunder, and very much resembles gunpowder.

That there are nitrous particles † raised into the air is evident from the nourishment which rain gives to vegetables more than any other water; and also by the collection of nitre or saltpetre in heaps of earth, out of which it has been extracted, if they be exposed to the air, so as to be kept from rain, not to mention other efforts, wherein the nitrous spirit in the air shows itself.

Clouds are the greatest and most considerable of all the meteors, as furnishing matter and plenty to the earth. They consist of very small drops of water, and are elevated a good distance above the surface of the earth; for a cloud is nothing but a mist flying high in the air, as a mist is nothing but a cloud here below.

How vapours are raised into the air in invisible steams by the heat of the sun out of the sea and moist parts of the earth, is easily understood, and there is a visible instance of it in ordinary distillations. But how these steams are collected into drops, which bring back the water again, is not so easy to determine.

---

* See Dr. Well's Treatise on the Production and Nature of Dew.—ED.
† The presence of nitre in the atmosphere is nowhere perhaps so palpable as in Egypt, where it occasions the sudden chilliness of the nights, and may be the cause of that corrosiveness of the air which had already been remarked in the time of Herodotus. (Book ii. § 12.)—ED.

To those that will carefully observe, perhaps it will appear probable that it is by that which the chemists call precipitation, to which it answers in all its parts.

The air may be looked on as a clear and pellucid menstruum, in which the insensible particles of dissolved matter float up and down, without being discerned or troubling the pellucidity of the air; when on a sudden, as if it were by a precipitation, they gather into the very small but visible misty drops that make clouds.

This may be observed sometimes in a very clear sky, when, there not appearing any cloud or anything opaque in the whole horizon, one may see on a sudden clouds gather, and all the hemisphere overcast; which cannot be from the rising of new aqueous vapours at that time, but from the precipitation of the moisture, that in invisible particles floated in the air, into very small, but very visible drops, which by a like cause being united into greater drops, they become too heavy to be sustained in the air, and so fall down in rain.

Hail* seems to be the drops of rain frozen in their falling.

Snow is the small particles of water frozen before they unite into drops.

The regular figures, which branch out in flakes of snow, seem to show that there are some particles of salt mixed with the water, which makes them unite in certain angles.

The rainbow is reckoned one of the most remarkable meteors, though really it be no meteor at all, but the reflection of the sunbeams from the smallest drops of a cloud or mist, which are placed in a certain angle made by the concurrence of two lines, one drawn from the sun, and the other from the eye, to these little drops in the cloud, which reflect the sunbeams; so that two people, looking upon a rainbow at the same time, do not see exactly the same rainbow.

CHAPTER VII.

OF SPRINGS, RIVERS, AND THE SEA.

Part of the water that falls down from the clouds runs away upon the surface of the earth into channels, which con-

* On the physical causes of congelation see Hobbes' Elements of Natural Philosophy, Part IV. c. xxviii. § 9.—Ed.

vey it to the sea; and part of it is imbibed in the spongy shell of the earth, from whence, sinking lower by degrees, it falls down into subterranean channels, and so underground passes into the sea; or else, meeting with beds of rock or clay, it is hindered from sinking lower, and so breaks out in springs,* which are most commonly in the sides or at the bottom of hilly ground.

Springs make little rivulets; those united make brooks; and those coming together make rivers, which empty themselves into the sea.

The sea is a great collection of waters in the deep valleys of the earth. If the earth were all plain, and had not those deep hollows, the earth would be all covered with water; because the water, being lighter than the earth, would be above the earth, as the air is above the water.

The most remarkable thing in the sea is that motion of the water called tides.† It is a rising and falling of the water of the sea. The cause of this is the attraction of the moon, whereby the part of the water in the great ocean which is nearest the moon, being most strongly attracted, is raised higher than the rest; and the part opposite to it on the contrary side, being least attracted, is also higher than the rest. And these two opposite rises of the surface of the water in the great ocean, following the motion of the moon from east to west, and striking against the large coasts of the continents that lie in its way, from thence rebounds back again, and so makes floods and ebbs in narrow seas, and rivers remote from the great ocean. Herein we also see the reason of the times of the tides, and why they so constantly follow the course of the moon.

* On the origin of springs and rivers see Hobbes' Elements of Philosophy, Part IV. c. xxviii. § 18. Connected with this subject, however, there are several difficulties which had not apparently presented themselves to the mind of the great philosopher of Malmesbury. See in Spallanzani's Travels in the Kingdom of the Two Sicilies, vol. iv. p. 136; and in M. M. Dolomieu's Voyage aux Isles de Lipari, p. 120, the account of a perennial spring in the Eolian Islands, the existence of which can scarcely be explained according to the principles laid down by Hobbes and Locke.—ED.

† On the subject of tides see the somewhat rare treatise of Isaac Vossius concerning the motion of the Seas and the Winds, c. viii. p. 96 and compare with his theory the notions of Hobbes. (Elements of Philosophy, Part IV. c. xxvi. § 10.)—ED.

CHAPTER VIII.

OF SEVERAL SORTS OF EARTH, STONES, METALS, MINERALS, AND OTHER FOSSILS.

THIS solid globe we live upon is called the earth, though it contains in it a great variety of bodies, several whereof are not properly earth; which word, taken in a more limited sense, signifies such parts of this globe as are capable, being exposed to the air, to give rooting and nourishment to plants, so that they may stand and grow in it. With such earth as this, the greatest part of the surface of this globe is covered; and it is, as it were, the storehouse from whence all the living creatures of our world have originally their provisions; for from thence all the plants have their sustenance, and some few animals, and from these all the other animals.

Of earth, taken in this sense, there are several sorts, v. g., common mould, or garden earth, clay of several kinds, sandy soils.

Besides these, there is medicinal earth; as that which is called terra lemnia, bolus armena, and divers others.

After the several earths, we may consider the parts of the surface of this globe, which are barren; and such, for the most part, are sand, gravel, chalk, and rocks, which produce nothing, where they have no earth mixed among them. Barren sands are of divers kinds, and consist of several little irregular stones without any earth; and of such there are great deserts to be seen in several parts of the world.

Besides these, which are most remarkable on the surface of the earth, there are found, deeper in this globe, many other bodies, which, because we discover by digging into the bowels of the earth, are called by one common name, fossils; under which are comprehended metals, minerals, or half metals, stones of divers kinds, and sundry bodies that have the texture between earth and stone.

To begin with those fossils which come nearest the earth: under this head we may reckon the several sorts of ochre, chalk, that which they call black-lead, and other bodies of this kind, which are harder than earth, but have not the consistency and hardness of perfect stone.

Next to these may be considered stones of all sorts,

whereof there is almost an infinite variety. Some of the most remarkable, either for beauty or use, are these: marble of all kinds, porphyry, granite, freestone, &c., flints, agates, cornelians, pebbles, under which kind come the precious stones, which are but pebbles of an excessive hardness, and when they are cut and polished they have an extraordinary lustre. The most noted and esteemed are diamonds, rubies amethysts, emeralds, topazes, opals.

Besides these, we must not omit those which, though of not so much beauty, yet are of greater use, viz., loadstones, whetstones of all kinds, limestones, calamine, or lapis calaminaris, and abundance of others.

Besides these, there are found in the earth several sorts of salts, as eating or common salt, vitriol, sal gemma, and others.

The minerals, or semi-metals that are dug out of the bowels of the earth, are antimony, cinnabar, zink, &c., to which may be added brimstone.

But the bodies of most use that are sought for out of the depths of the earth are the metals; which are distinguished from other bodies by their weight, fusibility, and malleableness; of which there are several sorts: gold, silver, copper, tin, lead, and, the most valuable of them all, iron; to which one may join that anomalous body, quicksilver, or mercury.

He that desires to be more particularly informed concerning the qualities and properties of these subterraneous bodies, may consult natural historians and chemists.

What lies deeper towards the centre of the earth we know not, but a very little beneath the surface of this globe; and whatever we fetch from underground is only what is lodged in the shell of the earth.

All stones, metals, and minerals, are real vegetables; that is, grow organically from proper seeds, as well as plants.

CHAPTER IX.

OF VEGETABLES, OR PLANTS.

NEXT to the earth itself, we may consider those that are maintained on its surface; which, though they are fastened to it, yet are very distinct from it; and those are the whole tribe of vegetables, or plants. These may be divided into three sorts: herbs, shrubs, and trees.

Herbs are those plants whose stalks are soft, and have nothing woody in them: as grass, sowthistle, and hemlock. Shrubs and trees have all wood in them; but with this difference, that shrubs grow not to the height of trees, and usually spread into branches near the surface of the earth; whereas trees generally shoot up in one great stem or body, and then, at a good distance from the earth, spread into branches; thus gooseberries and currants are shrubs, oaks and cherries are trees.

In plants, the most considerable parts are these: the root, the stalk, the leaves, the flower, and the seed. There are very few of them that have not all these parts; though some few there are that have no stalk, others that have no leaves, and others that have no flowers; but without seed or root I think there are none.

In vegetables, there are two things chiefly to be considered: their nourishment and propagation.

Their nourishment is thus: the small and tender fibres of the roots, being spread under ground, imbibe, from the moist earth, juice fit for their nourishment; this is conveyed by the stalk up into the branches and leaves, and, in some plants, imperceptible tubes, and from thence, by the bark, returns again to the root; so that there is in vegetables, as well as in animals, a circulation of the vital liquor. By what impulse it is moved is somewhat hard to discover. It seems to be from the difference of day and night, and other changes in the heat of the air; for the heat dilating and the cold contracting those little tubes, supposing there be valves in them, it is easy to be conceived how the circulation is performed in plants, where it is not required to be so rapid and quick as in animals.

Nature has provided for the propagation of the species of plants several ways. The first and general is by seed. Besides this, some plants are raised from any part of the root set in the ground; others by new roots that are propagated from the old ones, as in tulips; others by offsets; and in others, the branches set in the ground will take root and grow; and last of all, grafting and inoculation, in certain sorts, are known ways of propagation. All these ways of increasing plants make one good part of the skill of gardening; and from the books of gardeners may be best learned.

CHAPTER X.
OF ANIMALS.

THERE is another sort of creatures belonging to this our earth, rather as inhabitants than parts of it. They differ in this from plants, that they are not fixed to any one place, but have a freedom of motion up and down; and besides, have sense to guide them in their motions.

Man and brute divide all the animals of this our globe.

Brutes may be considered as either aërial, terrestrial, aquatic, or amphibious. I call those aërial which have wings, wherewith they can support themselves in the air. Terrestrial are those whose only place of rest is upon the earth. Aquatic, are those whose constant abode is upon the water. Those are called amphibious, which live freely in the air upon the earth, and yet are observed to live long in the water, as if they were natural inhabitants of that element; though it be worth the examination to know, whether any of those creatures that live at their ease, and by choice, a good while or at any time upon the earth, can live a long time together perfectly under water.

Aërial animals may be subdivided into birds and flies.

Fishes, which are the chief part of aquatic animals, may be divided into shell-fishes, scaly fishes, and those that have neither apparent scales nor shells.

And the terrestrial animals may be divided into quadrupeds or beasts, reptiles, which have many feet, and serpents, which have no feet at all.

Insects, which in their several changes belong to several of the before-mentioned divisions, may be considered together as one great tribe of animals. They are called insects, from a separation in the middle of their bodies, whereby they are, as it were, cut into two parts, which are joined together by a small ligature; as we see in wasps, common flies, and the like.

Besides all these there are some animals that are not perfectly of these kinds, but placed, as it were, in the middle betwixt two of them, by something of both; as bats, which have something of beasts and birds in them.

Some reptiles of the earth, and some of aquatics, want one or more of the senses, which are in perfecter animals; as worms, oysters, cockles, &c.

Animals are nourished by food, taken in at the mouth, digested in the stomach, and thence by fit vessels distributed over the whole body, as is described in books of anatomy.

The greatest part of animals have five senses: viz., seeing, hearing, smelling, tasting, and feeling. These, and the way of nourishment of animals, we shall more particularly consider, because they are common to man with beasts.

The way of nourishment of animals, particularly of man, is by food taken in at the mouth, which being chewed there, is broken and mixed with the saliva, and thereby prepared for an easier and better digestion in the stomach.

When the stomach has performed its office upon the food, it protrudes it into the guts, by whose peristaltic motion it is gently conveyed along through the guts, and, as it passes, the chyle, which is the nutritive part, is separated from the excrementitious by the lacteal veins: and from thence conveyed into the blood, with which it circulates till itself be concocted into blood. The blood, being by the vena cava brought into the right ventricle of the heart,* by the contraction of that muscle, is driven through the arteria pulmonaris into the lungs; where the constantly inspired air mixing with it enlivens it; and from thence being conveyed by the vena pulmonaris into the left ventricle of the heart, the contraction of the heart forces it out, and, by the arteries, distributes it into all parts of the body; from whence it returns by the veins into the right ventricle of the heart, to take the same course again. This is called the circulation of the blood, by which life and heat are communicated to every part of the body.

In the circulation of the blood, a good part of it goes up into the head; and by the brains are separated from it, or made out of it, the animal spirits; which, by the nerves, impart sense and motion to all parts of the body.

The instruments of motion are the muscles; the fibres

* Vid. Blumenbach's Comparative Anatomy, c. xii. On the Heart and Blood-vessels in Mammalia, Birds, &c. Physiology, § 7, p. 81.— ED.

whereof, contracting themselves, move the several parts of the body.

This contraction of the muscles is, in some of them, by the direction of the mind, and in some of them without it; which is the difference between voluntary and involuntary motions in the body.

CHAPTER XI.
OF THE FIVE SENSES.
Of Seeing.

THE organ of seeing is the eye;* consisting of variety of parts wonderfully contrived for the admitting and refracting the rays of light, so that those that come from the same point of the object, and fall upon different parts of the pupil, are brought to meet again at the bottom of the eye, whereby the whole object is painted on the retina that is spread there.

That which immediately affects the sight, and produces in us that sensation which we call seeing, is light.

Light† may be considered either, first, as it radiates from luminous bodies directly to our eyes; and thus we see luminous bodies themselves, as the sun, or a flame, &c.; or, secondly, as it is reflected from other bodies; and thus we see a man or a picture by the rays of light reflected from them to our eyes.

Bodies, in respect of light, may be divided into three sorts: first, those that emit rays of light, as the sun and fixed stars; secondly, those that transmit the rays of light, as the air; thirdly, those that reflect the rays of light, as iron, earth, &c. The first are called luminous, the second pellucid, and the third opaque.

The rays of light themselves are not seen; but by them the bodies from which they originally come, as the sun or a fixed star; or the bodies from which they are reflected, as a horse or a tulip. When the moon shines, we do not see the rays which come from the sun to the moon, but by them we see the moon, from whence they are reflected.

* Blumenbach's Physiology, § 17, p. 246. Comparative Anatomy, c. xxi. p. 287.—ED.
† Hobbes' Elements of Natural Philosophy, Part IV. c. xxvii § 2, seq —ED.

If the eye be placed in the medium through which the rays pass to it, the medium is not seen at all; for instance, we do not see the air through which the rays come to our eyes. But if a pellucid body, through which the light comes, be at a distance from our eye, we see that body, as well as the bodies from whence the rays come that pass through them to come to our eyes. For instance, we do not only see bodies through a pair of spectacles, but we see the glass itself. The reason whereof is, that pellucid bodies being bodies, the surfaces of which reflect some rays of light from their solid parts, these surfaces, placed at a convenient distance from the eye, may be seen by those reflected rays; as, at the same time, other bodies beyond those pellucid ones may be seen by the transmitted rays.

Opaque bodies are of two sorts, specular or not specular. Specular bodies, or mirrors, are such opaque bodies whose surfaces are polished; whereby they, reflecting the rays in the same order as they come from other bodies, show us their images.

The rays that are reflected from opaque bodies always bring with them to the eye the idea of colour; and this colour is nothing else, in the bodies, but a disposition to reflect to the eye more copiously one sort of rays than another. For particular rays are originally endowed with particular colours: some are red, others blue, others yellow, and others green, &c.

Every ray of light, as it comes from the sun, seems a bundle of all these several sorts of rays; and as some of them are more refrangible than others, that is, are more turned out of their course in passing from one medium to another, it follows that after such refraction they will be separated, and their distinct colour observed. Of these the most refrangible are violet, and the least, red; and the intermediate ones, in order, are indigo, blue, green, yellow, and orange. This separation is very entertaining, and will be observed with pleasure in holding a prism in the beams of the sun.

As all these rays differ in refrangibility, so they do in reflexibility; that is, in the property of being more easily reflected from certain bodies than from others; and hence arise, as hath been said, all the colours of bodies; which are, in a manner, infinite, as an infinite number of compositions and proportions of the original colours may be imagined.

The whiteness of the sun's light is compounded of all the original colours, mixed in due proportion.

Whiteness in bodies is but a disposition to reflect all colours of light nearly in the proportion they are mixed in the original rays; as, on the contrary, blackness is only a disposition to absorb or stifle, without reflection, most of the rays of every sort that fall on the bodies.

Light is successively propagated with an almost inconceivable swiftness; for it comes from the sun to this our earth in about seven or eight minutes of time, which distance is about 80,000,000 English miles.

Besides colour, we are supposed to see figure: but, in truth, that which we perceive when we see figure, as perceivable by sight, is nothing but the termination of colour.

Of Hearing.

NEXT to seeing, hearing* is the most extensive of our senses. The ear is the organ of hearing, whose curious structure is to be learned from anatomy.

That which is conveyed into the brain by the ear is called sound; though, in truth, till it come to reach and affect the perceptive part, it be nothing but motion.

The motion which produces in us the perception of sound is a vibration of the air, caused by an exceeding short but quick tremulous motion of the body from which it is propagated; and therefore we consider and denominate them as bodies sounding.

That sound is the effect of such a short, brisk, vibrating motion of bodies from which it is propagated, may be known from what is observed and felt in the strings of instruments, and the trembling of bells, as long as we perceive any sound come from them, for as soon as that vibration is stopped, or ceases in them, the perception ceases also.

The propagation of sound is very quick, but not approaching that of light. Sounds move about 1140 English feet in a second of time; and in seven or eight minutes of time, they move about one hundred English miles.

* On the organ of hearing see Blumenbach's Comparative Anatomy, c. xx. p. 278. Physiology, § 16, p. 240. To avoid constant reference to the same works, the reader is here requested to consult them on the organs and operations of the senses generally.—ED.

Of Smelling.

SMELLING is another sense that seems to be wrought on by bodies at a distance; though that which immediately affects the organ, and produces in us the sensation of any smell, are effluvia, or invisible particles, that, coming from bodies at a distance, immediately affect the olfactory nerves.

Smelling bodies seem perpetually to send forth effluvia, or steams, without sensibly wasting at all. Thus a grain of musk will send forth odoriferous particles for scores of years together without its being spent; whereby one would conclude that these particles are very small; and yet it is plain that they are much grosser than the rays of light, which have a free passage through glass; and grosser also than the magnetic effluvia, which pass freely through all bodies, when those that produce smell will not pass through the thin membranes of a bladder, and many of them scarce ordinary white paper.

There is a great variety of smells, though we have but a few names for them; sweet, stinking, sour, rank, and musty are almost all the denominations we have for odours; though the smell of a violet and of musk, both called sweet, are as distinct as any two smells whatsoever.

Of Taste.

TASTE is the next sense to be considered. The organ of taste is the tongue and palate.

Bodies that emit light, sounds, and smells are seen, heard, and smelt at a distance; but bodies are not tasted but by immediate application to the organ; for till our meat touch our tongues or palates we taste it not, how near soever it be.

It may be observed of tastes, that though there be a great variety of them, yet, as in smells, they have only some few general names; as sweet, bitter, sour, harsh, rank, and some few others.

Of Touch.

THE fifth and last of our senses is touch; a sense spread over the whole body, though it be most eminently placed in the ends of the fingers.

By this sense the tangible qualities of bodies are dis

cerned; as hard, soft, smooth, rough, dry, wet, clammy, and the like.

But the most considerable of the qualities that are perceived by this sense are heat and cold.

The due temperament of those two opposite qualities is the great instrument of nature, that she makes use of in most, if not all, her productions.

Heat is a very brisk agitation of the insensible parts of the object, which produces in us that sensation from whence we denominate the object hot; so what in our sensation is heat, in the object is nothing but motion. This appears by the way whereby heat is produced; for we see that the rubbing of a brass nail upon a board will make it very hot; and the axle-trees of carts and coaches are often hot, and sometimes to a degree that it sets them on fire, by the rubbing of the nave of the wheel upon it.

On the other side, the utmost degree of cold is the cessation of that motion of the insensible particles, which to our touch is heat.

Bodies are denominated hot and cold in proportion to the present temperament of that part of our body to which they are applied; so that feels hot to one which seems cold to another; nay, the same body, felt by the two hands of the same man, may at the same time appear hot to the one and cold to the other, because the motion of the insensible particles of it may be more brisk than that of the particles of the other.

Besides the objects before mentioned, which are peculiar to each of our senses, as light and colour of the sight, sound of hearing, odours of smelling, savours of tasting, and tangible qualities of the touch, there are two others that are common to all the senses; and those are pleasure and pain, which they may receive by and with their peculiar objects. Thus, too much light offends the eye; some sounds delight and others grate the ear; heat in a certain degree is very pleasant, which may be augmented to the greatest torment; and so the rest.

These five senses are common to beasts with men; nay, in some of them, some brutes exceed mankind. But men are endowed with other faculties, which far excel anything that is to be found in the other animals in this our globe.

Memory, also, brutes may be supposed to have, as well as men.

CHAPTER XII.
OF THE UNDERSTANDING OF MAN.

THE understanding of man does so surpass that of brutes, that some are of opinion brutes are mere machines, without any manner of perception at all. But letting this opinion alone, as ill-grounded, we will proceed to the consideration of human understanding, and the distinct operations thereof.

The lowest degree of it consists in perception, which we have before in part taken notice of, in our discourse of the senses; concerning which it may be convenient further to observe, that, to conceive a right notion of perception, we must consider the distinct objects of it, which are simple ideas; v. g., such as are those signified by these words, scarlet, blue, sweet, bitter, heat, cold, &c., from the other objects of our senses; to which we may add the internal operations of our own minds as the objects of our own reflection, such as are thinking, willing, &c.

Out of these simple ideas are made, by putting them together, several compounded or complex ideas; as those signified by the words pebble, marigold, horse.

The next thing the understanding doth in its progress to knowledge, is to abstract its ideas, by which abstraction they are made general.

A general idea is an idea in the mind, considered there as separated from time and place; and so capable to represent any particular being that is conformable to it. Knowledge, which is the highest degree of the speculative faculties, consists in the perception of the truth of affirmative or negative propositions.

This perception is either immediate or mediate. Immediate perception of the agreement or disagreement of two ideas is when, by comparing them together in our minds, we see, or, as it were, behold, their agreement or disagreement. This, therefore, is called intuitive knowledge. Thus we see that red is not green; that the whole is bigger than a part; that two and two are equal to four.

The truth of these and the like propositions we know by a bare simple intuition of the ideas themselves, without any more ado; and such propositions are called self-evident.

The mediate perception of the agreement or disagreement of two ideas is when, by the intervention of one or more other ideas, their agreement or disagreement is shown. This is called demonstration, or rational knowledge. For instance, the inequality of the breadth of two windows, or two rivers, or any two bodies that cannot be put together, may be known by the intervention of the same measure applied to them both; and so it is in our general ideas, whose agreement or disagreement may be often shown by the intervention of some other ideas, so as to produce demonstrative knowledge; where the ideas in question cannot be brought together and immediately compared, so as to produce intuitive knowledge.

The understanding doth not know only certain truth, but also judges of probability, which consists in the likely agreement or disagreement of ideas.

The assenting to any proposition as probable is called opinion, or belief.

We have hitherto considered the great and visible parts of the universe, and those great masses of matter, the stars, planets, and particularly this our earth, together with the inanimate parts and animate inhabitants of it; it may be now fit to consider what these sensible bodies are made of, and that is of inconceivably small bodies or atoms,* out of whose various combinations bigger moleculæ are made; and so, by a greater and greater composition, bigger bodies; and out of these the whole material world is constituted.

By the figure, bulk, texture, and motion of these small and insensible corpuscles, all the phenomena of bodies may be explained.

* On the subject of atoms, &c., the reader may be amused by a little treatise, entitled, Man in Quest of Himself, p. 185, in Metaphysical Tracts, by English Philosophers of the Eighteenth Century, collected and edited by Dr. Parr.—ED.

SOME THOUGHTS

CONCERNING

READING AND STUDY,

FOR A GENTLEMAN.

Although this brief tract cannot, strictly speaking, be denominated philosophical, it contains several useful and excellent observations, which render it worthy to be preserved. In the opening remarks Locke touches slightly upon a topic which the reader will find more fully discussed in the Treatise concerning the Conduct of the Understanding; but it is useful, and at all events entertaining, to compare the different expressions made use of by the philosopher in delivering at different times the same thoughts. The course of reading recommended may at first sight appear somewhat too limited, though very few men of the world, perhaps, would care to go through it completely. Some few of the books enumerated are now no longer in use, their place being supplied by more modern compilations; but the works on which Locke himself set any particular value are as deserving of study now as they were then; I mean those which treat of eloquence, ethics, and politics. Even the books of Voyages and Travels which he considered of sufficient value to be mentioned, continue for the most part to be popular, as far as popularity can be said to belong to any such productions. The political treatises which Locke desired to behold in the hands of gentlemen are every one of them such as still to merit the same distinction, more particularly Sir Ralph Sadlier's Rights of the Kingdom, which, with Algernon Sydney's Discourses, Harrington's political works, and Milton's Tenure of Kings, and Defence of the People of England, may be said to contain an almost complete development of the science. The few foreign works which ought perhaps to be added, are Aristotle's Politics, Macchiavelli's Prince and Discourses on Livy, and Montesquieu's Esprit des Loix.—Ed.]

Reading is for the improvement of the understanding. The improvement of the understanding is for two ends: first, for our own increase of knowledge; secondly, to enable us to deliver and make out that knowledge to others.

The latter of these, if it be not the chief end of study in a gentleman, yet it is at least equal to the other, since the greatest part of his business and usefulness in the world is by the influence of what he says or writes to others.

The extent of our knowledge cannot exceed the extent of our ideas; therefore, he who would be universally knowing, must acquaint himself with the objects of all sciences. But this is not necessary to a gentleman, whose proper calling is the service of his country, and so is most properly concerned in moral and political knowledge; and thus the studies which more immediately belong to his calling are those which treat of virtues and vices, of civil society, and the arts of government, and will take in also law and history.

It is enough for a gentleman to be furnished with the ideas belonging to his calling, which he will find in the books that treat of the matters above mentioned.

But the next step towards the improvement of his understanding, must be, to observe the connexion of these ideas in the propositions which those books hold forth and pretend to teach as truths; which, till a man can judge whether they be truths or no, his understanding is but little improved; and he doth but think and talk after the books that he hath read, without having any knowledge thereby. And thus men of much reading are greatly learned but may be little knowing.

The third and last step, therefore, in improving the understanding, is to find out upon what foundation any proposition advanced bottoms; and to observe the connexion of the intermediate ideas by which it is joined to that foundation upon which it is erected, or that principle from which it is derived. This, in short, is right reasoning; and by this way alone true knowledge is to be got by reading and studying.

When a man, by use, hath got this faculty of observing and judging of the reasoning and coherence of what he reads, and how it proves what it pretends to teach; he is then, and not till then, in the right way of improving his understanding and enlarging his knowledge by reading.

But that, as I have said, being not all that a gentleman should aim at in reading, he should further take care to improve himself in the art also of speaking, that so he may be able to make the best use of what he knows.

The art of speaking well consists chiefly in two things, viz., perspicuity and right reasoning.

Perspicuity consists in the using of proper terms for the ideas or thoughts which he would have to pass from his own mind into that of another man. It is this that gives them an easy entrance; and it is with delight that men hearken to those whom they easily understand; whereas what is obscurely said, dying as it is spoken, is usually not only lost, but creates a prejudice in the hearer, as if he that spoke knew not what he said, or was afraid to have it understood.

The way to obtain this is to read such books as are allowed to be writ with the greatest clearness and propriety, in the language that a man uses. An author excellent in this faculty, as well as several others, is Dr. Tillotson, late Archbishop of Canterbury, in all that is published of his. I have chosen rather to propose this pattern for the attainment of the art of speaking clearly, than those who give rules about it, since we are more apt to learn by example than by direction. But if any one hath a mind to consult the masters in the art of speaking and writing, he may find in Tully "De Oratore," and another treatise of his, called Orator, and in Quintilian's Institutions, and Boileau's "Traité du Sublime,"* instructions concerning this and the other parts of speaking well.

Besides perspicuity, there must be also right reasoning; without which perspicuity serves but to expose the speaker. And for the attaining of this I should propose the constant reading of Chillingworth, who by his example will teach both perspicuity and the way of right reasoning, better than any book that I know; and therefore will deserve to be read on that account over and over again; not to say anything of his argument.

Besides these books in English, Tully, Terence, Virgil, Livy, and Cæsar's Commentaries may be read to form one's mind to a relish of a right way of speaking and writing.

The books I have hitherto mentioned have been in order only to writing and speaking well; not but that they will deserve to be read on other accounts.

The study of morality I have above mentioned as that

* This treatise is a translation from Longinus.

that becomes a gentleman; not barely as a man, but in order to his business as a gentleman. Of this there are books enough writ both by ancient and modern philosophers; but the morality of the gospel doth so exceed them all, that, to give a man a full knowledge of true morality, I shall send him to no other book but the New Testament. But if he hath a mind to see how far the heathen world carried that science, and whereon they bottomed their ethics, he will be delightfully and profitably entertained in Tully's Treatises "De Officiis."

Politics contains two parts, very different the one from the other: the one containing the original of societies, and the rise and extent of political power; the other the art of governing men in society.

The first of these hath been so bandied amongst us, for these sixty years backward, that one can hardly miss books of this kind. Those which I think are most talked of in English are the first book of Mr. Hooker's "Ecclesiastical Polity," and Mr. Algernon Sydney's "Discourses concerning Government." The latter of these I never read. Let me here add, "Two Treatises of Government," printed in 1690;* and a treatise of "Civil Polity," printed this year.† To these one may add, Puffendorf "De Officio Hominis et Civis," and "De Jure Naturali et Gentium;" which last is the best book of that kind.

As to the other part of politics, which concerns the art of government, that, I think, is best to be learned by experience and history, especially that of a man's own country. And therefore I think an English gentleman should be well versed in the history of England, taking his rise as far back as there are any records of it; joining with it the laws that were made in the several ages, as he goes along in his history; that he may observe from thence the several turns of state, and how they have been produced. In Mr. Tyrrel's History of England, he will find all along those several authors which have treated of our affairs, and which he may have recourse to, concerning any point which either his curiosity or judgment shall lead him to inquire into.

* These two treatises are written by Mr. Locke himself.—ED.
† "Civil Polity. A Treatise concerning the Nature of Government," &c London, 1703, in 8vo. Written by Peter Paxton, M.D.—ED.

With the history, he may also do well to read the ancient lawyers, such as Bracton, "Fleta," Henningham, "Mirror of Justice," my Lord Coke's "Second Institutes," and the "Modus, tenendi Parliamentum;" and others of that kind which he may find quoted in the late controversies between Mr. Petit, Mr. Tyrrel, Mr. Atwood, &c., with Dr. Brady; as also, I suppose, in Sadlier's Treatise of "Rights of the Kingdom, and Customs of our Ancestors," whereof the first edition is the best; wherein he will find the ancient constitution of the government of England.

There are two volumes of "State Tracts," printed since the revolution, in which there are many things relating to the government of England.

As for general history, Sir Walter Raleigh and Dr. Howell are books to be had. He who hath a mind to launch further into that ocean, may consult Whear's "Methodus Legendi Historias," of the last edition; which will direct him to the authors he is to read and the method wherein he is to read them.

To the reading of history, chronology and geography are absolutely necessary.

In geography, we have two general ones in English, Heylin and Moll; which is the best of them I know not, having not been much conversant in either of them. But the last I should think to be of most use, because of the new discoveries that are made every day tending to the perfection of that science; though I believe that the countries which Heylin mentions are better treated of by him, bating what new discoveries since his time have added.

These two books contain geography in general; but whether an English gentleman would think it worth his time to bestow much pains upon that; though without it he cannot well understand a Gazette; it is certain he cannot well be without Camden's "Britannia," which is much enlarged in the last English edition. A good collection of maps is also necessary.

To geography, books of travels may be added. In that kind, the collections made by our countrymen Hackluyt and Purchas are very good. There is also a very good collection made by Thevenot, in folio, in French; and by Ramuzio, in Italian; whether translated into English or no

I know not. There are also several good books of travels of Englishmen published, as Sandys, Rowe, Brown, Gage, and Dampier.

There are also several voyages in French, which are very good, as Pyrard,* Bergeron,† Sagard,‡ Bernier,§ &c., whether all of them are translated into English, I know not.

There is at present a very good "Collection of Voyages and Travels," never before in English, and such as are out of print, now printing by Mr. Churchill.‖

There are besides these a vast number of other travels; a sort of books that have a very good mixture of delight and usefulness. To set them all down, would take up too much time and room. Those I have mentioned are enough to begin with.

As to chronology, I think Helvicus the best for common use; which is not a book to be read, but to lie by, and be consulted upon occasion. He that hath a mind to look further into chronology, may get Tallent's "Tables," and Strauchius's "Breviarium Temporum," and may to those add Scaliger's "De Emendatione Temporum," and Petavius, if he hath a mind to engage deeper in that study.

Those who are accounted to have writ best particular parts of our English history, are Bacon, of Henry VII.; and Herbert, of Henry VIII. Daniel also, is commended; and Burnet's "History of the Reformation."

Mariana's "History of Spain," and Thuanus's "History of his Own Time," and Philip de Comines are of great and deserved reputation.

There are also several French and English memoirs and collections, such as La Rochefoucault, Melvil, Rushworth,

---

* "Voyage de François Pyrard de Laval. Contenant sa Navigation aux Indes Orientales, Maldives, Moluques, Bresil." Paris, 1619, 8vo., third edition.

† "Relation des Voyages en Tartarie, &c. Le tout recueilli par Pierre Bergeron." Paris, 1634, 8vo.

‡ "Le grand Voyage des Hurons, situés en l'Amerique, &c. Par F. Gab. Sagard Theodat." Paris, 1632, 8vo.

§ "Memoires de l'Empire du Grand Mogol, &c., par François Bernier." Paris. 1670 and 1671. 3 vols. 12mo.

‖ A collection of voyages and travels published in 1704, in 6 vols. folio.

&c., which give a great light to those who have a mind to look into what hath past in Europe this last age.

To fit a gentleman for the conduct of himself, whether as a private man or as interested in the government of his country, nothing can be more necessary than the knowledge of men; which, though it be to be had chiefly from experience, and, next to that, from a judicious reading of history; yet there are books that of purpose treat of human nature, which help to give an insight into it. Such are those treating of the passions, and how they are moved; whereof Aristotle, in his second book of Rhetoric, hath admirably discoursed, and that in a little compass. I think this rhetoric is translated into English; if not, it may be had in Greek and Latin together.

La Bruyere's "Characters" are also an admirable piece of painting; I think it is also translated out of French into English.

Satirical writings, also, such as Juvenal and Persius, and, above all, Horace, though they paint the deformities of men, yet they thereby teach us to know them.

There is another use of reading, which is for diversion and delight. Such are poetical writings, especially dramatic, if they be free from profaneness, obscenity, and what corrupts good manners; for such pitch should not be handled.

Of all the books of fiction, I know none that equals "Cervantes' History of Don Quixote" in usefulness, pleasantry, and a constant decorum. And, indeed, no writings can be pleasant which have not nature at the bottom, and are not drawn after her copy.

There is another sort of books, which I had almost forgot, with which a gentleman's study ought to be well furnished, viz., dictionaries of all kinds. For the Latin tongue, Littleton, Cooper, Calepin, and Robert Stephens's "Thesaurus Linguæ Latinæ," and Vossii "Etymologicum Linguæ Latinæ." Skinner's "Lexicon Etymologicum," is an excellent one of that kind for the English tongue. Cowel's "Interpreter" is useful for the law terms. Spelman's "Glossary" is a very useful and learned book. And Selden's "Titles of Honour" a gentleman should not be without. Baudrand hath a very good "Geographical Dictionary." And there are several historical ones which are of use; as Lloyd's, Hoffman's, Moreri's; and Bayle's incomparable dictionary is something of the same kind. He that hath occasion to look into books written in Latin since the decay of the Roman empire and the purity of the Latin tongue, cannot be well without Du Cange's "Glossarium Mediæ et Infimæ Latinitatis."

Among the books above set down I mentioned Vossius's "Etymologicum Linguæ Latinæ;" all his works are lately printed in Holland, in six tomes. They are fit books for a gentleman's library, containing very learned discourses concerning all the sciences.

END OF VOLUME II.

INDEX.

ABBOT of St. Martin, ii. 57, s. 26
Abstraction, i. 274, s. 9
  Puts a perfect distance betwixt men and brutes, 275, s. 10
  What, 275, s. 9
Abstract ideas, why made, i. 522, s. 6, 7, 8
  Terms cannot be affirmed one of another, ii. 77, s. 1
Abstract and concrete terms, ii. 77
Abstruse ideas, whence derived, i. 282
Abuse of words, ii. 94; causes of, 95; logic and dispute have much contributed to it, 97; remedies, 113
Accident, i. 423, s. 2
Action, but two sorts of, thinking and motion, i. 362, s. 4; 421, s. 11
Actions, the best evidence of men's principles, i. 161, s. 7
  Unpleasant may be made pleasant, and how, 406, s. 69
  Cannot be the same in different places, 459, s. 2
  Considered as modes, or as moral, 494, s. 15
Adequate ideas, i. 510, s. 1, 2
  We have not, of any species of substances, ii. 162, s. 26
Affirmations are only inconcrete, ii. 77, s. 1
Aged, murder of the, among certain nations, i. 163
Agreement and disagreement of our ideas fourfold, ii. 129, s. 3-7
Alteration, i. 454, s. 2
Analogy, useful in natural philosophy, ii. 279, s. 12
Angels, on the nature of, i. 360; ii. 48, 163
Anger, i. 356, 357, s. 12-14
Animals, identity of, i. 462
Antipathy and sympathy, whence, i. 535, s. 7
Archetypes, ii. 175

Arguments of four sorts:
  1. Ad verecundiam, ii. 300, s. 19
  2. Ad ignorantiam, ii. 301, s. 20
  3. Ad hominem, ib., s. 21
  4. Ad judicium, ib., s. 22. This alone right, ib.
Arithmetic, systems of, nearly all founded on the decimal progression, i. 328
  The use of ciphers in arithmetic, ii. 155, s. 19
Artificial things are most of them collective ideas, i. 448, s. 3
  Why we are less liable to confusion about artificial things, than about natural, ii. 67, s. 40
  Have distinct species, 67, s. 41
Assent, a mark of self-evidence, i. 145, s. 18
  Not of innate, 145, s. 18-20; 197, s. 19
Assent to maxims, i. 139, s. 10
  Upon hearing and understanding the terms, 144, 145, s. 17, 18
Assent to probability, ii. 269, s. 3
  Ought to be proportioned to the proofs, 271, s. 1
Association of ideas, i. 531, s. 1, &c.
  This association how made, 534, s. 6
  Ill effects of it, as to antipathies, 535, 536, s. 7, 8; 538, s. 15
  And this in sects of philosophy and religion, 539, s. 18
  Its ill influence as to intellectual habits, 539, s. 17
Assurance, ii. 275, s. 6
Atheism in the world, i. 184, s 8
Atom, what, i. 460, s. 3
Authority; relying on others' opinions, one great cause of error, ii. 335, s. 17
Axioms. See Maxims.

Bat, question whether a bird or no, ii. 116

Bats, observations on, i. 260
Baxter, his idea that the happiness of a future would mainly consist in enlarged knowledge, ii. 147
Beings, but two sorts, ii. 235, s. 9
　The eternal being must be cogitative, 236, s. 10
Belief, what, ii. 269, s. 3
　To believe without reason, is against our duty, 302, s. 24
　Best in our opinion, not a rule of God's actions, i. 190, s. 12
Berkeley, his denial of the existence of the visible world, an extension of an idea of Locke, i. 247
Blind man, if made to see, would not know which a globe, which a cube, by his sight, though he knew them by his touch, i. 256, s. 8
Blood, how it appears in a microscope, i. 430, s. 11
Bodies and spirits, i. 231; no science of, ii. 162, 163
Body. We have no more primary ideas of body than of spirit, i. 435, s. 16
　The primary ideas of body, 436, s. 17
　The extension or cohesion of body, as hard to be understood, as the thinking of spirit, 437—440, s. 23-7
　Moving of body by body, as hard to be conceived as by spirit, 441, s. 28
　Operates only by impulse, 245, s. 11
　What, 288, s. 11
　The author's notion of the 'body,' 2 Cor. v. 10, ii. 360, and of 'his own body,' 1 Cor. xv. 35, &c., 360. The meaning of 'the same body,' 360. Whether the word body be a simple or complex term, 361. This only a controversy about the sense of a word, 376.
Brimha, or the Supreme Intelligence, temples to, i. 190

Brutes have no universal ideas, i. 275, s. 10, 11
　Abstract not, 275, s. 10
　But, its several significations, ii. 76, s. 5
Cannibalism, instances of, among various nations, i. 162
Capacity, ii. 284, s. 3
Capacities, to know their extent, useful, i. 130, s. 4
　To cure scepticism and idleness, 132, s. 6
　Are suited to our present state, 131, s. 5
Cassowary, the, described, ii. 64
Castellan, Pierre, his devotion to study, i. 385
Cause, i. 454, s. 1
　And effect, 454, s. 1
Certainty depends on intuition, ii. 134, s. 1
　Wherein it consists, 181, s. 18
　Of truth, 181, s. 1
　To be had in very few general propositions, concerning substances, 270, s. 6
　Where to be had, 201, s. 16
　Verbal, 186, s. 8
　Real, 186, s. 8
　Sensible knowledge, the utmost certainty we have of existence, 244, s. 2
　The author's notion of it not dangerous, &c., 382
　How it differs from assurance, 275, s. 6
Changelings, whether men or no, ii. 176, 177, s. 13, 14
Changes in animals and plants removed from their native climes, ii. 196
Children, systematic exposure of, among some nations, i. 162, 167
　Have ideas in the womb, but not innate ones, 254
Chillingworth, his style commended, ii. 499
Civil law, the measure of crime and innocence, i. 487

Clearness alone hinders confusion of ideas, i. 272, s. 3
Clear and obscure ideas, i. 499, s. 2
Cogitative and incogitative beings, ii. 236
Colours, modes of, i. 345, s. 4
Comments upon law, why infinite, ii. 84, s. 9
Comparing ideas, i. 273, s. 4
　Herein men excel brutes, 275, s. 3
Complex ideas how made, i. 273, s. 6; 279, s. 1
　In these the mind is more than passive, 280, s. 2
　Ideas reducible to modes, substances, and relations, 280, s. 3
Compounding ideas, i. 273, s. 6
　In this is a great difference between men and brutes, 273, s. 7
Compulsion, i. 368, s. 13
Concrete terms, ii. 77
Confidence, ii. 275, s. 7
Confused ideas, i. 499, s. 4
Confusion of ideas, wherein it consists, i. 500, s. 5-7
　Causes of confusion in ideas, 500, 501, s. 7-9; 503, s. 12
　Of ideas, grounded on a reference to names, 503, s. 10-12
　Its remedy, 503, s. 12
Conscience is our own opinion of our own actions, i. 161, s. 8
Consciousness makes the same person, i. 467, s. 10; 473, s. 16
　Probably annexed to the same individual, immaterial substance, 478, s. 25
　Necessary to thinking, 211, s. 10, 11; 219, s. 19
　What, 219, s. 19
Contemplation, i. 262, s. 1
Creation, i. 454, s. 2
　Not to be denied, because we cannot conceive the manner how, 342, s. 19

Darius, anecdote of, i. 163
Defining of terms would cut off a great part of disputes, ii. 101, s. 15
Definition, why the genus is used in definitions, ii. 13, s. 10

Demonstration, ii. 136, s. 3
　Not so clear as intuitive knowledge, 136, s. 4-6; 137, s. 7
　Intuitive knowledge necessary in each step of a demonstration, 137, s. 7
　Not limited to quantity, 138, s. 9
　Why that has been supposed, 138, s. 10
　Not to be expected in all cases, 249, s. 10
　What, 486, s. 15
Demonstrative knowledge, ii. 135
Descartes, his classification of ideas, i. 134
Desire, i. 353, s. 6
　Is a state of uneasiness, 377, s. 31, 32
　Is moved only by happiness, 383, s. 41
　How far, 384, s. 43
　How to be raised, 389, s. 46
　Misled by wrong judgment, 399, s. 60
Despair, i. 356, s. 11
Dictionaries, how to be made, ii. 126, s. 25
Discerning, i. 270, s. 1
　The foundation of some general maxims, 270, s. 1
Discourse cannot be between two men, who have different names for the same idea, or different ideas for the same name, i. 233, s. 5
Discoveries, extent of men's, how limited, i. 200
Disembodied souls, notion of, i. 214
Disposition, i. 420, s. 10
Disputation. See Logic.
Disputing: the art of disputing prejudicial to knowledge, i. 514, s. 6-9
　Destroys the use of language, 523, s. 10
Disputes, whence, s. 28
Disputes, multiplicity of them, owing to the abuse of words, ii. 107, s. 22
　Are most about the signification of words, 116, s. 7

Distance, i. 284, s. 3
Distinct ideas, i. 499, s. 4
Divine law the measure of sin and duty, i. 486
Divisibility of matter incomprehensible, i. 443, s. 31
Dreaming, i. 215, s. 13
 Seldom in some men, i. 215, s. 14
Dreams for the most part irrational, i. 217, s. 16
 In dreams no ideas but of sensation or reflection, 218, s. 17
Duelling, condemnation of, i. 494
Duration, i. 300, s. 1, 2
 Whence we get the idea of duration, 300, s. 3-5
 Not from motion, 307, s. 16
 Its measure, 307, s. 17, 18
 Any regular periodical appearance, 308, s. 19, 20
 None of its measures known to be exact, 310, s. 21
 We only guess them equal by the train of our ideas, 310, s. 21
 Minutes, days, years, &c., not necessary to duration, 312, s. 23
 Change of the measures of duration, change not the notion of it, 312, s. 23
 The measures of duration, as the revolutions of the sun, may be applied to duration before the sun existed, 313—315, s. 24, 25, 28
 Duration without beginning, i. 313, s. 26
 How we measure duration, 314, s. 27-9,
 Recapitulation, concerning our ideas of duration, time, and eternity, 316, s. 31
Duration and expansion compared, i. 317, s. 1
 They mutually embrace each other, 324, s. 12
 Considered as a line, 324, s. 11
 Duration not conceivable by us without succession, 324, s. 12

Education, partly the cause of unreasonableness, i. 533, s. 3

Effect, i. 454 s. 1.
Enormities practised without remorse, instances of, i. 162
Enthusiasm, ii. 311, s. 1
 Described, 314, s. 6
 Its rise, 313, s. 5
 Ground of persuasion must be examined, and how, 316, s. 10
 Firmness of it, no sufficient proof, 318, s. 12, 13
 Fails of the evidence it pretends to, 317, s. 11
Envy, i. 357, s 13, 14
Error, what, ii. 321, s. 1
 Causes of error, 321, s. 1
 1. Want of proofs, 322, s. 2
 2. Want of skill to use them, 324, s. 5
 3. Want of will to use them, 325, s. 6
 4. Wrong measures of probability, 326, s. 7
 Fewer men assent to errors, than is supposed, 335, s. 18
Essence, real and nominal, ii.17, s.15
 Supposition of unintelligible, real essences of species, of no use, 18, s. 17
 Real and nominal essences, in simple ideas and modes always the same, in substance always different, 19, s. 18
 Essences, how ingenerable and incorruptible, 20, s. 19
 Specific essences of mixed modes are of men's making, and how, 30, s. 3
 Though arbitrary, yet not at random, 33, s. 7
 Of mixed modes, why called notions, 37, s. 12
 What, 41, s. 2
 Relate only to species, 42, s. 4
 Real essences, what, 44, s. 6
 We know them not, 46, s. 9
 Our specific essences of substances, nothing but collections of sensible ideas, 52, s. 21
 Nominal are made by the mind, 56, s. 26
 But not altogether arbitrarily, 58, s. 28

Essence—
Nominal essences of substances, how made, 58, s. 28, 29
Are very various, 60, s. 30, 31
Of species, are the abstract ideas, the names stand for, 49, s. 12; 52, s. 19
Are of man's making, 49, s. 12
But founded in the agreement of things, 50, s. 13
Real essences determine not our species, 51, s. 18
Every distinct, abstract idea, with a name, is a distinct essence of a distinct species, 51, s. 14
Real essences of substances, not to be known, 198, s. 12
Essential, what, 41, s. 2; 43, s. 5
Nothing essential to individuals, 42, s. 4
But to species, 44, s. 6
Essential difference, what, 43, s. 5

Eternal verities, ii. 251, s. 14
Eternal Wisdom, proof of an, ii. 238
Eternity, in our disputes and reasonings about it, why we are apt to blunder, i. 505, s. 15
Whence we get its idea, 314, s. 27
Evil, what, i. 384, s. 42
Existence, an idea of sensation and reflection, i. 239, s. 7
Our own existence we know intuitively, ii. 230, s. 2
And cannot doubt of it, 230, s. 2
Of creatable things, knowable only by our senses, 243, s. 1
Past existence known only by memory, 250, s. 11
Expansion, boundless, i. 318, s. 2
Should be applied to space in general, 297, s. 27
Experience often helps us, where we think not that it does, i. 255, s. 8
Extasy, i. 351. s. 1
Extension: we have no distinct ideas of very great, or very little, i. 505, s. 16

Extension—
Of body, incomprehensible, 437, s. 23, &c.
Denominations from place and extension are many of them relatives, i. 457, s. 5
And body not the same thing, 289, s. 11
Its definition in signification, 290, s. 15
Of body and of space how distinguished, 232, s. 5; 297, s. 27

Faculties, discoveries dependent on the different application of, men's, i. 200
Faculties of discovery suited to our state, i. 430
Faculties of the mind first exercised, i. 277, s. 14
Are but powers, 370, s. 17
Operate not, 370, s. 18, 20
Fairy money, borrowed knowledge likened to, i. 203
Faith, what, ii. 281, s. 14
Not opposite to reason, 302, s. 24
As contra-distinguished to reason, what, 303, s. 2
Cannot convince us of anything contrary to our reason, 306—308, s. 5, 6, 8
Matter of faith is only divine revelation, 309, s. 9
Things above reason are only proper matters of faith, 308, s. 7; 309, s. 9
Faith and justice not owned as principles by all men, i. 156
Faith and knowledge, their difference, 269, s. 3
Faith and opinion, as distinguished from knowledge, what, ii. 268, 269, s. 2, 3 [i. 291
Fallacy of taking words for things,
Falsehood, what it is, ii. 187, s. 9
Fancy, ii. 186, s. 8
Fantastical ideas, i. 508, s. 1.
Fear, i. 356, s. 10
Fetiches, ii. 220
Figurative speech, an abuse of language, ii. 112, s. 34

Figure, i. 285, s. 5, 6
Finite, and infinite, modes of quantity, i. 330, s. 1
   All positive ideas of quantity finite, 335, s. 8
Fire, nations ignorant of the use of, i. 30
Forms, substantial, distinguish not species, ii. 47, s. 10
Free, how far a man is so, i. 372, s. 21
   A man not free to will, or not to will, 373, s. 22-24
Freedom belongs only to agents, i. 371, s. 19
   Wherein it consists, 375, s. 27
Free will, an improper term, i. 390
   Liberty belongs not to the will, 368, s. 14.
   Wherein consists that which is called free will, 373, s. 24; 389, s. 47

Genera and species, abstract ideas are the essences of, ii. 15; made in order to naming, 66
General assent the great argument for innate ideas, i. 135; insufficient, 135
   Ideas, how made, i. 274, s. 9
   Knowledge, what, ii. 169, s. 31
   Propositions cannot be known to be true, without knowing the essence of the species, 189, s. 4
   Words, how made, 7, s. 6-8
   Belong only to signs, 14, s. 11
General and universal are creatures of the understanding, ii. 14
Generation, i. 454, s. 2
Gentlemen should not be ignorant, ii. 325, s. 6
Genus is but a partial conception of what is in the species, ii. 62 s. 32
Genus and species, what, ii. 13, s. 10
   Are but Latin names for sorts, 35, s. 9   [63, s. 33
   Adjusted to the end of speech,
   Are made in order to general names, 66, s. 39

God immovable, because infinite, i. 437, s. 21
Fills immensity as well as eternity, 318, s. 3
His duration not like that of the creatures, 324, s. 12
An idea of God, not innate, 183, s. 8
The existence of a God evident, and obvious to reason, 187, s. 9
The notion of a God once got, is the likeliest to spread and be continued, 187, s. 9, 10
Idea of God late and imperfect, 192, s. 13
Contrary, 193—196, s. 15, 16
Inconsistent, 193, s. 15
The best notions of God, got by thought and application, 193, s. 15
Notions of God frequently not worthy of him, 195, s. 16
The being of a God certain, s. 16, 195; proved, ii. 229, s. 1
As evident, as that the three angles of a triangle are equal to two right ones, i. 200, s. 22
Yea, as that two opposite angles are equal, 196, s. 16
More certain than any other existence without us, ii. 231, s. 6
The idea of God not the only proof of his existence, 231, s. 7
The being of a God the foundation of morality and divinity, 231, s. 7
How we make our idea of God, i. 444, 445, s. 33, 34
Gold is fixed; the various significations of this proposition, ii. 73, s. 50
Water strained through it, i. 231, s. 4
Good and evil, what, i. 351, s. 2; 384, s. 42
The greater good determines not the will, 379, s. 35; 380, s. 38; 386, s. 44

Good and evil—
  Why, 386, s. 44; 389, s. 46;
    398—405, s. 59, 60, 64, 65-68
  Twofold, 400, s. 61
  Works on the will only by desire, 389, s. 46
  Desire of good, how to be raised, 389, s. 46, 47
  Government of our passions the right improvement of liberty, i. 393

Habit, i. 419, s. 10
Habitual actions pass often without our notice, i. 258, s. 10
Hair, how it appears in a microscope, i. 430, s. 11
Happiness, what, i. 384, s. 42
  What happiness men pursue, i. 384, s. 43
  How we come to rest in narrow happiness, 399, s. 59, 60
Hardness, what, i. 231, s. 4
Hatred, i. 353, s. 5; 357, s. 14
Heat and cold, how the sensation of them both is produced, by the same water, at the same time, i. 249, s. 21
Herbert, Lord, innate principles of, examined, i. 170
History, what history of most authority, ii. 278, s. 11
Hobbes's definition of conscience, i. 161; his argument for the existence of a Deity, ii. 233
Hope, i. 355, s. 9
Hume, his criticism on Locke's theory of the origin of ideas, i. 8, 146
Hypotheses, their use, ii. 261, s. 13
  Are to be built on matter of fact, 211, s. 10

Ice and water whether distinct species, ii. 50, s. 13
Idea, what, i. 255, s. 8
Ideas, their original in children, i. 179, s. 2; 192, s. 13
  None innate, 196, s. 17
  Because not remembered, 197, s. 20

Ideas—
  Are what the mind is employed about in thinking, 205, s. 1
  All from sensation or reflection, 205, s. 2, &c.
  How this is to be understood, 207
  Their way of getting, observable in children, i. 208, s. 6
  Why some have more, some fewer, ideas, 209, s. 7
  Of reflection got late, and in some very negligently, 210, s. 8
  Their beginning and increase in children, 221—223, s. 21-24
  Their original in sensation and reflection, 222, s. 24
  Of one sense, 226, s. 1
  Want names, 227, s. 2
  Of more than one sense, 233
  Of reflection, 234, s. 1
  Of sensation and reflection, 234, s. 1
  As in the mind, and in things, must be distinguished, 239, s. 7
  Not always resemblances, 246, s. 15, &c.
  Which are first, is not material to know, 255, s. 7
  Of sensation often altered by the judgment, 255, s. 8
  Principally those of sight, 257, s. 9
  Of reflection, 277, s. 14
  Simple ideas men agree in, 298, s. 28
  Moving in a regular train in our minds, 304, s. 9
  Such as have degrees, want names, 346, s. 6
  Why some have names, and others not, 346, s. 7
  Original, 414, s. 73
  All complex ideas resolvable into simple, 419, s. 9
  What simple ideas have been most modified, 420, s. 10
  Our complex idea of God, and other spirits, common in every thing, but infinity, 446, s. 36
  Clear and obscure, 499, s. 2

Ideas—
    Distinct and confused, 499, s. 4
    May be clear in one part, and obscure in another, 504, s. 13
    Real and fantastical, 508, s. 1
    Simple are all real, 508, s. 2
    And adequate, 511, s. 2
    What ideas of mixed modes are fantastical, 509, s. 4
    What ideas of substances are fantastical, 510, s. 5
    Adequate and inadequate, 510, s. 1
    How said to be in things, 511, s. 2
    Modes are all adequate ideas, 512, s. 3
    Unless as referred to names, 513, 514, s. 4, 5
    Of substances inadequate, 518, s. 11
        1. As referred to real essences, 514, s. 6; 516, s. 7
        2. As referred to a collection of simple ideas, 516, s. 8
    Simple ideas are perfect ἔκτυπα, 519, s. 12
    Of substances are perfect ἔκτυπα, 519, s. 13
    Of modes are perfect archetypes, 520, s. 14
    True or false, 520, s. 1, &c.
    When false, 529, 530, s. 21-5
    As bare appearances in the mind, neither true nor false, 521, s. 3
    As referred to other men's ideas, or to real existence, or to real essences, may be true or false, 521, s. 4, 5
    Reason of such reference, 522, 523, s. 6-8
    Simple ideas referred to other men's ideas, least apt to be false, 523, s. 9
    Complex ones, in this respect more apt to be false, especially those of mixed modes, 523, s. 10
    Simple ideas referred to existence, are all true, 525, s. 14; 526, s. 16
    Though they should be different in different men, 525, s. 15

Ideas—
    Complex ideas of modes are all true, 527, s. 17
    Of substances when false, 529, s. 21, &c.
    When right or wrong, 530, s. 26
    That we are incapable of, ii. 160, s. 23
    That we cannot attain, because of their remoteness, ii. 160, s. 24
    Because of their minuteness, 161, s. 25
    Simple have a real conformity to things, 171, s. 4
    And all others, but of substances, 171, s. 5
    Simple cannot be got by definition of words, 25, s. 11
    But only by experience, 28, s. 14
    Of mixed modes, why most compounded, 28, s. 13
    Specific, of mixed modes, how at first made: instance in kinneah and niouph, 69, s. 44
    Of substances: instance in zahab, 71, s. 46; 72, s. 47
    Simple ideas and modes have all abstract, as well as concrete, names, 78, s. 2
    Of substances, have scarce any abstract names, 78
    Different in different men, 86, s. 13
    Our ideas almost all relative, i. 361, s. 3
    Particulars are first in the mind, ii. 83, s. 9
    General are imperfect, 83, s. 9
    How positive ideas may be from privative causes, i. 241, s. 4
    The use of this term not dangerous, i. 242, s. 1, &c. It is fitter than the word notion, i. 242, s. 6. Other words as liable to be abused as this, i. 242, s. 6. Yet it is condemned, both as new and not new, 243, s. 1. The same with notion, sense, meaning, &c., ii. 129, s. 1

Identical propositions teach nothing, ii. 219, s. 2
Identity, not an innate idea, i. 180-182, s. 3-5
 Of a plant, wherein it consists, 461, s. 4
 Of animals, 462, s. 5
 Of a man, 462, s. 6; 463, s. 8
 Unity of substance does not always make the same identity, 463, s. 7
 Personal identity, 466, s. 9
 Depends on the same consciousness, 467, s. 10
 Continued existence makes identity, 481, s. 29
 And diversity, in ideas, the first perception of the mind, ii. 129, s. 4
Idiots and madmen, i. 276, s. 12, 13
Idolatry, origin of, i. 177
Incogitative beings, ii. 236
Ignorance, our ignorance infinitely exceeds our knowledge, ii.158, s. 22
 Causes of ignorance, 159, s. 23
 1. For want of ideas, 159, s. 23
 2. For want of a discoverable connexion between the ideas we have, 164, s. 28
 3. For want of tracing the ideas we have, 167, s 30
Illation, what, ii. 282, s. 2
Immensity, i. 284, s. 4
 How this idea is got, 331, s. 3
Immoralities of whole nations, i. 162, s. 9; 165, s. 11
Immortality, not annexed to any shape, ii. 178, s. 15
Impenetrability, i. 179, s. 1
Imposition of opinions unreasonable, ii. 273, s. 4
Impossibile est idem esse et non esse, not the first thing known, i. 151, s. 25
Impossibility, not an innate idea, i. 180, s. 3
Impression on the mind, what, i. 136, s. 5
Inadequate ideas, i. 498, s. 1

Incompatibility, how far knowable, ii. 151, s. 15
Individuationis principium, is existence, i. 460, s. 3
Infallible judge of controversies, i. 190, s. 12
Inference, what, ii. 266, 267, s. 2-4
Infinite, why the idea of infinite not applicable to other ideas as well as those of quantity, since they can be as often repeated, i. 333, s. 6
 The idea of infinity of space or number, and of space or number infinite, must be distinguished, 334, s. 7
 Our idea of infinite, very obscure, 335, s. 8
 Number furnishes us with the clearest ideas of infinite, 336, s. 9
 The idea of infinite, a growing idea, 337, s. 12
 Our idea of infinite, partly positive, partly comparative, partly negative, 339, s. 15
 Why some men think they have an idea of infinite duration, but not of infinite space, 342, s. 20
 Why disputes about infinity are usually perplexed, 343, s. 21
 Our idea of infinity has its original in sensation and reflection, 344, s. 22
 We have no positive idea of infinite, 338, s. 13, 14; 340, s. 16
Infinity, why more commonly allowed to duration than to expansion, i. 319, s. 4
 How applied to God by us, 330, s. 1
 How we get this idea, 331, s. 2, 3
 The infinity of number, duration, and space, different ways considered, 325, 326, s. 10, 11
Innate truths must be the first known, i. 152, s. 26
 Principles to no purpose, if men can be ignorant or doubtful of them, 167, s. 13

2 L

Innate—
　Principles of my Lord Herbert examined, 170, s. 15, &c.
　Moral rules to no purpose, if effaceable, or alterable, 173, s. 20
　Propositions must be distinguished from other by their clearness and usefulness, 203, s. 24
　The doctrine of innate principles of ill consequence, 203, s. 24
Instant, what, i. 305, s. 10
　And continual change, 306, s. 13-15
Intuitive knowledge, ii. 134, s. 1
　Our highest certainty, 298, s. 14
Invention, wherein it consists, i. 267, s. 8
Iron, of what advantage to mankind, ii. 260, s. 11

Joy, i. 354, s. 7
Judgment: wrong judgments, in reference to good and evil, i. 398, s. 58
　Right judgment, ii. 273, s. 4
　One cause of wrong judgment, 272, s. 3
　Wherein it consists, 265-267
Judgment, day of, speculations on the, i. 477
Justice, Locke's narrow and imperfect view of, ii. 154

Kinneah and niouph, ii. 70
Knowledge has a great connexion with words, ii. 109, s. 25
　The author's definition of it explained and defended, *note.*
　How it differs from faith, 268, s. 2, 3; *note*
　What, 129, s. 2
　How much our knowledge depends on our senses, 124, s. 23
　Actual, 131, s. 8
　Habitual, 131, s. 8
　Habitual, twofold, 132, s. 9
　Intuitive, 134, s. 1
　Intuitive, the clearest, 134, s. 1
　Intuitive, irresistible, 134, s. 1
　Demonstrative, 135, s. 2

Knowledge—
　Of general truths, is all either intuitive or demonstrative, 140, s. 14
　Of particular existences, is sensitive, 140, s. 14
　Clear ideas do not always produce clear knowledge, 142, s. 15
　What kind of knowledge we have of nature, 322, s. 2
　Its beginning and progress, i. 277, s. 15-17; 142, s. 15, 16
　Given us, in the faculties to attain it, 190, s. 12
　Men's knowledge according to the employment of their faculties, 200, s. 22
　To be got only by the application of our own thought to the contemplation of things, 202, s. 23
　Extent of human knowledge, 134
　Our knowledge goes not beyond our ideas, 134, s. 1
　Nor beyond the perception of their agreement or disagreement, 135, s. 2
　Reaches not to all our ideas, 136, s. 3
　Much less to the reality of things, 137, s. 6
　Yet very improvable if right ways are taken, 137, s. 6
　Of co-existence very narrow, 148, 149, s. 9-11
　And therefore, of substances very narrow, 150, s. 14
　Of other relations indeterminable, 153, s. 18
　Of existence, 158, s. 21
　Certain and universal, where to be had, 166, s. 29
　Ill use of words, a great hinderance of knowledge, 168, s. 30
　General, where to be got, 169, s. 31
　Lies only in our thoughts, 198, s. 13
　Reality of our knowledge, 169—181
　Of mathematical truths, how real, 172, s. 6

Knowledge—
Of morality, real, 172, s. 7
Of substances, how far real, 175, s. 12
What makes our knowledge real, 170, s. 3
Considering things, and not names, the way to knowledge, 176, s. 13
Of substance, wherein it consists, 175, s. 11
What required to any tolerable knowledge of substances, 199, s. 14
Self-evident, 201, s. 2
Of identity and diversity, as large as our ideas, 148, s. 8; 202, s. 4
Wherein it consists, 202
Of co-existence, very scanty, 204, s. 5
Of relations of modes, not so scanty, s. 6, 204
Of real existence, none, 205, s. 7
Begins in particulars, 205, s. 9
Intuitive of our own existence, 229, s. 3
Demonstrative of a God, 228, s. 1
Improvement of knowledge, 252—263
Not improved by maxims, 252, s. 1
Why so thought, 253, s. 2
Knowledge improved only by perfecting and comparing ideas, 256, s. 6; 262, s. 14
And finding their relations, 256, s. 7
By intermediate ideas, 262, s. 14
In substances, how to be improved, 257, s. 9
Partly necessary, partly voluntary, 263, 264, s. 1, 2
Why some, and so little, 264, s. 2
How increased, 275, s. 6

Language, why it changes, ii. 94, s. 1
Wherein it consists, 1, s. 1-3
Its use, 33, s. 7
Its imperfections, 79, s. 1

Language—
Double use, 79, s. 1
The use of language destroyed by the subtilty of disputing, 98, s. 6; 98, s. 8
Ends of language, 108, s. 23
Its imperfections not easy to be cured, 114, s. 2; 114, s. 4-6
The cure of them necessary to philosophy, 114, s. 3
To use no word without a clear and distinct idea annexed to it, is one remedy of the imperfections of language, 117, s. 8, 9
Propriety in the use of words, another remedy, 118, s. 11
Law of nature generally allowed, i. 160, s. 6
There is, though not innate, 167, s. 13
Its enforcement, 485, s. 6
Learning—the ill state of learning in these latter ages, ii. 79, &c.
Of the schools, lies chiefly in the abuse of words, 83, &c.
Such learning of ill consequence, 84, s. 10
Liberty, what, i. 365, s. 8-12; 369, s. 15
Belongs not to the will, 368, s. 14
To be determined by the result of our own deliberation, is no restraint of liberty, 390—392, s. 48-50
Founded in a power of suspending our particular desires, 389, s. 47; 392, s. 51, 52
Light, its absurd definitions, ii. 24, s. 10
In the mind, what, 319, s. 13
Excess of, destructive to the organs of vision, i. 237; Sir I. Newton's experiments, 237
Logic has introduced obscurity into languages, ii. 97, s. 6, 7
And hindered knowledge, 97, s. 7
Love, i. 352, s. 4
Lucian's burlesque history of Pythagoras, i. 182

Madness, i. 276, s. 13. Opposition

Madness—
    to reason deserves that name.
    534, s. 4
Magisterial, the most knowing are
    least magisterial, ii. 273, s. 4
Making, i. 454, s. 2
Malebranche, examination of his
    opinion of seeing all things in
    God, ii. 413, 459
Malotru, the abbot, notice of, ii. 57
Man not the product of blind
    chance, ii. 231, s. 6
The essence of man is placed in
    his shape, 179, s. 16
We know not his real essence,
    41, s. 3; 53, s. 22; 57, s. 27
The boundaries of the human species not determined, 57, s. 27
What makes the same individual
    man, i. 476, s. 21; 481, s. 29
The same man may be different
    persons, 475, s. 19
Mathematics, their methods, ii.
    256, s. 7. Improvement, 262,
    s. 15
Matter, incomprehensible, both in
    its cohesion and divisibility, i.
    437, s. 23; 442, 443, s. 30, 31
What, ii 87, s. 15
Whether it may think, is not to
    be known, 143, s. 6
Cannot produce motion, or any
    thing else, 236, s. 10
And motion cannot produce
    thought, 236, s. 10
Not eternal, 241, s. 18
Maxims, ii. 214—217, s. 12-15
Not alone self-evident, 202, s. 3
Are not the truths first known,
    205, s. 9
Not the foundation of our knowledge, 206, s. 10
Wherein their evidence consists,
    206, s. 10
Their use, 208—215, s. 11, 12
Why the most general self-evident propositions alone pass
    for maxims, 208, s. 11
Are commonly proofs, only where
    there is no need of proofs,
    216, s. 15

Maxims—
    Of little use, with clear terms,
    218, s. 19
Of dangerous use, with doubtful
    terms, 214, s. 12; 219, s. 20
When first known, i. 138, &c.,
    s. 9-13; 141, s. 14; 143, s. 16
How they gain assent, 143, s.
    21, 22
Made from particular observations, 143, s. 21, 22
Not in the understanding before
    they are actually known, 148,
    s. 22
Neither their terms nor ideas
    innate, 149, s. 23
Least known to children and illiterate people, 152, s. 27
Memory, i. 262, s. 2
Attention, pleasure, and pain,
    settled ideas in the memory,
    263, s. 3
And repetition, 264, s. 4; 266,
    s. 6
Difference of, 264, s. 4, 5
In remembrance, the mind sometimes active, sometimes passive, 266, s. 7
Its necessity, 264, s. 5; 267, s. 8
Defects, 267, s. 8, 9
In brutes, 269, s. 10
Men must know and think for
    themselves, i. 202
Metaphysics, and school divinity,
    filled with uninstructive propositions, ii. 225, s. 9
Method used in mathematics, ii.
    256, s. 7
Mind, the quickness of its actions,
    i. 258, s. 10
Steps by which it attains several
    truths, i. 142
Operations of the, one source of
    ideas, 207
Minutes, hours, days, not necessary to duration, i. 312, s. 23
Miracles, ii. 281, s. 13
Misery, what, i. 384, s. 42
Misnaming disturbs not the certainty of our knowledge, ii 174
Modes, mixed, i. 415, s. 1

Modes—
  Made by the mind, 415, s. 2
  Sometimes got by the explication of their names, 416, s. 3
  Whence its unity, 417, s. 4
  Occasion of mixed modes, 417, s. 5
  Their ideas, how got, 419, s. 9
  Simple and complex, 281, s. 5
  Simple modes, 282, s. 1
  Of motion, 345, s. 2
Mole, popular error regarding the, ii. 159
Monsters, ii. 17, 179
Moral good and evil, what, ii. 485, s. 5
  Three rules whereby men judge of moral rectitude, 486, s. 7
  Beings, how founded on simple ideas of sensation and reflection, 493, 494, s. 14, 15
Moral rules not self-evident, i. 158, s. 4
  Variety of opinions concerning moral rules, 159, s. 5, 6
  If innate, cannot with public allowance be transgressed, 166, 167, s. 11, 13
Moral truth, ii. 187
Morality, capable of demonstration, ii. 299, s. 16; 153, s. 18; 257, s. 8
  The proper study of mankind, 259, s. 11
  Of actions, in their conformity to a rule, i. 494, s. 15
  Mistakes in moral notions, owing to names, 495, s. 16
  Discourses in morality, if not clear, the fault of the speaker, ii. 121, s. 17
  Hinderances of demonstrative treating of morality: 1. Want of marks; 2. Complexedness, 155, s. 19; 3. Interest, 157, s. 20
  Change of names in morality, changes not the nature of things, 187, s. 9
  And mechanism, hard to be reconciled, i. 170, s. 14
  Secured amidst men's wrong judgments, 407, s. 70

Motion, slow or very swift, why not perceived, i. 304, 305, s. 7-11
  Voluntary, inexplicable, ii. 242, s. 19
  Its absurd definitions, 23, s. 8, 9
Mureti, his account of a person with an extraordinary memory, i. 265
Mutual charity and forbearance inculcated, ii. 273

Naming of ideas, i. 274, s. 8
Names, moral, established by law, not to be varied from, ii. 174, s. 10
  Of substances, standing for real essences, are not capable to convey certainty to the understanding, 184, s. 5
  For nominal essences will make some, though not many, certain propositions, 185, s. 6
  Why men substitute names for real essences, which they know not, 104, s. 19
  Two false suppositions, in such an use of names, 106, s. 21
  A particular name to every particular thing impossible, 9, s. 2
  And useless, 9, s. 3
  Proper names, where used, 5, 10, s. 4
  Specific names are affixed to the nominal essence, 18, s. 16
  Of simple ideas and substances, refer to things, 21, s. 2
  What names stand for both real nominal essence, 22, s. 3
  Of simple ideas not capable of definitions, 22, s. 4
  Why, 23, s. 7
  Of least doubtful signification, 28, s. 15
  Have few accents *in linea prædicamentali*, 29, s. 16
  Of complex ideas, may be defined, 26, s. 12
  Of mixed modes stand for arbitrary ideas, 30, s. 2, 3; 69, s. 44
  Tie together the parts of their complex ideas, 36, s. 10

Names—
    Stand always for the real essence, 38, s. 14
    Why got, usually, before the ideas are known, 38, s. 15
    Of relations comprehended under those of mixed modes, 39, s. 16
    General names of substances stand for sorts, 40, s. 1
    Necessary to species, 66, s. 39
    Proper names belong only to substances, 68, s. 42
    Of modes in their first application, 69, s. 44, 45
    Of substances in their first application, 71, s. 46, 47
    Specific names stand for different things in different men, 72, s. 48
    Are put in the place of the thing supposed to have the real essence of the species, 73, s. 49
    Of mixed modes, doubtful often, 81, s. 6
    Because they want standards in nature, 81, s. 7
    Of substances, doubtful, 85—87, s. 11, 14
    In their philosophical use, hard to have settled significations, 87, s. 15
    Instance, liquor, 88, s. 16; gold, 89, s. 17
    Of simple ideas, why least doubtful, 90, s. 18
    Least compounded ideas have the least dubious names, 91, s. 19
Natural philosophy, not capable of science, ii. 162, s. 26; 258, s. 10
    Yet very useful, 260, s. 12
    How to be improved, i. 363, s. 12
    What has hindered its improvement, i. 363, s. 12
Navarrete, uncharitable judgment of, ii. 323
Necessity, i. 368, s. 13
Negative terms, ii. 2, s. 4
    Names signify the absence of positive ideas, i. 242, s. 5
Nervous fluid, hypothesis of the, i. 241; ii. 89

Newton's, Sir Isaac, dangerous experiment on his eyes, i. 237
Norris, his assertion of Malebranche's opinion, remarks on, ii. 459
Nothing; that nothing cannot produce any thing, is demonstration, ii. 230, s. 3
Notions, i. 415, s. 2
Number, i. 325
    Modes of, the most distinct ideas, 416, s. 3
    Demonstrations in numbers, the most determinate, 417, s. 4
    The general measure, 330, s. 8
    Affords the clearest idea of infinity, 336, s. 9
    Numeration, what, 327, s. 5
    Names necessary to it, 327, s. 5, 6
    And order, 329, s. 7
    Why not early in children, and in some never, 329, s. 7

Obscurity, unavoidable in ancient authors, ii. 84, s. 10
    The cause of it in our ideas, i. 499, s. 3
Obstinate, they are most, who have least examined, ii. 272, s. 3
Opal, description of the, ii. 151
Opinion, what, ii. 269, s. 3
    How opinions grow up to principles, i. 175, s. 22-26
    Of others, a wrong ground of assent, ii. 270, s. 6; 335, s. 17
Organs; our organs suited to our state, i. 430, s. 12, 13
Ostracism, the Grecian, explained, i. 418

Pain, present, works presently, i. 402, s. 64
    Its use, 236, s. 4
Paley, his false definition of virtue, i. 159
Parrot mentioned by Sir W. T., i. 464, s. 8
    Holds a rational discourse, 465
Particles join parts, or whole sentences, together, ii. 74, s. 1

Particles—
    In them lies the beauty of well speaking, ii. 74, s. 2
    How their use is to be known, 76, s. 6
    They express some action or posture of the mind, 75, s. 4; i. 268
Pascal, his great memory, i. 26, s. 9
Passion, i. 421, s. 11
Passions, how they lead us into error, ii. 279, s. 11
    Turn on pleasure and pain, i. 352, s. 3
    Are seldom single, 382, s. 39
Perception threefold, i. 363, s. 5
    In perception, the mind for the most part passive, 253, s. 1
    Is an impression made on the mind, 253, s. 3, 4
    In the womb, 254, s. 5
    Difference between it, and innate ideas, 254, s. 6
    Puts the difference between the animal and vegetable kingdom, 258, s. 11
    The several degrees of it, show the wisdom and goodness of the Maker, 259, s. 12
    Belongs to all animals, 259, s. 12-14
    The first inlet of knowledge, 261, s. 15
Person, what, i. 466, s. 9
    A forensic term, 479, s. 26
    The same consciousness alone makes the same person, 469, s. 13; 477, s. 23
    The same soul without the same consciousness, makes not the same person, 470, s. 14, &c.
    Reward and punishment follow personal identity, 474, s. 18
Phantastical ideas, i. 508, s. 1
Philosophical law, the measure of virtue and vice, i. 487
Pictures, use of, in giving clear ideas of objects, ii. 127
Place, i. 286, s. 7, 8
    Use of place, 287, s. 9
    Nothing but a relative position, 288, s. 10

Place—
    Sometimes taken for the space body fills, 288, s. 10
    Twofold, 320, s. 6, 7
Pleasure and pain, i. 351, s. 1; 357, s. 15, 16
    Join themselves to most of our ideas, 235, s 2
Pleasure, why joined to several actions, i. 235, s. 3
Positive ideas from privative causes, i. 240, 242
Power, how we come by its idea, i. 359, s. 1
    Active and passive, 360, s. 2
    No passive power in God, no active in matter; both active and passive in spirits, 360, s. 2
    Our idea of active power clearest from reflection, 362, s. 4
    Powers operate not on powers, 370, s. 18
    Make a great part of the ideas of substances, 427, s. 7
    Why, 428, s. 8
    An idea of sensation and reflection, 239, s. 8
Practical principles not innate, i. 154, s. 1
    Not universally assented to, 156, s. 2
    Are for operation, 156, s. 3
    Not agreed, 169, s. 14
    Different, 174, s. 21
Principium individuationis, i. 460
Principles, not to be received without strict examination, ii. 254, s. 4; 327, s. 8
    The ill consequences of wrong principles, 327, s. 9, 10
    None innate, i. 134, s. 1
    None universally assented to, 135, s. 2-4
    How ordinarily got, 175, s. 22, &c.
    Are to be examined, 177, s. 26, 27
    Not innate, if the ideas they are made up of, are not innate, 179, s. 1
Privative terms, ii. 2, s. 4
Probability, what, ii. 267, s. 1, 3
    The grounds of, 269, c. 4

Probability.—
  In matter of fact, 270, s. 6
  How we are to judge in probabilities, 269, s. 5
  Difficulties in probabilities, 277, s. 9
  Grounds of probability in speculation, 279, s. 12
  Wrong measures of probability, 326, s. 7
  How evaded by prejudiced minds, 332, s. 13, 14
Proofs, ii. 136, s. 3
Properties of specific essences, not known, ii. 52, s. 19
  Of things very numerous, i. 518, s. 10 ; 529, s. 24
Propositions, identical, teach nothing, ii. 244, s. 2
  Generical, teach nothing, 222, s. 4; 227, s. 13
  Wherein a part of the definition is predicated of the subject, teach nothing, 223, s. 5, 6
  But the signification of the word, 224, s. 7
  Concerning substances, generally either trifling or uncertain, 225, s. 9
  Merely verbal, how to be known, 227, s. 12
  Abstract terms, predicated one of another, produce merely verbal propositions, 227, s. 12
  Or part of a complex idea, predicated of the whole, 222, s. 4; 227, s. 13
  More propositions, merely verbal, than is suspected, 227, s. 13
  Universal propositions concern not existence, 228, s. 1
  What propositions concern existence, 228
  Certain propositions, concerning existence, are particular; concerning abstract ideas, may be general, 238, s. 13
  Mental, 183, s. 3; 184, s. 5
  Verbal, 183, s. 3; 184, s. 5
  Mental, hard to be treated, 183, s. 3, 6

Punishment, what, i. 485, s. 5
  And reward, follow consciousness, 474, s. 18 ; 26, s. 489
  An unconscious drunkard, why punished, 476, s. 22
Pythagoras, his doctrine of the transmigration of souls, i. 180 ; Lucian's burlesque, 182

Qualities: secondary qualities, their connexion, or inconsistence, unknown, ii. 149, s. 11
  Of substances, scarce knowable, but by experience, 150—153 s. 14, 16,
  Of spiritual substances less than of corporeal, 153, s. 17
  Secondary, have no conceivable connexion with the primary, that produce them, 149, 150, s. 12, 13; 164, s. 28
  Of substances, depend on remote causes, 175, s. 11
  Not to be known by descriptions, 124, s. 21
  Secondary, how far capable of demonstration, 139, s. 11-13
  What, i. 244, s. 13
  How said to be in things, 508, s. 2
  Secondary, would be other, if we could discover the minute parts of bodies, 429, s. 11
  Primary, 243, s. 9
  How they produce ideas in us, 245, s. 11, 12
  Secondary qualities, 243, s.13-15
  Primary qualities resemble our ideas, secondary not, 246, s. 15, 16
  Three sorts of qualities in bodies, 250, s. 23, i.e., primary, secondary, immediately perceivable; and secondary, mediately, perceivable, 252, s. 26
  Secondary are bare powers, 250, s. 23-25
  Secondary have no discernible connexion with the first, 251, s. 25
Quotations, how little to be relied on, ii. 278, s. 11

INDEX. 521

Reading and study, thoughts concerning, ii. 497
Real ideas, i. 520, s. 1, 2
Reality of knowledge, ii. 169; demonstration, 170
Reason, its various significations, ii. 282, s. 1
  What, 282, s. 2
  Reason is natural revelation, 313, s. 4
  It must judge of revelation, 332, s. 14, 15
  It must be our last guide in every thing, 332, s. 14, 15
  Four parts of reason, 283, s. 3
  Where reason fails us, 296, s. 9
  Necessary in all but intuition, 298, s. 15
  As contra-distinguished to faith, what, 303, s. 2
  Helps us not to the knowledge of innate truths, i. 136, s. 5-8
  General ideas, general terms, and reason, usually grow together, 142, s. 15
Reasoning, ii. 282; its four parts, 283; syllogism not the great instrument of, 284; causes of its failure, 296
Recollection, i. 343, s. 1
Reflection, i. 207, s. 4
Related, i. 449, s. 1
Relation, i. 449, s. 1
  Proportional, 482, s. 1
  Natural, 482, s. 2
  Instituted, 483, s. 3
  Moral, 483, s. 4
  Numerous, 496, s. 17
  Terminate in simple ideas, 496, s. 18
  Our clear ideas of relation, 497, s. 19
  Names of relations doubtful, 497, s. 19
  Without correlative terms, not so commonly observed, 449, s. 2
  Different from the things related, 449, s. 4
  Changes without any change in the subject, 451, s. 5
  Always between two, 451, s. 6

Relation—
  All things capable of relation, 451, s. 7
  The idea of the relation, often clearer than of the things related, 452, s. 8
  All terminate in simple ideas of sensation and reflection, 453, s. 9
Relative, i. 449, s. 1
  Same relative terms taken for external denominations, 449, s. 2
  Some for absolute, 450, s. 3
  How to be known, 453, s. 10
  Many words, though seeming absolute, are relatives, 451, s. 3-5
Religion, all men have time to inquire into, ii. 323, s. 3
  But in many places are hindered from inquiring, 324, s. 4
Remembrance, of great moment in common life, i. 267, s. 8
  What, 197, s. 20; 266, s. 7
  Accounted a sixth sense, by Hobbes, 263
Reputation, of great force in common life, ii. 492, s. 12
Restraint, i. 368, s. 13
Resurrection, the author's notion of it, ii. 357
  Not necessarily understood of the same body, &c., 357. The meaning of "his body," 2 Cor. v. 10, 357
  The same body of Christ arose, and why, 357. How the scripture speaks about it, 376
Retention, i. 262
Revelation, an unquestionable ground of assent, ii. 282, s. 14
  Belief, no proof of it, 320, s. 15
  Traditional revelation cannot convey any new simple ideas, 304, s. 3
  Not so sure as our reason or senses, 305, s. 4
  In things of reason, no need of revelation, 306, s. 5
  Cannot over-rule our clear knowledge, 306, s. 5; 309, s. 10

Revelation—
Must over-rule probabilities of reason, 308, s. 8, 9
Revenge, instance of, i. 381
Reward, what, i. 485, s. 5
Rewards and punishments, future, i. 407, 477
Rhetoric, an art of deceiving, ii. 112, s. 34

Sagacity, ii. 136, s. 3
Hobbes' account of, ii. 137
Saints, pretended, among the Turks, their execrable lives, i. 164
Locke's inference disputed, 165
Same, whether substance, mode, or concrete, i. 481, s. 28
Sand, white to the eye, pellucid in a microscope, i. 430, s. 11
Scarlet, a blind man's definition of, ii. 26
Sceptical, no one so sceptical as to doubt his own existence, ii. 230, s. 2
Schools, wherein faulty, ii. 97, s. 6, &c.
Science, divided into a consideration of nature, of operation, and of signs, ii. 337
No science of natural bodies, s. 26, 162
Scripture; interpretations of scripture not to be imposed, ii. 93, s. 23
Self, what makes it, i. 475, s. 20; 477, s. 23-5
Self-love, i. 533, s. 2
Partly cause of unreasonableness in us, i. 533, s. 2
Self-evident propositions, where to be had, ii. 201, &c.
Neither needed nor admitted proof, 218, s. 19
Sensation, i. 206, s. 3
Distinguishable from other perceptions, ii. 140, s. 14
Explained, i. 249, s. 21
What, 347, s. 1
Senses: why we cannot conceive other qualities, than the objects of our senses, i. 125, s. 3

Senses—
Learn to discern by exercise, i. 124, s. 21
Much quicker would not be useful to us, i. 430, s. 12
Our organs of sense suited to our state, 430, s. 12, 13,
Sensible knowledge is as certain as we need, ii. 248, s. 8
Goes not beyond the present act, 249, s. 9
Shame, i. 358, s. 17
Siamese, unjustly accused of impiety, i. 186; their belief, 194
Sick and aged, murder of, among certain nations, i. 163
Simple ideas, i. 224, s. 1
Not made by the mind, i. 224, s. 2
Power of the mind over them 282, s. 1
The materials of all our knowledge, 239, s. 10
All positive, 239, s. 10
Very different from their causes, 241, s. 2, 3
Sin, with different men, stands for different actions, i. 172, s. 19
Sleepwalking, i. 350
Smell, nature of the sense of, i. 227
Solidity, i. 228, s. 1
Inseparable from body, i. 228, s. 1
By it body fills space, 230, s. 2
This idea got by touch, 228, s. 1
How distinguished from space, 230, s. 3
How from hardness, 231, s. 4
Something from eternity, demonstrated, ii. 233, s. 8
Sorrow, i. 354, s. 8
Sorts, the common names of substances stand for, ii. 40; the essence of each sort is the abstract idea, 41
Soul thinks not always, i. 210, s. 9, &c.
Not in sound sleep, 212, s. 11, &c.
Its immateriality, we know not, ii. 143, s. 6
Religion, not concerned in the soul's immateriality, 145, s. 6

Soul—
    Our ignorance about it, i. 480, s. 27
    The immortality of it, not proved by reason, ii. 145, *et seq.*
    It is brought to light by revelation, ii. 145

Sound, its modes, i. 345, s. 3

Space, its idea got by sight and touch, i. 283, s. 2
    Its modification, 284, s. 4
    Not body, 289, s. 11, 12
    Its parts inseparable, 289, s. 13
    Immovable, 290, s. 14
    Whether body, or spirit, 291, s. 16
    Whether substance, or accident, 291, s. 17
    Infinite, 294, s. 21; 332, s. 4
    Ideas of space and body distinct, 296, s. 24, 25
    Considered as a solid, 324, s. 11
    Hard to conceive any real being void of space, 324, s. 11

Species; why changing one simple idea of the complex one, is thought to change the species in modes but not in substances, ii. 104, s. 19
    Of animals and vegetables, distinguished by figure, 59, s. 29
    Of other things, by colour, 59, s. 29
    Made by the understanding, for communication, 35, s. 9
    No species of mixed modes without a name, 36, s. 11
    Of substances, are determined by the nominal essence, 45-50, &c., s. 7, 8, 11, 13
    Not by substantial forms, 47, s. 10
    Nor by the real essence, 50, s. 13; 55, s. 25
    Of spirits, how distinguished, 47, s. 11
    More species of creatures above than below us, 49, s. 12
    Of creatures very gradual, 49, s. 12
    What is necessary to the making of species, by real essences, 51, s. 14, &c.
    Of animals and plants, not distinguished by propagation, 54, s. 23
    Of animals and vegetables, distinguished principally by the shape and figure; of other things, by the colour, 59, s, 29
    Of man, likewise in part, 56, s. 26
    Instance, Abbot of St. Martin, 57, s. 26
    Is but a partial conception of what is in the individuals, 62, s. 32
    It is the complex idea which the name stands for, that makes the species, 64, s. 35
    Man makes the species, or sorts, 65, s. 35-37
    The foundation of it is in the similitude found in things, 65, s. 35-37
    Every distinct abstract idea, a different species, 66, s. 38

Speech, its end, ii. 1, s. 1, 2
    Proper speech, 8, s. 8
    Intelligible, 8, s. 8

Spirits, the existence of, not knowable, ii. 250, s. 12
    How it is proved, 250, s. 12
    Operation of spirits on bodies, not conceivable, 164, s. 28
    What knowledge they have of bodies, 124, s. 23
    Separate, how their knowledge may exceed ours, i. 268, s. 9
    We have as clear a notion of the substance of spirit, as of body, 425, s. 5
    A conjecture concerning one way of knowledge wherein spirits excel us, 432, s. 13
    Our ideas of spirit, 434, s. 14
    As clear as that of body, 434, s. 14; 437, s. 22
    Primary ideas belonging to spirits, 436, s. 18
    Move, 436, s. 19
    Ideas of spirit and body, compared, 437, s. 22; 442, s. 30
    Existence of, as easy to be admitted as that of bodies, 440, s. 28

Spirits—
  We have no idea how spirits communicate their thoughts, 446, s. 36
  How far we are ignorant of the being, species, and properties of spirits, ii. 163, s. 27
  The word spirit, does not necessarily denote immateriality, 388
  The scripture speaks of material spirits, 388
Strasburg, the great clock at, ii. 42
Study, stories of extraordinary passion for, i. 385
Stupidity, i. 267, s. 8
Substance, i. 422, s. 1
  No idea of it, 196, s. 18
  Not very knowable, 196, s. 18
  Our certainty, concerning substances, reaches but a little way, ii. 175, s. 11, 12; 216, s. 15
  The confused idea of substance in general, makes always a part of the essence of the species of substances, 52, s. 21
  In substances, we must rectify the signification of their names, by the things, more than by definitions, 125, s. 24
  Their ideas single, or collective, i. 281, s. 6
  We have no distinct idea of substance, 291, s. 18, 19
  We have no idea of pure substance, 423, s. 2
  Our ideas of the sorts of substances, 424, 425, s. 3, 4; 426, s. 6
  Observable, in our ideas of substances, 446, s. 37
  Collective ideas of substances, 447, &c.
  They are single ideas, 448, s. 2
  Three sorts of substances, 459, s. 2
  The ideas of substances, have a double reference, 514, s. 6
  The properties of substances, numerous, and not all to be known, 518, s. 9, 10

Substance—
  The perfectest ideas of substances, 427, s. 7
  Three sorts of ideas make our complex one of substances, 428, s. 9
  Idea of it obscure, ii. 144
  Not discarded by the Essay, 351
  The author's account of it clear as that of noted logicians, 351
  We talk like children about it, 356
  The author makes not the being of it depend on the fancies of men, 352
  The author's principles consist with the certainty of its existence, 352
Subtilty, what, ii. 98, s. 8
Succession, an idea got chiefly from the train of our ideas, i. 239, s. 9; 303, s. 6
Which train is the measure of it, 306, s. 12
Summum bonum, wherein it consists, i. 395, s. 55
Sun, the name of a species, though but one, ii. 40, s. 1
Syllogism, no help to reasoning, ii. 284, s. 4
  The use of syllogism, 284, s. 4
  Inconveniences of syllogism, 284, s. 4
  Of no use in probabilities, 293, s. 5
  Helps not to new discoveries, 294, s. 6
  Or the improvement of our knowledge, 294, s. 7
  Whether in syllogism, the middle terms may not be better placed, 295, s. 8
  May be about particulars, 295, s. 8

Taste and smells, their modes, i. 346, s. 5
Taylor, Jeremy, on diversity of opinion, ii. 273
Tears and weeping, i. 354

INDEX. 525

Testimony, how it lessens its force, ii. 277, s. 10
Thinking, i. 347
 Modes of thinking, i. 347, s. 1; 348, s. 2
 Men's ordinary way of thinking, ii. 269, s. 4
 An operation of the soul, i. 211, s. 10
 Without memory useless, 216, s. 15
Thoughts concerning reading and study, ii. 497
Time, what, i. 307, s. 17, 18
 Not the measure of motion, 312, s. 22
 And place, distinguishable portions of infinite duration and expansion, 320, s. 5, 6
 Twofold, 320, s. 6, 7
 Denominations from time are relatives, 455, s. 3
Toleration, necessary in our state of knowledge, ii. 273, s. 4
Tradition, the older the less credible, ii. 277, s. 10
Transmigration of souls, doctrine of, i. 180
Travellers, early, their accounts of nations of atheists to be received with doubt, i. 184
Trifling propositions, ii. 219
 Discourses, ii. 225—227, s. 9, 10, 11
True and false ideas, i. 520
Truth, what, ii. 183, s. 2; 185, s. 6
 Of thought, 183, s. 3; 187, s. 9
 Of words, 183, s. 3
 Verbal and real, 186, s. 8, 9
 Moral, 187, s. 11
 Metaphysical, 521, s. 2
 General, seldom apprehended, but in words, ii. 188, s. 2
 In what it consists, 190, s. 5
 Love of it necessary, 311, s. 1
 How we may know we love it, 311, s. 1

Vacuum possible, i. 294, s. 22
 Motion proves a vacuum, 295, s. 23

Vacuum—
 We have an idea of it, 230, s. 3; 232, s. 5
Variety in men's pursuits, accounted for, i. 240, s. 10
Vegetables, identity of, i. 461
Velleity, what, i. 353
Vice lies in wrong measures of good, ii. 334, s. 16
Virtue, what, in reality, i. 172, s. 18
 What in its common application, 165, s. 10, 11
 Is preferable, under a bare possibility of a future state, 406, s. 70
 How taken, 171, s. 17, 18
Volition, what, i. 363, s. 5; 369, s. 15; 375, s. 28
 Better known by reflection than words, 376, s. 30
Voluntary, what, i. 363, s. 5; 367, s. 11; 375, s. 27

Understanding, what, i. 363, s. 5, 6
 Like a dark room, 278, s. 17
 When rightly used, 131, s. 5
 Three sorts of perception in, 363, s. 5
 Wholly passive in the reception of simple ideas, 223, s. 25
Uneasiness alone determines the will to a new action, i. 376, s. 29, 31, 33, &c.
 Why it determines the will, 379, s. 36, 37
 Causes of it, 397, s. 57, &c.
Unity, an idea, both of sensation and reflection, i. 239, s. 7
 Suggested by every thing, 325, s. 1
Universal consent, argument of, examined, i. 135
Universality, is only in signs, ii. 14
Universals, how made, i. 274, s. 9

Weeping. *See* Tears.
What is, is, is not universally assented to, i. 136, s. 4
Where and when, i. 321, s. 8
Whole, bigger than its parts, its use, ii. 208, s. 11
 And part not innate ideas, i. 182, s. 6

Will, what, i. 363, s 5, 6; 369, s. 16; 375, s. 28
What determines the will, 37, s. 29
Often confounded with desire, 37, s. 30
Is conversant only about our own actions, 37, s. 30
Terminates in them, 383, s. 40
Is determined by the greatest, present, removable uneasiness, 383, s. 40
Wit and judgment, wherein different, i. 270, s. 2
Wolf, his theory of innate ideas, i. 140
Worcester, Locke's controversy with the bishop of, ii. 339
Words, an ill use of, one great hinderance of knowledge, ii. 167, s. 30
Abuse of words, i. 94, s. 1
Sects introduce words without signification, 94, s. 2
The schools have coined multitudes of insignificant words, 94, s. 2
And rendered others obscure, 97, s. 6
Often used without signification, 95, s. 3
And why, 96, s. 5
Inconstancy in their use, an abuse of words, 96, s. 5
Obscurity, an abuse of words, 97, s. 6
Taking them for things, an abuse of words, 101, s. 14, 15
Who most liable to this abuse of words, 101, s. 14, 15
This abuse of words is a cause of obstinacy in error, 103, s. 16
Making them stand for real essences we know not, is an abuse of words, 103, s. 17, 18
The supposition of their certain evident signification, an abuse of words, 107, s. 22
Use of words is, 1. To communicate ideas; 2. With quick-

Words—
ness; 3. To convey knowledge, 108, s. 23, 24
How they fail in all these, 109, s. 26, et seq.
How in substances, 110, 111, s. 32
How in modes and relations, 110, 111, s. 33
Misuse of words, a great cause of error, 114, s. 4
Of obstinacy, 115, s. 5
And of wrangling, 115, s. 6
Signify one thing in inquiries, and another in disputes, 116, s. 7
The meaning of words is made known, in simple ideas, by showing, 120, s. 14
In mixed modes, by defining, 120, s. 15
In substances, by showing and defining too, 123, s. 19; 124, s. 21, 22,
The ill consequence of learning words first, and their meaning afterwards, 125, s. 24
No shame to ask men the meaning of their words where they are doubtful, 126, s. 25
Are to be used constantly in the same sense, 128, s. 26
Or else to be explained, where the context determines it not, 128, s. 27
How made general, ii. 1, s. 3
Signifying insensible things, derived from names of sensible ideas, 2, s. 5
Have no natural signification, 4, s. 1
But by imposition, 8, s. 8
Stand immediately for the ideas of the speaker, 4, s. 1-3
Yet with a double reference:—
1. To the ideas in the hearer's mind, 6, s. 4
2. To the reality of things, 7, s. 5
Apt, by custom, to excite ideas, 7, s. 6
Often used without signification, 7, s. 7

Words—
  Most general, 9, s. 1
  Why some words of one language cannot be translated into those of another, 34, s. 8
  Why I have been so large on words, 39, s. 16
  New words, or in new significations, are cautiously to be used, 73, s. 51
  Civil use of words, 75, s. 3
  Philosophical use of words, 75, s. 3
  These very different, 87, s. 15
  Miss their end when they excite not, in the hearer, the same idea as in the mind of the speaker, 80, s. 4

Words—
  What words most doubtful, and why, 80, s. 5
  What unintelligible, 80, s. 5
  Fitted to the use of common life, 81, s. 7
  Not translatable, 34, s. 8
Worship not an innate idea, i. 183, s. 7
Wrangle, about words, ii. 227, s. 13
Writings, ancient, why hardly to be precisely understood, ii. 93, s. 22

Zahab, ii. 71

FUNDERBURG LIBRARY
MANCHESTER COLLEGE

192
L79p
v.2

WITHDRAWN
from
Funderburg Library